会计学精选教材·双语注释版

U0362623

审计
以风险导向法实施高质量审计

9E AUDITING

A RISK-BASED APPROACH TO CONDUCTING A QUALITY AUDIT

卡拉·M. 约翰斯通 (Karla M. Johnstone)

〔美〕奥德丽·A. 格拉姆林 (Audrey A. Gramling) 著

拉里·E. 里滕伯格 (Larry E. Rittenberg)

曹强 译注

第9版

北京大学出版社
PEKING UNIVERSITY PRESS

著作权合同登记号 图字：01-2015-4543

图书在版编目(CIP)数据

审计：以风险导向法实施高质量审计：第9版/(美)约翰斯通(Johnstone,K. M.)，(美)格拉姆林(Gramling, A. A.)，(美)里滕伯格(Rittenberg, L. E.)著；曹强译注. —北京：北京大学出版社，2016.6
(会计学精选教材·双语注释版)
ISBN 978-7-301-26762-2

Ⅰ. ①审… Ⅱ. ①约… ②格… ③里… ④曹… Ⅲ. ①审计学—双语教学—高等学校—教材 Ⅳ. ①F239.9

中国版本图书馆 CIP 数据核字（2016）第 011012 号

书 名	审计：以风险导向法实施高质量审计（第9版） SHENJI: YI FENGXIANDAOXIANGFA SHISHI GAOZHILIANGSHENJI
著作责任者	〔美〕卡拉·M. 约翰斯通（Karla M. Johnstone） 奥德丽·A. 格拉姆林（Audrey A. Gramling） 拉里·E. 里滕伯格（Larry E. Rittenberg） 著，曹强 译注
责 任 编 辑	刘誉阳
标 准 书 号	ISBN 978-7-301-26762-2
出 版 发 行	北京大学出版社
地 址	北京市海淀区成府路 205 号 100871
网 址	http://www.pup.cn
电 子 信 箱	em@pup.cn QQ：552063295
新 浪 微 博	@北京大学出版社 @北京大学出版社经管图书
电 话	邮购部 62752015 发行部 62750672 编辑部 62752926
印 刷 者	北京大学印刷厂
经 销 者	新华书店
	787 毫米×1092 毫米 16 开本 42 印张 839 千字 2016 年 6 月第 1 版 2016 年 6 月第 1 次印刷
印 数	0001—4000 册
定 价	89.00 元

出 版 者 序

作为一家致力于出版和传承经典、与国际接轨的大学出版社,北京大学出版社历来重视国际经典教材,尤其是经管类经典教材的引进和出版。自2003年起,我们与圣智、培生、麦格劳-希尔、约翰-威利等国际著名教育出版机构合作,精选并引进了一大批经济管理类的国际优秀教材。其中,很多图书已经改版多次,得到了广大读者的认可和好评,成为国内市面上的经典。例如,我们引进的世界上最流行的经济学教科书——曼昆的《经济学原理》,已经成为国内最受欢迎、使用面最广的经济学经典教材。

呈现在您面前的这套"引进版精选教材",是主要面向国内经济管理类各专业本科生、研究生的教材系列。经过多年的沉淀和累积、吐故和纳新,本丛书在各方面正逐步趋于完善:在学科范围上,扩展为"经济学精选教材""金融学精选教材""国际商务精选教材""管理学精选教材""会计学精选教材""营销学精选教材"六个子系列;在课程类型上,基本涵盖了经管类各专业的主修课程,并延伸到不少国内缺乏教材的前沿和分支领域;即便针对同一门课程,也有多本教材入选,或难易程度不同,或理论和实践各有侧重,从而为师生提供了更多的选择。同时,我们在出版形式上也进行了一些探索和创新。例如,为了满足国内双语教学的需要,对于部分影印版图书,我们改变了之前的单纯影印形式,在其基础上,由资深授课教师根据该课程的重点,添加重要术语和重要结论的中文注释,使之成为双语注释版。此次,我们更新了丛书的封面和开本,将其以全新的面貌呈现给广大读者。希望这些内容和形式上的改进,能够为教师授课和学生学习提供便利。

在本丛书的出版过程中,我们得到了国际教育出版机构同行们在版权方面的协助和教辅材料方面的支持。国内诸多著名高校的专家学者、一线教师,更是在繁重的教学和科研任务之余,为我们承担了图书的推荐、评审和翻译工作;正是每一位推荐者和评审者的国际化视野和专业眼光，帮助我们书海拾慧，汇集了各学科的前沿和经典；正是每一位译者的全心投入和细致校译，保证了经典内容的准确传达和最佳呈现。此外，来自广大读者的反馈既是对我们莫大的肯定和鼓舞，也总能让我们找到提升的空间。本丛书凝聚了上述各方的心血和智慧，在此，谨对他们的热忱帮助和卓越贡献深表谢意！

　　"千淘万漉虽辛苦，吹尽狂沙始到金。"在图书市场竞争日趋激烈的今天，北京大学出版社始终秉承"教材优先，学术为本"的宗旨，把精品教材的建设作为一项长期的事业。尽管其中会有探索，有坚持，有舍弃，但我们深信，经典必将长远传承，并历久弥新。我们的事业也需要您的热情参与！在此，诚邀各位专家学者和一线教师为我们推荐优秀的经济管理图书（em@pup.cn），并期待来自广大读者的批评和建议。您的需要始终是我们为之努力的目标方向，您的支持是激励我们不断前行的动力源泉！让我们共同引进经典，传播智慧，为提升中国经济管理教育的国际化水平做出贡献！

北京大学出版社

经济与管理图书事业部

关 于 本 书

适用对象

本书适合作为"审计学"课程本科生或硕士生的教材,也可以作为对审计领域相关知识感兴趣的业界人士或一般读者的参考读物。

内容简介

当下,审计环境在持续不断地变化着,而大学毕业生在参加实际工作前要具备高度的专业水平。《审计:以风险导向法实施高质量审计》(第9版)包含最新的专业指导,并涵盖详细的审计准则和最新的 PCAOB 准则。该书还讨论了 COSO 的最新《内部控制——整合框架》,而且对舞弊风险的探讨贯穿全书。总之,该书能够帮助学生理解变化的全球环境下全方面的审计事项。

主要特色

- 加强和整合对审计质量的讨论,并在各章强调舞弊调查的重要性。
- 涉及交易循环的各章(第九章至第十三章)基于一个统一的框架,以使读者有整体概念。
- 章末习题丰富且全面更新,从易到难,实用性更强。

本版更新

- 全书更新了 AICPA 和 IAASB 的所有审计标准。读者将会学习到最新的审计准则和实践。
- 第二章加强了对舞弊风险的介绍,以后各章也对这一重点问题不断强化。
- 第三章更新了与财务报告内部控制有关的内容。
- 全书强调审计质量,以第一章介绍的《审计质量框架》(*Audit Quality Framework*)为主线,并在第十四章进行了总结。

教辅资源

本书配套的教辅资源包括教师手册、PPT 课件、试题库软件。教师请填写并反馈书后的教辅资料申请表,以获得相关教辅资源的下载权限。

改编说明

在第9版中,我们根据教学需要,删除了原书第八章、第十六章、第十七章的内容,部分习题以及附录内容。读者可基于本书内容,自行扩展阅读。感谢中央财经大学会计学院曹强副教授为本书提供了审慎而细致的改编方案和中文注释。欢迎广大读者在使用中提出意见和建议。

简 明 目 录

Dedication

We dedicate this book to our families who encourage and support us through many hours of development, to our students who inspire us to always improve, to our mentors who guide us, to our professional friends who continue to educate us, and to our colleagues who challenge us.

KARLA M. JOHNSTONE
AUDREY A. GRAMLING
LARRY E. RITTENBERG

BRIEF CONTENTS

CONTENTS

CHAPTER 2

The Risk of Fraud and Mechanisms to Address Fraud: Regulation, Corporate Governance, and Audit Quality, 31

CHAPTER 3

Internal Control over Financial Reporting: Management's Responsibilities and Importance to the External Auditors, 67

CHAPTER 4

Professional Liability and the Need for Quality Auditor Judgments and Ethical Decisions, 109

CHAPTER 5

Professional Auditing Standards and the Audit Opinion Formulation Process,   149

CHAPTER 8

Specialized Audit Tools: Sampling and Generalized Audit Software (本章删除)

CHAPTER 9

Auditing the Revenue Cycle, 299

CHAPTER **12**

Auditing Long-Lived Assets: Acquisition, Use,
Impairment, and Disposal,   477

CHAPTER 14

Activities Required in Completing a Quality Audit, 537

Audit Reports on Internal Control Over Financial Reporting, 620

CHAPTER 16

Advanced Topics Concerning Complex Auditing Judgments (本章删除)

CHAPTER 17

Other Services Provided by Audit Firms (本章删除)

The auditing environment continues to change in dramatic ways, and university graduates entering the profession must be prepared for a high standard of responsibility. Here are only three examples of these changes:

- The American Institute of Certified Public Accountants (AICPA) and the International Auditing and Assurance Standards Board (IAASB) have issued clarifications that harmonize auditing standards in the United States (for nonpublic entities) and internationally.
- The Committee of Sponsoring Organizations (COSO) of the Treadway Commission has issued an updated *Internal Control–Integrated Framework*.
- The AICPA recently issued new audit sampling guidance.

The ninth edition of *Auditing: A Risk-Based Approach to Conducting a Quality Audit* represents the most up-to-date professional guidance available, and reflects the clarified auditing standards and the newest PCAOB standards. It discusses COSO's updated *Internal Control–Integrated Framework* and integrates discussions of fraud risk throughout the textbook. In short, the ninth edition helps students understand the full range of auditing issues in the evolving global environment.

Just as significantly, the ninth edition features entirely new and significantly revised end-of-chapter materials that have been developed to help students prepare for exams and understand real-life auditing scenarios. This material is updated, streamlined, and user friendly, with each problem linked to a specific learning objective. In addition, students will gain valuable experience by using the professional ACL auditing software that is packaged with each new textbook.

Revision Themes of the Ninth Edition

1. **Enhance and integrate discussion of audit quality and the importance of fraud detection throughout all chapters.** Many instructors indicate that they support an increased focus of the ninth edition on audit quality. And fraud detection is a recurring theme of importance among auditing instructors. Accordingly, the authors **thoroughly revised Chapter 2** to focus on audit quality and the importance of fraud detection. Significant fraud-related

material from the eighth edition's Chapter 9 was moved to Chapter 2, which enables the early introduction of this topic and allows for integration of the topic of fraud throughout the chapters dealing with audit risk, audit evidence, and auditing specific cycles. Moreover, the authors introduced the Financial Reporting Council's *Audit Quality Framework* in Chapter 1. Elements of this framework are applied throughout subsequent chapters of the textbook, with particular focus continuing in the chapter on completing the audit (Chapter 14). Finally, a section of each relevant chapter includes a new fraud-related discussion with both U.S. and international examples and applications.

2. **Implement a unifying framework for the chapters containing transaction cycles to provide users with a big picture perspective (Chapters 9–13).** Each chapter covering one of the primary transaction cycles has been restructured and contains a unifying framework to address key audit activities. This unifying framework is initially introduced in Chapter 5. The activities comprising the framework include identifying significant accounts, disclosures, and relevant assertions; identifying and assessing inherent risks, fraud risks, and control risks; using preliminary analytical procedures to identify possible material misstatement; determining appropriate responses to identified risks of material misstatement; determining appropriate tests of controls and considering results of tests of controls; and determining and applying sufficient appropriate substantive audit procedures.

3. **Restructure and streamline end-of-chapter materials.** The end-of-chapter materials have been thoroughly updated and streamlined to be much more user friendly. They are organized into the following categories: True-False Questions, Multiple-Choice Questions, Review and Short Case Questions, Contemporary and Historical Cases. Further, each end-of-chapter item is linked to a specific learning objective identified at the beginning of the chapter.

4. **Appropriately balance increased international focus.** A significant number of auditing instructors plan to increase coverage of international auditing standards and practices as U.S. and international standards converge. However, an equally large number of instructors counsel caution, saying that until the standards converge they will continue to moderate their international coverage. In response to these diverse opinions, the authors include more cases, examples, and descriptions of frauds containing international coverage, and they have updated coverage of international auditing standards. All the while, the revised textbook continues with extensive coverage of U.S. trends in standards and practices.

New, Revised, and Enhanced Ninth Edition

The ninth edition reflects the evolving nature of the auditing profession and the environment in which it operates.

New: Incorporates all AICPA and IAASB clarified auditing standards. Users of the ninth edition can be sure that they will be fully up-to-date in all auditing rules and practices. The textbook has been significantly revised to reflect the clarified standards.

Revised: Advanced topics in Chapter 16 concerning complex audit judgments. This revised Chapter 16 covers a variety of important, complex audit judgments, including determining materiality; resolving detected financial statement misstatements; distinguishing between material weaknesses and significant deficiencies in internal control; assessing the quality of a client's internal audit function; identifying and describing concepts of fair value and impairment, including goodwill impairment; and considering approaches to auditing significant management estimates.

Revised: **Emphasis on internal control.** A newly revised Chapter 3 discusses the importance of internal control to quality reporting and auditing and provides complete coverage of the *Committee of Sponsoring Organizations* of the *Treadway Commission's* updated *Internal Control–Integrated Framework* issued in 2013.

Enhanced: **Emphasis on fraud.** A newly revised Chapter 2 introduces the topic of fraud very early in the textbook, and this important topic is emphasized in relevant chapters and their end-of-chapter materials throughout the textbook. Chapter 2 covers the risk of fraud and mechanisms to address fraud, including regulation, corporate governance, and audit quality.

Enhanced: **Emphasis on audit quality.** As reflected in the new subtitle, the ninth edition focuses on *audit quality*, including the determinants of audit quality that are introduced through the Financial Reporting Council's *Audit Quality Framework* in Chapter 1. This edition applies elements of this framework throughout selected chapters, with a particular focus in Chapter 14 on completing the audit.

Enhanced: **Research analysis problems.** Because academic research yields insights on auditor decisions, the end-of-chapter materials in the ninth edition provide at least one problem related to an academic research paper addressing a relevant topic. Each research analysis problem requires the student to obtain an identified research paper, read it, and answer a set of uniform questions tied to the chapter's topics. These activities help students link the topical theory of the chapter with relevant contemporary academic research. The new research analysis problems are ideal for instructors who wish to extend students' theoretical understanding of the chapter concepts, particularly for graduate-level classes. Academic research articles have been selected that are approachable to students and yet highlight the complexities in the real practice of auditing. These research analysis problems address the recommendation of the recent report from the Pathways Commission to embed academic research into learning experiences for all accounting students.

Hallmark Pedagogical Features

Continued emphasis on professional skepticism. This emphasis provides students with the tools to learn how to apply the concept of professional skepticism. This textbook contains an introduction to this topic in Chapter 1 as well as in end-of-chapter materials throughout the textbook. This emphasis helps students see the practical application of this concept.

Continued emphasis on professional judgment. In addition to the focus on professional judgment in this textbook, numerous exercises emphasize this key auditing skill, including analyses of Ford and Toyota's SEC filings and proxy statements. Further, this textbook contains end-of-chapter materials to help ensure that students understand the link between mandatory financial reporting and auditing, risk assessment, transaction cycles, and analytical procedures.

Professional Judgment in Context feature. Each chapter opens with a real-life example from practice that illustrates the judgments involved in auditing. The examples tie to the learning objectives in the chapter and address important topics such as fraud, regulation, audit quality, and internal control. The following provides an example from Chapter 1.

PROFESSIONAL JUDGMENT IN CONTEXT

The Importance of Conducting a Quality Audit and Complying with Professional Standards

On December 20, 2011, the Public Company Accounting Oversight Board (PCAOB) revoked the ability of Bentleys Brisbane Partnership (an external audit firm) to audit public company audits, and the Board imposed a monetary penalty of $10,000 on Robert Forbes, the audit partner in charge of the audit of Alloy Steel International. These penalties were imposed because the PCAOB concluded that Bentleys and Forbes failed to exercise due professional care (a standard of care expected to be demonstrated by a competent auditing professional), failed to exercise professional skepticism (an attitude that includes a questioning mind and critical assessment of audit evidence), and failed to obtain sufficient evidence necessary to issue an audit opinion on the financial statements of Alloy Steel's 2006 fiscal year end financial statements. The PCAOB also concluded that Bentleys violated PCAOB quality control standards because the firm did not develop policies to ensure that the work performed by its personnel met PCAOB auditing standards and the Board said that the firm did not undertake audits that the firm could reasonably expect to be completed with professional competence.

Alloy Steel International is an American company headquartered in Malaga, Australia. Alloy's stock was traded on the Over the Counter (OTC) Bulletin Board and as such was subject to Securities and Exchange Commission (SEC) rules and requirements. Its auditors were subject to PCAOB rules and requirements. On the audit of Alloy, Bentleys and Forbes made a number of critical quality control mistakes. Bentleys and Forbes used an unregistered audit firm in Australia to actually perform the audit work, rather than performing the audit work themselves. Bentleys' and Forbes' involvement on the engagement was limited to reviewing the unregistered audit firm's workpapers. The unregistered audit firm's personnel had no training or experience in conducting audits that complied with PCAOB standards. Despite these factors, Bentleys and Forbes issued and signed an unqualified audit report on Alloy's 2006 financial statements. For further information about this scenario, see PCAOB disciplinary proceedings in Release No. 105-2011-007.

As you read through this chapter, consider the following questions:

- What is the objective of auditing, and what process should auditors follow to accomplish this objective? (LO 1)
- Why do companies obtain audited financial statements? (LO 1)
- Who are the users of audited financial statements? (LO 1)
- What skills and knowledge are needed to be a competent audit professional? (LO 3)
- Why is it vital to perform an audit in a quality manner? (LO 5)
- Why are low quality audits, like those performed in this case, harmful? (LO 5)

Professional decision-making and ethical decision-making frameworks. Decision-making frameworks, complete with a chapter-opening Professional Judgment in Context feature, require students to think about real-life professional and ethical decisions associated with that chapter. End-of-chapter materials continue the use of these professional and ethical decision-making frameworks to help students address contemporary issues.

Continued emphasis on the audit opinion formulation process to help organize study. A chapter-opening *Audit Opinion Formulation Process* figure helps students identify the major phases in the audit process and see how those steps within that process relate to specific chapters.

This textbook describes how auditors go through a structured judgment process to issue an audit opinion. This process is referred to as the *Audit Opinion Formulation Process*, and it serves as the foundation for this textbook. The process consists of five phases. **Phase I** concerns client acceptance and continuance. Once a client is accepted (or the audit firm decides to continue to provide services to a client), the auditor needs to perform risk assessment procedures to thoroughly understand the client's business (or update prior knowledge in the case of a continuing client), its industry, its competition, and its management and governance processes (including internal controls) to determine the likelihood that financial accounts might be materially misstated (**Phase II**). In some audits, the auditor also obtains evidence about internal control operating effectiveness through testing those controls (**Phase III**). Much of what most people think of as auditing, the obtaining of substantive evidence about accounts, disclosures, and assertions occurs in **Phase IV**. The information gathered in Phases I through III greatly influences the amount of testing to be performed in Phase IV. Finally, in **Phase V**, the auditor completes the audit and makes a decision about what type of audit report to issue.

Also fundamental to students' understanding is the framework's inclusion of the auditing profession, fraud, regulation, corporate governance, and audit quality. Further fundamentals highlighted in the *Audit Opinion Formulation Process* include discussion of professional liability and the need for quality audit judgments and ethical decisions, as depicted below.

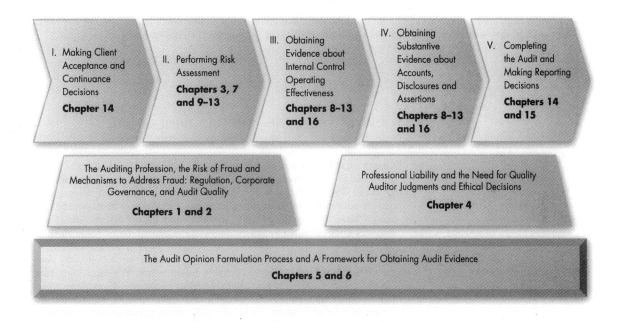

Auditing in Practice **features and chapter exhibits.** Each chapter contains multiple *Auditing in Practice* features and exhibits that highlight important, relevant, and practical examples and information related to chapter topics. Selected end-of-chapter materials require students to review these features and exhibits to answer related questions. Below is an example of an *Auditing in Practice* feature from Chapter 1.

Why Is Owning Stock in an Audit Client Unacceptable?

In 2005, Susan Birkert was an audit senior working for KPMG on the audit engagement of Comtech Corporation. One of Susan's friends asked her whether she thought that Comtech stock was a good investment. She responded that, indeed, it was a good investment. At that point, her friend asked if she would like him to purchase Comtech stock on her behalf. She agreed, and gave her friend $5,000 to make the purchase under his name rather than hers. She did so because she was aware that owning stock in one's audit client is not allowed because of independence concerns. If auditors own stock in their audit clients, they are not independent of their clients because they are part owners. Therefore, rather than acting in an unbiased manner during the conduct of the audit, they might make judgments that favor the

client company rather than external users of the financial statements. Even if the auditor does not actually behave in a biased manner and is independent in fact, external users may *perceive* an independence conflict—the auditor would not be independent in appearance.

Susan continued working on the Comtech engagement well into 2006, and she lied when she responded to KPMG's yearly written requirements to comply with the firm's independence policies. Prompted by an anonymous tip later in 2006, KPMG launched an internal investigation into the matter and terminated her employment. The PCAOB barred her from serving as an external auditor for a period of at least one year. For further details on this case, see PCAOB Release No. 105-2007-003.

Organization of the Ninth Edition

The ninth edition is organized as follows:

Chapters 1 and 2: A Foundational Understanding of the Role of Auditing as Integral to the Economy; Implications of Fraud; *and* The Importance of Regulation, Corporate Governance, and Audit Quality. Chapters 1 and 2 provide the foundation for students to understand the economic context in which external auditing exists. Chapter 1 defines the objective of external auditing and describes its role in meeting society's demands for reliable financial and internal control information. Chapter 1 identifies parties involved in preparing and auditing financial statements, lists the types of audit service providers, identifies organizations that affect the external auditing profession, defines audit quality and introduces the Financial Reporting Council's *Audit Quality Framework*, and identifies professional requirements that help to achieve high quality and minimize auditor exposure to lawsuits. Chapter 2 defines the types of fraud and the fraud triangle, describes examples of recent financial reporting frauds, explains the findings of the third COSO report on fraud, discusses users' expectations of auditors' fraud-related responsibilities, explains how the requirements of the Sarbanes-Oxley Act of 2002 reflect frauds perpetrated in the late 1990s and early 2000s, and defines corporate governance and identifies parties involved in corporate governance.

Chapter 3: Internal Control over Financial Reporting: Management's Responsibilities and Importance to the External Auditors. Chapter 3 articulates the importance of internal control over financial reporting, defines management's responsibility related to internal control, defines internal control as presented in COSO's updated *Internal Control–Integrated Framework*, identifies and describes the components and principles of internal control as presented in that framework, identifies management's responsibilities related to documenting internal control over financial reporting, and describes management's responsibility to evaluate and report on internal controls.

Chapter 4. Professional Liability and the Need for Quality Auditor Judgments and Ethical Decisions. Chapter 4 discusses the liability environment in which auditors operate and explores the effects of lawsuits on audit firms; lists laws from which auditor liability is derived; and describes possible causes of action, remedies or sanctions, and auditor defenses under both common and statutory law. **Chapter 4** also articulates frameworks for making quality professional and ethical decisions and illustrates how to apply these frameworks in selected audit settings. Finally, **Chapter 4** describes and applies the IESBA's Code of Ethics and the AICPA's Code of Professional Conduct.

Chapter 5. Professional Auditing Standards and the Audit Opinion Formulation Process. Chapter 5 identifies and compares the various auditing standards, discusses the foundational principles underlying the auditing standards, lists the phases and related activities in the audit opinion formulation process, explains the concept of accounting cycles, describes the assertions that are inherent to financial statements, defines audit evidence and the purpose and types of audit procedures used to obtain audit evidence, and discusses the importance of audit documentation.

Chapter 6. A Framework for Audit Evidence. Chapter 6 discusses the importance of the evidence concepts of sufficiency and appropriateness, identifies factors affecting the sufficiency and appropriateness of audit evidence, illustrates professional judgments about the type and timing of audit procedures, discusses the use and application of substantive analytical procedures, identifies issues relating to audit evidence needed for accounts involving management estimates, and discusses issues involving specialists and related-party transactions. **Chapter 6** also describes the characteristics of quality audit documentation and explains the nature, design, and purposes of audit programs.

Chapter 7. Planning the Audit: Identifying and Responding to the Risks of Material Misstatement. Chapter 7 defines the concept of *material misstatement* and discusses the importance of materiality judgments in the audit context. **Chapter 7** also identifies the risks of material misstatement and describes how they relate to audit risk and detection risk. **Chapter 7** illustrates the use of preliminary analytical procedures and brainstorming to identify areas of heightened risk of material misstatement, along with describing how auditors respond to assessed risks of material misstatement.

Chapter 8. Specialized Audit Tools: Sampling and Generalized Audit Software. Chapter 8 conveys all the new terminology and approaches recommended in the AICPA's 2012 sampling guidance. **Chapter 8** describes how auditors use sampling and generalized audit software, explains the objectives of sampling for testing controls and account balances, compares and contrasts nonstatistical and statistical sampling, describes attribute sampling, describes the sampling process used to gather evidence about misstatements in account balances and assertions, describes monetary unit sampling, and explains how to use generalized audit software to automate the audit process.

Chapters 9–13. Performing Audits Using the Transaction Cycle Approach: Revenue; Cash and Marketable Securities; Inventory, Goods and Services, and Accounts Payable; Long-Lived Assets; *and* **Debt Obligations and Stockholders' Equity Transactions. Chapters 9–13** focus on the application of concepts developed earlier for assessing risk, identifying and testing controls designed to address those risks, and using substantive approaches to testing account balances. Each chapter contains topic-relevant discussion of identifying significant accounts, disclosures, and relevant assertions; identifying and assessing inherent risks, fraud risks, and control risks; using preliminary analytical procedures to identify possible material misstatement; determining appropriate responses to identified risks of material misstatement; determining appropriate tests of controls and considering results of tests of controls; and determining and applying sufficient appropriate substantive audit procedures.

Chapters 14–15. Activities Required in Completing a Quality Audit *and* **Audit Reporting Decisions. Chapter 14** discusses numerous tasks that are conducted as part of completing the audit. These include reviewing activities relating to detected misstatements, loss contingencies, accounting estimates, disclosure adequacy, noncompliance with laws or regulations, going-concern considerations, analytical review, management representations, subsequent events, omitted audit procedures, and engagement quality review; audit committee and management communications; and issues relating to audit firm portfolio management (client acceptance and continuance decisions), audit partner rotation, and audit firm rotation. Once these activities are completed, the auditor makes a reporting decision, which is described in **Chapter 15**. This chapter identifies the principles underlying audit reporting on financial statements, describes the information that is included in a standard unqualified audit report, and describes financial statements requiring the following report modifications: unqualified audit report with explanatory language, qualified report, adverse report, and a disclaimer of opinion. **Chapter 15** also describes the information that is included in a standard unqualified audit report on internal control over financial reporting and identifies the appropriate audit report modifications for situations requiring other than an unqualified report on internal control over financial reporting.

Chapter 16. Advanced Topics Concerning Complex Auditing Judgments. Chapter 16 discusses the nature and types of complex judgments that permeate audit engagements and identifies complex audit judgments based on a review of a company's financial statements. **Chapter 16** describes a process for making judgments about materiality and assessing whether misstatements are material. It also describes audit considerations for long-term liabilities involving subjectivity, merger and acquisition activities, and assessing management's fair value estimates and related impairment judgments. It describes audit considerations for financial instruments, distinguishing between material weaknesses and significant deficiencies in internal control over financial reporting, and understanding and evaluating the client's internal audit function.

Chapter 17. Other Services Provided by Audit Firms. Chapter 17 describes other services provided by audit firms. This chapter explains review and compilation engagements, procedures and reporting requirements for providing assurance on interim financial information, special considerations for unique financial statement audit situations, and attestation engagements. **Chapter 17** also discusses forensic accounting and distinguishes between forensic accounting and auditing. Finally, **Chapter 17** describes sustainability reporting and articulates the auditor's role in providing assurance on management sustainability reports.

Supplements

CengageBrain. Instructors and students can find most of the textbook's support materials online at CengageBrain (www.cengagebrain.com), including the solutions manual, PowerPoint slides, ACL data spreadsheet files, and other resources.

Solutions Manual. The Solutions Manual contains the solutions to all end-of-chapter assignments. It is available on the instructor's page at www.cengagebrain.com and may be ordered in print form using this ISBN number.

ISBN-13: 9781133962281

PowerPoint Slides: Instructors can bring their lectures to life with engaging PowerPoint slides that are interesting, visually stimulating, and paced for student comprehension. These slides are ideal as lecture tools and provide a clear guide for student study and note-taking. PowerPoint slides are downloadable by chapter on the instructor's page at www.cengagebrain.com

ExamView Computerized Testing Software: This easy-to-use test-creation program contains all questions from the Test Bank, making it simple to customize tests to instructors' specific class needs as they edit or create questions and store customized exams. This is an ideal tool for online testing. This software is available only on the Instructor's Resource CD.

ISBN-13: 9781133962311

Test Bank in Word: A proven Test Bank features the questions instructors need to efficiently assess students' comprehension. These files are available along with the ExamView on the Instructor's Resource CD. These files are not accessible on the textbook Web site for security reasons.

Example Syllabi. The authors' syllabi for this edition of the textbook are available at the instructor's page at www.cengagebrain.com. These may be helpful to instructors as they consider alternative ways to use the textbook and alternative presentation formats for the syllabi. Instructors should feel free to update these to individual uses.

ACKNOWLEDGMENTS

We are grateful to members of the staff at Cengage Learning for their help in developing the ninth edition: Sharon Oblinger, acquisitions editor; Craig Avery, senior developmental editor; Kristen Hurd, senior brand manager; and Natalie Livingston, senior market development manager; Joseph Malcolm, content project manager; Stacy Shirley, art director; and A.J. Smiley, editorial assistant.

We are appreciative of LuAnn Bean (Florida Institute of Technology), Jason McGregor (Baylor University), and Amy Sue Sexton (Morehead State University) for their work on the ExamView test bank. We thank Sean Dennis and Kara Obermire (both at the University of Wisconsin) for their assistance with revisions to the academic research cases and the ACL case. We are again grateful to our students and to the instructors who have used the previous editions and have given their thoughtful feedback. We appreciate the assistance of Monica Weaver in helping us integrate new examples, exhibits, and features into this edition.

The following instructors provided invaluable feedback to the publisher, and we wish to thank them for their insights:

George R. Aldhizer, III, Wake Forest University
Erick O. Bell, University of San Francisco
Katherine Boswell, University of Louisiana at Monroe
Barry Bryan, Southern Methodist University
Susan R. Cockrell, Austin Peay State University
Frank Daroca, Loyola Marymount University
Roger S. Debreceny, University of Hawai'i at Manoa
Todd DeZoort, The University of Alabama
Magdy Farag, California State Polytechnic University, Pomona
Bill Fowler, Abilene Christian University

Marvin Gordon, Northwestern University
Carl W. Hollingsworth, Clemson University
Mary Jepperson, College of Saint Benedict/Saint John's University
Mary Lewis Haley, Cumberland University
Ralph D. Licastro, The Pennsylvania State University
Jason MacGregor, Baylor University
Brian W. Mayhew, University of Wisconsin
Paul H. Mihalek, Central Connecticut State University
Michael J. Miller, Sullivan University
Andreas Nicolaou, Bowling Green State University
D. Robert Okopny, Eastern Michigan University
Denise M. Patterson, California State University, Fresno
Marshall K. Pitman, University of Texas at San Antonio

Lydia Radnik, University of North Texas
Michael A. Ridenour Jr., Pennsylvania State University–Fayette
Cindy Seipel, New Mexico State University
Amy Sexton, Morehead State University
Mike Shapeero, Bloomsburg University of Pennsylvania
Joel M. Strong, St. Cloud State University

Judy A. Thomas, Columbia College of Missouri
Jerry L. Turner, Texas Christian University
Michael Ulinski, Pace University
Kelly Ann Ulto, Fordham University
Donna L. Whitten, Purdue University North Central
Jeffrey Wong, University of Nevada, Reno
Laura M. Zellers, Wichita State University

We are very grateful to ACL Services, Ltd., for permission to distribute its software and tutorials and for permission to reprint related images.

Karla M. Johnstone
Audrey A. Gramling
Larry E. Rittenberg

ABOUT THE AUTHORS

KARLA M. JOHNSTONE

Karla M. Johnstone, PhD, CPA, is a Professor of Accounting and Information Systems at the University of Wisconsin Madison School of Business. She teaches auditing, and her research investigates auditor decision making, including auditors' client acceptance and continuance decisions, how fraud risk and fraud brainstorming affects audit planning and audit fees, client–auditor negotiation, and audit budget-setting processes. She has also published various articles on accounting curriculum effectiveness. Professor Johnstone serves on the editorial boards of several academic journals and is active in the Auditing Section of the American Accounting Association (AAA), currently serving on the Executive Committee in the role of Treasurer. She has worked as a corporate accountant and as a staff auditor, and she was a doctoral fellow in residence at Coopers & Lybrand.

AUDREY A. GRAMLING

Audrey A. Gramling, PhD, CPA, CIA, is the Fr. Raymond J. Treece Endowed Chair and Accounting Department Professor and Chair at Bellarmine University. Professor Gramling's research investigates both internal and external auditing issues, with a focus on decision behavior of auditors, external auditor independence, internal control reporting, and other factors affecting the market for audit and assurance services. Prior to earning her PhD at the University of Arizona, Professor Gramling worked as an external auditor at a predecessor firm of Deloitte and as an internal auditor at Georgia Institute of Technology. She has also served a one-year appointment as an Academic Accounting Fellow in the Office of the Chief Accountant at the U.S. Securities and Exchange Commission. She is the past President of the Auditing Section of the AAA and has served in an advisory role to the COSO.

LARRY E. RITTENBERG

Larry E. Rittenberg, PhD, CPA, CIA, is Professor Emeritus, Department of Accounting and Information Systems, at the University of Wisconsin, Madison, where he taught courses in auditing, risk management, and corporate governance. He is also Chair Emeritus of the COSO of the Treadway Commission, where he has provided oversight of the development of the COSO Enterprise Risk Management Framework as well as the COSO Guidance for Smaller Businesses. He has served as Vice-Chair of Professional Practices for the Institute of Internal Auditors

(IIA) and President of the IIA Research Foundation; and has been a member of the Auditing Standards Committee of the AAA Auditing Section, the AICPA's Computer Audit Subcommittee, the Information Technology Committee, and the NACD Blue Ribbon Commission on Audit Committees; and Vice-President and Treasurer of the AAA. He is a member of an audit committee, the board, and the governance committee of Woodward Governor, a publicly traded company, and has consulted on audit committee, risk, and control issues with the largest public company in China. More recently, he has been named as one of the seven members of the International Oversight Council for Professional Practice of the IIA. Professor Rittenberg served as Staff Auditor for Ernst & Young and has coauthored five books and monographs and numerous articles.

Recommendations from Instructors Who Have Used This Textbook

"I selected this textbook because I believe that it presents a realistic approach to the integrated audit. Having worked with several of the Global Seven firms, it is evident to me that the authors have been diligent in writing a book that mirrors the risk-based approach to the audit. In addition, my students have enjoyed outstanding success on the AUD Exam having used this text as their primary study resource."

Professor Barry J. Bryan
Southern Methodist University

"I have used [this] text for four years now and it has been an outstanding resource for teaching my students the fundamentals of contemporary auditing. Text discussions and end-of-chapter applications help me to develop students' critical analysis and judgment skills, sensitivity and responses to ethical dilemmas, and understanding and appreciation of the essential role of professional skepticism in auditing.... My impression based on use of successive editions of the text is that the authors have worked very hard to ensure it is up-to-date as auditing standards and related guidance evolve and audit-relevant events occur in the rapidly-changing business environment. Without reservation, I highly recommend this text."

Professor Tim Bell
University of North Florida

"As a former auditor and current audit professor, I find the book very easy to follow and well written. The content is organized in a similar fashion to the audit process itself, which I think is essential for students' understanding. The authors also include topics that I have not found in any other auditing textbook (e.g., an entire chapter on corporate governance, sections on upcoming changes or changes soon to be integrated into the profession). This textbook simply *feels* more up to date about current events in auditing."

Professor Kim Westermann
Florida International University

"This textbook hits the sweet spot of the bat! As far as I am concerned it hits a home run! Not too complex yet not too simple, the right amount of standards presentation/explanation then a great example to illustrate the standard in the real world. This textbook is well organized and presents the materials and issues as an auditor would confront them in an actual audit. I like the inclusion of ACL on the disc that accompanies the book. The ACL materials are presented in such a manner that tech savvy students can do the assignments with a minimum of instruction."

Professor Douglas E. Ziegenfuss
Old Dominion University

Auditing: Integral to the Economy

CHAPTER OVERVIEW AND LEARNING OBJECTIVES

Capital markets depend on reliable information about organizations. This information provides a basis for making many types of decisions, including investing and lending decisions. If the capital markets do not receive reliable information, investors and others lose confidence in the system, make poor decisions, and may lose a great deal of money. The external auditing profession helps enhance the reliability of information throughout the capital markets. Individual external auditors are asked to make professional and ethical judgments about the information provided by business organizations. Professional judgment and the processes used to make such judgments are critical to the usefulness of the external audit profession and to individual auditors as they conduct quality audits.

Through studying this chapter, you will be able to achieve these learning objectives:

通过本章的学习，你将能够实现以下学习目标：

1. Define the objective of external auditing and describe its role in meeting society's demands for reliable financial and internal control information.

   明确外部审计的目标，描述外部审计如何满足社会对可靠财务与内部控制信息的需求。

2. Identify parties involved in preparing and auditing financial statements and briefly describe their roles.

   识别参与编制和审计财务报表的各方，简要描述它们的作用。

3. List the types of audit service providers and the skills and knowledge needed by professionals entering the external auditing profession.

   列示出审计服务提供者的类型和从事外部审计职业所需的知识和技能。

4. Identify organizations that affect the external auditing profession and the nature of their effects.

   识别影响外部审计职业的组织和这些组织影响的性质。

5. Define audit quality and identify drivers of audit quality as specified by the Financial Reporting Council's *Audit Quality Framework*.

   明确审计质量的含义，识别财务报告委员会《审计质量框架》中具体说明的审计质量驱动因素。

6. Identify professional requirements that help to achieve audit quality and minimize auditor exposure to lawsuits.

   识别能够帮助注册会计师实现审计质量并最小化诉讼风险的专业要求。

On December 20, 2011, the Public Company Accounting Oversight Board (PCAOB) revoked the ability of Bentleys Brisbane Partnership (an external audit firm) to audit public company audits, and the Board imposed a monetary penalty of $10,000 on Robert Forbes, the audit partner in charge of the audit of Alloy Steel International. These penalties were imposed because the PCAOB concluded that Bentleys and Forbes failed to exercise **due professional care** (a standard of care expected to be demonstrated by a competent auditing professional), failed to exercise **professional skepticism** (an attitude that includes a questioning mind and critical assessment of audit evidence), and failed to obtain sufficient evidence necessary to issue an audit opinion on the financial statements of Alloy Steel's 2006 fiscal year end financial statements. The PCAOB also concluded that Bentleys violated PCAOB quality control standards because the firm did not develop policies to ensure that the work performed by its personnel met PCAOB auditing standards and the Board said that the firm did not undertake audits that the firm could reasonably expect to be completed with professional competence.

Alloy Steel International is an American company headquartered in Malaga, Australia. Alloy's stock was traded on the Over the Counter (OTC) Bulletin Board and as such was subject to Securities and Exchange Commission (SEC) rules and requirements. Its auditors were subject to PCAOB rules and requirements. On the audit of Alloy, Bentleys and Forbes made a number of critical quality control mistakes. Bentleys and Forbes used an unregistered audit firm in Australia to actually perform the audit work, rather than performing the audit work themselves. Bentleys' and Forbes' involvement on the engagement was limited to reviewing the unregistered audit firm's workpapers. The unregistered audit firm's personnel had no training or experience in conducting audits that complied with PCAOB standards. Despite these factors, Bentleys and Forbes issued and signed an unqualified audit report on Alloy's 2006 financial statements. For further information about this scenario, see PCAOB disciplinary proceedings in Release No. 105-2011-007.

As you read through this chapter, consider the following questions:

- What is the objective of auditing, and what process should auditors follow to accomplish this objective? (LO 1)
- Why do companies obtain audited financial statements? (LO 1)
- Who are the users of audited financial statements? (LO 1)
- What skills and knowledge are needed to be a competent audit professional? (LO 3)
- Why is it vital to perform an audit in a quality manner? (LO 5)
- Why are low quality audits, like those performed in this case, harmful? (LO 5)

Overview of the External Auditing Profession

Introduction to the External Auditing Profession

A **financial statement audit** is a:

> systematic process of objectively obtaining and evaluating evidence regarding assertions about economic actions and events to ascertain the degree of correspondence between those assertions and established criteria; and communicating the results to interested users.[1]

The external auditing profession performs a unique task. While managers create the financial statements and design internal control systems, the objective of external auditing is to provide opinions on the reliability of the financial statements and, as part of an **integrated audit**, provide opinions on internal control effectiveness. For external auditing to have value, the public

外部审计职业概述
外部审计职业介绍

LO 1 Define the objective of external auditing and describe its role in meeting society's demands for reliable financial and internal control information.

---

[1] Auditing Concepts Committee, "Report of the Committee on Basic Auditing Concepts," *The Accounting Review*, 47, Supp. (1972), 18.

needs to have confidence in the objectivity and accuracy of the opinions provided by external auditors.

A free-market economy can exist only if there is sharing of reliable information among parties that have an interest in the financial performance of an organization. The market is further strengthened if the information is transparent and unbiased—that is, the data is not presented in such a way that it favors one party over another. An organization's reported information must reflect the economics of its transactions and the current economic condition of both its assets and any obligations owed. The external audit is intended to enhance the confidence that users can place on management-prepared financial statements. When the auditor has no reservations about management's financial statements or internal controls, the report is referred to as an **unqualified audit report**. Such a report is shown in Exhibit 1.1. You will note in Exhibit 1.1 that the audit firm PricewaterhouseCoopers has provided two opinions. One opinion states that the audit firm believes that the financial statements of Ford are fairly stated. The other opinion states that PricewaterhouseCoopers believes that Ford's internal control over financial reporting was effective as of Ford's year end, December 31, 2011. PricewaterhouseCoopers was able to provide these opinions after going through a systematic process of objectively obtaining and evaluating sufficient appropriate evidence. If the auditor had reservations about the fair presentation of the financial statements, the audit report would be modified to explain the nature of the auditor's reservations (covered in Chapter 15). And if the auditor had reservations about the effectiveness of the client's internal controls, the auditor would issue an **adverse opinion** on internal controls.

外部审计：一个特殊的功能

External Auditing: A Special Function

External auditing is a "special function" as described by Chief Justice Warren Burger in a 1984 Supreme Court decision:

> By certifying the public reports that collectively depict a corporation's financial status, the independent auditor assumes a public responsibility transcending any employment relationship with the client. The independent public accountant performing this special function owes ultimate allegiance to the corporation's creditors and stockholders, as well as to the investing public. This "public watchdog" function demands ... complete fidelity to the public trust.[2]

Chief Justice Burger's statement captures the essence of the external auditing profession. Auditors serve a number of parties, but the most important is the public, as represented by investors, lenders, workers, and others who make decisions based on financial information about an organization. Auditing requires the highest level of technical competence, freedom from bias, and concern for the integrity of the financial reporting process. In essence, auditors should view themselves as guardians of the capital markets.

The public expects auditors to (a) find fraud, (b) require accounting principles that best portray the spirit of the concepts adopted by accounting standard setters, and (c) be independent of management. When it comes to being independent, auditors must not only be independent *in fact*, but they must act in a manner that ensures that they are independent *in appearance*. For example, if an audit partner's uncle was the CEO at the partner's client company, users could reasonably worry about a conflict of interest. It is entirely possible that the audit partner has, in fact, an independent mental attitude. However, the audit partner would not be independent in appearance in this scenario. Further complicating matters, consider that management and the audit committee expect cost-effective audits. Thus, the auditing profession faces many pressures—keeping fees down, making careful decisions regarding

---

[2] *United States v. Arthur Young & Co. et ah*, U.S. Supreme Court, No. 82-687 [52 U.S.L.W.4355 (U.S., Mar. 21, 1984)].

| EXHIBIT **1.1** | Integrated Audit Report |

REPORT OF INDEPENDENT REGISTERED AUDIT FIRM

To the Board of Directors and Stockholders of Ford Motor Company

In our opinion, the accompanying consolidated balance sheets and the related consolidated statements of operations, of equity and of cash flows present fairly, in all material respects, the financial position of Ford Motor Company and its subsidiaries at December 31, 2011 and December 31, 2010, and the results of their operations and their cash flows for each of the three years in the period ended December 31, 2011 in conformity with accounting principles generally accepted in the United States of America. In addition, in our opinion, the accompanying financial statement schedule presents fairly, in all material respects, the information set forth therein when read in conjunction with the related consolidated financial statements. Also in our opinion, the Company maintained, in all material respects, effective internal control over financial reporting as of December 31, 2011, based on criteria established in *Internal Control—Integrated Framework* issued by the Committee of Sponsoring Organizations of the Treadway Commission (COSO). The Company's management is responsible for these financial statements and the financial statement schedule, for maintaining effective internal control over financial reporting and for its assessment of the effectiveness of internal control over financial reporting, included in Management's Report on Internal Control over Financial Reporting appearing under Item 9A. Our responsibility is to express opinions on these financial statements and on the Company's internal control over financial reporting based on our integrated audits. We conducted our audits in accordance with the standards of the Public Company Accounting Oversight Board (United States). Those standards require that we plan and perform the audits to obtain reasonable assurance about whether the financial statements are free of material misstatement and whether effective internal control over financial reporting was maintained in all material respects. Our audits of the financial statements included examining, on a test basis, evidence supporting the amounts and disclosures in the financial statements, assessing the accounting principles used and significant estimates made by management, and evaluating the overall financial statement presentation. Our audit of internal control over financial reporting included obtaining an understanding of internal control over financial reporting, assessing the risk that a material weakness exists, and testing and evaluating the design and operating effectiveness of internal control based on the assessed risk. Our audits also included performing such other procedures as we considered necessary in the circumstances. We believe that our audits provide a reasonable basis for our opinions.

Our audits were conducted for the purpose of forming an opinion on the basic financial statements taken as a whole. The accompanying sector balance sheets and the related sector statements of operations and of cash flows are presented for purposes of additional analysis and are not a required part of the basic financial statements. Such information has been subjected to the auditing procedures applied in the audit of the basic financial statements and, in our opinion, is fairly stated in all material respects in relation to the basic financial statements taken as a whole.

A company's internal control over financial reporting is a process designed to provide reasonable assurance regarding the reliability of financial reporting and the preparation of financial statements for external purposes in accordance with generally accepted accounting principles. A company's internal control over financial reporting includes those policies and procedures that (i) pertain to the maintenance of records that, in reasonable detail, accurately and fairly reflect the transactions and dispositions of the assets of the company; (ii) provide reasonable assurance that transactions are recorded as necessary to permit preparation of financial statements in accordance with generally accepted accounting principles, and that receipts and expenditures of the company are being made only in accordance with authorizations of management and directors of the company; and (iii) provide reasonable assurance regarding prevention or timely detection of unauthorized acquisition, use, or disposition of the company's assets that could have a material effect on the financial statements.

Because of its inherent limitations, internal control over financial reporting may not prevent or detect misstatements. Also, projections of any evaluation of effectiveness to future periods are subject to the risk that controls may become inadequate because of changes in conditions, or that the degree of compliance with the policies or procedures may deteriorate.

PricewaterhouseCoopers LLP
Detroit, Michigan
February 21, 2012

Why Is Owning Stock in an Audit Client Unacceptable?

In 2005, Susan Birkert was an audit senior working for KPMG on the audit engagement of Comtech Corporation. One of Susan's friends asked her whether she thought that Comtech stock was a good investment. She responded that, indeed, it was a good investment. At that point, her friend asked if she would like him to purchase Comtech stock on her behalf. She agreed, and gave her friend $5,000 to make the purchase under his name rather than hers. She did so because she was aware that owning stock in one's audit client is not allowed because of independence concerns. If auditors own stock in their audit clients, they are not independent of their clients because they are part owners. Therefore, rather than acting in an unbiased manner during the conduct of the audit, they might make judgments that favor the client company rather than external users of the financial statements. Even if the auditor does not actually behave in a biased manner and is independent in fact, external users may *perceive* an independence conflict—the auditor would not be independent in appearance.

Susan continued working on the Comtech engagement well into 2006, and she lied when she responded to KPMG's yearly written requirements to comply with the firm's independence policies. Prompted by an anonymous tip later in 2006, KPMG launched an internal investigation into the matter and terminated her employment. The PCAOB barred her from serving as an external auditor for a period of at least one year. For further details on this case, see PCAOB Release No. 105-2007-003.

---

independence, and conducting a quality audit. The *Auditing in Practice* feature "Why Is Owning Stock in an Audit Client Unacceptable?" is an example of a situation in which a young auditor violated independence rules, leading to her being sanctioned by the PCAOB and being fired by her audit firm employer.

无偏报告和独立鉴证的
需求

The Need for Unbiased Reporting and Independent Assurance

Effective capital markets require quality financial reporting. An organization's financial statements should reflect a true and fair view of the organization's financial results. The statements should not favor one user over another. However, the interests of the various users can conflict. Current shareholders might want management to use accounting principles that result in higher levels of reported income, while lending institutions generally prefer a conservative approach to valuation and income recognition. Exhibit 1.2 presents an overview of potential financial statement users and the decisions they make based on the financial reports.

Why do financial statement users need independent assurance about information provided by management? Shouldn't the information provided by management be reliable? The need for independent assurance arises from several factors:

- *Potential bias*—Management has incentives to bias financial information in order to convey a better impression of the financial data than real circumstances might merit. For example, management's compensation may be tied to profitability or stock price, so managers may be tempted to "bend" GAAP to make the organization's performance look better.
- *Remoteness*—An organization and the users of its financial information are often remote from each other, both in terms of geographic distance and the extent of information available to the both parties. Most users cannot interview management, tour a company's plant, or review its financial records firsthand; instead, they must rely on financial statements to communicate the results of management's performance. This

EXHIBIT **1.2**	Users of Audited Financial Statements
User	**Types of Decisions**
Management	Review performance, make operational decisions, report results to capital markets
Stockholders	Buy or sell stock
Bondholders	Buy or sell bonds
Financial Institutions	Evaluate loan decisions, considering interest rates, terms, and risk
Taxing Authorities	Determine taxable income and tax due
Regulatory Agencies	Develop regulations and monitor compliance
Labor Unions	Make collective bargaining decisions
Court System	Assess the financial position of a company in litigation
Vendors	Assess credit risk
Retired Employees	Protect employees from surprises concerning pensions and other post-retirement benefits

can tempt management to keep information from users or bend GAAP so the organization looks better.

- *Complexity*—Transactions, information, and processing systems are often very complex, so it can be difficult to determine their proper presentation. This provides an opportunity for management to deceive users.
- *Consequences*—During the past decade, many financial statement users— pension funds, private investors, venture capitalists, and banks—lost billions of dollars because financial information had become unreliable. As an example, the factors leading up to, and the consequences of, unreliable information can be seen in the subprime mortgage crisis in the United States. Many borrowers did not provide correct information on their loan applications and lenders sometimes did not perform adequate due diligence in making lending decisions. Consequently, various financial statement users and others suffered significant losses. When financial information is not reliable, investors and other users lose a significant source of information that they need to make decisions that have important consequences.

These factors suggest a role for external auditors who are independent. Independence requires objectivity and freedom from bias, and is often referred to as the *cornerstone* of the auditing profession. Without independence, audits would lack value.

Overall Objectives in Conducting an Audit

The overall objective of an audit is to obtain reasonable assurance about whether the financial statements are free from material misstatement and to report on the financial statements based on the auditor's findings. In completing these objectives, the auditor:

- Complies with relevant ethical requirements
- Plans and performs an audit with professional skepticism
- Exercises professional judgment
- Obtains sufficient appropriate evidence on which to base the auditor's opinion
- Conducts the audit in accordance with professional auditing standards

审计的总体目标

财务报表审计的总体目标包含两个方面：一是对财务报表是否不存在由于舞弊或者错误导致的重大错报获取合理保证，使得注册会计师能够对财务报表是否在所有重大方面按照适用的财务报告框架发表审计意见；二是按照审计准则的规定，根据审计结果对财务报表出具审计报告，并与管理层和治理层进行沟通。

审计意见形成过程概述 | Overview of the Audit Opinion Formulation Process

To be able to provide reasonable assurance, auditors go through a structured process, which we refer to as the Audit Opinion Formulation Process. That process is presented in Exhibit 1.3.

Phase I of the audit opinion formulation process concerns client acceptance and continuance. Auditors are not required to perform audits for any organization that asks; auditors choose whether or not to perform each individual audit. Audit firms have procedures to help them ensure that they are not associated with clients where management integrity is in question or where a company might otherwise present the audit firm with unnecessarily high risk (such as client financial failure or regulatory action against the client). Once a client is accepted (or the audit firm decides to continue to provide services to a client), the auditor needs to perform risk assessment procedures to thoroughly understand the client's business (or update prior knowledge in the case of a continuing client), its industry, its competition, and its management and governance processes (including internal controls) to determine the likelihood that financial accounts might be in error (Phase II). In some audits, the auditor will also obtain evidence about internal control operating effectiveness through testing those controls (Phase III). Much of what most people think of as auditing, the obtaining of substantive evidence about accounts, disclosures, and assertions, occurs in Phase IV. The information gathered in Phases I through III will greatly influence the amount of testing to be performed in Phase IV. Finally, in Phase V, the auditor will complete the audit and make a decision about what type of audit report to issue.

EXHIBIT 1.3   The Audit Opinion Formulation Process

I. Making Client Acceptance and Continuance Decisions
Chapter 14

II. Performing Risk Assessment
Chapters 3, 7 and 9–13

III. Obtaining Evidence about Internal Control Operating Effectiveness
Chapters 8–13 and 16

IV. Obtaining Substantive Evidence about Accounts, Disclosures and Assertions
Chapters 8–13 and 16

V. Completing the Audit and Making Reporting Decisions
Chapters 14 and 15

The Auditing Profession, the Risk of Fraud and Mechanisms to Address Fraud: Regulation, Corporate Governance, and Audit Quality
Chapters 1 and 2

Professional Liability and the Need for Quality Auditor Judgments and Ethical Decisions
Chapter 4

The Audit Opinion Formulation Process and A Framework for Obtaining Audit Evidence
Chapters 5 and 6

Parties Involved in Preparing and Auditing Financial Statements

Various parties are involved in preparation and audit of financial statements and related disclosures; these parties are depicted in Exhibit 1.4. Management has responsibilities for (a) preparing and presenting financial statements in accordance with the applicable financial reporting framework; (b) designing, implementing, and maintaining internal control over financial reporting; and (c) providing the auditors with information relevant to the financial statements and internal controls. The internal audit function provides management and the audit committee with assurance on internal controls and reports. The audit committee, a subcommittee of the organization's board of directors, oversees both management and the internal auditors, and they also hire the external auditor. The external auditor's job is to obtain reasonable assurance about whether management's statements are materially accurate and to provide a publicly available report. External auditors conduct their procedures and make judgments in accordance with professional standards (described in Chapter 5). The audited financial statements are provided to users who have an interest in the organization.

Providers of External Auditing Services

The external auditing profession includes sole-practitioner firms, local and regional firms, and large multinational professional services firms such as the Big 4. The Big 4 firms are KPMG, Deloitte Touche Tohmatsu (Deloitte in the United States), PricewaterhouseCoopers (pwc), and Ernst & Young. The organizational structure of these firms is quite complex. For example, each of the Big 4 firms is actually a network of member firms. Each of the member firms enters into agreements to share a common name, brand, and quality standards. In most cases, member firms are organized as a partnership or limited liability corporation within each country. Some smaller firms also practice internationally through an affiliation with a network of firms. For example, a number of regional or local firms belong to an affiliation of such firms under the name of Moore Stephens, and another group operates under the name of Baker Tilly. Many public accounting firms have also organized their practices along industry lines to better serve clients in those industries. These often include categories such as financial services, retailing, not-for-profit, manufacturing, and government.

参与编制和审计财务报表的各方

LO 2 Identify parties involved in preparing audited financial statements and briefly describe their roles.

外部审计服务的提供者

LO 3 List the types of audit service providers and the skills and knowledge needed by professionals entering the external auditing profession.

EXHIBIT 1.4 Parties Involved in Preparing and Auditing Financial Statements

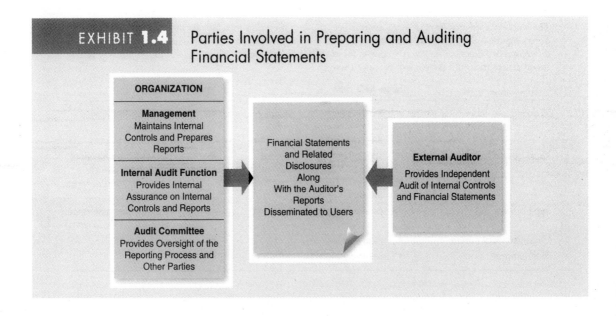

The organizational hierarchy of audit firms is structured with partners (or owners) at the top level; these individuals are responsible for the overall conduct of each audit. Next in the hierarchy are the managers, who review the audit work performed by seniors and staff personnel. Seniors are responsible for overseeing the day-to-day activities on a specific audit, and they oversee entry-level personnel who perform many of the basic auditing procedures. Partners and managers are responsible for many audit engagements that are being conducted simultaneously, whereas seniors and staff are usually assigned to fewer audits at one time.

从事外部审计职业所需的
知识和技能

Skills and Knowledge Needed to Enter the External Auditing Profession

The requirements of those entering the auditing profession are demanding. Audits are performed in teams where each auditor is expected to complete tasks requiring considerable technical knowledge and expertise, along with leadership, teamwork, and professional skills. In terms of technical knowledge and expertise, auditors must understand accounting and auditing authoritative literature, develop industry and client-specific knowledge, develop and apply computer skills, evaluate internal controls, and assess and respond to fraud risk.

In terms of leadership, teamwork, and professional skills, auditors make presentations to management and audit committee members, exercise logical reasoning, communicate decisions to users, manage and supervise others by providing meaningful feedback, act with integrity and ethics, interact in a team environment, collaborate with others, and maintain a professional personal presence. While external auditors at all types of audit firms need these skills, the work environment at larger versus smaller audit firms differs. *The Auditing in Practice* feature "Should I Work for a Large or a Small Audit Firm?" explores differences in the workplace at these types of firms.

Should I Work for a Large or a Small Audit Firm?

AUDITING IN PRACTICE

The workplace environment at large audit firms differs significantly from small audit firms. These differences are described below. Of course, these are broad generalities, and people will perceive these differences as relatively more or less appealing depending on their personalities and long-term career goals.

	Larger Audit Firms	Smaller Audit Firms
Working in a team environment	• multiple teams that typically disband after each audit engagement	• teams that overlap across engagements
Work specialization	• specialized by function, i.e., audit or tax, but usually not both • may also be specialized by industry	• less specialized by function; an individual may work across functions and industries
Type of work	• primarily external audit	• may include other assurance services
Organizational culture	• relatively formal	• relatively less formal
Staff turnover	• relatively higher	• relatively lower

Organizations Affecting the External Auditing Profession

External auditing is a profession with many organizations shaping and regulating the services provided by those in the profession.

Congress

During the early 2000s, various shocks affected the future of the auditing profession. Some of the major shocks included (a) the failure of one of the largest audit firms in the world (Arthur Andersen & Co.); (b) four of the largest bankruptcies in history—and each of the bankruptcies occurred in companies where fraud had taken place—that led to billions of dollars in investment and retirement fund losses by investors; (c) a sense that auditors were not independent of management; and (d) a question as to whether the auditing profession could sufficiently govern itself to ensure that it would always act in the public interest. In response to these shocks, Congress passed the **Sarbanes-Oxley Act of 2002**.[3] This legislation, which we expand upon in Chapter 2, has had a significant impact on audit firms through:

- Increasing auditor independence
- Enhancing the role and importance of the audit committee
- Requiring reporting on internal control over financial reporting
- Providing new oversight of the external auditing profession by the Public Company Accounting Oversight Board (PCAOB)

Public Company Accounting Oversight Board

The PCAOB (*www.pcaobus.org*) is a private sector, nonprofit organization that oversees auditors of public companies. The overall goal of the PCAOB is to "protect the interests of investors and further the public interest in the

LO 4 Identify organizations that affect the external auditing profession and the nature of their effects.

影响外部审计职业的组织

《萨班斯—奥克斯利法案》
(Sarbanes-Oxley Act of 2002)
是美国立法机构根据安然、世通等
财务舞弊事件暴露出来的公司和证
券监管问题所立的监管法规, 其全
称是《2002年公众公司会计改革和
投资者保护法案》。该法案共分11
章, 第1—6章主要涉及对会计职业
及公司行为的监管, 第8—11章的
主要目的是提高对公司高层主管及
白领犯罪的刑事责任的关注。

Who Are the Leaders of the PCAOB?

AUDITING IN PRACTICE

As of 2012, the five board members of the PCAOB include the following individuals:

Board Member Name	Prior Work Experience and Professional Credentials
James Doty, Chairman served since 2011	Attorney; General counsel of the SEC; partner in a law firm specializing in securities and corporate law.
Lewis Ferguson, served since 2011	Attorney; General counsel of the PCAOB; partner in a law firm specializing in securities regulation, disclosure issues, and corporate governance; senior vice president, general counsel and director of Wright Medical Technology; adjunct law professor.
Jay Hanson, served since 2011	CPA; partner at McGladrey & Pullen LLP and National Director of Accounting for that firm; served as Chairman of Financial Reporting Executive Committee of the AICPA.
Jeanette Franzel, served since 2012	CPA; Managing director of the Government Accountability Office.
Steven Harris, served since 2008	Attorney; Senior vice president and special counsel at APCO Worldwide, which specializes in advising clients on financial transactions, corporate governance, crisis management, and government affairs.

Board members are replaced on a planned, rotational basis in order to provide a fresh perspective periodically. Each term of service is five years, and no board member may serve more than two terms.

---

[3] Sarbanes-Oxley Act of 2002, H.R. Bill 3762.

preparation of informative, fair, and independent audit reports." The PCAOB has four primary responsibilities related to auditors of public companies: (1) registration of audit firms that audit public companies; (2) periodic inspections of registered audit firms; (3) establishment of auditing and related standards for registered audit firms; and (4) investigation and discipline of registered audit firms for violations of relevant laws or professional standards. The *Auditing in Practice* feature "Who Are the Leaders of the PCAOB?" describes the professional qualifications of the five board members of the PCAOB. It is interesting to note is that not all are external auditors. In fact, the rules for the PCAOB state that no more than two board members may be Certified Public Accountants (CPAs). This design choice was made deliberately to ensure that the Board was not unduly dominated by members of the external audit profession, thereby helping to assure users of financial statements that this important regulator is representing the broad interests of users, not just serving the preferences of the external audit profession.

The Securities and Exchange Commission

The **Securities and Exchange Commission** (SEC, *www.sec.gov*) was established by Congress in 1934 to regulate the capital market system. The SEC has oversight responsibilities for the PCAOB and for all public companies that are traded on U.S. stock exchanges. The SEC has the authority to establish GAAP for companies whose stock is publicly traded, although it has generally delegated this authority to the Financial Accounting Standards Board (FASB).

Actions by the SEC have important implications for public company auditors. In response to the independence requirements of Sarbanes-Oxley, the SEC made its auditor independence rules more stringent. The SEC also has a responsibility to prosecute public companies and their auditors for violating SEC laws, including fraudulent accounting. For example, in recent years, the SEC has brought actions against companies and auditors including (a) Dell for failing to disclose material information and for improper accounting related to the use of "cookie jar" reserves, (b) Lucent for inappropriate revenue recognition, (c) a former Deloitte & Touche partner for a lack of independence, and (d) Ernst & Young for allowing premature revenue recognition and improper deferral of costs in its audits of Bally Total Fitness Holding Corporation, among many others. The *Auditing in Practice* feature "Locating Enforcement Actions on the SEC Web Site" provides instructions on how to locate enforcement actions that the SEC is pursuing, and illustrates the ongoing efforts by the SEC to ensure both quality financial reporting and quality auditing.

Locating Enforcement Actions on the SEC Web Site

AUDITING IN PRACTICE

The SEC issues enforcement actions to penalize individuals and firms in the accounting and auditing professions for wrongdoings; these public disclosures are also intended to have a deterrence effect. Enforcement releases make for very interesting reading! Take these steps to see what enforcement releases have been made recently:

- Go to *www.sec.gov*.
- Go to the "Divisions and Offices" section and click "Enforcement."

- Click "Accounting and Auditing Enforcement Releases."
- Click the appropriate year.
- Click the enforcement release that you wish to read.

American Institute of Certified Public Accountants

The **American Institute of Certified Public Accountants** (AICPA, *www. aicpa.org*) has long served as the primary governing organization of the public accounting profession. That role has changed with the establishment of the PCAOB as the body for setting auditing standards for the audits of public companies. However, the AICPA continues to develop standards for audits of nonpublic companies. The ACIPA is responsible for a peer review program in which registered firms are subject to periodic peer review of their nonpublic audits. The AICPA also provides continuing education programs, and through its Board of Examiners, prepares and administers the Uniform CPA Examination.

The Center for Audit Quality

The **Center for Audit Quality** (CAQ, *www.thecaq.org*), an organization affiliated with the AICPA, is dedicated to enhancing investor confidence and trust in the financial markets. The CAQ is a thought leader in fostering high audit quality, collaborating with auditors and financial statement users about emerging issues and advocating for accounting and auditing standards that promote auditors' effectiveness.

International Auditing and Assurance Standards Board

The **International Auditing and Assurance Standards Board** (IAASB, *www.ifac.org/iaasb*) is a part of the International Federation of Accountants (IFAC), a global organization for the accounting profession. The IAASB sets International Standards on Auditing (ISAs) and facilitates the convergence of national and international auditing standards.[4]

Committee of Sponsoring Organizations

The **Committee of Sponsoring Organizations of the Treadway Commission** (COSO, *www.coso.org*) is a recognized provider of guidance on internal control, enterprise risk management, and fraudulent deterrence. COSO is sponsored by five organizations, including the Financial Executives International, the American Institute of Certified Public Accountants, the American Accounting Association, the Institute of Internal Auditors, and the Association of Accountants and Financial Professionals in Business (IMA). COSO provides the internal control framework that serves as the benchmark for auditors who assess the effectiveness of their client's internal controls.

Accounting Standard Setters

Generally accepted accounting principles (GAAP) in the United States have traditionally been set by the Financial Accounting Standards Board FASB, with approval by the Securities and Exchange Commission (SEC). International accounting standards (IFRS—International Financial Reporting Standards) are set by the IFRS Foundation of International Accounting Standards Board (IASB).[5] Their goal is to develop a single set of understandable, enforceable and globally accepted international financial reporting standards. During the past several years, the U.S. and international standard setters have worked towards global harmonization of U.S. and international accounting standards.

---

[4] When referring to external auditing standards, we will use the term generally accepted auditing standards (GAAS). We recognize that GAAS are set by several bodies, including the AICPA, the IAASB, and the PCAOB.

[5] When referring to financial reporting requirements, we will use the term generally accepted accounting principles (GAAP) for financial reporting, recognizing that the criteria may be developed by either FASB or the IASB. In some instances we will use the term applicable financial reporting framework. The auditor will determine which of the financial reporting frameworks is applicable to the audit and then apply that framework to determine whether the principles underlying that framework are properly applied.

State Boards of Accountancy

CPAs are licensed by state boards of accountancy, which are charged with regulating the profession at the state level. All state boards require passage of the Uniform CPA Examination as one criterion for licensure. However, education and experience requirements vary by state. In terms of education, most states require 150 college semester hours for CPA licensure, although in some states a candidate may be able to sit for the CPA exam with only 120 hours. Some states require candidates to have external auditing experience before issuing them a license to practice; other states give credit for audit experience related to private or governmental accounting. The work experience requirement can also vary with the level of education. Most states have reciprocal agreements for recognizing public accountants from other states; in some instances, however, a state may require either additional experience or coursework before issuing a license.

The Court System

The court system acts as a quality-control mechanism for the auditing profession. Third parties may sue CPAs under federal securities laws, various state statutes, and common law for substandard audit work. Although the profession often becomes alarmed when large damages are awarded to plaintiffs in suits against audit firms, the courts help ensure that the profession meets its responsibilities to third parties.

审计质量

LO 5 Define audit quality and identify drivers of audit quality as specified by the Financial Reporting Council's *Audit Quality Framework*.

美国审计总署（GAO）将高质量审计定义为："依据公认审计准则的要求为已审财务报表和相关披露遵循公认会计原则的要求编制，不存在由于错误或者舞弊导致的重大错报提提高合理保证。"英国财务报告委员会（FRC）的"审计质量框架"讨论了影响审计质量的五大因素。这些因素包括：会计师事务所文化、审计项目合伙人和员工的技能和素质、审计过程的效率、审计报告的可靠性和有用性及注册会计师无法控制的审计质量影响因素。

Audit Quality

Assuring that the audit is conducted in a quality manner is paramount to fulfilling users' expectations about the auditor's role in the capital markets. Throughout this textbook, we discuss approaches that are used to achieve audit quality. But before proceeding, it is worthwhile to take a moment to reflect on a very fundamental question: What is **audit quality**?

A definition published by the GAO (2003) states that a quality audit is one performed "in accordance with generally accepted auditing standards (GAAS) to provide reasonable assurance that the audited financial statements and related disclosures are presented in accordance with generally accepted accounting principles GAAP and (2) are not materially misstated whether due to errors or fraud."[6] The Financial Reporting Council (FRC) developed "The Audit Quality Framework" to provide guidance on specific drivers of audit quality. The FRC is the United Kingdom's independent regulator responsible for promoting investment in securities through good corporate governance and financial reporting.

The FRC's Audit Quality Framework states that there are five primary drivers of audit quality, including (1) audit firm culture, (2) the skills and personal qualities of audit partners and staff, (3) the effectiveness of the audit process, (4) the reliability and usefulness of audit reporting, and (5) factors outside the control of auditors that affect audit quality. An overview of the FRC framework is shown in Exhibit 1.5. The framework recognizes that effective audit processes, by themselves, are not sufficient to achieve audit quality. Rather, it is a package of factors that includes a culture that influences auditors who in turn influence audit procedures. However, there are other factors, outside of the control of the audit firm, that affect audit quality and thereby the overall quality of the audited financial statements. These factors include the robustness of the accounting framework as well as the regulatory and legal environment.

---

[6] Government Accountability Office (GAO). 2003. Public Accounting Firms: Required Study on the Potential Effects of Mandatory Audit Firm Rotation. GAO Report 04–216 (November).

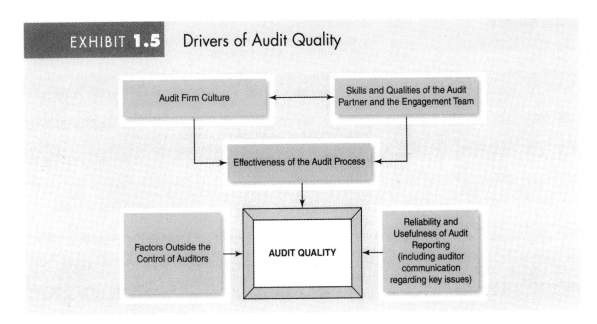

EXHIBIT **1.5** Drivers of Audit Quality

Audit Firm Culture

会计师事务所文化

According to the FRC, audit firm culture contributes positively to audit quality when the leadership of the firm completes the following types of activities:

- Creating a work culture where audit quality is valued and rewarded
- Emphasizing that 'doing the right thing' is appropriate from a public interest perspective, and that 'doing the right thing' helps to develop and maintain both individual and audit firm reputation
- Ensuring that audit firm employees have enough time and resources to address difficult issues that may arise
- Ensuring that monetary considerations do not adversely affect audit quality
- Promoting the benefits of having audit partners seek guidance on difficult issues and supporting their professional judgment
- Ensuring that the audit firm has quality systems in place for making client acceptance and continuation decisions
- Fostering evaluation and compensation practices that promote personal characteristics important to quality auditing
- Ensuring that audit quality is monitored within the audit firm and that appropriate consequences are taken when audit quality is found to be lacking

Skills and Qualities of the Engagement Team

项目组的技能和能力

The FRC notes that audit firm employees positively contribute to audit quality when they engage in the following types of activities:

- Understanding the clients' business and adhering to auditing and ethical standards
- Exhibiting professional skepticism and addressing issues identified during the audit
- Ensuring that staff performing audit work have appropriate levels of experience and that they are properly supervised by their superiors
- Ensuring that partners and managers provide lower level staff with mentoring and "on the job" training opportunities
- Attending to and learning during training intended to aid in understanding audit, accounting, and industry specialist issues

审计过程的效率

Effectiveness of the Audit Process

The FRC recognizes that the audit process itself contributes in a positive way to audit quality when the following activities and processes are in place:

- The audit methodology is well structured and:
  - Encourages partners and managers to be work diligently in planning the audit
  - Provides a framework and procedures to obtain sufficient appropriate audit evidence in an effective and efficient manner
  - Requires appropriate audit documentation
  - Provides for complying with auditing standards, but does not inhibit professional judgment
  - Ensuring that audit work is effectively reviewed
  - Audit quality control procedures are effective, understood, and applied.
- Quality technical support is available when auditors encounter unfamiliar situations in which they require assistance or guidance.
- Ethical standards are communicated and achieved, thereby aiding auditors' integrity, objectivity, and independence.
- Auditors' evidence collection is not constrained by financial pressures.

审计报告的可靠性和有用性

Reliability and Usefulness of Audit Reporting

According to the FRC, audit reports contribute to audit quality when they have the following attributes:

- Audit reports are written in a way that clearly and unambiguously convey the auditor's opinion on the financial statements and addresses the needs of users of financial statements.
- Auditors appropriately conclude as to the truth and fairness of the financial statements (for example, in the U.S. concluding that the financial statements are fairly presented in accordance GAAP.
- The auditor communicates with the audit committee about the following:
  - Audit scope (in other words, what the auditor is engaged to accomplish)
  - Threats to auditor objectivity
  - Important risks identified and judgments that were made in reaching the audit opinion
  - Qualitative aspects of the client's accounting and reporting and possible ways of improving financial reporting

注册会计师无法控制的审计
质量影响因素

Factors Outside the Control of Auditors That Affect Audit Quality

The FRC is realistic, and it explicitly recognizes that some factors that affect audit quality are outside of the direct control of the external auditor, such as client corporate governance and the regulatory environment. The FRC recognizes that good corporate governance includes audit committees that are robust in dealing with issues and a greater emphasis by the client on getting things right as opposed to getting done by a particular date. Further, a regulatory environment that emphasizes audit quality over all else is critical.

审计质量最大化和审计
诉讼最小化

Achieving Audit Quality and Minimizing Lawsuits

LO 6 Identify professional requirements that help to achieve audit quality and minimize auditor exposure to lawsuits.

If an audit is not conducted in a quality manner, the auditor and audit firm are susceptible to lawsuits. While we expand on legal implications for the external audit profession in detail in Chapter 4, we discuss here how certain professional requirements help to achieve audit quality, and thus how they can minimize the exposure of external auditors to lawsuits.

These requirements include (1) maintaining auditor independence, (2) participating in review programs, (3) issuing engagement letters, (4) making appropriate client acceptance/continuance decisions, (5) evaluating the audit firm's limitations, and (6) maintaining quality audit documentation.

Auditor Independence Requirements

注册会计师的独立性要求

The SEC, PCAOB, and AICPA all have requirements related to auditor independence that are intended to assist auditors in conducting a quality audit.

SEC and PCAOB Independence Requirements

The SEC and PCAOB's independence requirements are applicable to auditors of public companies. These two organizations have set complementary independence requirements. The PCAOB's independence requirements are designed to address specific requirements in the Sarbanes-Oxley Act of 2002 (see Chapter 4 for specific details).

The SEC's commitment to independence is summarized in the following two paragraphs:

> The independence requirement serves two related, but distinct, public policy goals. One goal is to foster high quality audits by minimizing the possibility that any external factors will influence an auditor's judgments. The auditor must approach each audit with professional skepticism and must have the capacity and the willingness to decide issues in an unbiased and objective manner, even when the auditor's decisions may be against the interests of management of the audit client or against the interests of the auditor's own accounting firm.
>
> The other related goal is to promote investor confidence in the financial statements of public companies. Investor confidence in the integrity of publicly available financial information is the cornerstone of our securities market ... Investors are more likely to invest, and pricing is more likely to be efficient, where there is greater assurance that the financial information disclosed by issuers is reliable ... [that] assurance will flow from knowledge that the financial information has been subjected to rigorous examination by competent and objective auditors.[7]

The SEC has taken a principles-based approach in dealing with independence issues. All of the SEC statements on independence follow from four basic principles that define when an auditor is in a position that impairs independence. Those principles dictate that auditor independence is impaired when the auditor has a relationship that:

- Creates a mutual or conflicting interest between the accountant and the audit client
- Places the accountant in the position of auditing his or her own work
- Results in the accountant acting as management or an employee of the audit client
- Places the accountant in a position of being an advocate for the audit client[8]

AICPA Requirements: A Conceptual Framework on Independence

The AICPA has articulated a conceptual framework on independence. That framework describes seven categories of threats to independence, which are circumstances that could lead to an auditor lacking independence in fact or in appearance. These various threats to independence include:

1. Self-review threat—occurs when the audit firm also provides non-audit work for the client, such as preparing source documents used to generate

---

[7] U.S. Securities and Exchange Commission, Final Rule: Revision of the Commission's Auditor Independence Requirements, February 5, 2001.

[8] Op. cit.

the client's financial statements. Independence is threatened because it may appear that the auditor is reviewing his or her own work.

2. Advocacy threat—occurs when the auditor acts to promote the client's interests, such as representing the client in tax court. Independence is threatened because it may appear that the auditor cares more about the client than external users of the financial statements.

3. Adverse interest threat—occurs when the auditor and the client are in opposition to one another, such as when either party has initiated litigation against the other. Independence is threatened because the auditor may take actions that are intended to weaken the client's chances in the litigation, and may appear to care more about the audit firm and its interests rather than those of the company or external users of the financial statements.

4. Familiarity threat—occurs when the auditor has some longstanding relationship with an important person associated with the client. Examples include:
    *   The audit partner's close relative is employed in a key position at the client.
    *   The audit partner has been assigned to the client for a long period of time and has developed very close personal relationships with top management.
    *   A member of the audit team has a close personal friend who is employed in a key position at the client.
    *   A member of the audit team was recently a director or officer at the client.

    In each of these examples, independence is threatened because the auditor may act in a way that favors the client or individual employed at the client rather than external users of the financial statements.

5. Undue influence threat—occurs when client management attempts to coerce or provide excessive influence over the auditor. Examples include:
    *   Top management threatens to replace the auditor or the audit firm because of a disagreement over an accounting issue.
    *   Top management pressures the auditor to reduce the amount of work they do on the audit in order to achieve lower audit fees.
    *   An employee of the client gives the auditor a gift that is clearly significant or economically important to the auditor.

    In each of these examples, independence is threatened because the auditor may act in a way that favors the client or individual employed at the client rather than external users of the financial statements.

6. Financial self-interest threat—occurs when the auditor has a direct financial relationship with the client, such as owning stock in the client company, owing money to the client company, or when the audit client makes up the vast majority of the audit firm's total revenue. Independence is threatened because the auditor's judgment may be unduly influenced by their own financial interests rather than acting in the best interests of external users of the financial statements.

7. Management participation threat—occurs when the auditor takes on the role of management or completes functions that management should reasonably complete, such as establishing internal controls or hiring/firing client employees. Independence is threatened because the auditor is acting as management, and so would in essence be reviewing his or her own work.

The AICPA also articulates safeguards to avoid the independence problems associated with these threats. These safeguards include:

1. Safeguards created by the profession or regulation. Examples include:
    *   Education, continuing education, and training requirements
    *   Professional standards and disciplinary punishments
    *   External review of audit firms' quality control systems

- Legislation concerning independence requirements
- Audit partner rotation requirements for publicly traded companies, which include mandatory partner rotation after five years of service
- Nonaudit (e.g., consulting) work not allowed for companies for which the auditor provides external audit work

2. Safeguards created by the audit client. Examples include:
- Client personnel with expertise to adequately complete necessary management and accounting tasks without the involvement or advice of the auditor
- Appropriate tone at the top of the client company
- Policies and procedures to ensure accurate financial reporting
- Policies and procedures to ensure appropriate relationships with audit firm

3. Safeguards created by the audit firm. Examples include:
- Audit firm leadership that stresses the importance of independence
- Audit firm quality control policies and procedures
- Audit firm monitoring processes to detect instances of possible independence violations
- Disciplinary mechanisms to promote compliance with independence policies and procedures
- Rotation of senior engagement personnel

Review Programs

复核程序

Three types of review programs exist:

- external inspections/peer reviews
- engagement quality reviews
- interoffice reviews

External Inspections/Peer Reviews

The PCAOB performs inspections of registered audit firms every year for audit firms that have over 100 public company audits and every three years for the other registered audit firms. You can access inspection reports on the PCAOB's Web site. Many of these reports identify audit performance deficiencies found by the inspectors.

The AICPA has a peer review program that reviews and evaluates those portions of an audit firm's accounting and auditing practice that are not inspected by the PCAOB; therefore, the focus of the peer reviews would be on the nonpublic clients of the audit firm. The reviews are conducted by auditors from another external audit firm and provide an objective assessment of the appropriateness of the firm's quality-control policies and procedures as well as of the degree of compliance with them. Peer review reports are issued to the audit firm and are available from the AICPA.

Engagement Quality Reviews

An audit partner not otherwise involved in the audit performs an **engagement quality review** (also referred to as **concurring partner review**) near the end of each audit to make sure that documented evidence supports the audit opinion. Such reviews are required for audits of public companies, and it is desirable for firms to conduct these reviews on all audits. The concurring partner should be familiar with the nature of the business being audited. Some single-partner audit firms arrange with other small firms to perform concurring reviews for each other before issuing audit reports.

会计师事务所应当制定政策和程序，要求对适当业务实施项目质量控制复核，以客观评价项目组做出的重大判断以及在编制报告时得出的结论。同时，会计师事务所应当制定与委派项目质量控制复核人员相关的政策和程序，明确项目质量控制复核人员的资格要求。

The AICPA has no formal requirement for engagement quality/concurring partner review on individual audit engagements. However, the AICPA does require that firms establish specific criteria by which they decide on a systematic basis the clients that should have such a review. The AICPA still requires the firms to undergo a quality review process at the overall audit firm level on a periodic basis and (a) the absence of specific criteria for engagement quality reviews, or (b) absence of adherence to those criteria would be considered a deficiency when overall audit firm reviews are performed. Recall that the AICPA standards concern nonpublicly traded entities, and many of the firm's clients may be very small and have only one or two people assigned to the total audit. Thus, in the view of the AICPA (and many smaller firms), it would not make economic sense to have an engagement quality review for clients that are both uncomplicated and small. Some of the criteria that the firms use to decide that an engagement quality review is needed include: riskiness of client, size of client, and the extent of outside distribution of audit report (and thus, potentially the legal liability for the auditor).

PCAOB guidance requires an engagement quality review, and the engagement quality reviewer must evaluate all significant judgments made by the engagement team and to consider their evaluation of the client's risks. The guidance specifically states that the engagement quality reviewer must have competence, independence, integrity, and objectivity, and the standard requires that all phases of the review be carefully documented.

Similar to the PCAOB, the IAASB requires that the engagement quality reviewer evaluate significant risks and the engagement team's responses to those risks, judgments made (particularly relating to addressing risks and materiality), the disposition of misstatements identified during the engagement (whether corrected or not), and matters communicated to management and others charged with governance over the organization.

Interoffice Reviews

An **interoffice review** is a review of one office of the audit firm by professionals from another office of the same firm to assure that the policies and procedures established by the firm are being followed. Like external inspections/peer reviews, interoffice reviews include selecting and reviewing a sample of audits to help assure that quality work was performed.

审计业务约定书

Engagement Letters

The **engagement letter** states the scope of the work to be done on the audit so that there should be no doubt in the mind of the client, external auditor, or the court system as to the expectations agreed to by the external auditor and the client. The engagement letter, which includes the audit fee, also includes a description of the timing of the external auditor's work and a description of documentation that the client is expected to provide to the external auditor. In writing an engagement letter, care should be taken when describing the degree of responsibility the auditor takes with respect to discovering fraud and misstatements. If the client wants its auditors to go beyond the requirements of the auditing standards, the auditors should have their attorneys review the wording to make sure that it says not only what is intended but also what is possible.

客户接受/保留决策

Client Acceptance/Continuance Decisions

Another element of quality-control deals with accepting and retaining clients. This decision should involve more than just a consideration of management's integrity. Strict client acceptance/continuance guidelines should be established to screen out the following:

- *Clients that are in financial and/or organizational difficulty*—For example, clients that could go bankrupt or clients with poor internal accounting controls and sloppy records.
- *Clients that constitute a disproportionate percentage of the firm's total practice*—Clients may attempt to influence the auditor into allowing unacceptable accounting practices or issuing inappropriate opinions.

- *Disreputable clients*—External audit firms cannot afford to have their good reputation tarnished by serving a disreputable client or by associating with a client that has disreputable management.
- *Clients that offer an unreasonably low fee for the auditor's services*—In response, the auditor may attempt to cut corners imprudently or lose money on the engagement. Conversely, auditors may bid for audits at unreasonably low prices.

Audit Firm Limitations

对会计师事务所的限制

An external audit firm should not undertake an engagement that it is not qualified to handle. Doing so is especially important for smaller, growing firms that may be tempted to agree to conduct an audit for which they are not qualified or not large enough to perform. Statistics show that firms covered by an AICPA professional liability insurance plan that are most susceptible to litigation are those with staffs of eleven to twenty-five auditors. They appear to become overzealous, leading to low audit quality and exposure to subsequent litigation.

Audit Documentation

审计工作底稿

The audit team should document everything done on the audit. It is difficult to persuade a jury or a regulator such as the PCAOB that something was done that is not documented. Audit documentation should clearly show evidence of supervisory review, particularly in those areas with the greatest potential for improprieties, such as inventories, revenue recognition, and accounting estimates. The documentation should indicate what tests were performed, who performed them, and any significant judgments made (along with the rationale for those judgments). We provide significant detail on audit documentation in Chapter 6.

编制审计工作底稿的主要目的有两个：一是提供注册会计师得出实现总体目标结论的基础和证据；二是提供注册会计师按照审计准则和适用的法律法规的要求计划和执行了审计工作的证据。

SUMMARY AND NEXT STEPS

By now, you can appreciate the role that external auditing plays in providing independent assurance on financial information. You should have a basic understanding of the audit opinion formulation process and of the skills and knowledge needed by auditing professionals. Most notably, we hope that you recognize the importance of audit quality, understand the drivers of audit quality, and know the professional requirements that help to achieve audit quality and minimize auditor exposure to lawsuits.

One of the big concerns for auditors in conducting a quality audit is the existence of fraud. In the next chapter, we provide examples of fraud and describe auditors' responsibilities for detecting fraud. We also discuss the many mechanisms that are in place to help prevent fraud and to help ensure that financial information is accurate and reliable.

SIGNIFICANT TERMS

Adverse opinion An adverse opinion should be expressed when the auditor believes that the financial statements taken as a whole are *not presented fairly* in conformity with GAAP or when the auditor believes that the client's internal controls are not effective.

American Institute of Certified Public Accountants (AICPA) The primary professional organization for CPAs, it has a number of committees to develop professional standards for the conduct of nonpublic company audits and other services performed by its members and to self-regulate the profession.

Audit quality Performing an audit in accordance with generally accepted auditing standards (GAAS) to provide reasonable assurance that the audited financial statements and related disclosures are presented in accordance with GAAP and providing assurance that those financial statements are not materially misstated whether due to errors or fraud.

Center for Audit Quality (CAQ) An organization affiliated with the AICPA that is dedicated to enhancing investor confidence and trust in the financial markets.

Committee of Sponsoring Organizations of the Treadway Commission (COSO) An organization that provides thought leadership and guidance on enterprise risk management, internal control and fraud deterrence.

Concurring partner review Occurs when an audit partner not otherwise involved in the audit independently reviews each audit to make sure that documented evidence supports the audit opinion. Otherwise known as an engagement quality review.

Due professional care A standard of care expected to be demonstrated by a competent professional in his or her field of expertise, set by the generally accepted auditing standards but supplemented in specific implementation instances by the standard of care expected by a reasonably prudent auditor.

Engagement letter States the scope of the work to be done on the audit so that there can be no doubt in the mind of the client, external auditor, or the court system as to the expectations agreed to by the external auditor and the client.

Engagement quality review Occurs when an audit partner not otherwise involved in the audit independently reviews each audit to make sure that documented evidence supports the audit opinion. Otherwise known as a concurring partner review.

Financial statement audit A systematic process of objectively obtaining evidence regarding assertions about economic actions and events to ascertain the degree of correspondence between those assertions and established criteria and communicating the results to interested users.

Generally accepted accounting principles (GAAP) GAAP refers to generally accepted accounting principles for financial reporting. Throughout the text we recognize that the criteria may be developed by either FASB or the IASB. GAAP has general acceptance and provides criteria by which to assess the fairness of a financial statement presentation.

Generally accepted auditing standards (GAAS) GAAS refers to professional external auditing standards that are followed by auditors when conducting a financial statement audit. Throughout the text, when we refer to professional external auditing standards, we will use the term GAAS (generally accepted auditing standards). We recognize that GAAS are set by several bodies, including the AICPA, the IAASB, and the PCAOB.

Integrated audit Type of audit provided when an external auditor is engaged to perform an audit of the effectiveness of internal control over financial reporting ("the audit of internal control over financial reporting") that is integrated with an audit of the financial statements.

International Accounting Standards Board (IASB) This organization issues IFRS (International Financial Reporting Standards) and is working to be the one provider of accounting standards around the world.

International Auditing and Assurance Standards Board (IAASB) A part of the International Federation of Accountants that is responsible for issuing auditing and assurance standards. Its goal is to harmonize auditing standards on a global basis.

International Standards for Auditing (ISAs) Standards issued by the IAASB for all auditors who are following international auditing standards.

Interoffice review A review of one office of the audit firm by professionals from another office to assure that the policies and procedures established by the firm are being followed.

Professional skepticism An attitude that includes a questioning mind and critical assessment of audit evidence.

Public Company Accounting Oversight Board (PCAOB) A quasi-public board, appointed by the SEC, to provide oversight of the firms that audit public companies registered with the SEC. It has the authority to set auditing standards for the audits of public companies.

Sarbanes-Oxley Act of 2002 Broad legislation mandating new standard setting for audits of public companies and new standards for corporate governance.

Securities and Exchange Commission (SEC) The governmental body with the oversight responsibility to ensure the proper and efficient operation of capital markets in the United States.

Unqualified audit report The standard three-paragraph audit report that describes the auditor's work and communicates the auditor's opinion that the financial statements are fairly presented in accordance with GAAP.

TRUE-FALSE QUESTIONS

1-1 `LO 1` When the auditor has no reservations about management's financial statements or internal controls, the audit opinion is said to be unqualified.

1-2 `LO 1` Independence is referred to as the cornerstone of the auditing profession.

1-3 `LO 2` The sole responsibility of management with regard to financial reporting involves preparing and presenting financial statements in accordance with the applicable financial reporting framework.

1-4 `LO 2` The internal audit function is designed primarily to assist the external auditor in providing assurance to third party users of the financial statements.

1-5 `LO 3` The Big 4 audit firms are the only types of firms that conduct financial statement audits.

1-6 `LO 3` With regard to working in a team environment, larger audit firms have teams with more continuity and overlap across engagements, whereas smaller audit firms have multiple teams that typically disband after each engagement.

1-7 [LO 4] Congress passed the Sarbanes-Oxley Act of 2002 in response to a variety of major economic shocks during the early 2000s.

1-8 [LO 4] The AICPA sets auditing standards for nonpublic companies in the United States.

1-9 [LO 5] Audit quality is achieved when the audit is performed in accordance with GAAS and when it provides reasonable assurance that the financial statements have been presented in accordance with GAAP and are not materially misstated due to errors or fraud.

1-10 [LO 5] One of the key drivers of audit quality is the gross margin achieved by the audit firm and the ability of the engagement partner to maintain those margins over the duration of the audit engagement.

1-11 [LO 6] There exist three types of review programs: (1) external inspections/peer reviews, (2) engagement quality reviews, and (3) interoffice reviews.

1-12 [LO 6] The engagement letter states the scope of the work to be done on the audit so that there should be no doubt in the mind of the client, external auditor, or the court system as to the expectations agreed to by the external auditor and the client.

MULTIPLE-CHOICE QUESTIONS

1-13 [LO 1] Which of the following factors does not create a demand for external audit services?
a. Potential bias by management in providing information.
b. Requirement of the Center for Audit Quality (CAQ).
c. Complexity of the accounting processing systems.
d. Remoteness between a user and the organization.

1-14 [LO 1] Which of the following expectations can users of the audit report reasonably expect with regards to the audited financial statements?
a. The financial statements include all financial disclosures desired by users.
b. The financial statements are presented fairly according to the substance of GAAP.
c. The financial statements are free from all errors.
d. All of the above are reasonable expectations.
e. None of the above are reasonable expectations.

1-15 [LO 2] Which of the following parties are involved in preparing and auditing financial statements?
a. Management.
b. Audit committee.
c. Internal audit function.
d. External auditor.
e. All of the above.

1-16 [LO 2] Which of the following are the responsibilities of the external auditor in auditing financial statements?
a. Maintaining internal controls and preparing financial reports
b. Providing internal assurance on internal control and financial reports
c. Providing internal oversight of the reporting process
d. All of the above.
e. None of the above.

1-17 ☐3 In which of the following categories do Big 4 audit firms operate?
a. Sole-practitioner firms.
b. Local firms.
c. Regional firms.
d. Multinational firms.

1-18 ☐3 In terms of technical knowledge and expertise, which of the following should external auditors do?
a. Understand accounting and auditing authoritative literature.
b. Develop industry and client-specific knowledge.
c. Develop and apply computer skills.
d. All of the above.
e. None of the above.

1-19 ☐4 The AICPA remains a valuable organization to the external auditing profession because of its continuing involvement in which of the following activities?
a. The audit standard setting process for audits of publicly traded companies.
b. Regulation and enforcement of the internal audit profession.
c. Education and administration of the CPA exam.
d. Promulgation of financial accounting standards.

1-20 ☐4 Which of the following organizations is the primary organization that performs inspections of registered external audit firms that audit public companies?
a. PCAOB
b. CAQ
c. AICPA
d. FASB

1-21 ☐5 Audit quality involves which of the following?
a. Performing an audit in accordance with GAAS to provide reasonable assurance that the audited financial statements and related disclosures are presented in accordance with GAAP and providing assurance that those financial statements are not materially misstated whether due to errors or fraud.
b. Performing an audit in accordance with GAAP to provide reasonable assurance that the audited financial statements and related disclosures are presented in accordance with GAAS and providing assurance that those financial statements are not materially misstated, whether due to errors or fraud.
c. Performing an audit in accordance with GAAS to provide absolute assurance that the audited financial statements and related disclosures are presented in accordance with GAAP and providing assurance that those financial statements are not materially misstated whether due to errors or fraud.
d. Performing an audit in accordance with GAAS to provide reasonable assurance that the audited financial statements and related disclosures are presented in accordance with GAAP and providing assurance that those financial statements contain no misstatements due to errors or fraud.

1-22 ☐5 Which of the following factors is not a driver of audit quality as discussed by the FRC?
a. Audit firm culture.
b. Skills and personal qualities of client management.
c. Reliability and usefulness of audit reporting.
d. Factors outside the control of auditors.

1-23 [LO 6] Strict client acceptance/continuance guidelines should be established by external auditors to screen out which of the following types of clients?
a. Those that are in financial and/or organizational difficulty.
b. Those that constitute a disproportionate percentage of the audit firm's total practice.
c. Those that are disreputable.
d. Those that offer an unreasonably low fee for the auditor's services.
e. All of the above.

1-24 [LO 6] The PCAOB performs external inspections of audit firms registered to audit publicly traded clients. Which of the following is accurate regarding the timing of those inspections?
a. Inspections occur once a year for audit firms that conduct over 50 public clients in a given year.
b. Inspections occur once every three years for audit firms that conduct over 100 public clients in a given year.
c. Inspections occur once a year for audit firms that conduct over 100 public clients in a given year.
d. Inspections occur once every five years for audit firms that conduct over 50 public clients in a given year.

REVIEW AND SHORT CASE QUESTIONS

NOTE: Completing Review and Short Case Questions does not require the student to reference additional resources and materials.

NOTE: For the remaining problems, we make special note of those addressing fraud, international issues, professional skepticism, and ethics.

1-25 [LO 1] What is the objective of external auditing? Describe the role of external auditing in meeting society's demands for unbiased financial and internal control information.

1-26 [LO 1] What is the "special function" that auditors perform? Whom does the external auditing profession serve in performing this special function?

1-27 [LO 1] What factors create a demand for an independent external audit?

1-28 [LO 1] How does an audit enhance the quality of financial statements and management's reports on internal control? Does an audit guarantee a fair presentation of a company's financial statements?

1-29 [LO 1] Why is it important that users perceive auditors to be independent? What is the difference between being independent in fact and being independent in appearance?

1-30 [LO 1] It has been stated that auditors must be independent because audited financial statements must serve the needs of a wide variety of users. If the auditor were to favor one group, such as existing shareholders, there might be a bias against another group, such as prospective investors.
a. What steps has the external auditing profession taken to minimize potential bias toward important users and thereby encourage auditor independence?
b. Refer to Exhibit 1.2 and describe the users of audited financial statements and the decisions that they need to make based on reliable information.

ETHICS **1-31** [LO 1] Refer to the *Auditing in Practice* feature "Why Is Owning Stock in an Audit Client Unacceptable?" and answer the following:
a. Describe the unethical actions of Susan Birkert.
b. Compare and contrast the ideas of independence in fact and independence in appearance in the context of this case.
c. Do you think that Susan's punishments were appropriate? Defend your answer.

1-32 `LO 1, 3` Green Day Golf Distributors is a relatively small, privately held golf distributing company that operates in the Midwest and handles several product lines, including shoes, clothing, and golf clubs. It sells directly to golf shops and does not sell to the big retailers. It has approximately $8 million in sales and wants to grow at about 20% per year for the next five years. It is also considering a takeover or a merger with another golf distributorship that operates in the same region.

a. Explain why management might want an independent audit of its financial statements.

b. What are the factors that Green Day might consider in deciding whether to seek an audit from a large national audit firm, a regional audit firm, or a local firm?

c. What types of users might be interested in Green Day's financial results?

1-33 `LO 2` Refer to Exhibit 1.4 and identify the primary parties involved in preparing and auditing financial statements, and then briefly describe their roles.

1-34 `LO 3` List the various types of audit service providers. What types of audit firms are best suited for auditing large multinational companies versus small, regional companies that are not publicly traded?

1-35 `LO 3` What types of skills and knowledge are needed by professionals entering the external auditing profession?

1-36 `LO 3` Refer to the *Auditing in Practice* feature "Should I Work for a Large or a Small Audit Firm?" Compare and contrast the workplace environments at larger versus smaller audit firms. Explain which type of environment you think would best fit your needs.

1-37 `LO 4` Briefly describe the various roles of the following organizations that affect the external auditing profession and the nature of those effects:

a. Congress

b. Public Company Accounting Oversight Board (PCAOB)

c. Securities and Exchange Commission (SEC)

d. American Institute of Certified Public Accountants (AICPA)

e. Center for Audit Quality (CAQ)

f. International Auditing and Assurance Standards Board (IAASB)

g. Committee of Sponsoring Organizations (COSO)

1-38 `LO 4` Distinguish between the roles of the PCAOB and the AICPA in (a) setting audit standards, (b) performing quality-control reviews of member firms, and (c) setting accounting standards.

1-39 `LO 4` The PCAOB has the authority to set audit standards for all audits of public companies registered in the United States. The AICPA continues to set audit standards for nonpublic companies through its Auditing Standards Board (ASB).

a. What are the pros and cons of having the same auditing standards for both public and nonpublic entities?

b. In what ways might you expect auditing standards for audits of nonpublic companies to differ from the standards for public companies?

c. What difficulties might this dual structure for auditing standards create?

1-40 `LO 4` Refer to the *Auditing in Practice* feature "Who are the Leaders of the PCAOB?." Why is there a requirement that no more than two of the board members are CPAs?

1-41 |LO 5| Define audit quality. What are the five primary drivers of audit quality as articulated by the Financial Reporting Council's "Audit Quality Framework"?

1-42 |LO 5| Refer to Exhibit 1.5, the "Audit Quality Framework."
a. How does positive audit firm culture, along with expert skills and qualities of both the audit partner and the engagement team affect audit quality?
b. What factors outside the control of the external auditor affect audit quality?
c. Why do users care about audit quality? Are there certain users who might care more about audit quality than others? Explain.

1-43 |LO 6| Auditing standards emphasize the importance of independence. Explain why independence is often considered the cornerstone of the auditing profession. Explain why independence issues were a primary concern of Congress when it developed the Sarbanes-Oxley Act.

1-44 |LO 6| Describe the following requirements that help to achieve audit quality and thereby help to minimize the exposure of external auditors to lawsuits:
a. Maintaining auditor independence
b. Participating in review programs
c. Issuing engagement letters
d. Making appropriate client acceptance/continuance decisions
e. Evaluating the audit firm's limitations
f. Maintaining high quality audit documentation

1-45 |LO 6| Describe the seven threats to independence articulated in the AICPA's independence conceptual framework.

1-46 |LO 6| Describe the safeguards to independence articulated in the AICPA's independence conceptual framework, and provide examples of each.

CONTEMPORARY AND HISTORICAL CASES

INTERNATIONAL

PROFESSIONAL SKEPTICISM

1-47 **PCAOB**
|LO 1, 3, 4, 5| Refer to the *Professional Judgment in Context* feature at the outset of the chapter, which discusses the PCAOB enforcement action related to the audit of Alloy Steel International. As you will recall, Robert Forbes was the audit partner in charge of the Alloy Steel engagement, and he made several critical mistakes that adversely affected audit quality.
a. What is the objective of auditing, and how did Forbes' and Bentley's actions fail to achieve that objective?
b. Why did Alloy Steel require an independent audit on its financial statements?
c. Which parties are likely users of Alloy Steel's financial statements? How might they have been adversely affected by Forbes' actions?
d. What skills and knowledge were required to do a quality audit of Alloy Steel's financial statements? How did the individuals who actually performed the audit work on the Alloy Steel engagement fail in this regard?
e. Refer to Exhibit 1.5. Explain how the facts in this case relate to each of the drivers of audit quality identified in the Exhibit. If a particular driver is not applicable to this case, state why.

FRAUD

PROFESSIONAL SKEPTICISM

1-48 **ENRON AND ARTHUR ANDERSEN LLP**
|LO 1, 2, 5| Enron was an energy company based in Houston, Texas that made energy trades. It was

formed in 1985 with the merger of Houston Natural Gas and InterNorth. After an aggressive expansion plan that involved risky financing transactions outside the original, fundamental business model of the company, Enron was billions of dollars in debt. Enron concealed this debt through hidden transactions with related party partnerships, fraudulent accounting, and illegal loans. Enron is considered to be one of the largest and most important financial reporting frauds in history. The company ultimately filed for bankruptcy in 2001.

One of the reasons that Enron was able to get away with the fraud for some time was because of a low quality audit by its external audit firm, Arthur Andersen. Prior to the failure of Enron in 2001, Arthur Andersen had been involved in two other major audit failures. These failed audits, related to frauds at Waste Management (1996) and Sunbeam (1997), should have raised red flags for management and any outside observers that some of the audit firm's internal quality assurance processes were not working. When the federal government uncovered Enron's fraud along with the string of poor quality audits at Arthur Andersen, the government forced the audit firm out of business.

Internal documentation at Arthur Andersen showed that there were conflicts between the auditors and the audit committee of Enron, and that even though there were many individuals concerned about the accounting and disclosure practices at Enron, nothing was done by Andersen to report these problems. In fact, the leading partner on the audit, David Duncan, actively worked to ensure that Enron's fraudulent financial reporting went uncovered. It appears that Duncan was motivated by the fact that Arthur Andersen was earning enormous consulting fees on the Enron engagement; Enron was a hugely important client for him personally and for the Houston office of Arthur Andersen. Together, these conflicts of interest clouded his independent judgment and professional skepticism.

Around the time that Enron declared bankruptcy in late 2001, Arthur Andersen personnel in the Houston office began aggressively destroying documentation relating to the Enron engagement. This action enabled the federal government to file charges against Arthur Andersen that ultimately led to the downfall of the audit firm. The Sarbanes-Oxley Act of 2002 was enacted partially in response to the Enron fraud and the revelation of the poor audit conducted by Arthur Andersen, which is why this case is of particular historical relevance. Considering these facts, answer the following questions:

a. Members of Enron management were the individuals who perpetrated the financial statement fraud. Given this, why do you think auditors were held responsible when they are not the ones actually making the fraudulent journal entries?

b. Explain why the consulting fees and importance of Enron to David Duncan and the Houston office of Arthur Andersen might have affected Duncan's independence, and thus the quality of the audits he supervised.

c. Describe the likely users of Enron's audited financial statements. How were these various user groups likely affected by the fraud?

d. How might the sequential list of frauds perpetrated by Arthur Andersen clients (Waste Management, Sunbeam, and finally Enron) have affected the decision by the SEC and federal prosecutors to aggressively seek Arthur Andersen's legal demise?

2

The Risk of Fraud and Mechanisms to Address Fraud: Regulation, Corporate Governance, and Audit Quality

CHAPTER OVERVIEW AND LEARNING OBJECTIVES

When conducting a quality audit, auditors are particularly concerned about the occurrence of fraud. There are various types of fraud, and many motivations, opportunities, and rationalizations explaining why people perpetrate fraud. In this chapter, we provide examples of both historical and more recent fraud schemes, and we discuss implications for auditors of recent regulations designed to prevent and detect fraud. We also describe corporate governance, a process by which the owners and creditors of an organization exert control through requiring accountability for the resources entrusted to the organization, and we explain how effective corporate governance can reduce fraud risk.

Through studying this chapter, you will be able to achieve these learning objectives:

通过本章的学习，你将能够实现以下学习目标：

1. Define the various types of fraud that affect organizations.

   定义影响组织的各种舞弊的类型。

2. Define the fraud triangle and describe the three elements of the fraud triangle.

   明确舞弊三角的含义，描述舞弊三角的三个要素。

3. Describe implications for auditors of recent fraudulent financial reporting cases and the third COSO report on fraud.

   描述近期的财务报表舞弊案例和第三个COSO舞弊报告对注册会计师的启示。

4. Discuss auditors' fraud-related responsibilities and users' related expectations.

   讨论注册会计师与舞弊相关的责任和使用者的相关预期。

5. Explain how various requirements in the Sarbanes–Oxley Act of 2002 are designed to help prevent the types frauds perpetrated in the late 1990s and early 2000s.

   解释2002年《萨班斯—奥克斯利法案》中的各种要求是如何防止如19世纪末和20世纪初发生的各种类型的舞弊的。

6. Define corporate governance, identify the parties involved, and describe their respective activities.

   界定公司治理的含义，识别相关各方并描述它们各自的活动。

THE AUDIT OPINION FORMULATION PROCESS

I. Making Client Acceptance and Continuance Decisions **Chapter 14**	II. Performing Risk Assessment **Chapters 3, 7 and 9-13**	III. Obtaining Evidence about Internal Control Operating Effectiveness **Chapters 8-13 and 16**	IV. Obtaining Substantive Evidence about Accounts, Disclosures and Assertions **Chapters 8-13 and 16**	V. Completing the Audit and Making Reporting Decisions **Chapters 14 and 15**

The Auditing Profession, the Risk of Fraud and Mechanisms to Address Fraud: Regulation, Corporate Governance, and Audit Quality
Chapters 1 and 2

Professional Liability and the Need for Quality Auditor Judgments and Ethical Decisions
Chapter 4

The Audit Opinion Formulation Process and A Framework for Obtaining Audit Evidence
Chapters 5 and 6

PROFESSIONAL JUDGMENT IN CONTEXT

Examples of Fraud in Organizations

Milwaukee-based Koss Corporation reported an embezzlement of funds orchestrated by its CFO of approximately $31 million over a five-year period of time when the company's reported earnings were only $26 million. The CFO used the funds to buy personal goods, such as expensive coats, jewelry, and other personal items that were mostly kept in storage facilities. Interestingly, the CFO was neither an accountant nor a CPA; the CEO had a college degree in anthropology; most of the board members had served on the board for 20-30 years; and the company made highly technical products that were in very competitive markets. In another recent fraud, a senior benefits executive at Hitachi America, Inc. diverted approximately $8 million from Hitachi by creating a separate bank account that included the Hitachi name, but that was controlled by him. The funds that were diverted included payments from health providers and insurance companies intended for the Hitachi's employee benefit plans. The executive used the $8 million in the new account to purchase an expensive vacation home and a new Lexus automobile, among other items.

In addition to outright thefts, fraud can also involve inaccurate financial reporting. For example, WorldCom orchestrated its fraud, in part, by capitalizing items that should have been recorded as expenses, thereby increasing current-period income. Charter Communications inflated revenue by selling control boxes back to its supplier and then repurchasing them later. Dell, Inc. admitted to manipulating its reported income by not accurately disclosing payments that it received from computer-chip maker Intel. The payments were in exchange for Dell's agreement not to use chips from Intel's rival, Advanced Micro Devices. These payments accounted for 76% of Dell's operating income in early 2007. Dell also covered earnings shortages by dipping into reserves and claimed the seemingly strong financial results were due to high quality management and efficient operations.

Fraudulent financial reporting can also involve financial-related reports that are not a formal part of the financial statements. As an example, publicly traded oil companies are required to report changes in their proved reserves each year. A proved reserve is the discovery of an oil field in which the company has determined it is economically feasible to extract the oil from the field at current oil prices. The amount of proved reserves are a best estimate of the millions (or billions) of barrels of crude oil that can economically be extracted from the field. During 2004, the SEC successfully brought action against Shell Oil Company, alleging that the company had falsely reported its proved reserves in an effort to make the company look more successful and to maintain the stock price. As you read through this chapter, consider the following questions:

• What are the major types of fraud? What are the major characteristics of fraud that auditors should consider? (LO 1, 2)

• To what extent should the auditor be responsible for identifying the risk of fraud, and then determining whether material fraud actually exists? How can a quality audit prevent or detect these types of frauds? (LO 4)

• How can society as a whole, and the external auditing profession in particular, act to prevent and detect fraud? (LO 4, 5, 6)

• What is corporate governance, and how can effective corporate governance prevent these types of frauds? (LO 6)

舞弊的定义

LO 1 Define the various types of fraud that affect organizations.

舞弊(fraud)
是指被审计单位的管理层、治理层、员工或第三方中的一人或者多人使用欺骗手段获取不当或非法利益的故意行为。

侵占资产导致的错报

编制虚假财务报告导致的错报

Fraud Defined

Fraud is an intentional act involving the use of deception that results in a material misstatement of the financial statements. Two types of misstatements are relevant to auditors' consideration of fraud: (a) misstatements arising from misappropriation of assets, and (b) misstatements arising from fraudulent financial reporting. Intent to deceive is what distinguishes fraud from errors. Auditors routinely find financial errors in their clients' books, but those errors are *not* intentional.

Misstatements Arising From Misappropriation of Assets

Asset misappropriation occurs when a perpetrator steals or misuses an organization's assets. Asset misappropriations are the dominant fraud scheme perpetrated against small businesses and the perpetrators are usually employees. Asset misappropriations can be accomplished in various ways, including embezzling cash receipts, stealing assets, or causing the company to pay for goods or services that were not received. Asset misappropriation commonly occurs when employees:

• Gain access to cash and manipulate accounts to cover up cash thefts
• Manipulate cash disbursements through fake companies
• Steal inventory or other assets and manipulate the financial records to cover up the fraud

An important contemporary example of asset misappropriation is the famous Madoff Ponzi scheme, which is described in Exhibit 2.1.

Misstatements Arising from Fraudulent Financial Reporting

The intentional manipulation of reported financial results to misstate the economic condition of the organization is called **fraudulent financial reporting**. The *Auditing in Practice* feature "The Great Salad Oil Swindle of 1963" is an example of fraudulent financial reporting. The perpetrator of such a fraud generally seeks gain through the rise in stock price and the commensurate increase in personal wealth. Sometimes the perpetrator does not seek direct personal gain, but instead uses the fraudulent financial reporting to "help" the organization avoid bankruptcy or to avoid some other negative financial outcome. Three common ways in which fraudulent financial reporting can take place include:

1. Manipulation, falsification, or alteration of accounting records or supporting documents

EXHIBIT **2.1**	The Bernie Madoff Ponzi Scheme

A **Ponzi scheme** occurs when the deposits of current investors are used to pay returns on the deposits of previous investors; no real investment is happening. A Ponzi scheme will collapse if new investors do not join, or their deposits are too small to pay an adequate return to previous investors. Ponzi schemes are based on two fundamentals: trust and greed. The trust comes from building a relationship with the potential victims. Usually, in Ponzi schemes, the person perpetrating the fraud has gained trust through (a) direct, observable actions by others, (b) professional or other affiliations, or (c) through personal references by others. The greed comes from the investors who see an opportunity to obtain higher than usual returns, and because the trust is there, they do not perform their normal due diligence. Both trust and greed were prevalent in the Madoff scheme.

In March 2009, Madoff pleaded guilty to 11 federal crimes and admitted to turning his wealth management business into a massive Ponzi scheme that defrauded thousands of investors of billions of dollars. Madoff said he began the Ponzi scheme in the early 1990s. However, federal investigators believe the fraud began as early as the 1980s, and that the investment operation may never have been legitimate. The amount missing from client accounts, including fabricated gains, was almost $65 billion. On June 29, 2009, Madoff was sentenced to 150 years in prison, the maximum allowed.

Madoff built a veil of trust by running a legitimate brokerage firm, and at one time was the Chair of NASDAQ. He often appeared on CNBC talking about the securities industry. Madoff took advantage of his unique ties to the investment community to encourage further investment, and he always sold the idea of an investment into his company as one of "special privilege". He conducted the scheme by hiring individuals who were paid commissions to bring in more investors. Obviously, the scheme can only work as long as the funds brought into the scheme in future years are sufficient to continue to pay all the previous investors. Ponzi schemes always become too big and collapse. However, until the collapse, Madoff led an extremely lavish lifestyle.

Madoff conducted the scheme by keeping all of the transactions off his formal books. He employed a CPA firm to audit the books, but the firm consisted of only one employee and there is no indication that the CPA firm ever visited Madoff's offices or that any real audit was actually performed. However, note that the investors never asked for such audit reports. This is where the importance of greed plays a part. The investors felt they were part of something special, and they enjoyed earning high investment returns. They trusted Madoff, so they let down their guard by not asking for typical due diligence information of which an external audit is an important part.

Although not verified, a rumor (as reported on a CNBC prime-time special) alleges that Madoff chose to surrender and plead guilty because one of the investors was with the Russian mob and Madoff feared for both his life and that of his sons. Madoff is currently serving his life sentence in federal prison, and one of his sons committed suicide two years after the fraud was revealed. During the time of this fraud, the PCAOB did not require that hedge funds like Madoff's be audited by audit firms registered with the PCAOB. Following the Madoff fraud, in July 2010 Congress gave the PCAOB oversight of the audits of SEC-registered brokers and dealers.

2. Misrepresentation or omission of events, transactions, or other significant information
3. Intentional misapplication of accounting principles

The Fraud Triangle

The term **fraud triangle** was introduced by career criminologist Don Cressey more than 30 years ago. Cressey started by identifying patterns in fraud cases, and he identified three factors that were consistently present in all frauds. Research over the past two decades has reinforced the validity of the fraud triangle.

The three elements of the fraud triangle, as shown in Exhibit 2.2, include:

- Incentive to commit fraud
- Opportunity to commit and conceal the fraud
- Rationalization—the mindset of the fraudster to justify committing the fraud

舞弊三角

LO 2 Define the fraud triangle and describe the three elements of the fraud triangle.

舞弊的产生是由动机（或压力）、机会以及借口（或自我合理化）三要素组成，就像必须同时具备一定的热度、燃料、氧气这三要素才能燃烧一样，缺少了上述任何一项要素都不可能真正形成舞弊。

The Great Salad Oil Swindle of 1963

The Great Salad Oil Swindle was one of the first modern large-scale frauds involving financial reporting. It was perpetrated by Allied Crude Vegetable Oil in New Jersey. The concept was simple: the company could overstate its financial position by claiming that it had more inventory than it actually had. Overstated assets provide the company the opportunity to understate expenses and to overstate income. The fraud ultimately cost creditors and suppliers about $150 million (over $1 billion in current dollars).

The fraud was fairly simple. The company stored salad oil in large tanks. It issued numerous receipts all showing that it owned a large amount of salad oil inventory. The auditor did observe part of the inventory, but did so by checking the various tanks one after another. The company accomplished the fraud by doing the following:

- First, it filled the tanks with a large inside container of water.
- Second, it created an outer layer with salad oil, so if the auditor checked the oil from an opening on top, the auditor would find oil.
- Third, the company pumped the oil underground from one tank to another in anticipation of the auditor's planned inspection route.

This is a historically relevant fraud and has practical application today, because fraud perpetrators continue to use inventory manipulation to commit fraud.

EXHIBIT **2.2**   The Fraud Triangle

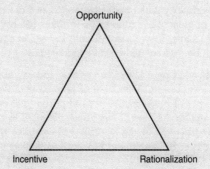

Factors associated with these elements are referred to as fraud risk factors or **red flags**.

We illustrate the fraud triangle with a simple example from a fraud that took place in a construction company. The company did paving, sewer, and gutter work. It started small, but grew to about $30 million in annual revenue. The construction work was performed at various locations throughout Michigan and Colorado. The company often purchased supplies at the job location, which were signed for by a construction employee and forwarded to the accountant for payment. The company had one accountant, but the president of the company approved all payments and formally signed off on them. When the president retired, he was replaced by his son, who spent more time growing the paving business than on accounting. He trusted the accountant because of the work the accountant had done for his father; therefore, he spent considerably less time in reviewing and signing off on payments than his father had done.

Now let us consider how the fraud triangle worked in this case. The essence of the fraud was that the accountant prepared bogus invoices for a bogus vendor, set the account up in his name, and prepared receiving slips and purchase orders to gain approval for the payments. First, what were the *incentives* for the fraud? Like many similar situations, the accountant faced considerable personal financial problems, mostly associated with taking care of his elderly parents, who had unpaid medical bills. Second, because the new president no longer reviewed items for payment, the *opportunity* (deficiencies in controls) presented itself. Third, the *rationalization* was a little more complex. Like most frauds, the fraudster thought that it would be a one-time extra payment to get him over the difficult times, and like most frauds, when the fraud was not detected, there was a further opportunity to grow it. The other part of the rationalization was more subtle. When the new president furnished all of the vice-presidents and job supervisors with new pickup trucks, the accountant did not receive one, nor did he receive a very substantial bonus, as compared to the job superintendents. The accountant felt that the amount of money he was taking was no different than what the job superintendents and vice-presidents were getting. In other words, he rationalized his actions to himself by believing that he "deserved" the payments.

If any one of these three elements of the fraud triangle were not present (medical "need," poor internal controls, rationalization), then it is less likely that the fraud would have taken place. Thus, when the auditor starts to consider the likelihood of fraud—either through misappropriation of assets or through fraudulent financial reporting—the auditor should start with consideration of the three elements of the triangle.

Incentives or Pressures to Commit Fraud

舞弊的动机或压力

The audit team should consider the incentives or pressures to commit fraud on each engagement, including the most likely areas in which fraud might take place. These incentives include the following for fraudulent financial reporting:

- Management compensation schemes
- Other financial pressures for either improved earnings or an improved balance sheet
- Debt covenants
- Pending retirement or stock option expirations
- Personal wealth tied to either financial results or survival of the company
- Greed—for example, the backdating of stock options was performed by individuals who already had millions of dollars of wealth through stock

Incentives relating to asset misappropriation include:

- Personal factors, such as severe financial considerations
- Pressure from family, friends, or the culture to live a more lavish lifestyle than one's personal earnings allow for
- Addictions to gambling or drugs

Opportunities to Commit Fraud

舞弊的机会

One of the most fundamental and consistent findings in fraud research is that there must be an opportunity for fraud to be committed. Although this may sound obvious—that is, "everyone has an opportunity to commit fraud"—it really conveys much more. It means not only that an opportunity exists, but either there is a lack of controls or the complexities associated with a transaction are such that the perpetrator assesses the risk of being caught as low. Some of the opportunities to commit fraud that the auditor should consider include the following:

- Significant related-party transactions
- A company's industry position, such as the ability to dictate terms or conditions to suppliers or customers that might allow individuals to structure fraudulent transactions

- Management's inconsistency involving subjective judgments regarding assets or accounting estimates
- Simple transactions that are made complex through an unusual recording process
- Complex or difficult to understand transactions, such as financial derivatives or special-purpose entities
- Ineffective monitoring of management by the board, either because the board of directors is not independent or effective, or because there is a domineering manager
- Complex or unstable organizational structure
- Weak or nonexistent internal controls

合理化的解释

Rationalizing the Fraud

Rationalization is a crucial component in most frauds. Rationalization involves a person reconciling unlawful or unethical behavior, such as stealing, with the commonly accepted notions of decency and trust. For fraudulent financial reporting, the rationalization can range from "saving the company" to personal greed, and includes thoughts such as:

- This is a one-time thing to get us through the current crisis and survive until things get better.
- Everybody cheats on the financial statements a little; we are just playing the same game.
- We will be in violation of all of our debt covenants unless we find a way to get this debt off the financial statements.
- We need a higher stock price to acquire company XYZ, or to keep our employees through stock options, and so forth.

For asset misappropriation, personal rationalizations often revolve around mistreatment by the company or a sense of entitlement (such as, "the company owes me!") by the individual perpetrating the fraud. Following are some common rationalizations for asset misappropriation:

- Fraud is justified to save a family member or loved one from financial crisis.
- We will lose everything (family, home, car, and so on) if we don't take the money.
- No help is available from outside.
- This is "borrowing," and we intend to pay the stolen money back at some point.
- Something is owed by the company because others are treated better.
- We simply do not care about the consequences of our actions or of accepted notions of decency and trust; we are out for ourselves.

财务报告舞弊的近期历史

LO 3 Describe implications for auditors of recent fraudulent financial reporting cases and the third COSO report on fraud.

近期财务报告舞弊的案例以及对外部注册会计师的启示

Recent History of Fraudulent Financial Reporting

We now turn to a discussion of recent frauds, their implications for external auditors, a report by the Committee of Sponsoring Organizations (COSO) on the general characteristics of major financial reporting frauds, and a detailed discussion of the Enron fraud.

Examples of Recent Frauds and Implications for External Auditors

Examples of fraudulent financial reporting in the recent past are described in Exhibit 2.3. Of course, there are many more frauds that were discovered during this time, but this is a glimpse of a few notable instances.

EXHIBIT **2.3**	Examples of Recent Fraudulent Financial Reporting
Company	**Nature of the Fraud**
Enron (2001) 安然舞弊案被认为是21世纪初影响最严重的舞弊事件。该公司成立于1930年，曾连续四年获《财富》杂志评选的"美国最具创新精神的公司"称号。其主要通过"特别目的实体"高估利润、低估负债；通过空挂应收票据，高估资产和股东权益；通过设立众多的有限合伙企业，进行自我交易，操纵利润。	Considered by many to be one of the most significant frauds of the early 2000s, Enron was initially a utility company that management converted into an energy trading company. When energy trades went bad, management covered up financial problems by: • Shifting debt to off-balance sheet special entities • Recognizing revenue on impaired assets by selling them to special-purpose entities that they controlled • Engaging in round-tripping trades, which are trades that eventually found the assets returning to Enron after initially recognizing sales and profits • Numerous other related-party transactions
WorldCom (2002)	In what would end in one of the largest bankruptcies of all time, WorldCom was the second-largest U.S. long distance phone company (after AT&T). The company pursued an aggressive growth strategy of acquiring other telecommunications companies. When the financial results of these acquisitions faltered, management decreased expenses and increased revenues through the following: • Recorded bartered transactions as sales; for example, trading the right to use lines in one part of the world to similar rights to another part of the world • Used restructuring reserves established through acquisitions to decrease expenses; for example, over-accrued reserves upon acquiring a company and later "releasing" those reserves to decrease expenses of future periods • Capitalized line costs (rentals paid to other phone companies) rather than expensing them as would have been appropriate
Parmalat (2003)	Parmalat is an Italian multinational company specializing in milk, fruit juice, and other food products. In the late 1990s, the company acquired various international subsidiaries and funded the acquisitions with debt. Ultimately, the fraud led to the largest bankruptcy in Europe. The company siphoned cash from subsidiaries through a complex scheme that: • Overstated cash and included the false recording of cash ostensibly held at major banks • Understated debt by entering into complex transactions with off-shore subsidiaries in tax-haven places such as countries in the Caribbean
HealthSouth (2003)	HealthSouth runs the largest group of inpatient rehabilitation hospitals in the U.S. Top management directed company employees to grossly exaggerate earnings in order to meet shareholder and analyst expectations. A wide variety of schemes were used including: • Billing group psychiatric sessions as individual sessions; for example, with ten people in a group session, billing for ten individual sessions instead of one group session • Using adjusted journal entries to both reduce expenses and enhance revenues
Dell (2005)	Dell is a U.S. computer maker that ultimately was forced to pay the SEC $100 million to settle fraud charges against the company. The fraud included various disclosure inaccuracies, including: • Misleading investors by miscategorizing large payments from Intel, which were essentially bribes to ensure that Dell would not use central processing units manufactured by Intel's main rival • Misrepresenting the Intel payments as involving operations, enabling the company to meet its earnings targets • Failing to disclose the true reason for the company's profitability declines that occurred after Intel refused to continue making the payments

(continued)

EXHIBIT **2.3**	Examples of Recent Fraudulent Financial Reporting (*continued*)
Company	**Nature of the Fraud**
Koss Corp. (2009)	Koss Corporation is a U.S. headphone manufacturer. The CFO misappropriated approximately $31 of funds for her personal use during a period of time in which reported earnings was $26 million. Ultimately, she had to pay $34 million in restitution and is currently serving an 11-year prison sentence. She perpetrated the fraud through a process consisting of: • Intimidation of lower-level employees • Sole approval for large expenditures made through American Express and other corporate credit cards • Lack of supervisory review and approval by CEO • Lack of audit committee oversight • Lack of an effective internal audit function
Olympus (2011)	Olympus is a large multinational manufacturer involved in the medical, life science, industrial, and imaging industries. Its top level executives and boards: • Concealed large losses related to securities investments for over two decades • Switched audit firms during the period because company management clashed with their external auditor over accounting issues • Committed fraud, which was eventually revealed when the company's president was fired after discovering and objecting to accounting irregularities
Longtop Financial Technologies (2011)	Longtop was the first Chinese software company to be listed on the NYSE and was the leading software development provider in the financial services industry in that country. This fraud highlighted the risks that investors face when investing their money in Chinese companies with weak corporate governance. The company: • Exaggerated profit margins by shifting staffing expenses to another entity • Recorded fake cash to cover up fake revenue that had been previously recognized • Threated the audit firm personnel and tried to physically retain the audit firm's workpapers when the auditors uncovered the fraud

The patterns evident across the frauds presented in Exhibit 2.3 imply the following regarding the conduct of the audit:

• The auditor should be aware of the pressure that analyst following and earnings expectations create for top management.
• If there are potential problems with revenue, the audit cannot be completed until there is sufficient time to examine major year-end transactions.
• The auditor must understand complex transactions to determine their economic substance and the parties that have economic obligations.
• The auditor must clearly understand and analyze weaknesses in an organization's internal controls in order to determine where and how a fraud may take place.
• Audit procedures must be developed to address specific opportunities for fraud to take place.

保持职业怀疑要求注册会计师对获取的信息和审计证据是否表明可能存在由于舞弊导致的重大错报风险始终保持警惕，包括考虑拟用作审计证据的信息的可靠性，并考虑与信息的生成和维护相关的控制。

These examples also illustrate that auditors must exercise professional skepticism in analyzing the possibility of fraud and must be especially alert to trends in performance, or results that are not consistent with other companies, in determining whether extended audit procedures should be performed. Further, those procedures cannot simply be an expansion of normal procedures. Rather, the procedures must be targeted at discovering potential fraud when there are red flags suggesting a heightened risk of

Professional Skepticism

What is professional skepticism, and how does an auditor maintain proper professional skepticism in an environment in which the auditor's personal experiences might consist only of audits in which no fraud was ever found? After all, we are all products of our experiences, and many times our audit experience will tell us that we spent extra time investigating something that showed nothing was wrong, resulting in increased audit time, but no discovery of wrongdoing. How do we approach each situation as something unique, and not the total culmination of our past experiences?

The Center for Audit Quality (CAQ), in its 2010 report on fraud, describes professional skepticism as follows:

> Skepticism involves the validation of information through probing questions, the critical assessment of evidence, and attention to inconsistencies. Skepticism is not an end in itself and is not meant to encourage a hostile atmosphere or micromanagement; it is an essential element of the professional objectivity required of all participants in the financial reporting supply chain. Skepticism throughout the supply chain increases not only the likelihood that fraud will be detected, but also the perception that fraud will be detected, which reduces the risk that fraud will be attempted.

Similar to the CAQ report, international auditing standards define professional skepticism as follows:

> Professional skepticism is an attitude that includes a questioning mind and a critical assessment of audit evidence. Professional skepticism requires an ongoing questioning of whether the information and audit evidence obtained suggests that a material misstatement due to fraud may exist.
> (ISA 240, para. 23)

The Standard goes on to state:

> The auditor's previous experience with the entity contributes to an understanding of the entity. However, although the auditor cannot be expected to fully disregard past experience with the entity about the honesty and integrity of management and those charged with governance, the maintenance of an attitude of professional skepticism is important because there may have been changes in circumstances. When making inquiries and performing other audit procedures, the auditor exercises professional skepticism and is not satisfied with less-than-persuasive audit evidence based on a belief that management and those charged with governance are honest and have integrity. With respect to those charged with governance, maintaining an attitude of professional skepticism means that the auditor carefully considers the reasonableness of responses to inquiries of those charged with governance, and other information obtained from them, in light of all other evidence obtained during the audit.
> (ISA 240, para. 25)

The key elements to successfully exercising professional skepticism include obtaining strong evidence and analyzing that evidence through critical assessment, attention to inconsistencies, and asking probing (often open-ended) questions. The essence of auditing is to bring professional skepticism to the audit and to be alert to all of the possibilities that may cause the auditor to be misled.

fraud. The *Auditing in Practice Feature* "Professional Skepticism" provides definitions and further explanation of this important concept.

The Third COSO Report

第三个COSO报告

COSO has conducted three major studies on fraudulent financial reporting. The most recent study, published in 2010, was of companies that were cited by the SEC during the time period of 1998-2007 for fraudulent financial reporting. The analysis identified the major characteristics of companies that had perpetrated fraud. The analysis also focused on comparing fraud and nonfraud companies of similar sizes and in similar industries to determine which factors were the best in discriminating between the fraud and the nonfraud companies. Some of the major findings were:

- The amount and incidence of fraud remains high. The total amount of fraud was more than $120 billion spread across just 300 companies.
- The median size of company perpetrating the fraud rose tenfold to $100 million during the 1998-2007 period (as compared to the previous ten years).
- There was heavy involvement in the fraud by the CEO and/or CFO, with at least one of them named in 89% of the cases.
- The most common fraud involved revenue recognition—60% of the cases during the latest period compared to 50% in previous periods.
- One-third of the companies changed auditors during the latter part of the fraud (with the full knowledge of the audit committee) compared to less than half that amount of auditor changes taking place with the non-fraud companies.
- Consistent with previous COSO studies, the majority of the frauds took place at companies that were listed on the Over-The-Counter (OTC) market, rather than those listed on the NYSE or NASDAQ.

Overall, the third COSO report shows that fraudulent financial reporting remains a very significant problem. Commonly cited motivations for fraud included the need to meet internal or external earnings expectations, an attempt to conceal the company's deteriorating financial condition, the need to increase the stock price, the need to bolster financial performance for pending equity or debt financing, or the desire to increase management compensation based on financial results.[1]

安然舞弊案：监管改革的一个重要驱动力

The Enron Fraud: A Key Driver of Regulatory Change

Enron is perhaps the most famous fraud of the early 2000s, representing almost everything that was wrong at the time with corporate governance, accounting, financial analysts, banking, and the external auditing profession. How did it happen? Enron was a utility company that developed a new concept and rode the new concept to unbelievable stock market highs. Just prior to its collapse, it had a stock value of $90 per share, which eventually became worthless. The concept: it would increase market efficiency by developing the most sophisticated system in the world to trade electricity, natural gas, and related resources. It would separate the production of energy—a capital intensive process—from the trading and use of the resources. It would improve market efficiency by increasing the scope of energy production and expanding the output of the local utility to the nation and the world. Energy would flow where the highest market bid for it, which is a fundamental concept of economics. Enron hired MBA traders who were provided lucrative bonuses for meeting profit objectives. Competition among the traders was encouraged, and risks were encouraged; but most of all, reported profits were rewarded. However, much of the company, at its heart, remained a utility. It needed heavy amounts of cash to support its trading position and it needed to continually report higher profits to sustain stock market valuations. Most of the top executives of the company were compensated primarily through stock.

The nature of fraud that took place was widespread. Most of the frauds involved Special Purpose Entities (SPEs), partnerships that often involved substantial loans from banks to be secured by assets transferred to the SPE, partners dominated by Enron executives, and a small outside interest (exceeding 3% per the accounting rule). The company transferred devalued assets to the SPEs and

---

[1] COSO, Fraudulent Financial Reporting: 1998–2007, An Analysis of U.S. Public Companies, 2010, available at *www.coso.org*.

recognized gains on the books. It kept borrowing off the books by having the SPEs borrow from banks and purchase Enron assets. It even recognized over $100 million in anticipated sales that it hoped would occur with a joint venture with Blockbuster on rental movies over the Internet. The SPEs were used such that Enron's balance sheet looked healthy because it minimized the debt on the balance sheet; the SPEs also increased reported income by hiding all losses.

What were the failures that allowed the Enron fraud to occur? Unfortunately, the answer is that the failures were widespread and include:

- *Management Accountability.* Management was virtually not accountable to anyone as long as the company showed dramatic stock increases justified by earnings growth. Company management had a "good story," and anyone who questioned them was viewed as being stupid. Compensation was based on stock price. And, apparently stock price was based on a good story and fictitious numbers.
- *Corporate Governance.* Although the board appeared to be independent, most of the board members had close ties to management of the company through philanthropic organizations. Some board members hardly ever attended a meeting, and they certainly did not ask hard questions. Finally, the board waived a "conflict of interest" provision in their code of ethics that allowed Andy Fastow, the treasurer of the company, to profit handsomely from related-party transactions.
- *Accounting Rules.* Accounting became more rule-oriented and complex. Accounting allowed practitioners to take obscure pronouncements, such as those dealing with Special Purpose Entities that were designed for leasing transactions, and apply the pronouncement to other entities for which such accounting was never intended. Accounting was looked at as a tool to earn more money, not as a mechanism to portray economic reality.
- *The Financial Analyst Community.* Financial analysts that were riding the bubble of the dot-com economy concluded they did not have tools to appropriately value many of the emerging companies. Rather than analyze the underlying fundamentals, the analysts relied too much on "earnings guidance" by management. Managers that achieved the projected guidance were rewarded; those who did not were severely punished. Analysts came to accept "pro forma accounting statements," more aptly described as what would occur as long as nothing bad happened.
- *Banking and Investment Banking.* Many large financial institutions were willing participants in the process because they were rewarded with large underwriting fees for other Enron work. Enron management was smart enough to know that the investment bankers were also rewarded on the amount of fees they generated.
- *The External Auditing Profession and Arthur Andersen.* At the time of Enron, the largest five external audit firms referred to themselves as professional service firms with diverse lines of business. All of the firms had large consulting practices. Arthur Andersen performed internal audit work for Enron, in addition to performing the external audit. The consulting fees of many clients dramatically exceeded the audit fees. Partners were compensated on revenue and profitability. Worse yet, auditors were hired by management who sometimes succeeded in pressuring auditors to acquiesce to aggressive financial reporting preferences. In short, there is a perception that audit quality was low during this period of time. The final straw for Arthur Andersen was that when federal authorities began investigating the bankruptcy of Enron, the Houston office auditors on the Enron engagement began aggressively destroying documentation and evidence related to their failed audit. Ultimately, this action was what enabled federal authorities to force the downfall of Arthur Andersen.

注册会计师与舞弊相关
的责任和使用者的预期

LO 4 Discuss auditors' fraud-related responsibilities and users' related expectations.

An Overview of the Auditor's Fraud-Related Responsibilities and Users' Expectations

Given the prevalence of fraud, it is important to consider the auditor's role related to fraud detection. In October 2010, the Center for Audit Quality (CAQ) issued a paper titled *Deterring and Detecting Financial Reporting Fraud—A Platform for Action.*[2] The CAQ views fraud-related responsibilities as the key means to improve the external auditor's contribution to society and to gain respect for the auditing profession. However, the CAQ also recognizes that preventing and detecting fraud cannot be the job of the external auditor alone; all the parties involved in preparing and opining on audited financial statements need to play a role in preventing and detecting fraud. The CAQ report identifies three ways in which individuals involved in the financial reporting process (management, the audit committee, internal audit, external audit, and regulatory authorities) can mitigate the risk of fraudulent financial reporting:

- These individuals need to acknowledge that there needs to exist a strong, highly ethical tone at the top of an organization that permeates the corporate culture, including an effective fraud risk management program.
- These individuals need to continually exercise professional skepticism, a questioning mindset that strengthens professional objectivity, in evaluating and/or preparing financial reports.
- These individuals need to remember that strong communication among those involved in the financial reporting process is critical.

Auditing standards historically have reflected a belief that it is not reasonable to expect auditors to detect cleverly implemented frauds. However, it is increasingly clear that the general public, as reflected in the orientation of the PCAOB, expects that auditors have a responsibility to detect and report on material frauds, as noted below:

> The mission of the PCAOB is to restore the confidence of investors, and society generally, in the independent auditors of companies. There is no doubt that repeated revelations of accounting scandals and audit failures have seriously damaged public confidence. The detection of material fraud is a reasonable expectation of users of audited financial statements. Society needs and expects assurance that financial information has not been materially misstated because of fraud. *Unless an independent audit can provide this assurance, it has little if any value to society.* [emphasis added][3]

The users' message to auditors is clear: auditors must assume a greater responsibility for detecting fraud and providing assurance that the financial statements are free of material fraud. Professional auditing standards do require the auditor to plan and perform an audit that will detect material misstatements resulting from fraud. As part of that requirement, auditors should begin an audit with a brainstorming session that focuses on how and where fraud could occur within the organization. Auditors also need to communicate with the audit committee and management about the risks of fraud and how they are addressed. The auditor should then plan the audit to be responsive to an organization's susceptibility to fraud. In subsequent chapters, we discuss specific ways that auditors can respond to fraud in various phases of the audit.

---

[2] Center for Audit Quality, *Deterring and Detecting Financial Reporting Fraud—A Platform for Action,* available at *www.thecaq.org/Anti-FraudInitiative/CFraudReport.pdf.*

[3] Douglas R. Carmichael, *The PCAOB and the Social Responsibility of the Independent Auditor,* Chief Auditor, Public Accounting Oversight Board, speech given to Midyear Auditing Section meeting of the American Accounting Association, January 16, 2004.

The Sarbanes–Oxley Act of 2002 as a Regulatory Response to Fraud

The financial scandals and associated stock market declines in the late 1990s and early 2000s dramatically illustrated the costs of inappropriate ethical decisions by various parties, of weak corporate governance, of low audit quality, and of insufficient auditor independence. The bankruptcy of Enron and the subsequent collapse of Arthur Andersen were such dramatic events that Congress was compelled to respond, and it did so in the form of the **Sarbanes-Oxley Act of 2002**. Exhibit 2.4 summarizes the major provisions of the Sarbanes-Oxley Act. Note that the Sarbanes-Oxley Act applies to publicly traded companies, not privately held organizations. However, since the Sarbanes-Oxley Act was enacted, privately held organizations often view the requirements of the Act as "best practice" and sometimes try to adhere to the requirements even though they are not legally required to do so.

2002年的《萨班斯–奥克斯利法案》：监管机构对舞弊的反应

LO 5 Explain how various requirements in the Sarbanes–Oxley Act of 2002 are designed to help prevent the types frauds perpetrated in the late 1990s and early 2000s.

EXHIBIT 2.4   Significant Provisions of the Sarbanes–Oxley Act of 2002

Section	Requirements

TITLE 1: Public Company Accounting Oversight Board

101 *Establishment and administrative provisions.* The Board:
- Is a nonprofit corporation, not an agency of the U.S. government
- Will have five financially literate members who are prominent individuals of integrity and reputation with a commitment to the interests of investors and the public
- Has authority to set standards related to audit reports and to conduct inspections of registered public accounting firms

102 *Registration with the Board.* Accounting firms auditing public companies must register with the PCAOB.

103 *Auditing, quality control, and independence standards and rules.* The Board will:
- Establish or adopt rules regarding the conduct of audits and regarding audit firm quality control standards
- Require audit firms to describe the scope of testing of issuers' internal control structure

104 *Inspections of registered public accounting firms.* The Board will:
- Inspect annually registered accounting firms that audit 100 or more issuers
- Inspect at least every three years registered accounting firms that audit fewer than 100 issuers
- Publicly report results of its inspections

105 *Investigations and disciplinary proceedings.* The Board will:
- Adopt procedures for disciplining registered accounting firms
- Require registered accounting firms to provide documentation and testimony that the Board deems necessary to conduct investigations
- Be able to sanction registered accounting firms for noncooperation with investigations

106 *Foreign public accounting firms.* Foreign accounting firms must comply with the same rules related to the PCAOB as domestic accounting firms.

107 *Commission oversight of the Board.* The SEC has oversight and enforcement authority over the Board, including in processes involving standards setting, enforcement, and disciplinary procedures.

108 *Accounting standards.* The SEC will recognize as "generally accepted" accounting principles that are established by a standard setter that meets the Act's criteria.

109 *Funding.* Registered accounting firms and issuers will pay for the operations of the Board.

(continued)

EXHIBIT **2.4**   Significant Provisions of the Sarbanes–Oxley Act of 2002 (*continued*)

Section	Requirements

TITLE II: Auditor Independence

201   *Services outside the scope of practice of auditors.* There exist a variety of services that registered accounting firms may not perform for issuers, such as bookkeeping, systems design, appraisal services, and internal auditing, among others. Tax services may be performed, but only with pre-approval by the audit committee.

202   *Preapproval requirements.* All audit and nonaudit services (with certain exceptions based on size and practicality) must be approved by the audit committee of the issuer.

203   *Audit partner rotation.* The lead partner and reviewing partner must rotate off the issuer engagement at least every five years.

204   *Auditor reports to audit committees.* Registered accounting firms must report to the audit committee issues concerning:

- Critical accounting policies and practices
- Alternative treatments of financial information within generally accepted accounting principles that have been considered by management, as well as the preferred treatment of the accounting firm
- Significant written communications between the accounting firm and management

205   *Conforming amendments.* This section details minor wording changes between the Sarbanes–Oxley Act and the Securities Act of 1934.

206   *Conflicts of interest.* Registered accounting firms may not perform audits for an issuer whose CEO, CFO, controller, chief accounting officer, or other equivalent position was employed by the accounting firm during the one–year period preceding the audit. This is known as a "cooling off period."

207   *Study of mandatory rotation of registered public accounting firms.* The Comptroller General of the United States shall conduct a study addressing this issue.

TITLE III: Corporate Responsibility

301   *Public company audit committees.*

- Audit committees are to be directly responsible for the appointment, compensation, and oversight of the work of registered accounting firms.
- Each audit committee member shall be independent.
- Audit committees must establish "whistleblowing" mechanisms within issuers.
- Audit committees have the authority to engage their own independent counsel.
- Issuers must provide adequate funding for audit committees.

302   *Corporate responsibility for financial reports.* The signing officers (usually the CEO and CFO):

- Will certify in quarterly and annual reports filed with the SEC that the report does not contain untrue statements of material facts, and that the financial statements and disclosures present fairly (in all material respects) the financial condition and results of operations of the issuer
- Must establish and maintain effective internal controls to ensure reliable financial statements and disclosures
- Are responsible for designing internal controls, assessing their effectiveness, and disclosing material deficiencies in controls to the audit committee and to the registered accounting firm

303   *Improper influence on conduct of audits.* Officers of issuers may not take action to fraudulently influence, coerce, manipulate, or mislead the registered accounting firm or its employees.

TITLE IV: Enhanced Financial Disclosures

401   *Disclosures in periodic reports.*

- Financial reports must be in accordance with generally accepted accounting principles, and must reflect material correcting adjustments proposed by the registered accounting firm.

<table>
<tr><td>EXHIBIT **2.4**</td><td>Significant Provisions of the Sarbanes–Oxley Act of 2002 (*continued*)</td></tr>
</table>

Section	Requirements

- Material off–balance–sheet transactions and other relationships with unconsolidated entities or persons must be disclosed.
- The SEC must issue new rules on *pro forma* figures, and must study the issues of off–balance–sheet transactions and the use of special–purpose entities.

402   *Enhanced conflict of interest provisions.* Issuers may not extend credit to directors or executive offers.

403   *Disclosures of transactions involving management and principal stockholders.* Requires that any director, officer, or shareholder who owns more than 10 percent of the company's equity securities publicly disclose that fact.

404   *Management assessment of internal controls.*

- Annual reports must state the responsibility of management for establishing and maintaining an adequate internal control structure and procedures for financial reporting.
- Annual reports must contain an assessment of the effectiveness of the internal control structure and procedures of the issuer for financial reporting.
- Each registered accounting firm must attest to and report on the assessment made by the management of the issuer, and such attestation must not be the subject of a separate engagement (in other words, requires an integrated audit).

404条款要求公众公司管理当局定期对企业内部控制的有效性进行评价，并披露评价报告；注册会计师则需要对该份报告进行审计。

406   *Code of ethics for senior financial officers.* The SEC must issue rules requiring issuers to disclose whether or not the issuer has adopted a code of ethics for senior financial officers (and if not, the issuer must explain the rationale).

407   *Disclosure of audit committee financial expert.* The SEC must issue rules to require issuers to disclose whether or not the audit committee of the issuer is comprised of at least one member who is a financial expert (and if not, the issuer must explain the rationale).

SECTION V: Analyst Conflicts of Interest

501   *Treatment of securities analysts.* Registered securities associations and national securities exchanges must adopt rules to address concerns about conflicts of interest for analysts that recommend equity securities.

SECTION VI: Commission Resources and Authority

601   *Enhanced funding for the SEC.* The SEC's budget is increased to enable stronger enforcement and regulation of parties involved in the securities markets.

602   *Appearance and practice before the Commission.* The SEC may censure any person, or deny, temporarily or permanently, the privilege of appearing or practicing before the SEC if that person is found:

- Not to possess the requisite qualifications to represent others
- To be lacking in character or integrity, or to have engaged in unethical or improper professional conduct
- To have willfully violated or willfully aided and abetted the violation of any provision of the securities laws

SECTION VII: Studies and Reports

701   *GAO study and report regarding consolidation of public accounting firms.* The Comptroller General of the United States shall conduct a study addressing factors leading to consolidation of public accounting firms since 1989 and the reduction in the number of firms capable of providing audit services to large national and multinational businesses subject to the securities laws.

702   *Commission study and report regarding credit rating agencies.* The SEC shall conduct a study on the role and function of credit rating agencies in the operation of the securities market.

(*continued*)

| EXHIBIT **2.4** | Significant Provisions of the Sarbanes–Oxley Act of 2002 (*continued*) |

Section	Requirements
703	*Study and report on violators and violations.* The SEC shall conduct a study to determine the number of securities professionals (public accountants, public accounting firms, investment bankers, brokers, dealers, attorneys, and so on) who have aided and abetted a violation of the federal securities laws, but have not been sanctioned, disciplined, or otherwise penalized.
704	*Study of enforcement actions.* The Comptroller General of the United States shall review and analyze all enforcement actions by the SEC involving violations of reporting requirements imposed under the securities laws and restatements over the five–year period preceding the Sarbanes–Oxley Act.
705	*Study of investment banks.* The Comptroller General of the United States shall conduct a study on whether investment banks and financial advisers assisted public companies in manipulating their earnings and obfuscating their true financial condition.

SECTION VIII: Corporate and Criminal Fraud Accountability

Section	Requirements
802	*Criminal penalties for altering documents.* Stronger penalties are now imposed for crimes involving the destruction, alteration, falsification, or destruction of financial records or corporate audit records.
805	*Review of federal sentencing guidelines for obstruction of justice and extensive criminal fraud.* Sentencing guidelines are enhanced for fraud and obstruction of justice sentences.
806	*Protection for employees of publicly traded companies who provide evidence of fraud.* This section provides whistleblower protection to protect against retaliation in fraud cases.
807	*Criminal penalties for defrauding shareholders of publicly traded companies.* Stronger penalties are now imposed for crimes involving securities fraud.

TITLE IX: White–Collar Crime Penalty Enhancements

Section	Requirements
903	*Criminal penalties for mail and wire fraud.* This section increases penalties for these violations.
904	*Criminal penalties for violations of the Employee Retirement Income Security Act of 1974.* This section increases penalties for violations of this Act.
905	*Amendment to sentencing guidelines relating to certain white–collar offenses.* The United States Sentencing Commission shall review and amend Federal Sentencing Guidelines related to provisions of the Sarbanes–Oxley Act.
906	*Corporate responsibility for financial reports.* This section provides penalties for corporate directors who knowingly provide incorrect certifications of financial statements and reports.

TITLE X: Corporate Tax Returns

Section	Requirements
1001	*Sense of the Senate regarding the signing of corporate tax returns by chief executive officers.* The CEO must sign the corporate tax return.

TITLE XI: Corporate Fraud and Accountability

Section	Requirements
1102	*Tampering with a record or otherwise impeding an official proceeding.* This section provides penalties for whoever corruptly alters, destroys, mutilates, or conceals a record, document, or other object (or attempts to do so) with the intent to impair the object's integrity and availability for use in an official proceeding. It also provides penalties for whoever otherwise obstructs, influences, or impedes any official proceeding, or attempts to do so.
1105	*Authority of the Commission to prohibit persons from serving as officers or directors.* The SEC may prohibit from serving before it as an officer or director any individual who has violated Section 10(b) of the Securities Act of 1934 or Section 8A of the Securities Act of 1933.
1106	*Increased criminal penalties under Securities Act of 1934.* This section provides increased penalties for violations of the Securities Act of 1934.

As is clear from reading Exhibit 2.4, many sections of the Sarbanes–Oxley Act were written to respond to various abuses of the financial reporting process in the late 1990s and early 2000s, and many provisions affect auditors and the auditing profession directly through requirements intended to increase audit quality. For example, Title I and its relevant sections effectively remove self–regulation of the auditing profession and replace it with independent oversight by the Public Company Accounting Oversight Board (PCAOB). Section 201 prevents audit firms from providing many consulting services to audit clients, which was an issue cited as a significant driver of the failed audits of Enron. Sections 204, 301, and 407 significantly expand the power, responsibilities, and disclosures of corporate audit committees, thereby addressing concerns over weak corporate governance. Audit committees are directly responsible for the oversight of the company's external auditors and have the power to hire and fire the auditors. Section 404 requires management assessment and external audit firm attestation regarding the effectiveness of internal control over financial reporting—a key structural problem in many organizations experiencing fraud. Finally, many sections of the Sarbanes–Oxley Act significantly enhance the penalties for criminal wrongdoing that affects the securities markets, individual shareholders, and the general public.

The Post Sarbanes-Oxley World: A Time of Improved Corporate Governance

后《萨班斯–奥克斯利法案》世界：公司治理改善的时代

With the requirements of the Sarbanes-Oxley Act and the realization that many of the frauds of the late 1990s and early 2000s might have been prevented or detected earlier, the overall environment for doing business changed toward enhanced accountability and governance. Most notably, the business environment now includes a greater focus on corporate governance, the role of corporate governance in preventing fraud, and the important role that audit committees play in ensuring reliable financial reporting.

LO 6 Define corporate governance, identify the parties involved, and describe their respective activities.

What Is Corporate Governance?

什么是公司治理？

Corporate governance is a process by which the owners (stockholders) and creditors of an organization exert control and require accountability for the resources entrusted to the organization. The owners elect a board of directors to provide oversight of the organization's activities and accountability to stakeholders.

Exhibit 2.5 portrays the various parties involved in corporate governance. Governance starts with the owners delegating responsibilities to management through an elected **board of directors**—including a subcommittee of the board that serves as an **audit committee**. In turn, responsibilities are handed to operating units with oversight and assistance from internal auditors. The board of directors and its audit committee oversee management, and, in that role, are expected to protect the stockholders' rights and ensure that controls exist to prevent and detect fraud. However, it is important to recognize that management is part of the governance framework; management can influence who sits on the board and the audit committee, as well as other governance controls that might be put into place.

In return for the responsibilities (and power) given to management and the board, governance demands accountability back through the system to the owners and other stakeholders. **Stakeholders** include anyone who is influenced, either directly or indirectly, by the actions of a company. Management and the board have responsibilities to act within the laws of

EXHIBIT **2.5** Overview of Corporate Governance Responsibilities and Accountabilities

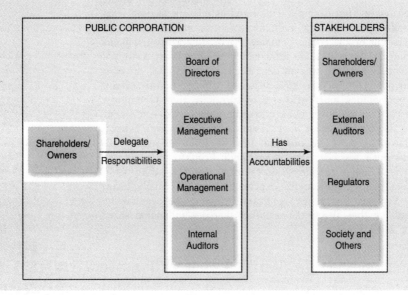

society and to meet various requirements of creditors and employees and other stakeholders.

Exhibit 2.6 describes the responsibilities of major parties involved in corporate governance. Importantly, note that these parties each have unique responsibilities, but they rely on the other parties to do their share to help ensure quality financial reporting through effective corporate governance.

有效公司治理的原则 ## Principles of Effective Corporate Governance

What characteristics and actions on the part of organizations are important to quality corporate governance? In 2010, a commission sponsored by the New York Stock Exchange (NYSE) issued a report identifying key core governance principles. This report was in response to the financial crisis of 2008 and 2009. The principles related to boards and management include:

- The board's fundamental objective should be to build long-term sustainable growth in shareholder value for the corporation.
- Successful corporate governance depends upon successful management of the company, as management has the primary responsibility for creating a culture of performance with integrity and ethical behavior.
- Effective corporate governance should be integrated with the company's business strategy and not viewed as simply a compliance obligation.
- Transparency is a critical element of effective corporate governance, and companies should make regular efforts to ensure that they have sound disclosure policies and practices.
- Independence and objectivity are necessary attributes of board members; however, companies must also strike the right balance in the appointment of independent and nonindependent directors to ensure an appropriate range and mix of expertise, diversity, and knowledge on the board.

EXHIBIT **2.6**	Corporate Governance Responsibilities
Party	**Overview of Responsibilities**
Shareholders/Owners	**Broad Role:** Provide effective oversight through election of board members, through approval of major initiatives (such as buying or selling stock), and through annual reports on management compensation from the board
Board of Directors	**Broad Role:** The major representatives of stockholders; they ensure that the organization is run according to the organization's charter and that there is proper accountability. **Specific activities include:** • Selecting management • Reviewing management performance and determining compensation • Declaring dividends • Approving major changes, such as mergers • Approving corporate strategy • Overseeing accountability activities
Executive Management	**Broad Role:** Manage the organization effectively; provide accurate and timely accountability to shareholders and other stakeholders **Specific activities include:** • Formulating strategy and risk management • Implementing effective internal controls • Developing financial and other reports to meet public, stakeholder, and regulatory requirements • Managing and reviewing operations • Implementing an effective ethical environment
Audit Committees of the Board of Directors	**Broad Role:** Provide oversight of the internal and external audit function and over the process of preparing the annual financial statements and public reports on internal control **Specific activities include**: • Selecting the external audit firm • Approving any nonaudit work performed by the audit firm • Selecting and/or approving the appointment of the Chief Audit Executive (Internal Auditor) • Reviewing and approving the scope and budget of the internal audit function • Discussing audit findings with internal and external auditors, and advising the board (and management) on specific actions that should be taken
Regulators and Standards Setters SEC, AICPA, FASB, PCAOB, IAASB	**Broad Role:** Set accounting and auditing standards dictating underlying financial reporting and auditing concepts; set the expectations of audit quality and accounting quality **Specific activities include:** • Establishing accounting principles • Establishing auditing standards • Interpreting previously issued standards • Enforcing adherence to relevant standards and rules for public companies and their auditors

In addition to these types of broad principles, the NYSE has mandated certain corporate governance guidelines that registrants must follow, including:

- Boards need to consist of a majority of independent directors.
- Boards need to hold regular executive sessions of independent directors without management present.
- Boards must have a nominating/corporate governance committee composed entirely of independent directors.
- The nominating/corporate governance committee must have a written charter that addresses the committee's purpose and responsibilities, and there must be an annual performance evaluation of the committee.
- Boards must have a compensation committee composed entirely of independent directors.
- The compensation committee must have a written charter that addresses the committee's purpose and responsibilities, which must include (at a minimum) the responsibility to review and approve corporate goals relevant to CEO compensation, to make recommendations to the Board about nonCEO compensation and incentive-based compensation plans, and to produce a report on executive compensation; there must also be an annual performance evaluation of the committee.
- Boards must have an audit committee with a minimum of three independent members.
- The audit committee must have a written charter that addresses the committee's purpose and responsibilities, and the committee must produce an audit committee report; there must also be an annual performance evaluation of the committee.
- Companies must adopt and disclose corporate governance guidelines addressing director qualification standards, director responsibilities, director access to management and independent advisors, director compensation, director continuing education, management succession, and an annual performance evaluation of the Board.
- Companies must adopt and disclose a code of business conduct and ethics for directors, officers, and employees.
- Foreign companies must disclose how their corporate governance practices differ from those followed by domestic companies.
- CEOs must provide an annual certification of compliance with corporate governance standards.
- Companies must have an internal audit function, whether housed internally or outsourced.

Effective governance is important to the conduct of an audit for one very simple reason: companies with effective corporate governance are less likely to experience fraud and are therefore less risky to audit. For that reason, most audit firms are not willing to accept potential audit clients unless the clients demonstrate a strong commitment to effective corporate governance. The auditor is in a much better position to provide a quality audit when governance mechanisms, such as the board and the audit committee, adhere to and embrace fundamental principles of effective governance. At those types of organizations, the auditor can serve as an independent party working with other governance parties such as management, the board, and the audit committee, to help ensure reliable financial reporting. However, in organizations where governance is not well developed or is heavily influenced by management, the auditor may decide that the risk of fraud is unduly high and that audit firm is going to have to bear too much responsibility for assuring reliable financial reporting. In essence, ineffective corporate governance increases fraud risk to an extent that at some point the client is not auditable from a risk-mitigation standpoint.

Responsibilities of Audit Committees

Section 301 of the Sarbanes-Oxley Act outlines the responsibilities of audit committee members for publicly traded companies, stating that audit committees are to be directly responsible for the appointment, compensation, and oversight of the work of registered accounting firms; they must be independent; they must establish whistleblowing mechanisms within the company; they must have the authority to engage their own independent counsel; and companies must provide adequate funding for audit committees.

In addition to these broad responsibilities, the NYSE has mandated certain specific responsibilities of audit committees, including:

- Obtaining each year a report by the external auditor that addresses the company's internal control procedures, any quality control or regulatory problems, and any relationships that might threaten the independence of the external auditor
- Discussing the company's financial statements with management and the external auditor
- Discussing in its meetings the company's earnings press releases, as well as financial information and earnings guidance provided to analysts
- Discussing in its meetings policies with respect to risk assessment and risk management
- Meeting separately with management, internal auditors, and the external auditor on a periodic basis
- Reviewing with the external auditor any audit problems or difficulties that they have had with management
- Setting clear hiring policies for employees or former employees of the external auditors
- Reporting regularly to the board of directors

Further, in many companies the audit committee also has the authority to hire and fire the head of the internal audit function, set the budget for the internal audit activity, review the internal audit plan, and discuss all significant internal audit results. Other responsibilities might include performing or supervising special investigations, reviewing policies on sensitive payments, and coordinating periodic reviews of compliance with company policies such as corporate governance policies.

审计委员会的责任

《萨班斯–奥克斯利法案》的301条款强调了公众公司审计委员会的责任。例如，审计委员会对于会计师事务所的选聘、审计费用的确定和审计工作的监督方面负有直接的责任。

SUMMARY AND NEXT STEPS

Fraud raises important concerns for external auditors, and they have clear professional obligations to perform an audit that provides reasonable assurance that the financial statements are free from material misstatement, including fraud. Various types of fraud exist, and the fraud triangle characterizes incentives, opportunities, and rationalizations that enable fraud to exist. Recent high-profile frauds ultimately led to the regulatory reforms enacted through the Sarbanes-Oxley Act of 2002. Corporate governance plays an important role in mitigating the risk of fraud.

While the possibility of fraud and the associated need for effective corporate governance are of utmost importance to the external auditor, management also seeks to provide reasonable assurance that the financial statements are free from material misstatements from either fraud or errors. In the next chapter, we discuss management's role in assuring reliable financial reporting through their responsibilities for internal control over financial reporting.

SIGNIFICANT TERMS

Asset misappropriation   A fraud that involves the theft or misuse of an organization's assets. Common examples include skimming cash, stealing inventory, and payroll fraud.

Audit committee   A subcommittee of the board of directors responsible for monitoring audit activities and serving as a surrogate for the interests of shareholders; it should be composed of outside members of the board, that is, members who are independent of the organization.

Board of directors   The major representative of stockholders to help ensure that the organization is run according to the organization's charter and that there is proper accountability.

Corporate governance   A process by which the owners and creditors of an organization exert control and require accountability for the resources entrusted to the organization. The owners (stockholders) elect a board of directors to provide oversight of the organization's activities and accountability to stakeholders.

Fraudulent financial reporting   The intentional manipulation of reported financial results to misstate the economic condition of the organization.

Fraud   An intentional act involving the use of deception that results in a material misstatement of the financial statements.

Fraud triangle   A model that includes incentives, opportunity, and rationalization to commit fraud; if one of these elements is absent then fraud is much less likely.

Ponzi scheme   This type of fraud occurs when the deposits of current investors are used to pay returns on the deposits of previous investors; no real investment is happening.

Red flags   Risk factors suggesting a heightened risk of fraud.

Sarbanes-Oxley Act of 2002   Broad legislation mandating new standard setting for audits of public companies and new standards for corporate governance.

Stakeholders   Anyone who is influenced, either directly or indirectly, by the actions of a company; stakeholders extend beyond the shareholders of a company.

TRUE-FALSE QUESTIONS

2-1   [LO 1]   The Great Salad Oil Swindle of 1963 could best be categorized as an asset misappropriation fraud.

2-2   [LO 1]   The Koss Corporation fraud could best be categorized as fraudulent financial reporting.

2-3   [LO 2]   The three elements of the fraud triangle include incentive, opportunity, and rationalization.

2-4   [LO 2]   Management compensation schemes that heavily emphasize stock-based compensation most affect the opportunity to commit fraud.

2-5   [LO 3]   In the Enron fraud, one of the key ways that management covered up the fraud was to shift debt off the balance sheet to special purpose entities.

2-6   [LO 3]   Professional skepticism involves the validation of information through probing questions, critical assessment of evidence, and attention to inconsistencies.

2-7   [LO 4]   The investing public generally recognizes that it is very difficult for auditors to detect fraud, and so it does not hold auditors accountable when auditors fail to detect it.

2-8   [LO 4]   Auditing standards historically have reflected the belief that it is not reasonable to expect auditors to detect cleverly hidden frauds.

2-9   [LO 5]   The Sarbanes-Oxley Act of 2002 was written by Congress to address problems revealed in frauds that were committed in the late 1980s.

2-10   [LO 5]   An important change caused by the Sarbanes-Oxley Act is that auditors are no longer allowed to provide most consulting services for their public company audit clients.

2-11   [LO 6]   Corporate governance is the process by which the owners and creditors of an organization exert control over and require accountability for the resources entrusted to the organization.

2-12   [LO 6]   Companies with effective corporate governance are more risky to audit.

MULTIPLE-CHOICE QUESTIONS

2-13   [LO 1]   What is the primary difference between fraud and errors in financial statement reporting?
a.   The materiality of the misstatement.
b.   The intent to deceive.
c.   The level of management involved.
d.   The type of transaction effected.

2-14   [LO 1]   Which of the following best represents fraudulent financial reporting?
a.   The transfer agent issues 40,000 shares of the company's stock to a friend without authorization by the board of directors.
b.   The controller of the company inappropriately records January sales in December so that year-end results will meet analysts' expectations.
c.   The in-house attorney receives payments from the French government for negotiating the development of a new plant in Paris.
d.   The accounts receivable clerk covers up the theft of cash receipts by writing off older receivables without authorization.

2-15   [LO 2]   Which of the following creates an opportunity for fraud to be committed in an organization?
a.   Management demands financial success.
b.   Poor internal control.
c.   Commitments tied to debt covenants.
d.   Management is aggressive in its application of accounting rules.

2-16 **LO 2** Which of the following is a common rationalization for fraudulent financial reporting?

a. This is a one-time transaction and it will allow the company to get through the current financial crisis, but we'll never do it again.

b. We are only borrowing the money; we will pay it back next year.

c. Executives at other companies are getting paid more than we are, so we deserve the money.

d. The accounting rules don't make sense for our company, and they make our financial results look weaker than is necessary, so we have a good reason to record revenue using a nonGAAP method.

e. a. and d.

2-17 **LO 3** Which of the following types of transactions did WorldCom management engage in as part of that company's fraudulent financial reporting scheme?

a. Recorded bartered transactions as sales.

b. Used restructuring reserves from prior acquisitions to decrease expenses.

c. Capitalized line costs rather than expensing them.

d. All of the above.

e. None of the above.

2-18 **LO 3** Which of the following is a valid conclusion of the third COSO report?

a. The most common frauds involve outright theft of assets.

b. The individuals most often responsible for fraud include low-level accounting personnel, such as accounts payable clerks.

c. The majority of frauds took place at companies that were listed on the Over-The-Counter market rather than those listed on the NYSE.

d. All of the above.

e. None of the above.

2-19 **LO 4** Which of the following statements is accurate regarding the Center for Audit Quality's 2010 paper on deterring and detecting fraud in financial reporting?

a. It recognizes that preventing and detecting fraud is the job of the external auditor alone.

b. It notes that an effective fraud risk management program can be expected to prevent virtually all frauds, especially those perpetrated by top management.

c. It illustrates that communication among those involved in the financial reporting process is critical.

d. All of the above.

e. None of the above.

2-20 **LO 4** Which of the following statements are true?

a. Unless an independent audit can provide assurance that financial information has not been materially misstated because of fraud, it has little if any value to society.

b. Repeated revelations of accounting scandals and audit failures related to undetected frauds have seriously damaged public confidence in external auditors.

c. A strong ethical tone at the top of an organization that permeates corporate culture is essential in preventing fraud.

d. All of the above.

e. None of the above.

2-21 **LO 5** The Sarbanes-Oxley Act enacted which of the following provisions as a response to a growing number of frauds?

a. The PCAOB was established, and it has the power to conduct inspections of audits for external audit firms that audit more than 100 publicly traded companies in a given year.

b. The lead audit partner and reviewing partner must rotate off the audit of a publicly traded company at least every 10 years.

c. Annual reports must state the responsibility of management for establishing and maintaining an adequate internal control structure and procedures for financial reporting, and management must have the company's internal audit function attest to the accuracy of the annual reports.

d. All of the above.

e. None of the above.

2-22 **LO 5** Which of the following statements is correct regarding the Public Company Accounting Oversight Board (PCAOB)?

a. The PCAOB is a nonprofit corporation, not an agency of the U.S. government.

b. The PCAOB will have five financially literate members who are prominent individuals of integrity and reputation with a commitment to the interests of investors and the public.

c. The PCAOB has authority to set standards related to public company audit reports and to conduct inspections of registered external audit firms.

d. All of the above.

e. None of the above.

2-23 **LO 6** Audit committee activities and responsibilities include which of the following?

a. Selecting the external audit firm.

b. Approving corporate strategy.

c. Reviewing management performance and determining compensation.

d. All of the above.

e. None of the above.

2-24 **LO 6** Which of the following audit committee responsibilities has the NYSE mandated?

a. Obtaining each year a report by the internal auditor that addresses the company's internal control procedures, any quality control or regulatory problems, and any relationships that might threaten the independence of the internal auditor.

b. Discussing in its meetings the company's earnings press releases, as well as financial information and earnings guidance provided to analysts.

c. Reviewing with the internal auditor any audit problems or difficulties that they have had with management.

d. All of the above.

e. None of the above.

REVIEW AND SHORT CASE QUESTIONS

NOTE: Completing Review and Short Case Questions does not require the student to reference additional resources and materials.

NOTE: For the remaining problems, we make special note of those addressing international issues, professional skepticism, and ethics. We do not make special note of fraud-related problems in this chapter because of the heavy emphasis on that topic throughout this chapter.

2-25 **LO 1** Define fraud, and explain the two types of misstatements that are relevant to auditors' consideration of fraud.

2-26 **LO 1** What are the most common approaches that perpetrators use to commit fraudulent financial reporting?

2-27 **LO 1** You are asked to be interviewed by a student newspaper regarding the nature of accounting fraud. The reporter says, "As I understand it, asset misappropriations are more likely to be found in small organizations, but not in larger organizations. On the other hand, fraudulent financial reporting is more likely to be found in larger organizations." How would you respond to the reporter's observation?

2-28 **LO 1** Refer to Exhibit 2.1 and answer the following questions.
a. What is a Ponzi scheme?
b. Describe the key elements of the Bernie Madoff fraud.
c. Is this fraud primarily a case of asset misappropriation or fraudulent financial reporting?

2-29 **LO 2** Refer to the *Auditing in Practice* feature, "The Great Salad Oil Swindle of 1963," and answer the following questions.
a. How did management perpetrate the fraud?
b. What was management's incentive to perpetrate the fraud?
c. Is this fraud primarily a case of asset misappropriation or fraudulent financial reporting?

2-30 **LO 2** The fraud triangle identifies incentives, opportunities, and rationalizations as the three elements associated with most frauds. Describe how each of these elements is necessary for fraud to occur.

2-31 **LO 2** If one of the three elements of the fraud triangle is not present, can fraud still be perpetrated? Explain.

2-32 **LO 2** Identify factors (red flags) that would be strong indicators of opportunities to commit fraud.

2-33 **LO 2** Is the ability to rationalize the fraud an important aspect to consider when analyzing a potentially fraudulent situation? What are some of the common rationalizations used by fraud perpetrators?

2-34 **LO 2** Each of the following scenarios is based on facts in an actual fraud. Categorize each scenario as primarily indicating (1) an incentive to commit fraud, (2) an opportunity to commit fraud, or (3) a rationalization for committing fraud. Also state your reasoning for each scenario.
a. There was intense pressure to keep the corporation's stock from declining further. This pressure came from investors, analysts, and the CEO, whose financial well-being was significantly dependent on the corporation's stock price.
b. A group of top-level management was compensated (mostly in the form of stock-options) well in excess of what would be considered normal for their positions in this industry.
c. Top management of the company closely guards internal financial information, to the extent that even some employees on a "need-to-know basis" are denied full access.
d. Managing specific financial ratios is very important to the company, and both management and analysts are keenly observant of variability in key ratios. Key ratios for the company changed very little even though the ratios for the overall industry were quite volatile during the time period.

e. In an effort to reduce certain accrued expenses to meet budget targets, the CFO directs the general accounting department to reallocate a division's expenses by a significant amount. The general accounting department refuses to acquiesce to the request, but the journal entry is made through the corporate office. An accountant in the general accounting department is uncomfortable with the journal entries required to reallocate divisional expenses. He brings his concerns to the CFO, who assures him that everything will be fine and that the entries are necessary. The accountant considers resigning, but he does not have another job lined up and is worried about supporting his family. Therefore, he never voices his concerns to either the internal or external auditors.

f. Accounting records were either nonexistent or in a state of such disorganization that significant effort was required to locate or compile them.

2-35 **LO 3** Refer to Exhibit 2.3 and briefly describe the frauds that were perpetrated at the following companies. For each company, categorize the fraud as involving primarily (1) asset misappropriation, or (2) fraudulent financial reporting.

a. Enron
b. WorldCom
c. Parmalat
d. HealthSouth
e. Dell
f. Koss Corporation
g. Olympus
h. Longtop Financial Technologies

2-36 **LO 3** Refer to the *Auditing in Practice* feature, "Professional Skepticism."

a. What is professional skepticism?
b. Why is professional skepticism necessary to detecting fraud?
c. What are the key behaviors needed to successfully exercise professional skepticism during the performance of the audit?
d. Why is it sometimes difficult for auditors to exercise appropriate levels of professional skepticism in practice?
e. Imagine that you are working on an audit engagement. What are the personal characteristics and behaviors of management or other company employees that might make you skeptical about whether or not they are providing you accurate audit evidence? Aside from personal observations, what publicly available information about management or other company employees could you obtain to determine whether you should exercise heightened professional skepticism in your dealings with these individuals?

2-37 **LO 3** For each of the following situations indicating heightened fraud risk, discuss how a professionally skeptical auditor might interpret the situation.

a. The company is not as profitable as its competitors, but it seems to have good products. However, it has a deficiency in internal control over disbursements that makes it subject to management override.

b. The company is doing better than its competitors. Although sales are about the same as competitors, net income is significantly more. Management attributes the greater profitability to better control of expenses.

PROFESSIONAL SKEPTICISM

PROFESSIONAL SKEPTICISM

    c. The company is financially distressed and is at some risk of defaulting on its debt covenants. The company improves its current ratio and other ratios by making an unusually large payment against its current liabilities, accompanied by highly discounted sales if their customers paid before year end.

    d. A smaller public company has a CFO who has centralized power under her. Her style is very intimidating. She is not a CPA; and she has limited accounting experience. The company has not been able to increase profitability during her time with the company.

2-38 [LO 3] The Committee of Sponsoring Organizations released its third study on fraudulent financial reporting in 2010. Describe major findings of the study.

2-39 [LO 3] The Enron fraud is considered by many to be one of the most significant frauds of the early 2000s.

    a. Describe the various failures and environmental characteristics during this time period that enabled the Enron fraud to happen.

    b. What elements of the fraud triangle seem most relevant to the Enron fraud?

2-40 [LO 4] What is the responsibility of the external auditor to detect material fraud?

2-41 [LO 4] The Center for Audit Quality (CAQ) issued a paper in 2010 on deterring and detecting fraud. The CAQ report identifies three ways in which individuals involved in the financial reporting process (management, the audit committee, internal audit, external audit, and regulatory authorities) can mitigate the risk of fraudulent financial reporting. Describe these three ways, and articulate your opinion on whether these will be effective given your knowledge of frauds that have happened in the relatively recent past (such as Enron, WorldCom, Parmalat, and Koss).

2-42 [LO 5] Refer to Exhibit 2.4 and answer the following questions.

    a. (Sections 101, 104, and 105) How does the establishment and operation of the PCAOB help to ensure quality external audits? How will audit firm inspections and investigations by the PCAOB help ensure high audit quality?

    b. (Sections 201-203) What do Sections 201-203 do to address auditor independence concerns?

    c. (Section 206) What is a cooling off period, and how does it address auditor independence concerns?

    d. (Section 301) How do the audit committee requirements help ensure effective corporate governance?

    e. (Sections 302 and 906) How do the officer certification requirements help to address the risk of fraud in publicly traded organizations? What is the likelihood that a CFO who is committing fraudulent financial reporting would sign the certification falsely, and what are your reactions to that possibility?

    f. (Section 401) How does this section relate to the Enron fraud?

    g. (Section 404) How do the management assessment and auditor attestation of internal controls contained in this section help to address the risk of fraud in publicly traded organizations?

    h. (Section 407) Why is it important that at least one member of the audit committee be a financial expert? What are the financial reporting implications if the audit committee does not have any individuals serving on it that possess financial expertise?

i.   (Section 802) How does this section relate to the Enron fraud?

2-43 [LO 5] Are nonpublic organizations required to adhere to the requirements of the Sarbanes-Oxley Act? Explain.

2-44 [LO 6] Corporate governance is the process by which the owners and creditors of an organization exert control over and require accountability for the resources entrusted to the organization. Refer to Exhibits 2.5 and 2.6 and answer the following questions.

a.   List the major parties involved in corporate governance.

b.   Describe the general roles and activities for each party.

2-45 [LO 6] Describe the five key principles of effective corporate governance articulated in the 2010 report of the NYSE.

2-46 [LO 6] Below is a summary of the NYSE corporate governance requirements of companies listed on this stock exchange. For each requirement, state how it is intended to help to address the risk of fraud in publicly traded organizations.

a.   Boards need to consist of a majority of independent directors.

b.   Boards need to hold regular executive sessions of independent directors without management present.

c.   Boards must have a nominating/corporate governance committee composed entirely of independent directors.

d.   The nominating/corporate governance committee must have a written charter that addresses the committee's purpose and responsibilities, and there must be an annual performance evaluation of the committee.

e.   Boards must have a compensation committee composed entirely of independent directors.

f.   The compensation committee must have a written charter that addresses the committee's purpose and responsibilities, which must include (at a minimum) the responsibility to review and approve corporate goals relevant to CEO compensation, make recommendations to the Board about nonCEO compensation and incentive-based compensation plans, and produce a report on executive compensation; there must also be an annual performance evaluation of the committee.

g.   Boards must have an audit committee with a minimum of three independent members.

h.   The audit committee must have a written charter that addresses the committee's purpose and responsibilities, and the committee must produce an audit committee report; there must also be an annual performance evaluation of the committee.

i.   Companies must adopt and disclose corporate governance guidelines addressing director qualification standards, director responsibilities, director access to management and independent advisors, director compensation, director continuing education, management succession, and an annual performance evaluation of the Board.

j.   Companies must adopt and disclose a code of business conduct and ethics for directors, officers, and employees.

k.   Foreign companies must disclose how their corporate governance practices differ from those followed by domestic companies

l.   CEOs need to provide an annual certification of compliance with corporate governance standards.

m.   Companies must have an internal audit function, whether housed internally or outsourced.

2-47 [LO 6] Below is a summary of the NYSE listing requirements for audit committee responsibilities of companies listed on this stock exchange. For each requirement, state how it is intended to help to address the risk of fraud in publicly traded organizations.

a. Obtaining each year a report by the external auditor that addresses the company's internal control procedures, any quality control or regulatory problems, and any relationships that might threaten the independence of the external auditor

b. Discussing the company's financial statements with management and the external auditor

c. Discussing in its meetings the company's earnings press releases, as well as financial information and earnings guidance provided to analysts

d. Discussing in its meetings policies with respect to risk assessment and risk management

e. Meeting separately with management, internal auditors, and the external auditor on a periodic basis

f. Reviewing with the external auditor any audit problems or difficulties that they have had with management

g. Setting clear hiring policies for employees or former employees of the external auditors

h. Reporting regularly to the board of directors

2-48 [LO 6] Audit committees are an important corporate governance party and have taken on additional responsibilities following the passage of the Sarbanes-Oxley Act.

a. Describe the changes in audit committee membership, and list duties that were mandated by the Sarbanes-Oxley Act. Also, describe any other increased responsibilities of audit committees following the passage of the Sarbanes-Oxley Act.

b. The audit committee now has ownership of the relationship with the external auditor. What are the implications of this change for the audit committee and for the external auditor?

c. Assume that management and the auditor disagree on the appropriate accounting for a complex transaction. The external auditor has conveyed the disagreement to the audit committee and provided an assessment that the disagreement is on the economics of the transaction and has nothing to do with earnings management. What is the responsibility of the audit committee? What skills of audit committee members do you think might be helpful in this type of situation?

2-49 [LO 6] The following factors describe a potential audit client. For each factor, indicate whether it is indicative of poor corporate governance. Explain the reasoning for your assessment. Finally, identify the risks associated with each factor.

a. The company is in the financial services sector and has a large number of consumer loans, including mortgages, outstanding.

b. The CEO's and CFO's compensation is based on three components: (a) base salary, (b) bonus based on growth in assets and profits, and (c) significant stock options.

c. The audit committee meets semiannually. It is chaired by a retired CFO who knows the company well because she had served as the CFO of a division of the firm. The other two members are local community members—one is the president of the Chamber of Commerce and the other is a retired executive from a successful local manufacturing firm.

d. The company has an internal auditor who reports directly to the CFO and makes an annual report to the audit committee.

e. The CEO is a dominating personality—not unusual in this environment. He has been on the job for six months and has decreed that he is streamlining the organization to reduce costs and centralize authority (most of it in him).

f. The company has a loan committee. It meets quarterly to approve, on an ex-post basis, all loans over $300 million (top 5% for this institution).

g. The previous auditor has resigned because of a dispute regarding the accounting treatment and fair value assessment of some of the loans.

CONTEMPORARY AND HISTORICAL CASES

2-50 | **KOSS CORPORATION AND GRANT THORNTON** **LO 2, 3, 4, 6**   In the *Professional Judgment in Context* feature at the outset of the chapter, we introduced you to the Koss Corporation fraud. In this problem we provide you with further details about that fraud. During the fall of 2009, Koss Corporation, a Wisconsin–based manufacturer of stereo headphone equipment, revealed that its Vice President of Finance (Sujata "Sue" Sachdeva) had defrauded the company of approximately $31 million over a period of at least five years. Grant Thornton LLP was the company's auditor, and the firm issued unqualified audit opinions for the entire period in which they worked for Koss. According to reports, Sachdeva's theft accelerated over a period of years as follows:

FY 2005:	$2,195,477
FY 2006:	$2,227,669
FY 2007:	$3,160,310
FY 2008:	$5,040,968
FY 2009:	$8,485,937
Q1 FY 2010:	$5,326,305
Q2 FY 2010:	$4,917,005

PROFESSIONAL SKEPTICISM

ETHICS

To give you a sense of the magnitude of the fraud, annual revenues for Koss Corporation are in the range of $40—$45 million annually. Previously reported pre–tax income for fiscal years 2007 and through Q1 2010 was as follows:

FY 2007:	$8,344,715
FY 2008:	$7,410,569
FY 2009:	$2,887,730
FY 2010:	$ 928,491

How could Sachdeva have stolen so much money and fooled so many people over a long period? It is thought that Sachdeva hid the theft in the company's cost of goods sold accounts, and that weak internal controls and poor corporate governance and oversight enabled her to conceal the theft from corporate officials. Certainly, there must have been questions raised about the company's deteriorating financial condition. But any number of excuses could have been used by Sachdeva to explain the missing money. For example, she might have blamed higher cost of goods sold on a change in suppliers or rising raw materials prices.

Another contributing factor in Sachdeva's ability to conceal her thefts was that top-management of Koss had a high degree of trust in her, so they did not monitor the accounts that she controlled at the company.

Sachdeva's total compensation for fiscal year 2009 was $173,734. But according to published reports, Sachdeva was known for her unusually lavish lifestyle and shopping sprees. It is reported that she spent $225,000 at a single Houston, Texas, jewelry store. Another report describes a $1.4 million shopping spree at Valentina Boutique in Mequon, Wisconsin. People familiar with her spending habits assumed that she used family money and that her husband's job as a prominent pediatrician funded her extravagant lifestyle. The fraud was ultimately uncovered because American Express became concerned when it realized that Sachdeva was paying for large balances on her personal account with wire transfers from a Koss Corporation account. American Express notified the FBI and relayed its concerns.

Upon learning of the fraud, Koss Corporation executives fired Sachdeva, along with the company's audit firm, Grant Thornton LLP. Koss Corporation is attempting to recover its monetary losses through the recovery and sale of merchandise that was purchased by Sachdeva as part of the unauthorized transactions, and through insurance proceeds and possible claims against third parties (including Grant Thornton LLP). Law enforcement authorities notified Koss Corporation that at least 22,000 items—including high-end women's clothing, shoes, handbags, and jewelry—have been recovered to date. Sachdeva stored the bulk of the items she purchased in rented storage units in order to conceal the items from her husband.

After considering this situation, answer the following questions:

a. Why might Koss management have placed so much trust in Sachdeva, along with providing only minimal supervision and monitoring?

b. What was Grant Thornton's obligation to uncover the fraud?

c. Why should Sachdeva's lavish lifestyle have raised suspicions? Why might it have been ignored or explained away by her professional colleagues?

d. How could management, the audit committee, and the auditors have been more professionally skeptical in this situation?

e. What was the audit committee's responsibility to notice that something looked amiss in the financial statements?

f. Sachdeva paid for her purchases using corporate credit cards. What internal controls could the company have used to prevent inappropriate use of the credit cards?

g. Some reports have described Sachdeva as having a very dominating personality, and revelations were made about the fact that she would often be verbally abusive of her subordinates in front of top-level managers at Koss. How should top-level managers have responded to this behavior? What actions could the subordinates have taken to respond to this behavior? Why might this behavior be a red flag indicating a heightened risk of fraud?

2-51 KOSS CORPORATION

LO **3, 5, 6**   Read the facts of the case in Problem 2–51 to become familiar with the fraud involving Koss Corporation. From the Company's October 7, 2009, proxy statement (Def 14A filing with the SEC), we know the following facts about the Company's audit committee. Members, ages, and descriptions of the audit committee members are as follows:

THOMAS L. DOERR 65, has been a director of the Company since 1987. In 1972, Mr. Doerr co-founded Leeson Electric Corporation and served as its President and Chief Executive Officer until 1982. The company manufactures industrial electric motors. In 1983, Mr. Doerr incorporated Doerr Corporation as a holding company for the purpose of acquiring established companies involved in distributing products to industrial and commercial markets. Currently, Mr. Doerr serves as President of Doerr Corporation. Mr. Doerr owns no stock in Koss Corporation, and received $24,000 in cash compensation during 2009 to serve on the audit committee.

LAWRENCE S. MATTSON 77, has been a director of the Company since 1978. Mr. Mattson is the retired President of Oster Company, a division of Sunbeam Corporation, which manufactures and sells portable household appliances. Mr. Mattson is the designated audit committee financial expert. Mr. Mattson owns no stock in Koss Corporation, and received $23,000 in cash compensation during 2009 to serve on the audit committee.

THEODORE H. NIXON 57, has been a director of the Company since 2006. Since 1992, Mr. Nixon has been the Chief Executive Officer of D.D. Williamson, which is a manufacturer of caramel coloring used in the food and beverage industries. Mr. Nixon joined D.D. Williamson in 1974 and was promoted to President and Chief Operating Officer in 1982. Mr. Nixon is also a director of the non-profit Center for Quality of Management. Mr. Nixon owns 2,480 shares of common stock of the Company (less than 1% of outstanding shares), and received $21,000 in cash compensation during 2009 to serve on the audit committee.

JOHN J. STOLLENWERK 69, has been a director of the Company since 1986. Mr. Stollenwerk is the Chairman of the Allen–Edmonds Shoe Corporation, an international manufacturer and retailer of high–quality footwear. He is also a director of Allen–Edmonds Shoe Corporation; Badger Meter, Inc.; U.S. Bancorp; and Northwestern Mutual Life Insurance Company. Mr. Stollenwerk owns 13,551 shares of common stock of the Company (less than 1% of outstanding shares), and received $23,000 in cash compensation during 2009 to serve on the audit committee.

- The Audit Committee met three times during the fiscal year ended June 30, 2009. The independent accountants (Grant Thornton LLP) were present at two of these meetings to discuss their audit scope and the results of their audit.
- Koss claims that each member of the Audit Committee is independent as defined in Nasdaq Marketplace Rule 4200.
- The proxy statement describes the responsibilities of the audit committee as follows: "The Audit Committee, among other things, monitors the integrity of the financial reporting process, systems of internal controls, and financial statements and reports of the Company; appoints, compensates, retains, and oversees the Company's independent auditors, including reviewing the qualifications, performance and independence

of the independent auditors; reviews and preapproves all audit, attest and review services and permitted nonaudit services; oversees the audit work performed by the Company's internal accounting staff; and oversees the Company's compliance with legal and regulatory requirements. The Audit Committee meets twice a year with the Company's independent accountants to discuss the results of their examinations, their evaluations of the Company's internal controls, and the overall quality of the Company's financial reporting."

a. Does the description of the audit committee members warrant a conclusion that its members appear to be professionally qualified for their positions? Do they meet enough times during the year to accomplish their responsibilities? What additional information might you need to answer this question, and how would the auditor obtain that information?

b. Who was the audit committee financial expert? Do you think that the experiences of this individual as described should ensure that he is truly a financial expert capable of fulfilling his roles in this regard? Why is financial expertise important for audit committee members in general?

c. In your opinion, was the compensation that the audit committee members received for their services adequate?

d. Based on the information that you have learned in Parts a-c of this problem, what weaknesses in the audit committee governance structure existed at Koss Corporation immediately preceding the discovery of fraud?

2-52 **DELL INC.**
LO 1, 3, 4, 6 In August 2010, Michael Dell, Dell Inc.'s CEO and chairman of the board, was reelected to Dell's board of directors by Dell's shareholders. However, not all of the shareholders were happy with Mr. Dell's reappointment. Specifically, two labor groups that own shares of Dell stock wanted Mr. Dell removed from the board because of a Securities and Exchange Commission (SEC) action and settlement involving the company and Mr. Dell. The SEC complaint alleged various accounting manipulations that called into question Dell's reported financial success from 2002 to 2006. In July 2010, Dell, Inc. agreed to pay $100 million to settle SEC charges, without admitting or denying guilt. Mr. Dell agreed to pay a $4 million fine, also without admitting or denying guilt. Consider the principles of effective corporate governance presented in this chapter and answer the following questions.

a. What principles of corporate governance appear to have been missing at Dell?

b. Given the apparent actions of Mr. Dell, along with his management and board roles, should Dell's external auditor expect the corporate governance at Dell to be effective?

c. How might Dell's external auditor respond to concerns about the quality of governance at Dell?

d. Given the SEC settlement, should Dell's board have an independent chair?

e. Given the SEC settlement, should Mr. Dell be removed from his CEO position?

3

Internal Control over Financial Reporting: Management's Responsibilities and Importance to the External Auditors

CHAPTER OVERVIEW AND LEARNING OBJECTIVES

This chapter focuses on understanding a client's internal control over financial reporting (Phase II of the audit opinion formulation process). An important part of an organization's corporate governance is its system of internal control. All organizations need effective internal control over financial reporting so that they can produce reliable financial statements. For example, internal control is needed to provide reasonable assurance that all sales are recorded, all cash receipts are collected and properly deposited in the organization's bank accounts, and all assets and liabilities are properly valued. Management has the responsibility to design, implement, and maintain effective internal control over financial reporting. Management of public companies will also evaluate and publicly report on the effectiveness of the company's internal control. The external auditor needs to understand a client's internal control over financial reporting and how management has fulfilled its internal control responsibilities. This chapter helps you identify aspects of a client's internal controls that you need to understand in order to plan and conduct an audit.

Through studying this chapter, you will be able to achieve these learning objectives:

通过本章的学习，你将能够实现以下学习目标：

1. Articulate the importance of internal control over financial reporting for organizations and their external auditors.

   认识财务报告内部控制对组织和它们的外部注册会计师的重要性。

2. Define internal control as presented in COSO's updated *Internal Control–Integrated Framework* and identify the components of internal control.

   明确COSO更新的《内部控制——整合框架》中描述的内部控制的含义，识别内部控制的要素。

3. Describe the control environment component of internal control, list its principles, and provide examples of each principle.

   描述内部控制的控制环境要素，列示它的原则并提供每个原则的案例。

4. Describe the risk assessment component of internal control, list its principles, and provide examples of each principle.

   描述内部控制的风险评估要素，列示它的原则并提供每个原则的案例。

5. Describe the control activities component of internal control, list its principles, and provide examples of each principle.

   描述内部控制的控制活动要素，列示它的原则并提供每个原则的案例。

6. Describe the information and communication component of internal control, list its principles, and provide examples of each principle.

   描述内部控制的信息与沟通要素，列示它的原则并提供每个原则的案例。

7. Describe the monitoring component of internal control, list its principles, and provide examples of each principle.

   描述内部控制的监控要素，列示它的原则并提供每个原则的案例。

8. Identify management's responsibilities related to internal control over financial reporting, including the factors management considers when assessing control deficiencies.

   识别管理层与财务报告内部控制相关的责任，包括当评估控制缺陷时管理层考虑的因素。

THE AUDIT OPINION FORMULATION PROCESS

I. Making Client Acceptance and Continuance Decisions **Chapter 14**	II. Performing Risk Assessment **Chapters 3, 7 and 9–13**	III. Obtaining Evidence about Internal Control Operating Effectiveness **Chapters 8–13 and 16**	IV. Obtaining Substantive Evidence about Accounts, Disclosures and Assertions **Chapters 8–13 and 16**	V. Completing the Audit and Making Reporting Decisions **Chapters 14 and 15**

The Auditing Profession, the Risk of Fraud and Mechanisms to Address Fraud: Regulation, Corporate Governance, and Audit Quality **Chapters 1 and 2**	Professional Liability and the Need for Quality Auditor Judgments and Ethical Decisions **Chapter 4**

The Audit Opinion Formulation Process and A Framework for Obtaining Audit Evidence
Chapters 5 and 6

PROFESSIONAL JUDGMENT IN CONTEXT

The Importance of Internal Control for Safeguarding Assets at Chesapeake Petroleum and Supply, Inc.

Most companies, presumably, have reliable financial reporting as one of their objectives. This objective would include safeguarding assets. However, to achieve this objective, organizations need to have effective controls in place. Such controls were not in place at Chesapeake Petroleum and Supply, Inc., where the chief financial officer (CFO) pled guilty to embezzling more than $2.7 million from the company. The CFO—employed by Chesapeake Petroleum for 30 years—authorized and signed company checks made payable to him and to the bank that held the mortgage to one of his properties. The CFO had both authorizing and signing control over company checks. This executive also had exclusive control over petty cash and stole thousands of dollars from the company's petty cash fund. These situations represent classic examples of control deficiencies related to an inadequate segregation of duties.

As you read through this chapter, consider the following questions:

- Why is internal control over financial reporting important to an organization? (LO 1)
- How does internal control help an organization achieve reliable financial reporting? (LO 1)
- Why does an external auditor need to know about a client's internal control? (LO 1)
- What is internal control over financial reporting, and what are its components? (LO 2)
- What type of control is segregation of duties, and what risks is that control intended to mitigate? (LO 5)

财务报告内部控制的重要性

Importance of Internal Control Over Financial Reporting

LO 1 Articulate the importance of internal control over financial reporting for organizations and their external auditors.

Internal control helps an organization mitigate the risks of not achieving its objectives. Examples of objectives include achieving profitability, ensuring efficiency of operations, manufacturing high-quality products or providing high-quality service, adhering to governmental and regulatory requirements, providing users with reliable financial information, and conducting operations and employee relations in a socially responsible manner. While an organization has these multiple objectives, the external auditor is most interested in the objective of reliable financial reporting. Organizations face many risks of not achieving reliable financial reporting. For example, a salesperson may overstate sales to improve the likelihood of receiving a bonus. Employees in the receiving area may be too busy to accurately record inventory when it is received. Management may misapply judgment and overvalue intangible assets. Management needs to identify the risks to their organization of not achieving reliable financial reporting. Once these risks to reliable financial reporting are identified, management implements controls to provide reasonable assurance that material misstatements do not occur in the financial statements.

Internal control over financial reporting provides many benefits to organizations, including providing confidence regarding the reliability of their financial information and helping reduce unpleasant surprises. Effective internal control improves the quality of information, thereby allowing for more informed decisions by internal and external users of the financial information. The *Auditing in Practice* feature "Control Deficiencies and Poor Decisions at Reliable Insurance Co." illustrates how poor internal controls can result in poor decision making.

内部控制对外部审计的重要性

Importance of Internal Control to the External Audit

Professional auditing standards require the auditor, as part of planning an audit, to identify and assess a client's risks of material misstatement, whether

Control Deficiencies and Poor Decisions at Reliable Insurance Co.

AUDITING IN PRACTICE

Reliable Insurance Co. of Madison, Wisconsin, introduced a new insurance policy to provide supplemental coverage to Medicare benefits for the elderly. The insurance was well received by elderly policyholders, many of whom were in nursing homes. The insurance policy was competitively priced and sold very well. To estimate reserves (liabilities) for future claims against the policies, the client used initial claims data to estimate costs and to build a model to estimate the reserves. For example, claims data for the first year could be compared with premiums for the same time period to estimate the needed reserve for claims. Unfortunately, the client's accounting system had control deficiencies that delayed the processing of claims. As a result, the internal estimation model was comparing claims

data for one month with premiums for three months, which resulted in the model significantly underestimating the needed reserves for future claims.

Because the internal control system failed to record claims on a timely basis, the company underpriced the policies and misrepresented its financial condition to shareholders and lenders. The low price attached to the policies allowed the company to greatly expand its sales. Unfortunately, the company was forced into bankruptcy when it could not meet policyholder claims. Had the internal control processes been properly designed, implemented, and maintained, management would have made better decisions. The internal control deficiency led not only to unreliable financial statements, but ultimately to the failure of the business.

due to fraud or error. This assessment is based on an understanding of the organization and its environment, including its internal control over financial reporting. The auditor needs to understand a company's internal controls in order to anticipate the types of material misstatements that may occur and then develop appropriate audit procedures to determine whether those misstatements exist in the financial statements. If a client has ineffective internal controls, the auditor will plan the audit with this in mind. For example, if an auditor notes that a client does not have effective controls to provide reasonable assurance that all sales are recorded in the correct time period, then the auditor needs to develop sufficient and appropriate audit procedures to test whether sales and receivables are materially misstated because of the absence of effective controls.

Auditors of large public companies have an additional interest in their client's internal controls. When conducting a financial statement audit for these companies, the auditor performs an **integrated audit**, which includes providing an opinion on the effectiveness of the client's internal control over financial reporting in addition to the opinion on the financial statements.

Defining Internal Control

Just as a U.S. company might refer to generally accepted accounting principles (GAAP) as a framework for determining whether its financial statements are fairly presented, companies need to refer to a framework of internal control when assessing the effectiveness of internal control over financial reporting. The most widely used framework in the United States is the *Internal Control–Integrated Framework* published by COSO (Committee of Sponsoring Organizations of the Treadway Commission). The sponsoring organizations first came together in the 1980s to address the increasing fraudulent financial reporting that was occurring at that time. COSO released the original **COSO's updated *Internal Control–Integrated Framework*** in 1992. The framework gained widespread acceptance following the financial failures of the early 2000s. In 2013 COSO updated, enhanced, and clarified the framework. Today, *Internal Control–Integrated Framework* (often referred to simply as "COSO") is the most widely used internal control framework in the United States, and is also used throughout the world.

COSO defines **internal control** as:

> a process, effected by an entity's board of directors, management, and other personnel, designed to provide reasonable assurance regarding the achievement of objectives relating to operations, reporting, and compliance.

Important elements of the definition recognize that internal control is:

- A *process* consisting of ongoing tasks and activities.
- *Effected by people* and is not just about policy manuals, systems, and forms. People at every level of the organization, ranging from shipping clerks to the internal auditor to the chief financial officer (CFO), chief executive officer (CEO), and the board of directors, impact internal control.
- Able to *provide reasonable assurance*, but not absolute assurance, regarding the achievement of objectives. Limitations of internal control preclude absolute assurance. These limitations include faulty human judgment, breakdowns because of mistakes, circumventing controls by collusion of multiple people, and management ability to override controls.
- Geared toward the *achievement of multiple objectives*. The definition highlights that internal control provides reasonable assurance

内部控制的定义

LO 2 Define internal control as presented in COSO's updated *Internal Control–Integrated Framework* and identify the components of internal control.

内部控制(internal control)
被审计单位为了合理地保证财务报告的可靠性、经营的效率和效果，以及对法律法规的遵守，由治理层、管理层和其他人员设计和执行的政策和程序。

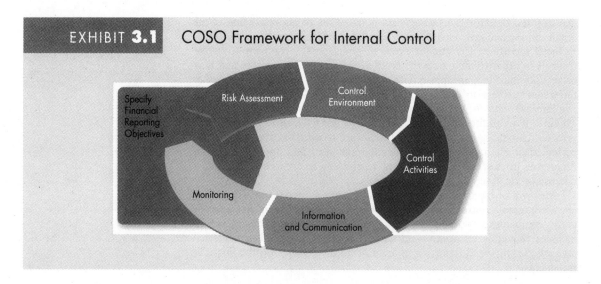

EXHIBIT **3.1** COSO Framework for Internal Control

regarding three categories of objectives. However, the external auditor is primarily interested in the objective related to the reliability of financial reporting.

COSO identifies five components of internal control that support an organization in achieving its objectives. These components of the COSO's updated *Internal Control–Integrated Framework* are shown in Exhibit 3.1, which highlights that internal control starts with setting the organization's *financial reporting objectives*, that is, to produce financial statements that are free from material misstatement. The five components include:

内部控制包括风险评估、控制环境、控制活动、信息与沟通和对控制的监督五要素。内部控制设计、执行和维护的方式因被审计单位规模和复杂程度的不同而不同。

1. **Risk Assessment** involves the process for identifying and assessing the risks that may affect an organization from achieving its objectives. Risk assessment needs to be conducted before an organization can determine the other necessary controls.
2. **Control Environment** is the set of standards, processes and structures that provides the basis for carrying out internal control across the organization. It includes the tone at the top regarding the importance of internal control and the expected standards of conduct. The control environment has a pervasive impact on the overall system of internal control.
3. **Control Activities** are the actions that have been established by policies and procedures. They help ensure that management's directives regarding internal control are carried out. Control activities occur at all levels within the organization.
4. **Information and Communication** recognizes that information is necessary for an organization to carry out its internal control responsibilities. Information can come from internal and external sources. Communication is the process of providing, sharing, and obtaining necessary information. Information and communication help all relevant parties understand internal control responsibilities and how internal controls are related to achieving objectives.
5. **Monitoring** is necessary to determine whether the controls, including all five components, are present and continuing to function effectively.

Effective internal control requires that all five components be implemented and operate effectively. Specifically, the controls need to (1) be effectively designed and implemented, and (2) operate effectively; that is, procedures are consistent with the design of the controls. These considerations are necessary for internal control to achieve the intended benefits.

Terminology: Entity-Wide Controls and Transaction Controls

Some components of internal control operate across an entity and are referred to as entity-wide controls. Entity-wide controls affect multiple processes, transactions, accounts, and assertions. The following are typically considered entity-wide controls:

- Controls related to the control environment
- Controls over management override
- The organization's risk assessment process
- Centralized processing and controls, including shared service environments
- Controls to monitor results of operations
- Controls to monitor other controls, including activities of the internal audit function, the audit committee, and self-assessment programs
- Controls over the period-end financial reporting process
- Policies that address significant business control and risk management practices

To illustrate why these controls are described as entity-wide, consider controls over management override. If the CFO is able to override controls, the CFO could record erroneous transactions in multiple processes affecting multiple accounts. Thus, controls over management override have an entity-wide effect.

In contrast, other controls such as control activities typically affect only certain processes, transactions, accounts, and assertions. These types of controls are sometimes referred to as transaction controls, and they are not expected to have a pervasive effect throughout the organization. For example, an organization might require that a supervisor approve an employee expense report after reviewing it for reasonableness and compliance with policy. This control provides assurance about employee expenses, but will not provide assurance on other types of transactions and accounts throughout the entity. The following are common examples of transaction controls:

- Segregation of duties over cash receipts and recording
- Authorization procedures for purchasing
- Adequately documented transaction trail for all sales transactions
- Physical controls to safeguard assets such as inventory
- Reconciliations of bank accounts

We provide additional information on transaction controls as part of our discussion on control activities later in this chapter.

Components and Principles of Internal Control

The guidance issued by COSO in 2013 recognizes that each of the five internal control components includes principles representing the fundamental concepts associated with the component. Further, supporting the 17 principles are points of focus, representing important characteristics typically associated with principles. While the COSO framework provides examples of points of focus, management needs to determine suitable and relevant points of focus that reflect the organization's unique industry, operations, and regulatory environment. The five components and their seventeen associated principles are summarized in Exhibit 3.2, and discussed next. The discussion focuses on components and principles from the perspective of the objective related to the reliability of financial reporting, which is the objective most relevant to the external auditor.

内部控制的构成要素和基本原则

LO 3 Describe the control environment component of internal control, list its principles, and provide examples of each principle.

COSO要素：控制环境

控制环境包括治理职能和管理职能，以及治理层和管理层对内部控制及其重要性的态度、认识和行动。控制环境设定了被审计单位内部控制的基调，影响员工的内部控制意识。

COSO Component: Control Environment

The control environment is seen as the foundation for all other components of internal control. It starts with the leadership of the organization, including the board of directors, the audit committee, and management, and is often referred to as the "tone at the top" or the "internal control culture." The board of directors and management establish the tone regarding the importance of internal control and expected standards of conduct. These expectations should be reinforced throughout the organization. A strong control environment is an important line of defense against the risks related to the reliability of financial statements. As highlighted in the *Auditing in*

EXHIBIT **3.2**	Internal Control Components and Principles

Components	Principles
Control Environment	1. The organization demonstrates a commitment to integrity and ethical values.
	2. The board of directors demonstrates independence from management and exercises oversight for the development and performance of internal control.
	3. Management establishes, with board oversight, structures, reporting lines, and appropriate authorities and responsibilities in the pursuit of objectives.
	4. The organization demonstrates a commitment to attract, develop, and retain competent individuals in alignment with objectives.
	5. The organization holds individuals accountable for their internal control responsibilities in the pursuit of objectives.
Risk Assessment	6. The organization specifies objectives with sufficient clarity to enable the identification and assessment of risks relating to objectives.
	7. The organization identifies risks to the achievement of its objectives across the entity and analyzes risks as a basis for determining how the risks should be managed.
	8. The organization considers the potential for fraud in assessing risks to the achievement of objectives.
	9. The organization identifies and assesses changes that could significantly impact the system of internal control.
Control Activities	10. The organization selects and develops control activities that contribute to the mitigation of risks to the achievement of objectives to acceptable levels.
	11. The organization selects and develops general control activities over technology to support the achievement of objectives.
	12. The organization deploys control activities through policies that establish what is expected and in procedures that put policies into action.
Information and Communication	13. The organization obtains or generates and uses relevant, quality information to support the functioning of other components of internal control.
	14. The organization internally communicates information, including objectives and responsibilities for internal control, necessary to support the functioning of other components of internal control.
	15. The organization communicates with external parties regarding matters affecting the functioning of other components of internal control.
Monitoring	16. The organization selects, develops, and performs ongoing and/or separate evaluations to ascertain whether the components of internal control are present and functioning.
	17. The organization evaluates and communicates internal control deficiencies in a timely manner to those parties responsible for taking corrective action, including senior management and the board of directors, as appropriate.

Practice feature "Ethical Values and the Control Environment at HealthSouth," a weak control environment enables fraud to occur.

Deficiencies in the control environment have been associated with many financial frauds that are likely familiar to you. For example, the failures of major financial institutions such as Lehman Brothers and Bear Stearns were linked to problems in the control environment, including weak board oversight. Each organization had an ineffective board of directors that was dominated by top management. Management teams were driven to increase the stock price, either as a basis for expanding the company or for personally enriching themselves through stock compensation. Other examples of control environment deficiencies include:

- A low level of control consciousness within the organization
- An audit committee that does not have independent members
- The absence of an ethics policy or a lack of reinforcement of ethical behavior within the organization
- An audit committee that is not viewed as the client of the external auditor
- A management that overrides controls over accounting transactions
- Personnel who do not have the competencies to carry out their assigned tasks

The five control environment principles are summarized in Exhibit 3.2 and discussed next.

Commitment to Integrity and Ethical Values (COSO Principle 1)

An organization's commitment to integrity and ethical values is demonstrated through the tone set by the board and management throughout the organization. Do the directives, actions, and behaviors of the board and management highlight the importance of integrity and ethical values? The organization should have standards of conduct regarding expectations for integrity and ethical values. An organization should also have processes in place to determine if individuals are performing in accordance with

Ethical Values and the Control Environment at HealthSouth

In testimony before the House Subcommittee in October 2003, the director of internal audit of HealthSouth testified that she had inquired about expanding her department's work and that she needed access to corporate records. She reported directly to the HealthSouth CEO, Richard Scrushy. She told a congressional committee that Mr. Scrushy reminded her that she did not have a job before she came to HealthSouth and she should do the job she was hired to do. When asked by a congressman whether she had thought about reporting rumors of fraud to Ernst & Young (HealthSouth's external auditors), she indicated that she had run her concerns through the chain of command within the

company and had done all she could do. Unfortunately, the chain of command was run by the CEO.

The internal auditor did not follow up with Ernst & Young. Others testified to the same effect—if they wanted to keep their jobs, they continued to do the work they were hired to do and let management take care of other items. The tone at the top sent a clear message: "Don't question management!" In the case of HealthSouth, it did not matter that the organization had a code of ethics for its employees. The company and its board were dominated by management. The unwritten message was stronger than any written message: "Do what we want you to do or lose your job."

expected standards of conduct. Importantly, deviations in expected conduct should be identified and addressed in an appropriate, timely, and consistent matter.

The importance of an appropriate tone cannot be overstated. As indicated in the *Auditing in Practice* feature "Inappropriate Tone Regarding Internal Controls Leads to Other Deficiencies at NutraCea," an inappropriate tone about the importance of internal control can lead to deficiencies throughout the internal control system.

The Board of Directors Exercises Oversight Responsibility (COSO Principle 2)

Members of the board of directors are the elected representatives of shareholders. At public organizations and other larger organizations, the board will include committees that specialize in certain areas. For example, the audit committee of the board should oversee management, have responsibility for the overall reliability of financial reporting, and oversee the external auditor. The compensation committee should review and approve the compensation of the organization's CEO and other top officers, oversee the organization's benefit plans (for example, incentive compensation plans), and make recommendations to the full board regarding board compensation.

The board of directors, primarily through the audit committee, is expected to exercise objective oversight for the development and performance of internal control. For example, the board, as part of its oversight responsibilities, might require discussions with senior management on areas where controls have not been operating effectively. The board should have sufficient

Inappropriate Tone Regarding Internal Controls Leads to Other Deficiencies at NutraCea

AUDITING IN PRACTICE

Management at NutraCea identified the following material weaknesses in the company's internal control over financial reporting as of December 31, 2008:

The Company did not maintain an effective control environment based on the criteria established in the COSO framework. The Company failed to design controls to prevent or detect instances of inappropriate override of, or interference with, existing policies, procedures and internal controls. The Company did not establish and maintain a proper tone as to internal control over financial reporting. More specifically, senior management failed to emphasize, through consistent communication and behavior, the importance of internal control over financial reporting and adherence to the Company's code of business conduct and ethics, which, among other things, resulted in information being withheld from, and improper explanations and inadequate supporting documentation being provided to the Company's Audit Committee, its Board of Directors and independent registered public accountants.

Presumably the weak control environment led to other material weaknesses in internal control. For example, NutraCea management failed to properly analyze, account for, and record significant sales contracts for proper revenue recognition. The company also failed to retain the resources necessary to analyze significant transactions, prepare financial statements, and respond to regulatory comments in a timely manner.

knowledge and skills to fulfill its oversight responsibilities. Necessary knowledge and skills would include market and company knowledge, financial expertise, legal and regulatory expertise, knowledge of systems and technology, and problem-solving skills. Importantly, the board needs a sufficient number of members who are independent of the organization to help ensure the board's objectivity. A board and its committees are most effective when they can provide unbiased oversight consisting of evaluations, guidance, and feedback.

Management Establishes Structure, Authority, and Responsibility (COSO Principle 3)

A well-controlled organization has an appropriate structure and clearly defined lines of responsibility and authority. Everyone in the organization has some responsibility for the effective operation of internal control. COSO has identified the following internal control responsibilities:

- *The board of directors* retains authority over significant decisions and reviews management's assignments.
- *Senior management* establishes directives, guidance, and controls to help employees understand and carry out their internal control responsibilities.
- *Management* guides and facilitates senior management's directives.
- *Personnel* understand internal control requirements relative to their position in the organization.
- *Outsourced service providers* adhere to management's definition of the scope of authority and responsibility for all nonemployees engaged.

The Organization Demonstrates Commitment to Competence (COSO Principle 4)

An organization needs to attract, develop, and retain competent individuals. Competence is the knowledge and skills necessary to accomplish tasks that define the individual's job. Commitment to competence includes management's consideration of the competence levels for particular jobs and how those levels translate into requisite skills and knowledge. This commitment is demonstrated through policies and procedures to attract, train, mentor, evaluate, and retain employees.

The Organization Enforces Accountability (COSO Principle 5)

An organization should hold individuals accountable for their internal control responsibilities. Accountability mechanisms include establishing and evaluating performance measures and providing appropriate incentives and rewards. Management and the board should be sensitive to, and address as appropriate, pressures that could cause personnel to circumvent controls or undertake fraudulent activity. Excessive pressures could include unrealistic performance targets or an imbalance between short-term and long-term performance measures. For example, pressures to generate unrealistic levels of sales might cause sale managers to book fraudulent sales entries, thereby reducing the reliability of financial reporting.

LO 4 Describe the risk assessment component of internal control, list its principles, and provide examples of each principle.

COSO Component: Risk Assessment

All organizations face risks of material misstatement in their financial reports. Risk is the possibility that an event will adversely affect the

COSO要素：风险评估

被审计单位的风险评估过程为管理层需要管理的风险提供了基础。如果这一过程对于具体情况是适当的，则有助于注册会计师识别重大错报风险。

organization's achievement of its objectives. Risk comes from both internal and external sources. Examples of internal risks include:

- Changes in management responsibilities
- Changes in internal information technology
- A poorly conceived business model that makes it difficult for the organization to remain profitable

Examples of external risks include:

- Economic recessions that decrease product or service demand
- Increases in competition or substitute products or services
- Changes in regulation that make the business model of the organization unsustainable
- Changes in the reliability of source goods that reduce profitability and interrupt the supply chain

An organization that ignores these risks will subject both the organization and its auditors to potential bankruptcy and litigation, respectively. Risk assessment is a robust process for identifying and assessing the risks associated with the objective of reliable financial reporting. This process also requires considering how changes in either the external environment or within the organization's business model may impact the controls necessary to mitigate risk.

The four principles of the risk assessment are summarized in Exhibit 3.2 and discussed below.

Specifies Relevant Objectives (COSO Principle 6)

An organization has many reasons for having reliable financial reporting as one of its objectives. Reliable financial reporting is important for accessing capital markets, being awarded sales contracts, and dealing with vendors, suppliers, and other third parties. When specifying this objective, management should take steps so that the financial reporting reflects the underlying transactions and events of the organization. Financial reporting objectives should be consistent with the accounting principles that are suitable for the organization. As appropriate, the broad reporting objective should be cascaded down to various business units. Further, management should consider the level of materiality when specifying objectives. For example, management might have an objective that revenue be accurately reported. Management does not likely mean that revenue needs to be accurate to the nearest dollar. Rather, management's objective would likely be that any misstatements in revenue not be material, or important, to the overall financial statement presentation. For example, if the revenue account of a large company had an error that caused revenue to be overstated by $1,000, most users of the financial statement would not consider that misstatement to be material, or important, to their decisions. Materiality is a topic that we explore further in Chapter 7.

Identifies and Analyzes Risk (COSO Principle 7)

This principle highlights the importance of an organization identifying the risks that it will not achieve its financial reporting objective and serves as a basis for determining how the risks should be mitigated. Appropriate levels of management need to be involved in the identification and analysis of risk. Risk identification should include both internal and external factors. For example, economic changes may impact barriers to competitive entry or a new financial reporting standard may require different or additional reporting. Internally, a change in management responsibilities could affect the way certain controls operate, or the expiration of labor agreements can affect the availability of competent personnel. Identified risks—whether internal or external—should be analyzed to include an estimate of the potential significance of the risks and consideration of how each risk should be managed.

Assesses Fraud Risk (COSO Principle 8)

As part of assessing risks, the organization considers fraud risks—risks related to misappropriation of assets and fraudulent financial reporting (as discussed in Chapter 2). This assessment recognizes that an individual's actions may not align with expected standards of conduct. Assessment of fraud risk considers ways that fraud could occur, fraud risk factors that impact financial reporting, incentives and pressures that might lead to fraud in the financial statements, opportunities for fraud, and whether personnel might engage in or rationalize fraud activities, that is, the fraud triangle. The *Auditing in Practice* feature "Ineffective Internal Control Over Financial Reporting Leads to Embezzlement at Citigroup" highlights the importance of identifying fraud risks as a basis for determining the controls necessary to mitigate such risks.

Identifies and Analyzes Significant Change (COSO Principle 9)

As internal and external conditions change, an organization's internal controls may need to change. Internal control that is considered effective in one condition may not be effective when that condition changes. For example, when an organization alters its lines of business or business model, new controls may be needed because the organization may have taken on new risks. Another example of change impacting controls would be the introduction of new information system technologies. The organization also needs to consider changes in management and other personnel and their respective attitudes and philosophies on the system of internal control. Overall, the key principle is that an organization needs a process for identifying and assessing changes in internal and external factors that can affect its ability to produce reliable financial reports.

COSO Component: Control Activities

Control activities are the actions that are established through policies and procedures that help ensure that management's directives regarding controls are accomplished. Control activities are performed within processes, for example, segregation of duties required in processing transactions, and over the technology

COSO要素：控制活动

LO 5 Describe the control activities component of internal control, list its principles, and provide examples of each principle.

Ineffective Internal Control Over Financial Reporting Leads to Embezzlement at Citigroup

AUDITING IN PRACTICE

Gary Foster was a mid-level accountant in Citigroup's Long Island City office, with an annual salary of about $100,000. His embezzlement of about $19 million from the company was revealed in June 2011. It appears that Foster transferred money from various Citigroup accounts to his personal bank account at JPMorgan Chase. He did so by making adjusting journal entries from interest expense accounts and debt adjustment accounts to Citigroup's main cash accounts. Then, on at least eight occasions, he transferred the money to a personal bank account at Chase. To conceal the transactions, he used a false contract number in the

reference line of the wire transfer. This series of actions continued for at least a year, undetected by the company's internal controls. During that time, Foster traveled extensively internationally, owned six expensive homes, and owned Maserati and BMW automobiles.

The revelation of this fraud serves as another embarrassment to the embattled Citigroup, which lost billions during the financial crisis and was criticized for taking over a month to disclose that hackers stole data from over 360,000 Citigroup credit card accounts. Clearly, the internal controls at Citigroup are causing major problems for the company.

控制活动是指有助于确保管理层的指令得以执行的政策和程序。审计工作的重点是了解和识别重大错报风险较高的领域的控制活动。

environment. They are performed at all levels of the organization. The three principles of control activities are summarized in Exhibit 3.2 and discussed next.

Selects and Develops Control Activities (COSO Principle 10)

Although some control activities are seen in many organizations—segregation of duties, independent reconciliations, authorizations and approvals, verifications—no universal set of control activities is applicable to all organizations. Rather, organizations select and develop control activities that are specific to the risks they identify during risk assessment. For example, highly regulated organizations generally have more complex control activities than less-regulated entities. As another example, an organization with decentralized operations and an emphasis on local autonomy and innovation will have different control activities than another whose operations are constant across locations and highly centralized.

Transaction Controls Transaction controls (also referred to as **application controls**) represent an important type of control activities. They are control activities implemented to mitigate transaction processing risk, and they affect certain processes, transactions, accounts, and assertions. Three types of transactions that have a significant effect on the quality of data in the financial statement account balances and disclosures are shown in Exhibit 3.3. They include transactions related to:

- Business processes
- Accounting estimates
- Adjusting, closing, and unusual entries

During transaction processing an organization wants reasonable assurance that the information processing is complete, accurate, and valid. The organization wants to achieve the following control objectives:

- Recorded transactions exist and have occurred.
- All transactions are recorded.
- Transactions are properly valued.
- Transactions are properly presented and disclosed.
- Transactions relate to rights or obligations of the organization.

Various transaction controls performed within specific business processes—such as purchasing and sales—are developed and implemented to provide reasonable assurance that these processing objectives are achieved. Control activities related to business transaction processing include verifications such as computer matching or reasonableness checks, reconciliations such as checking for agreement between detailed subsidiary accounts and control accounts, and authorizations and approvals such as a supervisor approving an expense report.

EXHIBIT **3.3**   Transaction Processing

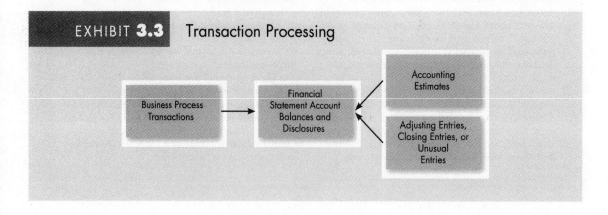

Accounting estimates, such as those used in developing the allowance for doubtful accounts, pension liabilities, environmental obligations, and warranty reserves, are subject to significant management judgment. These estimates should be based on underlying processes and data that have been successful in providing accurate estimates in the past. Controls should be built around the processes to provide reasonable assurance that the data are accurate, the estimates are faithful to the data, and the underlying estimation model reflects current economic conditions and has proven to provide reasonable estimates in the past.

Controls over adjusting, closing, and other unusual entries include:

- Documented support for all entries
- Reference to underlying supporting data with a well-developed transaction trail that includes the documents and records that allow a user (or auditor) to trace a transaction from its origination through to its final disposition, or vice versa
- Review by the CFO or controller

Automated and Manual Transaction Controls Transaction controls include manual control activities, automated control activities, and a combination of the two. An example of an automated application control activity is an automated matching and edit check to examine data entered online. If the data do not match or are entered in the wrong format, feedback is provided so that appropriate corrections can be made. In some cases that feedback and correction occur automatically. In other cases, a combination of manual and automated controls is present such that the system automatically detects the data transmission error, but an individual is needed to manually retransmit the data. Transaction controls, whether automated or manual, mitigate risks associated with data input, processing, and output.

Input controls are designed to ensure that authorized transactions are correct and complete, and that only authorized transactions can be input. Two common types of input controls are input validation tests and self-checking digits. Input validation tests are often referred to as edit tests because they are control tests built into an application to examine or edit input data for obvious errors. Input validation tests are designed to review transactions much like experienced personnel do in manual systems in which an employee would know, for example, that no one worked more than 70 hours in the past week. If an item entered online does not meet the required criteria, the user is notified and a correction is made or a decision is made about whether the transaction should be processed or reviewed further before processing. Self-checking digits are a type of input validation test that have been developed to test for transposition errors associated with identification numbers. Self-checking digits operate by computing an extra digit, or several digits, that are added (or inserted) into a numeric identifier. The algorithms are designed to detect the common types of mistakes. Whenever the identifier is entered into the system, the application recalculates the self-checking digit to determine whether the identifier is correct.

Processing controls are designed to provide reasonable assurance that the correct program is used for processing, all transactions are processed, and the transactions update appropriate files. For example, processed payroll transactions should update the payroll sub-ledger.

Output controls are designed to provide reasonable assurance that all data are completely processed and that output is distributed only to authorized recipients. Typical controls include reconciliation of control totals, output distribution schedules and procedures, and output reviews. For critical data, the user may perform a detailed review and reconciliation of the output data with the input to determine the completeness of a crucial process. The organization should also develop policies for protecting privacy and retaining records.

Other Important Control Activities Other important control activities include **segregation of duties** and **physical controls over assets**. Segregation of duties is an important control activity that is designed to protect against the risk that an individual could both perpetrate and cover up a fraud. Proper segregation of duties requires that at least two employees be involved such that one does not have (a) the authority and ability to process transactions and (b) custodial responsibilities. Separating these functions prevents someone from authorizing a fictitious or illegal transaction and then covering it up through the accounting process. Separating record keeping and physical custody of assets is designed to prevent someone with custodial responsibilities from taking assets and covering it up by making fictitious entries to the accounting records. Refer to the *Professional Judgment in Context* feature at the beginning of the chapter, "The Importance of Internal Control for Safeguarding Assets at Chesapeake Petroleum and Supply, Inc." for an example of where segregation of duties was lacking, thereby allowing an individual to misappropriate assets.

Physical controls are necessary to protect and safeguard assets from accidental or intentional destruction and theft. Examples of physical controls include security locks to limit access to inventory warehouses and vaults, safes, and similar items to limit access to cash and other liquid assets. An additional control is a periodic count of the physical assets, such as inventory, and a reconciliation of this count with recorded amounts.

Preventive and Detective Controls The appropriate mix of control activities includes both preventive and detective controls. **Preventive controls** are designed to prevent the occurrence of a misstatement. For example, edit tests may prevent some inappropriate transactions from being recorded. Preventive controls are usually the most cost-efficient. **Detective controls** are designed to discover errors that occurred during processing. For example, continuous monitoring techniques detect transactions that should not have been processed.

Selects and Develops General Controls Over Technology (COSO Principle 11)

Nearly all organizations depend on information technology to facilitate reliable financial reporting. As part of selecting control activities, management needs to determine the extent to which automated control activities and **general computer controls** are part of the mix of control activities. For automated application controls to work properly, an organization needs to have effective general computer controls (sometimes referred to as **information technology general controls**). General computer controls are pervasive control activities that affect multiple types of information technology systems, from mainframe computers, to desktop computers, to laptop computers, to the mobile devices that you use to organize your everyday life. General computer controls include control activities—either manual or automated—over technology infrastructure, security management, and technology acquisition, development, and maintenance.

Technology Infrastructure Technology infrastructure provides the support for information technology to effectively function. It includes the communication network that links technologies together, the computing resources needed for applications to operate, and even the electricity needed to power the technology. Control activities are necessary to check the technology for any problems and take corrective action as necessary. Two other important control activities related to the infrastructure include backup procedures and disaster recovery plans.

Security Management Security management includes control activities that limit access to technologies. These control activities include policies that restrict authorized users to applications that are related to their job responsibilities, update access when employees change jobs or leave the organization, and require a periodic review of access rights to determine if they remain appropriate. Security controls over technology protect the organization from inappropriate and unauthorized access, thereby protecting data and program integrity.

Important considerations in security management related to user access include the following:

- Access to any data item is limited to those *with a need to know.*
- The ability to change, modify, or delete a data item is restricted to those *with the authorization to make such changes.*
- The access control system has the *ability to identify and verify any potential users* as authorized or unauthorized for the data item and function requested.
- *A security department should actively monitor* attempts to compromise the system and prepare periodic reports to those responsible for the integrity of data and access to the data.

Techniques for controlling user access include passwords, cards with magnetic strips (often combined with a password requirement), and required identification on the basis of physical characteristics (for example, fingerprint or retina scan).

Technology Acquisition, Development, and Maintenance An organization needs to select and develop control activities over the acquisition, development, and maintenance of technology. Some organizations may develop their technology in-house, while other organizations may obtain their technology through packaged software or through outsourcing arrangements. If an organization chooses to use packaged software, it should have policies about selecting and implementing these packages. If an organization develops and maintains its technology in-house, the organization should have polices on documentation requirements, approval requirements, authorization of change requests, and appropriate protocols and testing of whether changes are made properly.

Deploys through Policies and Procedures (COSO Principle 12)

An important principle of control activities is that an organization needs to have policies that outline what is expected and procedures that put the policies into action. For example, a policy might require monthly reconciliations of all bank accounts by appropriate personnel who do not have access to cash. The procedure would be the reconciliation itself. Policies can be communicated orally or in writing, but in either case, they should establish clear responsibility and accountability. Further, the procedures should be performed diligently, consistently, and by appropriate and competent personnel in a timely manner.

COSO Component: Information and Communication

An organization needs information, from both internal and external sources, to carry out its internal control responsibilities. Communication is the process of providing, sharing, and obtaining information. Information is communicated internally throughout the organization. And there should be two-way communication with relevant parties external to the organization. The internal control component of information and communication refers to the process of identifying, capturing, and exchanging information in a timely fashion to enable accomplishment of the organization's objectives. It includes the organization's accounting system and methods for recording and reporting on transactions, as well as other communications such as key policies, code of conduct, and strategies. The three principles of information and communication are summarized in Exhibit 3.2 and discussed next.

COSO要素：信息与沟通

LO 6 Describe the information and communication component of internal control, list its principles, and provide examples of each principle.

Uses Relevant Information (COSO Principle 13)

An organization needs to identify and obtain relevant internal and external information to support its internal control and achieve its objective of reliable financial reporting. For example, an organization may conduct a periodic survey of its employees to determine whether they had been asked to behave in a manner that was inconsistent with the organization's standards of conduct, for example, record a journal entry without adequate supporting documentation. This survey produces information about the functioning of the control environment and can be used to determine if other controls are needed. Other sources of internal information include the accounting system, internal emails, minutes from meetings, and time reporting systems. Examples of external sources of information include industry research reports, whistleblower hotlines, and competitor earnings releases.

Communicates Internally (COSO Principle 14)

Internal communication of information occurs throughout the organization, including up, down, and across the organization. For example, all personnel should receive a clear message that internal control responsibilities should be taken seriously. This communication could occur through periodic newsletters, posters in the break rooms, or more formal communications from senior management and the board. In some cases, a special line of communication is needed for anonymous or confidential communications, particularly when an employee is concerned that something is inappropriate in the company's operations. This is referred to as a "whistleblower function" and often includes processes such that reporting can be anonymous. Further, employers should not be permitted to take adverse actions against employee whistleblowers. The whistleblower program should include a process to bring important ethical and financial issues to the audit committee. The *Auditing in Practice* feature "Reporting of Financial Improprieties at The William and Flora Hewlett Foundation: Excerpt from Its Whistleblower Policy" provides an example of a whistleblower policy highlighting the importance of employee involvement and the absence of any fear of retaliation for being a whistleblower employee.

Communicates Externally (COSO Principle 15)

Organizations have a need for two-way communication with parties external to the organization, including shareholders, business partners, customers, and regulators. Management's external communication should send a message about the importance of internal control and the organization's values and culture. Organizations should also have mechanisms so that external parties can provide information to the organization. For example, customers may provide feedback about product quality and vendors may have questions about payments for goods sold or complaints about possibly inappropriate behavior. As another example, large retailers often have relationships with many vendors. Many of these retailers establish a hotline where a vendor can communicate directly with the internal audit department or other appropriate party if the vendor finds any inappropriate action by a purchasing agent of the company, for example, a suggestion of a kickback if a large order is placed.

COSO要素：监控

LO 7 Describe the monitoring component of internal control, list its principles, and provide examples of each principle.

COSO Component: Monitoring

Monitoring is defined as a process that provides feedback on the effectiveness of each of the five components of internal control. Management selects a mix of ongoing evaluations, separate evaluations, or some combination of the two to accomplish monitoring. Monitoring requires that identified deficiencies in internal control be communicated to appropriate personnel and follow-up action be taken.

The two principles of monitoring are summarized in Exhibit 3.2 and discussed next.

Conducts Ongoing and/or Separate Evaluations (COSO Principle 16)

Ongoing evaluations are procedures built into the normal recurring activities of an entity. The *Auditing in Practice* feature "*Monitoring Controls in Fast-Food Franchises*" provides an example of ongoing evaluations. Computerized monitoring of transactions is an approach many organizations take to review a large volume of transactions at a relatively low cost. An organization may use software to automate the review of all payment transactions and identify anomalies that are investigated further.

Separate evaluations are conducted periodically, typically by objective management personnel, internal auditors, or external consultants. For example, an organization's internal auditors may perform an annual audit of all disbursements at selected operating units. As part of that audit, the internal auditors will identify instances in which a control is not operating effectively. Consider an organization that has a policy requiring approvals from appropriate personnel for disbursements over a certain dollar amount. During its annual audit, the internal auditor might find several instances when disbursements were made without the required approval. Since separate evaluations take place periodically, they are not as timely as ongoing evaluations in identifying control deficiencies. But separate evaluations do allow for a fresh, objective look at control effectiveness.

对控制的监督是指被审计单位评价内部控制在一段时间内运行有效性的过程，涉及及时评估内部控制的有效性并采取必要的补救措施。

Monitoring Controls in Fast-Food Franchises

AUDITING IN PRACTICE

A company such as Wendy's or McDonald's that serves fast food across thousands of locations must be able to monitor the workings of its controls at each location. The company has written policies and procedures dealing with control issues ranging from product acceptance (must be from authorized vendor), waste disposal, recording sales (must offer a cash register receipt or the meal is free), and employee supervision. The companies have standardized procedures for counting cash, reconciling cash with the cash register, depositing the cash daily, and transferring cash to corporate headquarters. From previous statistics and industry averages, the company knows that food costs should equal approximately 37% of revenue.

The company develops a performance-monitoring process that results in daily and weekly reports on:

- Store revenue compared with expected revenue and previous year's revenue for the same week
- Special promotions in effect
- Gross margin

The company then uses the monitoring reports to follow up with local stores and to determine which stores, if any, need further investigation.

For example, the company identifies a group of stores—all managed by one person—for which store revenue is lower than expected; but more important, the gross margin is significantly less than expected (63% expected, but 60% attained). The monitoring report indicates that one of the following explanations may represent the problems at the stores: (a) not all revenue is being recorded, (b) product is unnecessarily wasted, (c) product is diverted to other places (or stolen), or (d) some combination of these. Although the original focus is on operating data, the implication is that a breakdown of internal controls exists at those specific locations. The monitoring of performance has led to the monitoring of controls. The report leads management to determine the cause of the problem and to take corrective action.

Evaluates and Communicates Deficiencies (COSO Principle 17)

Control deficiencies identified through monitoring or other activities need to be communicated to appropriate personnel such as management or the board of directors so that appropriate corrective action can be taken. Recall the previous example in which internal auditors, conducting a separate evaluation, identified a deficiency in controls over disbursement. Internal audit should provide this information to parties responsible for taking appropriate corrective action. Included in this principle is the need for an organization to implement a system to track whether deficiencies are corrected on a timely basis.

管理层对财务报告内部控制的责任

Management's Responsibilities Related to Internal Control Over Financial Reporting

LO 8 Identify management's responsibilities related to internal control over financial reporting, including the factors management considers when assessing control deficiencies.

Management can be thought of as providing the first line of defense in achieving reliable financial reporting. Management is responsible for designing, implementing, and maintaining effective internal control over financial reporting. Further, management should maintain adequate documentation related to internal control over financial reporting. Management of U.S. public companies also has a responsibility to provide users with a report on the effectiveness of the organization's internal control based on the requirements in the Sarbanes-Oxley Act of 2002.

内部控制的记录

Documentation of Internal Control

Management needs to maintain sufficient and appropriate internal control documentation. This documentation should provide clarity and communicate standards and expectations related to internal control. Documentation is also useful in training new personnel or serving as a reference tool for all employees. Further, documentation provides evidence that the controls are operating, enables proper monitoring activities, and supports reporting on internal control effectiveness. The external auditor can use this documentation to obtain an understanding of the client's internal control system. Further, for clients like Ford Motor Company where the external auditor issues an opinion on the effectiveness of the client's controls, management will need to provide the auditor with documentation supporting management's assessment, and the auditor may use that documentation as part of the audit evidence. The nature and extent of internal control documentation will vary across organizations, but should be sufficient to support the design and operating effectiveness of controls.

In terms of documentation supporting financial transactions, an organization should have documentation, for example, that provides evidence of the authorization of transactions, the existence of transactions, the support for journal entries, and the financial commitments made by the organization. Documentation of controls is often thought of as existing on paper. However, the documentation can be either paper or electronic. The information technology system may have an automated application that is programmed to pay for merchandise when an electronic copy of receipt of merchandise is available. The computer program compares receipts with a purchase order and may or may not require a vendor invoice before payment.

The following are some guidelines for developing reliable documentation related to internal control. These guidelines apply to both paper and electronic documents.

- *Prenumbered paper or computer-generated documents* facilitate the control of, and accountability for, transactions and are crucial to the completeness assertion.
- *Timely preparation* improves the credibility and accountability of documents and decreases the rate of errors on all documents.
- *Authorization* of a transaction should be clearly evident in the records.
- A *transaction trail* should exist such that a user (or auditor) could trace a transaction from its origination through to its final disposition, or vice versa. A transaction trail serves many purposes, including providing information in order to respond to customer inquiries and identify and correct errors. An overview of important aspects of an electronic transaction trail is shown in Exhibit 3.4.

Reporting on Internal Control Over Financial Reporting   财务报告内部控制的报告

The Sarbanes-Oxley Act of 2002 requires public company management to annually report on the design and operating effectiveness of the organization's controls. The U.S. Securities and Exchange Commission (SEC) has provided guidelines to assist management in its evaluation of the effectiveness of internal controls over financial reporting. The SEC guidelines require that suitable criteria, for example, COSO, be used as the benchmark in assessing internal control effectiveness. Determining whether internal control is effective requires an assessment of whether each of the five internal control components, and their principles, are present and operating effectively. The components should be viewed as part of an integrated system in making the assessment. Management's annual assessment of internal control effectiveness is provided in a public report.

EXHIBIT 3.4 Electronic Transaction Trail

Unique identification of transaction—Examples include assigning a unique number by the computer. The unique identifier could be assigned sequentially or could consist of a location identifier and unique number within a location. Sales invoices, for example, are sequentially numbered by the computer application.

Date and time of transaction—These could be assigned automatically by the computer application.

Individual responsible for the transaction—The log-in to the system identifies the party authorizing or initiating the transaction.

Location from which the transaction originated—The log-in to the system can identify the source of the transaction.

Details of the transaction—These should be noted in a system log. Essentially, all the details normally found in a paper document, such as the quantities ordered, back-order provisions, can also be captured and saved as electronic trail.

Cross-reference to other transactions—When applicable, all cross-referencing to other transactions should be captured. For example, if a payment cross-references a specific invoice, the information needed to complete the cross-reference should be captured.

Authorization or approval of the transaction—If the transaction requires authorization by a party other than the one initiating the transaction, the proper electronic authorization should be captured.

An example of a management report from Ford Motor Company is shown in Exhibit 3.5. Note that management, including the CEO and CFO, both supervised and participated in the evaluation of internal controls. Further, they concluded that their internal control over financial reporting was effective as of December 31, 2011. A review of Exhibit 3.5 highlights important features of management's report. Management's report:

- Provides a statement that management is responsible for internal control
- Includes a definition of internal control
- Discusses the limitations of internal control
- Identifies the criteria (COSO) used in assessing internal control
- Concludes as to the effectiveness of internal control at a point in time (year-end)
- References the report on internal control provided by the company's external auditors

Note that Ford's external auditors have audited Ford's internal controls. Only larger public companies are required to have an external audit opinion on the effectiveness of internal control. However, management in smaller public companies still needs to evaluate and report on the effectiveness of their companies' internal controls over financial reporting.

财务报告内部控制的评价   Evaluating Internal Control Over Financial Reporting

What does management, or parties acting on management's behalf, need to do to be able to provide a report on internal control effectiveness? Management is responsible for evaluating internal control in order to report on its design and operating effectiveness. However, management may use external consultants or internal employees, such as internal auditors, to help fulfill its responsibility. These individuals need to be sufficiently competent and objective.

The SEC's guidance on management evaluation encourages a risk-based approach to evaluation. The steps involved in management's evaluation of

---

EXHIBIT 3.5   Ford Motor Company Management Report on Internal Control Over Financial Reporting (2011)

Our management is responsible for establishing and maintaining adequate internal control over financial reporting, as such term is defined in Exchange Act Rule 13a-15(f). The Company's internal control over financial reporting is a process designed to provide reasonable assurance regarding the reliability of financial reporting and the preparation of financial statements for external purposes in accordance with generally accepted accounting principles.

Because of its inherent limitations, internal control over financial reporting may not prevent or detect misstatements. Also, projections of any evaluation of effectiveness to future periods are subject to the risk that controls may become inadequate because of changes in conditions or because the degree of compliance with policies or procedures may deteriorate.

Under the supervision and with the participation of our management, including our CEO and CFO, we conducted an assessment of the effectiveness of our internal control over financial reporting as of December 31, 2011. The assessment was based on criteria established in the framework *Internal Control—Integrated Framework*, issued by the Committee of Sponsoring Organizations of the Treadway Commission. Based on this assessment, management concluded that our internal control over financial reporting was effective as of December 31, 2011.

The effectiveness of the Company's internal control over financial reporting as of December 31, 2011 has been audited by PricewaterhouseCoopers LLP, an independent registered public accounting firm, as stated in its report included herein.

internal control over financial reporting are summarized in Exhibit 3.6. Management begins by identifying the significant risks to reliable financial reporting. For example, a computer chip manufacturer would likely consider inventory to be a **significant account** because of the materiality of the inventory account. Further, the substantial judgment required by accounting personnel in valuing the inventory suggests that valuation is a particularly **relevant assertion**. Management then focuses on the design and operating effectiveness of the controls intended to mitigate the risks to reliable financial reporting for the significant accounts and their relevant assertions. Management will likely conduct a **walkthrough**, following a transaction from origination to when it is reflected in the financial records to determine if the controls are effectively designed and have been implemented. Management then gathers evidence through various procedures (for example, inquiry, observation, review of documentation, reperformance) as to whether the controls are operating effectively. For example, within its purchasing process, an organization may require approvals for all purchases over a stated dollar amount. As part of its testing, management could inquire of personnel who provide such approval and review documentation for an indication of the required approval by appropriate personnel. Exhibit 3.7 provides other examples of approaches management might use to test the operating effectiveness of various controls. After testing is completed, management evaluates any identified control deficiencies and provides its management report as part of its filings with the SEC.

EXHIBIT **3.6**   Steps in Management's Evaluation of Internal Control Over Financial Reporting

Identify Financial Reporting Risks and Controls Implemented to Mitigate those Risks

Identify financial reporting risks
Identify controls that mitigate financial reporting risks
Assess design effectiveness (possibly via walkthroughs)

Evaluate the Operating Effectiveness of Internal Control over Financial Reporting

Select and perform testing procedures to evaluate the operating effectiveness
Document operating effectiveness

Provide Report on Effectiveness of Internal Control over Financial Reporting

Evaluate control deficiencies
Provide public disclosure of management report, including any material weaknesses

---

EXHIBIT **3.7**	Examples of Approaches to Management Testing of Operating Effectiveness of Control

Control to Be Tested	Possible Management Testing Approach
As part of the organization's risk assessment process, formal forecasts are prepared and updated during the year to reflect changes in conditions, estimates, or current knowledge.	Obtain and review the most recent corporate budget, including current forecasts. Inquire of those that are responsible for preparing and updating the forecasts.
The organization has a documented and approved disaster recovery plan, which includes off-site storage controlled by a third-party vendor.	Review disaster recovery plan and third-party vendor contract. Confirm off-site storage arrangement with third-party vendor. Obtain evidence of approval of the disaster recovery plan.
The organization has a policy requiring that a revenue recognition review be performed by the revenue accountant before revenue from complex contracts is recorded.	Review the policy. For selected transactions, review documentation that substantiates the review or reperform the review.
Surveys of internal users of financial reports are conducted to obtain information on user satisfaction with the reliability and timeliness of the reporting.	Obtain and review user surveys. Interview users.

内部控制存在的缺陷包括设计缺陷和运行缺陷。设计缺陷是指缺少实现控制目标所必需的控制，或现有控制设计不恰当，即使正常运行也难以实现预期的控制目标。运行缺陷是指现存设计适当的控制没有按设计意图运行，或者执行人员没有获得必要授权或缺乏胜任能力，无法有效地实施内部控制。

Assessing Internal Control Deficiencies

As part of its evaluation, management may become aware of deficiencies in internal control design or operating effectiveness. A **control deficiency** is some shortcoming in internal controls such that the objective of reliable financial reporting may not be achieved. A deficiency in *design* exists when a control necessary to meet the control objective is missing, or when an existing control is not properly designed so that, even if the control operates as designed, the control objective would not be met. A deficiency in *operation* exists when a properly designed control does not operate as designed, or when the person performing the control does not possess the necessary authority or competence to perform the control effectively. Management will assess the severity of all identified control deficiencies. Two categories of deficiencies are noteworthy: material weakness and significant deficiency.

Material Weakness in Internal Control A **material weakness** is a deficiency, or a combination of deficiencies, in internal control over financial reporting, such that there is a *reasonable possibility* that a *material* misstatement of the company's annual or interim financial statements will not be prevented or detected on a timely basis. For these deficiencies, the likelihood and magnitude of potential misstatement are such that the company cannot conclude that its internal control over financial reporting is effective. A material weakness does not mean the control deficiency resulted in a material, or even immaterial, misstatement in the financial statements. Rather, a reasonable possibility is that this type of control deficiency *could* lead to a material misstatement. However, when management has to restate published financial statements because of a material misstatement, management will likely conclude a material weakness in internal control existed.

An organization that has one or more material weaknesses will issue a report indicating the internal control over financial reporting is not effective. The report will describe the identified material weaknesses. Examples of internal control material weaknesses that have been identified in management reports are shown in Exhibit 3.8. Note that the material weaknesses can be in either the design or operation of the control. Exhibit 3.8 highlights material weakness primarily related to control activities over information processing. But recall from the various examples provided throughout this chapter that material weaknesses can include deficiencies in other components of internal control, including the control environment, risk assessment, information and communication, and monitoring.

Significant Deficiency in Internal Control A significant deficiency is a deficiency, or a combination of deficiencies, in internal control over financial reporting that is less severe than a material weakness, yet important enough to merit attention by those responsible for oversight of the organization's financial reporting. A significant deficiency is important enough that it should be brought to the attention of management and the audit committee, but it does not need to be reported to external users. Significant deficiencies would not be included in management's report on internal control effectiveness.

EXHIBIT 3.8   Examples of Material Weaknesses in Internal Control Over Financial Reporting

Weaknesses in the Design of Controls
- Absence of appropriate segregation of duties over important processes
- Absence of appropriate reviews and approvals of transactions, accounting entries, or systems output
- Inadequate controls to safeguard assets
- Absence of controls to ensure that all items in a population are recorded
- Inadequate processes to develop significant estimates affecting the financial statements, for example, estimates for pensions, warranties, and other reserves
- Undue complexity in the design of the processing system that obfuscates an understanding of the system by key personnel
- Inadequate controls over access to computer systems, data, and files
- Inadequate controls over computer processing
- Inadequate controls built into computer processing

Weaknesses in the Operation of Controls
- Independent tests of controls at a division level indicate that the control activities are not working properly; for example, purchases have been made outside of the approved purchasing function
- Controls fail to prevent or detect significant misstatements of accounting information
- Misapplication of accounting principles
- Credit authorization processes overridden by the sales manager to achieve sales performance goals
- Reconciliations (a) not performed on a timely basis or (b) performed by someone independent of the underlying process
- Testing reveals evidence that accounting records have been manipulated or altered
- Evidence of misrepresentation by accounting personnel
- Computerized controls leading to items identified for nonprocessing systematically overridden by employees to process the transactions
- The completeness of a population, for example, prenumbered documents or reconciling items logged on to the computer with those processed, not accounted for on a regular basis

Differences between Material Weaknesses and Significant Deficiencies Management uses professional judgment in assessing whether identified control deficiencies rise to the level of a significant deficiency or material weakness. The severity of a deficiency depends on the magnitude of the potential misstatement resulting from the deficiency and whether there is a reasonable possibility that the organization's controls will fail to prevent, or detect and correct a misstatement of an account balance or disclosure. Management will need to consider the specific facts and circumstances surrounding the identified deficiency. Exhibit 3.9 describes two control deficiencies—one that would likely be assessed as a material weakness and one that would likely be assessed as a significant deficiency. Chapter 16 contains discussion of complex judgments relating to classifying a deficiency as a material weakness or a significant deficiency.

EXHIBIT 3.9   Assessing Identified Control Deficiencies

Likely Material Weakness

An organization has a new product line whereby the total annual revenue for this product line is large enough that a misstatement in the revenue account could be material to the financial statements overall. The revenue from this product line is based on contracts that have complex multi-element arrangements. The organization initiates a significant number of new contracts for this product line each week across multiple regions. When preparing these new contracts, a standard contract is used, and modifications to the standard contract are made based on the specific characteristics of the transaction.

When a new contract is entered into the computerized billing system, client accounting personnel at the regional office are to verify that revenue recognition conforms to GAAP. As part of the control procedure, the client accounting personnel who perform the verification are to complete and sign off on a revenue checklist. It appears that the control is effectively designed. However, when management tested the control they found that these control procedures had not been consistently documented or performed for the new product line. The control had not been operating effectively. Based only on these facts, management would likely determine that this deficiency represents a material weakness for the following reasons: (1) the magnitude of a financial statement misstatement resulting from this deficiency could reasonably be expected to be material as many new significant sales transactions occur each week and (2) the total sales transactions over the year are material. Management could conclude that the likelihood of material misstatements occurring is reasonably possible. Taken together, the magnitude and likelihood of misstatement that could occur in the financial statements resulting from this internal control deficiency meet the definition of a material weakness.

Likely Significant Deficiency

Consider the same scenario as described earlier with the following additional facts. The organization has implemented an additional procedure whereby the revenue accounting manager at the company headquarters verifies the revenue recognition provisions of a random sample of new contracts on a weekly basis. The manager examines documents that indicate regional accounting personnel have verified the revenue recognition provisions. The manager also reperforms the verification procedure to ensure that revenue recognition provisions have been properly entered into the billing system. A test of this control by management indicates that the control has been operating effectively. Based only on these facts, management now would likely determine that the deficiency represents a significant deficiency because the weekly verifications by the revenue accounting manager constitute a compensating control that is likely to detect and prevent material misstatements in revenue recognition. Thus, the control deficiency should likely be reported to the audit committee, but does not rise to the level of a material weakness.

SUMMARY AND NEXT STEPS

An important part of an organization's corporate governance is its system of internal control. All organizations need effective internal control over financial reporting so they can produce reliable financial statements that are free from material misstatement. Auditors should expect their clients to design, implement, and maintain effective internal control over financial reporting, and for public clients, to evaluate and report publicly on the effectiveness of its internal control over financial reporting. In the United States, the primary benchmark for assessing internal control effectiveness is the COSO's updated *Internal Control–Integrated Framework*.

Now that you understand the role of the external auditor (see Chapter 1), the elements of quality auditing (see Chapter 2), and the expectations for clients to implement mechanisms to provide reasonable assurance about the reliability of their reporting (see Chapters 2 and 3), it is time to focus on the external auditor. The next chapter provides information on the professional liability of external auditors and steps they can take to make quality professional and ethical judgments throughout the audit opinion formulation process.

SIGNIFICANT TERMS

Application controls   See transaction controls.

Control activities   The component of internal control that includes control actions that have been established by policies and procedures. They help ensure that management's directives regarding internal control are carried out.

Control deficiency   A shortcoming in internal controls such that the objective of reliable financial reporting may not be achieved.

Control environment   The component of internal control that includes the set of standards, processes, and structures that provides the basis for carrying out internal control across the organization. It includes the "tone at the top" regarding the importance of internal control and the expected standards of conduct.

COSO's updated *Internal Control–Integrated Framework*   A comprehensive framework of internal control used to assess the effectiveness of internal control over financial reporting, as well as controls over operational and compliance objectives.

Detective controls   Controls designed to discover errors that occur during processing.

Edit tests   See input validation tests.

Entity-wide controls   Controls that operate across an entity and affect multiple processes, transactions, accounts, and assertions.

General computer controls   Pervasive control activities that affect multiple types of information technology systems and are necessary for automated application controls to work properly (also referred to as information technology general controls).

Information and communication The component of internal control that refers to the process of identifying, capturing, and exchanging information in a timely fashion to enable accomplishment of the organization's objectives.

Information technology general controls See general computer controls.

Input controls Controls designed to ensure that authorized transactions are correct and complete, and that only authorized transactions can be input.

Input validation tests Control tests built into an application to examine input data for obvious errors (also referred to as edit tests).

Integrated audit An audit in which the same auditor provides an opinion on both the financial statements and the effectiveness of internal control over financial reporting.

Internal control A process, effected by an entity's board of directors, management, and other personnel, designed to provide reasonable assurance regarding the achievement of objectives relating to operations, reporting, and compliance.

Material weakness in internal control A deficiency, or a combination of deficiencies, in internal control over financial reporting such that there is a reasonable possibility that a material misstatement of the company's annual or interim financial statements will not be prevented or detected on a timely basis.

Monitoring The component of internal control that determines whether the controls, including all five components, are present and continuing to function effectively.

Ongoing evaluations Monitoring procedures that are built into the normal recurring activities of an entity.

Output controls Controls designed to provide reasonable assurance that all data are completely processed and that output is distributed only to authorized recipients.

Physical controls over assets Controls designed to protect and safeguard assets from accidental or intentional destruction and theft.

Preventive controls Controls designed to prevent the occurrence of a misstatement.

Processing controls Controls designed to provide reasonable assurance that the correct program is used for processing, all transactions are processed, and the transactions update appropriate files.

Relevant assertion A financial statement assertion, for a given account, is most relevant to determining whether there is a reasonable possibility that the account could contain a material misstatement, without considering the effect of internal controls.

Risk assessment The component of internal control that is the process for identifying and assessing the risks that may affect an organization from achieving its objectives.

Segregation of duties A control activity that is designed to protect against the risk that an individual could both perpetrate and cover up a fraud.

Self-checking digits A type of input test that has been developed to test for transposition errors associated with identification numbers.

Separate evaluations Monitoring procedures that are conducted periodically, typically by objective management personnel, internal auditors, or external consultants.

Significant account An account that has a reasonable possibility of containing a material misstatement, without considering the effect of internal controls.

Significant deficiency in internal control A deficiency, or a combination of deficiencies, in internal control over financial reporting that is less severe than a material weakness, yet important enough to merit attention by those responsible for oversight of the company's financial reporting.

Transaction controls Control activities implemented to mitigate transaction processing risk that typically affect only certain processes, transactions, accounts, and assertions These are controls that do not have an entity-wide effect.

Transaction trail Includes the documents and records that allow a user (or auditor) to trace a transaction from its origination through to its final disposition, or vice versa.

Walkthrough A process whereby management (or the auditor) follows a transaction from origination through the organization's processes until it is reflected in the organization's financial records. This process includes a combination of inquiry, observation, inspection of documentation making up the transaction trail, and reperformance of controls.

TRUE-FALSE QUESTIONS

3-1 [LO 1] Effective internal control allows for more informed decisions by internal and external users of the financial information.

3-2 [LO 1] While understanding a client's internal control over financial reporting may help the external auditor plan the audit, the external auditor is not required to obtain this understanding for all audit engagements.

3-3 [LO 2] Internal control is intended to provide absolute assurance that an organization will achieve its objective of reliable reporting.

3-4 [LO 2] Setting financial reporting objectives is a prerequisite for an organization designing and implementing internal control over financial reporting.

3-5 [LO 3] The control environment component of internal control is considered a pervasive or entity-wide control because it affects multiple processes and multiple types of transactions.

3-6 [LO 3] The control environment is seen as the foundation for all other components of internal control.

3-7 [LO 4] Only organizations in high-risk industries face a risk that they will not achieve their objective of reliable financial reporting.

3-8 [LO 4] An organization's risk assessment process should identify risks to reliable financial reporting from both internal and external sources.

3-9 [LO 5] There is one set of control activities that all organizations should implement.

3-10 [LO 5] Control activities include both preventive and detective controls.

3-11 [LO 6] An organization's accounting system is part of its information and communication component of internal control.

3-12 [LO 6] An organization needs information from both internal and external sources to carry out its internal control responsibilities.

3-13 [LO 7] As part of monitoring, an organization will select either ongoing evaluations or separate evaluations, but not both.

3-14 [LO 7] Communicating identified control deficiencies is a principle of monitoring.

3-15 [LO 8] If management identifies even one material weakness in internal control, then management will conclude that the organization's internal control over financial reporting is not effective.

3-16 [LO 8] Management will classify a control deficiency as a material weakness only if there has been a material misstatement in the financial statements.

MULTIPLE-CHOICE QUESTIONS

3-17 [LO 1] The quality of an organization's internal controls affects which of the following?
a. Reliability of financial data.
b. Ability of management to make good decisions.
c. Ability of the organization to remain in business.
d. Approach used by the auditor in auditing the financial statements.
e. All of the above.

3-18 [LO 1] Which of the following creates an opportunity for committing fraudulent financial reporting in an organization?
a. Management demands financial success.
b. Poor internal control.
c. Commitments tied to debt covenants.
d. Management is aggressive in its application of accounting rules.

3-19 [LO 2] What are the components of internal control per COSO's updated *Internal Control–Integrated Framework*?
a. Organizational structure, management philosophy, planning, risk assessment, and control activities.
b. Control environment, risk assessment, control activities, information and communication, and monitoring.
c. Risk assessment, control structure, backup facilities, responsibility accounting, and natural laws.
d. Legal environment of the firm, management philosophy, organizational structure, control activities, and control assessment.

3-20 [LO 2] Which of the following statements regarding internal control is false?

a. Internal control is a process consisting of ongoing tasks and activities.

b. Internal control is primarily about policy manuals, forms, and procedures.

c. Internal control is geared toward the achievement of multiple objectives.

d. A limitation of internal control is faulty human judgment.

e. All of the above statements are true.

3-21 [LO 3] Which of the following would not be considered a principle of an organization's control environment?

a. Independence and competence of the board.

b. Competence of accounting personnel.

c. Structures, reporting lines, and authorities and responsibilities.

d. Commitment to integrity and ethical values.

e. They would all be considered principles of the control environment.

3-22 [LO 3] Which one of the following components of internal control over financial reporting sets the tone for the organization?

a. Control risk assessment.

b. Control environment.

c. Information and communication.

d. Monitoring.

3-23 [LO 4] Which of the following statements is false regarding the risk assessment component of internal control?

a. Risk assessment includes assessing fraud risk.

b. Risk assessment includes assessing internal and external sources of risk.

c. Risk assessment includes the identification and analysis of significant changes.

d. Economic changes would not be considered a risk that needed to be analyzed as part of the risk assessment process.

3-24 [LO 4] Which of the following is not part of management's fraud risk assessment process?

a. The assessment considers ways the fraud could occur.

b. The assessment considers the role of the external auditor in preventing fraud.

c. Fraud risk assessments serve as an important basis for determining the control activities needed to mitigate fraud risks.

d. The assessment considers pressures that might lead to fraud in the financial statements.

3-25 [LO 5] Segregation of duties is best achieved in which of the following scenarios?

a. Employees perform only one job, even though they might have access to other records.

b. The internal audit department performs an independent test of transactions throughout the year and reports any errors to departmental managers.

c. The person responsible for reconciling the bank account is responsible for cash disbursements but not for cash receipts.

d. The payroll department cannot add employees to the payroll or change pay rates without the explicit authorization of the personnel department.

3-26 `LO 5` Which of the following statements about application controls is true?

a. Organizations can have manual application controls or automated application controls, but not a combination of the two.

b. Application controls are intended to mitigate risks associated with data input, data processing, and data output.

c. Application controls are a part of the monitoring component of internal control.

d. Self-checking digits are an output control.

3-27 `LO 6` Which of the following would be considered an effective implementation of the information and communication component of COSO's updated *Internal Control–Integrated Framework*?

a. The organization has one-way communication with parties external to the organization.

b. The organization has a whistleblower function that allows parties internal and external to the organization to communicate concerns about possible inappropriate actions in the organization's operations.

c. The organization has a robust process for assessing risks internal and external to the organization.

d. The organization builds in edit checks to determine whether all purchases are made from authorized vendors.

e. All of the above.

3-28 `LO 6` Which of the following is not a principle of the information and communication component of COSO's updated *Internal Control–Integrated Framework?*

a. The organization identifies, obtains, and uses relevant information.

b. The organization communicates internally.

c. The organization communicates externally.

d. All of the above.

3-29 `LO 7` Which of the following would *not* be considered an effective implementation of the monitoring component of COSO's updated *Internal Control–Integrated Framework*?

a. Internal audit periodically performs an evaluation of internal controls that have been documented and tested in prior years.

b. Management reviews current economic performance against expectations and investigates to determine causes of significant deviations from the expectations.

c. The company implements software that captures all instances in which the underlying program is designed to capture processed transactions that exceed company-authorized limits.

d. The company builds in edit checks to determine whether all purchases are made from authorized vendors.

3-30 `LO 7` Which of the following is the most accurate statement related to the monitoring component of COSO's updated *Internal Control–Integrated Framework?*

a. Monitoring is a process that is relevant only to the control activities component of COSO's updated *Internal Control–Integrated Framework*.

b. Separate evaluations are more timely than ongoing evaluations in identifying control deficiencies.

    c. Monitoring is a process that provides feedback on the effectiveness of each component of internal control.

    d. Monitoring includes automated edit checks to determine whether all purchases are made from authorized vendors.

3-31 [LO 8] Assume that an organization sells software. The sales contracts with the customers often have nonstandard terms that impact the timing of revenue recognition. Thus, there is a risk that revenue may be recorded inappropriately. To mitigate that risk, the organization has implemented a policy that requires all nonstandard contracts greater than $1 million to be reviewed on a timely basis by an experienced and competent revenue accountant for appropriate accounting, prior to the recording of revenue. Management tested this control and found several instances in which the control was not working. Management has classified this deficiency as a material weakness. Which of the following best describes the conclusion made by management?

    a. There is more than a remote possibility that a material misstatement could occur.

    b. The likelihood of misstatement is reasonably possible.

    c. There is more than a remote possibility that a misstatement could occur.

    d. There is a reasonable possibility that a material misstatement could occur.

    e. There is a reasonable possibility that a misstatement could occur.

3-32 [LO 8] Which one of the following represents a control deficiency?

    a. A missing control that is required for achieving objectives.

    b. A control that operates as designed.

    c. A control that provides reasonable, but not absolute assurance, about the reliability of financial reporting.

    d. An immaterial individual misstatement in internal control.

REVIEW AND SHORT CASE QUESTIONS

3-33 [LO 1] Why do external auditors need to understand their client's internal control over financial reporting?

NOTE: Completing Review and Short Case Questions does not require the student to reference additional resources and materials.

3-34 [LO 1] How does internal control benefit an organization?

3-35 [LO 1] How are the concepts of risk and internal control related?

3-36 [LO 2] Using COSO's updated *Internal Control–Integrated Framework* define internal control and describe important elements of the definition.

3-37 [LO 2] Refer to Exhibit 3.1. Identify the components of internal control and describe the prerequisite for designing and implementing internal control over financial reporting.

NOTE: For the remaining problems, we make special note of those addressing fraud, international issues, professional skepticism, and ethics.

3-38 [LO 2] Distinguish between entity-wide and transaction controls. Which components of internal control are typically entity-wide controls? Which components of internal control are typically transaction controls?

3-39 [LO 3] Refer to Exhibit 3.2. List the principles representing the fundamental concepts of the control environment component.

ETHICS

3-40 [LO 3] Refer to Exhibit 3.2. For each control environment principle, provide an example of how that principle might be applied in an organization.

ETHICS

3-41 [LO 3] What functions do an organization's board of directors and the audit committee of the board of directors perform in promoting a strong control environment?

ETHICS

FRAUD   **3-42** [LO 3]   As part of assessing the control environment management might consider the compensation programs that the organization has in place. Why would management consider these programs?

FRAUD   **3-43** [LO 4]   Refer to Exhibit 3.2. List the principles representing the fundamental concepts of the risk assessment component.

FRAUD   **3-44** [LO 4]   Refer to Exhibit 3.2. For each risk assessment principle, provide an example of how that principle might be applied in an organization.

3-45 [LO 5]   Refer to Exhibit 3.2. List the principles representing the fundamental concepts of the control activities component.

3-46 [LO 5]   Refer to Exhibit 3.2. For each control activities principle, provide an example of how that principle might be applied in an organization.

3-47 [LO 5]   Refer to Exhibit 3.3. Describe the three types of transactions subject to transaction processing risk. For each type of transaction, indicate a control activity that could be implemented to mitigate that risk.

3-48 [LO 5]   What are the important considerations in security management related to user access?

3-49 [LO 5]   What are general computer controls? What is the relationship between general computer controls and application controls? Why is management concerned about the effectiveness of these controls?

3-50 [LO 5]   Brown Company provides office support services for more than 100 small clients. These services include supplying temporary personnel, providing monthly bookkeeping services, designing and printing small brochures, copying and reproduction services, and preparing tax reports. Some clients pay for these services on a cash basis, some use 30-day charge accounts, and others operate on a contractual basis with quarterly payments. Brown's new office manager was concerned about the effectiveness of control procedures over sales and cash flow. At the manager's request, the process was reviewed by conducting a walkthrough. The following facts were identified. Review the identified facts (listed as A. through L. below) and complete the following.

a. What is a walkthrough, and why would it be useful for assessing controls over sales and cash flow?

b. List at least eight elements of ineffective internal control at Brown Company.

c. List at least six elements of effective internal control at Brown Company.

   A. Contracts were written by account executives and then passed to the accounts receivable department, where they were filed. Contracts had a limitation (ceiling) on the types of services and the amount of work covered. Contracts were payable quarterly in advance.

   B. Client periodic payments on contracts were identified on the contract, and a payment receipt was placed in the contract file.

   C. Periodically, a clerk reviewed the contract files to determine their status.

   D. Work orders relating to contract services were placed in the contract file. Accounting records showed Debit Cost of Services; Credit Cash or Accounts Payable; or Accrued Payroll.

   E. Monthly bookkeeping services were usually paid for when the work was complete. If not paid in cash, a copy of the financial statement (marked "Unpaid _____") was put into cash-pending file. It was removed when cash was received, and accounting records showed Debit Cash; Credit Revenue.

F. Design and printing work was handled like bookkeeping's work. However, a design and printing order form was used to accumulate costs and compute the charge to be made to the client. A copy of the order form served as a billing to the client and, when cash was received, as a remittance advice.

G. Reproduction (copy) work was generally a cash transaction that was rung up on a cash register and balanced at the end of the day. Some reproduction work was charged to open accounts. A billing form was given to the client with the work, and a copy was put in an open file. It was removed when paid. In both cases, when cash was received, the accounting entry was Debit Cash; Credit Revenue.

H. Tax work was handled like the bookkeeping services.

I. Cash from cash sales was deposited daily. Cash from receipts on account or quarterly payments on contracts was deposited after being matched with the evidence of the receivable.

J. Bank reconciliations were performed using the deposit slips as original data for the deposits on the bank statements.

K. A cash log of all cash received in the mail was maintained and used for reference purposes when payment was disputed.

L. Monthly comparisons were made of the costs and revenues of printing, design, bookkeeping, and tax service. Unusual variations between revenues and costs were investigated. However, the handling of deferred payments made this analysis difficult.

3-51 `LO 5` The following items represent errors that often occur in an automated environment. For each error (listed as A. through I. below), identify a control activity that would have been effective in either preventing or detecting the error.

A. The selling price for all products handled by a particular company salesperson was reduced from authorized prices by 25% to 40%. The salesperson was paid commission on gross sales made. Subsequently, management found that other sales personnel also reduced prices in order to meet sales targets.

B. Duplicate paychecks were prepared for all employees in the company's warehouse for the week ended July 31. This occurred because the data processing department processed employee time cards twice.

C. An employee in the sales order department who was upset about an inadequate pay raise copied the client's product master file and sold it to a competitor. The master file contained information on the cost and sales price of each product, as well as special discounts given to customers.

D. An individual in the sales department accessed the product master file and, in an attempt to change prices for a specific customer, ended up changing prices for the products for all customers.

E. A nonexistent part number was included in the description of goods on a shipping document. Fortunately, the individual packing the item for shipment was able to identify the product by its description and included it in the order. The item was not billed, however, because it was not correctly identified in the system.

F. A customer account number was transposed during the order-taking process. Consequently, the shipment was billed to another customer. By the time the error was identified, the original customer decided to take its business elsewhere.

G. An accounts receivable clerk with access to entering cash remittances misappropriated the cash remittances and recorded the credit to the customer's account as a discount.

H. An employee consistently misstated his time card by returning at night and punching out then, rather than when his shift was over at 3:30 p.m. Instead of being paid for 40 hours per week, he was paid, on average, for over 60 hours per week for almost one year. When accused of the error, he denied any wrongdoing and quit.

I. A customer order was filled and shipped to a former customer, who had already declared bankruptcy and already owed a large amount to the company that was most likely uncollectible. The company's standard billing terms are 2%, 10 days, or net 30.

FRAUD **3-52** **LO 5** Authorization of transactions is considered a key control in most organizations. Authorizations should not be made by individuals who have incompatible functions. For each transaction (listed as A. through I. below), indicate the individual or function (e.g., the head of a particular department) that should have the ability to authorize that transaction. Briefly provide rationale for your answer.

A. Writing off old accounts receivable.

B. Committing the organization to acquire another company that is half the size of the existing company.

C. Paying an employee for overtime.

D. Shipping goods on account to a new customer.

E. Purchasing goods from a new vendor.

F. Temporarily investing funds in common stock investments instead of money market funds.

G. Purchasing a new line of manufacturing equipment to remodel a production line at one of the company's major divisions (the purchase represents a major new investment for the organization).

H. Replacing an older machine at one of the company's major divisions.

I. Rewriting the company's major computer program for processing purchase orders and accounts payable (the cost of rewriting the program will represent one quarter of the organization's computer development budget for the year).

3-53 **LO 5** For each of the following situations (indicated A. through G. below), evaluate the segregation of duties implemented by the company and indicate the following:

a. Any deficiency in the segregation of duties described. (Indicate "None" if no deficiency is present.)

b. The potential financial statement misstatements that might occur because of the inadequate segregation of duties.

c. Compensating, or other, controls that might be added to mitigate potential misstatements.

A. The company's payroll is computerized and is handled by one person in charge of payroll who enters all weekly time reports into the system. The payroll system is password protected so that only the payroll person can change pay rates or add/delete company personnel to the payroll file. Payroll checks are prepared weekly, and the payroll person batches the checks by supervisor or department head for subsequent distribution to employees.

B. A relatively small organization has segregated the duties of cash receipts and cash disbursements. However, the employee responsible for handling cash receipts also reconciles the monthly bank account.

C. Nick's is a small family-owned restaurant in a northern resort area whose employees are trusted. When the restaurant is very busy, any of the servers have the ability to operate the cash register and collect the amounts due from the customer. All orders are tabulated on "tickets." Although each ticket has a place to indicate the server, most do not bother to do so, nor does management reconcile the ticket numbers and amounts with total cash receipts for the day.

D. A sporting goods store takes customer orders via a toll-free phone number. The order taker sits at a terminal and has complete access to the customer's previous credit history and a list of inventory available for sale. The order clerk has the ability to input all the customer's requests and generate a sales invoice and shipment with no additional supervisory review or approval.

E. The purchasing department of Big Dutch is organized around three purchasing agents. The first is responsible for ordering electrical gear and motors, the second orders fabrication material, and the third orders nuts and bolts and other smaller supplies that go into the assembly process. To improve the accountability to vendors, all receiving slips and vendor invoices are sent directly to the purchasing agent placing the order. This allows the purchasing agent to better monitor the performance of vendors. When approved by the purchasing agent for payment, the purchasing agent must forward (a) a copy of the purchase order, (b) a copy of the receiving slip, and (c) a copy of the vendor invoice to accounts payable for payment. Accounts payable will not pay an invoice unless all three items are present and match as to quantities, prices, and so forth. The receiving department reports to the purchasing department.

3-54 **LO 5** Cabelas is a catalog retailer emphasizing outdoor gear, with a focus on fishing and hunting equipment and clothing. It prints an annual catalog containing over 200 pages of products, as well as approximately six special sale catalogs during the year. Products range from fishing lures retailing for just over a $1.00 to boat packages for over $25,000. Cabelas also has both a significant Internet presence and a number of large retail locations. Purchases can be made through the mail, on the Internet, or at the retail store. There will sometimes be online specials that are not available elsewhere (e.g., closeouts). Merchandise can be paid for by personal check, credit card, or cash. Customers can (a) order online, (b) mail in their order (with check or credit card information included), or (c) place an order by calling the company's toll-free number.

Focusing on catalog operations, assume the company has implemented an order-entry system by which computer operators take the customer order, check the availability of items for shipment, and confirm the invoice amount with the customer. Once an order is taken, the system generates a shipping-and-packing document, places a hold on the inventory, and prepares an invoice (and recording of sales) when items are shipped.

a. Identify the application control procedures (including edit controls) you would recommend for orders coming in over the Internet or through calls to the online order taker.

b. Briefly indicate how control procedures might differ for the orders that are made directly over the Internet.

c. For each control procedure identified in your response to (a), briefly indicate the potential types of misstatements that could occur because the control is not present or is not operating effectively.

3-55 [LO 6] Refer to Exhibit 3.2. List the principles representing the fundamental concepts of the information and communication component.

3-56 [LO 6] Refer to Exhibit 3.2. For each information and communication principle, provide an example of how that principle might be applied in an organization.

3-57 [LO 7] Refer to Exhibit 3.2. List the principles representing the fundamental concepts of the monitoring component.

3-58 [LO 7] Refer to Exhibit 3.2. For each monitoring principle, provide an example of how that principle might be applied in an organization.

3-59 [LO 7] Companies can gain efficiencies by implementing effective ongoing monitoring of their internal control processes. Identify the important ongoing monitoring procedures that an organization might use in assessing its controls over revenue recognition in each of the following situations:

a. A convenience store such as 7-Eleven.

b. A chain restaurant such as Olive Garden.

c. A manufacturing division of a larger company that makes rubberized containers for the consumer market.

3-60 [LO 8] What are management's responsibilities related to internal control over financial reporting?

3-61 [LO 8] Refer to Exhibit 3.4 What is a transaction trail? List important aspects of an electronic transaction trail. What are management's responsibilities related to maintaining a transaction trial?

3-62 [LO 8] Refer to Exhibit 3.5. What are the important features of management's report on internal control over financial reporting?

ETHICS **3-63** [LO 8] Refer to Exhibits 3.6 and 3.7. Describe management's process for evaluating internal control over financial reporting. For the control environment principles, identify evidence that management might obtain to assess the operating effectiveness of the control environment.

3-64 [LO 8] Refer to Exhibits 3.8 and 3.9. Define the terms significant deficiency and material weakness. What factors does management consider when assessing identified control deficiencies?

3-65 [LO 8] Should management's assessment of internal control over financial reporting consider all of the COSO components, or could it be based on the controls over the processing of transactions? Explain.

3-66 [LO 8] What role can internal auditors have in assisting management in evaluating the effectiveness of internal control over financial reporting?

3-67 [LO 8] One principle of the control environment is the organization's commitment to develop, attract, and retain competent individuals. How would management go about evaluating the competency of accounting department personnel and the competencies of those making judgments on financial reporting issues?

3-68 [LO 8] Assume that management had determined that its organization's audit committee is not effective. For example, Lehman Brothers, Inc., had weak directors with little financial knowledge, and those directors were not independent of management. How do the weaknesses in audit committee affect management's evaluation of internal control over financial reporting? Would an ineffective audit committee constitute a material weakness in internal control over financial reporting? State the rationale for your response.

3-69 **LO 8** Assume that management is gathering evidence as part of its process for assessing the effectiveness of internal control over financial reporting. The company is a manufacturing company with high-dollar specialized machines used in the medical profession. The following table identifies important controls that management is testing regarding accounts related to revenue recognition, accounts receivable, and other sales-related activities. The first column describes the control, and the second column describes the test results. Based on the test results, determine the conclusion that management should make about the deficiency (is it a control deficiency, a significant deficiency, or a material weakness?).

CONTROL TESTING OVER REVENUE

Control Tested	Test Results
A. All sales over $10,000 require computer check of outstanding balances to see if approved balance is exceeded.	Tested throughout year with a sample size of 30. Only three failures, all in the last quarter, and all approved by sales manager.
B. The computer is programmed to record a sale only when an item is shipped.	Sampled 10 items during the last month. One indicated that it was recorded before it was shipped. Management was aware of the recording.
C. All prices are obtained from a standardized price list maintained within the computer and accessible only by the marketing manager.	Management selected 40 invoices and found 5 instances in which the price was less than the price list. All of the price changes were initiated by salespeople.
D. Sales are shipped only upon receiving an authorized purchase order from customer.	Management selects 15 transactions near the end of each quarter. On average, 3–4 are shipped each quarter based on salesperson's approval and without a customer purchase order.

3-70 **LO 8** The following scenario describes PPC, a small plastics producer with $250 million in revenue and approximately 300 employees. PPC is a public company that first became listed three years ago. It has been hit hard by the recent recession, and its sales have dropped from $1,375 million to $1,250 million. It is barely profitable and is just meeting some of its most important debt covenants. During the past year, John Slade, CEO and owner of 22% of the company's shares, has taken the following actions (listed as A. through I. below) to reduce costs. For each action, complete the following.

a. Would the action be considered an operational issue and not a control deficiency, or would it likely constitute a material weakness or significant deficiency in internal control? Provide brief rationale for your assessment. If additional information is needed in order to assess whether the item is a control deficiency, briefly indicate what information would be required.

b. Considering all of the indicated actions (A. through I. below), how has the risk related to the objective of reliable financial reporting changed during the year?

   A. Laid off approximately 75 factory workers and streamlined receiving and shipping to be more efficient.

   B. Cut hourly wages by $3 per hour.

   C. Reduced the size of the board by eliminating three of the four independent directors and changed the compensation of remaining board members to 100% stock options to save cash outflow. The company granted options to the remaining six directors with a market value of $100,000 per director, but no cash outlay.

   D. Eliminated the internal audit department at a savings of $450,000. The process owners (e.g., those responsible for accounts payable) are now required to objectively evaluate the quality of controls over their own areas and thus to serve as a basis for management's report on the effectiveness of internal control.

   E. Changed from a Big 4 audit firm to a regional audit firm, resulting in an additional audit savings of $300,000. This is the first public company audit for the new firm.

   F. Because internal audit no longer exists, the CEO relies on monitoring as the major form of control assessment. Most of the monitoring consists of comparing budget with actual results. Management argues this is very effective because the CEO is very much involved in operations and would know if there is a reporting problem.

   G. Set tight performance goals for managers and promised a bonus of 20% of their salary if they meet the performance objectives. The performance objectives relate to increased profitability and meeting existing volumes.

   H. The purchasing department has been challenged to move away from single-supplier contracts to identify suppliers that can significantly reduce the cost of products purchased.

   I. Put a freeze on all hiring, in spite of the fact that the accounting department has lost its assistant controller. This has required a great deal of extra overtime for most accounting personnel, who are quite stressed.

CONTEMPORARY AND HISTORICAL CASES

FRAUD   **3-71**   **CHESAPEAKE PETROLEUM AND SUPPLY, INC.**
LO 1, 2, 5   Refer to the *Professional Judgment in Context* feature at the outset of the chapter, which describes the embezzlement at Chesapeake Petroleum and Supply.

a. Why is internal control important to an organization?

b. How does internal control help an organization achieve reliable financial reporting?

c. Why does an external auditor need to know about a client's internal control?

d. What is internal control over financial reporting and what are its components?

e. What type of control is segregation of duties and what risks is that control intended to mitigate?

f. What controls could Chesapeake have implemented that may have prevented the embezzlement?

3-72 DIAMOND FOODS, INC.
LO 8   FRAUD

In February 2012, the *Wall Street Journal* reported that Diamond Foods Inc. fired its CEO and CFO, and would restate financial results for two years. The restatement was required after the company found that it had wrongly accounted for crop payments to walnut growers. The investigation focused primarily on whether payments to growers in September 2011 of approximately $60 million and payments to growers in August 2010 of approximately $20 million were accounted for in the correct periods. Shareholders suing the company allege the payments may have been used to shift costs from a prior fiscal year into a subsequent fiscal year. As part of the internal investigation, the audit committee did not uncover any evidence of intent to deceive shareholders. Rather, the situation was described as a breakdown of controls. In a February 2012 filing with the SEC, the audit committee stated that Diamond has one or more material weaknesses in its internal control over financial reporting.

a. Does the restatement suggest that the company's internal controls contained a material weakness? Explain your rationale.

b. In September 2011, the company filed its annual report with the SEC for its fiscal year ended July 31, 2011. As part of that filing the company maintained that it had effective internal controls over financial reporting as of its year-end date. Do you believe that management's report on internal control over financial reporting was accurate?

c. In February 2012, the audit committee indicated that the company had ineffective internal controls. What types of material weaknesses do you think might exist at Diamond?

4

Professional Liability and the Need for Quality Auditor Judgments and Ethical Decisions

CHAPTER OVERVIEW AND LEARNING OBJECTIVES

The past three chapters have introduced you to the external auditing profession, the need for audit quality, the challenges that fraud poses for auditors, and management's responsibility to ensure reliable financial reporting through effective internal controls. In this chapter, we discuss the legal environment in which auditors operate and we explore what litigation they might face, should they fail to perform quality audits. Even though most audits are performed in a quality manner, a large percentage of the revenues of external audit firms is spent on litigation-related costs. Litigation costs have caused some of the world's largest audit firms to declare bankruptcy, so it is extremely important that auditors use due professional care and provide quality audits to minimize such costs. Following the discussion on litigation, we introduce a framework for professional decision making and a framework for ethical decision making that, when applied effectively, help auditors to avoid the risk of litigation.

Through studying this chapter, you will be able to achieve these learning objectives:

通过本章的学习，你将能够实现以下学习目标：

1. Discuss the liability environment in which auditors operate and explore the effects of lawsuits on audit firms.

   讨论注册会计师面临的法律环境和诉讼对会计师事务所的影响。

2. List laws from which auditor liability is derived and describe the causes of legal action against auditors.

   列示出涉及注册会计师责任的法律，描述针对注册会计师的法律诉讼的原因。

3. Describe possible causes of action, remedies or sanctions, and auditor defenses under both common law and statutory law.

   描述诉讼、赔偿或处罚的可能原因，以及注册会计师在普通法和成文法下的抗辩。

4. Articulate a framework for making quality professional decisions and apply this framework in selected audit settings.

   认识为做出高质量职业决策所构建的框架，并在选定的审计环境下运用这个框架。

5. Articulate a framework for making quality ethical decisions and apply this framework in selected settings.

   描述为做出高质量道德决策所构建的框架，并在选定的审计环境下运用这个框架。

6. Describe and apply the IESBA's Code of Ethics and the AICPA's Code of Professional Conduct.

   描述和应用国际会计师职业道德准则理事会（IESBA）的职业道德规范和美国注册会计师协会（AICPA）的职业行为规范。

THE AUDIT OPINION FORMULATION PROCESS

| I. Making Client Acceptance and Continuance Decisions **Chapter 14** | II. Performing Risk Assessment **Chapters 3, 7 and 9–13** | III. Obtaining Evidence about Internal Control Operating Effectiveness **Chapters 8–13 and 16** | IV. Obtaining Substantive Evidence about Accounts, Disclosures and Assertions **Chapters 8–13 and 16** | V. Completing the Audit and Making Reporting Decisions **Chapters 14 and 15** |

| The Auditing Profession, the Risk of Fraud and Mechanisms to Address Fraud: Regulation, Corporate Governance, and Audit Quality **Chapters 1 and 2** | Professional Liability and the Need for Quality Auditor Judgments and Ethical Decisions **Chapter 4** |

The Audit Opinion Formulation Process and A Framework for Obtaining Audit Evidence
Chapters 5 and 6

PROFESSIONAL JUDGMENT IN CONTEXT

KPMG LLP served as the external auditor for some of the largest subprime mortgage lenders in the United States leading up to and during the housing market crisis of the mid-2000s. The audits of two of their largest lending clients, New Century Financial Corporation and Countrywide, ultimately led the firm to settle litigation charges in 2010 for $44.7 million and $24 million, respectively. The business model of these two subprime mortgage lenders consisted of providing loans to borrowers with weak credit histories. The business model had begun to fail during a short period of time in 2007, when the economy weakened, borrowers began defaulting, and home prices declined drastically. New Century filed for bankruptcy and Countrywide was purchased by Bank of America, which subsequently suffered massive losses related to business failures at Countrywide.

Just before the housing crash of 2007 put the companies in severe financial crises, KPMG had given both companies unqualified audit opinions. In both cases, KPMG was subsequently accused of violating professional standards, lacking independence, and being negligent. KPMG defended itself by arguing that its audits were not the cause of the financial woes at New Century and Countrywide. Rather, the firm contended that it was the failed business model of the two companies that led to investor losses. As you read through this chapter, consider the following questions:

- How does the business environment affect the litigation risk faced by audit firms? (LO 1)
- Should auditors be held liable when their client's business fails or its financial statements contain a fraud that the auditors did not detect? (LO 2)
- What defenses do auditors use in response to litigation? (LO 3)
- What actions can auditors take to minimize litigation exposure? (LO 3, 4, 5, 6)

法律环境和诉讼对会计师事务所的影响

LO 1 Discuss the liability environment in which auditors operate and explore the effects of lawsuits on audit firms.

"深口袋"理论
(deep-pocket theory)
任何看上去拥有赔偿能力的个体或者组织都可能受到起诉，不论其应当受到惩罚的程度如何。

责任原则

The Legal Environment and the Effects of Lawsuits on Audit Firms

Litigation cases are expensive for audit firms—whether they win or lose—because they result in monetary losses, take up the time of audit firm members, and can hurt the reputation of the audit firm. In fact, audit firms report that practice protection costs, such as insurance, legal fees, and litigation settlements, are the second-highest costs faced by audit firms, behind only employee compensation costs. When auditors agree to perform audits, they purport to be experts in assessing the fairness of financial statements on which the public relies. In conducting most audits, auditors use great care, perform professionally, issue appropriate opinions, and serve the interests of the public. In short, most audits are conducted in a quality manner. Even so, audit firms continue to experience high levels of litigation. Reasons for this include the following:

- Liability doctrines that include joint and several liability statutes permitting a plaintiff to recover the full amount of a settlement from an external audit firm, even though that firm is found to be only partially responsible for the loss (often referred to as the **deep-pocket theory**, meaning we sue those who can pay)
- Class action suits and associated user awareness of the possibilities and rewards of litigation
- Contingent-fee-based compensation for law firms, especially in class action suits
- The misunderstanding by some users of financial statement that an unqualified audit opinion represents an insurance policy against investment losses

Liability Doctrines

Auditors may be subject to either joint and several liability or proportionate liability. **Joint and several liability** concepts are designed to protect users who suffer losses because of misplaced reliance on materially misstated financial statements. Users suffer real losses, but sometimes those primarily responsible for the losses, such as management, do not have the monetary resources to compensate users. Under joint and several liability, users suffering a loss are able to recover full damages from any defendant, including an audit firm, regardless of the level of fault of the party. For example, if a jury decided that management was 80% at fault and the auditor was 20% at fault, the damages would be apportioned 80% to management and 20% to auditors. Unfortunately, in many lawsuits involving auditors, the client is in bankruptcy, management has few monetary resources, and the auditor is the only party left with adequate resources to pay the damages. Joint and several liability then apportions the damages over the remaining defendants in proportion to the relative damages. Under joint and several liability, if management has no resources and there are no other defendants, 100% of the damages are then apportioned to the audit firm. In federal suits, Congress has limited the extent of joint and several liability damages to actual percentage of responsibility (if auditors are found liable for less than 50% of damages).

In 1995, Congress passed the Private Securities Litigation Reform Act (PSLRA), which is designed to curb frivolous securities class action lawsuits brought under federal securities laws against companies whose stock performs below expectations. Under this Act, liability is proportional rather than joint and several, unless the violation is willful—that is, unless the auditor knowingly participated in a fraud. In some situations, a defendant may have to cover some of the obligation of another defendant who is unable to pay his or her share. Under **proportionate liability**, a defendant must pay a proportionate share of the damage, depending on the degree of fault determined by the judge or jury. Because the PSLRA applies only to lawsuits brought in federal courts, many lawyers filed their cases in state courts. This loophole was closed by the Securities Litigation Uniform Standards Act of 1998, which says, "Any covered class action brought into any state court involving a covered security...shall be removable to the federal district court for the district in which the action is pending." The 1998 Act is designed to require potential plaintiffs to adhere to the spirit, as well as the letter, of the PLSRA Act of 1995.

Class Action Lawsuits

集体诉讼

Class action lawsuits are designed to prevent multiple lawsuits that might result in inconsistent judgments and to encourage litigation when no individual plaintiff has a claim large enough to justify the expense of litigation. These types of lawsuits are especially appropriate for securities litigation because they enable a number of shareholders to combine claims that they could not afford to litigate individually. Often in these cases, the lawyers are working on a contingent fee basis and will work very diligently to identify every potential member of the class. Damages to audit firms in such cases can be extremely large, thus the fees for the lawyers are also usually quite large.

Contingent-Fee Compensation for Lawyers

对律师的或有费用补偿

Contingent fees for lawyers have evolved in our society to allow individuals who cannot afford high-priced lawyers to seek compensation for their damages. Lawyers take **contingent-fee cases** with an agreement that a client who loses a case owes the lawyer nothing; however, if the case is won, the lawyer receives an agreed-upon portion (usually one-third to one-half) of the damages awarded. This arrangement protects the underprivileged and encourages lawsuits by a wide variety of parties. The plaintiffs have little to lose, while the lawyers have a large incentive to successfully pursue such cases.

Audits Viewed as an Insurance Policy: The Expectations Gap

被视为保险的审计：期望差距

As you know from your readings, an audit report accompanying a financial statement is not a guarantee that an investment in the audited company is free of risk. Unfortunately, some investors mistakenly view the unqualified audit report as an insurance policy against any and all losses from a risky investment. When they do suffer losses, these investors believe that they should be able to recover their losses from the auditor. This misperception has elements of an **"expectations gap,"** whereby shareholders believe that they are entitled to recover losses on investments for which the auditor provided an unqualified opinion on the financial statements. This misperception, coupled with joint and several liability, class action lawsuits, and contingent-fee compensation for lawyers, encourages large lawsuits against auditors, even for cases in which the auditor is only partially at fault or is not at fault.

Applicable Laws and Causes of Legal Action

适用的法律和法律诉讼的原因

Laws from Which Auditor Liability Is Derived and Causes of Legal Action

导致注册会计师责任的法律和法律诉讼的原因

Liability that affects external audit firms is derived from the following laws:

- **Common law**—Liability concepts are developed through court decisions based on negligence, gross negligence, or fraud.
- **Contract law**—Liability occurs where there is a breach of contract. The contract is usually between the external auditor and the client for the performance of the financial statement audit.
- **Statutory law**—Liability is based on federal securities laws or state statutes. The most important of these statutes to the auditing profession

LO 2 List laws from which auditor liability is derived and describe the causes of legal action against auditors.

are the Securities Act of 1933 (1933 Act), the Securities Exchange Act of 1934 (1934 Act), and the Sarbanes-Oxley Act of 2002.

Parties that bring suit against auditors usually allege that the auditors did not meet the standard of due care in performing the audit. Auditors are responsible for due care. The specific responsibility in a particular case depends on whether there is a breach of contract, negligence, gross negligence, or fraud.

Breach of contract occurs when a person fails to perform a contractual duty. As an example, an auditor was hired to find a material fraud. If reasonable procedures would have detected the fraud and the auditor failed to uncover the fraud, the auditor would have breached the contract. As another example, if the auditor agreed to provide the audit report by a certain date, but did not, the auditor would have breached the contract.

Negligence is the failure to exercise reasonable care, thereby causing harm to another or to property. If an auditor, for example, did not detect an embezzlement scheme because of a failure to follow up on evidence that would have brought it to light, but a prudent auditor would have performed such follow-up, the auditor is negligent. The profession's standards require that audits be conducted in accordance with professional auditing standards; thus, a failure to meet these standards could be construed as negligence on the part of the auditor.

Gross negligence is the failure to use even minimal care, a reckless disregard for the truth, or reckless behavior. Expressing an opinion on a set of financial statements with careless disregard of professional auditing standards is an example of gross negligence. Gross negligence is more than failing to comply with professional standards; it is such complete disregard for due care that judges and juries are allowed to infer intent to deceive, even though there may be no direct evidence of intent to deceive.

Fraud is an intentional concealment or misrepresentation of a material fact that causes damage to those deceived. In an action for fraud, scienter must generally be proved. **Scienter** means knowledge on the part of a person making false representations, at the time they are made, that they are false. An auditor perpetrates a fraud on investors, for example, by expressing an unqualified opinion on financial statements that the auditor knows, in reality, are not fairly presented. In such a situation, the purpose of expressing the unqualified audit opinion is to deceive.

可能对注册会计师提起诉讼的各方

Parties that May Bring Suit against Auditors

In most cases, anyone who can support a claim that damages were incurred based on misleading audited financial statements can bring a claim against the auditor. We refer to these parties as the client and third-party users. They may accuse the auditor of breach of contract or of a tort. A **tort** is a civil wrong, other than breach of contract, based on negligence, gross negligence, or fraud. Exhibit 4.1 lists the parties to whom the external auditor is held liable, and it outlines the applicable law from which auditor liability is derived. We expand on these topics in the subsequent section.

EXHIBIT **4.1**	Overview of Auditor Liability

(AUDITOR HELD LIABLE? Y = YES, N = NO, NA = NOT APPLICABLE)

Who Can Sue?	Client		3rd Parties		
				Statutory Law	
Under What Law?	Contract Law	Common Law	Common Law	1933 Act	1934 Act
For What?					
Breach of contract	Y	NA	NA	NA	NA
Negligence	Y	Y	*	Y	N
Gross negligence	Y	Y	Y	Y	Unclear
Fraud	Y	Y	Y	Y	Y

*Depends on the test used:
- Identified User
- Foreseen User
- Foreseeable User

Auditor Liability under Common Law and Contract Law

Auditor liability under common law includes breach of contract and liability to third parties. Important concepts include foreseeability, negligence, and the implications of different types of users of the financial statements.

Common-Law Liability to Clients: Breach of Contract

When a client contracts with an auditor to perform specific services, a contract is drawn up that says the services will be performed in accordance with professional auditing standards and will be completed on a timely basis. Auditors are expected to fulfill these contractual responsibilities to clients. Auditors can be held liable to clients under contract law and/or under common law for breach of contract, and they can be sued under the concepts of negligence, gross negligence, and fraud.

Breach of contract may occur when there is nonperformance of a contractual duty. Causes for action against the auditor for breach of contract may include, but are not limited to, the following:

- Violating client confidentiality
- Failing to provide the audit report on time
- Failing to discover a material error or employee fraud
- Withdrawing from an audit engagement without justification

A client seeking to recover damages from an auditor in an action based on negligence must show that the auditor had a duty not to be negligent. In determining this duty, courts use as criteria the standards and principles of the profession, including professional auditing standards and financial accounting principles. Liability may be imposed for lack of due care either in performing the audit or in presenting financial information. The auditor must have breached that duty by not exercising due professional care. The client must show there was a causal relationship between the negligence and damage. The client must prove actual damages. The amount of damages must be established with reasonable certainty, and the client must demonstrate that the auditor's acts or omissions were the cause of the loss. See the *Auditing in Practice* feature,

普通法和契约法下的审计师责任

LO 3 Describe possible causes of action, remedies or sanctions, and auditor defenses under both common law and statutory law.

对客户的普通法责任：违约

违约是指注册会计师在职业过程中未能达到审计业务约定书的要求，如未能及时提交审计报告，违反了与被审计单位订立的保密协议等。

Moss Adams and the Meridian Mortgage Funds Fraud

Although management is responsible for the preparation of financial statements, it is possible that the statements contain material misstatements that should have been discovered by the auditor. For example, the auditor may have failed to discover a fraud that was being perpetrated against the management of the company. The auditor will usually argue that the client was negligent because client management contributed to the fraud in some way (for example, the auditor might argue that the damage was intentional or was at least in part caused by management's carelessness or lack of internal controls). Nonetheless, clients have brought litigation against auditors when financial statements were misleading or frauds were not detected.

As an example, in late 2011, the trustee for the bankrupt Meridian Mortgage funds sued the audit firm Moss Adams for $150 million for failing to detect the founder's Ponzi scheme. The founder, Frederick Berg, pleaded guilty, admitting to stealing about $100 million of Meridian's funds for personal use and to perpetuating the Ponzi scheme. Moss Adams had issued unqualified audit opinions for the funds, and the trustee argued that it was a series of low quality audits that allowed the Ponzi scheme to continue undetected. The trustee alleged that Moss Adams acted intentionally and recklessly. They also argued that the audit firm was not independent, as Berg was paying the firm large sums of money to perform consulting and personal tax services for him. This case illustrates the serious litigation risk that audit firms face when their clients are acting fraudulently and when the audit firm conducts the audits in a way that allows those relying on the financial statements to question audit quality.

"Moss Adams and the Meridian Mortgage Funds Fraud," for an example of a case in which the audit firm was sued for breach of contract.

The remedies for breach of contract include the following:

- Requiring specific performance of the contract agreement
- Granting an injunction to prohibit the auditor from doing certain acts, such as disclosing confidential information
- Providing for recovery of amounts lost as a result of the breach

When specific performance or an injunction is not appropriate, the client is entitled to recover compensatory damages. In determining the amounts of compensation, courts try to put the client in the position in which it would have been had the contract been performed as promised.

The auditor can use the following arguments as defenses against a breach of contract suit:

- The auditor exercised due professional care in accordance with the contract.
- The client was contributory negligent.
- The client's losses were not caused by the breach.

对第三方的普通法责任   Common-Law Liability to Third Parties

In most engagements, the auditor does not know specifically who will be using the financial statements but is aware that third parties will be using them. The courts generally have held auditors liable to injured third parties when the auditor has been found guilty of gross negligence or fraud. Courts differ, however, as to what third parties the auditor should be held liable to for ordinary negligence. Common law has developed through court decisions, custom, and usage without written legislation. To win a claim against the auditor, third parties suing under common law must generally prove that:

- They suffered a loss.
- The loss was due to reliance on misleading financial statements.

- The auditor knew, or should have known, that the financial statements were misleading.

Differing Requirements for Auditor Liability to Third Parties under Common Law

The auditor's liability depends on the jurisdiction of the case, along with whether the auditor could foresee that different types of users would be relying upon the audit report and audited financial statements.

Foreseeability and Negligence: Common Law The fundamental issue is whether the plaintiff has to prove negligence or gross negligence in order to obtain damages from an auditor. Courts in different jurisdictions have taken different approaches to determining a plaintiff's standing to bring a suit for negligence. The critical point in determining the type of claim to be made against the auditor is the likelihood that an auditor could reasonably foresee that a user might have relied upon the audited financial statements. Generally, less foreseeable plaintiffs need to establish a gross negligence claim, whereas foreseeable users, in some jurisdictions, have to establish only a negligence claim.

The Ultramares Case: The Third-Party Beneficiary Test The landmark case of *Ultramares Corporation v. Touche,* decided by the New York Court of Appeals in 1931, set the precedent for an auditor's liability to third parties. The court held that auditors are liable to third parties for fraud and gross negligence, but not for negligence. For liability to be established, a **third-party beneficiary** must be specifically identified in the engagement letter as a user for whom the audit is being conducted. If, for example, a bank requires an audit as part of a loan application and is named in the engagement letter, the auditor may be held liable to the bank for negligence. If the bank had not been named in the engagement letter, however, such liability would not exist. This precedent dominated judicial thinking for many years and is still followed in many jurisdictions.

Expansion of Ultramares: The Identified User Test In the 1985 case of *Credit Alliance Corp. v. Arthur Andersen & Co.,*[1] the New York Court of Appeals extended auditor liability for ordinary negligence to identified users. An **identified user** is a specific third party whom the auditor knows will use the audited financial statements for a particular purpose, even though the identified user is not named in the engagement letter.

Foreseen User Test The 1965 Restatement (Second) of Torts[2] expanded auditor liability for negligence to identified users and to any individually unknown third parties who are members of a known or intended class of third parties, called **foreseen users**. The client must have informed the auditor that a third party or class of third parties intends to use the financial statements for a particular transaction. The auditor does not have to know the identity of the third party. For example, the client tells the auditor that it plans to include the audited financial statements in an application to some financial institution for a loan. The auditor would be liable to the bank that ultimately makes the loan, even though its identity was not known at the time of the audit.

---

[1] *Credit Alliance Corp. v. Arthur Andersen & Co.,* 483 N.E. 2d 110 (N.Y. 1985).

[2] The *Restatement (Second) of Torts* is published by the American Law Institute. Courts may refer to this treatise when considering an issue of outdated precedent. It offers a unique perspective on the law because its purpose is to state the law as the majority of courts would decide it today. It does not necessarily reflect the rules of the common law as adopted by the courts. Rather, it represents principles of common law that the American Law Institute believes would be adopted if the courts reexamined their common-law rules.

EXHIBIT **4.2**	Foreseeability Concepts for Auditor's Common-Law Liability to Third Parties

FORSEEABLE USER

FORSEEN USER

IDENTIFIED USER

The auditor knows the user's identity and specific transaction involved.	The user is a member of a limited class of users for a specific transaction. Identity of the specific user may or may not be known to the auditor.	The user is a member of a group who could foreseeably use the financial statements.
Example: The auditor knows that the First National Bank wants audited financial statements as part of the client's application for a loan.	*Example:* The auditor knows that the client wants audited financial statements to obtain a loan from one of several possible banks.	*Example:* The auditor knows that current and prospective creditors and stockholders are likely to use the audited statements.

在"可预见的使用者"这一标准下，注册会计师需要对任何可以预见到的将依赖其审计报告的第三方所遭受的损失承担责任。

Foreseeable User Test Some courts have extended auditor liability to **foreseeable users** (as opposed to foreseen users) of audited financial statements. In *Citizens State Bank v. Timm, Schmidt & Co.*, the Wisconsin Supreme Court extended auditor liability to creditors who could foreseeably use the audited financial statements.[3] A similar position was taken in *Rosenblum, Inc. v. Adler*, where the New Jersey Supreme Court noted that the nature of the economy had changed since the *Ultramares* case and that auditors are indeed acting as if a number of potential users rely on their audit opinion. This court made it clear that for liability to be established, foreseeable users must have obtained the financial statements from the client for proper business purposes,[4] but this is not true in all jurisdictions.

Exhibit 4.2 provides a summary of foreseeability concepts under common law, along with practical examples. The current liability status depends on the state and court involved and on the precedent the court determines is appropriate.

成文法下的注册会计师责任

Auditor Liability under Statutory Law

For public companies, audited financial statements are required to be included in information provided to current and prospective investors. The Securities Act of 1933, the Securities Exchange Act of 1934, and the Sarbanes-Oxley Act of 2002 are the primary federal statutes affecting auditor liability for public clients. These laws were enacted to assure that investors in public companies have access to full and adequate disclosure of relevant information. Auditors found to be unqualified, unethical, or in willful violation of any provision of the federal securities laws can be disciplined by the Securities and Exchange Commission (SEC). Possible sanctions available to the SEC include:

- Temporarily or permanently revoking the firm's registration with the Public Company Accounting Oversight Board (PCAOB), meaning that the SEC will not accept its audit reports
- Imposing a civil penalty of up to $750,000 for each violation
- Requiring special continuing education of firm personnel

---

[3] *Citizens State Bank v. Timm, Schmidt & Co.*, 335 N.W. 2d 361 (Wis. Sup. Ct. 1983).
[4] *Rosenblum, Inc. v. Adler*, 461 A. 2d 138 (N.J. 1983).

Securities Act of 1933

The Securities Act of 1933 requires companies to file registration statements with the SEC before they may issue new securities to the public. A registration statement contains, among other things, information about the company itself, lists of its officers and major stockholders, and plans for using the proceeds from the new securities issue. Part of the registration statement, called the **prospectus**, includes audited financial statements. The most important liability section from the perspective of external auditors in the 1933 Act is Section 11 because it imposes penalties for misstatements contained in registration statements.

For purposes of Section 11, the accuracy of the registration statement is determined at its effective date, which is the date the company can begin to sell the new securities. Because the effective date may be several months after the end of the normal audit fieldwork, the auditors must perform certain audit procedures covering events between the end of the normal fieldwork and the effective date.

In understanding the liability provisions of the 1933 Act, it is important to know that the intent of the SEC is to assure full and fair disclosure of public financial information. Anyone receiving the prospectus may sue the auditor based on damages due to alleged misleading financial statements or inadequate audits. Under the 1933 Act, an auditor may be held liable to purchasers of securities for negligence, or even gross negligence and fraud. Purchasers need to prove only that they incurred a loss and that the financial statements were materially misleading or not fairly stated. They do not need to prove reliance on the financial statements, that such statements had been read or even seen, or that the auditors were negligent. In terms of defenses, the burden of proof shifts to the auditors, who must prove that (1) they used due professional care, (2) the statements were not materially misstated, or (3) the purchaser did not incur a loss caused by the misleading financial statements.

Securities Exchange Act of 1934

The 1934 Act regulates the trading of securities after their initial issuance. Regulated companies are required to file periodic reports with the SEC and stockholders. The following are the most common periodic reports:

- *Annual reports* to shareholders and *10-Ks*, which are annual reports filed with the SEC, both containing audited financial statements. 10-Ks must be filed within 60 to 90 days of the end of the fiscal year. Smaller companies have up to 90 days to file; larger companies must file within 60 days.
- *Quarterly financial reports* to shareholders and *10-Qs*, which are quarterly reports filed with the SEC. 10-Qs must be filed within 40 to 45 days of the end of each of the first three quarters and must be reviewed by the auditors. Smaller companies have up to 45 days to file; larger companies must file within 40 days.
- *8-Ks*, which are reports filed with the SEC describing the occurrence of important events, such as a change in auditors. Other important events required to be reported include changes in the company's business and operations, changes in financial status (such as an acquisition or disposal of assets), and major changes in corporate governance elements (such as the departure of a senior member of management), among others. These disclosures generally must occur within four business days of the event.

The most important liability section from the perspective of external auditors in the 1934 Act is Section 10, and specifically Rule 10b-5. This rule prohibits material misrepresentations or omissions and fraudulent conduct and provides a general antifraud remedy for purchasers and sellers of securities. Under the 1934 Act, an auditor may be held liable for fraud when a plaintiff alleges that in making decisions on purchasing or selling securities, it was misled by misstatements in financial statements. The Act explicitly makes it unlawful to make any untrue statement of a material fact or to omit to state a material fact that is necessary for understanding the financial statements. In order to bring a successful case for securities fraud, a private party must prove six basic elements: (1) a material misrepresentation or omission, (2) fraudulent conduct in connection with the purchase or sale of a security, (3) a wrongful state of mind, known as scienter, when making the misrepresentation or omission, (4) reliance upon the fraudulent conduct, (5) measurable monetary damages, and (6) a causal connection between the misrepresentation or omission and the economic loss. Each of these elements has been interpreted by the courts over the years; court decisions continue to shape how the elements are applied.

In *Herzfeld v. Lauenthol, Krekstein, Horwath & Horwath* (1974), the auditors were found liable under the 1934 Act for failure to fully disclose the facts and circumstances underlying their qualified opinion. The judge on the case stated that the auditor cannot be content merely to see that the financial statements meet minimum requirements of GAAP, but that the auditor has a duty to inform the public if adherence to GAAP does not fairly portray the economic results of the company being audited. More specifically, the trial court judge stated:

> The policy underlying the securities laws of providing investors with all the facts needed to make intelligent investment decisions can only be accomplished if financial statements fully and fairly portray the actual financial condition of the company. In those cases where application of generally accepted accounting principles fulfills the duty of full and fair disclosure, the accountant need go no further. But if application of accounting principles alone will not adequately inform investors, accountants, as well as insiders, the auditor must take pains to lay bare all the facts needed by investors to interpret the financial statements accurately.[5]

Federal courts have struggled with the negligence standard implied by the 1934 Act. The standard of holding auditors responsible for gross negligence had essentially eroded to a standard of negligence. In 1976, the U.S. Supreme Court provided greater guidance in its review of *Ernst & Ernst v. Hochfelder*. The Court held that under the 1934 Act, Congress had intended the plaintiff to prove that an auditor acted with scienter in order to hold the auditor liable. The Court reserved judgment as to whether reckless disregard for the truth (gross negligence) would be sufficient to impose liability.

In situations of alleged fraud, historically, investors have sued both the parties who carried out the fraud and those, such as auditors, who assisted, or aided and abetted, the fraud. It appears recent cases might be limiting civil liability related to Rule 10b-5 against auditors. For example, in June 2011, the Supreme Court ruled in *Janus Capital Group, Inc. v. First Derivative Traders* that an investment adviser could not be held liable for mere participation in the drafting and dissemination of false and misleading prospectuses issued by its client. Rather, the Court found that the client, not the adviser, made the fraudulent statement, and thus the adviser was not liable. It remains to be seen how various courts will implement this Supreme Court decision. It seems that parties, such as auditors, who merely assist in preparing a statement will not face liability as primary violators. Such parties, however, would continue to face exposure to enforcement actions brought by the SEC for violations of the federal securities laws.

Showing compliance with GAAP is an acceptable defense by the auditor. However, as shown in the *Herzfeld v. Lauenthol, Krekstein, Horwath & Horwath* case, the auditor must take care to make sure that GAAP are not being manipulated to achieve a specific financial presentation result that is not in accord with the substance of the transaction. Both the 1933 and 1934 Acts provide for criminal actions against auditors who willfully violate provisions of either Act and related rules or regulations or for those who know that financial

---

[5] *Herzfeld v. Laventhol, Krekstein, Horwath & Horwath* [1973–1974] Transfer Binder CCH FED. Sec. Law Reporter #94,574, at 95,999 (S.D.N.Y. May 29, 1974).

statements are false and misleading and who issue inappropriate opinions on such statements. In the PSLRA, Congress expressly authorized the SEC to pursue persons who knowingly provide substantial assistance to primary violators of the securities laws. In 2010, the Dodd-Frank Act amended the pleading standard in the 1934 Act from "knowingly" to "knowingly or recklessly." The lower pleading standard may enable the SEC to more easily bring cases for aiding and abetting securities fraud. The possible resolutions in these cases include, among other remedies, injunctions, disgorgement orders, civil penalties, and orders barring or suspending individuals from serving as officers or directors of securities issuers or participating in the securities industry.

Summary of Auditor Liability to Third Parties under Common and Statutory Law

普通法和成文法下注册会计师对第三方责任的小结

Auditors are clearly liable to injured third parties for fraud under both common law and statutory law. Because third parties are likely to sue under both common law and statutory law in a specific lawsuit, auditors are essentially liable for gross negligence as well. Auditors are liable for negligence under the Securities Act of 1933 and possibly under common law, depending on the precedent used by the court.

Third parties must prove the auditor's guilt under common law and the Securities Exchange Act of 1934. Under the Securities Act of 1933, however, auditors must prove their innocence. Auditor defenses include the following:

- Due diligence; that is, the auditor did what a prudent auditor would have done.
- The audit was not the cause of the plaintiff's loss.
- The financial statements were not materially misstated.

In order to make the first of these two defenses actually work in practice, auditors need to make fundamentally good professional and ethical decisions while conducting a quality audit. We next introduce frameworks designed to help you understand how to make quality professional and ethical decisions.

A Framework for Professional Decision Making

一个职业决策框架

Auditors add value to the financial markets by making quality decisions associated with their evaluation of client financial statements. Quality decisions are unbiased, meet the expectations of users, are in compliance with professional standards, and are based on sufficient factual information to justify the decision that is rendered. For example, auditors have to make decisions about the types of evidence to gather, how to evaluate that evidence, when to gather additional evidence, and what conclusions are appropriate given the evidence they have obtained. Ultimately, auditors have to decide whether the client's financial statements contain any material departures from generally accepted accounting principles that would affect the judgment of users of the financial statements.

LO 4 Articulate a general framework for making quality professional decisions and apply this framework in selected audit settings.

This type of decision making situation is common among professionals. For example, consider a doctor trying to diagnose the illness of a patient. The doctor must decide what tests to order, how to interpret the test results, and when to order additional tests (how many and what type), and must ultimately diagnose any potential illness in the patient. In order to make complex, difficult, and important decisions such as these, professionals can benefit from a structured approach to their decision making, as depicted in Exhibit 4.3.

In **Step 1,** the auditor structures the problem, which includes considering the relevant parties to involve in the decision process, identifying various feasible alternatives, considering how to evaluate the alternatives, and identifying uncertainties or risks. To illustrate these tasks, consider a common decision that auditors face—determining whether a client's inventory values are fairly stated in accordance with generally accepted accounting principles. In terms of identifying relevant parties, auditors work within an organizational hierarchy with clearly

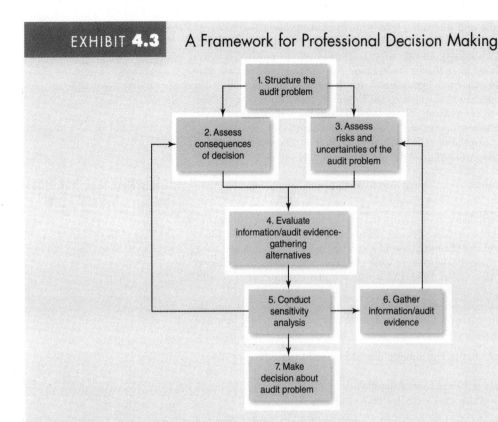

EXHIBIT **4.3**   A Framework for Professional Decision Making

Source: Adapted from "Judgment and Choice" by Robin Hogarth.

defined roles about appropriate types of auditors that should participate in inventory testing (for example, less experienced auditors may conduct inventory test counts, but industry experts may consider the valuation of complex inventory items). In addition, auditors consider which individuals at the client are most qualified to assess inventory values. Auditors also identify feasible alternatives about the inventory balance. For example, is it fairly stated, overstated, understated? Consideration will also be given to the evidence necessary to determine accurate inventory valuation (such as observing the inventory, consulting outside prices of the inventory, and evaluating potential obsolescence). Auditors also have to evaluate the risk that the evidence they collect may not necessarily be diagnostic of the true, underlying value of the inventory. In other words, there is a risk that despite the work that they perform, their conclusions may be incorrect.

In **Step 2,** the auditor assesses the consequences of the potential alternatives. Considerations at this stage include determining the dimensions on which to evaluate the alternatives and how to weight those dimensions. Continuing the preceding example, the auditor will have to consider the consequences of various inventory valuation alternatives and whether a particular valuation alternative is more or less appropriate than the other available alternatives. If the auditor decides that the inventory is properly valued, and that is in fact the case, then there are no negative consequences to the decision. However, if the auditor reaches an incorrect conclusion, then stakeholders may be misled, exposing auditors to litigation and reputation damage.

In **Step 3,** the auditor assesses the risks and uncertainties in the situation. Those risks and uncertainties are related to (a) the risks the audit client faces, (b) the quality of evidence the auditor gathers, and (c) the sufficiency of audit evidence gathered. In other words, there are risks related to a particular client, and there are risks in gathering sufficient audit evidence. All of these risks need to be assessed in determining the appropriate audit evidence to gather.

In **Step 4**, the auditor evaluates the various information/audit evidence gathering alternatives against an appropriate decision rule. For auditors, decision rules are often articulated in terms of generally accepted accounting principles or generally accepted auditing standards. In our example, inventory valuation rules under generally accepted accounting principles may provide necessary guidance to assist in the decision–making process. Further, generally accepted auditing standards articulate rules regarding appropriate evidence gathering strategies that must be followed when auditing inventory values.

In **Step 5**, the auditor considers the sensitivity of the conclusions reached in Steps 2, 3, and 4 to incorrect assumptions. It may be, given the results of the earlier steps, the auditor can determine enough evidence has been gathered to support (or not support), at a convincing level of certainty, and that the audit problem being evaluated can be answered appropriately. Continuing the preceding example, it may be that the auditor's initial evidence gathering and risk analysis enable a definitive conclusion. In that case, the auditor can move on to Step 7. However, there may still be significant uncertainties to resolve. For example, in the case of inventory, there may be variation in available market values used to value the client's inventory. As such, the true inventory value may fall within a range, so the client and auditor will have to use their **professional judgment** to determine a value that is most reflective of economic reality. In such a situation, the auditor will move to Step 6 of the process. The *Auditing in Practice* feature "What is Professional Judgment?" provides additional insights on the importance of professional judgment.

审计中的职业判断是指注册会计师在审计准则的框架下，运用专业知识和经验在备选方案中做出决策。由于被审计单位的情况千差万别，在审计准则中不可能针对所有可能遇到的情况规定对应的审计程序。因此，在审计职业过程中合理运用职业判断至关重要。

In **Step 6**, the auditor gathers information and audit evidence in an iterative process that affects considerations about the consequences of potential alternatives and the uncertainties associated with those judgments. Importantly, the auditor considers the costs and benefits of information acquisition, knowing that gathering additional evidence requires time, effort, and money. Given that an audit is a for-profit enterprise, cost-benefit considerations in evidence gathering are particularly important. A good auditor knows "when to say when"—to stop collecting evidence at the right time. In contrast, some auditors stop evidence collection too soon, thereby yielding inadequate evidence on which to make a decision. Still others continue evidence collection even though the current evidence is adequate, thereby contributing to inefficiency and reduced profitability in the audit.

What is Professional Judgment?

AUDITING IN PRACTICE

Professional judgment involves applying relevant professional knowledge and experience to unique and potentially uncertain facts and circumstances in order to reach a conclusion or make a decision. Thus, a first part of professional judgment is determining when the auditor has sufficient, appropriate evidence to make a decision. Then, when an auditor makes quality professional judgments, he or she competently applies auditing and/or accounting principles and makes decisions that are appropriate given the evidence that should be known to the auditor at the time of the judgment. Importantly, professional judgment cannot be used to justify conclusions or decisions that would otherwise not be supported by the existing evidence. Documenting a professional judgment is critical. Professional standards in the United States and internationally require that documentation is sufficient to enable an experienced auditor, having no previous connection with the audit, to understand the significant judgments made in reaching conclusions on significant matters arising during the audit. Professional judgment is the key to conducting a quality audit.

The auditor iterates through Steps 1 through 6 repeatedly until satisfied that a decision can prudently be made.

Finally, in **Step 7** of the professional decision making framework, the auditor needs to make the difficult determination of whether the problem has been sufficiently analyzed and whether the risk of making an incorrect decision has been minimized to an acceptable level by collecting adequate, convincing evidence. Ultimately, the auditor must make and document the decision reached. Throughout the text and chapter problems, we will illustrate other applications of this professional decision making framework.

在做职业判断时职业怀疑
的重要性

Importance of Professional Skepticism in Making Professional Judgments

When completing the steps in Exhibit 4.3, it is imperative that the auditor exercise professional skepticism. Recall from Chapter 2 that professional skepticism is an attitude that includes a questioning mind and a critical assessment of audit evidence. Professional skepticism is important because without it auditors are susceptible to accepting weak or inaccurate audit evidence. By exercising adequate professional skepticism, auditors are less likely to overlook unusual circumstances, to over-generalize from limited audit evidence, or to use inappropriate assumptions in determining the nature, timing, and extent of audit procedures. An auditor who is professionally skeptical will:

- Critically question contradictory audit evidence
- Carefully evaluate the reliability of audit evidence, especially in situations in which fraud risk is high and/or only a single piece of evidence exists to support a material financial accounting transaction or amount
- Reasonably question the authenticity of documentation, while accepting that documents are to be considered genuine unless there is reason to believe the contrary
- Reasonably question the honesty and integrity of management, individuals charged with governance, and third party providers of audit evidence

Given that auditors operate in an environment of significant litigation risk and one in which there is ample evidence of past frauds involving deception against auditors, it may seem that auditors will intuitively act with professional skepticism. However, the difficulty that auditors face is one inherent in the human condition—we are taught to trust others and to accept information and assertions as the truth. Further, if an auditor did not trust management, for example, that auditor would presumably cease to perform audit services for the client. These difficulties sometimes cause auditors to be less professionally skeptical than is optimal. The PCAOB's Report on its 2004–2007 inspections of domestic annually inspected audit firms reveals that the Board finds a lack of professional skepticism to be an important weakness in the current practice of auditing. For example, the Report notes "certain of the deficiencies also raised concerns about the sufficiency of firms' application of professional skepticism.... In some instances, firms did not sufficiently test or challenge management's forecasts, views, or representations that constituted critical support for the amounts recorded in the financial statements. In many of these instances, they limited their audit procedures to obtaining management's oral representations."

This view regarding professional skepticism is not limited to U.S. regulators. In a July 2010 periodical release, the United Kingdom Financial Services Authority (the chief regulator in the UK) stated, "In some cases that the FSA has seen, the auditor's approach seems to focus too much on gathering and accepting evidence to support management's assertions" *(Accountancy Age,* June 29, 2010). This is a human bias: if we think someone has integrity, then there is a tendency to overweight information that favors that person's view and underweight other evidence. Therefore, developing a "balanced" approach to gathering and evaluating evidence regarding management assertions is the fundamental value associated with an audit.

So how can audit firms and individual auditors be sure that they maintain and exercise professional skepticism? At the audit firm level, leaders must ensure that auditors receive training on how to be skeptical, and they must create firm policies and procedures to encourage skepticism. At the individual auditor level, the following tips can encourage a skeptical mindset:

- Be sure to collect sufficient evidence so that judgments are not made in haste or without adequate support.
- When evidence is contradictory, be particularly diligent in evaluating the reliability of the individuals or processes that provided that evidence.
- Generate independent ideas about reasons for unexpected trends or financial ratios rather than simply relying on management's explanations.

What Was He Thinking? An Example of Poor Professional Judgment and Low Audit Quality

AUDITING IN PRACTICE

On June 15, 2009, the PCAOB issued disciplinary proceedings against Lawrence Scharfman, CPA. Scharfman, a 76 year old auditor licensed in the State of New York, issued audit opinions for three companies: Prospero Minerals, Cal-Bay International, and LitFunding Corporation. Each of these companies was traded on the OTC Bulletin Board and the Pink Sheets. The PCAOB questioned Scharfman's professional judgments in the conduct of the audits of each of these three companies. These low quality decisions are summarized below:

The Prospero Minerals Audit

- Scharfman accepted the audit engagement on August 14, 2006 and issued an unqualified audit opinion on August 16, 2006.
- Scharfman provided no documentation that he planned the audit or that he performed any audit procedures on significant balance sheet items.
- Scharfman provided no documentation that he addressed disclosure issues, valuation issues, or material related-party transactions.
- While conducting the audit, Scharfman committed to acquire 200,000 shares of Prospero stock in exchange for services that he agreed to perform for the shareholder and the Company.

The Cal-Bay Audit

- Scharfman accepted the audit engagement on March 29, 2006 and issued an unqualified opinion on April 12, 2006.
- Scharfman provided no documentation that he performed adequate audit procedures to test a material real estate purchase transaction.
- Scharfman provided no documentation that he gathered audit evidence necessary to value a material acquired asset.
- Scharfman failed to alert the SEC or the PCAOB that he had requested Cal-Bay to subsequently restate its financial statements and that Cal-Bay had refused.

- Scharfman failed to alert the SEC or the PCAOB that he had become aware of an illegal act at Cal-Bay.

The LitFunding Audit

- Scharfman accepted the audit engagement on April 28, 2006 and issued an unqualified opinion on May 3, 2006.
- Scharfman provided no documentation that he gathered audit evidence regarding a reserve for legal costs and a review of a significant accounting estimate.
- Much of the documentation that Scharfman provided to the PCAOB was added to the engagement file after completion of the audit, and it was unclear who prepared the documents. The inference is that Scharfman added the documents to the file upon learning that he was being reviewed by PCAOB inspectors.

After conducting its review of Scharfman's work on these audits, the PCAOB revoked his CPA firm's registration and barred him from performing audits for public entities permanently. What was Scharfman thinking? It appears that he was simply doing "sham" audits for cash payments. These small companies required unqualified audit opinions, and Scharfman was willing to accept the engagements, do little or no audit work, and issue an opinion within just a few days. He clearly did not exhibit professional skepticism. His actions are an extreme example of low quality auditing and poor professional decision making. Auditors often face pressure over budgets and schedules, and all people are subject to the tendency to rationalize away unpleasant or unwanted issues. Scharfman's actions, however, seem to go beyond normal rationalizations and reflect the worst possible intentions associated with such forces.

For further details on this case, see PCAOB Release No. 105-2009-005.

- Question trends or outcomes that appear "too good to be true."
- Wait to make professional judgments until all the relevant facts are known.
- Have confidence in your own knowledge or in your own ability to understand complex situations; do not assume that the client's explanation for unexpected trends or financial ratios simply reflects your lack of understanding.

We encourage you to keep these ideas in mind as you proceed throughout this textbook. Because of the importance of professional skepticism to making quality auditing judgments, we will return to this concept throughout the textbook, including examples and problems to help you learn about and apply this concept. The *Auditing in Practice* feature, "What Was He Thinking? An Example of Poor Professional Judgment and Low Audit Quality," provides an extreme example of low (likely nonexistent) professional skepticism and its implications.

一个道德决策框架

L0 5 Articulate a framework for making quality ethical decisions and apply this framework in selected settings.

A Framework for Ethical Decision Making

The auditing profession has worked hard to gain the public trust, and it benefits monetarily from that trust as the sole legally acceptable provider of audit services for companies and other organizations. For that trust and economic advantage to be maintained, it is essential that professional integrity be based on personal moral standards and reinforced by codes of conduct. Whenever a scandal surfaces, the profession is diminished and auditors' reputations may be tarnished beyond repair. It is not difficult to find oneself in ethically compromising situations without realizing it. During the course of an audit, for example, an auditor may become aware of a client's plans that will likely double the market value of its stock. Suppose the auditor has a roommate from college who would like to know about the investment opportunity. The roommate does not have a large investment portfolio, so sharing this knowledge would not affect the market. Should the auditor share the information with the roommate? Consider Susan Birkert in the Auditing *in Practice* feature, "A Young Auditor Makes an Ethical Mistake in Professional Judgment." Imagine that you were Birkert's friend and colleague—would you have made the difficult ethical decision to alert KPMG personnel to her deception?

解决道德两难问题

Resolving Ethical Dilemmas

Auditors working through professional decisions using the framework in Exhibit 4.3 will at times encounter decisions that have ethical implications. For example, consider a situation in which your senior on the engagement is already worried about the time that it has taken you to complete your work. Would you take the time needed to diligently follow up on evidence suggesting that something might be wrong with the financial statements? Would you consider

A Young Auditor Makes an Ethical Mistake in Professional Judgment

AUDITING IN PRACTICE

We introduced the following case to you in Chapter 1, and we return to it now from a professional and ethical judgment perspective. Recall that Susan Birkert was a lead senior on the KPMG audits of Comtech during fiscal years 2004–2006. During this time, an acquaintance of Birkert agreed to purchase $5,000 of Comtech stock for her, in violation of professional rules regarding auditor independence. In May 2006, Birkert falsely asserted to KPMG that she was in compliance with audit firm and professional rules regarding

independence. Following an anonymous tip and an ensuing KPMG internal investigation, Birkert admitted to the deception, and KPMG fired her. The anonymous tipster in that case was rumored to be a friend and fellow auditor on the Comtech engagement. Subsequently, the PCAOB barred her from serving before it for a period of at least one year.

For further details on this case, see the facts disclosed in PCAOB Release No. 105–2007–003, November 14, 2007.

concluding that a client's decision to extend the life of its assets is appropriate, even if you have serious reservations about this decision? Auditing professionals are often faced with these types of difficult ethical decisions. In such situations, a defined methodology is helpful in resolving the situation in a thoughtful, quality manner. An **ethical dilemma** occurs when there are conflicting moral duties or an individual is ethically required to take an action that may conflict with his or her immediate self-interest. Complex ethical dilemmas do not lend themselves to simple "right" or "wrong" decisions. Ethical theories are helpful in assisting individuals in dealing with both ethical dilemmas. Two such theories—the utilitarian theory and the rights theory—have help developed codes of conduct that can be used by professionals in dealing with ethically challenging situations.

Utilitarian Theory

Utilitarian theory holds that what is ethical is the action that achieves the greatest good for the greatest number of people. Actions that result in outcomes that fall short of the greatest good for the greatest number and those that represent inefficient means to accomplish such ends are less desirable. Utilitarianism requires the following:

- An identification of the potential problem and possible courses of action
- An identification of the potential direct or indirect impact of actions on each affected party (often referred to as **stakeholders**) who may have a vested interest in the outcome of actions taken
- An assessment of the desirability (goodness) of each action
- An overall assessment of the greatest good for the greatest number

Utilitarianism requires that individuals not advocate or choose alternatives that favor narrow interests or that serve the greatest good in an inefficient manner. There can be honest disagreements about the likely impact of actions or the relative efficiency of different actions in attaining desired ends. There are also potential problems in measuring what constitutes "the greatest good" in a particular circumstance. One problem with the utilitarian theory is the implicit assumption that the "ends achieved" justify the means to attain those ends. Unfortunately, such an approach can lead to disastrous courses of actions when those making the decisions fail to adequately measure or assess the potential costs and benefits. Thus, ethicists generally argue that utilitarian arguments should be mitigated by some "value–based" approach. The rights theory approach presents such a framework.

Rights Theory

Rights theory focuses on evaluating actions based on the fundamental rights of the parties involved. However, not all rights are equal. In the hierarchy of rights, higher order rights take precedence over lower order rights. The highest order rights include the right to life, to autonomy, and to human dignity. Second-order rights include rights granted by the government, such as civil rights, legal rights, rights to own property, and license privileges. Third-order rights are social rights, such as the right to higher education, to good health care, and to earning a living. The fourth-order rights are related to one's nonessential interests or one's personal tastes.

Rights theory requires that the "rights" of affected parties should be examined as a constraint on ethical decision making. The rights approach is most effective in identifying outcomes that ought to be automatically eliminated, such as the "Robin Hood approach" of robbing from the rich to give to the poor; in these situations, the utilitarian answer is at odds with most societal values.

Applying the Ethical Decision Making Framework

应用道德决策框架

Exhibit 4.4 contains a framework derived from the utilitarianism and rights theories that can help individuals resolve ethical dilemmas in a quality manner.

The following case, based on an actual situation, is presented as an application of this framework to auditing situations.

EXHIBIT **4.4**	A Framework for Ethical Decision Making

Step 1

Identify the ethical issue(s).

Step 2

Determine the affected parties and identify their rights.

Step 3

Determine the most important rights.

Step 4

Develop alternative courses of action.

Step 5

Determine the likely consequences of each proposed course of action.

Step 6

Assess the possible consequences, including an estimation of the greatest good for the greatest number. Determine whether the rights framework would cause any course of action to be eliminated.

Step 7

Decide on the appropriate course of action.

Step 1. Identify the ethical issue(s). The external auditor for Payroll Processors, Inc., believes that the company might go bankrupt. Several clients of the audit firm use the payroll processing services of Payroll Processors. Should the other clients be provided with this **confidential information** prior to the information being publicly available through the audit report—which might be delayed as auditors further assess the potential for bankruptcy?

Step 2. Determine the affected parties and identify their rights. The relevant parties to the issue include the following:

- Payroll Processors and its management
- Payroll Processors' current and prospective customers, creditors, and investors
- The audit firm and its other clients
- The external auditing profession

Listing those potentially affected by the decision is easier than identifying their rights. The following, however, are some of the rights involved:

- Company management has the right to assume that confidential information obtained by its auditors will remain confidential unless disclosure is permitted by the company or is required by accounting, auditing, or legal standards.
- Payroll Processors' current and prospective customers, creditors, and investors have a right to receive reliable information and not be denied important information that could adversely affect their operations.
- The audit firm has the right to expect its employees to follow the professional standards. However, some may argue that the firms' existing clients have a right to information that might protect them from financial crises.
- The external auditing profession has the right to expect all its members to uphold the Code of Professional Conduct (described in the following section of the chapter) and to take actions that enhance the general reputation and perception of the integrity of the profession.

Step 3. Determine the most important rights. Many auditors would assess that the rights listed in order of importance are (1) the client to not have confidential information improperly disclosed, (2) other affected parties to receive important information that will affect their operations, (3) the profession to retain its reputation for conducting quality audits.

Step 4. Develop alternative courses of action. The possible courses of action are (1) share the confidential information with the other clients of the audit firm prior to issuing an audit opinion on the client's financial statements, or (2) do not share that information prior to issuing an audit opinion on the client's financial statements. The audit firm was performing audit work, and the professional standards require that the reservations about Payroll Processors remaining a going concern in their audit report, not in private information given to selected entities.

Step 5. Determine the likely consequences of each proposed course of action. These could include:

1. *Prior to Issuing the Audit Opinion.* Sharing this information with the other clients prior to issuing an audit report with a going concern reservation may cause these other clients to take their business away from Payroll Processors, thus increasing the likelihood of bankruptcy for Payroll Processors. It might also increase the possibility of the audit firm being found in violation of the rules of conduct and being sued by Payroll Processors or others for inappropriately providing confidential information to selected parties outside of the public role that external auditors fulfill. The auditor may also have his or her license suspended or revoked. Other Payroll Processors' clients who do not receive the information because they are not the audit firm's clients will be put at a competitive disadvantage, and they may sue the auditor because of discriminatory disclosure.
2. *Do Not Share the Information Until the Audit Report Has Been Issued.* If the information is not shared with the other clients, those clients might take their audit business elsewhere if they find out the auditors knew of this problem and did not share it with them. Other clients of Payroll Processors may suffer losses because of the financial problems of Payroll Processors.

Step 6. Assess the possible consequences, including an estimation of the greatest good for the greatest number. Determine whether the rights framework would cause any course of action to be eliminated. Sharing the information may help other clients move their payroll processing business to other service providers in a more orderly manner and more quickly than would happen if they had to wait until the audit opinion was issued. However, other Payroll Processors' customers may be placed at a disadvantage if Payroll Processors does go bankrupt and their payroll processing is disrupted. Payroll Processors' employees will lose their jobs more quickly, and its investors are likely to lose more money more quickly. Its right to have confidential information remain confidential will be violated. There may be less confidence in the profession because of discriminatory or unauthorized disclosure of information. Management of other companies may be reluctant to share other nonfinancial information with audit firms. After assessing the relative benefits of disclosing versus not disclosing the information prior to issuing the audit opinion, it appears that the greatest good is served by not sharing the information selectively with current audit clients, but to complete the audit and issue the audit opinion in a timely manner.

Step 7. Decide on the appropriate course of action. The auditor should not share the information prior to issuing the audit opinion. The auditor may encourage Payroll Processors to share its state of affairs with its clients but cannot dictate that it do so. The need for equity and confidentiality of information dictates that the auditor's primary form of communication is through formal audit reports associated with the financial statements.

Consolidata Services v. Alexander Grant

The actual court case used to develop the example above was *Consolidata Services v. Alexander Grant.* In that case, the court found the audit firm guilty of providing confidential information to its other clients. Alexander

Grant (now Grant Thornton) did tax work for Consolidata Services, a company that provided computerized payroll services to other companies. On learning that Consolidata was in financial trouble, Grant warned some of its other clients, who were also Consolidata customers. Consolidata sued Grant, charging that the audit firm's disclosures effectively put it out of business. The jury ruled in favor of Consolidata. Grant was also found guilty of providing the information only to selected parties; that is, it provided the information only to its clients—not all customers of Consolidata.

决策的职业指导
国际会计师职业道德准则理事会的职业道德规范

LO 6 Describe and apply the IESBA's Code of Ethics and the AICPA's Code of Professional Conduct.

Professional Guidance on Decision Making
IESBA's Code of Ethics

The International Ethics Standards Board for Accountants (IESBA) outlines fundamental principles that should guide auditor decision making in every situation. The Code of Ethics requires auditors to adhere to five fundamental principles:[6]

- *Integrity*—A professional accountant should be straightforward and honest in performing professional services.
- *Objectivity*—A professional accountant should not allow bias, conflict of interest, or undue influence of others to override professional or business judgments.
- *Professional Competence and Due Care*—A professional accountant has a continuing duty to maintain professional knowledge and skill at the level required to assure that a client or employer receives competent professional service based on current developments. A professional accountant should act diligently and in accordance with applicable technical and professional standards when providing professional services.
- *Confidentiality*—A professional accountant should respect the confidentiality of information acquired as a result of professional and business relationships and should not disclose any such information to third parties without proper and specific authority unless there is a legal or professional right or duty to disclose. Confidential information acquired as a result of professional and business relationships should not be used for the personal advantage of the professional accountant or of third parties.
- *Professional Behavior*—A professional accountant should comply with relevant laws and regulations and should avoid any action that discredits the profession.

美国注册会计师协会的职业行为规范

美国注册会计师协会的职业行为规范包含六个职业行为原则，分别是责任、公众利益、正直、客观和独立、应有的谨慎和服务的范围和性质。这些行为原则为具体的职业行为守则提供了基础。

AICPA Code of Professional Conduct

Although the frameworks for professional and ethical decision making clearly help the auditor in resolving difficult professional situations, the auditing profession via the AICPA has developed a code of professional conduct to aid in making these judgments. The AICPA's Code of Professional Conduct is made up of a set of **principles of professional conduct** that provide the basis for the specific **rules of conduct**. The principles of professional conduct express the auditing profession's recognition of its responsibilities to the users of the financial statements. The principles provide high-level guidance to auditors about their professional and ethical responsibilities.

---

[6] **Source:** © 2008 by The International Federation of Accountants (IFAC). All rights reserved. Used with permission of IFAC. This text is an extract from the Handbook of International Standards on Auditing, Assurance, and Ethics Pronouncements of the International Auditing and Assurance Standards Board (IAASB), published by the International Federation of Accountants (IFAC) in April 2009 and is used with permission of IFAC.

We expand on some of these rules in the discussion below.

Independence—Rule 101

The external auditor is required to be independent when providing services to either public or private entities. Independence is considered the cornerstone of the auditing profession. There are several interpretations of Rule 101; many specific rulings provide detailed guidance on such matters as financial interests in the client, family relationships, loans with a client, and performance of nonaudit services.

Financial Interests An important point concerning Rule 101 is that it applies only to a **covered member**. A covered member is, among other things, defined as:

- An individual on the audit engagement team
- An individual in a position to influence the audit engagement
- A partner in the office in which the lead attest audit partner primarily practices in connection with the auditor engagement

A covered member's immediate family is also subject to Rule 101. If you are a new staff person, manager, or partner working on an audit, you and your immediate family should not have any direct or material indirect financial interest in that client. A **direct financial interest** is a financial interest owned directly by, or under the control of, an individual or entity or beneficially owned through an investment vehicle, estate, or trust when the beneficiary controls the intermediary or has the authority to supervise or participate in the intermediary's investment decisions. An **indirect financial interest** occurs when the beneficiary neither controls the intermediary nor has the authority to supervise or participate in the intermediary's investment decisions.

确定经济利益是直接的还是间接的，取决于受益人能否控制投资工具或具有影响投资决策的能力。如果受益人能够控制投资工具或具有影响投资决策的能力，则这种经济利益被界定为直接经济利益；反之，则为间接经济利益。

For example, suppose an auditor has an investment in a mutual fund that has an investment in an audit client. The auditor does not make the decisions to buy or sell the security held by the mutual fund. The ownership of mutual fund shares is a direct financial interest. The underlying investments of a mutual fund are considered to be indirect financial interests. If the mutual fund is diversified, a covered member's ownership of 5% or less of the outstanding shares of the mutual fund would not be considered to constitute a material indirect financial interest in the underlying investments. For purposes of determining materiality, the financial interests of the covered member and immediate family should be aggregated. No partner or professional employee of the audit firm, whether a covered member or not, may be employed by an attest client or own more than 5% of an attest client's outstanding equity securities or other ownership interests.

Family Relationships A covered member's independence would be considered impaired if an immediate family member was employed by an audit client in a key position in which he or she can exercise influence over the contents of the financial statements, such as the CEO, CFO, chief accountant, member of the board of directors, chief internal audit executive, or treasurer. Independence is impaired if a covered member has a close relative who has a key position with the client or has a material financial interest in the client of which the CPA has knowledge.

Loans There are limits on the types and amounts of loans covered members may obtain from a financial institution that is also an audit client. Essentially, auditors cannot obtain large loans, or loans for investment purposes, from a client. However, auditors are permitted to obtain normal loans if they are at standard terms, such as automobile loans or leases.

Performing Nonaudit Services The AICPA's code does not prohibit auditors from performing other services such as bookkeeping for their private clients, but auditors must take care to assure that working too closely with the client does not compromise the appearance of independence. If, for example, the auditor does bookkeeping, prepares tax returns, and performs management consulting services, the appearance of independence has disappeared, even if independence in fact remains. A fundamental premise in these standards is that management must not concede decision making authority to the accountant or auditor. For example, it is acceptable for the auditor of a nonpublic company to design, install, or integrate a client's information system, provided the client makes all management decisions. It is not acceptable to supervise client personnel in the daily operation of a client's information system.

Importantly, recall that Sarbanes-Oxley Act requires that external auditors may not provide the following nonaudit services to their publicly traded clients because of concerns that doing so would impair independence in fact or in appearance:

- Bookkeeping services
- Financial information systems design and implementation
- Appraisal or valuation services
- Actuarial services
- Internal audit outsourcing services
- Management functions or human resources
- Broker or dealer, investment adviser, or investment banking services
- Legal services and expert services unrelated to the audit

Integrity and Objectivity—Rule 102

Rule 102 requires the AICPA member to act with integrity and objectivity in all services that may be provided to a client. Note that this applies also to CPAs who are not in public practice. For example, if the CFO of a company knowingly makes or permits others to make materially false and misleading entries in the financial statements or records, fails to correct an entity's financial statements or records, or signs—or directs another to sign—a document containing materially false and misleading information, that person has violated the AICPA Code of Ethics. A CPA is a special certificate that holds its owner to a high standard of ethical conduct, no matter where the individual is in his or her career.

Confidentiality—Rule 301

During the course of an audit, the auditor develops a complete understanding of the client and obtains confidential information, such as its operating strengths, weaknesses, and plans for financing or expanding into new markets. To assure a free flow and sharing of information between the client and the auditor, the client must be assured that the auditor will not communicate confidential information to outside parties. **Privileged communication** means that confidential information obtained about a client cannot be subpoenaed by a court of law to be used against that client. Most states allow privileged communication for lawyers, but not for auditors.

The only exceptions to this general rule are that auditors are not precluded from communicating information for any of the following purposes:

- To assure the adequacy of accounting disclosures required by GAAP
- To comply with a validly issued and enforceable subpoena or summons or to comply with applicable laws and government regulations
- To provide relevant information for an outside quality review of the firm's practice under PCAOB, AICPA, or state board of accountancy authorization
- To initiate a complaint with, or respond to an inquiry made by, the AICPA's professional ethics division or by the trial board or investigative or disciplinary body of a state CPA society or board of accountancy

Contingent Fees—Rule 302

A **contingent fee** is defined as a fee established for the performance of any service in which a fee will not be collected unless a specified finding or result is attained, or in which the amount of the fee depends on the finding or results of such services. An example of a contingent fee is a consulting firm agreeing to perform an information systems project for a fee of 50% of the defined cost savings attributable to the system for a period of three years. Contingent fees are attractive to clients because they do not pay unless the consultant delivers real value. Consulting firms often use contingent fees to compete with each other.

Contingent fees are prohibited from any client for whom the auditor performs audit services. However, an auditor's fees may vary, depending on the complexity of services rendered or the time taken to perform the services. Contingent fees have not been prohibited for services provided to non-audit clients. However, the auditor must still assure that the use of such fees does not impair the auditor's objectivity or need to uphold the public trust.

或有收费是指收费与否或收费多少取决于交易的结果或所执行工作的结果。会计师事务所在提供审计服务时，以直接或间接形式取得或有收费，将因自身利益产生非常严重的不利影响，导致没有防范措施能够将其降低至可接受的水平。会计师事务所不得采用这种收费安排。

Enforcement of the Code of Professional Conduct

Compliance with the Code depends primarily on the voluntary cooperation of AICPA members and secondarily on public opinion, reinforcement by peers, and ultimately, on disciplinary proceedings by the Joint Ethics Enforcement Program, sponsored by the AICPA and state CPA societies. Disciplinary proceedings are initiated by complaints received by the AICPA's Professional Ethics Division.

Audit and other attestation reports on financial statements can be signed only by those who are licensed as CPAs by their state board of accountancy. Anyone can provide consulting, bookkeeping, and tax services. To become a licensed CPA, a person must pass the CPA exam, meet specific education and experience requirements, and agree to uphold the profession and its code of professional conduct. The member's CPA certificate may be suspended or revoked by the state board of accountancy. Without that certificate or license, a person is legally prohibited from issuing an audit opinion or a review report on financial statements. The state board may also require additional continuing education to retain or reinstate the CPA certificate.

SUMMARY AND NEXT STEPS

The liability environment has significant implications for auditors and it is important for you to understand the environment and its implications. You should now understand the auditors' legal environment and specific laws from which auditor liability is derived, along with possible causes of action against auditors and auditor legal defenses. The frameworks for both general professional decision making and ethical decision making should assist auditors in behaving in ways that minimize litigation exposure. Finally, by following the IESBA's Code of Ethics and the AICPA's Code of Professional Conduct, auditors can minimize their litigation exposure. In the next chapter we turn to a discussion of the specific steps in the audit opinion formulation process and the professional auditing standards that guide that process.

SIGNIFICANT TERMS

Breach of contract Failure to perform a contractual duty that has not been excused; for audit firms, the parties to a contract normally include clients and designated third-party beneficiaries.

Class action lawsuits   Lawsuits that are brought on behalf of a large group of plaintiffs to consolidate suits and to encourage consistent judgments and minimize litigation costs; plaintiff shareholders may bring suit for themselves and all others in a similar situation, that is, all other shareholders of record at a specific date.

Common law   Liability concepts are developed through court decisions based on negligence, gross negligence, or fraud.

Confidential information   Information obtained during the conduct of an audit related to the client's business or business plans; the auditor is prohibited from communicating confidential information except in very specific instances defined by the Code or with the client's specific authorization.

Contingent fee   A fee established for the performance of any service in which a fee will not be collected unless a specified finding or result is attained, or in which the amount of the fee depends on the finding or results of such services.

Contingent-fee cases   Lawsuits brought by plaintiffs with compensation for their attorneys being contingent on the outcome of the litigation.

Contract law   Liability occurs where there is a breach of contract. The contract is usually between the external auditor and the client for the performance of the financial statement audit.

Covered member   An individual on the audit engagement team, an individual in a position to influence the audit engagement, or a partner in the office in which the lead audit engagement partner primarily practices in connection with the audit engagement.

Deep-pocket theory   The practice of suing another party not based on the level of their true fault in a legal action, but based instead on the perceived ability of that party to pay damages.

Direct financial interest   A financial interest owned directly by, or under the control of, an individual or entity or beneficially owned through an investment vehicle, estate, or trust when the beneficiary controls the intermediary or has the authority to supervise or participate in the intermediary's investment decisions.

Ethical dilemma   A situation in which moral duties or obligations conflict; an ethically correct action may conflict with an individual's immediate self-interest.

Expectations gap   A misunderstanding whereby shareholders mistakenly believe that they are entitled to recover losses on investments for which the auditor provided an unqualified opinion on the financial statements.

Foreseeable user   Those not known specifically by the auditor to be using the financial statements, but recognized by general knowledge as current and potential creditors and investors who will use them.

Foreseen user   Individually unknown third parties who are members of a known or intended class of third-party users who the auditor, through knowledge gained from interactions with the client, can foresee will use the statements.

Fraud   Intentional concealment or misrepresentation of a material fact with the intent to deceive another person, causing damage to the deceived person.

Gross negligence Failure to use even minimal care or evidence of activities that show a recklessness or careless disregard for the truth; evidence may not be present, but may be inferred by a judge or jury because of the carelessness of the defendant's conduct.

Identified user Third-party beneficiaries and other users when the auditor has specific knowledge that known users will be utilizing the financial statements in making specific economic decisions.

Indirect financial interest A financial interest in which the beneficiary neither controls the intermediary nor has the authority to supervise or participate in the intermediary's investment decisions.

Joint and several liability A type of liability that apportions losses among all defendants who have an ability to pay for the damages, regardless of the level of fault.

Negligence Failure to exercise reasonable care, thereby causing harm to another or to property.

Objectivity An impartial, unbiased mental attitude that auditors should maintain.

Privileged communication Information about a client that cannot be subpoenaed by a court of law to be used against a client; it allows no exceptions to confidentiality.

Principles of professional conduct Broad principles that articulate auditors' responsibilities and their requirements to act in the public interest, to act with integrity and objectivity, to be independent, to exercise due care, and to perform an appropriate scope of services.

Professional judgment The application of relevant professional knowledge and experience to the facts and circumstances in order to reach a conclusion or make a decision.

Proportionate liability Payment by an individual defendant based on the degree of fault of the individual.

Prospectus The first part of a registration statement filed with the SEC, issued as part of a public offering of debt or equity and used to solicit prospective investors in a new security issue containing, among other items, audited financial statements. The Securities Act of 1933 imposes liability for misstatements in a prospectus.

Rights theory An ethical theory that identifies a hierarchy of rights that should be considered in solving ethical dilemmas.

Rules of conduct Detailed guidance to assist the auditor in applying the broad principles contained in the AICPA's Code of Professional Conduct; the rules have evolved over time as members of the profession have encountered specific ethical dilemmas in complying with the principles of the Code.

Scienter Knowledge on the part of the person making the representations, at the time they are made, that they are false; intent.

Stakeholders   Those parties who have a vested interest in, or are affected by, the decision resulting from an ethical dilemma.

Statutory law   Laws developed through legislation, such as the Securities Act of 1933 and the Securities Exchange Act of 1934.

Third-party beneficiary   A person who was not a party to a contract but is named in the contract as one to whom the contracting parties intended that benefits be given.

Tort   A civil wrong, other than breach of contract, based on negligence, constructive fraud, or fraud.

Utilitarian theory   An ethical theory that systematically considers all the potential stakeholders who may be affected by an ethical decision and seeks to measure the effects of the decision on each party; it seeks to facilitate decisions resulting in the greatest amount of good for the greatest number of people.

TRUE-FALSE QUESTIONS

4-1   [LO 1]   Litigation costs are the largest single cost faced by audit firms.

4-2   [LO 1]   The expectations gap includes a misperception by shareholders that they are entitled to recover losses on investments for which the auditor provided an unqualified opinion on the financial statements.

4-3   [LO 2]   The three laws from which auditor liability is derived include common law, contract law, and statutory law.

4-4   [LO 2]   Negligence occurs when a person fails to perform a contractual duty.

4-5   [LO 3]   Examples of breach of contract include violating client confidentiality, failing to provide the audit report on time, and failing to discover material error or employee fraud.

4-6   [LO 3]   To win a claim against the auditor, third parties suing under common law must generally prove that they suffered a loss, that the loss was due to lack of reliance on misleading financial statements, and that the auditor knowingly participated in the financial misrepresentation.

4-7   [LO 4]   Professional judgment involves applying relevant professional knowledge and experience to unique and potentially uncertain facts and circumstances in order to reach a conclusion or make a decision.

4-8   [LO 4]   An auditor who is professionally skeptical will reasonably question the honesty and integrity of management.

4-9   [LO 5]   Utilitarian theory holds that what is ethical is the action that achieves the greatest good for the least number of people.

4-10   [LO 5]   In rights theory, the highest order rights are those granted by the government, such as civil rights, legal rights, rights to own property, and license privileges.

4-11   [LO 6]   The AICPA's principles of professional conduct articulate auditors' responsibilities and their requirements to act in the public interest, to act with integrity and objectivity, to be independent, to exercise due care, and to perform an appropriate scope of services.

4-12 [LO 6] An auditor's independence would be considered to be impaired if his or her immediate family member were employed by the audit client in any capacity or personnel level.

MULTIPLE-CHOICE QUESTIONS

4-13 [LO 1] Which of the following is not a reason that audit firms continue to experience high levels of litigation?
a. Joint and several liability statutes.
b. Class action lawsuits.
c. Contingent fee compensation for audit firms.
d. A misunderstanding by some users that an unqualified audit opinion represents an insurance policy against investment losses.

4-14 [LO 1] The shareholders of a bank sue Karen Frank, CPA, for malpractice due to an audit failure that preceded the bank's financial failure. The jury determines that Frank is 40 percent at fault and that management is 60 percent at fault. The bank has no financial resources, nor does its management. Under joint and several liability, Frank will pay what percentage of the damages?
a. 100%.
b. 50%.
c. 40%.
d. None of the above.

4-15 [LO 2] Which of the following statements is false?
a. Breach of contract occurs when a person competently performs a contractual duty.
b. Negligence is the failure to exercise reasonable care, thereby causing harm to another person or to property.
c. Gross negligence is operating with a reckless disregard for the truth, or the failure to use even minimal care.
d. Fraud is an intentional concealment or misrepresentation of a material fact with the intent to deceive another person, causing damage to the deceived person.

4-16 [LO 2] An audit client can sue the auditor under contract law for which of the following?
a. Breach of contract.
b. Negligence.
c. Gross negligence.
d. Fraud.
e. All of the above.

4-17 [LO 3] The remedies for breach of contract include which of the following?
a. Requiring specific performance of the contract agreement.
b. Granting an injunction to prohibit the auditor from doing certain acts, such as disclosing confidential information.
c. Providing for recovery of amounts lost as a result of the breach.
d. All of the above.

4-18 [LO 3] An example of a foreseen user would include which of the following?
a. The auditor knows that the First National Bank wants audited financial statements as part of the client's application for a loan.

b. The auditor knows that the client needs audited financial statements because it wants to obtain a loan from one of several possible banks.

c. Current and prospective creditors and stockholders are likely to use the audited financial statements.

d. None of the above.

4-19 `LO 4` Which of the following is not a step in the framework for professional decision making?

a. Structure the audit problem.

b. Assess consequences of decision.

c. Assess the likelihood of fraud.

d. Gather information and audit evidence.

e. Conduct sensitivity analysis.

4-20 `LO 4` An auditor who is professionally skeptical will do which of the following?

a. Critically question contradictory evidence.

b. Carefully evaluate the reliability of audit evidence.

c. Reasonably question the authenticity of documentation.

d. Reasonably question the honesty and integrity of management.

e. All of the above.

4-21 `LO 5` Utilitarianism does not require which of the following when a person considers how to resolve an ethical dilemma?

a. Identification of the potential problem and courses of action.

b. Identification of the potential direct or indirect impact of actions on each affected party who has an interest in the outcome.

c. Identification of the motivation of the person facing the ethical dilemma.

d. Assessment of the desirability of each action for each affected party.

4-22 `LO 5` Which of the following statements related to rights theory is false?

a. The highest order rights include the rights to life, autonomy, and human dignity.

b. The second order rights include rights granted by the government, such as civil rights and legal rights.

c. The third order rights include social rights, such as the right to higher education, to good health care, and to earning a living.

d. The fourth order rights include one's nonessential interests or personal tastes.

4-23 `LO 6` Rule 201 of the AICPA Rules of Conduct requires the auditor to do which of the following?

a. Undertake only those professional services that the auditor or audit firm can reasonably expect to be completed with professional competence.

b. Exercise due professional care in the performance of professional services.

c. Adequately plan and supervise the performance of professional services.

d. Obtain sufficient relevant data to afford a reasonable basis for conclusions in relation to professional services performed.

e. All of the above.

4-24 [LO 6] Which of the following statements is false?
a. An auditor in public practice shall be independent in the performance of professional services.
b. In performing audit services, the auditor shall maintain objectivity and integrity, be free of conflicts of interest, and not knowingly misrepresent facts or subordinate his or her judgment to others.
c. In performing audit services, the auditor may accept only contingent fees for publicly-traded audit clients.
d. An auditor in public practice shall not seek to obtain clients by advertising or other forms of solicitation in a manner that is false, misleading, or deceptive.

REVIEW AND SHORT CASE QUESTIONS

4-25 [LO 1] Describe the forces that continue to cause audit firms to experience high rates of litigation.

4-26 [LO 2] Compare and contrast the concepts of breach of contract, negligence, gross negligence, and fraud.

FRAUD

4-27 [LO 2] Distinguish between the development of common law versus statutory law.

NOTE: Completing Review and Short Case Questions does not require the student to reference additional resources and materials.

4-28 [LO 3] What are the potential causes of action against an auditor under a breach of contract lawsuit?

4-29 [LO 3] What are some remedies for a breach of contract?

4-30 [LO 3] What defenses might an auditor use in successfully defending a:
a. Suit brought about because of breach of contract?
b. Suit brought under statutory law?

4-31 [LO 3] Refer to the *Auditing in Practice* feature "Moss Adams and the Meridian Mortgage Funds Fraud."
a. Describe why Moss Adams was sued by the trustee for the bankrupt Meridian Mortgage.
b. What is the trustee going to have to prove in order for the courts to hold Moss Adams liable for damages?

FRAUD

NOTE: In problem materials including Review and Short Case Questions and beyond, we make special note of those problems addressing fraud, international issues, and professional skepticism. We do not make special note of problems on ethics because of the heavy number of those problems based on chapter content.

4-32 [LO 3] Three tests have been used by various courts in common-law decisions to determine which third-party users can successfully bring a suit against the auditor for negligence. Identify each of these tests and describe the parties that are defined in each of these tests.

4-33 [LO 3] What are some sanctions the SEC can bring against auditors who have violated statutory law?

4-34 [LO 3] Briefly explain the primary purpose of the:
a. Securities Act of 1933
b. Securities Exchange Act of 1934

FRAUD

4-35 [LO 3] How does the auditor's liability to third parties differ under the 1933 Act and the 1934 Exchange Act? What is the importance of the *Hochfelder* case as it relates to the 1934 Act?

4-36 [LO 3] Is there a conceptual difference between an error on the part of the auditor and ordinary negligence? Explain.

4-37 [LO 3] What precedent was set in the *Ernst & Ernst vs. Hochfelder* case described in the chapter? What actions would be necessary to change the precedent?

4-38 `LO 3` An auditor was sued for and found guilty of negligence. For each of the following situations, indicate the likelihood the plaintiff would win if the plaintiff is:

a. A financial institution that was known to the auditor as the primary beneficiary of the audit, suing under common law.

b. A stockholder suing under common law.

c. A financial institution that was unknown to the auditor loaned money to the client based on the audit financial statements, but the auditor knew only that the client would use the statements to obtain a loan from some financial institution. The plaintiff is suing under common law.

d. An investor suing under the 1934 Securities Exchange Act.

e. An investor suing under the 1933 Securities Act.

4-39 `LO 3`

a. Compare an auditor's liability to third parties for negligence under *Ultramares, Credit Alliance, 1965 Restatement (Second) of Torts*, and *Rosenblum*. Then indicate which approach you think auditors prefer, and why.

b. Which approach do you think is best for society? Why?

4-40 `LO 3` An auditor issued an unqualified opinion on financial statements that failed to disclose that a significant portion of the accounts receivable was uncollectible. The auditor also failed to follow professional auditing standards with respect to inventory. The auditor knew that the financial statements would be used to obtain a loan. The client subsequently declared bankruptcy. Under what concepts might a creditor, who loaned money to the client on the basis of the financial statements, recover losses from the auditor?

4-41 `LO 3` An investor is suing an auditor for issuing an unqualified opinion on the financial statements of Duluth Industries, which contained a material error. The auditor was negligent in performing the audit. The investor had reason to believe the statements were wrong prior to purchasing stock in the company. In the subsequent period, Duluth Industries sustained operating losses, the stock price went down by 40%, and the investor sold the stock at a loss. During the period that the investor held this stock, the Dow Jones Industrial Average declined 10%. What defenses might the auditor use against the investor's lawsuit to recover losses?

`FRAUD` **4-42** `LO 3` A client applied for a bank loan from First Bank. In connection with the loan application, the client engaged an auditor to audit its financial statements, and the auditor issued an unqualified opinion. On the basis of those statements, First Bank loaned money to the client. Shortly thereafter, the client filed for bankruptcy, and First Bank sued the auditor for damages. The audit documentation showed negligence and possible other misconduct in performing the audit.

a. Under what circumstances is First Bank an identified user?

b. What exceptions to the identified user test might First Bank argue?

`FRAUD` **4-43** `LO 3` The Monicker Co. engaged the audit firm of Gasner & Gasner to audit the financial statements to be used in connection with a public offering of securities. Monicker's stock is regularly traded on the NASDAQ. The audit was completed and an unqualified opinion was expressed on the financial statements, which were submitted to the SEC along with the registration statement. Three hundred thousand shares of Monicker common stock were sold to the public at $13.50 per share. Eight months later, the stock fell to $2 per share when it was disclosed that several large loans to two "paper" companies owned by one of the directors were worthless. The loans were secured by the stock of the borrowing corporation and by Monicker stock owned by the director. These facts were not disclosed in the financial statements. The director and the two corporations are insolvent. Considering these facts, indicate whether each of the following statements is true or false, and briefly explain the rationale for your choice.

a. The Securities Act of 1933 applies to the preceding public offering of securities.

b. The audit firm has potential liability to any person who acquired the stock described in connection with the public offering.

c. An investor who bought shares in Monicker would make a reasonable case if he or she alleged that the failure to explain the nature of the loans in question constituted a false statement or misleading omission in the financial statements.

d. The auditors could avoid liability if they could show that they were not fraudulent in the conduct of the audit.

e. The auditors could avoid or reduce the damages asserted against them if they could establish that the drop in price was due in whole or in part to other causes.

f. The SEC would establish contributory negligence as a partial defense for the auditor because the SEC approved the registration statement.

4-44 `L0 3`   To expand its operations, Dark Corporation raised $4 million by making a private interstate offering of $2 million in common stock and negotiating a $2 million loan from Safe Bank. The common stock was properly offered pursuant to Rule 505 of Regulation D, which exempts the offering from the 1933 Act, but not the antifraud provisions of the Federal Securities Acts.   `FRAUD`

In connection with this financing, Dark engaged Crea & Company, CPAs, to audit Dark's financial statements. Crea knew that the sole purpose for the audit was so that Dark would have audited financial statements to provide to Safe Bank and the purchasers of the common stock. Although Crea conducted the audit in conformity with its audit program, Crea failed to detect material committed by Dark's president. Crea did not detect the embezzlement because of its inadvertent failure to exercise due care in designing its audit program for this engagement.

After completing the audit, Crea rendered an unqualified opinion on Dark's financial statements. The financial statements were relied on by the purchasers of the common stock in deciding to purchase the shares. In addition, Safe Bank approved the loan to Dark based on the audited financial statements. Within 60 days after selling the common stock and obtaining the loan from Safe Bank, Dark was involuntarily petitioned into bankruptcy. Because of the president's embezzlement, Dark became insolvent and defaulted on its loan to Safe. Its common stock became virtually worthless. Actions have been commenced against Crea by the purchasers of the common stock (who have asserted that Crea is liable for damages under the Securities Exchange Act of 1934) and Safe Bank, based on Crea's negligence.

a. Discuss the merits of the actions commenced against Crea by the purchasers of the common stock and by Safe Bank, indicating the likely outcomes and the reasoning behind each outcome.

b. How would your answer be different if the client filed a registration statement and the purchasers of the common stock were able to bring suit under the 1933 Act?

4-45 `LO 3`

Part A

The common stock of Wilson, Incorporated is owned by twenty stockholders. Wilson's financial statements as of December 31, 2013, were audited by Doe & Company, CPAs, who rendered an unqualified opinion on the financial statements. In reliance on Wilson's financial statements, which showed net income for 2013 of $1,500,000, Peters purchased 10,000 shares of Wilson stock for $200,000 on April 10, 2014. Wilson's financial statements contained material misstatements. Because Doe did not carefully follow GAAP, it did not discover that the statements failed to reflect unrecorded expenses, which reduced Wilson's actual net income to $800,000. After disclosure of the corrected financial statements, Peters sold his shares for $100,000, which was the highest price he could obtain. Peters has brought an action against Doe under federal securities law and common law.

Answer the following, setting forth reasons for your conclusions:

a. Will Peters prevail on his federal securities-law claims?

b. Will Peters prevail on his common-law claims?

Part B

Able Corporation decided to make a public offering of bonds to raise needed capital. It publicly sold $2,500,000 of 12% debentures in accordance with the registration requirements of the Securities Act of 1933. The financial statements filed with the registration statement contained the unqualified opinion of Baker & Company, CPAs. The statements overstated Able's net income and net worth. Through negligence, Baker did not detect the overstatements. As a result, the bonds, which originally sold for $1,000 per bond, have dropped in value to $700. Ira is an investor who purchased $10,000 of the bonds. He promptly brought an action against Baker under the Securities Act of 1933.

Answer the following, setting forth reasons for your conclusions:

a. Will Ira likely prevail on his claim under the Securities Act of 1933?

b. Identify the primary issues that will determine the likelihood of Ira's prevailing on the claim.

4-46 `LO 4` Refer to Exhibit 4.3. Briefly explain the seven steps in the framework for professional decision making. Provide an example of a professionally oriented decision that you have recently made, and relate it to the seven steps (one example might be a decision about which apartment to rent for the next academic year, or a decision about whether to apply to a Master's program).

4-47 `LO 4` Refer to the *Auditing in Practice* feature "What is Professional Judgment?" Describe what is meant by the term *professional judgment*. Explain why documentation is critical to professional judgment.

4-48 `LO 4` Explain why professional skepticism is important in making professional judgments. What are the types of actions that a professionally skeptical auditor will take?

PROFESSIONAL SKEPTICISM

4-49 `LO 4` Refer to the *Auditing in Practice* feature "What Was He Thinking? An Example of Poor Professional Judgment and Low Audit Quality."

a. Briefly explain the common themes indicating poor professional judgment evident from the facts about the Prospero Minerals audit, the Cal Bay audit, and the LitFunding audit.

b. What do you think Scharfman's motivation was in explaining his conduct?

c. Why were Scharfman's actions so potentially harmful to external users of the audited financial statements?

4-50 `LO 5` Describe utilitarian theory and how it is used to resolve an ethical dilemma. What are the weaknesses of utilitarian theory?

4-51 `LO 5` Describe rights theory and list the four levels of rights. In what way is rights theory particularly helpful?

4-52 `LO 5` Refer to Exhibit 4.4. Briefly explain the seven steps in the framework for ethical decision making. Provide an example of a difficult ethical decision that you have recently made, and show how you would make a decision using the seven steps (an example might be a decision to challenge a friend who has done something wrong or a decision to report on a person that you know was cheating on an exam).

4-53 `LO 5` Refer to the *Auditing in Practice* feature "A Young Auditor Makes an Ethical Mistake in Professional Judgment."

a. What was the ethical dilemma faced by Susan Birkert's friend when that fellow auditor learned of Birkert's ethical wrongdoing?

b. What aspects of the framework for ethical decision making would the friend likely have considered in deciding to reveal Birkert's mistake?

4-54 `LO 5` As the auditor for XYZ Company, you discover that a material sale ($500,000 sale; cost of goods of $300,000) was made to a customer this year. Because of poor internal accounting controls, the sale was never recorded. Your client makes a management decision not to bill the customer because such a long time has passed since the shipment was made. You determine, to the best of your ability, that the sale was not fraudulent. Using the framework for ethical decision making, determine whether the auditor should require either a recording or a disclosure of the transaction. Explain your reasoning.

4-55 `LO 5` You have worked as a staff auditor for two and one-half years and have mastered your job. You will likely be promoted to a senior position after this busy season. Your current senior was promoted about a year ago. He appreciates your competence and rarely interferes with you. As long as he can report good performance to his manager on things she wants, he is satisfied. The manager has been in her position for three years. She is focused on making sure audits run smoothly and is good at this. She is not as strong on the softer skills. Although she is approachable, her attention span can be short if what you are saying does not interest her. You are aware that she expects her teams to perform excellently during this busy season and she hopes to be promoted to senior manager as a result, bringing her closer to her goal of making partner early.

ETHICS

The audit engagement on which you are working has become increasingly difficult since last year because of some complicated accounting transactions that the client made. There has also been unexpected turnover in accounting personnel at the client. This has made interacting with the client and getting the information you need in a timely manner problematic. However, the engagement time budget and the audit fee remain the same as last year's. Further, four staff auditors are assigned to the engagement, and there are no additional staff available to transfer in to ease the workload. Your senior now tells you that the manager has requested that you, he, and the other staff auditors do an additional analysis of a potential misstatement in one of the client's accounts. Even with your team's current workload there is significant danger that the engagement will run over budget. You know that if you do the analysis thoroughly, it will further endanger meeting the time budget the manager had planned. The more time you spend on the engagement, the less profitable it will be for the audit firm, which clearly will displease the manager and her superiors.

As a group, the staff auditors discuss the situation and express their concerns regarding the perceptions that running over budget will create and the reputational issues that short-circuiting the analysis could create. When your senior stops by to discuss the new plan, the group raises its concerns. He talks to the group and implies that he would be satisfied if the team did either of the following: complete the analysis and simply not record the hours (doing so would prevent the reported audit hours from going too far over budget) or do a minimal job on the analysis, which would save time and avoid having to question the client too much. You and a few other staff members express discomfort with both of these strategies. It is suggested that the ramifications of the new order be made clear to the manager. The senior wants nothing to do with this. He says, "She doesn't want to hear these details so just use one of the ideas I have already given you." When he leaves, several staff members start griping about what they are being asked to do. A couple say they are going to leave the firm after this busy season, so they don't really care about this issue. Another says, "We've been told what to do. Let's just get on with it."

a. Using the framework for ethical decision making, decide what you would do. Explain your rationale.

b. How can you do what you think is the right thing without undermining your senior or undermining the manager's confidence in your ability to get a job done?

INTERNATIONAL   **4-56**   **LO 6**   Summarize the five fundamental principles of ethics as articulated by the International Ethics Standards Board for Accountants (IESBA).

4-57   **LO 6**   Refer to Exhibit 4.5. Describe the AICPA's six principles of professional conduct.

4-58   **LO 6**   Refer to Exhibit 4.6, which describes the AICPA's rules of conduct. Read Rule 101 and answer the following questions.

a. Are auditors of publicly traded clients required to be independent?

b. Are auditors of privately held clients required to be independent?

c. Rule 101 applies only to covered members. What does it mean to be a covered member?

d. What is the difference between a direct financial interest and an indirect financial interest?

e. What services does the Sarbanes-Oxley Act of 2002 prohibit auditors from performing for their publicly traded clients?

4-59 [LO 6]   Refer to Exhibit 4.6, which describes the AICPA's rules of conduct. Read Rule 102 and answer the following questions.
a. What does Rule 102 require?
b. Does Rule 102 apply to just external auditors, or all CPAs?

4-60 [LO 6]   Refer to Exhibit 4.6, which describes the AICPA's rules of conduct. Read Rule 301 and answer the following questions.
a. Distinguish between confidential information and privileged communication.
b. Normally, the external auditor must keep client information confidential. Identify those circumstances in which this does not apply.

4-61 [LO 6]   Refer to Exhibit 4.6, which describes the AICPA's rules of conduct. Read Rule 302 and answer the following questions.
a. What is a contingent fee?
b. Why are external auditors not allowed to accept contingent fees?

4-62 [LO 6]   Describe the various ways in which the AICPA's Code is enforced.

4-63 [LO 6]   Would a CPA violate the AICPA's Code by serving a client both as its auditor and legal counsel? Explain your answer.

4-64 [LO 6]   The following are a number of scenarios that might constitute a violation of the AICPA Code of Professional Conduct. For each of the five situations, indicate which principle or rule would be violated.
a. Tom Hart, CPA, does the bookkeeping, prepares the tax returns, and performs various management services for Sanders, Incorporated, but does not do the audit. One management service involved the assessment of the computer needs and the identification of equipment to meet those needs. Hart recommended a product sold by Computer Company, which has agreed to pay Hart a 10% commission if Sanders buys its product.
b. Irma Stone, CPA, was scheduled to be extremely busy for the next few months. When a prospective client asked if Stone would do its next year's audit, she declined but referred them to Joe Rock, CPA. Rock paid Stone $2,000 for the referral.
c. Nancy Heck, CPA, has agreed to perform an inventory control study and recommend a new inventory control system for Ettes, Incorporated, a new client. Currently, Ettes engages another audit firm to audit its financial statements. The financial arrangement is that Ettes will pay Heck 50% of the savings in inventory costs over the two-year period following the implementation of the new system.
d. Brad Gage, CPA, has served Hi-Dee Company as auditor for several years. In addition, Gage has performed other services for the company. This year, the financial vice president has asked Gage to perform a major computer system evaluation.
e. Due to the death of its controller, an audit client had its external auditor, Gail Klate, CPA, perform the controller's job for a month until a replacement was found.

CONTEMPORARY AND HISTORICAL CASES

FRAUD **4-65** **KPMG**

LO 1, 2, 3, 4, 5, 6 Refer to the *Professional Judgment in Context* feature at the outset of the chapter, which features the litigation charges against KPMG for its audit failures during the subprime mortgage crisis.

a. How does the business environment affect the litigation risk faced by audit firms?

b. Should auditors be held liable if their client's business fails or if the financial statements contain a fraud that the auditors did not detect?

c. What defenses do auditors use in response to litigation?

d. What actions can auditors take to minimize litigation exposure?

4-66 **THOMAS FLANAGAN OF DELOITTE**

LO 4, 5, 6 Thomas Flanagan was an audit partner and key member of management (Vice Chairman) at Deloitte LLP, based out of the firm's Chicago office. During the latter part of his career, he managed a large number of public company audit engagements. Based on knowledge obtained from key members of management of one of his audit clients, Flanagan learned that the client would soon be purchasing another company. Knowing that the value of the acquired company would rise upon the news of the purchase, Flanagan purchased stock in the acquired company. As such, he engaged in insider trading. As the subsequent investigation would reveal, Flanagan traded in securities of at least 12 of his audit clients during 2005–2008. In fact, he made more than 300 trades in shares of the firm's clients over this period. He concealed his actions by lying on his independence disclosure filings with Deloitte, not revealing the existence of several of his brokerage accounts that would have identified his actions. Ultimately, the SEC uncovered his actions and notified Deloitte. Flanagan resigned from the firm, and Deloitte subsequently sued him for breach of fiduciary duty, fraud, and breach of contract based upon his misconduct. The firm ultimately won a judgment against him. A spokesperson for the firm stated "Deloitte unequivocally condemns the actions of this individual, which are unprecedented in our experience. His personal trading activities were in blatant violation of Deloitte's strict and clearly stated policies for investments by partners and other professional personnel."

In August 2010 the Securities and Exchange Commission charged Thomas Flanagan and his son with insider trading in the securities of several of the firm's audit clients. The SEC alleges that Flanagan's illegal trading resulted in profits of more than $430,000. On four occasions, Flanagan shared the nonpublic information with his son, who then traded based on that information for illegal profits of more than $57,000. The SEC also instituted administrative proceedings against Thomas Flanagan, finding that he violated the SEC's auditor independence rules on 71 occasions between 2003 and 2008. The Flanagans agreed to pay more than $1.1 million to settle the SEC's charges.

a. Why is owning stock in one's client considered inappropriate?

b. Why is it important that auditors be independent of their clients?

c. Why did Deloitte take Flanagan's actions so seriously?

d. What do you think might have led Flanagan to make such poor professional and ethical decisions?

e. Assume that you were working on one of Flanagan's engagements and you discovered that insider trading was occurring. What procedures should the audit firm have in place to encourage you to report the inappropriate behavior and yet protect your career?

5 Professional Auditing Standards and the Audit Opinion Formulation Process

CHAPTER OVERVIEW AND LEARNING OBJECTIVES

Professional standards for auditors provide guidance on the many judgments and decisions they make throughout the audit opinion formulation process. These standards help auditors properly plan, perform, document, and supervise audits. Auditors who follow the professional auditing standards are viewed as conducting a quality audit. This chapter will help you identify the relevant guidance to follow in your auditing career and help you explore the various activities you will be completing each time you perform an audit.

Through studying this chapter, you will be able to achieve these learning objectives:

通过本章的学习，你将能够实现以下学习目标：

1. Identify and compare the various auditing standards that provide guidance on the audit opinion formulation process.
   识别和比较为审计意见形成过程提供指导的各种审计准则。

2. List and discuss the foundational principles underlying the auditing standards.
   列示和讨论审计准则的基本原则。

3. List the phases and related activities in the audit opinion formulation process.
   列示审计意见形成过程中经历的阶段和相关的活动。

4. Explain the concept of accounting cycles and discuss their importance to the audit opinion formulation process.
   解释会计循环的概念，讨论它们对审计意见形成过程的重要性。

5. Describe the assertions that are inherent to financial statements and explain their importance to the audit opinion formulation process.
   描述财务报表固有的认定，解释它们对审计意见形成过程的重要性。

6. Define audit evidence and describe the purpose and types of audit procedures used to obtain audit evidence.
   明确审计证据的含义，描述用于获得审计证据的审计程序的目的和类型。

7. Discuss the importance of audit documentation and provide examples.
   讨论审计工作底稿的重要性并举例说明。

8. Discuss audit activities in Phase I of the audit opinion formulation process.
   讨论审计意见形成过程第一阶段的审计活动。

9. Discuss audit activities in Phase II of the audit opinion formulation process.
   讨论审计意见形成过程第二阶段的审计活动。

10. Discuss audit activities in Phase III of the audit opinion formulation process.
    讨论审计意见形成过程第三阶段的审计活动。

11. Discuss audit activities in Phase IV of the audit opinion formulation process.
    讨论审计意见形成过程第四阶段的审计活动。

12. Discuss audit activities in Phase V of the audit opinion formulation process.
    讨论审计意见形成过程第五阶段的审计活动。

13. Apply the concepts related to the auditor's assessment of internal control design effectiveness, implementation, and operating effectiveness.
    应用与注册会计师评估内部控制设计与运行有效性相关的概念。

14. Apply the frameworks for professional decision making and ethical decision making to issues involving conducting an audit.
    应用职业决策和道德决策框架解决执行审计时遇到的问题。

THE AUDIT OPINION FORMULATION PROCESS

| I. Making Client Acceptance and Continuance Decisions **Chapter 14** | II. Performing Risk Assessment **Chapters 3, 7 and 9–13** | III. Obtaining Evidence about Internal Control Operating Effectiveness **Chapters 8–13 and 16** | IV. Obtaining Substantive Evidence about Accounts, Disclosures and Assertions **Chapters 8–13 and 16** | V. Completing the Audit and Making Reporting Decisions **Chapters 14 and 15** |

| The Auditing Profession, the Risk of Fraud and Mechanisms to Address Fraud: Regulation, Corporate Governance, and Audit Quality **Chapters 1 and 2** | Professional Liability and the Need for Quality Auditor Judgments and Ethical Decisions **Chapter 4** |

The Audit Opinion Formulation Process and A Framework for Obtaining Audit Evidence
Chapters 5 and 6

PROFESSIONAL JUDGMENT IN CONTEXT

The Importance of Adhering to Professional Auditing Standards as Illustrated in the Audits of Thornton Precision Components, Limited performed by Ernst & Young, LLP UK

Auditors who adhere to the professional auditing standards are viewed as conducting a quality audit. A lack of adherence to the professional auditing standards heightens the risk that the auditor will provide an unqualified audit opinion on financial statements that are materially misstated. This lesson is highlighted in the 2004-2006 audits of Thornton Precision Components, Limited (TPC) performed by Ernst & Young, LLP UK (E&Y UK).

TPC became a wholly owned UK subsidiary of Symmetry Medical, Inc. in 2003. Symmetry became a public company in 2004 and was listed on a United States stock exchange. Its consolidated financial statements included TPC's financial data. Beginning in 2003, Ernst & Young, LLP (E&Y US) became Symmetry's audit firm. In connection with the 2004-2006 audits of Symmetry, E&Y US engaged E&Y UK to perform audits of TPC, using Public Company Accounting Oversight Board (PCAOB) auditing standards. During the 2004-2006 audits, E&Y US relied on E&Y UK's audits to issue unqualified audit opinions for Symmetry.

From 1999 through September 2007, TPC's management participated in multiple schemes to increase TPC's revenues, net income, and other performance indicators. These schemes included booking fictitious revenues, understating costs of goods sold, creating fictitious inventories, and improperly capitalizing certain expenses. The fraud at TPC was not discovered by the auditors, but only came to light in 2007 when a TPC employee alerted Symmetry's CEO to the fraud. In 2008, Symmetry restated its financial statements, which included among other items, significant reductions in Symmetry's net income.

In 2012, the Securities and Exchange Commission (SEC) concluded that E&Y UK (a firm registered with the PCAOB) had conducted its audits in such a way that the audits did not adhere to the relevant professional auditing standards. Deficiencies in E&Y UK's 2004-2006 audits of TPC included a failure to perform appropriate procedures to audit the accounts receivable balances, adequately review top-side journal entries, properly audit inventory, and a failure to plan, staff, and supervise the audits. During the audit, the audit partner and manager did not appropriately question management's representations, did not fully document the results of testing, did not appropriately consider the risks of misstatements due to fraud, and did not exercise due professional care and professional skepticism.

The SEC prohibited both the audit manager and partner of TPC from auditing U.S. public companies for two years.

As you read through this chapter, consider the following questions:

- What is the role of auditing standards and their underlying principles in promoting a quality audit? (LO 1, 2)
- How does the fundamental concept of professional skepticism relate to audit quality? (LO 2)
- What audit evidence is necessary for opining on a client's financial statements? (LO 6)

- How does audit documentation provide evidence related to audit quality? (LO 7)
- What audit activities are conducted during the audit opinion formulation process to provide reasonable assurance about a client's financial statements? (LO 8, 9, 10, 11, 12)
- How does professional judgment and ethical decision making contribute to audit quality? (LO 14)

For further details on this case, see Securities and Exchange Commission Accounting and Auditing Enforcement Release No. 3359 (January 2012).

审计准则

Professional Auditing Standards

LO 1 Identify and compare the various auditing standards that provide guidance on the audit opinion formulation process.

在美国，注册会计师主要遵循美国注册会计师、国际审计与鉴证准则委员会和美国公众公司会计监督委员会发布的审计准则。组织的性质不同，注册会计师所遵循的审计准则也不同。在审计公众公司时应依据美国公众公司会计监督委员会发布的审计准则。在审计非公众公司时应依据美国注册会计师协会发布的公认审计准则。

Auditors in the United States follow auditing guidance issued by the American Institute of Certified Public Accountants (AICPA), the PCAOB, and the International Auditing and Assurance Standards Board (IAASB). Auditing standards set by these various authorities have a common objective—to provide reasonable assurance to the public that audits are conducted in a quality manner. Auditing standards apply to the auditor's task of developing and communicating an opinion on financial statements and, as part of an integrated audit, on a client's internal control over financial reporting. The auditing standards used will vary according to the nature of the organization audited, such as whether an entity is public or nonpublic. For example, U.S. public companies are subject to SEC regulation and must be audited in accordance with the auditing standards established by the PCAOB, while U.S. nonpublic companies will have an audit performed in accordance with generally accepted auditing standards that have been established by the AICPA. Further, the domicile of the organization that is being audited and, more importantly, where its stock is publicly traded (if applicable), determine whether the auditor must comply with PCAOB or AICPA standards or those developed by IAASB.

美国注册会计师协会发布的审计准则

Auditing Standards Issued by the AICPA

In 2004, the AICPA's Auditing Standards Board (ASB) began a project to redraft its standards for clarity. The AICPA's Clarity Project was intended to make the standards easier to read, understand, and apply. As part of the project, the ASB also worked on converging its standards with the International Standards on Auditing (ISAs), issued by the IAASB. The ASB has written its standards using a drafting convention called the clarity format. The clarity format presents each standard in the following sections:

- *Introduction* explains the purpose and scope of the standard.
- *Objective* defines the context in which the requirements are set.
- *Definitions* include, where relevant, specific meanings of terms in the standards.
- *Requirements* identify what the auditor is required to do to achieve the objective of the standard. Requirements are expressed using the words "the auditor should" or "the auditor must."
- *Application and Other Explanatory Material* include cross-references to the requirements and provide further guidance for applying the requirements of the standard.

The ASB issued most of its clarified standards in a single Statement on Auditing (SAS No. 122) in 2012. These clarified standards became effective for audits of financial statements for periods ending on or after December

15, 2012. Throughout the text, and as presented in the Appendix to this chapter, we reference the AICPA's clarified auditing standards by referring to "AU-C" and a section number (for example AU-C 200).

Auditing Standards Issued by the IAASB

国际审计与鉴证准则委员会发布的审计准则

The IAASB states that its objective is to "serve the public interest by setting high-quality auditing, assurance, and other related standards and by facilitating the convergence of international and national auditing and assurance standards, thereby enhancing the quality and consistency of practice throughout the world and strengthening public confidence in the global auditing and assurance profession." The IAASB recognizes that standards need to be understandable, clear, and consistent. Accordingly, in 2004, the IAASB began a program to enhance the clarity of its ISAs. The IAASB's Clarity Project was completed in 2009, and as of 2013, the set of IAASB's clarified standards comprises 36 ISAs and International Standard on Quality Control (ISQC) 1. The ISAs are structured so that information is consistently presented in the following separate sections, which is very similar to the format of the AICPA's standards:

- *Introduction* includes information regarding the purpose, scope, and subject matter of the ISA, in addition to the responsibilities of the auditors and others.
- *Objective* contains a clear statement of the objective of the auditor.
- *Definitions* for applicable terms are included.
- *Requirements* for each objective are provided. Requirements are indicated by the phrase "the auditor shall."
- *Application and Other Explanatory Material* explains more precisely what a requirement means or is intended to cover, or includes examples of procedures that may be appropriate under given circumstances.

Throughout the text, and as presented in the Appendix to this chapter, we reference the IAASB's auditing standards by referring to "ISA" and a section number (for example, ISA 200).

Auditing Standards Issued by the PCAOB

美国公众公司会计监督委员会发布的审计准则

The PCAOB, which came into existence in 2002, issues auditing standards that apply to auditors of U.S. public companies. As of 2013, the PCAOB had issued sixteen Auditing Standards (ASs). Further, the PCAOB adopted the AICPA standards that were in place on April 16, 2003 (referred to as PCAOB interim standards). Thus, PCAOB requires public company auditors to follow these standards of the AICPA, unless they have been superseded by a PCAOB standard. Standards issued by the AICPA after April 16, 2003, are not part of PCAOB's interim standards.

Throughout the text, and as presented in the Appendix to this chapter, we reference the PCAOB's promulgated auditing standards by referring to "AS" and a section number (for example, AS 1). We refer to the PCAOB's interim auditing standards by referring to "AU" and a section number (for example, AU 110).

Comparison of the Auditing Standards

审计准则的比较

Fortunately, there is a great deal of commonality among the auditing standards. All of the standards start from fundamental principles on how an audit engagement should be planned and performed and how the results should be communicated. An overview of these auditing standards is shown in Exhibit 5.1. The Appendix to this chapter provides a summary of the relevant standards for each phase of the audit opinion formulation process.

Principles Underlying the Auditing Standards

制定审计准则的基本原则

Auditing standards in the United States have historically been based on ten generally accepted auditing standards (commonly referred to as the ten

LO 2 List and discuss the foundational principles underlying the auditing standards.

EXHIBIT **5.1**	Comparison of U.S. and International Auditing Standards		
	IAASB	**PCAOB**	**AICPA**
Authority	International Federation of Accountants, and as agreed-upon by countries who abide by these standards	U.S Congress, as expressed in the Sarbanes-Oxley Act of 2002	Historical, as a self-regulatory profession
Terminology	International Standards on Auditing (ISA)	Auditing Standards (AS) and Interim Standards (AU)	Statements on Auditing Standards (AU-C)
Scope of Applicability of Standards	Audits in countries for which international standards are required, including most of Europe and many emerging markets	Audits of U.S. public companies	Audits of most U.S. nonpublic entities
Convergence of Auditing Standards	Committed to international convergence	Does not currently have a mandate for international convergence	Committed to international convergence

standards) that have served as the foundation for the audit of financial statements. Currently, however, the PCAOB is the only standard setter that still incorporates these ten standards (they were adopted by the PCAOB as part of its interim standards). The AICPA has replaced the ten standards with seven principles. While the wording differs, the fundamental tenant is that audits must be conducted in a quality manner.

PCAOB Guidance—The Ten Standards

The ten standards fall within three categories:

- *General standards* are applicable to the auditor and audit firm and provide guidance in selecting and training its professionals to meet the public trust. The general standards require the following:
  1. The audit is to be performed by individuals having adequate technical training and proficiency as an auditor.
  2. Auditors are to be independent in their mental attitude in conducting the audit (independence *in fact*) and be perceived by users as independent of the client (independence *in appearance*).
  3. The audit is to be conducted with due professional care which is a standard of care that would be expected of a reasonably prudent auditor.
- *Fieldwork standards* are applicable to the conduct of the audit and require that:
  4. An audit is properly planned and supervised.
  5. Auditors develop an understanding of the client's controls as an important prerequisite to developing specific audit tests.
  6. Auditors obtain sufficient appropriate audit evidence by performing audit procedures to provide a reasonable basis for the audit opinion being provided.
- *Reporting standards* are applicable to communicating the auditor's opinion and require that:
  7. The auditor will state explicitly whether the financial statements are fairly presented in accordance with the applicable financial reporting framework, which may be Generally Accepted Accounting Principles (GAAP) or International Financial Reporting Standards (IFRS).

8. The auditor will identify in the auditor's report, those circumstances in which accounting principles have not been consistently observed in the current period in comparison to the preceding period.
9. The auditor will review disclosures for adequacy, and if the auditor concludes that informative disclosures are not reasonably adequate, the auditor must so state in the auditor's report.
10. The auditor will express an opinion on the financial statements as a whole or state that an opinion cannot be expressed.

AICPA Guidance: Principles Governing an Audit

In place of the ten standards, the AICPA developed seven fundamental principles that govern audits. The four categories, with their specific principles, are:

Purpose of an Audit and Premise upon Which an Audit Is Conducted
1. The purpose of an audit is to enhance the degree of confidence that users can place in the financial statement. This purpose is achieved when an auditor expresses an opinion on the financial statements.
2. An audit is based on the premise that management has responsibility to prepare the financial statements, maintain internal control over financial reporting, and provide the auditor with relevant information and access to personnel.

Responsibilities
3. Auditors are responsible for having the appropriate competence and capabilities to perform the audit, should comply with ethical requirements, and maintain professional skepticism throughout the audit.

Performance
4. The auditor needs to obtain reasonable assurance as to whether the financial statements are free from material misstatement.
5. Obtaining reasonable assurance requires the auditor to plan and supervise the work, determine materiality levels, identify risks of material misstatement, and design and implement appropriate audit responses to the assessed risks.
6. An audit has inherent limitations such that the auditor is not able to obtain absolute assurance about whether the financial statements are free from misstatement.

Reporting
7. The auditor expresses an opinion as to whether the financial statements are free of material misstatement or states that an opinion cannot be expressed.

The Audit Opinion Formulation Process　　　　　　审计意见的形成过程

As an auditor you may be performing an audit of an organization's financial statements only, or you may be performing an integrated audit that combines the audits of an organization's financial statements and its internal control over financial reporting. Although an integrated audit is required only for larger public companies listed in the U.S., the concepts underlying it are generally applicable to any financial statement audit. As indicated in the *Auditing in Practice* feature, "Benefits of Integrating the Audits," audit efficiencies can result from integrating the audits of the financial statements and internal control.

The audit opinion formulation process is basically the same for the financial statement only audit and the integrated audit. However, in an integrated audit, the auditor provides on opinion on the effectiveness of internal control over financial reporting and does additional audit work to be able to issue that opinion, along with the opinion on the financial statements. Specifically,

Benefits of Integrating the Audits

Integrating the audits of internal controls and of the financial statements makes sense because both the tests of controls and the direct tests of account balances provide evidence related to each other. For example, tests of controls provide indirect evidence on the likelihood that the financial statements are free from misstatement. If the controls are effective, it is more likely that the financial statements are free from material misstatement. Further, if the auditor finds material misstatements in account balances or disclosures, those misstatements imply that there were material weaknesses in internal controls. Integrating the work promotes audit efficiency.

the auditor plans and performs the audit to obtain reasonable assurance about whether a material weakness in internal control exists as of the client's balance sheet date.

审计意见形成过程的阶段概述

LO 3 List the phases and related activities in the audit opinion formulation process.

An Overview of the Phases in the Audit Opinion Formulation Process

An important aspect of the audit opinion formulation process is the client's responsibilities related to internal controls and the financial statements.

Exhibit 5.2 provides an overview of the client's preparation of its financial statements and management report on internal control. An important implication of Exhibit 5.2 is that the quality of internal control, which is the responsibility of the client, affects the reliability of the client's financial statement data. If controls over input, process, and output activities are effective, there is a higher likelihood that the financial statements are free from material

| EXHIBIT **5.2** | Overview of the Client's Preparation of Financial Statements and Management Report on Internal Control |

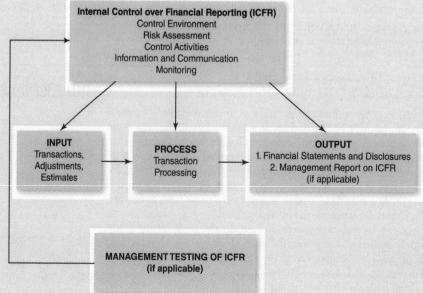

misstatement. This relationship has important implications for planning and performing the audit. The *Audit Opinion Formulation Process* diagram presented at the beginning of this chapter summarizes the phases of an audit performed for purposes of providing an opinion on the client's financial statements and internal control effectiveness. These phases include:

Phase I   Making Client Acceptance and Continuance Decisions
Phase II   Performing Risk Assessment
Phase III   Obtaining Evidence about Internal Control Operating Effectiveness
Phase IV   Obtaining Substantive Evidence about Accounts, Disclosures, and Assertions
Phase V   Completing the Audit and Making Reporting Decisions

審計意見的形成過程包含五個階段：做出客戶接受與保留決策，實施風險評估，獲取內部控制有效性的證據，獲取賬戶、披露和認定的實質性證據，以及完成審計並做出報告決策。

Within each of these phases the auditor performs various activities, most of which are the same whether the auditor is performing a financial statement only audit or an integrated audit. Exhibit 5.3 lists these activities. These activities are influenced by the auditing profession, regulation, and professional liability. When performing each of the activities in Exhibit 5.3, the auditor is expected to make quality professional judgments and ethical decisions.

Important Concepts Affecting the Audit Opinion Formulation Process

影響審計意見形成過程的重要概念

A number of important audit concepts that are pervasive throughout the audit opinion formulation process include:

* Accounting cycles
* Management assertions
* Audit evidence and audit procedures
* Documentation

Accounting Cycles

LO 4 Explain the concept of accounting cycles and discuss their importance to the audit opinion formulation process.

Financial statements are made up of accounts, such as revenue or accounts receivable, and they represent a summary of an organization's transactions. Similar transactions that are linked by procedures and controls and that affect

EXHIBIT 5.3   Activities of each Phase of the Audit Opinion Formulation Process

Phase of the Audit Opinion Formulation Process	Activities Within the Phase
Phase I Making Client Acceptance and Continuance Decisions	• Assess preconditions for an audit • Develop common understanding of the audit engagement with the client
Phase II Performing Risk Assessment	• Identify and assess risks of material misstatement • Respond to identified risks of material misstatement
Phase III Obtaining Evidence about Internal Control Operating Effectiveness, if applicable	• Select controls to test, if applicable • Perform tests of controls, if applicable • Consider the results of tests of controls, if applicable
Phase IV Obtaining Substantive Evidence about Accounts, Disclosures, and Assertions	• Perform appropriate substantive procedures
Phase V Completing the Audit and Making Reporting Decisions	• Complete review and communication activities • Determine the type(s) of opinion(s) to issue

EXHIBIT **5.4**	Illustrations of Cycles and Related Accounts

Cycle	Related Accounts
Acquisitions and Payments for Inventory, Goods, and Services	Accounts Payable Inventory Expenses Other Assets Cash
Acquisitions and Payments for Long-Lived Assets	Equipment Accumulated Depreciation Depreciation Expense Gain or Loss on Disposal Impairment Loss

related accounts are often grouped together for analysis (and audit) purposes and are referred to as an accounting **cycle** (or process). Many accounting transactions follow a defined cycle. For example, the revenue cycle includes transactions related to revenue, beginning with an initial customer order that flows through to an invoice, a recording of a receivable and a sale, and eventually the collection of cash. The cycle concept provides a convenient way to break the audit up into manageable sections of related accounts. Individual auditors or teams of auditors are typically assigned to audit a particular accounting cycle. Exhibit 5.4 lists two cycles and their related accounts.

For a particular cycle, the auditor focuses on the flow of transactions within that cycle, including how transactions are initiated, authorized, recorded, and reported. The auditor identifies points in the cycle where material misstatement can occur and controls that have been designed and implemented to mitigate those risks. Understanding the risks and controls within each cycle helps the auditor determine the specific audit procedures to use and the specific audit evidence to obtain. We cover the following cycles in this text:

- Revenue (Chapter 9)
- Cash and Marketable Securities (Chapter 10)
- Inventory, Goods, and Services, and Accounts Payable (Chapter 11)
- Long-Lived Assets (Chapter 12)
- Debt Obligations and Stockholders' Equity (Chapter 13)

LO 5 Describe the assertions that are inherent to financial statement and explain their importance to the audit opinion formulation process.

Financial Statement Assertions

Within each cycle, the audit is designed around management's assertions inherent in the financial statements. For example, if an organization asserts that it has property, plant, and equipment (PPE) net of depreciation of $42 million, the assertions being made by the organization are that:

- PPE is physically present *(existence)*.
- All purchases of PPE are fully recorded *(completeness)*.
- It owns the PPE and has title to the equipment *(rights and obligations)*.
- The PPE is properly valued at cost with applicable allowances for depreciation *(valuation)*.
- The PPE is appropriately classified and described *(presentation and disclosure)*.

The auditor's job is to obtain evidence related to these assertions for each significant account and disclosure in the financial statements. As part of this process, auditors identify the most relevant assertions associated with the accounts and disclosures. Relevant assertions are those assertions that have a meaningful bearing on whether a financial statement account is fairly stated. While multiple assertions likely have a bearing on a financial statement account or disclosure, certain financial statement assertions are "more" relevant than others for particular financial statement accounts. For example, valuation is not particularly relevant to the cash account, unless currency translation is involved. However, existence would be considered more relevant to the cash account. As another example, valuation is especially relevant for the inventory account. The type of account will impact the assertions considered most relevant. In general, assets and revenues are more likely to be overstated, so existence/occurrence is the more relevant assertion. In contrast, completeness would be the relevant assertion for liabilities and expenses, as management would be more likely to understate these accounts. Accounts that require subjective judgments by management (such as allowance for loan loss reserve or allowance for inventory obsolescence) will usually have valuation as a more relevant assertion, since the valuation assessment is subject to management bias. The five assertions identified in the PCAOB's standards are described in Exhibit 5.5.

The assertions listed in Exhibit 5.5 are the ones we refer to throughout the text. The AICPA and IAASB have a similar conceptual structure for their assertions, although in some cases the wording differs somewhat from the wording in Exhibit 5.5.

Audit Evidence and Audit Procedures

Audit evidence is information obtained by the auditor to support the audit opinion. Most of the auditor's work in forming an opinion consists of obtaining and evaluating audit evidence. This is done by performing **audit procedures**, which fall into three categories:

* **Risk assessment procedures**. Procedures performed by the auditor to obtain information for identifying and assessing the risks of material

LO 6 Define audit evidence and describe the purpose and types of audit procedures used to obtain audit evidence.

审计证据(audit evidence)
注册会计师为了得出审计结论、形成审计意见而获取的所有信息。充分性和适当性是审计证据的两个基本特征。

EXHIBIT **5.5** Management's Financial Statement Assertions in PCAOB Standards

Existence or Occurrence: Assertions about existence address whether assets and liabilities exist and assertions about occurrence address whether recorded transactions, such as sales transactions, have occurred.
Example: Management asserts that sales recorded in the income statement represent transactions in which the exchange of goods or services with customers for cash or other consideration had occurred.

Completeness: Assertions about completeness address whether all transactions and accounts that should be included in the financial statements are included.
Example: Management asserts that notes payable in the balance sheet include all such obligations of the organization.

Valuation or Allocation: Assertions about valuation or allocation address whether accounts have been included in the financial statements at appropriate amounts.
Example: Management asserts that trade accounts receivable included in the balance sheet are stated at net realizable value.

Rights and Obligations: Assertions about rights address whether assets are the rights of the organization, while assertions about obligations address whether liabilities are the obligations of the organization.
Example: Management asserts that amounts capitalized for leases in the balance sheet represent the cost of the entity's rights to leased property and that the corresponding lease liability represents an obligation of the entity.

Presentation and Disclosure: Assertions about presentation and disclosure address whether components of the financial statements are properly classified, described, and disclosed.
Example: Management asserts that obligations classified as long-term liabilities in the balance sheet will not mature within one year.

misstatement in the financial statements whether due to error or fraud. Risk assessment procedures by themselves do not provide sufficient appropriate evidence on which to base an audit opinion, but are used for purposes of planning the audit.

- **Tests of controls**. Audit procedures designed to evaluate the operating effectiveness of controls in preventing, or detecting and correcting, material misstatements, typically at the assertion level.
- **Substantive procedures**. Audit procedures designed to detect material misstatements in accounts which include tests of details and substantive analytical procedures.

The auditor has a responsibility to design and perform audit procedures to obtain **sufficient appropriate audit evidence** that supports the auditor's opinion. Auditors make decisions about the nature, timing, and extent of audit procedures to perform. The nature of an audit procedure refers to its purpose and its type. The purpose of an audit procedure determines whether it is a risk assessment procedure, a test of controls, or a substantive procedure. The types of audit procedures include inspection of documentation, inspection of assets, observation, external confirmation, recalculation, reperformance, analytical procedures, scanning, and inquiry. Exhibit 5.6 describes each of these types of procedures. Generally, each type of procedure may be used as a risk assessment procedure, a test of controls, or a substantive procedure, depending on the context in which it is applied by the auditor.

Timing of an audit procedure refers to when it is performed or the period or date to which the audit evidence applies. For example, procedures may be performed as of the client's year-end or at an interim date prior to the client's year-end. Extent of an audit procedure refers to the quantity to be performed (for example, a sample size or the number of observations of a control activity). The audit procedures that are performed during an audit are summarized in a document referred to as an **audit program**. In Chapter 6 we provide more detail on audit procedures and audit evidence.

EXHIBIT **5.6**	Types of Audit Procedures
Types of Audit Procedure	**Example**
Inspection of documentation	Examining a client document for evidence of authorization
Inspection of assets	Physically examining a client's equipment
Observation	Looking at a process or procedure, such as observing the client use of a restricted access area
External confirmation	Obtaining a direct written response to the auditor from a third party, such the client's customers, confirming the amount owed to the client
Recalculation	Checking the mathematical accuracy of a document or record, such as an inventory count sheet
Reperformance	Independently performing procedures or controls that were originally performed by the client, such as reperforming a bank reconciliation
Analytical procedures	Analyzing plausible relationships among both financial and nonfinancial data
Scanning	Performing a type of analytical procedure which involves reviewing accounting data to identify significant or unusual items, such as examining a credit balance in an account that typically has a debit balance
Inquiry	Seeking information of persons within or outside of the client organization, such as communicating with the CFO or general counsel about changes in accounting policy

Evidence Example: Substantive Audit Procedures to Obtain Evidence about Management Assertions The auditor's selection of audit procedures and evidence is based on the specific accounts and on the assertions being tested. Consider an audit of property, plant, and equipment (PPE) and the following valuation assertion implied in an organization's financial statement:

> The equipment shown on the financial statements is properly valued at cost, with applicable allowances for depreciation.

This assertion can be broken down into four major components:

- The valuation of new assets added this year
- The valuation of assets that were acquired in previous years
- The proper recording of depreciation
- Potential impairment of the existing assets

For illustration purposes, we focus on whether the current year's additions to equipment are properly valued. Audit procedures that would address this assertion include:

- *Auditing Additions to PPE through Inspection of Documentation*—Take a sample of all additions to property, plant, and equipment, verify the cost through vendor invoices, and determine that cost is accurately recorded. If there is a high risk that the valuation may be misstated, the auditor may choose to take a larger sample.
- *Assessing the Potential Impairment of the Asset Additions through Inquiry of Management and Inspection of Assets*—These procedures help the auditor determine if the assets should be written down to an impaired value. Current economic information and independent evidence as to the current market price of the assets can be used to corroborate management's statements.

Important elements in these audit procedures highlight the following:

- *Select a sample* of items to test. The auditor needs to take a representative sample because it is often too costly to examine all additions to PPE. The sample size could be increased in order to respond to a heightened risk of misstatement increases. Sampling is discussed further in Chapter 8.
- *Inspect documentary evidence* of cost. The auditor examines external, objective evidence of the amount paid and the nature of the equipment purchased, for example an invoice.
- *Inquire and corroborate with other procedures.* While the auditor will likely inquire of management to obtain some audit evidence, it is important that the auditor corroborate what management has said by obtaining complementary evidence, such as inspection of documentation or observation.

Audit Documentation

The auditor needs to prepare **audit documentation** that provides evidence that the audit was planned and performed in accordance with auditing standards. The terms *working papers* or *workpapers* are sometimes used to refer to audit documentation. The auditor should document the procedures performed, the audit evidence examined, and the conclusions reached with respect to relevant financial statement assertions. Auditing standards note that audit documentation serves other purposes, including:

- Assisting the engagement team in planning and performing the audit
- Assisting members of the engagement team responsible for supervising and reviewing the audit work
- Retaining a record of matters of continuing significance to future audits of the same organization

LO 7 Discuss the importance of audit documentation and provide examples.

- Enabling internal or external inspections of completed audits
- Assisting auditors in understanding the work performed in the prior year as an aid in planning and performing the current engagement

Examples of audit documentation include:

- Audit programs
- Analyses prepared by the client or the auditor
- Memorandums
- Summaries of significant findings or issues
- Letters of confirmation and representation
- Checklists
- Correspondence (including e-mail) concerning significant findings or issues

阶段1：做出客户接受和保留决策

LO 8 Identify audit activities in Phase I of the audit opinion formulation process.

Phase I Making Client Acceptance and Continuance Decisions

Phase I concerns client selection and continuance. No one requires auditors to perform audits for any organization that asks. Audit firms have procedures to help them ensure that they are not associated with clients where management integrity is in question or where an organization might otherwise present the audit firm with unnecessarily high risk (such as client financial failure or regulatory action against the client).

The auditor wants to accept audit engagements (whether for new or existing clients) only when the preconditions for an audit are present and when there is a common understanding of the terms of the engagement between the auditor and management and, when appropriate, those charged with governance. Generally, the preconditions for an audit include:

- *Management's use of an acceptable financial reporting framework.* Without an acceptable financial reporting framework, management does not have an appropriate basis for the preparation of the financial statements, and the auditor does not have suitable criteria for auditing the financial statements.
- *The agreement of management that it acknowledges and understands its responsibilities.* These responsibilities include the preparation and fair presentation of the financial statements, along with the design, implementation, and maintenance of internal control over financial reporting. (Refer to Exhibit 5.2 presented earlier.) Further, management needs to agree to provide the auditor with access to all relevant information, such as records, documentation, and so on, and unrestricted access to persons within the organization.

As highlighted in the *Auditing in Practice* feature "Accepting a New Audit Engagement," an additional procedure for new clients typically includes communication with the predecessor audit firm.

The agreed-upon terms of the audit engagement should be documented in an **audit engagement letter**. Items in the engagement letter typically include:

审计业务约定书
(audit engagement letter)
会计师事务所与被审计单位签订的，用以记录和确认审计业务的委托与受托关系、审计目标和范围、双方的责任以及报告的格式等事项的书面协议。

- The objective and scope of the audit of the financial statements
- The responsibilities of the auditor
- The responsibilities of management
- A statement that because of the inherent limitations of an audit, together with the inherent limitations of internal control, an unavoidable risk exists that some material misstatements may not be detected, even though the audit is properly planned and performed in accordance with relevant auditing standards
- Identification of the applicable financial reporting framework for the preparation of the financial statements

Accepting a New Audit Engagement

Before accepting a new audit client, the auditor should request that management authorizes the predecessor auditor to respond to the auditor's inquiries on issues that will assist the auditor in determining whether to accept the new client. If management refuses to authorize the predecessor auditor to respond, or limits the response, the auditor should inquire about the reasons and consider the implications in deciding whether to accept the engagement.

The communication with the predecessor auditor may be either written or oral, although obtaining the communication in writing is better. Matters addressed include:

- Information that might bear on the integrity of management

- Disagreements with management about accounting policies, auditing procedures, or other similarly significant matters
- Communications to those charged with governance regarding fraud and noncompliance with laws or regulations by the entity
- Communications to management and those charged with governance regarding significant deficiencies and material weaknesses in internal control
- The predecessor auditor's understanding about the reasons for the change of auditors

While U.S. auditing standards (AU-C 210; AU 325) require the auditor's communications with the predecessor auditors for an initial audit, international auditing standards (ISA 210) do not include this requirement.

- Reference to the expected form and content of any reports to be issued by the auditor and a statement about circumstances that may arise in which a report may differ from its expected form and content

阶段2：实施风险评估

LO 9 Identify audit activities in Phase II of the audit opinion formulation process.

Phase II Performing Risk Assessment

Once a client is accepted (or the audit firm decides to retain a continuing client), the auditor needs to thoroughly understand the client, with a focus on understanding the risks of material misstatement—due to either fraud or errors— in the financial statements and in related disclosures. For continuing clients, much of the information is available from the previous year's audit and can be updated for changes. For new clients, this process is more time-consuming. During Phase II, the auditor identifies the relevant risks and then determines the audit procedures needed to address those risks. Risk assessment procedures provide a basis for identifying and assessing risks of material misstatement at the financial statement and relevant assertion levels. Risk assessment procedures by themselves, however, do not provide sufficient appropriate audit evidence on which to base the audit opinion.

Identifying and Assessing Risks of Material Misstatement

Risk assessment underlies the entire audit process; identifying the risks of material misstatement is essential to planning an audit. A starting point for risk assessment is the identification of significant accounts, disclosures, and relevant assertions. These are the areas where the auditors will direct their risk assessment. Because the focus is on identifying material misstatements in the financial statements, the auditor establishes a materiality level for the financial statements overall and for specific accounts and disclosures. Materiality relates to the importance/significance of an amount, transaction, or discrepancy. Misstatements are material if they could reasonably be expected to influence the decisions of users made on the basis of the financial statements. Materiality considerations are the same for a financial statement audit and an integrated audit. The assessment of what is material is a matter of professional judgment; we discuss this concept further in Chapters 7 and 16.

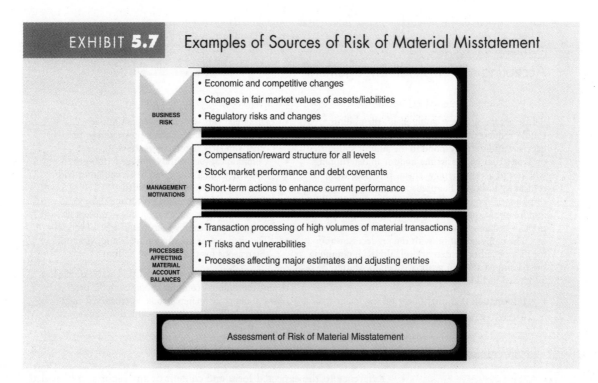

EXHIBIT **5.7**   Examples of Sources of Risk of Material Misstatement

BUSINESS RISK
• Economic and competitive changes
• Changes in fair market values of assets/liabilities
• Regulatory risks and changes

MANAGEMENT MOTIVATIONS
• Compensation/reward structure for all levels
• Stock market performance and debt covenants
• Short-term actions to enhance current performance

PROCESSES AFFECTING MATERIAL ACCOUNT BALANCES
• Transaction processing of high volumes of material transactions
• IT risks and vulnerabilities
• Processes affecting major estimates and adjusting entries

Assessment of Risk of Material Misstatement

注册会计师需要在财务报告层次和认定层次上评估客户的重大错报风险。财务报告层次的重大错报风险与财务报表整体广泛相关。而认定层次的重大错报风险则与特定的某类交易、账户余额、列报的认定相关。

Assessing risks of material misstatement begins during the client acceptance activities (Phase I) and continues into the risk assessment activities (Phase II). Exhibit 5.7 illustrates examples of sources of risk of material misstatement that the auditor should consider.

The auditor assesses the risk of material misstatement at both the financial statement level and the assertion level. Risks at the financial statement level could potentially affect many assertions. In looking at Exhibit 5.7, consider the presence of declining economic conditions and management pressure for good stock performance. These risks could affect multiple financial statement assertions, including the existence of sales, the valuation of receivables, and the completeness of expenses. At the assertion level, the auditor will consider both inherent and control risks. **Inherent risk** refers to the the susceptibility of an assertion about a class of transaction, account balance, or disclosure to a misstatement that could be material, either individually or when aggregated with other misstatements, before consideration of any related controls. For example, the valuation of the loan loss reserve for a financial institution will likely have a high level of inherent risk. **Control risk** refers to the risk that a misstatement that could occur in an assertion about a class of transaction, account balance, or disclosure and that could be material, either individually or when aggregated with other misstatements, will not be prevented, or detected and corrected, on a timely basis by the entity's internal control. For example, a small, non-profit client with few accounting personnel is likely to have a high level of control risk because of the lack of resources. Control risk is a function of the effectiveness of the design and operation of internal control. During Phase II, the auditor is focused on the design effectiveness of internal control.

Risk assessment procedures typically include:

• Inquiries of management and others within the entity who may have information to assist in identifying risks of material misstatement due to fraud or error
• Preliminary analytical procedures
• Observation (such as watching an organization's operations, facilities, or premises) and inspection of documentation (for example, going through business plans, internal control manuals, or management reports)

Controls to Address Fraud Risk

The PCAOB has identified the following as specific types of controls that the auditor should consider in evaluating whether or not an organization has sufficiently addressed fraud risk:

• Controls over significant, unusual transactions, particularly those that result in late or unusual journal entries

• Controls over journal entries and adjustments made in the period-end financial reporting process
• Controls over related-party transactions
• Controls related to significant management estimates
• Controls that mitigate incentives for, and pressures on, management to falsify or inappropriately manage financial results

Assessing Internal Control Design Effectiveness and Implementation An important aspect of risk assessment is obtaining an understanding of internal control over financial reporting. The quality of internal control directly affects the risk of material misstatement. The focus is on internal control design and implementation and includes entity-wide controls, transaction controls, and fraud-related controls. The *Auditing in Practice* feature "Controls to Address Fraud Risk" provides examples of fraud-related controls.

The auditor assesses control design effectiveness and implementation by determining whether the organization's controls, if they are operated as designed by persons possessing the necessary authority and competence, can reasonably prevent or detect material misstatements in the financial statements. This understanding will allow the auditor to make a preliminary control risk assessment. The auditor performs various types of procedures to assess design effectiveness, including inquiry of appropriate personnel, observation of the organization's operations, and inspection of relevant documentation. Auditors also perform walkthroughs, as discussed in Chapter 3, to evaluate design effectiveness and implementation. As described in the *Auditing in Practice* feature, "Documenting the Auditor's Understanding of an Organization's Internal Controls," the auditor should document the preliminary assessment of control design and the basis for that assessment.

Documenting the Auditor's Understanding of an Organization's Internal Controls

The auditor's documentation should clearly identify each important control and the auditor's assessment of the design and implementation of that control. The auditor may base the audit documentation on documentation prepared by the client. The assessment of design effectiveness and implementation is the basis for the auditor's preliminary control risk assessment. The documentation of the understanding of internal control is often captured using narratives and flowcharts that describe the control processes.

Some audit firms also use questionnaires to assist in identifying important areas where controls are expected. There is no one right approach; each audit firm chooses an approach that fits the nature of its technology, its clients, and its clients' risks. Once the overall internal control process has been initially documented, in subsequent years many audit firms focus only on changes in the system and the effectiveness of monitoring controls to signal potential breakdowns in the overall control design.

In some organizations (primarily public companies), management will have tested internal controls. The auditor considers how management tested the effectiveness of important controls, including who did the testing, the objectivity of the testing process, and the nature of samples taken for the testing (both representativeness and sample size). Further, the auditor needs to understand the approach management used for its conclusions on the effectiveness of internal control over financial reporting.

Based on obtaining an understanding through the various procedures and review of management's documentation, the auditor assesses control risk ranging from high (weak controls) to low (strong controls). Assessing control risk as high means the auditor does not have confidence that internal controls will prevent or detect material misstatements; assessing control risk as low has the opposite implication. This preliminary assessment, based on the auditor's understanding of the design and implementation of the controls, is important because it drives the planning for the rest of the audit. If control risk is assessed as high, the auditor cannot plan on relying on the controls to reduce substantive procedures for account balances. Therefore, the auditor will not perform tests of controls; instead, the auditor must plan for substantive procedures, with no reliance being placed on the client's internal controls. If control risk is assessed as low, the auditor will plan to test the operating effectiveness of those controls (see Phase III) in an effort to reduce substantive testing related to account balances. The *Auditing in Practice* feature "Weak Internal Control Design and Links to Substantive Audit Procedures" illustrates the linkage between control effectiveness and planned substantive audit procedures.

Additional Considerations for an Integrated Audit In an integrated audit, the risks of material misstatement of the financial statements are the same for both the audit of internal control over financial reporting and the audit of financial statements. The auditor's risk assessment procedures apply to both audits. The auditor uses a top-down approach to the audit of internal control over financial reporting to select the controls to test. A top-down approach begins at the financial statement level, with the auditor's

Weak Internal Control Design and Links to Substantive Audit Procedures

AUDITING IN PRACTICE

Scenario. The auditor finds that the client does not use prenumbered receiving slips to record the return of sales merchandise, nor does it have procedures to assure prompt recording of returned merchandise. To make things worse, sales returns have been high. The auditor is concerned that the overall control environment is weak and that management seems preoccupied with increasing earnings rather than accurate recording of returns.

Linkage to Substantive Audit Procedures. The auditor assesses internal control design as ineffective and makes a preliminary assessment of control risk as high. Accordingly, the auditor is not able to rely on controls when testing the balance of sales returns. Therefore, the auditor expands the substantive tests

for sales returns by (1) arranging to be on hand at the end of the year to observe the taking of physical inventory, observing items received during the inventory counting process, and the client's procedures for documenting receipts, (2) tracing receipts for items returned by customers to credit memos to determine if they are issued in the correct time period, (3) reviewing all credit memos issued shortly after year end to determine whether they are recorded in the correct time period, and (4) increasing the number of accounts receivable confirmations sent to the client's customers. All four of these procedures represent an expansion of tests beyond what would be required if the organization had effective internal controls over receiving returned goods.

understanding of the overall risks to internal control over financial reporting. The auditor then focuses on entity-wide controls and works down to significant accounts and disclosures and their relevant assertions. This approach directs the auditor's attention to accounts, disclosures, and assertions that present a reasonable possibility of material misstatement to the financial statements and related disclosures. The auditor selects for testing those controls that are designed to effectively address the assessed risk of misstatement to each relevant assertion.

Responding to Identified Risks of Material Misstatement

Once the auditor completes the risk assessment procedures, the next step is to determine the mix of tests of controls and substantive procedures for Phases III and IV of the audit opinion formulation process. The purpose of risk assessment procedures is to identify the risks of material misstatement, determine where misstatements in the financial statements may occur, and design the appropriate audit strategy (audit procedures) to respond to those risks and potential misstatements.

For a financial statement audit where the auditor wants to rely on controls as part of the basis for the audit opinion, the auditor designs a **controls reliance audit**—an audit that includes tests of controls and substantive procedures. For some audits, the auditor may determine that it is not efficient or effective to rely on the client's controls in forming the audit opinion. In those audits, the auditor designs a **substantive audit**—an audit that includes substantive procedures and does not include tests of controls. Within the same audit, the auditor can take different approaches across different cycles. For example, a controls reliance approach might be taken when auditing cash, but a substantive approach might be taken when auditing revenue.

如果注册会计师拟信赖被审计单位的控制并将其作为出具审计意见的基础，那么注册会计师应进行控制信赖审计。控制信赖审计包括控制测试和实质性程序。

In addition to selecting specific audit procedures to respond to identified risks, the auditor should consider the following overall responses to identified risks:

- Assembling an audit team that has the knowledge, skill, and ability needed to address the assessed risks of material misstatement
- Emphasizing to the audit team the need for professional skepticism
- Providing the level of supervision that is appropriate for the assessed risks of material misstatement
- Incorporating elements of unpredictability in the selection of audit procedures to be performed

An Analogy for Responding to Identified Risks of Material Misstatement   It can be helpful to view the response to identified risks of material misstatements as accumulating boxes of audit evidence. Two key considerations are the size of each evidence box and what type of evidence goes into each box. Accounts, disclosures, and assertions that have a higher level of identified risk of material misstatement would require larger boxes of evidence. Consider the three boxes in Panel A of Exhibit 5.8. An assertion with a low risk of material misstatement might require only enough evidence to fill Box A; an assertion with a high level of risk of material misstatement might require enough evidence to fill Box C; an assertion with a moderate level of risk of material misstatement might require enough evidence to fill Box B. There is not one right box size for every assertion. The appropriate size of the box will be based on the level of assessed risk of material misstatement.

The evidence that goes into each box will also vary. Consider an assertion where the auditor has assessed the risk of material misstatement as moderate. Again referring to Exhibit 5.8, the auditor needs to fill Box B in Panel A with audit evidence. Panel B illustrates alternative approaches that the auditor could use in filling that box. First, assume that the auditor has determined

EXHIBIT **5.8**   Responding to Identified Risks through Evidence Decisions

PANEL A: EXTENT OF EVIDENCE

Box A Low Risk	Box B Moderate Risk	Box C High Risk

Evidence Needs:

Low   Moderate   High

PANEL B: NATURE OF EVIDENCE

50% Tests of Controls	
50% Substantive Procedures	100% Substantive Procedures

Audit Approach:

Controls Reliance   Substantive

that the controls for that assertion are well designed. The auditor can fill the box with evidence from tests of controls and from substantive procedures (a controls reliance audit). For example, 50% of the evidence may come from tests of controls and 50% from substantive procedures. In contrast, assume that the auditor has determined that the controls related to that assertion are not well designed. The auditor should not obtain any evidence on operating effectiveness (why bother testing the operating effectiveness of a control that is poorly designed?), but instead should fill Box B with only evidence from substantive procedures (a substantive audit). That is, 100% of the evidence will come from substantive procedures. These same types of evidence decisions would also occur for assertions where the risk of material misstatement is high (Box C in Panel A of Exhibit 5.8) or low (Box A in Panel A of Exhibit 5.8)

Additional Considerations for an Integrated Audit In an integrated audit, the auditor should develop an audit strategy that includes tests of controls to accomplish the objectives of both audits. The auditor needs to obtain sufficient evidence related to operating effectiveness of controls to support the auditor's control risk assessments for purposes of the audit of financial statements and to support the auditor's opinion on internal control over financial reporting as of year-end.

Fraud Considerations The auditor should plan to perform tests of controls and substantive procedures that are specifically responsive to the assessed fraud risks. For example, when testing an account balance where there is a heightened risk of fraud, the auditor may decide to increase sample sizes or apply computer-assisted audit techniques to all items in an account. Further, the auditor should perform procedures related to the risk of management override of controls; such procedures include including examining journal entries (and other adjustments for evidence of possible material misstatement due to fraud), reviewing accounting estimates for biases that could result in material misstatement due to fraud), and evaluating the business rationale for significant unusual transactions.

Phase III Obtaining Evidence about Internal Control Operating Effectiveness

Phase III is relevant for integrated audits and for financial statement audits where the auditor wants to rely on controls as part of the evidence about the reasonableness of account balances and disclosures (in other words, a controls reliance audit). In an integrated audit, the auditor needs to opine on internal control effectiveness—including operating effectiveness—as of the client's year end. However, if the auditor wants to rely on controls as part of the audit evidence about account balances for the financial statement audit, the auditor needs to know whether controls were operating effectively throughout the year. To determine whether controls are operating effectively—at either year-end (for the internal control opinion) or throughout the year (for the financial statement opinion)—the auditor tests controls that are important to the conclusion about whether the organization's controls adequately address the risk of material misstatement. There is no need to test every control related to a relevant assertion; the auditor tests only those controls that are most important in reducing the risk.

In Phase II, the auditor performs procedures to assess the design effectiveness and implementation of controls. In Phase III, the auditor tests the operating effectiveness of controls, which is different from what was done in Phase II. However, as noted in the *Auditing in Practice* feature, "Risk Assessment Procedures and Tests of Operating Effectiveness of Controls," the risk assessment procedures might provide some evidence on the operating effectiveness of controls. The auditor tests the operating effectiveness of controls, determining whether the control is operating as designed and whether the person performing the control has the necessary authority and competence to perform the control effectively. In designing and performing tests of controls, the auditor should obtain more persuasive audit evidence as the reliance the auditor places on the effectiveness of a control increases.

阶段3：获取有关内部控制有效性的证据

LO 10 Identify audit activities in Phase III of the audit opinion formulation process.

Risk Assessment Procedures and Tests of Operating Effectivness of Controls

AUDITING IN PRACTICE

Although risk assessment procedures performed during Phase II may not have been specifically designed as tests of controls, they may still provide audit evidence about the operating effectiveness of the controls. In such cases, these procedures might serve as appropriate tests of controls. For example, the auditor's risk assessment procedures may include the following:

- Inquiring about management's use of budgets
- Inspecting documentation of management's comparison of monthly budgeted and actual expenses

- Inspecting reports pertaining to the investigation of variances between budgeted and actual amounts

These audit procedures provide knowledge about the design of the entity's budgeting policies and whether they have been implemented. However, these procedures also may provide audit evidence about the effectiveness of the operation of budgeting policies in preventing, or detecting and correcting, material misstatements in the classification of expenses. To the extent possible, the auditor should look for ways such as this to improve audit efficiency.

Selecting Controls to Test

The auditor selects controls that are important to the conclusion about whether the organization's controls adequately address the assessed risk of material misstatement for relevant assertions. The auditor selects both entity-wide and transaction controls for testing. The selection of control activities to be tested will depend, in part, on the results of testing the selected entity-wide controls. Effective entity-wide controls may reduce the number of control activities selected for testing. Overall, risks associated with significant accounts, disclosures, and their relevant assertions should lead to the identification of important controls that need to be tested.

In determining which controls to select for testing, the auditor should explicitly link controls and assertions. Exhibit 5.9 links the assertions of existence, completeness, and valuation to possible controls that the auditor may test.

Performing Tests of Controls

To obtain evidence about whether a control is operating effectively, the auditor directly tests the control in operation. The following tests of controls are presented in the order of their rigor, from least to most rigorous: inquiry, observation, inspection of relevant documentation, and reperformance of a control. Also note that inquiry alone does not provide sufficient evidence to support a conclusion about the effectiveness of a control. The type of audit procedure used varies with the process, the materiality of the account balance, and the control. For example, computerized edit controls built into a computer application could be tested by submitting test transactions. For manual controls, such as authorizations, the auditor might select a number of transactions to determine if there is documented evidence that proper authorization has taken place. For the reconciliation of shipments with recorded sales, the auditor could select a number of daily sales and review documentation to determine whether the reconciliations were performed appropriately. Or if a more rigorous test was needed because of the materiality of the account related to the reconciliation, the auditor may choose to reperform the reconciliation.

In selecting approaches to test control, there are several concepts that are important to consider. These concepts relate to testing various types of controls, including computerized controls, manual controls, controls over adjusting entries, and controls over accounting estimates. Exhibit 5.10 provides examples of important concepts and indicates possible tests of controls.

EXHIBIT 5.9	Linking Financial Statement Assertions and Selecting Controls to Test
Financial Statement Assertion	**Examples of Controls That Might Be Selected for Testing**
Existence/Occurrence	• Shipments recorded are reconciled with shipping documents daily. • Items cannot be recorded without underlying source documents and approvals.
Completeness	• Prenumbered shipping documents are used and reconciled with shipments recorded daily. • A list of cash receipts is developed when cash is collected and is reconciled with cash deposits and the debit to cash daily.
Valuation/Allocation	• Preauthorized sales prices are entered into the computer pricing table by authorized individuals. • Sales prices can be overridden only on the authorization of key management personnel. A record of overrides is documented and independently reviewed by management, internal audit, or other parties performing control analysis.

EXHIBIT **5.10**	Types of Controls and Examples of Concepts Affecting Control Testing

Types of Controls	Concepts Affecting Control Testing and Possible Tests of Controls
Computerized Controls	**Concept:** *Determine whether there have been changes to important computer applications during the year.* • Determine if there are changes in the computer program. If there are, test the integrity of the controls after the changes (inspection of relevant documentation and reperformance of control). • Consider submitting test transactions through the system to determine that it is working properly (reperformance of control). • Take a random sample of transactions and determine that (a) key controls are operating and (b) processing is complete (reperformance of control). • Review exception reports to determine that (a) proper exceptions are being noted and that (b) exceptions go to authorized personnel and there is adequate follow-up for proper processing (inspection of relevant documentation).
Manual Controls Authorizations Reconciliations Reviews for unusual transactions	**Concept:** *There should be documented evidence that a control is working. The auditor should take a sample of transactions to determine that there is evidence of the control's operation.* • Take a sample of transactions and examine evidence supporting that the controls are working. For example, review a document or a computer printout indicating proper approval (inspection of relevant documentation). • Take a sample of reconciliations to determine that (a) they were performed by an authorized person and that (b) they were performed properly (inspection of relevant documentation, re-performance of control). • Review documentation of selected transactions to determine whether they were properly authorized and recorded in the correct time period (inspection of relevant documentation). • Take a sample of reports that management uses to identify unusual transactions. Review to determine (a) that they are used regularly and that (b) unusual items are identified and investigated further (inspection of relevant documentation).
Controls over Adjusting Entries	**Concept:** *There should be documented evidence that there are controls over normal journal entries (such as depreciation) and that they are applied on a regular basis. All other adjusting entries should include documentation that spells out (a) the reason and support for the adjustment and (b) the authorization of the adjustment.* • Take a sample of adjusting entries and review to determine that (a) there is supporting documentation for the entry, (b) the entry is appropriate, (c) the entry is made to the correct accounts, and (d) the entry was properly authorized (inspection of relevant documentation). • Give special attention to significant entries made near year end (inquiry of management, inspection of relevant documentation).

Controls over Accounting Estimates	**Concept:** *There should be documented evidence regarding the estimate. Further, the auditor should determine that controls are sufficient to ensure that (a) the estimate is made based on accurate data, (b) the process of making the estimate is performed consistently, and (c) the model is updated for changing economic or business conditions. For example, estimates of a health care liability should be updated for changes in the trend of health care costs and required employee deductibles and co-pays.*
	
	• Review the process, noting that:
	
	   • All entries are properly authorized (inspection of relevant documentation).
	   • There are controls to ensure that estimates are updated for current market or economic conditions (inquiry of management and inspection of relevant documentation).
	   • There is evidence that data used to make the estimates come from reliable sources (inquiry of management and inspection of relevant documentation).

Example of Approaches to Testing Controls   As an example of alternative testing approaches, consider an important control in virtually every organization. That control is that the organization *requires a credit review and specific approval for all customers that are granted credit, and the amount of credit for any one company is limited by customer policy which is based on financial health of the customer, past collection experience, and current credit rating of the customer.* There are three approaches that an auditor might consider in testing the control:

1. Take a sample of customer orders and trace the customer orders through the system to determine whether (a) there was proper review of credit and (b) credit authorization or denial was proper.
2. Take a sample of recorded items (accounts receivable) and trace back to the credit approval process to determine that it was performed appropriately.
3. Use a computer audit program to read all accounts receivable and develop a print-out of all account balances that exceed their credit authorization.

Clearly, there are different costs and advantages associated with each of these three methods. The third method is dependent on proper input of the credit limits into the computer system. If there are no exceptions, the auditor could infer that the control is working even though the auditor did not directly test the control. This approach is cost-effective, but it requires an inference about the control and covers only the operation of the controls related to the current account balances. The first method is the most effective because it not only requires that the auditor look at documentary evidence, but that the auditor determine that the control did work effectively—it led to the correct conclusion, to either deny or provide credit. This method requires documentation of all credit applications and purchase orders and is based on audit sampling (not an examination of all transactions), whereas the third method was a 100% evaluation of each item currently recorded. The second method (sample from recorded items) can provide evidence on whether there was proper credit approval for all items that are presently recorded. However, it does not provide evidence as to whether other items should have been approved for credit, but had not been approved.

All three methods provide relevant evidence to the controls related to credit approval. Which one is the most appropriate? Auditors have to make decisions like this on every engagement. It seems trite to say "it depends," but the right choice does depend on the risk associated with the engagement, the auditor's experience with the credit level set by the organization (in other words, the credit approval level seems appropriate), the auditor's assessment of the control environment, the auditor's assessment of the quality of controls surrounding the computer applications, and the overall cost of the audit procedure. If other controls are good and risk is low, the auditor will most likely use the third approach because (a) it is the least costly and (b) it tests 100% of the recorded population. The auditor might reason further that the major risk is overstatement of accounts receivable through bad credit. The auditor is not very concerned about customers who were turned down for credit; on the other hand, management, in its assessment, might prefer to test the control by sampling from all customer orders because they do not want valid customers to be turned down for credit.

While the auditor has various options when testing controls, an important point is that the auditor has to perform tests of controls if the auditor plans to rely on those controls for the financial statement audit. Further, the auditor has to consider the results of tests of controls when designing substantive procedures. These points are highlighted in the *Auditing in Practice* feature, "The Need for Performing and Considering the Results of Tests of Controls."

The Need for Performing and Considering the Results of Tests of Controls

The PCAOB performs periodic inspections of audit firms that conduct audits of public companies. Following are excerpts from various firms' inspection reports, indicating that either the appropriate tests of controls had not been performed or the implications of the tests of controls were not reflected in the substantive procedures performed. A quality audit would require that such procedures be performed.

"The Firm failed to perform sufficient procedures to test the design and operating effectiveness of two important review controls on which it relied in evaluating internal controls over a number of significant accounts, including revenue, accounts receivable, inventory, and certain accruals."

"Further, for some Level 3 financial instruments, the Firm concluded that it did not need

to change the nature, timing, and extent of its procedures, notwithstanding certain issues that came to the Firm's attention regarding controls related to the valuation of these instruments."

"The Firm failed to sufficiently test controls over the issuer's revenue recognition for certain revenue arrangements, as the Firm focused its testing on verifying that the control activity had occurred without evaluating its effectiveness, including its level of precision. Further, in certain instances, the Firm performed procedures related to the issuer's transaction processes but failed to test controls over those processes."

Source: Public Company Accounting Oversight Board, 2010 Inspection Report of Deloitte & Touche LLP.

Testing the Operating Effectiveness of the Control Environment, Risk Assessment, Information and Communication, and Monitoring Components Auditors are often most comfortable testing control activities. However, research continues to show that fraud and other misstatements in financial statements are often caused by control deficiencies in other control components—especially deficiencies in the control environment. Similar to management's testing described in Chapter 3, the auditor tests the relevant principles of the components of control environment, risk assessment, information and communication and monitoring. For example, the auditor can test commitment to integrity and ethical values (Committee of Sponsoring Organizations, COSO, Principle 1) through first-hand knowledge of the client's attitude toward "pushing the accounting boundaries." As part of testing the risk assessment component, the auditor might test COSO Principle 6 ("The organization specifies objectives with sufficient clarity to enable the identification and assessment of risks relating to objectives."); this can be done by reviewing documentation of the organization's objectives. In testing the information and communication component, the auditor might inquire of personnel and review relevant documentation indicating how the organization internally communicates information, including objectives and responsibilities for internal control (COSO Principle 14). An important principle of the monitoring component is that the organization communicates internal control deficiencies in a timely manner to those parties responsible for taking corrective action (COSO Principle 17). Reviewing appropriate documentation and inquiring of appropriate personnel could provide audit evidence on the extent to which this principle is operating effectively.

Considering the Results of Tests of Controls

The auditor considers the results of the tests of controls before finalizing decisions about substantive procedures. For the financial statement audit, there are two potential outcomes, with associated alternative courses of action:

识别了控制缺陷否，评估这些缺陷
以确定是否需要对初步的控制风险
评估进行修正。同时，需要记录其
对实质性程序的影响。

1. If control deficiencies are identified, assess those deficiencies to determine whether the preliminary control risk assessment should be modified

(should control risk be increased from low to high?), and document the implications for substantive procedures (should the nature, timing, and extent of substantive procedures be modified?).

2. If no control deficiencies are identified, assess whether the preliminary control risk assessment is still appropriate, determine the extent that controls can provide evidence on the accuracy of account balances, and determine planned substantive audit procedures. The level of substantive testing in this situation will be less than what is required in circumstances where deficiencies in internal control were identified.

The results of the tests of controls will allow the auditor to determine how much assurance about the reliability of account balances can be obtained from the effective operation of controls. Using the previous analogy of accumulating a box of evidence, the auditor needs to determine if evidence from tests of operating effectiveness of controls can be used to partially fill the evidence box. Organizations with strong internal controls should require less substantive testing of account balances since more assurance is being obtained from internal controls. Within any audit, that level of assurance will vary across accounts, disclosures, and assertions. Even if the auditor can fill a box with a lot of evidence from tests of controls, for most accounts the auditor also needs to add some evidence from substantive procedures to the box.

Additional Considerations for an Integrated Audit   In an integrated audit, results of the tests of controls also have important implications for the auditor's opinion on internal control over financial reporting. The auditor evaluates the severity of each identified control deficiency to determine whether the deficiencies, individually or in combination, are material weaknesses. If any control deficiencies are severe enough to be considered material weaknesses, the auditor's report on internal control should describe the material weaknesses and include an opinion indicating that internal control over financial reporting is not effective.

执行实质性程序之前的审计决策小结

Summary of Audit Decisions Prior to Determining Substantive Procedures

The activities in Phases II and III of the audit opinion formulation process are important to determining the substantive procedures that need to be performed as a basis for the audit opinion on the financial statements.

Exhibit 5.11 provides a summary overview of important audit activities and decisions leading up to the performance of substantive procedures. The process begins with the identification of significant account balances and disclosures and their relevant assertions. For most organizations, the significant accounts and disclosures are obvious and include accounts such as revenue, cost of goods sold, inventory, receivables, and accounts payable. As part of identifying significant accounts and disclosures and their relevant assertions, the auditor identifies the types of risk that could cause a material misstatement to occur. The auditor should understand the controls that the client has implemented to address those risks of potential material misstatement. If the auditor plans to rely on those controls, the auditor should test their operating effectiveness. The results of these tests will influence the planned substantive procedures.

As an example, assume the auditor determines that a mid-sized public company has risk of material misstatement because the controller is not competent in addressing complex accounting issues. As a matter of policy, the company decided to mitigate the risks by (a) not engaging in complex business transactions and by (b) minimizing the percentage of management compensation that is directly attributed to reported profit. The auditor

EXHIBIT **5.11** Overview of Audit Decisions Leading up to Decisions about Substantive Procedures for the Financial Statement Audit

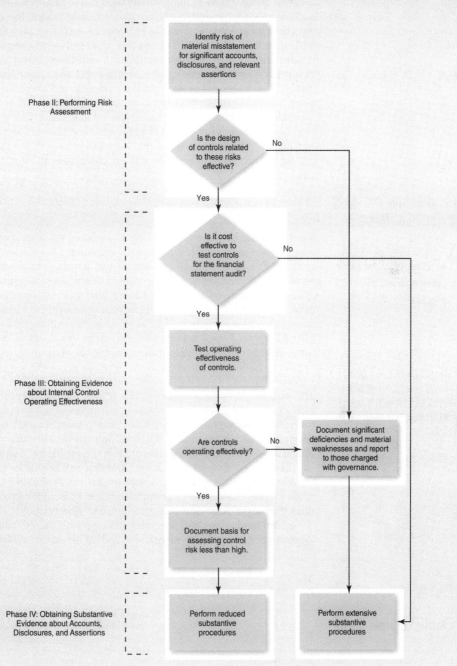

further reviews the revenue accounting process and determines that there are control activities designed to (a) prevent unauthorized transactions, (b) assure that revenue is recorded only when earned, and (c) require that all unusual contracts be reviewed and approved by the CEO. Further, because there is a risk of management override, the controller develops a list of unusual contracts to be reviewed with the chair of the audit committee and the lead director. Thus, while there is a risk of material misstatement, the controls are designed to mitigate the risks to the financial statements. If the auditor assesses the design of these controls as effective, the auditor should test their operating effectiveness. However, even if the controls are designed and operating effectively, the auditor may still have concerns about the residual risk of misstatements associated with revenue recognition because that process is most prone to misstatement related to poor accounting judgments. The auditor may respond by planning and performing more, and more rigorous, substantive procedures for revenue and receivables. For example, the auditor might extensively review and follow up on unusual transactions near year end and might examine unusual sales contracts as part of the substantive tests of the account balance. The auditor may also choose to increase the sample size of confirmations sent to the client's customers.

阶段4：获取与账户、披露和认定相关的实质性证据

[LO 11] Identify audit activities in Phase IV of the audit opinion formulation process.

不管评估的控制风险水平如何，注册会计师均需要对每一个重要账户和披露的相关认定实施实质性程序。这些程序包括实质性分析程序和账户余额的细节测试。

Phase IV Obtaining Substantive Evidence about Accounts, Disclosures, and Assertions

Much of what most people think of as auditing, the testing of account balances, occurs in Phase IV. As illustrated in Exhibit 5.11, the information gathered in Phases II and III influences the nature, extent, and timing of substantive procedures to be performed. The auditor plans substantive procedures of account balances (substantive analytical procedures and tests of details) based on the potential for material misstatement, including the effectiveness of internal controls. As described in the *Auditing in Practice* feature, "Dual-Purpose Tests," some audit efficiencies can result if the auditor performs substantive procedures at the same time as performing tests of controls.

Performing Substantive Procedures

The auditor performs substantive procedures for the relevant assertions of each significant account and disclosure, regardless of the assessed level of control risk. These procedures can include both substantive analytical procedures and tests of details of account balances. Substantive analytical procedures are optional, whereas tests of details would be necessary for significant accounts and disclosures. As indicated in the *Auditing in Practice* feature, "Not Performing Sufficient Appropriate Substantive Audit Procedures Leads To Low Audit Quality," a failure to perform sufficient substantive procedures is considered an audit deficiency, indicative of a low quality audit.

In determining appropriate substantive procedures, the auditor considers (a) the source of potential misstatement and (b) the extent and type of potential

---

Dual-Purpose Tests

AUDITING IN PRACTICE

In some situations, the auditor might perform a substantive procedure concurrently with a test of a control, if both are relevant to that assertion; this is called a **dual-purpose test**. In those situations, the auditor should design the dual-purpose test to achieve the objectives of both the test of the control and the substantive procedure. Also, when performing a dual-purpose test, the auditor should evaluate the results of the test in forming conclusions about both the assertion and the effectiveness of the control being tested. Dual purpose testing is an efficient way to perform an audit.

Not Performing Sufficient Appropriate Substantive Audit Procedures Leads To Low Audit Quality

The PCAOB performs periodic inspections of audit firms that conduct audits of public companies. Following are excerpts from various firms' inspection reports indicating that sufficient appropriate substantive audit procedures had not been performed. A quality audit requires that such procedures be performed.

"The Firm failed to perform sufficient substantive procedures to test a number of significant accounts, including revenue, accounts receivable, inventory, and certain accruals ..."

"The Firm failed to review contracts or perform other substantive procedures, beyond inquiry of management, to test the completeness of deferred sales and the completeness and accuracy of adjustments to revenue for promotional and rebate allowances."

"The Firm failed to sufficiently test the valuation of accounts receivable and net revenue."

"The Firm failed to perform sufficient procedures to test the issuer's evaluation of possible other-than-temporary impairment ('OTTI') of its securities. Specifically, the Firm failed to test whether the issuer had subjected to an evaluation of OTTI all securities that should have been subjected to such an evaluation and failed to test the assumptions and calculations used in this evaluation."

"In this audit, the Firm failed to perform sufficient procedures to evaluate the reasonableness of a significant assumption management used to calculate the gain on the sale of a business."

misstatement. This process can be illustrated by looking at the typical entries into accounts receivable, including the related allowance account, as follows:

Accounts Receivable

Previous Balance	Cash Receipts
Revenue (sales)	Write-Offs
Adjustments	Adjustments

Allowance for Uncollectible Accounts

Write-Offs	Previous Balance
	Current Provision

Note that multiple processes affect the account balances. Some of the processes contain subjectivity and are considered high risk—for example, determining how much of a receivable balance will ultimately be uncollectible. The following processes affect the accounts receivable balance:

- *Revenue*—The processing of normal transactions is usually computerized with consistent controls built into the process. However, because of recurring evidence that companies who want to boost reported sales and/or earnings often do so by overriding controls related to the recording of revenue, the SEC has designated revenue recognition as high risk, requiring the auditor to do some direct tests of account balances, including receivables. These problematic overrides often occur in the nature of special contracts or unusual shipments near the end of the year.
- *Cash Receipts*—The processing of cash receipts is usually automated with implementation of consistent controls. If an organization has good segregation of duties, the likelihood of misstatement is relatively small.

- *Current Provision for Uncollectible Accounts*—Most companies rely heavily on previous experience in making these estimates. Recent SEC cases indicate that the allowance is often subject to misstatements based on (a) inaccurate or nonrelevant data fed into the model and (b) motivation of management to meet earnings goals and therefore allowing subjectivity and bias to enter into the estimate.
- *Write-Offs*—The determination of when to write off account balances is subjective.
- *Adjustments*—Adjustments, other than those noted above, should be rare. If there are significant adjustments, the auditor should test the process or the adjustments to determine the correct balance.

Similar analyses will be made for other related accounts and will incorporate the following concepts:

- Assertions affected by highly subjective estimates usually require direct tests of the account balances.
- Nonstandard and large adjusting entries should be reviewed and tested using appropriate substantive procedures.
- The size of the account (materiality) influences, but does not totally dictate, the substantive procedures that should be performed.
- The extent and results of control testing performed by management, as well as the control testing performed by the auditor, will influence the substantive procedures of the account balance to be performed.
- The evidence the auditor has from risk assessment procedures and tests of controls influences the substantive procedures to be performed.
- The existence of other corroborating tests of the account balance, such as the knowledge gained from testing related accounts, affects substantive procedures to be performed.

The effects of some of these evidence factors on substantive procedures are summarized in Exhibit 5.12.

While performing substantive procedures, the auditor may identify misstatements—both material and immaterial— in the financial statements. The auditor accumulates a list of any identified misstatements for consideration prior to determining the appropriate audit opinion to issue.

Example: Effect of Nature of Misstatements on Audit Procedures
Ultimately, the auditor considers which account balances might be misstated and how they might be misstated. We demonstrate the audit process using the accounts receivable example. Assume the following scenario. Consistent with the relevant professional guidance, the auditor has assessed revenue to be high risk, even though management has concluded that internal controls over transactions processing are effective. A preliminary analytical review of the last quarter (conducted as part of the risk assessment procedures) led to the identification

---

EXHIBIT **5.12**   Factors Affecting Substantive Procedures to be Performed

Factor	If Auditor Assessment is:	Effect on Extent/Nature of Substantive Procedures
Subjectivity of accounting process	High	More / more rigorous
Materiality of account balance	High	More / more rigorous
Effectiveness of internal control as assessed by management and the auditor	Internal controls are effective	Less / less rigorous

of a large number of sales with nonstandard contractual terms. After reading a sample of the sales contracts and testing controls, the auditor concludes that there is an unacceptable level of residual risk in the revenue account. The auditor identified a number of ways in which the account could be misstated. For example, sales might:

- Be recorded in the wrong period
- Contain unusual rights-of-return provisions that have not been accounted for correctly
- Contain terms that are more consistent with a consignment rather than a sale
- Be concentrated in a very few customers, many of whom are international customers and may have different credit risks than most other customers

Given the identified risks, the auditor decides to expand substantive audit procedures of the recorded transactions that have unusual sales terms and focus on the existence and valuation assertions. The auditor has decided not to perform any substantive analytical procedures; the auditor will only perform substantive tests of details. In order to bring the residual risk to an acceptable level, the auditor gathers substantive evidence on the revenue (and receivables) associated with the unusual contracts and identifies sales that have these special terms. In testing receivables, the auditor decides to concentrate accounts receivable tests on a combination of large accounts, plus all of those that have unusual sales terms. Confirmations will be sent to both of those groups, with follow-up where confirmations are not returned, or where the auditor might suspect the validity of the contract, the customer, or the possibility of "side agreements" affecting the contracts.

Phase V Completing the Audit and Making Reporting Decisions

阶段5：完成审计工作和做出报告决策

LO 12 Identify audit activities in Phase V of the audit opinion formulation process.

In Phase V, the auditor (a) completes various review and communication activities and (b) makes a decision about what type(s) of opinion(s) should be issued. Examples of review and communication activities include assessing detected misstatements and identified control deficiencies, reviewing the adequacy of financial statement disclosures, performing final analytical review procedures, communicating with the audit committee and management about identified control deficiencies, and performing an engagement quality review.

After completing the required review and communication activities, the auditor then decides on the appropriate opinion(s) to issue. In an integrated audit, the auditor issues an opinion on both the financial statements and internal control. The opinions can be issued in one report or in two separate reports. However, if separate reports are issued, each report must refer to the other. In Chapter 1 we presented Ford's combined audit report, which included an unqualified opinion on the financial statements and an unqualified opinion on internal controls. If the auditor has reservations about the fair presentation of the financial statements, the audit opinion on the financial statements would be modified and expanded to explain the nature of the auditor's reservations. If the auditor has reservations about the effectiveness of the client's internal controls, the auditor would issue an adverse opinion on internal controls. Exhibit 5.13 provides an example of an audit report with an unqualified opinion on the financial statements and an adverse opinion on internal control. Important aspects of Exhibit 5.13 related to the opinion on internal controls include the following:

- The report describes the materials weaknesses, but does not discuss any actions being taken by management to remediate the problems.
- The report does not discuss whether the control weaknesses were first identified by management or by the auditor.
- The report recognizes the integrated nature of the audit in that the auditors considered the identified material weaknesses when planning the financial statement audit.

EXHIBIT **5.13**   Example of Adverse Opinion on Internal Control and Unqualified Opinion on the Financial Statements (bold emphasis added in report)

REPORT OF INDEPENDENT REGISTERED PUBLIC ACCOUNTING FIRM

To the Board of Directors and Stockholders of Powell Industries, Inc.:

In our opinion, **the consolidated financial statements listed in the accompanying index present fairly**, in all material respects, the financial position of Powell Industries, Inc. and its subsidiaries at September 30, 2011 and 2010, and the results of their operations and their cash flows for each of the three years in the period ended September 30, 2011 in conformity with accounting principles generally accepted in the United States of America. Also, in our opinion, the Company **did not maintain**, in all material respects, **effective internal control over financial reporting** as of September 30, 2011, based on criteria established in Internal Control—Integrated Framework issued by the Committee of Sponsoring Organizations of the Treadway Commission (COSO) because **material weaknesses in internal control over financial reporting** related to the **financial close and reporting process, the revenue recognition process for long-term construction projects, the cost accumulation process, and the revenue and accounts receivable process for service contracts**, existed as of that date. A material weakness is a deficiency, or a combination of deficiencies, in internal control over financial reporting, such that there is a reasonable possibility that a material misstatement of the annual or interim financial statements will not be prevented or detected on a timely basis. The material weaknesses referred to above are described in Management's Report on Internal Control Over Financial Reporting under Item 9A. **We considered these material weaknesses in determining the nature, timing, and extent of audit tests applied in our audit of the fiscal year 2011 consolidated financial statements**, and our opinion regarding the effectiveness of the Company's internal control over financial reporting does not affect our opinion on those consolidated financial statements. The Company's management is responsible for these financial statements, for maintaining effective internal control over financial reporting and for its assessment of the effectiveness of internal control over financial reporting included in management's report referred to above. Our responsibility is to express opinions on these financial statements and on the Company's internal control over financial reporting based on our integrated audits. We conducted our audits in accordance with the standards of the Public Company Accounting Oversight Board (United States). Those standards require that we plan and perform the audits to obtain reasonable assurance about whether the financial statements are free of material misstatement and whether effective internal control over financial reporting was maintained in all material respects. Our audits of the financial statements included examining, on a test basis, evidence supporting the amounts and disclosures in the financial statements, assessing the accounting principles used and significant estimates made by management, and evaluating the overall financial statement presentation. Our audit of internal control over financial reporting included obtaining an understanding of internal control over financial reporting, assessing the risk that a material weakness exists, and testing and evaluating the design and operating effectiveness of internal control based on the assessed risk. Our audits also included performing such other procedures as we considered necessary in the circumstances. We believe that our audits provide a reasonable basis for our opinions.

A company's internal control over financial reporting is a process designed to provide reasonable assurance regarding the reliability of financial reporting and the preparation of financial statements for external purposes in accordance with generally accepted accounting principles. A company's internal control over financial reporting includes those policies and procedures that (i) pertain to the maintenance of records that, in reasonable detail, accurately and fairly reflect the transactions and dispositions of the assets of the company; (ii) provide reasonable assurance that transactions are recorded as necessary to permit preparation of financial statements in accordance with generally accepted accounting principles, and that receipts and expenditures of the company are being made only in accordance with authorizations of management and directors of the company; and (iii) provide reasonable assurance regarding prevention or timely detection of unauthorized acquisition, use, or disposition of the company's assets that could have a material effect on the financial statements.

Because of its inherent limitations, internal control over financial reporting may not prevent or detect misstatements. Also, projections of any evaluation of effectiveness to future periods are subject to the risk that controls may become inadequate because of changes in conditions, or that the degree of compliance with the policies or procedures may deteriorate.

PricewaterhouseCoopers LLP

Houston, Texas

December 12, 2011

Audit Example: Assessing Control Design Effectiveness, Implementation, and Operating Effectiveness

To illustrate the concepts related to internal control introduced in this chapter, we provide an abbreviated example of an integrated audit focusing on cost of goods sold, inventory, and accounts payable. We assume that the organization purchases and distributes products; in other words, the organization is not a manufacturer, but it does hold a material amount of inventory. We focus our example on the purchasing cycle and significant accounts of Accounts Payable, Inventory, and Expenses.

Management Assessment of Controls

Management has identified the significant accounts and relevant assertions in the process of procuring goods and recording the related accounts payable and inventory. After selecting and testing controls designed to mitigate risk of misstatement in these accounts, management identifies the following control deficiencies:

- *Segregation of duties:* At one location, the controls are not well designed, as there is not proper segregation of duties. However, the location is very small, accounting for less than 1% of purchases.
- *Lack of approval:* At a second location that handles 62% of the organization's purchases, management found that approximately 17% of the purchase orders did not contain proper approval. The reason for the lack of approval was the rush to procure material in a timely fashion to meet a contract requirement. This represents an operating deficiency.

In deciding whether to categorize a deficiency as a significant deficiency or material weakness, management considers the following factors:

- The risk that is being mitigated and whether other controls operate effectively to mitigate the risk of material misstatement
- The materiality of the related account balances
- The nature of the deficiency
- The volume of transactions affected
- The subjectivity of the account balance that is subject to the control
- The rate at which the control fails to operate

Management concludes that the first deficiency (related to segregation of duties) did not rise to the level of either a significant deficiency or a material weakness. However, management decides to use this deficiency as a motivation to centralize purchases at headquarters.

The second deficiency (related to lack of approval) is more of a problem. Management determines this is a significant deficiency based on the following rationale:

- It is a major departure from an approved process.
- It could lead to the purchase of unauthorized goods.
- The unauthorized goods could lead to either (a) inferior products or (b) potential obsolescence.
- Those making the purchases could cause them to be shipped elsewhere (fraudulently) and could lead to a material misstatement in the financial statements.

Management determines that other controls are in place that test for inferior products and obsolescence, and that cycle counting of inventory would discover goods that are shipped to a different location. Accordingly, management believes that because of these controls, any potential misstatements in the financial statements would not be material. Management tests these controls and determines that they are operating effectively. If these

审计实例：评估控制设计和执行的有效性

LO 13 Apply the concepts related to the auditor's assessment of internal control design effectiveness, implementation, and operating effectiveness.

管理层对控制的评估

other controls were not in place and operating effectively, then management would have assessed the control deficiency as a material weakness.

注册会计师对控制的评估 ## Auditor Assessment of Controls

After determining significant accounts and relevant assertions, the auditor reviews management's documentation of its internal control and management's evaluation and findings related to internal control effectiveness. The auditor had previously reviewed and tested the control environment and other entity-wide controls and had evaluated them as effective. The auditor then determined that the following were the important controls in this process (for discussion purposes, we will again concentrate on the purchasing process and assume that the auditor did not find any material weaknesses in the other processes):

- Only authorized goods are purchased from authorized vendors.
- Purchase prices are negotiated by contract or from bids.
- All purchases are delivered to the organization and received by a separate receiving department.
- All purchases are recorded in a timely fashion and are appropriately classified.
- Payments are made only for goods that are received.
- Payments are made consistent with the purchase orders or contracts.
- Payments are made in a timely fashion.

The auditor gathers evidence on the operating effectiveness of these controls as of the client's year end for the opinion on internal control effectiveness and on operating effectiveness throughout the year for the financial statement audit. Because much of the process is computerized, the auditor performs computer security tests to assure that access controls are working properly and there is adequate control over program changes. The auditor determines that those controls are effective.

The auditor takes a sample of fifty purchase orders to examine whether purchases are authorized and processed properly. The auditor's sample size is influenced by previous information about the operation of the control. Although management had also taken a random sample of purchases and tested the operating effectiveness, the auditor needs to independently determine that the controls are working (or not working). The sample is randomly chosen and the auditor traces the transactions through the system to determine that the objectives identified above are addressed by controls.

The auditor's testing of controls identified the same two deficiencies identified by management. Management viewed the deficiency related to lack of approval as a *significant deficiency* because (a) the organization has a good ethical climate and (b) management's tests confirmed that all goods were delivered to the organization. The auditor's tentative conclusion is that this deficiency is a *material weakness* because:

- The location was responsible for ordering 62% of all of the organization's products.
- Management's tests showed a failure rate of over 17%.

The fact that all the goods were delivered to the organization is important and a testament to the ethical culture of the organization. However, not all individuals are ethical; someone with a lower commitment to ethical behavior could be in the purchasing position. Stated another way, a material weakness in internal control can exist even if there are no errors in processing and no misstatements in the current period. The potential for misstatement is high because the auditor believes that existing controls do not mitigate the risk of material misstatement.

More specifically, the auditor notes the following related to the auditor's tests of controls:

- One of the fifty purchases was made from an unauthorized vendor. Investigation reveals that the vendor was subsequently authorized and it was a timing problem; that is, the vendor should have been authorized earlier.
- Seven of the fifty did not have proper authorization, corroborating the earlier finding by management.
- Three of the fifty purchases were paid even though there was no receiving report.
- All of the other controls were found to work properly.

The auditor is concerned that the system allowed a purchase to be made before the vendor was authorized. The auditor's analysis is focused primarily on the risks that may be caused by unauthorized purchases. The auditor believes that unauthorized purchases could lead to a material misstatement of inventory; that is, goods were ordered and paid for, with no proof that they were actually received, and may have been delivered elsewhere. Based on this concern, the auditor decides that the deficiency related to lack of approval warrants a material weakness designation. Using this analysis, the auditor determines the following implications for substantive procedures in the financial statement audit:

- The auditor will do limited testing of inventory quantities at year end, primarily through random tests of the perpetual inventory system.
- The auditor will assess the year-end inventory for potential obsolescence by looking at industry trends and recent prices within the firm and by using audit software to analyze the aging of inventory.
- The auditor will continue to examine all adjusting entries at the end of the year to determine whether there are unusual entries to inventory and related accounts.

SUMMARY AND NEXT STEPS

This chapter has presented a detailed overview of the activities you will be performing throughout the audit opinion formulation process. These activities are based on guidance provided in the professional auditing standards. Adhering to the relevant auditing standards and performing the required activities in a professional manner are important to audit quality. Most of what occurs during the audit opinion formulation process is directed towards obtaining evidence to support the audit opinion(s) that will be issued. The next chapter provides you with additional discussion on important aspects of audit evidence.

SIGNIFICANT TERMS

Accounting cycle Recording and processing transactions that affect a group of related accounts. The cycle begins when a transaction occurs and ends when it is recorded in the financial statements.

Audit documentation The record of audit procedures performed, relevant audit evidence obtained, and conclusions the auditor reached (terms such as *working papers* or *workpapers* are also sometimes used).

Audit engagement letter A document that specifies the responsibilities of both the client and the auditor.

Audit evidence Information used by the auditor in arriving at the conclusions on which the auditor's opinion is based.

Appropriate audit evidence The measure of the quality of audit evidence (that is, its relevance and reliability in providing support for the conclusions on which the auditor's opinion is based).

Audit procedures Procedures designed to obtain audit evidence to support the audit opinion(s). Three categories of procedures include risk assessment procedures, tests of controls, and substantive procedures (including substantive analytical procedures and tests of details).

Audit program An audit document that lists the audit procedures to be followed in gathering audit evidence and helps those in charge of the audit to monitor the progress and supervise the work.

Control risk The risk that a misstatement due to error or fraud that could occur in an assertion and that could be material, individually or in combination with other misstatements, will not be prevented or detected on a timely basis by the organization's internal control. Control risk is a function of the effectiveness of the design and operation of internal control.

Controls reliance audit An audit that includes tests of controls and substantive procedures.

Dual-purpose test A substantive test and a related test of a relevant control that are performed concurrently, for example a substantive test of sales transactions performed concurrently with a test of controls over those transactions.

Inherent risk The susceptibility of an assertion to a misstatement, due to error or fraud, that could be material, individually or in combination with other misstatements, before consideration of any related controls.

Risk assessment procedure A procedure performed by the auditor to obtain information for identifying and assessing the risks of material misstatement in the financial statements whether due to error or fraud. Risk assessment procedures by themselves do not provide sufficient appropriate evidence on which to base an audit opinion, but are used for purposes of planning the audit.

Substantive audit An audit that includes substantive procedures and does not include tests of controls.

Substantive procedure An audit procedure designed to detect material misstatements at the assertion level. Substantive procedures comprise tests of details and substantive analytical procedures.

Sufficient audit evidence The measure of the quantity of audit evidence.

Test of controls An audit procedure designed to evaluate the operating effectiveness of controls in preventing, or detecting and correcting, material misstatements, typically at the assertion level.

TRUE-FALSE QUESTIONS

5-1 `LO 1` Auditors of U.S. public companies should follow the PCAOB's auditing standards.

5-2 `LO 1` There is not much commonality among the auditing standards set by the PCAOB, AICPA, and IAASB.

5-3 `LO 2` The ten standards underlying the PCAOB's auditing standards fall within four different categories.

5-4 `LO 2` The purpose of an audit is to enhance the degree of confidence that users can place on the financial statements.

5-5 `LO 3` As a precondition to applying the audit opinion formulation process, the auditor needs to understand the client's responsibilities for internal control over financial reporting and the financial statements.

5-6 `LO 3` The audit opinion formulation is described as consisting of five phases.

5-7 `LO 4` The cycle approach to auditing provides a way for breaking the audit up into manageable components.

5-8 `LO 4` Within a particular cycle, the auditor focuses on the flow of transactions within that cycle, including how transactions are initiated, authorized, recorded, and reported.

5-9 `LO 5` The completeness assertion is typically the more relevant assertion for assets.

5-10 `LO 5` Within each cycle, the audit is designed to test management assertions.

5-11 `LO 6` Risk assessment procedures alone provide sufficient appropriate audit evidence on which to base an audit opinion.

5-12 `LO 6` The auditor's selection of audit procedures depends on the accounts and assertions being tested.

5-13 `LO 7` Auditors are encouraged, but not required, to prepare audit documentation.

5-14 `LO 7` Audit checklists and audit programs are examples of audit documentation.

5-15 `LO 8` U.S. auditing standards require that an auditor communicate with a predecessor auditor for an initial audit engagement.

5-16 `LO 8` The agreed-upon terms of an audit engagement should be documented in an audit program.

5-17 `LO 9` During risk assessment, the auditor is focused on understanding the risks of all misstatements in the financial statements and related disclosures.

5-18 `LO 9` The auditor assesses the risk of material misstatement at only the assertion level.

5-19 `LO 10` The auditor is expected to obtain evidence about the operating effectiveness of internal control on all audits.

5-20 `LO 10` When testing controls, the auditor tests only transaction controls.

5-21 `LO 11` The auditor is expected to perform substantive procedures for each relevant assertion of each significant account and disclosure.

5-22 `LO 11` Substantive procedures include substantive analytical procedures and tests of details.

5-23 `LO 12` Once the auditor completes the substantive procedures in Phase IV, the auditor is in a position to issue the audit opinion.

5-24 [LO 12] If the auditor issues an opinion on the client's internal controls and the client's financial statements, the auditor is required to issue two separate reports.

5-25 [LO 13] In an integrated audit, the auditor reviews management's documentation of internal control and management's evaluation and findings related to internal control effectiveness.

5-26 [LO 13] The results of the auditor's tests of controls will likely have implications for the substantive procedures the auditor will perform.

MULTIPLE-CHOICE QUESTIONS

5-27 [LO 1] Which of the following statements is correct regarding the setting of auditing standards in the U.S.?
a. The AICPA is responsible for the setting auditing standards for audits of nonpublic entities.
b. The PCAOB is responsible for setting auditing standards for audits of public companies.
c. The AICPA is responsible for setting auditing standards for audits of both public and nonpublic entities.
d. The SEC sets auditing standards for auditors of public and nonpublic entities.
e. Both (a) and (b) are correct.

5-28 [LO 1] The following describes a situation in which an auditor has to determine the most appropriate standards to follow. The audited company is headquartered in Paris but has substantial operations within the United States (60% of all operations) and has securities registered with the SEC and is traded on the NYSE. The company uses International Financial Reporting Standards (IFRS) for its accounting framework. What would be the most appropriate set of auditing standards to follow?
a. PCAOB.
b. Either PCAOB or AICPA.
c. Either IAASB or AICPA.
d. Only the AICPA standards would be appropriate.

5-29 [LO 2] Which of the following is not required as part of the field-work standards?
a. An audit should be properly planned and supervised.
b. Auditors should develop an understanding of the client's controls as an important prerequisite to developing specific audit tests.
c. Auditors should obtain sufficient appropriate audit evidence by performing audit procedures to provide a reasonable basis for the audit opinion being provided.
d. All of the above are required by the fieldwork standards.

5-30 [LO 2] Which of the following is included as part of the AICPA's principles governing an audit?
a. Auditors need to obtain a high level of assurance that the financial statements are free of all misstatements.
b. An audit has inherent limitations such that auditor cannot provide absolute assurance about whether the financial statements are free of misstatement.
c. Auditors need to maintain professional skepticism only on audits where there is a high risk of material misstatement.
d. All of the above are included as part of the AICPA's principles governing an audit.

5-31 [LO 3] Which of the following statements is true about the audit opinion formulation process presented in this chapter?
a. The audit opinion formulation process is significantly different for the financial statement only audit and the integrated audit.
b. The audit opinion formulation process is based on the premise that management has responsibility to prepare the financial statements and maintain internal control over financial reporting.
c. The audit opinion formulation process is comprised of seven phases.
d. All of the above are true statements regarding the audit opinion formulation process.

5-32 [LO 3] Which of the following activities is not part of the activities within the audit opinion formulation process?
a. The auditor develops a common understanding of the audit engagement with the client.
b. The auditor determines the appropriate nonaudit consulting services to provide to the client.
c. The auditor identifies and assesses risks of material misstatements and then responds to those identified risks.
d. The auditor determines the appropriate audit opinion(s) to issue.

5-33 [LO 4] Which of the following is a reason that the auditor uses an accounting cycle approach when performing an audit?
a. The accounting cycle approach allows the auditor to focus exclusively on either the balance sheet or income statement.
b. COSO internal control components are based on the accounting cycles.
c. The accounting cycles provide a convenient way to break the audit up into manageable pieces.
d. The auditor needs to be able to provide an opinion related to each accounting cycle.

5-34 [LO 4] Which of the following accounts would not be included in the Acquisition and Payment for Long-Lived Assets Cycle?
a. Revenue.
b. Depreciation expense.
c. Gain on disposal.
d. Equipment.

5-35 [LO 5] Which of the following is not one of the management assertions?
a. Completeness.
b. Existence.
c. Rights and obligations.
d. Valuation.
e. They are all management assertions.

5-36 [LO 5] Which management assertion addresses whether the components of the financial statements are properly classified, described, and disclosed?
a. Completeness.
b. Existence.
c. Rights and obligations.
d. Presentation and disclosure.
e. None of the above address whether the components of the financial statements are properly classified, described, and disclosed.

5-37 [LO 6] Assume that an auditor is physically examining a client's equipment. What type of audit procedure is the auditor performing?
a. Inspection of documentation.
b. Inspection of assets.
c. External confirmation.
d. Observation.

5-38 [LO 6] Which of the following is a true statement regarding audit evidence and audit procedures?
a. The auditor has a responsibility to design and perform audit procedures to obtain sufficient appropriate audit evidence.
b. Inquiry is a type of audit procedure that typically does not require corroborating evidence.
c. The audit procedures that are performed during an audit are summarized in a document referred to as an audit engagement letter.
d. Reperformance involves checking the mathematical accuracy of a document or record, such as an inventory count sheet.

5-39 [LO 7] Which of the following items should be included in audit documentation?
a. Procedures performed.
b. Audit evidence examined.
c. Conclusions reached with respect to relevant financial statement assertions.
d. All of the above should be included.

5-40 [LO 7] Which of the following statements is a false statement regarding audit documentation?
a. An audit program is an example of audit documentation.
b. The only purpose of audit documentation is to provide evidence that the audit was planned and performed in accordance with auditing standards.
c. Audit documentation helps facilitate internal and external inspections of completed audits.
d. All of the above statements are true.

5-41 [LO 8] Which of the following statements is a true statement regarding client acceptance?
a. Auditors in the U.S. are required to communicate with the predecessor auditor before accepting a new client.
b. Audit firms are required to provide audits for any organization that requests one.
c. Communication with a predecessor audit must be written.
d. International auditing standards require auditors to communicate with the predecessor auditor before accepting a new client.

5-42 [LO 8] Which of the following documents contains the agreed-upon terms of the audit engagement?
a. Audit program.
b. Audit plan.
c. Audit engagement letter.
d. Audit documentation.

5-43 [LO 9] Which of the following statements is correct regarding the design of controls related to credit limits?
a. The effectiveness of the control design is contingent on the credit manager's process for establishing and reviewing credit limits.
b. Because the process of establishing credit limits is fairly time-consuming, the control should be designed so that the marketing manager has the ability to approve sales on an ad hoc basis while waiting for the credit approval.
c. The control should be designed so that the sales manager has final approval regarding credit limits.
d. All are correct statements regarding the design of controls related to credit limits.

5-44 [LO 9]   Which of the following tests of controls would not typically be used in assessing control design effectiveness?
a. Inquiry.
b. Observation.
c. Inspection of documentation.
d. Reperformance.

5-45 [LO 10]   The auditor is testing the operating effectiveness of controls in the revenue cycle and notes the following: (a) the organization does not regularly follow its credit policies; rather it often overrides the credit policy when divisional management needs to meet its performance goals; and (b) the sales manager has the ability to override the credit policy for important customers. Which of the following statements would be correct regarding an integrated audit of sales and receivables?
a. Based on the test of controls, the auditor would likely assess control risk as high.
b. The auditor would be able to perform less rigorous substantive procedures.
c. The auditor likely concluded that the controls were not effectively designed.
d. All of the above are correct statements.

5-46 [LO 10]   Assume the auditor concludes the controls related to accounts receivable are operating effectively based on inquiry and other appropriate tests. Which of the following is a correct inference regarding the auditor's conclusion?
a. The auditor *will not* need to perform direct tests on the valuation of accounts receivable.
b. The auditor *could not* have concluded that the internal controls over credit were effective unless the auditor determined that the credit limits are updated for changed conditions.
c. The auditor does *not* need to confirm accounts receivable because the risk of a material misstatement of receivables is mitigated by the controls.
d. The auditor does *not* need to perform any more direct tests of the account balances if the auditor has tested the IT general controls.

5-47 [LO 11]   In performing substantive procedures, which of the following statements provides appropriate guidance to the auditor?
a. The auditor can perform both substantive analytical procedures and substantive tests of details.
b. The auditor should perform substantive procedures for all assertions of all financial statement accounts.
c. The auditor should perform more (or more rigorous) substantive procedures when control risk is low than when control risk is high.
d. All of the above statements provide appropriate guidance.

5-48 [LO 11]   In which of the following scenarios is the auditor likely to obtain more (or more rigorous) substantive evidence?
a. When subjectivity related to the assertion is low.
b. When controls are determined to be operating effectively.
c. When the account is immaterial.
d. When the design of controls is determined to be ineffective.

5-49 [LO 12]   Which of the following procedures is least likely to be performed during Phase V of the audit opinion formulation process?
a. Assessment of misstatements detected during the performance of substantive procedures and tests of controls.
b. Performance of preliminary analytical review procedures.
c. Performance of an engagement quality review.
d. Determination of the appropriate audit opinion(s) to issue.

5-50 `LO 12` Which of the following statements is correct regarding the auditor's report on a public company's internal control over financial reporting?

a. A company cannot have a material weakness in internal controls if the auditor does a quality audit and does not find a material misstatement.

b. The auditor must explicitly reference the criteria for evaluating internal control, using the COSO framework, for example.

c. The audit is performed in conjunction with the auditing standards promulgated by the AICPA Auditing Standards Board.

d. The audit must report on whether management used the appropriate tools in its assessment of internal control over financial reporting.

5-51 `LO 13` The auditor discovers that there is a key control deficiency over sales contracts and that some contracts near the end of the year are not properly reviewed by management. Which of the following would be the best way for the auditor to respond to the control deficiency identified?

a. Expand the testing over the control with a larger sample from the last quarter of the year.

b. Wait to assess whether the deficiency is a material weakness or significant deficiency based on the actual number of errors or misstatements found in the related account balances.

c. Expand the sample size for substantive testing and review of contracts during the latter part of the year to determine if revenue is appropriately identified.

d. All of the above.

5-52 `LO 13` Assume the auditor has assessed the design of controls and determines that the company has an ineffective control design related to pricing and dating of sales. This assessment is due to an inadequate segregation of duties. Based on this information, which of the following actions should the auditor take?

a. Resign from the audit because the entity is not auditable.

b. Do not test controls over sales pricing and dating of sales transactions.

c. Expand the direct tests of related account balances by selecting recorded sales and tracing back to shipping documents and authorized price lists.

d. Answers (b) and (c) above.

REVIEW AND SHORT CASE QUESTIONS

`INTERNATIONAL`

5-53 `LO 1` Refer to Exhibit 5.1. Briefly describe the relevance of the following standard setters for auditors.

a. AICPA

b. PCAOB

c. IAASB

NOTE: Completing Review and Short Case Questions does not require the student to reference additional resources and materials.

5-54 `LO 1` The PCAOB has the authority to set audit standards for all audits of public companies registered in the U.S. The AICPA continues to set audit standards for nonpublic companies through its auditing standards board.

a. What are the pros and cons of having the same audit standards for both public and nonpublic entities?

b. In what ways might you expect auditing standards for audits of nonpublic companies to differ from the standards for public companies? Identify three ways and state your rationale.

NOTE: For the remaining problems, we make special note of those addressing fraud, international issues, professional skepticism, and ethics.

5-55 `LO 2` Ray, the owner of a small company, asked Holmes, CPA, to conduct an audit of the company's records. Ray told Holmes that the audit must be completed in time to submit audited financial statements to a bank as part of a loan application. Holmes immediately accepted the engagement and agreed to provide an auditor's report within three weeks. Ray agreed to pay Holmes a fixed fee plus a bonus if the loan was granted.

Holmes hired two accounting students to conduct the audit and spent several hours telling them exactly what to do. Holmes told the students not to spend time reviewing the controls, but instead to concentrate on proving the mathematical accuracy of the ledger accounts and to summarize the data in the accounting records that support Ray's financial statements. The students followed Holmes's instructions and after two weeks gave Holmes the financial statements, which did not include footnotes because the company did not have any unusual transactions. Holmes reviewed the statements and prepared an unqualified auditor's report. The report, however, did not refer to GAAP or to the year-to-year application of such principles.

Briefly describe each of the ten standards and indicate how the action(s) of Holmes resulted in a failure to comply with each standard.

5-56 `LO 2` Compare the ten generally accepted auditing standards currently used by the PCAOB with the AICPA's "Principles Governing an Audit in Accordance with Generally Accepted Auditing Standards."

5-57 `LO 3` Refer to Exhibit 5.2. What are the client responsibilities that are relevant to the auditor? How do those responsibilities affect the audit opinion formulation process?

5-58 `LO 3` Refer to Exhibit 5.3. List the phases of audit opinion formulation process. What are the primary activities within each of the five phases?

5-59 `LO 4` Professional guidance says that revenue recognition should always be considered to be high risk in planning an audit of a company's financial statements.
a. Identify the activities that affect the revenue cycle.
b. Identify the financial statement accounts normally associated with the revenue cycle.

5-60 `LO 4` Refer to Exhibit 5.4. Identify typical accounting cycles *not* listed in the Exhibit and list their associated accounts.

5-61 `LO 5` Refer to Exhibit 5.5. Assume that an organization asserts that it has $35 million in net account receivables. Using the assertions listed in Exhibit 5.5, describe specifically what management is asserting with respect to net accounts receivable.

5-62 `LO 6` Describe how auditing standards affect the design of audit programs.

5-63 `LO 6` What is an audit program? What information should an auditor gather before developing an audit program?

5-64 `LO 6` Exhibit 5.6 lists types of audit procedures. Describe how you would you use those procedures to test the inventory account. For each procedure, indicate the purpose of the procedure—is it a risk assessment procedure, a test of control, or a substantive procedure?

5-65 `LO 7` Define the term audit documentation and provide examples.

5-66 `LO 8` Refer the *Auditing in Practice* feature, "Accepting a New Audit Engagement." Assume that an auditor is following U.S. auditing standards. What communication must an auditor of a new client have? How does that requirement differ for auditors following international auditing standards?

INTERNATIONAL

5-67 **LO 9** Refer to Exhibit 5.7. How do the sources of risk of misstatement listed help the auditor plan the audit?

FRAUD **5-68** **LO 9** Refer to the *Auditing in Practice* feature, "Controls to Address Fraud Risk." When assessing control design effectiveness, what types of controls would an auditor expect a client to have in place to address fraud risk? Why are these controls important?

5-69 **LO 9** Refer to the *Auditing in Practice* feature, "Documenting the Auditor's Understanding of an Organization's Internal Controls." What should an auditor document with respect to the design of controls? Why is this documentation important?

5-70 **LO 9** Refer to the *Auditing in Practice* feature, "Weak Internal Control Design and Links to Substantive Audit Procedures." Explain how the auditor's preliminary assessment of control risk affects planned substantive audit procedures.

5-71 **LO 9** An important part of Phase II of the audit opinion formulation process is determining how to respond to identified risks of material misstatement. As indicated in Exhibit 5.8, the auditor might respond by modifying evidence decisions about the extent or nature of audit evidence. Using the box of evidence analogy, explain these responses to identified risks.

5-72 **LO 9** Segregation of duties is an important concept in internal control. However, this is often a challenge for smaller businesses because they do not have sufficient staff. Normally, the segregation of duties deficiencies identified below results in either a significant deficiency or a material weakness in internal control. For each segregation of duties deficiency identified below as (1) – (6), do the following three tasks:
a. Indicate the risk to financial reporting that is associated with the inadequacy of the segregation of duties.
b. Identify other controls that might mitigate the segregation of duties risks.
c. Identify possible tests of controls for the mitigating controls selected in b. above.
   The inadequate segregation of duty situations to be considered are as follows:
   1. The same individual handles cash receipts, the bank reconciliation, and customer complaints.
   2. The same person prepares billings to customers and also collects cash receipts and applies them to customer accounts.
   3. The person who prepares billings to customers does not handle cash, but does the monthly bank reconciliation, which, in turn, is reviewed by the controller.
   4. The controller is responsible for making all accounting estimates and adjusting journal entries. The company does not have a CFO and has two clerks who report to the controller.
   5. A start-up company has very few transactions, less than $1 million in revenue per year, and has only one accounting person. The company's transactions are not complex.
   6. The company has one computer person who is responsible for running packaged software. The individual has access to the computer to update software and can also access records.

5-73 **LO 10** Refer to the *Auditing in Practice* feature, "Risk Assessment Procedures and Tests of Operating Effectiveness of Controls." Can risk assessment procedures be used as tests of controls? Explain.

5-74 **LO 10** Refer to Exhibit 5.9. What controls might an auditor test related to the valuation assertion for the sales account?

5-75 `LO 10` A review of corporate failures as described in the financial press, such as the *Wall Street Journal*, often describes the control environment as one of the major contributors to the failure. Often the tone at the top at the failed companies reflects a disdain for controls and an emphasis on accomplishing specific financial reporting objectives such as reporting increased profitability. How will the auditor's assessment of the operating effectiveness of the control environment affect the design and conduct of an audit? Consider both a positive and negative assessment.

5-76 `LO 10` Auditing standards indicate that if the preliminary control risk assessment is low, the auditor must gain assurance that the controls are operating effectively.
a. What is meant by testing the operating effectiveness of control procedures? How does an auditor decide which controls to test?
b. How is the auditor's assessment of control risk affected if a documented control procedure is not operating effectively? Explain the effect of such an assessment on substantive audit procedures.

5-77 `LO 10` An important principle of the control environment is the organization's commitment to ethics and integrity (COSO Principle 1). How might an auditor test the organization's commitment to ethics and integrity?   `ETHICS`

5-78 `LO 10` Is the auditor required to test the operation of controls on every audit engagement? Explain.

5-79 `LO 10` What are the external auditor testing requirements of internal controls for:
a. Large, publicly held companies?
b. Nonpublic companies and small, publicly held companies?

5-80 `LO 10` When the auditor determines that controls are not operating effectively, the auditor needs to consider the kind of misstatements that could occur, how they might occur, and how the auditor would adjust substantive audit procedures Assume that the authorization process for ordering inventory was found to contain a material weakness. Identify the accounts that could contain misstatements, how the misstatements might occur, and how the auditor would adjust substantive audit procedures because of the material weakness.

5-81 `LO 10` In analyzing the results of the tests of controls, there are two potential outcomes: (a) deficiencies are identified and (b) deficiencies are not identified. What are alternative courses of action for the financial statement audit associated with each of these alternative outcomes?

5-82 `LO 10` If a company's control risk is assessed as low, the auditor needs to gather evidence on the operating effectiveness of the controls. For each of the following control activities listed as (1) – (10) below, do the following two tasks:
a. Describe the test of control that the auditor would use to determine the operating effectiveness of the control.
b. Briefly describe how substantive tests of account balances should be modified if the auditor finds that the control is not working as planned. In doing so, indicate (a) what misstatement could occur because of the control deficiency, and (b) how the auditor's substantive tests should be expanded to test for the potential misstatement.
The control activities to be considered are as follows:
1. Credit approval by the credit department is required before salespersons accept any order of more than $15,000 and for all customers who have a past-due balance higher than $22,000.

2. All merchandise receipts are recorded on prenumbered receiving slips. The controller's department periodically accounts for the numerical sequence of the receiving slips.

3. Payments for goods received are made only by the accounts payable department on receipt of a vendor invoice, which is then matched for prices and quantities with approved purchase orders and receiving slips.

4. The accounts receivable bookkeeper is not allowed to issue credit memos or to approve the write-off of accounts.

5. Cash receipts are opened by a mail clerk, who prepares remittances to send to accounts receivable for recording. The clerk prepares a daily deposit slip, which is sent to the controller. Deposits are made daily by the controller.

6. Employees are added to the payroll master file by the payroll department only after receiving a written authorization from the personnel department.

7. The only individuals who have access to the payroll master file are the payroll department head and the payroll clerk responsible for maintaining the payroll file. Access to the file is controlled by computer passwords.

8. Edit tests built into the computerized payroll program prohibit the processing of weekly payroll hours in excess of 53 and prohibit the payment to an employee for more than three different job classifications during a one-week period.

9. Credit memos are issued to customers only on the receipt of merchandise or the approval of the sales department for adjustments.

10. A salesperson cannot approve a sales return or price adjustment that exceeds 6% of the cumulative sales for the year for any one customer. The divisional sales manager must approve any subsequent approvals of adjustments for such a customer.

5-83 `LO 10` The auditor of a public company in the retailing industry is planning an integrated audit. The company has approximately 260 retail stores, primarily in the southeastern United States.
a. Explain why an analysis of the company's control environment is important to planning the integrated audit.
b. The company claims that it has a strong control environment, including a culture of high integrity and ethics (COSO Principle 1), a commitment to financial reporting competencies (COSO Principle 4), and an independent, active, and knowledgeable board of directors (COSO Principle 2). For each of these principles, develop an audit program to gather evidence that these principles are operating effectively. In developing your answer, be sure to indicate the type of audit procedures to use. You may want to refer to Exhibit 5.6.

5-84 `LO 10` Refer to Exhibit 5.10. Assume that you are going to test computerized controls that your client has put in place. Consider the concept related to program changes. What is the important concept for you to consider when doing that testing? What are some possible tests of controls that you could perform? What are the audit implications if the controls are not working effectively?

5-85 `LO 10` Assume that you are planning to test a client's reconciliation. You could test by either inspecting documentation of the reconciliation or by reperforming the reconciliation. What factors would cause you to choose reperformance instead of inspection of documentation?

5-86 `LO 10` Assume that you want to test an entity-wide control related to the control environment. Specifically, you want to obtain evidence that the audit committee has periodic discussions about fraud. Recall that tests of controls include inquiry, observation, inspection of documentation, and reperformance of the control. Which approaches do you think would be used when testing this control environment control? Explain your answer.

5-87 `LO 10` Refer to Exhibit 5.11 What are some of the key decisions that influence the substantive testing to be performed by the auditor?

5-88 `LO 11` Refer to the *Auditing in Practice* feature, "Dual-Purpose Tests." What is a dual-purpose test, and why might an auditor choose to perform dual purpose tests?

5-89 `LO 11` Refer to Exhibit 5.12. Explain how the factors in the first column affect the auditor's decision about substantive testing.

5-90 `LO 11` What substantive procedures could an auditor use to determine that all purchases debited to a fixed asset account in the current year are properly valued?

5-91 `LO 11` Audits of financial statements are designed determine whether account balances are materially correct. Assume that your client is a construction company that has the following assets on its balance sheet:

- Construction equipment: $1,278,000
- Accumulated depreciation: $386,000
- Leased construction equipment: $550,000

a. Describe a substantive audit procedure that can used to determine that all leased equipment that should have been capitalized during the year was actually capitalized (as opposed to being treated as a lease expense).

b. The construction equipment account shows that the company purchased approximately $400,000 of new equipment this year. Identify a substantive audit procedure that will determine whether the equipment account was properly accounted for during the year.

c. Assuming the auditor determines the debits to construction equipment were proper during the year, what other information does the auditor need to know to have reasonable assurance that the construction equipment—net of depreciation—is properly reflected on the balance sheet?

d. How can an auditor determine that the client has assigned an appropriate useful life to the equipment and has depreciated it accurately?

5-92 `LO 12` The auditor provides an opinion on internal control over financial reporting for one of its public companies.

a. Is the auditor also required to audit the company's financial statements at the same time? Explain.

b. Does an unqualified report on internal controls over financial reporting imply that the company does not have any significant deficiencies in controls? Explain.

c. If the auditor did not detect any material misstatements in the financial statements, can the auditor conclude that there are no material weaknesses in internal control? Explain.

5-93 `LO 12` Review the external auditor's report on the integrated audit, presented in Exhibit 5.13. What are the important elements in that report related to internal control?

5-94 `LO 13` To what extent can the auditor use management's process in evaluating internal control, including evidence gathered, to plan and execute the auditor's integrated audit?

5-95 [LO 13] When testing internal controls, does the auditor test the same transactions that management and the internal auditors tested, or does the auditor test different transactions? Explain your rationale.

5-96 [LO 13] What are the factors that should be considered by management and the auditor in determining whether a control deficiency is a significant deficiency or a material weakness?

ETHICS

5-97 [LO 14] The auditor is evaluating the internal control of a new client. Management has prepared its assessment of internal control and has concluded that it has some deficiencies, but no significant deficiencies and no material weaknesses. However, in reviewing the work performed by management, the auditor observes the following:

- Sample sizes taken were never more than ten transactions, and most of the tests of operating effectiveness were based on a sample of one, performed as part of a walkthrough of a transaction.
- Management has fired the former CFO and a new CFO has not been appointed, but management indicates it is searching for a new CFO, and it currently has depth in the accounting area.
- The company has no formal whistleblowing function because management has an open-door policy so that anyone with a problem can take it up the line.
- Management's approach to monitoring internal control is to compare budget with actual expenses and investigate differences.

In response to inquiries by the auditor, management responds that its procedures are sufficient to support its report on internal control.

The auditor's subsequent work yields the following:

- Many controls do not operate in the way described by management, and the procedures are not effective.
- There is no awareness of, or adherence to, the company's code of conduct.
- The accounting department does not have a depth of talent; moreover, although the department can handle most transactions, it is not capable of dealing with new contracts that the firm has entered into. The response of management is, "That is why we pay you auditors the big bucks—to help us make these decisions."

The auditor reaches a conclusion that there are material weaknesses in internal control, thus differing from management's assessment. Management points out that every issue where there is a disagreement is a subjective issue, and there is no one position that is better than the others. Management's position is that these are management's financial statements, and the auditor should accommodate management's view because there are no right answers.

a. The partner in charge of the job appears to be persuaded that the differences are indeed subjective and is proposing that an unqualified opinion on internal controls be issued. Recognize that this is a first-year client—and an important one to the office. Apply the ethical framework presented in Chapter 4 to explore the actions that should be taken by the audit manager regarding (1) whether to disagree with the partner and (2) if there is a disagreement, to what level it should be taken in the firm.

b. Given the deficiencies noted, does the information support that there is a material weakness in internal control? If yes, what are the major factors that lead you to that conclusion?

c. Assume that the engagement team makes a decision that there is a material weakness in internal controls. Write two or three paragraphs describing those weaknesses that could be included in the audit report.

CONTEMPORARY AND HISTORICAL CASES

5-98 **ERNST & YOUNG-UK**
LO 1, 2, 6, 7, 8, 9, 10, 11, 12, 14 Refer to the *Professional Judgment in Context* feature at the outset of the chapter, which features details on the Ernst&Young-UK audits of Thornton Precision Components from 2004-2006.

PROFESSIONAL SKEPTICISM

ETHICS

FRAUD

INTERNATIONAL

a. What is the role of auditing standards and their underlying principles in promoting a quality audit?
b. How does the fundamental concept of professional skepticism relate to audit quality?
c. What audit evidence is necessary for opining on a client's financial statements?
d. How does audit documentation provide evidence related to audit quality?
e. What audit activities are conducted during the audit opinion formulation process to provide reasonable assurance about a client's financial statements?
f. How does professional judgment and ethical decision making contribute to audit quality?

5-99 **ERNST & YOUNG-UK**
LO 14 Refer to the *Professional Judgment in Context* feature at the outset of the chapter, which features details on the Ernst & Young-UK audits of Thornton Precision Components from 2004-2006. Use the ethical framework presented in Chapter 4 to analyze the judgments made by the E&Y-UK audit partner responsibility for the 2004-2006 audits of TPC.

PROFESSIONAL SKEPTICISM

ETHICS

FRAUD

5-100 **GENERAL MOTORS**
LO 9, 10, 13 In March 2006, General Motors (GM) announced that it needed to restate its prior year's financial statements. Excerpts from the *Wall Street Journal* describing the restatements include the following:

- GM, which already faces an SEC probe into its accounting practices, also disclosed that its 10-K report, when filed, will outline a series of accounting mistakes that will force the car maker to restate its earnings from 2000 to the first quarter of 2005. GM also said it was widening by $2 billion the loss it reported for 2005.
- Many of the other GM problems relate to rebates, or credits, from suppliers. Typically, suppliers offer an upfront payment in exchange for a promise by the customer to buy certain quantities of products over time. Under accounting rules, such rebates can't be recorded until after the promised purchases are made.
- GM said it concluded it had mistakenly recorded some of these payments prematurely. The biggest impact was in 2001, when the company said it overstated pretax income by $405 million as a result of prematurely recording supplier credits. Because the credits are being moved to later years, the impact in those years was less, and GM said it would have a deferred credit of $548 million that will help reduce costs in future periods. The issue of how to book rebates and other credits from suppliers is

a thorny one that has tripped up other companies, ranging from the international supermarket chain Royal Ahold, N.V. to the U.S.-based Kmart Corporation.

- GM also said it had wrongly recorded a $27 million pretax gain from disposing of precious-metals inventory in 2000, which it was obliged to buy back the following year.
- GM told investors not to rely on its previously reported results for the first quarter of 2005, saying it had underreported its loss by $149 million. GM said it had prematurely boosted the value it ascribed to cars it was leasing to rental-car companies, assuming they would be worth more after the car-rental companies were done with them. GM previously had reported a loss of $1.1 billion, or $1.95 a share, for the first quarter. (March 18, 2006)

You may assume the amounts are material.

a. Without determining whether the errors in accounting judgment were intentional or unintentional, discuss how the nature of the errors affects the auditor's judgment of the control environment and whether the auditor should conclude there are material weaknesses in internal control. What would your judgment be if the accounting treatment were deemed acceptable, but aggressive by the company's CFO and CEO? How would those judgments affect the auditor's assessment of the control environment?

b. Describe the nature of the accounting judgment made by the company regarding the residual value of the cars it leases. What information and communication system should exist regarding the residual value of the cars returned from leasing? What controls should be in place? What evidence would the auditor need to evaluate the reasonableness of the change made by the company?

c. Explain the rebates, or up-front rebates, from the company's suppliers. Why would the suppliers pay the up-front credits? What is the proper accounting for the up-front credits? What controls should be in place to account for the up-front credits? How would the auditor test (1) the controls over the accounting for the up-front credits and (2) the expense-offset account, or the liability account?

CHAPTER

A Framework for Audit Evidence

CHAPTER OVERVIEW AND LEARNING OBJECTIVES

Auditing is a process of objectively gathering and evaluating evidence pertaining to assertions. The auditor needs to obtain sufficient appropriate audit evidence. As the auditor plans an audit, the auditor needs to address two basic evidence-related questions: *What audit evidence is appropriate? How much audit evidence is sufficient?* The auditor will also need to determine when to gather the audit evidence. Audit programs detail how these decisions result in specific audit procedures performed during the audit opinion formulation process. The specific audit procedures performed must address the risk of

material misstatement in the financial statements or the likelihood that internal control over financial reporting contains material weaknesses. The auditor's process of gathering and assessing the evidence must be documented, clearly laying out the evidence gathered, the auditor's evaluation of that evidence, and the conclusions reached. In this chapter, we build on the concept of audit evidence presented in Chapter 5 by further discussing the type, extent, and timing of audit procedures typically performed during a financial statement or integrated audit.

Through studying this chapter, you will be able to achieve these learning objectives:

通过本章的学习，你将能够实现以下学习目标：

1. Discuss the importance of the evidence concepts of appropriateness and sufficiency.
   讨论审计证据的适当性和充分性概念的重要性。

2. Identify factors affecting the appropriateness of audit evidence.
   识别影响审计证据适当性的因素。

3. Make professional judgments about the type and timing of audit procedures to use to obtain audit evidence.
   对审计程序的类型和时间做出职业判断，以获得相关的审计证据。

4. Discuss the use of, and apply, substantive analytical procedures.
   讨论实质性分析程序的使用，并在实践中应用实质性分析程序。

5. Identify factors affecting the sufficiency of audit evidence.
   识别影响审计证据充分性的因素。

6. Identify issues related to audit evidence needed for accounts involving management estimates.
   对于涉及管理层估计的账户，识别与这些账户所需审计证据有关的问题。

7. Determine situations requiring the auditor to use a specialist/expert and describe the auditor's responsibilities related to that specialist/expert.
   确定注册会计师需要相关专家的情形，并描述注册会计师对相关专家的责任。

8. Describe the evidence needs for related-party transactions.
   描述关联方交易所需的审计证据。

9. Describe the characteristics of quality audit documentation.
   描述高质量审计工作底稿的特征。

10. Explain the nature, design, and purposes of audit programs.
    解释审计计划的性质、设计和目的。

11. Apply the frameworks for professional decision making and ethical decision making to issues involving audit evidence.
    运用职业决策和职业道德决策框架解决涉及审计证据的问题。

THE AUDIT OPINION FORMULATION PROCESS

I. Making Client Acceptance and Continuance Decisions
Chapter 14

II. Performing Risk Assessment
Chapters 3, 7 and 9–13

III. Obtaining Evidence about Internal Control Operating Effectiveness
Chapters 8–13 and 16

IV. Obtaining Substantive Evidence about Accounts, Disclosures and Assertions
Chapters 8–13 and 16

V. Completing the Audit and Making Reporting Decisions
Chapters 14 and 15

The Auditing Profession, the Risk of Fraud and Mechanisms to Address Fraud: Regulation, Corporate Governance, and Audit Quality
Chapters 1 and 2

Professional Liability and the Need for Quality Auditor Judgments and Ethical Decisions
Chapter 4

The Audit Opinion Formulation Process and A Framework for Obtaining Audit Evidence
Chapters 5 and 6

PROFESSIONAL JUDGMENT IN CONTEXT

Evidence-Related Findings in PCAOB Inspection Reports

The PCAOB performs annual inspections of each of the large public company audit firms. Following are excerpts from recently issued PCAOB annual inspection reports of some of these firms. Each excerpt describes an audit deficiency related to evidence, that is, a failure by the firm to perform, or to perform sufficiently, certain necessary audit procedures and to obtain sufficient appropriate audit evidence.

PCAOB Release No. 104-2012-095 notes that:

The Firm failed to sufficiently test inventory. Specifically, the Firm failed to test the existence of a significant portion of inventory and failed to test the completeness and accuracy of the system-generated reports that it used in its substantive procedures related to the valuation of inventory. Further, the Firm failed to test the completeness of inventory.

PCAOB Release No. 104-2011-289 states:

The Firm failed to sufficiently test the valuation of accounts receivable and net revenue. During the year, the issuer revised its policy for calculating its allowance for doubtful accounts, including changing certain significant assumptions used in its calculation. The Firm failed to evaluate the reasonableness of the issuer's revised assumptions. In addition, there

was no evidence in the audit documentation, and no persuasive other evidence, that the Firm had tested the completeness and accuracy of the data used in the calculation of the allowance for doubtful accounts as well as in the determination of the contractual revenue allowances.

PCAOB Release No. 104-2011-288 indicates:

In this audit, the Firm failed to obtain sufficient appropriate audit evidence to support its opinion on the effectiveness of ICFR [internal control over financial reporting].

PCAOB Release No. 104-2012-109 discloses:

The Firm failed to sufficiently test revenue. The Firm's planned approach for testing revenue included the performance of substantive analytical procedures. The analytical procedures consisted of comparing the current year's revenue to the prior year's revenue, but the Firm did not establish that the prior year's revenue could be expected to be predictive of the current year's revenue. In addition, the Firm failed to establish the amount of the difference from the prior year's revenue that could be accepted without further investigation, and failed to obtain corroboration of management's explanations of certain significant differences between the prior year's revenue and the current year's revenue. The Firm also failed to test the completeness and accuracy of certain of the data used in the analytical procedures. As a result of these failures, the analytical procedures provided little to no substantive assurance.

As you read through this chapter, consider the following questions:

• What is sufficient appropriate evidence, and how does it differ across clients? (LO 1, 2, 5)

• What are substantive analytical procedures, and when is evidence from these procedures appropriate? (LO 4)

• What are the unique evidence challenges for accounts such as allowance for doubtful accounts that are based on management estimates? (LO 6)

• How could the use of a standardized audit program lead to some of the problems identified in the PCAOB Releases introduced earlier? (LO 10)

获取充分的与适当的审计证据

Obtaining Sufficient Appropriate Audit Evidence

LO 1 Discuss the importance of the evidence concepts of appropriateness and sufficiency.

The auditor's job is to obtain sufficient appropriate audit evidence on which to base the audit opinion. The auditor wants to reduce the risk of issuing an unqualified opinion on financial statements containing a material misstatement or on internal control that has a material weakness. AS 15 defines audit evidence as

[A]ll the information, whether obtained from audit procedures or other sources, that is used by the auditor in arriving at the conclusions on which the auditor's opinion is based. Audit evidence consists of both information that supports and corroborates management's assertions regarding the financial statements or internal control over financial reporting and information that contradicts such assertions.

This definition is very similar to those used by the American Institute of Certified Public Accountants (AICPA) and the International Auditing and Assurance Standards Board (IAASB).

While the auditor is to obtain sufficient appropriate evidence before issuing an opinion, determining what is "appropriate" and "sufficient" is not an easy task. The AICPA's AU-C 500 defines the appropriateness of audit evidence as "[t]he measure of the quality of audit evidence (that is, its relevance and reliability in providing support for the conclusions on which the auditor's opinion is based)" and defines the sufficiency of audit evidence as "[t]he measure of the quantity of audit evidence. The quantity of the audit evidence needed is affected by the auditor's assessment of the risks of material misstatement and also by the quality of such audit evidence."

The relationship between risk, appropriateness, and sufficiency of audit evidence is shown in Exhibit 6.1.

What is determined to be appropriate and sufficient will be affected by the client's risk of material misstatement (in other words, its inherent and control risks) or risk of material weakness in internal control, and will vary across accounts and assertions. Both the U.S. and international auditing standards encourage auditors to focus on accounts and assertions with the greatest likelihood of material misstatement. With that in mind, study the relationships in Exhibit 6.1. There are cost implications associated with differences in appropriateness and sufficiency of evidence for accounts and assertions with varying risk levels. For example, consider an account in which there is little risk of misstatement, internal controls are effective, and the client has relatively noncomplex transactions. Here, the available audit evidence is relevant and reliable, and the quality of that evidence is high. In such a case, the auditor could likely perform less rigorous substantive procedures or only a minimal amount of substantive procedures, and the audit would therefore be less costly to conduct. Conversely, consider an account where there is high risk of misstatement and internal controls over that account are not effective. Here, the available audit evidence from

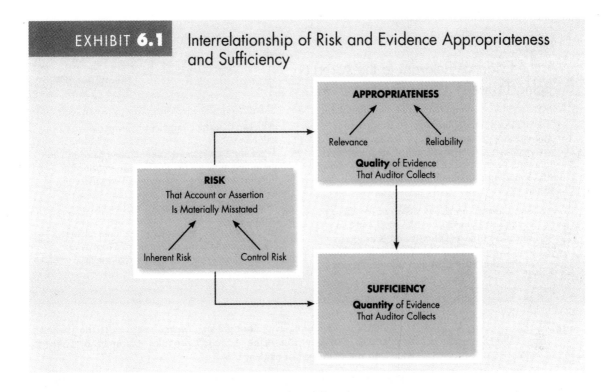

EXHIBIT 6.1 Interrelationship of Risk and Evidence Appropriateness and Sufficiency

the client is of lower quality. Therefore, the auditor will have to find other high quality evidence to corroborate evidence obtained from within the client's systems. Ultimately, these factors require the auditor to perform more, and more rigorous, substantive procedures, which are costly.

A frequent criticism of audits described in Public Company Accounting Oversight Board (PCAOB) inspection reports is that auditors often address high risk audit areas by simply gathering more of the same type of evidence. ISA 500 on audit evidence is very explicit that gathering more of the same evidence will not meet either the appropriateness or sufficiency criteria. For example, if high risk exists regarding the valuation of accounts receivable, increasing the sample size for confirmations, which are focused on the existence assertion, would not be very useful. Rather, the auditor will need to expand procedures related to the allowance account. Auditors need to tailor the gathering of evidence–both the appropriateness and sufficiency–to identified risks for each disclosure, account, or assertion.

Appropriateness of Audit Evidence

Appropriateness of audit evidence is a measure of its quality, including the **relevance** of the evidence, that is, whether it provides insight on the validity of the assertion being tested, and the **reliability** of the evidence, that is, whether it is convincing. The relevance of evidence relates to the connection between the audit procedure being performed and the assertion being audited. The reliability of evidence is influenced by its source and nature and depends on the circumstances under which it is obtained.

Relevance of Audit Evidence

The relevance of audit evidence considers the assertion being tested and is affected by several factors, including the purpose of the procedure being performed, the direction of testing, and the specific procedure or set of procedures being performed. Additionally, evidence can be directly or indirectly

审计证据的适当性

LO 2 Identify factors affecting the appropriateness of audit evidence.

审计证据的适当性 (appropriateness of audit evidence) 对审计证据质量的衡量，即审计证据在支持审计意见所依据的结论方面具有相关性和可靠性。相关性和可靠性是审计证据适当性的核心内容，只有既相关又可靠的审计证据才是高质量的。

审计证据的相关性

Is the Evidence Relevant to the Assertion Being Tested?

The auditor should guard against unwarranted inferences in gathering audit evidence. The following are examples of inappropriate inferences that auditors may make because they use evidence that is not entirely relevant to the assertion being tested:

• The auditor tests the existence of the client's equipment by inspecting the asset and concludes that the asset exists and is properly valued. However, evidence about the existence of the equipment does not provide relevant

evidence that the equipment is properly valued.

• The auditor examines documentation related to the largest accounts payable balances recorded in the client's financial statements and concludes that the accounts payable balance recorded in the financial statements is reasonable. But such evidence is relevant to the existence assertion (overstatements). In many situations, the more relevant evidence would relate to the completeness assertion and *understatements*, not overstatements.

relevant to an assertion. The *Auditing in Practice* feature "Is the Evidence Relevant to the Assertion Being Tested?" provides examples of concerns related to the relevance of evidence.

Purpose of an Audit Procedure   Recall that audit procedures fall into three categories: risk assessment, tests of controls, and substantive procedures. Risk assessment procedures are used during audit planning to identify the risks of material misstatement. Tests of controls are relevant when the auditor wants to evaluate the operating effectiveness of controls in preventing, or detecting and correcting, material misstatements. Substantive procedures are relevant when the auditor wants to obtain direct evidence about the presence of material misstatements in the financial statements.

Direction of Testing   The relevance of evidence obtained through audit procedures may be affected by the direction of testing. **Directional testing** involves testing balances primarily for either overstatement or understatement (but not both). For example, if the auditor wants to test the existence assertion for accounts payable, the auditor is concerned as to whether all of the recorded accounts payable actually exist, that is, overstatement of accounts payable. In that case, the auditor's starting point for testing would be all of the recorded accounts payable, and the auditor would perform procedures to obtain evidence supporting the existence of the recorded accounts payable. For example, the auditor may look at supporting documentation such as vendor invoices. Conversely, if the auditor wants to test the completeness assertion for accounts payable, the auditor is concerned as to whether all of the accounts payable owed by the client are recorded, that is, understatement of accounts payable. In that case, obtaining evidence about the recorded accounts payable would not be relevant. Instead, the auditor would obtain evidence as to whether there were unrecorded accounts payable. Relevant evidence could include information such as subsequent disbursements, suppliers' statements, and unmatched receiving reports.

Exhibit 6.2 compares testing related to the existence and completeness assertions. Panel A illustrates the auditor's work flow when testing for existence. This process is referred to as **vouching**. Vouching involves taking a sample of recorded transactions and obtaining the original source documents supporting the recorded transaction. For example, for a sample of items recorded in the sales journal, the auditor will obtain the related shipping documents and customer orders. Vouching provides evidence on

EXHIBIT **6.2** Illustration of Testing for Existence (Vouching) and Completeness (Tracing)

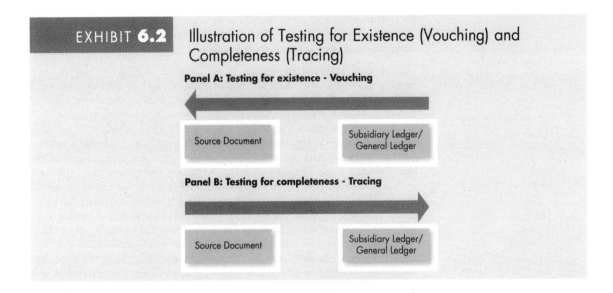

Panel A: Testing for existence - Vouching

Source Document

Subsidiary Ledger/ General Ledger

Panel B: Testing for completeness - Tracing

Source Document

Subsidiary Ledger/ General Ledger

the assertion that recorded transactions are valid (existence/occurrence). Panel B of Exhibit 6.2 illustrates the auditor's work flow when testing for completeness. This process is referred to as **tracing**. Tracing is sometimes referred to as reprocessing. Tracing involves taking a sample of original source documents and ensuring that the transactions related to the source documents have been recorded in the appropriate journal and general ledger. For example, the auditor might select a sample of receiving reports and trace them to the acquisitions journal and the general ledger.

In performing audit procedures, it is important to recognize that some assertions are directional by nature. The existence/occurrence assertion addresses overstatement, whereas the completeness assertion addresses understatement. Therefore, the assertion being tested determines the direction of testing and what type of evidence is relevant. Assets and revenues are most often tested for overstatement because the usual presumption is that managers would prefer to show superior financial results. Testing an asset for overstatement also provides corollary evidence on the potential overstatement of revenue and liabilities or the potential understatement of other asset or expense accounts. For example, if accounts receivable are overstated, it is likely that revenue is overstated or cash is understated.

Liabilities and expenses are most often tested for understatement because the usual presumption is that managers would prefer to show superior financial results. Testing liabilities for understatement provides evidence on the potential understatement of expenses or assets, or the potential overstatement of revenue and other liabilities. For example, if there are unrecorded liabilities, such as a failure to accrue payroll expense, the related payroll expense is understated, and possibly inventory is understated if payroll costs are not properly allocated to inventory.

Type of Procedure A specific audit procedure may provide audit evidence that is relevant to certain assertions, but not others. For example, if the auditor performs procedures to obtain evidence about the existence of an asset such as inventory or accounts receivable, the auditor would likely need to perform additional procedures to obtain evidence related to the rights assertion. If the auditor were to walk through the client's warehouse to inspect inventory, the auditor would be obtaining evidence related to the existence of inventory, but this procedure would not provide evidence relevant to the rights assertion. In some cases, a procedure may provide evidence relevant to multiple assertions. For example, if the auditor inspects documents related to the collection of accounts receivable after the year end, this procedure will likely provide audit evidence relevant to both the existence and valuation of accounts receivable.

Direct and Indirect Evidence Some evidence is directly relevant to a specific assertion. For example, communicating with a client's customers about whether the customer owes payment for goods to the client provides **direct evidence** about the existence of an accounts receivable balance.

Indirect evidence is not as directly relevant to an assertion. For example, the auditor might perform substantive analytical procedures on an account balance, such as analyzing expenses and comparing the expense account with those of previous years. Assuming the auditor does not find unexpected results, the auditor has indirect evidence about the valuation of expenses. In some cases, this indirect evidence may be sufficient. In other cases, where a high risk of material misstatement exists, the auditor may need to also obtain direct evidence about expenses. For example, the auditor might also examine invoices supporting the amount of expenses.

As another example, tests of controls provide direct evidence about the operating effectiveness of controls and indirect evidence about accounts and assertions. If the auditor finds that controls over the existence of inventory are operating effectively, the auditor has direct evidence about the effectiveness of those controls. The auditor also has indirect evidence indicating a high likelihood that the inventory existence assertion is not materially misstated. The auditor will likely need to also obtain direct evidence related to inventory existence through substantive procedures.

审计证据的可靠性

审计证据的可靠性是指审计证据的可信程度。审计证据的可靠性受其来源和性质的影响，并取决于获取审计证据的具体环境。

Reliability of Audit Evidence

The reliability of audit evidence is judged by its ability to provide convincing evidence related to the audit objective being evaluated. In considering the reliability of audit evidence, review the text of ISA 500 (A31), which states:

> The reliability of information to be used as audit evidence, and therefore of the audit evidence itself, is influenced by its source and its nature, and the circumstances under which it is obtained, including the controls over its preparation and maintenance where relevant. Therefore, generalizations about the reliability of various kinds of audit evidence are subject to important exceptions. Even when information to be used as audit evidence is obtained from sources external to the entity, circumstances may exist that could affect its reliability. For example, information obtained from an independent external source may not be reliable if the source is not knowledgeable, or a management's expert may lack objectivity. (ISA 500, A31)

This statement highlights the importance of considering the source of the evidence in assessing its reliability. The IAASB, in ISA 500, has established the following generalizations about the reliability of audit evidence:

More Reliable	Less Reliable
Directly obtained evidence (for example, observation of a control)	Indirectly obtained evidence (for example, an inquiry about the working of a control)
Evidence derived from a well-controlled information system	Evidence derived from a poorly controlled system or easily overridden information system
Evidence from independent outside sources	Evidence from within the client's organization
Evidence that exists in documentary form	Verbal evidence
Evidence from original documents	Evidence obtained from photocopies or facsimiles, or digitized data (would depend on the quality of controls over their preparation and maintenance)

The specific evidence choices depend on the assertion being tested, and evidence reliability can be influenced by multiple considerations. For example, if the auditor is testing warranty liabilities, most of the information likely resides internally—some in the client's accounting system and some in operational data. While internal documentation is generally less reliable than external documentation, internal documentation can be quite reliable when the underlying internal control system is effective and the original documentation cannot be easily manipulated by management.

Internal Documentation Internal documentation includes the following types of documents: legal, business, accounting, and planning and control. Exhibit 6.3 provides examples of these types of internal documents. As you review these examples, consider that the reliability of internal documentation varies because it is influenced by the following:

- Effectiveness of internal controls
- Management motivation to misstate individual accounts (fraud potential)
- Formality of the documentation, such as acknowledgment of its validity by parties outside the organization or independent of the accounting function
- Independence of those preparing the documentation from those recording transactions

External Documentation External documentation is generally considered to be highly reliable, but the reliability varies depending on whether the documentation (a) was prepared by a knowledgeable and independent outside party, and (b) is received directly by the auditor. Most external documentation,

EXHIBIT **6.3**	Examples of Internal Documents
Legal documents	Labor and fringe benefit agreements
	Sales contracts
	Lease agreements
	Royalty agreements
	Maintenance contracts
Business documents	Sales invoices
	Purchase orders
	Canceled checks
	Payment vouchers
	EDI agreements
Accounting documents	Estimated warranty liability schedules
	Depreciation and amortization schedules
	Standard cost computations and schedules
	Management exception reports
	Employee time cards
Other planning and control documents	Shipping and receiving reports
	Inventory movement documents such as scrap reports and transfer receipts
	Market research surveys
	Pending litigation reports
	Variance reports

EXHIBIT **6.4**	Examples of External Documents
Business documents	Vendor invoices and monthly statements
	Customer orders
	Sales or purchase contracts
	Loan agreements
	Other contracts
Third-party documents	Confirmation letters from legal counsel
	Confirmation statements from banks
	Confirmation replies from customers
	Vendor statements requested by auditors
General business information	Industry trade statistics
	Credit-rating reports
	Data from computer service bureaus

however, is directed to the client. For example, a customer order that specifies prices and quantities is external documentation received by the client, not the auditor. Therefore, in high-risk situations the auditor should confirm the contents of the document with the pertinent outside party.

Exhibit 6.4 provides examples of external documentation. External documentation can range from business documents normally found in the client's possession (vendor invoices and monthly statements), to confirmations received directly from the client's legal counsel, banker, or customer, to trade and credit information. One common business document in the client's possession is a vendor invoice. A vendor's invoice shows the purchase price (cost) of items in the client's inventory, dates of invoice and shipment, payment and ownership terms, shipping address (inventory location), purchase order reference, purchasing agent (evidence of authorization), and amount due (liability as well as asset valuation evidence). A vendor invoice is external documentation, but the auditor will typically obtain it from the client. Formal documents of this type are generally considered reliable except for situations in which the auditor questions management's integrity and has assessed the client and account balance being tested as high risk. Recognize that with the current state of technology, invoices often exist in electronic form. Thus, the auditor must assure that the data shown in an electronic invoice are safeguarded and well-controlled in the client's computer system and that they cannot be easily manipulated.

Evidence from a Management's Specialist

Some of the evidence that auditors receive from the client is prepared by a management's specialist that was hired by the client. AU-C 500 defines a **management's specialist** as "an individual or organization possessing expertise in a field other than accounting or auditing, whose work in that field is used by the entity to assist the entity in preparing the financial statements." In preparing its financial statements, a client may require expertise in a field other than accounting or auditing, such as actuarial calculations, valuations, or engineering data. If the client does not have the expertise needed to prepare the financial statements, the client will likely use a management's specialist in these fields to obtain the needed expertise to prepare the financial statements. In fact, failure to do so when such expertise is necessary increases the risks of material misstatement and may be a significant deficiency or material weakness in internal control.

If information to be relied upon as audit evidence has been prepared by a management's specialist, the auditor should consider the following factors as they affect the reliability and relevance of information produced by a management's specialist:

- Competence, capabilities, and objectivity of that specialist
- Work performed by that specialist
- Appropriateness of that specialist's work as audit evidence for the relevant assertion

Type and Timing of Audit Procedures

Type of Audit Procedures

Auditors' judgments about the type of audit procedures to perform in order to obtain evidence are critical to conducting a quality audit. Exhibit 6.5 identifies the types of audit procedures typically performed as tests of controls and substantive procedures, and provides relevant examples. We discuss audit procedures that are used as risk assessment procedures in Chapter 7.

审计程序的类型和时间

审计程序的类型

LO 3 Make professional judgments about the type and timing of audit procedures to use to obtain audit evidence.

EXHIBIT 6.5 Types of Audit Procedures

Categories of Audit Procedures	Purpose	Types of Audit Procedures Typically Performed	Examples of Audit Procedures
Tests of controls	Evaluate the operating effectiveness of controls	Inspection of documentation	Review client-prepared internal control documentation
			Select purchase transactions and review documentation for required approval
		Observation	Observe whether controls designed to limit access to a secure area (e.g., ID card need to access storage room) are functioning
		Reperformance	Reperform a reconciliation performed by client personnel
		Inquiry	Inquire of management and supervisory personnel about their control-related responsibilities
Substantive procedures	Determine whether material misstatements exist in the financial statements	Inspection of documentation	Review shipping documents as evidence of a sale having occurred
		Inspection of assets	Tour the manufacturing facility and inspect client's equipment
		External confirmation	Obtain confirmations from client's customers regarding amount owed by the customer to the client
		Recalculation	Recalculate the total amount included on a sales invoice
		Analytical procedures	Estimate the expected amount of interest income to be recorded by the client and follow up on significant unexpected differences between expectation and client's recorded balance
		Scanning	Scan the sales journal to identify unusual transactions posted to the sales account and follow up on the transactions
		Inquiry	Inquire of client management as to its valuation of the allowance for doubtful accounts

Evidence that the auditor obtains generally includes the client's underlying **accounting records** and corroborating information. The underlying accounting records include:

- Evidence of internal controls over financial reporting, as well as supporting records such as checks, invoices, contracts
- The general and subsidiary ledgers
- Journal entries
- Worksheets supporting cost allocations, computations, reconciliations, and disclosures

Corroborating information that validates the underlying accounting records includes evidence such as minutes of meetings, confirmations from independent parties, industry data, inquiry, observation, and inspection of documents.

Inspection of Documentation Much of the audit process involves examining documents, in either paper or electronic form. Common documents include invoices, payroll time cards, and bank statements. Auditors examine invoices from suppliers, for example, to establish the cost and ownership of inventory or various expenses. They also read contracts to help establish the potential existence of liabilities. Auditors should use original source documents rather than copies, because copies are easy for an unscrupulous management to falsify. Inspection of documents provides audit evidence of varying degrees of reliability. The reliability depends on the nature and source of the documentation, and, in the case of internal records and documents, the effectiveness of controls over their production.

Inspection of Assets Auditors will often inspect a client's assets, including inventory and long-term assets (for example, machinery or buildings). Inspection of tangible assets generally provides reliable evidence with respect to the existence of the asset, but not necessarily about the client's rights and obligations or completeness of the assets. For example, the inventory at a client location might be held on consignment from others and is therefore not owned by the audit client.

Observation Observation involves looking at a client's process or procedure. For example, an auditor might choose to observe whether unauthorized client personnel are prohibited from entering secure areas. A common practice is also to observe the client's process of taking physical inventory to establish existence and valuation. Although intuitively appealing, observation suffers from the following limitations:

- Observation of processing is rarely unobtrusive. Individuals who know they are being observed may act differently than when not observed.
- Observation of processing on one day does not necessarily indicate how the transactions were processed on a different day or over a relevant period of time.

External Confirmation Confirmations consist of sending an inquiry to an outside party to corroborate information. The outside parties are asked to respond directly to the auditor as to whether they agree or disagree with the information, or to provide additional information that will assist the auditor in evaluating the correctness of an account balance. Confirmations often include requests to legal counsel for an assessment of current litigation and the client's potential liability, letters to customers asking whether they owe the amount on the client's accounts receivable records, and letters to banks confirming bank balances and loans. In some cases, the auditor confirms the terms of sales agreements or other contracts.

The Parmalat Confirmation Fraud

The Parmalat fraud involved a large family-held Italian company that produced dairy products around the world. The company's management perpetrated a fraud that involved taking cash from the business for family purposes, but not recording the transactions in the books, thereby resulting in an overstatement of cash on the company's books. It also shifted monetary assets in and out of banks located in the Bahamas Islands. The audit firm decided it should independently confirm the existence of Parmalat's $3.2 billion account with the Bank of America in New York. Unfortunately, the audit senior was careless, and after preparing the confirmation, he put it in the client's mail room where it was intercepted by management. Management was able to scan the signature of a Bank of America employee from another document and put it on a copy of the confirmation form. A Parmalat employee then flew to New York from Italy just to mail that confirmation to the auditors with the appropriate postmark. The auditors received the fraudulent confirmation and concluded that the cash balance existed. There is an important point here: There are no trivial tasks in an audit. Each procedure must be completed in a professional manner and with due care.

Although confirmations can be a very reliable source of evidence, auditors must not rely on them unduly. The *Auditing in Practice* feature "The Parmalat Confirmation Fraud" provides an example where the confirmation process went terribly wrong. When using confirmations with outside parties, the auditor must assure that the outside party:

- Exists
- Is able to respond objectively and independently
- Is likely to respond conscientiously, appropriately, and in a timely fashion
- Is unbiased in responding

Professional auditing standards in the United States generally require that the auditor separately confirm accounts receivable. Confirmations must be sent independently of the client. The auditor often complements these types of confirmations with other sources of evidence, such as the customer's subsequent payment of the outstanding balance.

Recalculation Auditors often find it useful to recalculate a number of client computations. Various types of recalculations are summarized in Exhibit 6.6.

EXHIBIT 6.6 Types of Recalculations Performed by the Auditor

- **Footing** Adding a column of figures to verify the correctness of the client's totals.
- **Cross-footing** Checking the agreement of the cross-addition of a number of columns of figures that sum to a grand total. For example, the sum of net sales and sales discounts should equal total sales.
- **Tests of extensions** Recomputing items involving multiplication (for example, multiplying unit cost by quantity on hand to arrive at extended cost).
- **Recalculating estimated amounts** Recomputing an amount that the client has already estimated, such as recomputing the allowance for doubtful accounts based on a formula related to the aging of accounts receivable ending balances.

There are many court cases involving auditors where the details in the client's records did not agree with the balances in the financial statements. Moreover, clients often use spreadsheets to calculate accounting estimates. Auditors can test the accuracy of the estimates by recalculating them using an auditor-developed spreadsheet or evaluating the logic incorporated in the client's spreadsheet.

通常只有当询问、观察和检查程序结合在一起仍无法获得充分适当的证据时，注册会计师才考虑重新执行来证实控制是否有效运行。

Reperformance Reperformance involves the auditor's independent execution of controls that were originally performed as part of the client internal control. In other words, the auditor must not only inspect documents indicating that a control was performed; the auditor should do what is necessary to determine that the control actually worked. For example, rather than inspecting documents related to a bank reconciliation, the auditor may want to test a control requiring that bank reconciliations be performed. For selected months and bank accounts, the auditor may reperform the bank reconciliation and compare it to the reconciliations prepared by the client.

Analytical Procedures Analytical procedures consist of evaluations of financial information through analyzing plausible relationships among both financial and nonfinancial data. Later in this chapter we provide additional discussion on using analytical procedures as a substantive procedure. Chapter 7 provides discussion about using analytical procedures as a risk assessment procedure, while Chapter 14 discusses using analytical procedures when completing the audit.

Scanning Scanning is a type of analytical procedure involving the auditor's review of accounting data to identify significant or unusual items to test. Unusual individual items might include entries in transaction listings, subsidiary ledgers, general ledger control accounts, adjusting entries, reconciliations, or other detailed reports. For unusual or significant items, the auditor typically performs tests of details, such as client inquiry, inspection of documentation or assets, and, possibly, confirmations. While scanning can be conducted manually, electronic audit procedures may assist the auditor in identifying unusual items. We discuss these types of procedures in Chapter 8.

Inquiry Inquiry of appropriate individuals is used extensively to gain an understanding of the following:

- The accounting system
- Management's plans for such things as marketable investments, new products, disposal of lines of business, and new investments
- Pending or actual litigation against the organization
- Changes in accounting procedures or accounting principles
- Management's approach and assumptions used in the valuation of key accounts (for example, the collectibility of accounts receivable or the salability of inventory)
- Management's or the controller's assessment of complex financial matters

While inquiry is very helpful to understanding the client, the evidence obtained through inquiry typically needs to be corroborated through other audit procedures. Inquiry alone ordinarily does not provide sufficient audit evidence of the absence of a material misstatement, nor is inquiry alone sufficient to test the operating effectiveness of controls.

Application of Audit Procedures to Management Assertions

Recall that the auditor selects audit procedures to provide evidence relevant to a particular assertion. However, an audit procedure may provide evidence for one or more assertions affecting an account balance. Exhibit 6.7 presents

EXHIBIT **6.7**	Management Assertions and Examples of Related Audit Procedures	
Assertions	**Fixed Assets**	**Contingencies**
Existence	Inspect the assets. Select new assets that have been added to the subsidiary ledger/general journal and inspect supporting documentation (for example, invoices).	Inquire of management. Send confirmation request to legal counsel.
Completeness	Select source documents for repairs/ maintenance expense to determine if a fixed asset was inappropriately expensed. Inquire regarding process for determining whether an expenditure is an asset or an expense.	Inquire of management. Select source documents for legal expense and determine that the expenses were appropriately recorded.
Rights/obligations	Inspect documentation related to purchase contracts.	Inquire of management. Obtain confirmation from legal counsel. Inspect documentation of payments related to in-progress litigation.
Valuation/ allocation	Inspect vendor's invoice to establish purchase price. Determine that estimated life and salvage value are consistent with similar purchases, company policies, expected future use, and past experience. Recalculate depreciation expense. Develop an expectation of total depreciation using analytical procedures.	Inquire of management. Obtain confirmation from legal counsel. Recalculate potential damages sought by plaintiff. Review court filings.
Presentation/ disclosure	Review presentation within the financial statements to ensure completeness and conformance with the applicable financial reporting financial reporting framework. Review disclosures to ensure that they are adequate and understandable.	Review presentation within financial statements to ensure completeness and conformance with the applicable financial reporting framework. Review disclosures to ensure that they are adequate and understandable.

examples of procedures that address specific assertions regarding fixed assets and contingencies. The procedures are organized according to the assertion, and some of the procedures cover more than one assertion.

Assessing the Consistency of Evidence

In formulating an opinion about whether an account is materially correct, the auditor looks at the relative weight and internal consistency of evidence. AS 15 guides the auditor by stating:

> If audit evidence obtained from one source is inconsistent with that obtained from another, or if the auditor has doubts about the reliability of information to be used as audit evidence, the auditor should perform the audit procedures necessary to resolve the matter and should determine the effect, if any, on other aspects of the audit. (para. 29)

The key point in AS 15 is that the auditor needs to consider all sources of information, as well as the consistency of the information, in formulating a judgment as to whether the evidence clearly leads to a conclusion about the fairness of the financial statement presentation. In assessing the consistency of evidence, the auditor should do the following:

- Consider internal consistency of evidence gathered
- Consider the consistency of internal evidence generated with external evidence gathered that reflects economic conditions and client operations
- Expand evidence-gathering procedures for areas where results are inconsistent or where results raise questions on the correctness of account balances.
- Document conclusions based on the evidence gathered such that someone knowledgeable in auditing can follow the reasoning process.

Cost–Benefit Considerations When Selecting Audit Procedures

When considering the audit procedures to perform, keep in mind that audit firms have to balance two objectives: (a) be profitable, and (b) manage risk. Therefore, auditors must perform audits both efficiently and effectively. For example, they should not perform unnecessary procedures, and they should select procedures that maximize effectiveness while minimizing cost where possible.

Each of the audit procedures that an auditor could select takes time, effort, and ultimately money to perform. Audit procedures that are more rigorous, and that provide higher quality evidence, are generally more costly to perform. Exhibit 6.8 describes some generalizations about the cost-benefit trade-offs that auditors will make when they decide which mix of procedures to apply for specific accounts and assertions. In conducting the audit for a particular financial statement line item and related assertion, the auditor usually chooses multiple of these procedures, thereby enabling an assessment about whether or not the account balance is materially misstated. For example, in testing the existence and valuation of inventory, the auditor may initially use substantive analytical procedures to gain a sense of the reasonableness of the ending inventory amount. The auditor will inspect the client's inventory to establish existence, and will inspect documents to determine that the client actually owns the inventory. The auditor may scan material inventory transactions around year end to assess whether any unusual adjustments have been made to the account. As Exhibit 6.8 notes, each of these procedures has costs associated with it, as well as differential evidence quality. By using a mix of procedures, the auditor should ultimately gain a consensus opinion about the final, reported inventory amount reported on the balance sheet.

As ISA 500 notes, there are always exceptions to these generalizations, given each unique set of facts and characteristics of a particular client. The important point is that the types of substantive procedures selected depend on risk. For example, consider an account balance and related assertion with a low risk of misstatement. For this case, the auditor can obtain evidence using less rigorous and less costly procedures, such as inquiry, recalculation, and analytical procedures. In contrast, consider an account balance and related assertion with a high risk of misstatement. For this case, the auditor needs to rely on relatively more-rigorous and higher-cost procedures such as observation, inquiry, confirmations, reperformance, and inspection of documentation.

Many procedures are available to the auditor, and determining the appropriate mix of evidence for any particular account/assertion is an important decision, with cost, and therefore profitability implications. The decision about which audit procedures to perform is based on the auditor's professional judgment about the expected effectiveness and efficiency of the

EXHIBIT **6.8**	Cost of Audit Procedures and Evidence Quality	
Type of Substantive Procedure	**Cost of Procedure**	**Evidence Quality**
Inspection of documents (includes vouching and tracing)	Low to medium (depends on sample size)	Medium to high (assuming the documents are valid and unaltered, needs to consider source)
Inspection of physical assets	Low to high (depends on complexity, location of process, and expertise required)	High (existence) Low to medium (valuation, ownership)
Observation	Low to high (depends on complexity, location of process, and expertise required)	Medium (because people may change behavior while being observed)
External confirmations	Low to medium (can be performed manually or electronically; depends on sample size)	Medium to high (assuming that there is no fraud in the confirmation process)
Recalculation	Low to medium (can be performed manually or electronically; depends on sample size)	Medium to high
Reperformance	Low to high (depends on sample size and complexity of process)	Medium to high
Analytical procedures	Low to medium (depends on the type of analytical procedure)	Medium to high (if the auditor who is conducting the test is competent, and will generally have to obtain additional corroborating evidence)
Scanning	Low to medium (can be performed manually or electronically; depends on the length of document)	Low to medium (will need to follow on significant or unusual items using other procedures)
Inquiry of knowledgeable persons	Low	Low (will also need corroborating evidence)

available audit procedures. Depending on the circumstances, the auditor may determine the following with regard to substantive procedures:

- Performing only substantive analytical procedures would be appropriate, for example, when the auditor's assessment of risk is supported by audit evidence that the controls are operating effectively.
- Performing only substantive tests of details would be appropriate.
- Performing a combination of substantive analytical procedures and tests of details may be most responsive to the assessed risks.

However, irrespective of the assessed risks of material misstatement, the auditor should perform substantive procedures for all relevant assertions related to each material account balance and disclosure.

Timing of Procedures

In addition to determining which types of procedures to perform, the auditor must determine when to perform them—at the balance sheet date, earlier than the balance sheet date (referred to as an **interim date**), or after the balance sheet date. The decision of timing is based on the assessment of risk associated with the account, the effectiveness of internal controls, the nature of the account, and the availability of audit staff. Performing procedures after year end may provide the most convincing evidence; for example, a cash collection of an accounts receivable after year end is usually high quality evidence regarding both the existence and valuation of the receivable.

审计程序的时间

期中实施审计程序获取的审计证据不能直接作为期末财务报表认定的审计证据，注册会计师还需要进一步消耗审计资源使期中审计证据合理延伸到期末。

Performing procedures prior to the balance sheet date allows earlier completion of the audit and might require less overtime of the audit staff. It might also meet management's desire to distribute the financial statements shortly after year end. However, performing the procedures at an interim date increases the risk of material misstatements occurring between the interim date and the year end. When an organization has effective internal controls over financial reporting, the risk of misstatements occurring between the interim audit date and year end is decreased. There are several accounts for which the auditor can effectively and efficiently test transactions during the year rather than the final balance. For example, the auditor can test property, plant, and equipment additions and disposals during the year. Accounts receivable may be confirmed prior to year end. A similar approach can often be used for other noncurrent assets, long-term debt, and owners' equity transactions. However, when performing procedures at an interim date, the auditor needs to perform additional audit procedures at or after year end to make sure that no misstatements have occurred during the **roll-forward period** (the period between the interim date and the balance sheet date). These procedures could be substantive procedures, possibly combined with tests of controls for the intervening period. The auditor needs evidence that will provide a reasonable basis for extending the audit conclusions from the interim date to year end.

Another timing issue involves performing procedures during the cutoff period. The **cutoff period** is usually several days before and after the balance sheet date.

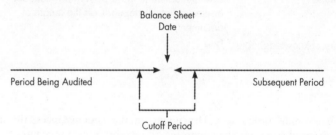

The greatest risk of recording transactions in the wrong period occurs during the cutoff period. For example, auditors are often concerned with whether sales, sales returns, and cash receipts transactions have been recorded in the proper period. To make this determination, the auditor performs **cutoff tests**, and the extent of cutoff tests depends on the auditor's assessment of the effectiveness of the client's cutoff controls. If the client has strong controls to assure that transactions are recorded in the correct period, the auditor can minimize such testing. However, it should be emphasized that controls can be overridden and that auditors have historically found a high degree of risk related to recording sales transactions in the correct period.

执行实质性分析程序

LO 4 Discuss the use of, and apply, substantive analytical procedures.

Performing Substantive Analytical Procedures

Both U.S. and international auditing standards allow the auditor the option of performing substantive analytical procedures; they are not required. A primary benefit of performing substantive analytical procedures is that they can reduce the need to perform additional, costly substantive tests of details. Exhibit 6.9 shows how the mix of tests may vary if the auditor performs substantive analytical procedures. In both Box A and Box B, the auditor is taking a controls reliance approach for a specific account or assertion, and part of the audit evidence is obtained from tests of controls. In Box A, the auditor will obtain the remainder of the audit evidence through substantive tests of details, which might include inspection of documentation, external confirmations,

EXHIBIT **6.9**   Alternative Approaches to Substantive Procedures

BOX A

25% Tests of
Controls

75% Substantive
Procedures: Only
tests of details

BOX B

25% Tests of
Controls

75% Substantive
Procedures: Both
tests of details
and analytical
procedures

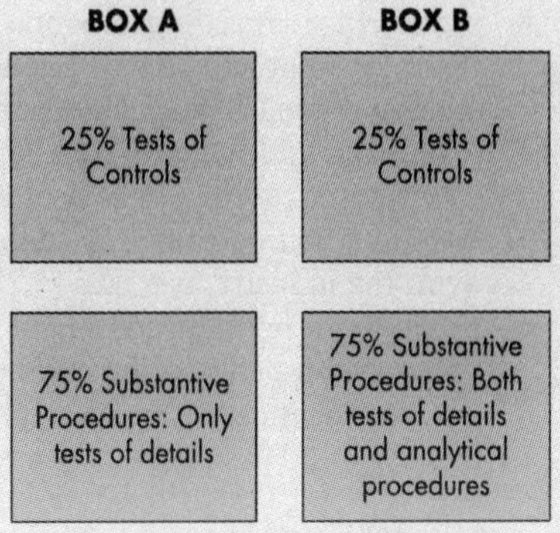

and recalculations. Conversely, in Box B, the auditor will obtain the remainder of the audit evidence from both substantive analytical procedures and substantive tests of details. Note that the relative percentages are judgmental in nature; the examples are simply intended to give you a sense of how an auditor might select an appropriate mix of procedures. As discussed next, if the substantive analytical procedures suggest that the account is materially correct, then the evidence needed from tests of details can be reduced.

In deciding to perform analytical procedures as a substantive audit procedure, the auditor considers the following:

- Does the company have adequate internal controls over the account? The more effective a client's internal controls, the greater reliance an auditor can place on substantive analytical procedures. Importantly, if a company does not have effective internal controls the auditor will rely more heavily on tests of details than on substantive analytical procedures as the auditor will have concerns about the quality of information that would be used in performing the analytical procedure.
- Is the risk of material misstatement low enough that inferences from indirect evidence such as substantive analytical procedures are appropriate to make conclusions about an account?
- Are the underlying data used in evaluating an account both relevant and reliable? External sources of data that might be used to help develop expectations include analyst reports and industry benchmarking data, while internal sources include budgets and forecasts, operational information for current and prior periods, and information from discussions with management.
- Are the relationships among the data logical and justified by current economic conditions? Plausible relationships among data may reasonably be expected to exist and continue in the absence of known conditions to the contrary. For example, a plausible relationship likely exists between store square footage and retail sales by store. Typical examples of other relationships and sources of data that might be used in analytical procedures include the following:
  - Financial information for equivalent prior periods, such as comparing the trend of fourth-quarter sales for the past three years and analyzing dollar and percent changes from the prior year, with prior expectations as to how the current results are expected to compare with these prior periods
  - Expected or planned results developed from budgets or other forecasts, such as comparing actual division performance with budgeted performance

- Comparison of linked account relationships, such as interest expense and interest-bearing debt
- Ratios of financial information, such as examining the relationship between sales and cost of goods sold or developing and analyzing common-sized financial statements
- Company and industry trends, such as comparing gross margin percentages of product lines or inventory turnover with industry averages, with a prior expectation as to how similar the client is with the industry averages
- Analysis of relevant nonfinancial information, such as analyzing the relationship between the numbers of items shipped and royalty expense or the number of employees and payroll expense

The Process for Performing Analytical Procedures

The process for performing analytical procedures includes the following four steps:

1. *Developing an expectation.* The expectation can be about an account balance, a ratio, or other expected relationship. For example, the auditor might develop an expectation about the client's revenue account, the gross profit margin, or the average payroll expenses per location. In developing an expectation, the auditor relies on information obtained during earlier activities in the audit opinion formulation process. Based on this information, the auditor, for example, may expect an account balance to increase or decrease from the prior period, the auditor may develop a range in which the account balance is expected to fall, or the auditor may develop a point estimate.
2. *Defining when the difference between the auditor's expectation and what the client has recorded would be considered significant.* When the auditor develops an expectation, it is unlikely that the expectation will be exactly the same as what the client has recorded, especially if the auditor's estimate is very precise (for example, a point estimate). Before comparing the auditor's expectation with what the client has recorded, the auditor should define the difference amount that would be considered significant; this will require consideration of the auditor's assessed materiality level.
3. *Computing the difference between the auditor's expectation and what the client has recorded.* Once this mechanical step is completed, the auditor will have identified any significant differences between the auditor's expectation and what the client has recorded. For example, the auditor might have developed an expectation that interest expense will be $1.5 million. If the client has a recorded balance of $1.75 million, the auditor will refer to the assessment made in Step 2 to determine if this difference is significant. As another example, the auditor might have expected the gross profit margin to be 23%. If the client's recorded gross profit margin is 25.5%, the auditor will refer to the assessment made in Step 2 to determine if this difference is significant.
4. *Following up on significant differences.* A significant difference between the auditor's expectation and what the client has recorded indicates an increased likelihood of material misstatement. In evaluating such a difference, the auditor may consider management's responses to the auditor's inquiries about why the difference may exist; but the auditor ordinarily should obtain other evidence to corroborate and quantify the information provided by management. If there is a significant difference, the auditor will likely need to perform sufficient and appropriate tests of details. If there is not a significant difference, the auditor may not have to perform any tests of details or may be able to reduce the amount and type of tests of details performed.

Improving the Effectiveness of Substantive Analytical Procedures The effectiveness of a substantive analytical procedure in providing reliable evidence depends on a number of factors, including (a) the nature of the assertion being tested, (b) the plausibility and predictability of the relationships in the data, (c) the availability and reliability of the data used to develop the expectation, (d) the precision of the expectation that the auditor develops, and (e) the rigor of the analytical procedure employed. While the first three of these factors are relatively self-explanatory, we expand on the latter two of these factors, precision and rigor, next.

In terms of the precision of the expectation, the auditor can develop a very general expectation, for example, that interest income will increase over the prior year. This expectation is likely not precise enough for a substantive analytical procedure. To develop a more precise expectation, the auditor may choose to use disaggregated data. **Disaggregation** involves breaking data down into their component parts, such as different time periods, geographical locations, customer type, or product lines. For example, in the case of interest income, the auditor could disaggregate interest rates based on the type of investment, because interest rates will likely vary across investment types. The more you disaggregate the information, the more precise the expectation.

In terms of the rigor of analytical procedures, note that there are various types of analytical procedures and these types vary in rigor. Three types of analytical procedures that tend to be less rigorous include trend analysis, ratio analysis, and scanning. Trend analysis involves the analysis of changes over time, and its rigor can be improved by including more periods in the trend, using disaggregated data, and using relevant external benchmarks (for example, industry averages). Ratio analysis involves the comparison of relationships between accounts and between an account and nonfinancial data. Similar to trend analysis, if ratio analysis is going to be used as a substantive analytical procedure, it is important to improve its rigor through the use of disaggregated data and relevant external benchmarks. Scanning could be used as a substantive analytical procedure, although its precision and rigor may not always be sufficient for the level required for substantive analytical procedures. When performing scanning, the auditor looks at account balances, listings of transactions, journals, and so on, in an effort to detect any unusual or unexpected balances or transactions. As with all analytical procedures, the auditor who is performing scanning has to have an idea of what is usual or expected. The expectation is based on the auditor's knowledge of the client, and of accounting, and just common sense. For example, the auditor would typically not expect to see several entries for round numbers in millions of dollars posted to the revenue journal at the end of each quarter. The auditor would consider such entries unusual and would follow up to investigate this unexpected finding.

A more rigorous approach to substantive analytical procedures is a reasonableness test. In a **reasonableness test**, the auditor develops an expected value of an account by using data partly or wholly independent of the client's accounting information system. For example, the auditor may develop an expectation of a client's interest income, which is equal to the average amount of investments held by the client for the year multiplied by the average interest rate paid on investments as determined by a source external to the client. While such simple models may be sufficient, the rigor of this analytic can be improved by disaggregating the data, possibly by investment type and time period (for example, a separate expectation for each month or quarter). A reasonableness test for revenue may be more detailed. For example, a reasonable test for sales could be based on the number of units sold, the unit price by product line, different pricing structures, and an understanding of industry trends.

Performing and Documenting Substantive Analytical Procedures by KBA Group

In its inspection of the audit firm KBA Group, the PCAOB noted that in one of KBA Group's audits, the audit team failed to perform and document adequate substantive analytical procedures relating to expenses. While substantive analytical procedures can provide important audit evidence related to income statement accounts, it is important for the audit team to appropriately document and adequately perform these procedures. Otherwise, reviewers of the workpapers, such as the PCAOB, might conclude that the audit team did not obtain sufficient appropriate evidence to support its audit opinion. U.S. auditing standards (AU-C and AU) require the auditor to document the process of substantive analytical procedures, including the expectation developed by the auditor, and follow up on unexpected differences between the auditor's expectation and the client's recorded account. In contrast, the international auditing standard (ISA z520) does not include specific documentation requirements for substantive analytical procedures.

For further details on the KBA Group inspection report, see PCAOB Release No. 104-2005-016.

One of the most rigorous approaches to analytical procedures is regression analysis. In performing regression analysis, the expected, or predicted, value is determined using a statistical technique whereby one or more factors are used to predict an account balance. For example, the auditor may develop a regression model that predicts revenue for a client that has hundreds of retail stores. The factors used in the model might include store square footage, economic factors such as employment data, and geographical location. Because of the amount of data and level of statistical knowledge required for such a procedure, many audit firms do not routinely perform regression analysis.

The *Auditing in Practice* feature "Performing and Documenting Substantive Analytical Procedures by KBA Group" provides an example in which the PCAOB took issue with one audit firm's performance and documentation of substantive analytical procedures.

Application of Substantive Analytical Procedures

Substantive analytical procedures are not simple techniques, but are part of a difficult decision-making process designed to provide evidence about the correctness of an account balance and should be used when the procedures are (a) reliable and (b) more cost-effective than other substantive procedures.

For example, consider the audit of natural gas revenue at a utility company. The auditor has tested controls over revenue recognition, including the processes of reading gas meters and the proper pricing of gas sold to customer homes. The auditor has concluded that internal controls are designed and operating effectively. Further, the auditor has concluded that consumers tend to pay their bills and that consumers do not have independent knowledge of the amount that should have been billed. Given these data, the auditor develops a regression model based on the following:

- Previous year's gas billings
- Changes in housing developments
- Changes in pricing of natural gas for the year
- Changes in the efficiency of energy use (index of efficiency considering new furnaces, insulation, etc.)
- Economic growth in the area

Based on these data, the auditor develops a regression model that predicts expected revenue within a tolerable range of error, with 95% accuracy.

Analytical Procedures Are Not Client Estimates AUDITING IN PRACTICE

There is sometimes confusion about the use of analytical procedures because they often look like client estimates. For example, in smaller businesses, the auditor's working papers may have the best data on bad-debt write-offs, percentage of bad debts as a percentage of sales, changes in credit policies, and changes in the volume of sales. The auditor may use these data in testing an estimate of the allowance for uncollectible accounts prepared by the client. However—and this is important—management is responsible for estimating the allowance. The auditor's work is to gather evidence on the accuracy of that estimate. The auditor's testing may come from

gathering evidence to support the client's underlying assumptions and recomputing the estimate. Alternatively, the auditor's testing may come from a substantive analytical procedure—using accumulated data in the auditor's workpapers, plus additional economic data, to come up with an independent estimate of the proper account balance. That estimate, however, represents audit evidence that the auditor should use in determining whether or not the client's account balance is correct. Substantive analytical procedures are designed to provide independent evidence about account balances—not to replace management's underlying estimation process.

If the auditor finds that the recorded revenue is within that range, further substantive testing of the account balance may not be necessary. Note that this conclusion is based on the assessment that the risk of material misstatement is low. In areas where significant risks of material misstatement exist, it is unlikely that audit evidence obtained from substantive analytical procedures alone will be sufficient. In those situations, the auditor will likely also need to perform substantive tests of details. However, if substantive analytical procedures provide reliable evidence, the auditor may be able to alter the nature, timing, or extent of substantive tests of details.

If a comparison of the auditor's expectation based on the regression analysis and the client's recorded revenue balance indicates a significant difference, the auditor follow up on this difference. The auditor should consider possible explanations for the difference, and even consider the possibility that the auditor's expectation might be flawed in some way (for example, the expectation did not incorporate important and recent economic events). Other causes for significant differences could be error or fraud in the client's accounting records. The auditor will also inquire of the client as to possible explanations. However, the auditor's follow-up needs to go beyond client inquiry and to include quantification and corroboration. **Quantification** involves determining whether an explanation for the difference can in fact account for the observed difference. If not, then additional explanations may be needed. **Corroboration** involves obtaining sufficient evidence that the explanation is accurate. The auditor must not just accept the client's explanation without corroborating that explanation. The *Auditing in Practice* feature "Analytical Procedures Are Not Client Estimates" provides important advice about the distinction between the work of the audit firm and the work of client management.

Sufficiency of Audit Evidence

Sufficiency of evidence is the measure of the quantity of audit evidence. The quantity of audit evidence needed is affected by the auditor's assessment of the risks of material misstatement (the higher the assessed risks, the more audit evidence is likely to be required) and also by the quality of such audit evidence (the higher the evidence quality, the less evidence may be required). The amount of evidence must be of sufficient quantity to convince the audit team of the effectiveness of internal control or the accuracy of an account

审计证据的充分性

LO 5 Identify factors affecting the sufficiency of audit evidence.

审计证据的充分性
(sufficiency of evidence)
是对审计证据数量的衡量，它是指审计证据的数量要足以支持注册会计师的审计意见。注册会计师判断证据是否充分，主要考虑其评估的重大错报风险和审计证据的质量。

balance or assertion. Similarly, the evidence must stand on its own such that another unbiased professional would reach the same conclusion. However, how much evidence is enough? This is partly a matter of experienced audit judgment, and it is also affected by client risk characteristics. Importantly, audit evidence is integrated from a number of sources. Documentation of that evidence from multiple sources and the demonstrated testing of account balances remain paramount and are the first things to be questioned when an audit fails.

The *Auditing in Practice* feature "When an Auditor Fails to Collect Sufficient Evidence: The Case at Ligand Pharmaceuticals" provides an example of the personal ramifications to the auditor of knowingly and recklessly not collecting sufficient evidence. In that feature, the audit partner was aware of factors that called into question the adequacy of Ligand's reserves for returns (for example, lack of actual return history, limited visibility into distribution channels, and significant increases in or excess levels of inventory), but he did not adequately analyze whether those factors impaired Ligand's ability to make reasonable estimates of returns. Consequently, the PCAOB concluded that the auditor in this case did not have a sufficient basis to support the conclusion that Ligand's revenue recognition was appropriate.

When an Auditor Fails to Collect Sufficient Evidence: The Case at Ligand Pharmaceuticals

AUDITING IN PRACTICE

James L. Fazio, age 46, was a CPA and partner in the San Diego office of Deloitte LLP. He was the partner-in-charge of the audit of Ligand Pharmaceuticals. At the time of the 2003 Ligand audit, Deloitte's audit policies required that each client's engagement risk be assessed annually as normal, greater than normal, or much greater than normal. In Ligand's case, the engagement team assessed engagement risk as "greater than normal" because of concerns regarding product sales and sales returns. Specifically, the engagement team documented concern in the audit workpapers that Ligand's estimates of sales returns and reserves were not sufficient to cover actual returns. Given the heightened risk, the written audit plan called for the engagement team to perform procedures to address the issue and to increase its professional skepticism regarding the returns issues.

However, the PCAOB found that James Fazio failed to obtain sufficient appropriate evidence to afford a reasonable basis for an opinion regarding the financial statements. Specifically, he failed to (1) adequately assess whether Ligand had gathered sufficient evidence to properly estimate future returns, (2) adequately evaluate the reasonableness of Ligand's estimates of returns, and (3) identify and address issues concerning Ligand's exclusion of certain returns from its estimates of returns.

The PCAOB concluded that Fazio's conduct met conditions warranting sanctions because of "intentional or knowing conduct, including reckless conduct." As a result of this conclusion, the PCAOB ordered that Fazio not be allowed to associate with a registered public accounting firm; but he may file a petition for PCAOB consent to have such an association after two years.

Ultimately, Ligand restated its financial statements for 2003 and other periods because its revenue recognition did not follow the applicable financial reporting framework. In its restatement, Ligand recognized about $59 million less in revenues (a 52% decrease from what was originally reported), and revealed a net loss that was more than 2.5 times the net loss originally reported. Thus, investors were misled by Ligand's misstated financial statements and by Fazio's failure to conduct sufficient audit tests in a manner that would have led to more accurate financial statements. The punishment that Fazio received highlights an evidence-sufficiency dilemma for auditors: No bright-line requirements tell auditors that they have collected enough evidence, yet if it is subsequently determined that they have not done so, then very severe ramifications can exist for what is subsequently deemed improper professional judgment.

For further information on this case, see PCAOB Release No. 105-2007–006, December 10, 2007.

Sample Sizes

For many tests of controls and substantive tests of details, the auditor will need to determine a sample size to use for testing. For example, assume that the auditor wants to send accounts receivable confirmations to a client's customers to obtain evidence related to the existence assertion. Or assume that the auditor wants to test the operating effectiveness of a control by inspecting purchase orders for the required approval. How many confirmations should be sent? How many purchases orders should be inspected? The sample size can be determined by applying a statistically based formula or using the auditor's professional judgment. When performing substantive tests of details, factors that would be considered in determining sample size include the risk of material misstatement and the assurance obtained from other procedures. When performing tests of controls, the extent of evidence necessary to persuade the auditor that the control is effective depends upon the risk associated with the control, that is, the risk that the control might not be effective and, if not effective, the risk that a material misstatement could occur. As the risk associated with the control being tested increases, the evidence that the auditor should obtain also increases. Issues related to determining appropriate sample sizes are discussed further in Chapter 8.

Additional Sample Size Considerations for Tests of Controls

When performing tests of controls, the amount of evidence the auditor needs to obtain depends on whether the client has tested controls as a basis for its assertion on the effectiveness of internal control. Further, the type of control being tested will affect the auditor's sample size. If the auditor is testing a manual control related to transaction processing, sample sizes will be based on guidelines developed for attribute testing using statistical sampling techniques (discussed in Chapter 8). For the most part, these sample sizes will vary between 30 and 100 transactions. In contrast, as discussed in Chapter 3, some controls related to transaction processing are automated controls built into computer applications. If the auditor has tested general computer controls, such as controls over program changes, and has concluded that those controls are effective, the tests of computerized application controls could be as small as one for each kind of control of interest to the auditor. However, in most cases, a control addresses a wide variety of circumstances, and the auditor may choose to examine exception reports to identify how unusual transactions are handled.

Another factor influencing sample sizes for tests of controls is the frequency with which a control is performed. For monthly controls, such as a bank reconciliation, the auditor could choose one month and perform a test of control, such as inspection of documentation or reperformance. In contrast, if a control is performed multiple times each day, such as controls over sales transactions, the auditor will use a larger sample.

Controls over adjusting entries require additional consideration as adjusting entries represent a high risk of material misstatement. The auditor's extent of tests of controls over adjusting entries will be inversely related to the control environment; in other words, the better the control environment, the smaller the sample size will be, and vice versa. The testing also varies directly with the materiality of the account balance and the auditor's assessment of risk that the account balance might be misstated. The auditor wants to review a number of transactions to determine that (a) other controls are not being overridden by management; (b) there is support for the adjusting entries, for example, underlying data analyses; and (c) the entries are properly approved by the appropriate level of management. If the number of transactions is high, the auditor might use statistical sampling. If the number of transactions is low, the auditor may choose to focus on the larger transactions.

对附加证据的考虑

审计管理层估计所需的证据

LO 6	Identify issues related to audit evidence needed for accounts involving management estimates.

Additional Evidence Considerations

Evidence Needed for Auditing Management Estimates

Many account balances are subject to estimates, appraisals, or other management assumptions. These accounts include estimated warranty liabilities, allowance for doubtful accounts or loan loss reserves, pension costs and liabilities, valuations of fixed assets, fair market value assessments, and analysis of goodwill for possible impairment. The auditor must determine that these management judgments are substantiated by independent, objective, and verifiable data that support the estimates. Unfortunately, accounting estimates have too often been subject to earnings management. As illustrated in the *Auditing in Practice* feature "A Description of Common Types of Earnings Management Techniques," auditors must take special care to exercise appropriate professional skepticism in evaluating the reasonableness of management estimates so that earnings management can be mitigated in a quality audit.

Objective and independent evidence must be gathered to evaluate management's accounting estimates. Auditors need to understand the processes used by management in developing estimates, including (a) controls over the process, (b) the reliability of underlying data in developing the estimate, (c) use of outside experts by management (for example, how they were used and their expertise), and (d) how management reviews the results of the estimates for reasonableness.

The auditor should evaluate, based on the audit evidence, whether the accounting estimates in the financial statements are reasonable. The auditor should also obtain sufficient appropriate audit evidence about whether

---

A Description of Common Types of Earnings Management Techniques

AUDITING IN PRACTICE

What types of earnings management related to estimates and other subjective assessments should auditors be prepared to detect and address? A summary of a variety of common types follows:

- *Cookie jar reserves techniques*—This approach involves management overaccruing expenses in the current period to set up a reserve that is reversed back into income in a future period. Examples of areas where cookie jar reserves are often created include accounts receivable allowance for doubtful accounts, sales returns and allowances, warranty allowances, and inventory allowance for valuation declines. This approach is typically used when management has already met its numbers and has extra cushion that can be saved for future periods that may not be as good.
- *Big bath techniques*—This approach is used when a company is already reporting bad news and involves charging as many potential future costs to expenses in the current bad

year, so that those costs will not have to be recognized in the future. While the current year stock price will be negatively affected, management thinks that a little more bad news will not be noticed, and future years will look particularly good and the stock price will rebound accordingly. Auditors should watch for the application of big bath techniques when companies report asset impairments, dispose of a significant part of their operations, or restructure debt.
- *Amortization, depreciation, and depletion techniques*—When a company has long-lived assets, those assets are expensed through amortization, depreciation, or depletion. The auditor should watch for management to exercise judgment in making selective decisions about the type of write-off method used, the write-off period, and the estimate of salvage value that might indicate earnings management.

disclosures in the financial statements related to accounting estimates are appropriate. Options for obtaining evidence include the following:

- Determine whether events occurring up to the date of the auditor's report provide audit evidence regarding the accounting estimate (for example, sale of a discontinued product shortly after the period end may provide audit evidence relating to the estimate of its net realizable value).
- Test how management made the accounting estimate and the data on which it is based. In doing so, the auditor should evaluate whether the method of measurement used is appropriate, the assumptions used by management are reasonable, the data on which the estimate is based are sufficiently reliable.
- Test the operating effectiveness of controls over the process management used to make the accounting estimate, together with appropriate substantive procedures.
- Develop a point estimate or range to evaluate management's point estimate.

Estimates that are based on industry-wide or economy-wide trends need to be independently evaluated. For example, earnings assumptions related to returns on pension funds should be based on how well stocks, as a whole, are doing within the economy and long-run predicted growth within the economy. Other pension data include actuarial reports on life expectancies and benefits that rely on experts. The auditor should review such evidence for consistency with economic reports and actuarial reports, and compare with the assumptions used by other clients and other companies in the same industry.

Using a Specialist/Expert to Assist with Obtaining Evidence

利用专家的帮助获取证据

When obtaining audit evidence for certain accounts, auditors may need to rely on work performed by an outside specialist/expert. (International auditing standards use the term *expert* rather than specialist; for simplicity we use the term *specialist* but acknowledge that both terms are appropriate.) It may be that for some accounts, expertise in a field other than accounting or auditing is necessary to obtain sufficient appropriate audit evidence. For example, using the work and relying on the valuation opinions of outside specialists are particularly relevant in auditing natural resources and other long-lived assets in which subject-matter expertise is required. The following are other examples where the auditor would likely rely on a specialist:

LO 7 Determine situations requiring the auditor to use a specialist/expert and describe the auditor's responsibilities related to that specialist/expert.

- The valuation of land and buildings, plant and machinery, jewelry, works of art, antiques, and intangible assets
- The estimation of oil and gas reserves
- The interpretation of contracts, laws, and regulations
- The analysis of complex or unusual tax compliance issues

The relevant auditing standards apply to situations in which the auditor has responsibilities relating to the work of an individual in a field of specialization other than accounting or auditing, and when the auditor uses that work to obtain sufficient appropriate audit evidence. Auditing standards require the auditor to understand the role, knowledge, and objectivity of the specialist and how the specialist's work affects important financial accounts.

When using the work of a specialist, the auditor needs to evaluate the professional qualifications of the individual. In making this evaluation, the auditor will consider:

- The professional certification, license, or other recognition of the competence of the specialist in his or her field, as appropriate
- The reputation and standing of the specialist in the views of peers and others familiar with the specialist's capability or performance

- The specialist's experience in the type of work under consideration

Further, the auditor needs to understand the nature of the work performed by the specialist. The auditor will:

- Obtain an understanding of the methods and assumptions used by the specialist
- Make appropriate tests of data provided to the specialist, taking into account the auditor's assessment of control risk
- Evaluate whether the specialist's findings support the related assertions in the financial statements

As indicated next, AU-C 620 notes that even when the auditor uses a specialist to obtain audit evidence, the auditor still has ultimate responsibility for the audit opinion.

> The auditor has sole responsibility for the audit opinion expressed, and that responsibility is not reduced by the auditor's use of the work of an auditor's specialist. Nonetheless, if the auditor using the work of an auditor's specialist, having followed this section, concludes that the work of that specialist is adequate for the auditor's purposes, the auditor may accept that specialist's findings or conclusions in the specialist's field as appropriate audit evidence.

审计关联方交易所需的证据

Evidence Needed for Related-Party Transactions

LO 8 Describe the evidence needs for related-party transactions.

Some transactions that an auditor will obtain evidence about are **related-party transactions**. These are transactions that a client has with other companies or people that may be related to either the client or client's senior management. Related-party transactions can occur between:

- Parents and subsidiaries
- An entity and its owners
- An entity and other organizations in which it has part ownership, such as joint ventures
- An entity and an assortment of special-purpose entities (SPEs), such as those designed to keep debt off the balance sheet

Many related-party transactions are conducted in the normal course of business and have no higher risk of material misstatement than similar transactions with unrelated parties. However, the nature of related-party relationships and transactions may give rise to higher risks of material misstatement of the financial statements than transactions with unrelated parties. For example, related-party transactions may be motivated primarily to engage in fraudulent financial reporting or to conceal misappropriation of assets. Or related-party transactions may not be conducted under normal market terms and conditions. These types of transactions present unique challenges for auditors.

When performing procedures for related-party transactions, the auditor should expect the client to have an information system, with effective internal controls, that can identify all related parties and account for all related-party transactions. The auditor should begin with an understanding of the information system developed by the client to identify such transactions. The auditor should be aware that in some cases, the client may not want to have related-party transactions discovered. Still, the auditor will work to obtain a list of all related parties and develop a list of all transactions with those parties during the year.

Once all related parties are identified, the auditor can use generalized audit software (discussed in Chapter 8) to read the client files and list all transactions that occurred with these parties. The auditor then investigates the transactions to determine whether they have been properly recorded. Finally, the auditor determines the appropriateness of management's disclosures. Exhibit 6.10 gives an overview of relevant audit procedures for related-party transactions.

| EXHIBIT **6.10** | Relevant Audit Procedures for Related-Party Transactions |

AUDIT OBJECTIVE: Determine if related-entity transactions occurred during the year and whether they are properly (a) authorized and (b) disclosed in the financial statements.

1. Inquire of the client about processes used to identify related-party transactions and the client's approach to accounting for related-party transactions.
2. Ask the client to prepare a list of all related parties. Supplement that list with disclosures that have been made to the Securities and Exchange Commission (SEC) of top officers and directors in the company. For smaller businesses, supplement the list with a listing of known relatives who may be active in the business or related businesses.
3. Ask the client for a list of all related-party transactions, including those with SPEs or variable interest entities, that occurred during the year.
4. Discuss the appropriate accounting for all identified related-party transactions with the client and develop an understanding of the appropriate disclosure for the financial statements.
5. Inquire of the client and its lawyers as to whether the client is under any investigation by regulatory agencies or law officials regarding related-party transactions.
6. Review the news media and SEC filings for any investigations of related-party transactions of the client.
7. Use generalized audit software to read the client's files and prepare a list of all transactions that occurred with related entities per the lists identified earlier. Compare the list to that developed by the client to help determine the quality of the client's information system.
8. Identify all unusual transactions using information specific to the client, including information on (a) unusually large sales occurring near the end of a period, (b) sales transactions with unusual terms, (c) purchase transactions that appear to be coming from customers, and (d) any other criteria the auditor might consider useful.
9. Review the transactions and investigate whether or not the transactions occurred with related entities. If related parties can be identified, determine the purpose of the transactions and consider the appropriate financial statement disclosure.
10. Determine whether any of the transactions were fraudulent or were prepared primarily to develop fraudulent financial statements. If there is intent to deceive, or if there is misuse of corporate funds, report the fraud or misuse to the board of directors. Follow up to determine if appropriate action is taken. If such action is not taken, consult with legal counsel.
11. Determine the appropriate accounting and footnote disclosure.
12. Prepare a memo on findings.

Performing audit procedures listed in Exhibit 6.10 is particularly important for related-party transactions because of the potential for undisclosed related-party relationships and transactions. In addition to the procedures in Exhibit 6.10, when performing audit procedures for accounts and assertions, the auditor should remain alert for information that may indicate the existence of related-party relationships or transactions that management has not previously identified or disclosed to the auditor.

Documenting Audit Evidence

记录审计证据

Audit documentation is the record that forms the basis for the auditor's representations and conclusions. Audit documentation facilitates the planning, performance, and supervision of the audit and forms the basis of the review of the quality of the work performed. Audit documentation includes records of the planning and performance of the work, the procedures performed, evidence obtained, and conclusions reached by the auditor.

Auditors like to assume that their work will never be questioned, but that is an unrealistic assumption. The documentation of audit work must stand on its own. The documentation should make it possible for an experienced auditor to evaluate the evidence independently of the individuals who performed the audit and reach the same conclusion. AS 3 notes that the documentation must also clearly show the auditor's reasoning process and the basis for conclusions reached on the audit. AS 3 states "Audit

LO 9 Describe the characteristics of quality audit documentation.

documentation should be prepared in sufficient detail to provide a clear understanding of its purpose, source, and the conclusions reached. Also, the documentation should be appropriately organized to provide a clear link to the significant findings or issues."

Audit documentation should include information about planning and risk assessment procedures (including the response to risk assessment procedures), audit work performed (including tests of controls and substantive procedures), and significant issues identified and their resolution.

记录审计计划和风险评估 程序

Documenting Planning and Risk Assessment Procedures

The planning process and risk assessment procedures form the foundation for the audit and should be carefully documented. For example, as part of performing the planning and the risk assessment procedures, the auditor should document the overall audit strategy and the audit plan. Further, the auditor should document the overall planned responses to address the assessed risks of material misstatement, and the nature, timing, and extent of the further audit procedures to be performed, as well as the linkage of those procedures with the assessed risks at the relevant assertion level. The documentation serves an important planning function for the audit; it also serves as evidence that the auditors took their responsibilities seriously in evaluating potential problems or special circumstances involved in, or related to, the audit. Exhibit 6.11 provides examples of information related to the risk assessment procedures that the auditor would typically document.

记录执行的审计工作

Documenting Audit Work Performed

After identifying risks of material misstatement and the plan for responding to those risks, auditors execute that plan. Documentation about audit work performed is critical in demonstrating at a later date that the audit was conducted in a quality manner. The following are typical types of documentation used to demonstrate the audit work that was performed:

- The client's trial balance and any auditor-proposed adjustments to it
- Copies of selected internal and external documents

EXHIBIT 6.11

Examples of Information Documented from Risk Assessment Procedures

- Interviews with key executives, with implications clearly drawn for the conduct of the audit
- Business risk analysis, fraud risk analysis, and analytical procedures, with a clear identification of accounts and assertions requiring special audit attention
- The auditor's assessment of materiality, overall audit approach, and personnel needed
- Evidence of planning (including identification of and response to risks of material misstatement), including the audit program
- Audit approach and basic data utilized to identify risk, including fraud risk
- Updates on how significant issues from previous year's audits are addressed during the current audit
- An analysis of the auditor's assessment of internal control and a linkage of control deficiencies to expanded (or different) audit tests for accounts where high risk of material misstatements exists
- Memoranda that describe the auditor's conclusions regarding risk associated with acceptance or continuance of the client
- Extent of involvement of professionals with specialized skills

- Memos describing the auditor's approach to gathering evidence and the reasoning process in support of account balances
- Results of analytical procedures and tests of client records, and the individuals responsible for performance, and subsequently the review, of the procedures
- Correspondence with specialists who provided evidence significant to the evaluation or accounting for assets/liabilities and the related revenue expense effects (for example, valuation specialists), including an analysis of the independence and credentials of the specialists
- Auditor-generated analysis of account balances (for example, audit software analysis of accounts and relationships)

Documenting Significant Issues and Their Resolution

Significant issues or **audit findings** are defined as substantive matters that are important to the analysis of the fair presentation of the financial statements. AS 3 provides the following examples of significant issues or audit findings:

记录重要的问题及其解决方法

- Significant matters involving the selection, application, and consistency of accounting principles, including related disclosures. Significant matters include, but are not limited to, accounting for complex or unusual transactions, accounting estimates, and uncertainties, as well as related management assumptions
- Results of auditing procedures that indicated a need for the modification of planned auditing procedures, or the existence of material misstatements, omissions in the financial statements, significant deficiencies, or material weaknesses in internal control over financial reporting
- Audit adjustments. An **audit adjustment** is a correction of a misstatement of the financial statements that was or should have been proposed by the auditor, whether or not recorded by management, which could, either individually or when aggregated with other misstatements, have a material effect on the company's financial statements

审计调整(audit adjustment)
对注册会计师在审计过程中发现的重要或重大审计差异进行的调整。

- Disagreements among members of the engagement team or with others consulted on the engagement about final conclusions reached on significant accounting or auditing matters
- Circumstances that cause significant difficulty in applying auditing procedures
- Significant changes in the assessed level of audit risk for particular audit areas and the auditor's response to those changes
- Any matters that could result in the modification of the auditor's report

The PCAOB requires that all audit engagements document significant issues or audit findings, as well as the actions taken to address them (including additional evidence obtained, where applicable). The following are typical types of documentation retained to demonstrate audit work related to the identification of significant issues and their resolution:

- Identification of significant accounting issues that were identified during the course of audit and how they were resolved, including any correspondence with national office experts
- A clear articulation of the auditor's judgment and the reasoning process that led to the judgment on the fairness of the financial statements

Copies of Documents

Some client documents are of such importance that a copy should be included in the audit documentation. Such documents usually have legal significance, such as lease agreements, bond covenant agreements, significant portions of the board of directors' minutes, government correspondence

记录的复印件

regarding client investigations, and loan agreements. Responses to the auditor's confirmation requests for accounts receivable, pending litigation, or bank loans are examples of documents from outside parties that are retained. Finally, management representations are formally documented in a management representation letter, which is signed by management to acknowledge the accuracy of its verbal or written assertions.

注册会计师的备忘录
Auditor-Generated Memos

Auditors assimilate diverse evidence to reach an opinion as to whether a particular account balance is fairly stated. The auditor's reasoning process in assembling and analyzing evidence is important and should be documented via auditor-generated memos. At first you might think that documenting your own opinion is unnecessary. After all, you will have documented all the evidence underlying that opinion. However, the documentation must stand on its own; in other words, another auditor must be able to understand the reasoning process by which you evaluated that evidence and formulated your opinion. In order to gain that understanding, another auditor will not be able to rely on just talking to you. Over time you will likely forget important details about how you reached your opinions; therefore, documenting them for the audit file via an auditor-generated memo is essential.

高质量审计工作底稿的特征
Characteristics of Quality Audit Documentation

Audit documentation serves as the primary evidence of an audit. Exhibit 6.12 provides an example of a workpaper related to an inventory price test.

EXHIBIT 6.12 Working Paper for Inventory Price Test

C-1/2

CMI Manufacturing Company — Prepared by: ACM

Inventory Price Test — Date: 1/21/14

Year Ended December 31, 2013 — Reviewed by: KMJ

Date: 1/30/14

Item No.	Item Name	Quantity	Cost Per Unit	Extended Cost
4287	Advanced Microstamping machine	22*	$5,128†	112,816.00‡
5203	1/4 HP electric motor	10*	$39†	390.00‡
2208	Assembly kit for motor housing	25*	$12†	300.00‡
1513	Micro stamping machine, Model 25	200*	$2,100†	420,000.00‡
0068	Rack & Pinion component	300*	$42†	12,600.00‡
8890	Repair kits for stamping machines	1,000*	$48†	48,000.00‡
	Total value of items tested			594,106.00
	Items not tested			1,802,000.00
	Balance per general ledger			2,396,106.00§

Sampled items were selected utilizing a dollar unit sampling technique with materiality of $50,000, and internal control assessed as effective (B-1).
*Quantities agree with client physical inventory tested earlier.
†Traced to client's standard cost system that was independently tested (B-2). Amount agrees with client's standard cost.
‡Tested extension, no exceptions.
§Footed, no exceptions; agrees with trial balance.
Conclusion: No significant issues were noted. In my opinion, the pricing and clerical accuracy of inventory is proper.

A review of Exhibit 6.12 indicates that audit documentation should contain the following:

- A heading that includes the name of the audit client, an explanatory title, and the balance sheet date
- The initials or electronic signature of the auditor performing the audit test and the date the test was completed
- The initials or electronic signature of the manager or partner who reviewed the documentation and the date the review was completed
- A workpaper page number (see C-1/2 in Exhibit 6.12)
- A description of the tests performed (including the items looked at) and the findings
- Tick marks and a tick mark legend indicating the nature of the work performed by the auditor
- An assessment of whether the tests indicate the possibility of material misstatement in an account
- A cross-reference to related documentation, when applicable (see references to other workpapers, including B-1 and B-2 in Exhibit 6.12)
- A section that identifies all significant issues that arose during the audit and how they were resolved
- A comprehensive and clear memorandum that delineates the auditor's analysis of the consistency of audit evidence and the conclusions reached regarding the fairness of the financial presentation (see references to other worked performed at B-1 and B-2 in Exhibit 6.12. A second page of this workpaper, C-2/2, would likely include a more comprehensive memo.)

Revisions and Retention of Audit Documentation

审计工作底稿的修改和保存

Audit documentation generally should be completed and assembled within 60 days following the audit report release date. After that date, the auditor must not delete or discard audit documentation before the end of the required retention period (generally seven years). Occasionally, because of an internal or external quality review process, it may be determined that procedures considered necessary were omitted from the audit or the auditor subsequently becomes aware of information related to financial statements that have already been issued. The auditor should then perform any necessary procedures and make the necessary changes to the audit documentation.

审计工作底稿的归档期限为审计报告日后60天内。除非有特殊情况，注册会计师不得在规定的保存期届满前修改、删除或废弃审计工作底稿。

Audit Programs

审计计划

An **audit program** documents the procedures to be performed in gathering audit evidence and is used to record the successful completion of each audit step. The auditor makes decisions on the best combination of procedures to use in gathering evidence to evaluate assertions for each client. The audit program provides an effective means for:

LO 10 Explain the nature, design, and purposes of audit programs.

- Organizing and distributing audit work
- Monitoring the audit process and progress
- Recording the audit work performed and those responsible for performing the work
- Reviewing the completeness and persuasiveness of procedures performed

Most audit firms have standardized audit programs that should be modified to fit a client's unique features, including risk factors. For example, the audit of accounts receivable might appear to be the same for most businesses. However, significant differences may exist in how each organization processes receivables and the related controls, or their credit terms, or in the economic health of their industry that might cause an audit team to modify a standard audit program to fit the particular circumstances of the client. A partial audit program for accounts receivable is presented in Exhibit 6.13.

EXHIBIT **6.13**	Partial Audit Program for Accounts Receivable		
Audit Procedures		**Performed by**	**Reference**
1. Test the accuracy and completeness of the underlying accounting records by footing the accounts receivable file and agreeing it to the general ledger (valuation).		_____	_____
2. Take a sample of recorded accounts receivable balances and confirm the balances with the customers (existence, valuation, rights).		_____	_____
3. Vouch aging details to supporting documents, discuss collectibility of receivables with responsible officials, and review correspondence with customers (valuation).		_____	_____
4. Analyze allowance for doubtful accounts; compare to past history and industry trends to determine adequacy (valuation).		_____	_____
5. Take a sample of recorded receivables and prepare a list of subsequent cash receipts to determine if they are fully paid before the end of the audit (existence, valuation, rights).		_____	_____
6. Verify cutoff for sales, cash receipts, and returns by examining transactions near the end of the year (completeness, existence).		_____	_____
7. Determine adequacy of disclosure of related-party, pledged, discounted, or assigned receivables (presentation).		_____	_____

SUMMARY AND NEXT STEPS

Each audit is unique, but the approach to all audits is essentially the same. Management makes assertions in financial statements about the existence/occurrence, completeness, rights or obligations, valuation, and presentation/disclosure of financial data. Management might also make an assertion about the effectiveness of its internal control over financial reporting. Evidence about these assertions is gathered, analyzed, and documented to enable the auditor to reach a justified opinion on the fairness of the financial statements. Auditing standards require the auditor to gather sufficient appropriate evidence. A quality audit combines this audit evidence to provide reasonable assurance that the financial statements are free of material misstatement. Now that you understand audit evidence and audit procedures, the next chapter turns to the planning phase of the audit, including risk assessment procedures.

SIGNIFICANT TERMS

Accounting records The records of initial accounting entries and supporting records.

Analytical procedures Evaluations of financial information through analyzing plausible relationships among both financial and nonfinancial data.

Appropriateness of audit evidence A measure of the quality of audit evidence, and includes both the relevance and reliability of the evidence.

Audit adjustment Correction of a misstatement of financial statements that was or should have been proposed by the auditor, whether or not recorded by management, that could, either individually or when aggregated with other misstatements, have a material effect on the company's financial statements.

Audit documentation The written record that forms the basis for the auditor's conclusions.

Audit program A workpaper that specifies the procedures to be performed in gathering audit evidence and is used to record the successful completion of each audit step.

Auditor's specialist An individual or organization possessing expertise in a field other than accounting or auditing, whose work in that field is used by the auditor to assist the auditor in obtaining sufficient appropriate audit evidence. An auditor's specialist may be either an auditor's internal specialist (who is a partner or staff, including temporary staff, of the auditor's firm or a network firm) or an auditor's external specialist.

Corroboration Obtaining sufficient evidence that management's explanation is accurate.

Cross-footing Checking the agreement of the cross-addition of a number of columns of figures that sum to a grand total.

Cutoff period A period of time usually covering several days before and after the client's balance sheet date.

Cutoff tests Procedures applied to transactions selected from those recorded during the cutoff period to provide evidence as to whether the transactions have been recorded in the proper period.

Direct evidence Audit evidence that requires only one inference to reach a conclusion about the assertion being tested. Usually that inference is that the sample taken is representative of the population as a whole.

Directional testing An approach to testing account balances that considers the type of misstatement likely to occur in the account balance and the corresponding evidence provided by other accounts that have been tested. The auditor normally tests assets and expenses for overstatement, and liabilities and revenues for understatement, because (1) the major risks of misstatements on those accounts are in those directions or (2) tests of other accounts provide evidence of possible misstatements in the other direction.

Disaggregation Breaking data down into their component parts, such as different time periods, geographical locations, customer type, or product lines.

Footing Adding a column of figures to verify the correctness of the client's totals.

Indirect evidence Audit evidence that requires a linkage of inferences to provide assurance about the assertion being tested, that is, one or more inferences are made. Examples include inferences made when using analytical procedures as audit evidence.

Interim date A date at which audit evidence is collected earlier than the balance sheet date.

Management's specialist An individual or organization possessing expertise in a field other than accounting or auditing, whose work in that field is used by the entity to assist the entity in preparing the financial statements.

Quantification Determining whether management's explanation for observed differences can in fact account for the observed difference.

Reasonableness test The development of an expected value of an account by using data partly or wholly independent of the client's accounting information system.

Recalculating estimated amounts Recomputing an amount that the client has already estimated, such as recomputing the allowance for doubtful accounts based on a formula related to the aging of accounts receivable ending balances.

Related-party transactions Transactions that a client has with other companies or people who may be related to either the client or client's senior management.

Relevance of audit evidence Evidence that provides insight on the validity of the assertion being tested; that is, the evidence bears directly on the assertion being tested.

Reliability of audit evidence A measure of the quality of the underlying evidence. It is influenced by risk, potential management bias associated with the evidence, and the quality of the internal control system underlying the preparation of the evidence.

Reperformance The auditor's independent execution of controls that were originally performed as part of the entity's internal control.

Roll-forward period The period between the confirmation date and the balance sheet date.

Scanning A type of analytical procedure involving the auditor's review of accounting data to identify significant or unusual items to test.

Significant issues or audit findings Substantive matters that are important to the procedures performed, evidence obtained, or conclusions reached on an audit.

Sufficiency of evidence Measure of the quantity of audit evidence.

Tests of extensions Recomputing items involving multiplication.

Tracing Taking a sample of original source documents and ensuring that the transactions related to the source documents have been recorded in the appropriate journal and general ledger.

Vouching Taking a sample of recorded transactions and obtaining the original source documents supporting the recorded transaction.

TRUE-FALSE QUESTIONS

6-1 **LO 1** The appropriateness of audit evidence refers to its relevance and reliability.

6-2 **LO 1** The sufficiency of evidence is a measure of evidence quality.

6-3 `LO 2` When testing for existence, the auditor will vouch recorded transactions.

6-4 `LO 2` Evidence that is obtained directly from the client is usually considered more reliable than evidence obtained from a source independent of the client.

6-5 `LO 3` A procedure that involves only inspection of documentation is usually considered to be of lower quality than a procedure involving reperformance.

6-6 `LO 3` All audit procedures need to be performed at or after the client's balance sheet date.

6-7 `LO 4` Substantive analytical procedures are required on every audit.

6-8 `LO 4` One of the most rigorous approaches to substantive analytical procedures is regression analysis.

6-9 `LO 5` The quantity of audit evidence needed when testing an account will be influenced by the risk of material misstatement in that account.

6-10 `LO 5` When testing the operating effectiveness of a control, the frequency with which the control is performed will influence the sample size to be used by the auditor.

6-11 `LO 6` Because management estimates are often subjective, the auditor does not need to test these estimates, but can rely solely on management's work.

6-12 `LO 6` When testing management estimates, the auditor should understand the process that management uses to develop its estimates.

6-13 `LO 7` When relying on the work of a specialist, the auditor should evaluate the professional qualifications of the specialist.

6-14 `LO 7` When the auditor uses the work of a specialist, the auditor's responsibility for the audit opinion is reduced.

6-15 `LO 8` The auditor may be able to use generalized audit software to identify transactions that have been entered into with related parties.

6-16 `LO 8` A primary concern for the auditor for related-party transactions is whether undisclosed related-party relationships and transactions exist.

6-17 `LO 9` The auditor should document significant issues that were identified and how they were resolved.

6-18 `LO 9` As part of the audit documentation, auditors should maintain copies of all client documents reviewed during the audit.

6-19 `LO 10` A standardized audit program, without any modifications, should be used for each client.

6-20 `LO 10` An audit program can be used to record the audit work performed and identify those responsible for performing the work.

MULTIPLE-CHOICE QUESTIONS

6-21 `LO 1` Which of the following statements best describes what is meant by the term *appropriateness of audit evidence*?
a. Appropriateness is a measure of the quality of audit evidence.
b. Appropriateness refers to the relevance and reliability of audit evidence.

    c. Appropriateness is a measure of the quantity of audit evidence.

    d. Both a. and b.

6-22 **LO 1** Which of the following statements is true regarding the relationship between risk and evidence sufficiency for substantive tests?

    a. Evidence sufficiency will be affected by inherent risk, but not control risk.

    b. Evidence sufficiency will be affected by control risk, but not inherent risk.

    c. Evidence sufficiency will be affected by both inherent and control risks.

    d. None of the above statements are true.

6-23 **LO 2** An auditor determines that management integrity is high, the risk of material misstatement is low, and the client's internal controls are effective. Which of the following conclusions can be reached regarding the need to obtain direct evidence regarding the account balances?

    a. Direct evidence can be limited to material account balances, and the extent of testing should be sufficient to corroborate the auditor's assessment of low risk.

    b. Direct evidence of account balances is not needed.

    c. Direct evidence can be obtained through analytical procedures.

    d. Direct evidence should be obtained for all accounts, regardless of the auditor's assessment of control risk.

6-24 **LO 2** Which of the following factors affects the relevance of audit evidence?

    a. The purpose of the audit procedure.

    b. The direction of testing.

    c. The type of procedure.

    d. All of the above factors affect the relevance of audit evidence.

6-25 **LO 3** The auditor wishes to test the completeness assertion. Which of the following statements is true regarding the auditor's work flow?

    a. The auditor would take a sample of recorded transactions and obtain supporting documentation for those transactions.

    b. The auditor would perform a process referred to as tracing.

    c. The auditor would take a sample of source documents and obtain additional supporting documents for those transactions.

    d. For a sample of items recorded in the sales journal, the auditor would obtain the related shipping documents and customer orders.

6-26 **LO 3** The auditor wishes to gather evidence to test the assertion that the client's capitalization of leased equipment assets is properly valued. Which of the following sources of evidence will the auditor generally find to be of the highest quality (most reliable and relevant)?

    a. Inspection of the leased equipment.

    b. Inspection of documents, including the lease contract and recalculation of capitalized amount and current amortization.

    c. Confirmation of the current purchase price for similar equipment with vendors.

    d. Confirmation of the original cost of the equipment with the lessor.

6-27 `LO 4`   Analytical procedures are best used as a substantive audit procedure in which of the following scenarios?
  a. The auditor's primary objective is to reduce audit costs to a minimum.
  b. Internal control risk is high, and therefore it is not efficient to test controls.
  c. Preliminary analytical procedures indicate that misstatements are likely to occur in significant account balances.
  d. Substantive analytical procedures would not be appropriate in any of the above scenarios.

6-28 `LO 4`   Which of the following statements is false regarding substantive analytical procedures?
  a. Substantive analytical procedures are not required to be performed on all audit engagements.
  b. If the results of substantive analytical procedures suggest that an account balance is materially correct, the evidence needed from tests of details can likely be reduced.
  c. Substantive analytical procedures would be performed after tests of details.
  d. All of the above statements are true.

6-29 `LO 5`   The sufficiency of audit evidence is affected by which of the following factors?
  a. The reliability of the audit evidence.
  b. The relevance of the audit evidence gathered.
  c. The risk of material misstatement of the assertion being examined.
  d. All of the above.

6-30 `LO 5`   Which of the following statements is true regarding the sufficiency of evidence needed to test an account?
  a. Evidence sufficiency is a measure of evidence quality.
  b. Evidence sufficiency is affected by the quality of evidence.
  c. A relationship does not exist between evidence sufficiency and evidence quality.
  d. For a specific client, evidence sufficiency will be the same across all accounts.

6-31 `LO 6`   Which of the following procedures would an auditor typically perform first when assessing the reasonableness of management's estimate of its pension liability?
  a. Inspect documentation related to the pension transactions that the client has recorded.
  b. Develop an understanding of management's process for developing the estimate.
  c. Identify sensitive management assumptions.
  d. Review transactions occurring prior to the report release date to assess the reasonableness of management estimates.

6-32 `LO 6`   Which of the following is a reason that accounts containing management estimates pose a high level of risk of material misstatement for auditors?
  a. Accounting estimates are especially susceptible to management bias.
  b. Accounting estimates are a means for management to manage or misstate the financial statements.
  c. Accounting estimates are sensitive to variations in management assumptions.
  d. All of the above are reasons that accounts containing management estimates pose a high level of risk of material misstatement for auditors.

6-33 **LO 7** For which of the following audit judgments would an auditor be least likely to use an audit specialist?
a. Existence of cash.
b. Valuation of works of art.
c. Valuation of oil and gas reserves.
d. Interpretation of laws and regulations.

6-34 **LO 7** Which of the following statements is true regarding the auditor's use of the work of a specialist?
a. The specialist, not the auditor, is responsible for evaluating whether the specialist's findings support the assertions in the financial statements.
b. Because the individual is considered a specialist, the auditor does not need to evaluate the professional qualifications of the specialist.
c. The auditor should obtain an understanding of the methods and assumptions used by the specialist.
d. All of the above statements are true.

6-35 **LO 8** Which of the following statements is most accurate regarding the auditor's primary focus on a client's related-party transactions?
a. The auditor wants reasonable assurance that all related-party transactions are accounted for differently than transactions with unrelated parties.
b. The auditor will want to confirm the existence of the related parties.
c. The auditor wants reasonable assurance that all related-party transactions have been appropriately disclosed.
d. The auditor will focus on verifying the valuation of the related-party transactions.

6-36 **LO 8** Which of the following transactions would be least likely to be a related-party transaction?
a. A purchase transaction between an entity and its owners.
b. A debt-related transaction between an entity and one of its SPEs.
c. An exchange of property between an entity and a joint venture in which the entity has part ownership.
d. Writing-off obsolete inventory prior to year end.

6-37 **LO 9** Which of the following statements is true regarding audit documentation?
a. Auditors document only those significant issues that have not been resolved by the audit report date.
b. Audit documentation provides the principal support for the audit opinion expressed by the auditor.
c. Audit documentation would identify who reviewed the audit work, but not who performed the audit work.
d. Documentation must be in paper format.

6-38 **LO 9** Which of the following items would typically not be included in the heading of a workpaper?
a. Client name.
b. Client balance sheet date.
c. Audit firm name.
d. A descriptive explanatory title.

6-39 **LO 10** Which of the following statements describes a purpose of an audit program?
a. An audit program is used to specify the procedures to be performed in obtaining audit evidence.
b. An audit program is used to record the completion of each audit step.

    c. An audit program is useful for monitoring the progress of the audit.

    d. All of the above statements describe the purpose of an audit program.

6-40 `LO 10` Which of the following items would typically not be included in an audit program?

    a. A list of audit procedures to be performed.

    b. An indication of who performed the procedure.

    c. A workpaper heading.

    d. All of the above would typically be included in an audit program.

REVIEW AND SHORT CASE QUESTIONS

6-41 `LO 1` Refer to Exhibit 6.1. Auditing standards require the auditor to gather sufficient appropriate evidence to ensure that the auditor has a reasonable basis for an opinion regarding the financial statements. What are the characteristics of (a) sufficient audit evidence and (b) appropriate audit evidence? How are sufficiency and appropriateness related?

6-42 `LO 1` Refer to Exhibit 6.1. Describe how the appropriateness and sufficiency of evidence for a specific account is influenced by the risk of material misstatement associated with that account. Contrast how appropriateness and sufficiency of evidence would be different for a high-risk and low-risk assertion.

6-43 `LO 2` Appropriateness of audit evidence considers what two evidence characteristics? Define these characteristics and identify factors that affect these characteristics.

6-44 `LO 2` What is directional testing? How is the concept of directional testing related to appropriateness of audit evidence?

6-45 `LO 2` Refer to Exhibit 6.2 and describe the differences between vouching and tracing.

6-46 `LO 2` Discuss the relative reliability of internal and external documentation. Give two examples of each type of documentation.

6-47 `LO 3` Refer to Exhibit 6.5 and identify the nine types of audit procedures. Assume that you are planning the audit of the PageDoc Company's inventory. PageDoc manufactures a variety of office equipment. Describe how each of the nine procedures could be used in the audit of inventory and identify the related assertion(s) the procedure is designed to test.

6-48 `LO 3` Refer to Exhibit 6.5 to identify the nine types of audit procedures used as part of the audit evidence-gathering process. Following is a list of audit procedures performed. For each procedure (listed as a. through p. below), classify the evidence gathered according to one (or more, if applicable) of the audit procedure types indicated in Exhibit 6.5 and identify the assertion(s) being tested. Organize your answer as follows:

Procedure	Type of Procedure	Assertion Tested
a.		
b.		

    a. Calculate the ratio of cost of goods sold to sales as a test of overall reasonableness of the balance for cost of goods sold.

NOTE: Completing Review and Short Case Questions does not require the student to reference additional resources and materials.

NOTE: For the remaining problems, we make special note of those addressing fraud, international issues, professional skepticism, and ethics.

b. Trace a sales transaction from the origination of an incoming sales order to the shipment of merchandise to an invoice and to the proper recording in the sales journal.

c. Test the accuracy of the sales invoice by multiplying the number of items shipped by the authorized price list to determine extended cost. Foot the total and reconcile it with the total invoiced.

d. Select recorded sales invoices and trace the corresponding shipping documents to verify the existence of goods shipped.

e. Examine canceled checks returned with the client's January bank statement as support of outstanding checks listed on the client's December year-end bank reconciliation.

f. Perform inspection and independently count a sample of the client's marketable securities held in a safe deposit box.

g. Tour the plant to determine that a major equipment acquisition was received and is in working condition.

h. Review a lease contract to determine the items it covers and its major provisions.

i. Request a statement from a major customer as to its agreement or disagreement with a year-end receivable balance shown to be due to the audit client.

j. Develop a spreadsheet to calculate an independent estimate of the client's warranty liability (reserve) based on production data and current warranty repair expenditures.

k. Meet with the client's internal legal department to determine its assessment of the potential outcome of pending litigation regarding a patent infringement suit against the company.

l. Review all major past-due accounts receivable with the credit manager to determine whether the client's allowance for doubtful accounts is adequate.

m. Make test counts of inventory items counted by client personnel.

n. Obtain information about the client's processing system and associated controls by asking the client's personnel to fill out a questionnaire.

o. Examine board of directors' minutes for the approval of a major bond issued during the year.

p. Have the client's outside law firm send a letter directly to the auditor providing a description of any differences between the lawyer's assessment of litigation and that of the client.

6-49 **LO 3** Assume that an automotive company discloses the following risk factors (labeled 1. through 7. below) that might affect the financial statements.

1. Continued decline in market share, and a market shift (or an increase in or acceleration of market shift) away from sales of trucks or sport utility vehicles, or from sales of other more profitable vehicles in the United States.

2. Continued or increased price competition resulting from industry overcapacity, currency fluctuations, or other factors.

3. Lower-than-anticipated market acceptance of new or existing products.

4. Substantial pension and postretirement health care and life insurance liabilities impairing our liquidity or financial condition.

5. Worse-than-assumed economic and demographic experience for our postretirement benefit plans (e.g., discount rates, investment returns, and health care cost trends).

6. The discovery of defects in vehicles resulting in delays in new model launches, recall campaigns, or increased warranty costs.

7. Unusual or significant litigation or governmental investigations arising out of alleged defects in our products or otherwise.
   a. For each risk factor, identify a related account balance that might be affected by the risk.
   b. For each account balance identified, indicate how the risk will affect the audit evidence that will be gathered. Include what specific assertion is being addressed.

6-50 `LO 3` An auditor has to determine both the reliability and the relevance of potential audit evidence in order to determine that appropriate audit evidence is gathered.

a. Explain the difference between relevance and reliability.
b. How does an auditor determine the reliability of potential audit evidence?
c. For each of the following items (labeled 1. through 6. below), identify whether or not the auditor has made a judgment error, and if there is a judgment error whether the error relates to evidence reliability or relevance. Organize your answer as follows:

Judgment Error	Nature of Error	Explanation
Yes or No	Relevance, Reliability, or Both	Description of error

1. The auditor receives only 20% of the confirmations that were sent to customers to verify their account balance. The auditor responds by taking another sample of receivables to send out in place of the first sample. The auditor is convinced the first sample is not representative of the population as a whole.
2. The auditor sent a confirmation to an independent warehouse to confirm the existence of inventory owned by the audit client. There was no response. The auditor decided to visit the warehouse to independently inspect the inventory on hand.
3. The auditor decides to test the completeness of accounts payable by taking a sample of recorded accounts payable and tracing to the source document evidencing receipt of the goods or services. No exceptions were noted so the audit or does not expand the audit work.
4. An auditor wishes to test the valuation of a marketable security and inquires about management's intent for using the securities. Management indicates that they are intending to hold the securities as a long-term investment. The auditor decides that no further evidence is needed and that the securities are properly valued at cost.
5. The auditor notes that there are some problems with segregation of duties over accounts receivable that could affect the existence assertion. The client is aware that the auditor normally sends out accounts receivable confirmations. The auditor decides to expand the audit work by sending additional confirmations.
6. During the observation of inventory, the auditor notes a number of items that look old and apparently not used. The auditor discusses each item with the marketing manager to determine whether or not the item is considered saleable at normal prices.

6-51 `LO 4` What are the basic assumptions that must hold for an auditor to justifiably use analytical procedures as a substantive audit procedure?

6-52 [LO 4] Refer to the *Auditing in Practice* feature "Analytical Procedures are Not Client Estimates." What is the relationship between the auditor's use of an analytical procedure and a client estimate?

6-53 [LO 4] Assume that the auditor proposes that sales be audited by examining the relationship of sales and cost of sales to that of the previous two years, as adjusted for an increase in gross domestic product. Further, the auditor has assessed the risk of material misstatement (inherent and control risk) for this account as high. Explain either why, or why not, this would be an effective test of the account balance.

6-54 [LO 4] Assume that an auditor wishes to use analytical procedures as a substantive procedure. Indicate how substantive analytical procedures could be used in assisting the auditor in testing the following accounts:

a. Interest expense related to bonds outstanding.
b. Natural gas expense for a public utility company.
c. Supplies expense for a factory.
d. Cost of goods sold for a fast-food franchisor (for example, Wendy's or McDonald's). Note that cost of goods sold tends to average about 35% of sales in fast food franchises.
e. Salary expense for an office (region) of a professional services firm.

PROFESSIONAL SKEPTICISM **6-55** [LO 4] Assume that you have finished your substantive analytical procedures in the area of revenue. You used trend analysis and a reasonableness test and conducted the procedures at a disaggregated level. You are very pleased that your expectations are almost identical to what the client has recorded. Specifically, revenue increased in line with prior period increases and with the industry increases. You let your senior know that you likely do not have any additional work to perform. Your senior asks you to reconsider your conclusion. What is likely the primary concern of your senior?

6-56 [LO 4] Review Exhibit 6.9 and describe how the two audit approaches presented in the Exhibit differ. What factors would lead to such a difference?

6-57 [LO 5] Sufficiency is a measure of the quantity of evidence. Identify factors that affect evidence sufficiency.

6-58 [LO 5] An auditor typically selects samples when testing controls. What are some factors that that affect the sample sizes used when testing controls?

PROFESSIONAL SKEPTICISM **6-59** [LO 6] Refer to the *Auditing in Practice* feature "Description of Common Types of Earnings Management Techniques." Why might it be difficult for auditors to disallow companies' preferences to decrease existing reserves? Explain the role of professional skepticism in the context of evaluating management's explanations for their accounting for reserves in this context.

6-60 [LO 6] When testing accounts that are based on management estimates, the auditor should understand the process management uses to develop those estimates. As part of obtaining that understanding, what aspects of the process should the auditor understand?

6-61 [LO 7] Why would an auditor need to use an outside specialist when performing an audit? Identify specific accounts or assertions where a specialist might be needed.

6-62 [LO 7] What factors should the auditor consider when evaluating the professional qualifications of a specialist?

6-63 `LO 8` What is a related-party transaction? Provide examples of transactions that would be considered related-party transactions.

6-64 `LO 8` Review Exhibit 6.10 and identify audit procedures that an auditor might use for related-party transactions.

6-65 `LO 9` What is audit documentation? Refer to Exhibit 6.12 and identify the key components that each audit document should contain.

6-66 `LO 9` What is meant by the statement *audit documentation ought to stand on its own*? What is the importance of this concept?

6-67 `LO 10` What are the purposes of an audit program? Review Exhibit 6.13 and identify the major items that should be included in an audit program.

CONTEMPORARY AND HISTORICAL CASES

6-68 **PCAOB**
`LO 1, 2, 3, 4, 5, 6, 10` The *Professional Judgment in Context* feature "Evidence-Related Findings in PCAOB Inspection Reports" presented at the beginning of the chapter provides excerpts of various PCAOB inspection reports issued in 2012 and 2011. Review the feature, consider the information you learned while reading this chapter, and answer the following questions.

PROFESSIONAL SKEPTICISM

a. What is sufficient appropriate evidence and how does it differ across clients? Can what is considered sufficient and appropriate differ across accounts within a specific client?

b. What are substantive analytical procedures, and when is evidence from these procedures appropriate?

c. What are the unique evidence challenges for accounts such as allowance for doubtful accounts? How is professional skepticism helpful when testing this type of account?

d. How could the use of a standardized audit program lead to some of the problems identified in the PCAOB inspection reports?

6-69 **PCAOB AND ERNST & YOUNG**
`LO 9, 11` In August 2011, the PCAOB barred two former Ernst & Young LLP (E&Y) employees from auditing public companies, alleging they provided misleading documents to PCAOB inspectors who were evaluating the audit firm's work. One partner was barred for three years, and a senior manager was barred for two years.

ETHICS

The PCAOB said that shortly before its inspectors were to inspect an E&Y audit of an unidentified company, the two auditors created, backdated, and placed in the audit files a document concerning the valuation of one of the audit client's investments. One of the auditors allegedly authorized other members of the audit team to alter other working papers in advance of the inspection. The changes were not disclosed to the PCAOB. E&Y indicated that the conduct of the two auditors had no impact on the client's financial statements or on E&Y's audit conclusions.

a. What is audit documentation, and why is it important to a quality audit?

b. Given that the conduct of the two auditors had no impact on the client's financial statements or on E&Y's conclusions, why was this situation over audit documentation of concern to the PCAOB?

c. Suppose that you are asked by a superior to add or alter an audit workpaper after completing an audit engagement. Use the framework for ethical decision making presented in Chapter 4 to consider your actions in this situation.

FRAUD

PROFESSIONAL SKEPTICISM

INTERNATIONAL

6-70 **LONGTOP FINANCIAL TECHNOLOGIES LIMITED AND DELOITTE TOUCHE TOHMATSU CPA LTD.**
LO 1, 2, 4, 5

In May 2011, Deloitte Touche Tohmatsu (DTT) resigned as the auditor for Longtop Financial Technologies Limited (Longtop). Excerpts from DTT's resignation letter are provided here:

As part of the process for auditing the Company's financial statements for the year ended 31 March 2011, we determined that, in regard to bank confirmations, it was appropriate to perform follow up visits to certain banks. These audit steps were recently performed and identified a number of very serious defects, including statements by bank staff that their bank had no record of certain transactions; confirmation replies previously received were said to be false; significant differences in deposit balances reported by the bank staff compared with the amounts identified in previously received confirmations (and in the books and records of the Group); and significant bank borrowings reported by bank staff not identified in previously received confirmations (and not recorded in the books and records of the Group).

In the light of this, a formal second round of bank confirmation was initiated on 17 May. Within hours however, as a result of intervention by the Company's officials including the Chief Operating Officer, the confirmation process was stopped amid serious and troubling new developments including: calls to banks by the Company asserting that Deloitte was not their auditor; seizure by the Company's staff of second round bank confirmation documentation on bank premises; threats to stop our staff leaving the Company premises unless they allowed the Company to retain our audit files then on the premises; and then seizure by the Company of certain of our working papers.

Then on 20 May the Chairman of the Company, Mr. Jia Xiao Gong called our Eastern Region Managing Partner, Mr. Paul Sin, and informed him in the course of their conversation that "there were fake revenue in the past so there were fake cash recorded on the books". Mr. Jia did not answer when questioned as to the extent and duration of the discrepancies. When asked who was involved, Mr. Jia answered: "senior management".

a. What audit evidence-related problems did DTT encounter during the audit of Longtop?

b. Review Exhibit 6.8. This chapter describes external confirmations as generally being a reliable, high quality type of evidence. When would that generality not be accurate? What assumptions should the auditor address concerning confirmations before concluding that using confirmations will result in reliable audit evidence?

c. Explain the role of professional skepticism in the context of evaluating evidence obtained from confirmations.

PROFESSIONAL SKEPTICISM

6-71 **PCAOB AND DELOITTE & TOUCHE**
LO 1, 2, 3, 5, 6, 10   On May 4, 2010, the PCAOB issued its public inspection of Deloitte & Touche, LLP, covering their inspection of audits conducted during 2009. In their summary comments, the PCAOB inspectors stated:

In some cases, the conclusion that the Firm failed to perform a procedure may be based on the absence of documentation and the absence of persuasive other evidence, even if the Firm claims to have performed the procedure. PCAOB Auditing Standard No. 3, *Audit Documentation* ('AS No. 3") provides that, in various circumstances including PCAOB inspections, a firm that has not adequately documented that it performed a procedure, obtained evidence, or reached an appropriate conclusion must demonstrate with persuasive other evidence that it did so, and that oral assertions and explanations alone do not constitute persuasive other evidence. (p. 3)

The report went on to say:

In some cases, the deficiencies identified were of such significance that it appeared to the inspection team that the Firm, at the time it issued its audit report, had not obtained sufficient competent evidential matter to support its opinion on the issuer's financial statements or internal control over financial reporting ("ICFR").

It is reasonable to ask: what is the nature of these deficiencies; could this criticism happen to me; why didn't the firm reviewing partners detect the deficiencies? In order to understand how to answer these questions, the following excerpts describe the nature of deficiencies found on individual audits:

In this audit, the Firm failed in the following respects to obtain sufficient competent evidential matter to support its audit opinion—

- The Firm failed to perform adequate audit procedures to test the valuation of the issuer's inventory and investments in joint ventures (the primary assets of which were inventory). Specifically, the Firm:
  - Failed to re-evaluate, in light of a significant downturn in the issuer's industry and the general deterioration in economic conditions, whether the issuer's assumption, which it had also used in prior years, that certain inventory required no review for impairment was still applicable in the year under audit;
  - Excluded from its impairment testing a significant portion of the inventory that may have been impaired, because the Firm selected inventory items for testing from those for which the issuer already had recorded impairment charges;
  - Failed to evaluate the reasonableness of certain of the significant assumptions that the issuer used in determining the fair value estimates of inventory and investments in joint ventures;
  - Failed to obtain support for certain of the significant assumptions that the Firm used when developing an independent estimate of the fair value of one category of inventory; and
  - Failed to test items in a significant category of inventory, which consisted of all items with book values per item below a Firm-specified amount that was over 70 percent of the Firm's planning materiality.
- The Firm failed to perform adequate audit procedures to evaluate the issuer's assertion that losses related to the issuer's guarantees of certain joint venture obligations were not probable, because the Firm's procedures were limited to inquiry of management.

a. What is the auditor's responsibility to consider information outside of the client's records and processing to develop sufficient and appropriate audit evidence?

b. Why are the items identified above by the PCAOB considered critical mistakes in performing an audit? What is the critical error of omission by the audit firm, and why would the specific problem lead to a deficiency in sufficient appropriate evidence?

c. Why is inquiry of management not considered sufficient information by itself?

d. Assumptions are assumptions! What is the auditor's responsibility regarding the questioning of the assumptions used by the client? In formulating your response, keep in mind that the client will claim that assumptions are just assumptions and it is difficult to say that one is more correct than another.

e. What do the deficiencies identified by the PCAOB suggest about the level of professional skepticism on the audit engagements? What might be reasons for decreased professional skepticism?

f. Presumably Deloitte used a standardized audit program. How could a standardized audit program lead to some of the problems identified earlier, such as failing to test a category of inventory that had book value in excess of 70% of the firm's planning materiality, or limiting the testing of impairment to inventory that had already been assessed as impaired by management?

6-72 **ADECCO SA**

LO 1, 2, 3, 5 Adecco SA is the world's largest temporary employment company. It lost several major accounts because customers felt it was not adequately serving their complex staffing needs. In lawsuits filed in the United States, shareholders alleged that the company filed false and misleading financial statements during the period 2000–2004, with problems relating to information technology security, payrolls, and revenue recognition. Ultimately, the company announced that it was not able to deliver its financial statements on schedule. Their auditors had raised questions about accounting and controls as part of an integrated audit as mandated by the Sarbanes-Oxley Act.

One of the revenue recognition problems that Adecco had was that its accountants recorded revenue for temporary services provided during the first several weeks in January as previous year's income. The company has a database in which it knows, at any point in time, which temporary employees are assigned to which clients, and the daily billing rates for those employees. The company bills each client at a rotating month end; for some clients, the billing is on the 5th of the month, others are on the 15th of the month, and so on. Each client receives only one bill per month and is expected to pay within 30 days after the billing date. The billing is computerized, and the client makes accruals for unbilled revenue at the end of each quarter and year end. Most of the bills are sent electronically, although a few are sent using paper documents.

a. One evidence-gathering option was to send out a confirmation to Adecco's clients as to the amount owed to Adecco as of year end. Explain why (or why not) this would be an effective audit procedure.

b. What other audit procedures could have been used to determine whether revenue was properly recorded?

FRAUD **6-73** **GATEWAY COMPUTERS**

LO 6 The SEC took action against Gateway Computers in 2001 because it believed that Gateway systematically understated the allowance for doubtful accounts to meet sales and earnings targets. This is essentially the way the alleged fraud took place:

- Gateway sold most of its computers over the Internet and had a strong credit department that approved sales.
- When sales dropped, management decided to go back to customers who had been rejected because of poor credit approval.
- During the first quarter, it went after the better of the previously rejected customers.
- As the need for more revenue and earnings remained, Gateway continued down the list to include everyone.
- However, it did not change any of its estimates for the allowance for uncollectible accounts.

At the end of the process, the poor credit customers represented about 5% of total income, but the SEC alleged that the allowance account was understated by over $35 million, which amounted to approximately $0.07 per share. In essence, Gateway wanted to show it was doing well when the rest of the industry was doing badly.

a. What is the requirement regarding proper valuation of the allowance for doubtful accounts? Does that requirement differ from account balances that are based on recording transactions as opposed to the allowance being an estimate? In other words, is more preciseness required on account balances that do not contain estimates?
b. What information should the company use in a system to make the estimate of the allowance for uncollectible accounts?
c. What evidence should the auditor gather to determine whether the client's estimate of the allowance for uncollectible accounts is fairly stated?
d. How should the expansion of sales to customers who had previously been rejected for credit affect the estimate of the allowance for doubtful accounts?
e. How important are current economic conditions to the process of making an estimate of the allowance for doubtful accounts? Explain.

6-74 CENDANT CORPORATION
LO 1, 2, 3, 5 Cendant Corporation, a company that sold travel and health club memberships, was the subject of an intensive fraud investigation that culminated in 1998. The company's Web site revealed the following statements contained in a report given to the SEC.

FRAUD
PROFESSIONAL SKEPTICISM

- *Irregular charges against merger reserves*—Operating results at the former Cendant business units were artificially boosted by recording fictitious revenues through inappropriately reversing restructuring charges and liabilities to revenues. Many other irregularities were also generated by inappropriate use of these reserves.
- *False coding of services sold to customers*—Significant revenues from members purchasing long-term benefits were intentionally misclassified in accounting records as revenue from shorter-term products. The falsely recorded revenues generated higher levels of immediately recognized revenues and profits for Cendant.

- *Delayed recognition of canceled memberships and chargebacks (a chargeback is a rejection by a credit-card-issuing bank of a charge to a member's credit card account)*—In addition to overstating revenues, these delayed charges caused Cendant's cash and working capital accounts to be overstated.
- *Quarterly recording of fictitious revenues*—Large numbers of accounts receivable entries made in the first three quarters of the year were fabricated; they had no associated clients or customers and no associated sale of services. This practice also occurred in the prior two years.

The company also had other accounting errors. Approximately 6 to 9 cents per share of the total estimated restatement of earnings resulted from the elimination of these errors. These accounting errors include inappropriate useful lives for certain intangible assets, delayed recognition of insurance claims, and use of accounting policies that do not conform to the applicable financial reporting framework.

a. Identify audit procedures (and audit evidence gathered) that could have detected the misstatement of revenues and intangible assets. Be specific about each of the four irregularities identified.

b. How would the auditor's assessment of management integrity and management motivation have affected the nature, timing, and extent of audit procedures identified? Explain the role of professional skepticism in this context.

FRAUD   **6-75**   **MINISCRIBE**

LO 1, 2, 3, 5   As reported in the *Wall Street Journal* (September 11, 1989), MiniScribe, Inc., inflated its reported profits and inventory through a number of schemes designed to fool the auditors. At that time, MiniScribe was one of the major producers of disk drives for personal computers. The newspaper article reported that MiniScribe used the following techniques to meet its profit objectives:

- An extra shipment of $9 million of disks was sent to a customer near year end and booked as a sale. The customer had not ordered the goods and ultimately returned them, but the sale was not reversed in the year recorded.
- Shipments were made from a factory in Singapore, usually by air freight. Toward the end of the year, some of the goods were shipped by cargo ships. The purchase orders were changed to show that the customer took title when the goods were loaded on the ship. However, title did not pass to the customer until the goods were received in the United States.
- Returned goods were recorded as usable inventory. Some were shipped without any repair work performed.
- MiniScribe developed a number of just-in-time warehouses and shipped goods to them from where they were delivered to customers. The shipments were billed as sales as soon as they reached the warehouse.

For each of the items described, identify the audit evidence that should have been gathered that would have enabled the auditor to uncover the fraud. As appropriate, indicate the timing of when the evidence should be obtained.

6-76 **LO 9, 11** Entry-level auditing staff often inspect client records and documentation supporting accounting transactions in order to gain evidence about the appropriate application of the applicable financial reporting framework. One of these tasks involves comparing original client records of transactions to client reports that summarize those transactions. In this way, auditors gain assurance that the transactions used to construct the financial statements are complete and accurate. Here we report a case related to this task that is based on an actual situation. However, names have been changed to achieve confidentiality concerning audit firm personnel issues.

 Elizabeth Jenkins was a staff auditor assigned to a large insurance client engagement. She was working on the portion of the audit concerning the client's claims loss reserves (reserves for future claims submitted by those insured by the insurance company). This reserve is analogous to the allowance for doubtful accounts of a company in the manufacturing or service sector. Essentially, the audit firm wants to provide assurance that the client's estimate of the amount of claims that will ultimately be filed is correctly stated on the balance sheet, with the appropriate write-off appearing on the income statement. Elizabeth was asked by the senior accountant on the engagement (Brett Stein) to tie out (in other words to compare) the client's claim loss reserve estimate (summarized on a large Excel worksheet) with the client's system-generated reports that provided the underlying data for the reserve estimate. The calculation is complex and involves inputs from several sources. Therefore, the tie-out process was very detail oriented and rather repetitive, involving a significant amount of time and patience to complete accurately. To demonstrate that she had compared the amount on the claims loss reserve Excel spreadsheet with that on the system-generated reports, Elizabeth was instructed to put a tick mark in both documents that would enable her senior to review her work. Along with each tick mark, Elizabeth was instructed to write a short note that described whether the two amounts did or did not agree. Elizabeth proceeded through the task, inserting tick marks where appropriate and noting agreement in all cases between the spreadsheet and the system-generated report. Because Elizabeth was feeling pressed for time and was exceedingly bored with her task, she skipped many of the comparisons and simply inserted tick marks indicating agreement even though she had not compared the numbers. She rationalized her actions by telling herself that this client had good internal controls and she had never found disagreements between source documents in other areas of the audit in which she was involved. In the audit profession, this action is known as ghost tick marking.

 After Elizabeth had completed the task, she moved on to other parts of the audit as instructed by Brett. Subsequently, Brett reviewed Elizabeth's work. During that review, he recomputed amounts on both the Excel spreadsheet and the system-generated reports. To his surprise, there were instances in which Elizabeth had noted agreement between the two documents when in fact the numbers were not the same.

 Brett met with Elizabeth and asked her about what had happened. She readily confessed to her actions. Brett counseled her that this behavior was unacceptable because it implies that audit work is being done when in fact the work is not being done. This puts the

ETHICS

audit firm at risk because it provides inappropriate assurance that the client's records are accurate, when in fact they are not accurate. Elizabeth was embarrassed and remorseful and promised not to engage in ghost tick marking in the future. Brett noted the situation in Elizabeth's personnel records and notified the manager and partner on the engagement, along with relevant human resource personnel. The matter was fully documented in Elizabeth's personnel file.

During the course of the year, the supervisory audit firm personnel on all of Elizabeth's engagements were notified of her actions, and her work was subjected to more thorough review as a result. The firm noted no problems with the quality of Elizabeth's work during that time. During her annual review, she was again coached on the severity of her mistake. However, during the annual review process of all staff accountants, the firm did consider firing her based upon the mistake, but ultimately decided that her confession, remorseful attitude, and subsequent high-quality work merited that she retain her employment.

a. Try to put yourself in Elizabeth's position for a moment. Have you ever been tempted to do a low-quality job on some task that you considered mundane? Have you ever thought that your low-quality work would remain undiscovered?

b. Why is Elizabeth's misrepresentation of her work so important to the firm?

c. What did Elizabeth ultimately do right in this situation, once her misrepresentation was discovered?

d. Do you agree with the outcome? Do you think the firm was too lenient? Too harsh? What would you recommend the firm do in this situation? Use the framework for ethical decision making from Chapter 4 to help you arrive at a conclusion.

7

Planning the Audit: Identifying and Responding to the Risks of Material Misstatement

CHAPTER OVERVIEW AND LEARNING OBJECTIVES

The financial statements of any organization are subject to certain risks of material misstatement; this fact creates risks for any auditor attempting to conduct a quality audit. Auditors first identify and assess the risks of material misstatement, and then they respond to those risks. In doing so, the auditor makes materiality assessments to determine which accounts require more audit effort and which accounts might require less audit effort. In terms of the audit opinion formulation process, this chapter focuses on Phase II—Performing Risk Assessment.

Through studying this chapter, you will be able to achieve these learning objectives:

通过本章的学习，你将能够实现以下学习目标：

1. Define the concept of material misstatement and discuss the importance of materiality judgments in the audit context.
   明确重大错报的概念，讨论注册会计师对重要性的判断在审计中的作用。

2. Identify the risks of material misstatement and describe how they relate to audit risk and detection risk.
   识别重大错报风险，描述它们与审计风险和检查风险的关系。

3. Assess factors affecting inherent risk.
   评估影响固有风险的因素。

4. Assess factors affecting control risk.
   评估影响控制风险的因素。

5. Use preliminary analytical procedures and brainstorming to identify areas of heightened risk of material misstatement.
   采用初步的分析性程序和集体研讨活动识别重大错报风险较高的领域。

6. Describe how auditors make decisions about detection risk and audit risk.
   描述注册会计师如何做出检查风险和审计风险的决策。

7. Respond to the assessed risks of material misstatement and plan the procedures to be performed on an audit engagement.
   应对评估的重大错报风险，计划在审计项目中将要实施的审计程序。

8. Apply the frameworks for professional decision making and ethical decision making to issues involving materiality, risk assessment, and risk responses.
   运用职业决策和职业道德决策框架解决涉及重要性、风险评估和风险反应的问题。

THE AUDIT OPINION FORMULATION PROCESS

| I. Making Client Acceptance and Continuance Decisions **Chapter 14** | II. Performing Risk Assessment **Chapters 3, 7 and 9–13** | III. Obtaining Evidence about Internal Control Operating Effectiveness **Chapters 8–13 and 16** | IV. Obtaining Substantive Evidence about Accounts, Disclosures and Assertions **Chapters 8–13 and 16** | V. Completing the Audit and Making Reporting Decisions **Chapters 14 and 15** |

| The Auditing Profession, the Risk of Fraud and Mechanisms to Address Fraud: Regulation, Corporate Governance, and Audit Quality **Chapters 1 and 2** | Professional Liability and the Need for Quality Auditor Judgments and Ethical Decisions **Chapter 4** |

The Audit Opinion Formulation Process and A Framework for Obtaining Audit Evidence
Chapters 5 and 6

PROFESSIONAL JUDGMENT IN CONTEXT

Risks Associated with Financial Statement Misstatements

Risk is a concept that is used to express uncertainty about events and/or their outcomes that could have a material effect on an organization. ISA 315 provides an excellent summary of the varied risks that may be present in an organization and that may be associated with material misstatements in the organization's financial statements. The existence of one or more of these risk factors does not necessarily mean that there is a material misstatement present, but it does indicate that the auditor should carefully consider and investigate that possibility, obviously leading to more audit work. As you read the list, notice that (1) the risks are associated with a wide range of both operational and financial reporting decisions, (2) the risks are sometimes hard to quantify and are judgmental in nature, and (3) many organizations have these risks but do *not* necessarily have material misstatements, thus making it difficult for auditors to know when a risk factor truly is leading to a material misstatement for their particular clients. The list is as follows:

- Operations in regions that are economically unstable, such as countries with significant currency devaluation or highly inflationary economies
- Operations exposed to volatile markets, such as futures trading

- Operations that are subject to a high degree of complex regulation
- Going concern and liquidity issues, including loss of significant customers or constraints on the availability of capital or credit
- Offering new products or moving into new lines of business
- Changes in the entity, such as acquisitions or reorganizations
- Entities or business segments likely to be sold
- The existence of complex alliances and joint ventures
- Use of off-balance sheet financing, special-purpose entities, and other complex financing arrangements
- Significant transactions with related parties
- Lack of personnel with appropriate accounting and financial reporting skills
- Changes in key personnel, including departure of key executives
- Deficiencies in internal control, especially those not addressed by management
- Changes in the Information Technology (IT) system or environment and inconsistencies between the entity's IT strategy and its business strategies
- Inquiries into the organization's operations or financial results by regulatory bodies

- Past misstatements, history of errors, or significant adjustments at period end
- Significant amount of nonroutine or non-systematic transactions, including intercompany transactions and large revenue transactions at period end
- Transactions that are recorded based on management's intent, such as debt refinancing, assets to be sold, and classification of marketable securities
- Accounting measurements that involve complex processes

- Pending litigation and contingent liabilities, such as sales warranties, financial guarantees, and environmental remediation

As you read through this chapter, consider the following questions:

- What conditions would cause these types of risks to lead to a material misstatement in the financial statements? (LO 1, 2, 3, 4, 5)
- What types of risks do these examples represent? (LO 2, 3, 4)
- How do these risks affect detection risk and audit risk? (LO 2, 7)

评估重要性

Assessing Materiality

LO 1 Define the concept of material misstatement and discuss the importance of materiality judgments in the audit context.

The auditor is expected to design and conduct an audit that provides reasonable assurance that material misstatements will be detected. Materiality is a concept that relates to the significance or importance of an item. Auditors and management sometimes have legitimate differences of opinion about the significance or importance of a misstatement. A **misstatement** is an error, either intentional or unintentional, that exists in a transaction or financial statement account balance. The auditor and management may disagree about whether a misstatement is material. Further, a dollar amount that may be significant to one person may not be significant to another. Despite these measurement difficulties, the concept of materiality is pervasive and guides the nature and extent of the audit opinion formulation process. Therefore, it is essential to understand materiality in the context of designing and conducting a quality audit. There are various definitions of materiality; we highlight several below that capture the essential elements of this concept.

重要性(materiality)
这是审计准则中的一个基本理念和原则。如果一项错报单独或者连同其他错报可能影响财务报表使用者依据财务报表做出的经济决策，则该项错报是重大的。

In Concepts Statement No. 2, the Financial Accounting Standards Board (FASB) defines **materiality** as "the magnitude of an omission or misstatement of accounting information that, in light of surrounding circumstances, makes it *probable* that the judgment of a reasonable person relying on the information would have been changed or influenced by the omission or misstatement." ISA 320, *Materiality in Planning and Performing an Audit*, makes the point that auditors' judgments about materiality should be made based on a consideration of the information needs of users as an overall group. The Supreme Court of the United States offers a somewhat different definition, stating that "a fact is material if there is a substantial likelihood that the ... fact would have been viewed by the reasonable investor as having significantly altered the 'total mix' of information made available" (see AS 11). These definitions make it clear that materiality includes both the nature of the misstatement as well as the dollar amount of misstatement and must be judged in relation to importance placed on the amount by financial statement users. Thus, auditors need to understand the needs of financial statements users in order to make appropriate materiality judgments.

重要性指导

Materiality Guidance

Most audit firms provide specific written guidance and decision aids to assist auditors in making consistent materiality judgments. The guidelines usually involve applying percentages to some base, such as total assets, total revenue, or net income. In choosing a base, the auditor considers the stability of the base from year to year, so that materiality does not fluctuate significantly between annual audits. Income is often more volatile than total assets or revenue.

A simple guideline for setting materiality for the financial statements as a whole is to use 1% of total assets or revenue (whichever is higher); another option is to use 5% of net income. Some audit firms have more complicated guidelines that may be based on the nature of the industry or a composite of materiality decisions made by experts in the firm. Still, any guideline is just that: a guideline. The auditor should use the guideline as a starting point and then adjust as necessary for qualitative characteristics of the particular audit client. For example, a company may have restrictive debt covenants that require the company to maintain a current ratio of at least 2:1, which would imply that current assets must be twice as large as current liabilities. If that ratio per the books is near the requirement, the auditor should set materiality at a lower level for auditing current asset and liability accounts.

Auditors consider materiality at two levels: (1) materiality for the financial statements as a whole, and (2) performance materiality for particular classes of transactions, account balances, or disclosures. The materiality level for the financial statements as a whole should be stated as a specific monetary amount. For purposes of planning the audit, auditors should consider overall materiality in terms of the smallest aggregate level of misstatements that could be material to any one of the financial statements. For example, if the auditor believes that misstatements aggregating approximately $100,000 would be material to the income statement, but misstatements aggregating approximately $200,000 would be material to the balance sheet, the auditor typically assesses overall materiality at $100,000 or less (not $200,000 or less).

After establishing overall materiality at the financial statement level, auditors set materiality that is relevant at the transaction or account balance level. **Performance materiality** refers to the amount or amounts set by the auditor at less than the materiality level for the financial statements as a whole or for particular classes of transactions, account balances, or disclosures. If the auditor plans the audit only to detect individual material misstatements, the auditor would be overlooking the fact that the aggregate of individually immaterial misstatements can cause the financial statements as a whole to be materially misstated. Performance materiality is used for assessing the risks of material misstatement and determining the nature, timing, and extent of audit procedures to perform during the audit opinion formulation process. If performance materiality is set too high, the auditor might not perform sufficient procedures to detect material misstatements in the financial statements. If performance materiality is set too low, the auditor might perform more substantive procedures than necessary. Performance materiality is different from, but relates to, the concept of tolerable misstatement. **Tolerable misstatement** is the amount of misstatement in an account balance that the auditor could tolerate and still not judge the underlying account balance to be materially misstated. Tolerable misstatement is the application of performance materiality to a particular sampling procedure, so it is always less than or equal to performance materiality.

Auditors need to aggregate all potential misstatements in a place where the audit team can assess the materiality of misstatements. The accumulation of such information is often based on whether those misstatements are clearly trivial. A **clearly trivial** amount, according to AU-C 450, is one that is "clearly inconsequential, whether taken individually or in the aggregate and whether judged by any criteria of size, nature, or circumstances". The term *clearly trivial* should not be used instead of *not material*. The materiality level for a clearly trivial item occurs where the auditor believes errors below that level would not, even when aggregated with all other misstatements, be material to the financial statements. For example, if amounts at or below $5,000 are considered clearly trivial, misstatements that the auditor detects that are below that amount would essentially be ignored for purposes of suggesting corrections to the client regarding misstatements that were detected during the course of the audit. Auditors have used the term **posting materiality** to refer to amounts that were clearly trivial.

美国证券交易委员会对重要性的意见

SEC Views on Materiality

The Securities and Exchange Commission (SEC) has been critical of the auditing profession for not sufficiently examining qualitative factors in making materiality decisions. In particular, the SEC has criticized the profession for:

- *Netting (offsetting) material misstatements.* This approach involves not making adjustments because the net effect may not be material to net income. However, each account item may have been affected by a material amount.
- *Not applying the materiality concept to swings in accounting estimates.* For example, an accounting estimate could be misstated by just under a material amount in one direction one year and just under a material amount in the opposite direction the next year. The SEC says the materiality amount should be determined by looking at the total swing in estimates over the two-year period, rather than by using the best estimate each year.
- *Consistently passing (in other words, refusing to adjust the financial statements to correct a detected misstatement) on individual adjustments that may not be considered material.* The SEC believes that the auditor should look at the qualitative nature of each misstatement and the potential aggregate effect of the misstatement. The SEC does not understand why a client would not be willing to adjust for a known error—even if it believes it is immaterial. The SEC often asks, if it is not material, why would management object to a change in the account balance?

The SEC provides guidance on situations in which a *quantitatively* small misstatement may still be considered material because *of qualitative* reasons. These qualitative reasons include the following:

- The misstatement hides a failure to meet analysts' consensus expectations for the company.
- The misstatement changes a loss into income, or vice versa.
- The misstatement concerns a segment or other portion of the company's business that plays a significant role in the company's operations or profitability.
- The misstatement affects the company's compliance with regulatory requirements.
- The misstatement affects the company's compliance with loan covenants or other contractual requirements.
- The misstatement has the effect of increasing management's compensation—for example, by satisfying requirements for the award of bonuses or other forms of incentive compensation.
- The misstatement involves the concealment of an unlawful transaction.

The above examples highlight situations in which management might argue that an amount is quantitatively immaterial and therefore should be allowed to remain uncorrected in the audited financial statements. This guidance from the SEC helps auditors to provide a rationale to managers about why such misstatements need to be corrected. Further, the auditors should consider these factors when setting planning materiality so that the audit is more likely to identify misstatements that might seem small but could make a difference to the user of the financial statements.

在审计意见形成过程中对重要性判断的变化

Changes in Materiality Judgments Throughout the Audit Opinion Formulation Process

The auditor makes judgments about materiality at the overall financial statement level, performance materiality, tolerable misstatements, and clearly trivial during the risk assessment phase of the audit. Sometimes these judgments need to be revised after more facts about the client and its circumstances become known during the audit. Situations that would necessitate a change in materiality judgments include the following:

- Initial materiality judgments were based on estimated or preliminary financial statement amounts that turn out to be different from the audited amounts.
- The financial statement amounts used in initially making the materiality judgments have changed significantly. For example, if during the course of the audit, the financial statements were adjusted significantly, then the initial materiality judgments might need to be adjusted accordingly.

If materiality judgments change during the course of the audit, then auditors must reassess any decisions that relied on these judgments. For example, if performance materiality turns out to have been set too high (such as $150,000 when it should have been $100,000), then the auditor might need to perform additional audit procedures designed to detect misstatements at this lower level. If performance materiality had been set too low (such as $100,000 when it should have been $150,000), then the auditor may have done more work than was really necessary, thereby leading to audit inefficiencies.

Ultimately, as auditors plan each audit, they make professional judgments about the size of misstatements that they judge to be material. These judgments, in turn, provide a basis for:

- Determining the nature and extent of risk assessment procedures
- Identifying and assessing the risks of material misstatement
- Determining the nature, timing, and extent of tests of controls and substantive audit procedures

注册会计师对重要性的判断是明确风险评估程序的性质和范围，识别和评估重大错报风险以及确定控制测试与实质性审计程序的性质、时间和范围的基础。

Identifying and Assessing Risks of Material Misstatement

识别和评估重大错报风险

Assessing and managing risks is fundamental to conducting a quality audit. Exhibit 7.1 provides a graphical depiction of the relationship between the risks of material misstatement and how they relate to audit risk. The definitions of the risks depicted in Exhibit 7.1 are as follows:

LO 2 Identify the risks of material misstatement and describe how they relate to audit risk and detection risk.

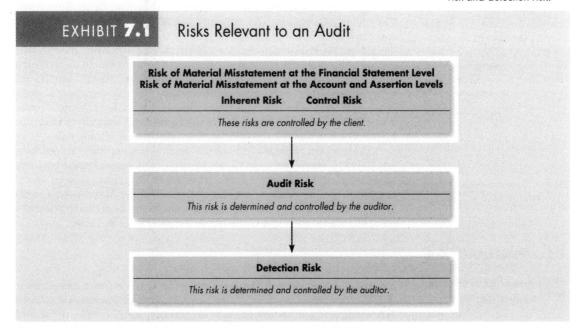

EXHIBIT 7.1   Risks Relevant to an Audit

Risk of Material Misstatement at the Financial Statement Level
Risk of Material Misstatement at the Account and Assertion Levels

Inherent Risk   Control Risk

These risks are controlled by the client.

Audit Risk

This risk is determined and controlled by the auditor.

Detection Risk

This risk is determined and controlled by the auditor.

- **Inherent Risk**—The susceptibility of an assertion about a class of transaction, account balance, or disclosure to a misstatement that could be material, either individually or when aggregated with other misstatements, before consideration of any related controls.
- **Control Risk**—The risk that a misstatement that could occur in an assertion about a class of transaction, account balance, or disclosure and that could be material, either individually or when aggregated with other misstatements, will not be prevented, or detected and corrected, on a timely basis by the entity's internal control.
- **Audit Risk**—The risk that the auditor expresses an inappropriate audit opinion when the financial statements are materially misstated.
- **Detection Risk**—The risk that the procedures performed by the auditor to reduce audit risk to an acceptably low level will not detect a misstatement that exists and that could be material, either individually or when aggregated with other misstatements.

审计风险(audit risk)
是指财务报表存在重大错报而注册会计师发表不恰当审计意见的可能性。

Exhibit 7.1 illustrates the relationships among these risks. The **risk of material misstatement** exists at the overall financial statement level and at the account and assertion levels, and within these levels, risk can be categorized as involving inherent risk and control risk. These risks originate with the audit client, are controllable by the audit client, and are related to characteristics of the organization, its environment, and its internal control. After assessing inherent and control risks, the auditor then determines the appropriate level of audit risk to accept. When the risk of material misstatement is higher, the auditor accepts less audit risk (as low as 1%); conversely, when the risk of material misstatement is lower, the auditor accepts more audit risk (such as 5%). For example, consider a client that is publicly traded, has a management team with questionable integrity (with a high inherent risk) that does not place high importance on the control environment (with a high control risk). In this case, the auditor should accept only low audit risk (1%) because the auditor is concerned that there exists a reasonable possibility that a material misstatement exists. Contrast this first example with a client that is privately held, has a management team with good integrity (a low inherent risk) that places importance on the control environment (a low control risk). In this case, the auditor accepts higher audit risk (5%) because a material misstatement is less likely.

Upon determining the level of acceptable audit risk, the auditor should determine detection risk. Detection risk is under the control of the auditor, and the level of audit effort that the auditor will expend on the engagement depends on the level of detection risk. When the risk of material misstatement is higher, detection risk is lower, in order to reduce audit risk to an acceptable level. The auditor reduces detection risk through the nature, timing, and extent of substantive audit procedures. As detection risk decreases, evidence obtained by the auditor through substantive audit procedures should increase. When the risk of material misstatement is lower, the auditor can accept a higher detection risk and still achieve an acceptable level of audit risk.

Auditing standards also discuss the term *significant risk*. According to AU-C 315, a **significant risk** is an identified and assessed risk of material misstatement that, in the auditor's professional judgment, requires special consideration. The *Auditing in Practice* feature, "What Makes a Risk Significant?," outlines factors that the auditor considers in determining whether a particular identified risk is significant to the conduct of the audit.

评估影响固有风险的因素

Assessing Factors Affecting Inherent Risk
Inherent Risk at the Account and Assertion Levels

LO 3 Assess factors affecting inherent risk.

Inherent risk relates to the susceptibility of an assertion to a misstatement, due to either error or fraud, before consideration of any related controls. When inherent risk at the account or assertion level is high, the auditor is concerned that a particular account balance is relatively more likely to

What Makes a Risk Significant?

AU-C 315 provides guidance to the auditor in terms of factors that the auditor should consider when determining if a risk is significant. The standard states:

> In exercising professional judgment about which risks are significant risks, the auditor should consider at least:

a. whether the risk is a risk of fraud;
b. whether the risk is related to recent significant economic, accounting, or other developments and, therefore, requires specific attention;
c. the complexity of transactions;
d. whether the risk involves significant transactions with related parties;
e. the degree of subjectivity in the measurement of financial information related to the risk, especially those measurements involving a wide range of measurement uncertainty; and
f. whether the risk involves significant transactions that are outside the normal course of business for the entity or that otherwise appear to be unusual.

contain a material misstatement than when inherent risk is low. Inherent risk reflects the fact that some assertions and related account balances are more susceptible to misstatement than others. For example, cash is more susceptible to theft than industrial equipment. In addition, accounts whose valuation is derived from accounting estimates are more likely to be misstated than accounts whose valuation is derived from routine, factual data. The following is a list of factors that should lead the auditor to assess inherent risk at the assertion level at a higher level:

- The account balance represents an asset that is relatively easily stolen, such as cash.
- The account balance is made up of complex transactions.
- The account balance requires a high level of judgment or estimation to value.
- The account balance is subject to adjustments that are not in the ordinary processing routine, such as year-end adjustments.
- The account balance is composed of a high volume of nonroutine transactions.

Inherent Risk at the Financial Statement Level: Business Risks

At the financial statement level, there exists inherent risk that affects the business operations and potential outcomes of organizational activities; these are referred to as **business risks**. When business risk is high, the auditor is concerned that the organization might have difficulty operating effectively or profitably. The overall economic climate—favorable or unfavorable—can have a tremendous effect on the organization's ability to operate effectively and profitably. Economic downturns are often associated with the failure of otherwise successful organizations. Technological change also presents risk. For example, companies that previously were not in the phone business, such as Google and Apple, added communication products and greatly affected the phone business of Motorola and Nokia. Competitor actions, such as discounting prices or adding new product lines, also affect inherent risk at the financial statement level. Finally, geographic locations of suppliers also affect inherent risk at the financial statement level. For example, sourcing products in China might offer a competitive advantage, but it might also expose the organization to business risk if it finds that its products contain lead and cannot be sold. It is up to management to properly manage its business risk. All organizations are subject to business risk; management reactions may exacerbate it (make it more likely) or, conversely, good management can mitigate it.

Each organization has key processes that give it a competitive advantage or disadvantage. The auditor should gather sufficient information to understand these processes, the industry factors affecting key processes, how management monitors the processes and performance, and the potential operational and financial effects associated with key processes. The following is a list of factors that would lead the auditor to assess inherent risk relating to operations at a higher level:

- The company lacks personnel or expertise to deal with the changes in the industry.
- New products and service offerings have uncertain likelihood of successful introduction and acceptance by the market.
- The use of information technology is incompatible across systems and processes.
- Expansion of the business for which the demand for the company's products or services has not been accurately estimated.
- A new business strategy is incompletely or improperly implemented.
- Financing is lost due to the company's inability to meet financing requirements.
- New regulatory requirements increase legal exposure.
- Alternative products, services, competitors, or providers pose a threat to current business.
- There are significant supply chain risks.
- The production and delivery processes are complex.
- The industry is mature and declining.
- The organization lacks ability to control costs with the possibility of unforeseen costs.
- The organization produces products that have multiple substitutes.

While these types of risk do not necessarily lead to material misstatements in the financial statements, they represent issues that threaten the fundamental financial viability of the organization. Further, these risks might provide incentives to management to misstate multiple accounts (for example, increase revenues or decrease expenses) in an attempt to make the organization look more financially sound than is accurate. The *Auditing in Practice* feature, "Pfizer Pharmaceuticals Risk Disclosures as an Example of Inherent Risk at the Financial Statement Level," illustrates the types of inherent risks that the company faces in competing in its complex, regulated, and research-driven industry. Auditors need to be aware of these risks, as they could have misstatement implications for multiple financial statement accounts.

Sources of Information for Assessing Business Risks The auditor makes use of a variety of tools to understand the client's business and associated risks. Much of the work is done by monitoring the financial press and SEC filings and broker analyses, developing a firm and industry-based knowledge management system, and utilizing other online information sources about a company. Some traditional approaches continue to be used, including inquiries of management, reviews of internal risk management documentation, inquiries of business people, and review of legal or regulatory proceedings against the company. The following describe some of the resources an auditor can use to learn more about a company:

- *Management inquiries*—The auditor should interview management to identify its strategic plans, its analysis of industry trends, the potential impact of actions it has taken or might take, and its management style.
- *Review of client's budget*—The budget, representing management's fiscal plan for the forthcoming year, provides insight into management's approach to operations and to risks the organization might face. The auditor looks for significant changes in plans and deviations from budgets, such

Pfizer Pharmaceuticals Risk Disclosures as an Example of Inherent Risk at the Financial Statement Level

Pfizer Pharmaceuticals discloses a variety of risks. Regulators encourage companies to make these types of disclosures so that investors can estimate the uncertainties inherent in the organization. Interesting inherent risk examples from Pfizer's FYE 2011 10-K are as follows:

"U.S. and foreign governmental regulations mandating price controls and limitations on patient access to our products impact our business, and our future results could be adversely affected by changes in such regulations or policies. In the U.S., many of our biopharmaceutical products are subject to increasing pricing pressures."

"Specialty pharmaceuticals are medicines that treat rare or life-threatening conditions that have smaller patient populations, such as certain types of cancer and multiple sclerosis. The growing availability and use of innovative specialty pharmaceuticals, combined with their relative higher cost as compared to other types of pharmaceutical products, is beginning to generate significant payer interest in developing cost-containment strategies targeted to this sector. While the impact on us of payers' efforts to control access to and pricing of specialty pharmaceuticals has been limited to date, our growing portfolio of specialty products, combined with the increasing use of health technology assessment in markets around the world and the deteriorating finances of governments, may lead to a more significant adverse business impact in the future."

"Risks and uncertainties apply particularly with respect to product-related, forward-looking statements. The outcome of the lengthy and complex process of identifying new compounds and developing new products is inherently uncertain. Drug discovery and development is time-consuming, expensive and unpredictable. The process from early discovery or design to development to regulatory approval can take many years. Drug candidates can fail at any stage of the process. There can be no assurance as to whether or when we will receive regulatory approval for new products or for new indications or dosage forms for existing products. Decisions by regulatory authorities regarding labeling, ingredients and other matters could adversely affect the availability or commercial potential of our products. As examples, there is no assurance that our late stage pipeline products, such as tofacitinib, bosutinib and *Eliquis* (apixaban) for prevention of stroke in patients with atrial fibrillation, will receive regulatory approval and/or be commercially successful or that recently approved products, such as *Prevnar 13/Prevenar 13* for use in adults 50 years of age and older, *Xalkori* (crizotinib) and *Inlyta* (axitinib) will be approved in other markets and/or be commercially successful. There is also a risk that we may not adequately address existing regulatory agency findings concerning the adequacy of our regulatory compliance processes and systems or implement sustainable processes and procedures to maintain regulatory compliance and to address future regulatory agency findings, should they occur."

as planned disposal of a line of business, significant research or promotion costs associated with a new product introduction, new financing or capital requirements, changes in compensation or product costs due to union agreements, and significant additions to property, plant, and equipment.

- *Tour of client's plant and operations*—A tour of the client's production and distribution facilities offers much insight into potential audit issues. The auditor can visualize cost centers as well as shipping and receiving procedures, inventory controls, potentially obsolete inventory, and possible inefficiencies. The tour increases the auditor's awareness of company procedures and operations, providing direct experience into sites and situations that are otherwise encountered only in company documents or observations of client personnel.
- *Review relevant government regulations and client's legal obligations*—Few industries are unaffected by governmental regulation, and much of that regulation affects the audit. For example, auditors need to determine potential liabilities associated with cleanup costs defined by the Environmental Protection Agency. The auditor normally seeks information on litigation risks

through an inquiry of management, but follows up that inquiry with an analysis of litigation prepared by the client's legal counsel.

- *Knowledge management systems*—Audit firms have developed these systems around industries, clients, and best practices. These systems also capture information about relevant accounting or regulatory requirements for the companies and can be used to develop risk alerts for the companies.
- *Online searches*—Internet search companies (such as Hoover's at *www.hoovers.com*) are an excellent source of information about companies. Other online searches can be conducted through other portals such as Google. Yahoo has two excellent sources of information: (1) a financial section that provides data about most companies and (2) a chat line that contains current conversations about the company (much of which, of course, might be unreliable).
- *Review of SEC filings*—The SEC filings can be searched online through the EDGAR system. The filings include company annual and quarterly reports, proxy information, and registration statements for new security issues. These filings contain substantial information about the company and its affiliates, officers, and directors. This information can be used to obtain an understanding of management's compensation arrangements, including incentive compensation that may provide important information about management incentives and bonus arrangements. Further, the auditor should monitor trading activity of the organization's securities, along with the relevant holdings of top-level management and/or board members.
- *Company Web sites*—A company's Web site can contain information that is useful in understanding its products and strategies. As companies provide more financial information online, auditors should review the information to keep informed of developments.
- *Economic statistics*—Most industry data, including regional data, can now be found online. The auditor can compare the results of a client with regional economic data. For example, the auditor would likely question why a company is growing at a rate of 50%, while the overall industry is growing at a significantly slower rate. That question arises only if the auditor has industry information.
- *Professional practice bulletins*—The American Institute of Certified Public Accountants (AICPA) publishes Audit Risk Alerts, and the SEC often issues practice bulletins to draw the profession's attention to important issues. Both the Public Company Accounting Oversight Board (PCAOB) and the International Auditing and Assurance Standards Board (IAASB) have also published several Staff Audit Practice Alerts dealing with topics such as significant unusual transactions, fair value measurements, and the economic environment.
- *Stock analysts' reports*—Brokerage firms invest significant resources in conducting research about companies, their strategies, competitors, quality of management, and likelihood of success. Many of the major investment analysts are granted access to top management and are the beneficiaries of frequent analysts' meetings. These reports may contain a wealth of useful information about a client.
- *Company earnings calls*—The auditor can observe or read the transcripts of management's earnings calls in order to understand the most up-to-date issues that the organization is facing, along with management's publicly disclosed plans.

Inherent Risk at the Financial Statement Level: Financial Reporting Risks

There is also inherent risk associated with the recording of transactions and the presentation of financial data in an organization's financial statements. When inherent risk relating to the recording of transactions and the presentation of financial data is high, the auditor is concerned that management has recorded transactions or presented financial data inaccurately. When assessing this risk, auditors consider all of the items on a company's financial statements that are subjective and based on judgment, such as asset impairments, mark-to-market accounting, warranties, returns, pensions, and estimates regarding the useful lives of assets, among others. Because of these estimates, inherent risk at the financial statement level is affected by the competence and integrity of management and potential incentives to misstate the financial statements.

当评估这类风险时，注册会计师需要考虑财务报表中所有主观的判断事项。例如，资产的减值、以市值计价、资产使用年限的估计等。

Sources of Information Regarding Management Integrity Evaluating management integrity is critical in assessing inherent risk at the financial statement level. However, making such an evaluation is difficult and subjective. To make this evaluation, auditors consider a variety of information sources:

- *Predecessor auditor*—Information obtained directly through inquiries is required by professional auditing standards. The predecessor is required to respond to the auditor unless such data are under a court order or if the client will not approve communicating confidential information.
- *Other professionals in the business community*—Examples include lawyers and bankers with whom the auditor normally has good working relationships and of whom the auditor makes inquiries as part of the process of getting to know the client.
- *Other auditors within the audit firm*—Other auditors within the firm may have dealt with current management in connection with other engagements or with other clients.
- *News media and Web searches*—Information about the company and its management might be available in financial journals, magazines, industry trade magazines, or on the Web.
- *Public databases*—Computerized databases can be searched for public documents dealing with management or any articles on the company. Similarly, public databases such as LEXIS can be searched for the existence of legal proceedings against the company or against key members of management.
- *Preliminary interviews with management*—Such interviews can be helpful in understanding the amount, extent, and reasons for turnover in key positions. Personal interviews can also be helpful in analyzing the frankness or evasiveness of management in dealing with important company issues affecting the audit.
- *Audit committee members*—Members of the audit committee might have been involved in disputes between the previous auditors and management and might have additional insight.
- *Inquiries of federal regulatory agencies*—Although this is not a primary source of information, the auditor might want to make inquiries of specific regulatory agencies regarding pending actions against the company or the history of regulatory actions taken with respect to the company and its management.
- *Private investigation firms*—Use of such firms is rare, but is increasingly being done when the auditor becomes aware of issues that merit further inquiry about management integrity or management's involvement in potential illegal activities.

The *Auditing in Practice* feature, "Stock Option Backdating Fraud as an Example of Inherent Risk at the Financial Statement Level," provides an example of a case where low management integrity led to fraud.

The following is a list of factors that lead auditors to assess inherent risk relating to financial reporting at a higher level:

- *Discrepancies in the accounting records*—for example, last-minute adjustments that significantly affect financial results, transactions that are not recorded in a complete or timely manner, and unsupported or unauthorized balances or transactions
- *Problematic or unusual relationships between the auditor and management*—for example, denial of access to records or facilities,

Stock Option Backdating Fraud as an Example of Inherent Risk at the Financial Statement Level

On April 23, 2010, a jury found Carl Jasper, the former CFO of Maxim Integrated Products, liable for securities fraud for engaging in a scheme to backdate stock option grants that allowed the company to conceal hundreds of millions of dollars of compensation costs and to thereby report significantly inflated income to investors. The jury found that Jasper engaged in fraud, lied to auditors, and aided Maxim's failure to maintain accurate accounting records, which resulted in inaccurate financial reporting. Evidence from the trial showed that, with his knowledge, Jasper's staff granted stock options by using hindsight to identify dates with historically low stock prices. The staff then drafted false documentation to make it seem that the options had been granted at earlier dates, which enabled the company to conceal its true compensation expenses.

Clearly, management integrity was a fundamental problem leading to this fraud. Assessing management integrity is no easy task; auditors must constantly consider how potential lapses therein could affect financial reporting.

For more information about this case, see SEC Litigation Release No. 20381.

undue time pressures imposed by management to resolve complex or contentious issues, or unusual delays by management in providing information
- *Lack of management competence*—for example, inappropriate knowledge in relation to responsibilities, inappropriate management authority, poor past performance, no succession planning
- *Company history of exactly meeting analyst estimates or high earnings growth expectations*
- *An impending initial public offering of stock*
- *Disagreements over financial reporting with prior auditors*
- *Auditor resignation*—due to refusal of the predecessor auditor to continue to provide services to the organization
- *Unusual transactions with outsiders or significant related party transactions*
- *Transactions for which most or all of the revenue or expense is recognized at the inception of the transaction*
- *Financial results that seem too good to be true*—for example, when financial results are significantly better than competitors, without substantive differences in operations between the organization and competitors
- *Complex business arrangements that appear to serve little practical purpose*
- *Hesitancy or evasiveness from management regarding questions about the financial statements*
- *Insistence by the CEO or CFO to be present at all meetings between the audit committee and internal or external auditors*
- *Accounting methods that appear to favor form over economic substance*

The *Auditing in Practice* feature, "Application of Accounting Principles and Related Disclosures," provides guidance to consider when assessing inherent risks relating to financial reporting.

Exhibit 7.2 provides examples of questions for an auditor to ask when assessing inherent risk relating to financial reporting.

EXHIBIT **7.2**	Questions to Ask When Assessing Financial Reporting Quality: Selected Excerpts from the NACD Blue Ribbon Commission on Audit Committees

- What are the significant judgment areas (reserves, contingencies, asset values, note disclosures) that affect the current-year financial statements? What considerations were involved in resolving these judgment matters? What is the range of potential impact on future reported financial results?
- What issues or concerns exist that could adversely affect the future operations and/or financial condition of the company? What is management's plan to deal with these future risks?
- What is the overall quality of the company's financial reporting, including the appropriateness of important accounting principles followed by the company?
- What is the range of acceptable accounting choices the company has available to it?
- Were there any significant changes in accounting policies, or in the application of accounting principles during the year? If yes, why were the changes made and what impact did the changes have on earnings per share (EPS) or other key financial measures?
- Were there any significant changes in accounting estimates, or models used in making accounting estimates during the year? If yes, why were the changes made and what impact did the changes have on earnings per share (EPS) or other key financial measures?
- Are there any instances where the company may be thought of as pushing the limits of revenue recognition? If so, what is the rationale for the treatment chosen?
- Have similar transactions and events been treated in a consistent manner across divisions of the company and across countries in which the company operates? If not, what are the exceptions and the reasons for them?
- Do the accounting choices made reflect the economic substance of transactions and the strategic management of the business? If not, where are the exceptions and why do they exist?
- To what extent are the financial reporting choices consistent with the manner in which the company measures its progress toward achieving its mission internally? If not, what are the differences?
- How do the significant accounting principles used by the company compare with leading companies in the industry, or with other companies that are considered leaders in financial disclosure? What is the rationale for any differences?
- Has there been any instance where short-run reporting objectives (e.g., achieving a profit objective or meeting bonus or stock option requirements) were allowed to influence accounting choices? If yes, what choices were made and why?

Assessing Factors Affecting Control Risk

Control risk relates to the susceptibility that a misstatement, due to either error or fraud, will not be prevented or detected on a timely basis by the organization's internal control system. During audit planning and risk assessment, the auditor makes a preliminary assessment of control risk. The control risk assessment can be made at the overall financial statement level. However, to facilitate planning, these assessments are also typically made at the account or assertion level because control effectiveness can vary across accounts and assertions. When control risk is high, the auditor is concerned that a misstatement may not be prevented or that if a misstatement exists in the organization's financial statements that it will not be detected and corrected by management. Some level of control risk is always present because of the inherent limitations in internal control. The following is a list of factors that lead auditors to assess control risk at a higher level:

- Poor controls in specific countries or locations
- Difficulty gaining access to the organization or determining the individuals who own and/or control the organization
- Little interaction between senior management and operating staff
- Weak tone at the top leading to a poor control environment
- Inadequate accounting staff, or staff lacking requisite expertise

评估影响控制风险的因素

LO 4 Assess factors affecting control risk.

控制风险(control risk)
是指组织的内部控制系统无法及时阻止或发现由于错误或者舞弊导致的错报的可能性。

Application of Accounting Principles and Related Disclosures

One issue critical to understanding the client's financial reporting risks involves an analysis of management's selection and application of accounting principles, including related disclosures. The auditor needs to determine whether management's decisions are appropriate for its business and are consistent with the applicable financial reporting framework for its industry. The auditor should develop expectations about the appropriate disclosures that are necessary and should compare those expectations to the disclosures made by management in assessing inherent risks relating to financial reporting.

For example, AS 12 requires that the auditor obtain an understanding of the following types of matters relevant to understanding management's application of accounting principles and related disclosures:

- Significant changes in the company's accounting principles, financial reporting policies, or disclosures and the reasons for such changes;
- The financial reporting competencies of personnel involved in selecting and applying significant new or complex accounting principles;
- The accounts or disclosures for which judgment is used in the application of significant accounting principles, especially in determining management's estimates and assumptions;
- The effect of significant accounting principles in controversial or emerging areas for which there is a lack of authoritative guidance or consensus;
- The methods the company uses to account for significant and unusual transactions; and
- Financial reporting standards and laws and regulations that are new to the company, including when and how the company will adopt such requirements.

- Inadequate information systems
- Growth of the organization exceeds the accounting system infrastructure
- Disregard for regulations or controls designed to prevent illegal acts
- No internal audit function, a weak internal audit function, or lack of respect for the internal audit function by management
- Weak design, implementation, and monitoring of internal controls
- Lack of supervision of accounting personnel

The last of these control risk factors is particularly relevant to the fraud scheme perpetrated by the comptroller of the city of Dixon, Illinois. Her crimes are described in the *Auditing in Practice* feature "Lack of Oversight as a Control Weakness Leads to Embezzlement."

Techniques to Understanding Management's Risk Assessment and Other Control Components

To have an appropriate level of understanding of the client's internal controls, the auditor needs to understand management's risk assessment process and the controls management has implemented to mitigate identified risks of material misstatement. As part of understanding risk assessment, the auditor typically uses some or all of the following techniques:

- Develop an understanding of the processes used by the board of directors and management to evaluate and manage risks
- Review the risk-based approach used by the internal audit function with the director of the internal audit function and with the audit committee
- Interview management about its risk approach, risk preferences, risk appetite, and the relationship of risk analysis to strategic planning
- Review outside regulatory reports, where applicable, that address the company's policies and procedures toward risk

Lack of Oversight as a Control Weakness Leads to Embezzlement

Rita Crundwell was the comptroller for the city of Dixon, Illinois from 1983 through early 2012. During that time, she is accused of stealing millions of dollars from the city to fund her extravagant lifestyle related to breeding and showing quarter horses. While maintaining this lavish, high-profile lifestyle, Crundwell received a relatively meager $80,000 per year salary from the city. Apparently the discrepancy between her salary and lifestyle went unnoticed by her supervisors or the city's auditors. Crundwell handled all of the city's finances, and it appears that she was left relatively unsupervised by the city's leadership. Most shocking is the magnitude of the theft—over $50 million—in relation to the size of the community. Dixon, a small town about 100 miles southwest of Chicago, has a population of just fewer than 16,000 people. It is difficult to understand how the leadership of a city so small could have not realized that the massive amount of funds was missing.

The fraud appears to have begun late in 1990, when Crundwell opened a bank account in the joint name of the city of Dixon and an acronym, RSCDA. The account holder was listed as "RSCDA, c/o Rita Crundwell." RSCDA was purportedly the city's capital development fund. Crundwell transferred funds from Dixon's money market account to the RSCDA fund, as well as to various other city-held bank accounts. Crundwell then wrote checks from the RSCDA account to pay for her personal expenses, including expenses relating to her horse business. To conceal the fraud, Crundwell created fictitious invoices from the state of Illinois, made to look as though the funds she was fraudulently depositing into the RSCDA account were being used for a legitimate city purpose.

To give a sense of the magnitude of the fraud, Crundwell charged about $2.5 million to her American Express card between January 2007 and March 2012; this included charges of $339,000 on jewelry alone. Between September 2011 and March 2012 she wrote 19 checks worth $3,558,000 from a city account payable to "Treasurer;" she deposited these checks into the RSCDA account. She then took $3,311,860 from the

RSCDA account by checks and online withdrawals, using only $74,274 for the city's actual operations. Crundwell used the remainder of those funds for personal and business expenses, including approximately $450,000 relating to her horse farming operations, $600,000 in online credit card payments, and $67,000 to purchase a 2012 Chevy Silverado pickup truck. After the fraud was discovered, the FBI seized, among other items, the following from Crundwell:

- 311 quarter horses
- 2009 Liberty Coach motor home: $2.1 million
- 2009 Kenworth T800 tractor truck: $146,000
- 2009 Freightliner truck: $140,000
- 2009 Chevrolet Silverado pickup truck: $56,646
- 2009 Featherlite horse trailer: $258,698

The fraud unraveled when Crundwell took a 12-week unpaid vacation during 2011. While she was away, a city employee who served as her replacement obtained bank statements from all of the city's bank accounts. After reviewing those statements, the employee contacted the city's mayor, Mayor Burke, to alert him that one particular account had unusual transactions within it. Specifically, the September 2011 statement for that account showed three deposits totaling $785,000, as well as 84 checks drawn totaling $360,493, and 40 withdrawals totaling $266,605. Burke was unaware that the account even existed, and it was apparent that the withdrawals had no legitimate purpose relating to the city's business. As of late May 2012, Crundwell pleaded not guilty to charges against her. If convicted of those charges, she faces up to 20 years in prison.

The implication for auditors is the need to be aware of weak internal controls and the negative consequences for a client's financial statements. A control risk assessment of high means that the auditor needs to perform additional substantive procedures. In contrast, when an auditor believes that controls are well designed and assesses control risk as low, the auditor needs to test those controls to see if they are operating effectively, and may need to modify the control risk assessment (to higher) if they are not operating effectively.

- Review company policies and procedures for addressing risk
- Gain a knowledge of company compensation schemes to determine if they are consistent with the risk policies adopted by the company
- Review prior years' work to determine if current actions are consistent with risk approaches discussed with management
- Review risk management documents
- Determine how management and the board monitor risk, identify changes in risk, and react to mitigate, manage, or control the risk

利用分析性程序和集体研
讨活动评估重大错报风险

[LO 5] Use preliminary analytical
procedures and brain-
storming to identify areas
of heightened risk of
material misstatement.

在计划阶段，注册会计师需要对客
户的未审财务报表和行业数据实施
初步的分析性程序，以更好地识别
特定账户中的重大错报风险。

Analytical Procedures and Brainstorming Activities to Assess the Risks of Material Misstatement

The auditor will use analytical procedures and brainstorming activities to assess the risks of material misstatement.

Preliminary Analytical Procedures

During planning, the auditor should apply preliminary analytical procedures using the client's unaudited financial statements and industry data to better identify risks of material misstatement in particular account balances. This analysis improves the auditor's understanding of the client's business and directs the auditor's attention to high-risk areas. It enables the auditor to be better informed when responding to the risks and planning the nature, timing, and extent of procedures to test the client's account balances.

Recall from Chapter 6 that a basic premise underlying the application of analytical procedures is that plausible relationships among data can be reasonably expected to exist and to continue in the absence of known conditions to the contrary. Further, as explained in Chapter 6, the process used by the auditor in performing analytical procedures involves four primary steps. First, the auditor develops an expectation. Developing informed expectations, and critically appraising client performance in relationship to those expectations, is fundamental to a quality audit. The auditor needs to understand developments in the client's industry, general economic factors, and the client's strategic development plans in order to generate informed expectations about client results. Critical analysis based on these expectations should help the auditor to identify accounts and assertions with potential material misstatements. The analytical results are important in implementing the risk-based approach to auditing. It is only when these expectations are properly developed that the auditor can determine the amount of residual risk in key account balances.

Second, the auditor determines when a difference between the auditor's expectation and what the client has recorded would be considered significant. Third, the auditor computes the difference between the auditor's expectation and what the client has recorded. Fourth, the auditor follows up on significant differences that highlight areas where there is a heightened risk of material misstatement requiring further investigation by the auditor. The auditor's response to identified risks of material misstatement needs to address these heightened areas of risk. The auditor plans the nature, timing, and extent of audit procedures in a way that will most effectively address those risks.

Types of Analytical Techniques Two of the most frequently used analytical techniques during risk assessment include trend analysis and ratio analysis. Most commonly, the auditor imports the client's unaudited data into a spreadsheet or a software program to calculate trends and ratios and help pinpoint areas for further investigation. These trends and ratios are compared with auditor expectations that were developed from knowledge obtained in previous years, industry trends, and current economic development in the geographic area served by the client.

Trend analysis includes simple year-to-year comparisons of account balances, graphic presentations, and analysis of financial data, histograms of ratios, and projections of account balances based on the history of changes in the account. It is imperative for the auditor to develop expectations and to establish decision rules, or thresholds, in advance in order to identify unexpected results for additional investigation. One potential decision rule, for example, is that dollar variances exceeding one-third or one-fourth of planning materiality should be investigated. Another decision rule, or threshold, is to investigate any change exceeding a specified percentage. Auditors often use a trend analysis over several years for key accounts, as shown in the following example in planning for the 2013 audit (2013 data are unaudited).

	2013	**2012**	**2011**	**2010**	**2009**
Gross sales ($000)	$29,500	$24,900	$24,369	$21,700	$17,600
Sales returns ($000)	600	400	300	250	200
Gross margin ($000)	8,093	6,700	6,869	6,450	5,000
Percent of prior year: Sales	118.5%	102.2%	112.3%	123.3%	105.2%
Sales returns	150.0%	133.3%	120.0%	125.0%	104.6%
Gross margin	132.8%	97.5%	106.5%	129.0%	100.0%
Sales as a percentage of 2009 sales	167.6%	141.5%	138.5%	123.3%	100.0%

In this example, the auditor's expectation might be that gross margin percentage and sales percentage would increase at about the same rate. Further, the auditor might have an expectation that sales returns would be relatively stable in comparison with the prior year. After setting a threshold and comparing the expectation to the client's data, the auditor in this example might conclude that the changes in gross margin and sales returns warrant further investigation. The auditor should gain an understanding about why gross margin is increasing more rapidly than sales and why sales returns are increasing. More importantly, the auditor should develop some potential hypotheses as to why there was an increase in gross margin along with the reason for the substantial increase in sales. Then, once the hypotheses are developed, the auditor should determine which set of hypotheses is most likely and then use those for prioritizing audit work. Potential hypotheses for the increase in gross margin include:

- The company has introduced a new product that is a huge market success (for example, the introduction of the iPad by Apple).
- The company has changed its product mix.
- The company has improved its operational efficiencies.
- The company has fictitious sales (and consequently no cost of goods associated with those sales).

Upon analysis, two of the hypotheses above would best explain the unaudited changes in sales and gross margin for 2013: (a) a significant new product introduction that allows higher margins or (b) fictitious sales. With this analysis, the auditor can prioritize which hypothesis to investigate first and thus achieve audit efficiency. For example, if the company has not introduced a new product and the company's sales growth and gross margin are significantly higher than the competition, then it is likely that the fictitious sales hypothesis is the most likely. Going through this process of preliminary analytical procedures helps the auditor identify areas where the risk of material misstatement is high and then allows the auditor to plan appropriate procedures to address those risks. Importantly, the auditor should determine potential hypotheses rather than just inquiring of management as to the reasons for the change. Behavioral research shows that once an individual is given a potential explanation, it is more difficult to identify alternative explanations.

As suggested above, trend analysis can incorporate **ratio analysis,** which takes advantage of economic relationships between two or more accounts. It is widely used because of its power to identify unusual or unexpected changes in relationships. Ratio analysis is useful in identifying significant differences between the client results and a norm (such as industry ratios) or between auditor expectations and actual results. It is also useful in identifying potential audit problems when ratios change between years (such as inventory turnover).

Comparing ratio data over time for the client and its industry can yield useful insights. The auditor could rely on industry data to develop expectations for preliminary analytics. For example, if a particular industry ratio increased over time, the auditor should expect that the client's ratio would also increase over time.

In the following example, the percentage of sales returns and allowances to net sales for the client does not vary significantly from the industry average for the current period, but comparing the trend over time yields an unexpected result.

Sales Returns as A % of Net Sales

	2013	2012	2011	2010	2009
Client	2.1%	2.6%	2.5%	2.7%	2.5%
Industry	2.3%	2.1%	2.2%	2.1%	2.0%

This comparison shows that even though the percentage of sales returns for 2013 is close to the industry average, the client's percentage declined significantly from 2012, while the industry's percentage increased. In addition, except for the current year, the client's percentages exceeded the industry average. The result is different from the auditor's expectation that the percentage would increase from the prior period- it likely exceeds the auditor's threshold, and thus the auditor should investigate the potential cause. Some possible explanations for the differences include:

- The client has improved its quality control.
- Fictitious sales have been recorded in 2013.
- The client is not properly recording sales returns in 2013.

The auditor must design audit procedures to identify the cause of this difference to determine whether a material misstatement exists.

Exhibit 7.3 shows several commonly used financial ratios. The first three ratios provide information on potential liquidity problems. The turnover and gross margin ratios are helpful in identifying fraudulent activity or items

EXHIBIT **7.3**	Commonly Used Ratios

Ratio	Formula
Short-term liquidity ratios:	
Current ratio	Current Assets/Current Liabilities
Quick ratio	(Cash + Cash Equivalents + Net Receivables)/Current Liabilities
Current debt-to-assets ratio	Current Liabilities/Total Assets
Receivable ratios:	
Accounts receivable turnover	Credit Sales/Accounts Receivable
Days' sales in accounts receivable	365/Turnover
Inventory ratios:	
Inventory turnover	Cost of Sales/Ending Inventory
Days' sales in inventory	365/Turnover
Profitability measures:	
Net profit margin	Net Income/Net Sales
Return on equity	Net Income/Stockholders' Equity
Financial leverage ratios:	
Debt-to-equity ratio	Total Liabilities/Stockholders' Equity
Liabilities to assets	Total Liabilities/Total Assets
Capital turnover ratios:	
Asset liquidity	Current Assets/Total Assets
Sales to assets	Net Sales/Total Assets
Net worth to sales	Stockholders' Equity/Net Sales

recorded more than once, such as fictitious sales or inventory. The leverage and capital turnover ratios help in evaluating going-concern problems or adherence to debt covenants. Although the auditor chooses the ratios deemed most useful for a client, many auditors routinely calculate and analyze the ratios listed in Exhibit 7.3 on a trend basis over time. Other ratios are designed for a specific industry. In the banking industry, for example, auditors calculate ratios on percentages of nonperforming loans, operating margin, and average interest rates by loan categories. Ratio and trend analysis are generally carried out through a comparison of client data with expectations:

- Based on industry data
- Based on similar prior-period data
- Developed from industry trends, client budgets, other account balances, or other bases of expectations

Comparison with Industry Data A comparison of client data with industry data may identify potential problems. For example, if the average collection period for accounts receivable in an industry is 43 days, but the client's average collection period is 65 days, this might indicate problems with product quality or credit risk. Or, as another example, a bank's concentration of loans in a particular industry may indicate greater problems if that industry is encountering economic problems. One potential limitation to using industry data is that such data might not be directly comparable to the client's. Companies may be quite different, but still classified within one broad industry. Also, other companies in the industry may use accounting principles different from the client's (for example, LIFO versus FIFO).

Comparison with Previous Year Data Simple ratio analysis comparing current and past data that is prepared as a routine part of planning an audit can highlight risks of misstatement. The auditor often develops ratios on asset turnover, liquidity, and product-line profitability to search for potential signals of risk. For example, an inventory turnover ratio might indicate that a particular product line had a turnover of four times for the past three years, but only three times this year. The change may indicate potential obsolescence problems or errors in the accounting records. Even when performing simple ratio analysis, it is important that the auditor go through each of the steps in the process, beginning with the development of expectations.

Brainstorming Techniques

Brainstorming is a group discussion designed to encourage auditors to creatively assess client risks, particularly those relevant to the possible existence of fraud in the organization. Brainstorming sessions occur predominantly during the early planning phases of the audit, but on occasion these sessions are repeated if actual fraud is detected or at the end of the audit to ensure that all ideas generated during brainstorming have been addressed during the audit opinion formulation process. Brainstorming sessions are attended by the entire engagement team and should be led by the audit partner or manager. These sessions are viewed by audit firms as a way to transfer knowledge from top-level auditors to less senior members of the audit team via interactive and constructive group dialogue and idea exchange.

To encourage interactive and constructive group dialogue and idea exchange, the following guidelines are typically followed during the brainstorming session:

- *Suspension of criticism*—Participants are requested to refrain from criticizing or making value judgments during the session.
- *Freedom of expression*—Participants are encouraged to try to overcome their inhibitions about expressing creative ideas, and every idea is noted and accepted as a possibility.
- *Quantity of idea generation*— Participants are encouraged to provide more ideas rather than fewer, with the intent to generate a variety of

possible risk assessment scenarios that can then be explored during the conduct of the audit.

- *Respectful communication*—Participants are encouraged to exchange ideas, further develop those ideas during the session, and to respect the opinions of others.

Brainstorming sessions normally include the following steps:

1. Review prior year client information.
2. Consider client information, particularly with respect to the fraud triangle (incentive, opportunity, and rationalization).
3. Integrate information from Steps 1 and 2 into an assessment of the likelihood of fraud in the engagement.
4. Identify audit responses to fraud risks.

Academic research reveals that during this process, most audit firms encourage participants in the brainstorming session to explicitly consider professional skepticism. For example, audit firms encourage the brainstorming group to answer questions such as, "How could someone commit fraud at this client?" Auditors are told to be skeptical about assurances that client personnel provide, to be sure that they verify the authenticity of documentation, and to choose new and different audit procedures each year even if the results of brainstorming in the current year are similar to those in prior years. Brainstorming sessions usually last up to an hour, but on occasion may last for as much as two or more hours, depending the complexity and risk profile of the client.

对识别的重大错报风险的反应

LO 6 Describe how auditors make decisions about detection risk and audit risk.

确定检查风险和审计风险

检查风险(detection risk)
是指某一认定存在错报，该错报单独或者连同其他错报是重大的，但注册会计师未能发现这种错报的可能性。检查风险取决于审计程序设计的合理性和执行的有效性。

Responding to Identified Risks of Material Misstatement

In responding to identified risks of material misstatement, the auditor makes decisions about detection risk and audit risk, which will then have implications for the audit work ultimately conducted.

Determining Detection Risk and Audit Risk

The auditor assesses the risk of material misstatement at the financial statement level and the account and assertion levels, which includes both control risk and inherent risk, for each significant component of the financial statements of the organization. From this assessment, and with consideration of the desired level of audit risk, the auditor determines the level of detection risk. Detection risk is affected by both the effectiveness of the substantive auditing procedures that the auditor performs and the extent to which those procedures were performed with due professional care. The auditor's determination of detection risk influences the nature, amount, and timing of substantive audit procedures to ensure that the audit achieves the desired audit risk.

A high level of detection risk means that the audit firm is willing to take a higher risk of not detecting a material misstatement. A low level of detection risk means that the audit firm is not willing to take as much of a risk of not detecting a material misstatement. If detection risk is at a high level, then audit risk is higher as well, because there is a greater chance of issuing an audit opinion that the financial statements are fairly presented when they are materially misstated. If detection risk is at a low level, then audit risk is lower as well, because there is a lower chance of issuing an audit opinion that the financial statements are presented when they are materially misstated. Audit risk is usually set at between 1% (low audit risk) and 5% (high audit risk). Based on the set level of audit risk and the assessed levels of risk of material misstatement (inherent and control risk), detection risk will range from 1% (low detection risk) to 100% (high detection risk), although it would be unusual to have an extremely high level of detection risk. The risks of material misstatement may range from 0% (unlikely) to 100% (highly likely). Exhibit 7.4 shows the directional relationships among the various risks, along with interpretations of their meanings.

EXHIBIT **7.4** Risks and Their Effects on Audit Work

Risk of Material Misstatement	Interpretation	Relationship to Audit Risk	Interpretation	Effect on Detection Risk	Interpretation	Effect on of Audit Work
Inherent Risk:						
High (100%)	Likely that transaction is recorded in error.	Set audit risk at low level (1%).	Auditor is willing to take only a 1% chance of expressing an audit opinion that the financial statements are fairly presented when they are materially misstated.	Detection risk must be at low level (1%).	Auditor is willing to take only a 1% chance that substantive audit procedures will not detect a material misstatement.	More work or more reliable work or more relevant work.
Low (30%)	Unlikely that a transaction is recorded in error.	Set audit risk at high level (5%).	Auditor is willing to take a 5% chance of expressing an audit opinion that the financial statements are fairly presented when they are materially misstated.	Detection risk can be at high level (17%), assuming control risk is 100%.	Auditor is willing to take a 17% chance that substantive audit procedures will not detect a material misstatement.	Less work or less reliable work or less relevant work.
Control Risk:						
High (100%)	Controls are ineffective.	Set audit risk at low level (1%).	Auditor is willing to take only a 1% chance of expressing an audit opinion that the financial statements are fairly presented when they are materially misstated.	Detection risk must be at low level (1%).	Auditor is willing to take only a 1% chance that substantive audit procedures will not detect a material misstatement.	More work or more reliable work or more relevant work.
Low (30%)	Controls are effective (note that the auditor needs to test controls to confirm this assessment).	Set audit risk at high level (5%).	Auditor is willing to take a 5% chance of expressing an audit opinion that the financial statements are fairly presented when they are materially misstated.	Detection risk can be at high level (17%), assuming inherent risk is 100%.	Auditor is willing to take a 17% chance that substantive audit procedures will not detect a material misstatement.	Less work or less reliable work or less relevant work.

Quantitative Examples of the Audit Risk Model

We provide examples of the audit risk model for situations involving high and low risks of material misstatement.

High Risk of Material Misstatement Assume an account with many complex transactions and weak internal controls. The auditor assesses both inherent risk and control risk at their maximum (100%), implying that the client does not have effective internal control related to this account and there is a high risk that transactions posted to this account would be recorded incorrectly. Also assume that the auditor has set audit risk at a low level (1%). This implies that the auditor is willing to take only a 1% chance of expressing an audit opinion that the financial statements are fairly presented when they are materially misstated. A numerical depiction of the relationship between inherent risk, control risk, detection risk, and audit risk is often called the **audit risk model**, and it is calculated as follows:

$$Audit\ Risk = Inherent\ Risk \times Control\ Risk \times Detection\ Risk$$
$$0.01 = 1.00 \times 1.00 \times Detection\ Risk$$

therefore

$$Detection\ Risk = 0.01/(1.0 \times 1.0) = 1\%$$

In this example, detection risk and audit risk are the same because the auditor cannot rely on internal controls to prevent or detect misstatements. The illustration yields an intuitive result: a high likelihood of material misstatement leads to extended audit work to maintain audit risk at an acceptable level.

Low Risk of Material Misstatement Assume an account with simple transactions, well-trained accounting personnel recording those transactions, no incentive to misstate the financial statements, and effective internal control over the account. The auditor's previous experience with the client and an understanding of the client's internal controls indicate a low risk of material misstatement existing in the accounting records. The auditor assesses inherent and control risk as low (at 50% and 20%, respectively). Audit risk has been set at 5%. The auditor's determination of detection risk for this engagement would be calculated as follows:

$$Audit\ Risk = Inherent\ Risk \times Control\ Risk \times Detection\ Risk$$
$$0.05 = 0.50 \times 0.20 \times Detection\ Risk$$

therefore

$$Detection\ Risk = 0.05/(0.50 \times 0.20) = 50\%$$

In other words, the auditor could design tests of the accounting records with a higher detection risk—in this case 50%. Thus, minimal substantive tests of account balances are needed to provide corroborating evidence on the expectations that the accounts are not materially misstated. Because inherent and control risk are relatively low, the auditor is willing to accept a greater risk that substantive audit procedures will not detect a material misstatement. However, because the auditor is planning on relying on controls, the auditor will need to test the operating effectiveness of controls to see if the lower control risk assessment is warranted. As in the prior illustration, this illustration yields an intuitive result: a low likelihood of misstatement leads to less extensive audit work to maintain audit risk at an acceptable level.

The *Auditing in Practice* feature, "An Expanded Version of the Audit Risk Model," provides information about how auditors may divide detection risk into subcomponents relating to types of testing.

An Expanded Version of the Audit Risk Model

Auditors may choose to think of the audit risk model in an expanded version that divides *detection risk* (DR) into two subcomponents. These subcomponents are the (1) *tests of details risk* (TD), and (2) *substantive analytical procedures risk* (AP).

This expanded model can be represented as:

$$AR = IR \times CR \times AP \times TD$$

When using this expanded model, the auditor would want to determine TD as follows:

$$TD = AR/(IR \times CR \times AP)$$

Assume a situation where:

AR = 5%
IR = 50%

CR = 30%
AP = 60%

In this setting, the auditor would determine TD as:

$$TD = 5\%/(50\% \times 30\% \times 60\%)$$
$$TD = 55.5\%$$

This expanded model recognizes that detection risk incorporates both types of substantive procedures—substantive analytical procedures and tests of details. In audits where both types of procedures will be used, this expanded model may be a more appropriate way to think about the risks and the auditor's responses to those risks.

Planning Audit Procedures to Respond to the Assessed Risks of Material Misstatement

計劃審計程序以應對評估的重大錯報風險

LO 7 Respond to the assessed risks of material misstatement and plan the nature of procedures to be performed on an audit engagement.

Recall from Chapter 5 that for a financial statement audit where the auditor wants to rely on controls as part of the basis for the audit opinion, the auditor should design a controls reliance audit—an audit that includes tests of controls and substantive procedures. For some audits, the auditor might determine that it is not efficient or effective to rely on the client's controls in forming the audit opinion. In those audits, the auditor designs a substantive audit—an audit that includes substantive procedures and does not include tests of controls.

When considering risk responses, the auditor should do the following:

1. Evaluate the reasons for the assessed risk of material misstatement.
2. Estimate the likelihood of material misstatement due to the inherent risks of the client.
3. Consider the role of internal controls, and determine whether control risk is relatively high or low, thereby determining whether the auditor should rely on controls (thereby necessitating tests of controls) or whether the auditor needs to conduct a more substantive audit.
4. Obtain more relevant and reliable audit evidence as the auditor's assessment of the risk of material misstatement increases.

A practical analogy to conceptualize these steps is to compare an umbrella in a rainstorm to effective internal controls. Risks might result in material misstatements (rain); management is responsible for keeping the financial statements free of material misstatements (dry). The auditor's objective is to gather enough information to objectively assess how well management is doing in keeping the financial statements free from material misstatement (dry). Exhibit 7.5 shows that Client A has effective internal controls (the umbrella without holes) that prevent material misstatements (rain) from getting into the accounting records. However, we know that umbrellas are not always perfect—they can spring leaks when least expected, or one of the supporting arms can fail, letting rain come through on one side. The auditor has to test the umbrella (controls) to see that it is working,

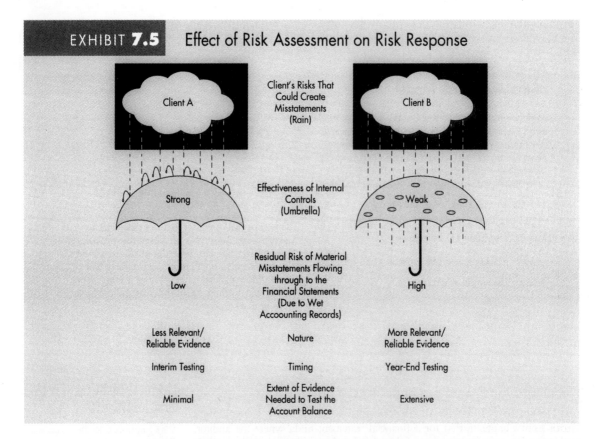

EXHIBIT **7.5** Effect of Risk Assessment on Risk Response

but must do enough substantive testing of the account balance to determine that leaks (misstatements) had not occurred in an amount that would be noticeable (material misstatement). Client B's umbrella has holes in it (weak internal controls), resulting in wet accounting records (they are likely to contain material misstatements). Because of the weak controls, it is unlikely that the auditor will perform any testing of controls, and the use of substantive analytical procedures will probably be limited. Thus, the auditor must perform extensive direct tests of the account balances to identify any misstatements.

Nature, Timing, and Extent of Risk Response Procedures

风险反应的性质
(nature of risk response)
是指将要实施的审计程序的类型，
强调的是审计程序的适当性。

The nature, timing, and extent of the auditor's risk response depend on the auditor's assessment of the risk of material misstatement. The **nature of risk response** refers to the types of audit procedures to be performed, with a focus on the appropriateness (relevance and reliability) of those procedures. For example, certain audit procedures may be more appropriate for some assertions than others. Assessing the existence of inventory is most effectively completed by inspecting the inventory, whereas assessing the valuation of inventory is most effectively completed by engaging a specialist. In addition, the nature of risk response could occur at a more global engagement level, and could include assembling an audit team that has more experienced auditors, auditors with specialized skills, or including on the audit team outside specialists to address assessed risks. Finally, another engagement level way to address assessed risks might be to put increased emphasis on professional skepticism or to conduct more detailed levels of review related to assessed risks.

The **timing of risk response** refers to when audit procedures are conducted and whether those procedures are conducted at announced or predictable times. When the risk of material misstatement is heightened, the auditor conducts the audit procedures closer to year end, on an unannounced basis, and includes some element of unpredictability in the timing. Some ways to introduce unpredictability include the following:

- Perform some audit procedures on accounts, disclosures, and assertions that would otherwise not receive scrutiny because they are considered low risk
- Change the timing of audit procedures from year to year
- Select items for testing that are outside the normal boundaries for testing that are lower than prior-year materiality
- Perform audit procedures on a surprise or unannounced basis
- Vary the location or procedures year to year for multilocation audits

Further, certain procedures can be completed only at or after period end. These include the following:

- Compare the financial statements to the accounting records
- Evaluate adjusting journal entries made by management in preparing the financial statements
- Conduct procedures to respond to risks that management may have engaged in improper transactions at period end

The **extent of risk response** refers to the sufficiency of evidence that is necessary given the client's assessed risks, materiality, and the level of acceptable audit risk. When the risk of material misstatement is heightened, the auditor increases the extent of audit procedures and demands more evidence. As an example of increasing the extent of risk response, one such response would be to increase the number of locations to be included in the scope of the audit (for example, supervising inventory counts at a greater number of warehouse locations).

The *Auditing in Practice* feature, "The City of Dixon, Illinois Sues Its Auditor for $50 Million Related to the Rita Crundwell Embezzlement," provides a chilling reminder to auditors of their obligation to accurately assess risk at the overall financial statement level and to respond accordingly.

The City of Dixon, Illinois Sues Its Auditor for $50 Million Related to the Rita Crundwell Embezzlement

AUDITING IN PRACTICE

Recall from earlier in the chapter that Rita Crundwell embezzled about $50 million from the city of Dixon, Illinois. On June 8, 2012, the city sued the accountants that had conducted the city's audit for the past five years: Samuel Card CPA and Janis Card Company LLC. In addition, the lawsuit names former Dixon auditor, CliftonLarsonAllen, as a respondent in discovery, which allows the city to request documents in order to determine whether or not to also sue the former auditor as well. The lawsuit alleges professional negligence and negligent misrepresentation, and it alleges certain deficiencies in how the auditors conducted the audit, including:

- Failing to identify inaccuracies in the city's financial statements and other financial documents
- Failing to properly perform audits and other financial services

- Failing to perform professional services and issue audits in conformance with nationally recognized standards and its own internal policies and procedures
- Failing to implement proper policies and procedures in order to perform the audits of the city
- Failing to properly train auditors and auditing staff to identify fraud, embezzlement, and criminal acts

Time will tell how the legal process will resolve this situation. But it is clear that the city of Dixon and its taxpayers are going to attempt to show that the auditors failed to perform their professional duty, thereby resulting in a massive financial loss. The message is clear: when auditors fail to assess and appropriately respond to the risk of material misstatement, there are severe consequences to all parties involved.

SUMMARY AND NEXT STEPS

This chapter has presented a discussion of the importance of materiality judgments in the audit process. This enables you to understand what constitutes a material misstatement in the financial statements. Certain risks associated with the client heighten the risk of material misstatements, including inherent and control risks. Audit risk and detection risk are determined by the auditor based upon inherent and control risks. The audit risk model is used by the auditor to respond to assessed risks, in terms of the nature, timing, and extent of audit procedures. In Chapter 8 we discuss specialized audit tools that you can use to respond to risk, including sampling and generalized audit software.

SIGNIFICANT TERMS

Audit risk The risk that the auditor expresses an inappropriate audit opinion when the financial statements are materially misstated.

Audit risk model A numerical depiction of the relationship between inherent risk, control risk, detection risk, and audit risk.

Brainstorming A group discussion designed to encourage auditors to creatively assess client risks, particularly those relevant to the possible existence of fraud in the organization.

Business Risk Inherent risk at the financial statement level that affects the business operations and potential outcomes of organizational activities.

Clearly trivial An amount that is clearly inconsequential, whether taken individually or in the aggregate and whether judged by any criteria of size, nature, or circumstances. This term is also referred to as posting materiality.

Control risk The risk that a misstatement that could occur in an assertion about a class of transaction, account balance, or disclosure and that could be material, either individually or when aggregated with other misstatements, will not be prevented, or detected and corrected, on a timely basis by the entity's internal control.

Detection risk The risk that the procedures performed by the auditor to reduce audit risk to an acceptably low level will not detect a misstatement that exists and that could be material, either individually or when aggregated with other misstatements.

Extent of risk response Refers to the amount of evidence that is necessary given the client's assessed risks, materiality, and the level of acceptable audit risk.

Inherent risk The susceptibility of an assertion about a class of transaction, account balance, or disclosure to a misstatement that could be material, either individually or when aggregated with other misstatements, before consideration of any related controls.

Materiality The magnitude of an omission or misstatement of accounting information that, in view of surrounding circumstances, makes it probable that the judgment of a reasonable person relying on the information would have been changed or influenced by the omission or misstatement.

Misstatement   An error, either intentional or unintentional, that exists in a transaction or financial statement account balance.

Nature of risk response   The types of audit procedures applied given the nature of the account balance and the most relevant assertions regarding that account balance.

Performance materiality   The amount or amounts set by the auditor at less than the materiality level for the financial statements as a whole or for particular classes of transactions, account balances, or disclosures.

Posting materiality   The amount below which errors are treated as inconsequential. This term is also referred to as clearly trivial.

Ratio analysis   An analytical technique that is useful in identifying significant differences between the client results and a norm (such as industry ratios) or between auditor expectations and actual results; ratio analysis is also useful in identifying potential audit problems that may be found in ratio changes between years.

Risk of material misstatement   Risk that exists at the overall financial statement level and at the assertion level, and within these levels risk can be categorized as involving inherent risk and control risk.

Risk   A concept used to express uncertainty about events and/or their outcomes that could have a material effect on the organization.

Significant risk   An identified and assessed risk of material misstatement that, in the auditor's professional judgment, requires special consideration.

Timing of risk response   Refers to when audit procedures are conducted and whether those procedures are conducted at announced or predictable times.

Tolerable misstatement   The amount of misstatement in an account balance that the auditor could tolerate and still not judge the underlying account balance to be materially misstated.

Trend analysis   An analytical technique that includes simple year-to-year comparisons of account balances, graphic presentations, and analysis of financial data, histograms of ratios, and projections of account balances based on the history of changes in the account.

TRUE-FALSE QUESTIONS

7-1 [LO 1]   Material misstatements refer only to intentional misstatements that exist in a transaction or financial statement account balance.

7-2 [LO 1]   Performance materiality is set less than overall materiality and helps the auditor determine the extent of audit evidence needed.

7-3 [LO 2]   Detection risk is the susceptibility of an assertion about a class of transaction, account balance, or disclosure to a misstatement that could be material before consideration of related controls.

7-4 [LO 2]   Audit risk is the risk that the auditor expresses an inappropriate audit opinion when the financial statements are materially misstated.

7-5 [LO 3] Inherent risks at the financial statement level include factors that could threaten the fundamental financial viability of the organization.

7-6 [LO 3] Inherent risk at the financial statement level is not affected by the competence and integrity of management or their potential incentives to misstate the financial statements.

7-7 [LO 4] Some level of control risk is always present in an organization because of the inherent limitations of internal control.

7-8 [LO 4] Each of the following factors would lead the auditor to assess control risk at a higher level: the company lacks personnel or expertise to deal with changes in the industry, there exist significant supply chain risks, the industry is mature and declining, and there exist regulatory requirements that increase legal exposure.

7-9 [LO 5] When conducting trend analysis, it is important that the auditor not develop expectations and establish decision rules in advance; doing so would make it more difficult for the auditor to identify unexpected results for additional investigation.

7-10 [LO 5] When performing preliminary analytical procedures and evaluating the results of those procedures, it is important that the auditor discusses the results with management before identifying hypotheses to explain the results; by discussing with management the auditor will be better able to identify alternative explanations.

7-11 [LO 6] A high level of detection risk means that the audit firm is willing to take accept a low risk of not detecting a material misstatement.

7-12 [LO 6] The interpretation of audit risk set at a low level (1%) is that the auditor is willing to take only a 1% chance of expressing an audit opinion that the financial statement are fairly presented when they are materially misstated.

7-13 [LO 7] The nature of risk response refers to the sufficiency and appropriateness of evidence that is necessary given the client's assessed risks, materiality, and the level of audit risk that is deemed acceptable.

7-14 [LO 7] In terms of the timing of the risk response, the following procedures can be completed only at or after period end: comparing the financial statements to the accounting records, evaluating adjusting journal entries made by management in preparing the financial statements, and conducting procedures to response to risks that management may have engaged in improper transactions at period end.

MULTIPLE-CHOICE QUESTIONS

7-15 [LO 1] Which of the following statements is true regarding the concept of materiality?

a. Materiality is the magnitude of an omission or misstatement of accounting information that, in light of surrounding circumstances, makes it probable that the judgment of a reasonable person relying on the information would have been changed or influenced by the omission or misstatement.

b. Materiality is the magnitude of an omission or misstatement of accounting information that, in light of surrounding circumstances, makes it possible that the judgment of a reasonable person relying on the information would have been changed or influenced by the omission or misstatement.

c. A fact is material if there is a substantial likelihood that the fact would have been viewed by the reasonable investor as having significantly altered the total mix of information made available.

d. Both (a) and (c) are correct.

e. Both (b) and (c) are correct.

7-16 [LO 1] Which of the following statements is true concerning the concept of performance materiality?

a. Performance materiality is set less than overall materiality and helps the auditor determine the extent of audit evidence.

b. If performance materiality is set too low, the auditor might not perform sufficient procedures to detect material misstatements in the financial statements.

c. If performance materiality is set too high, the auditor might perform more substantive procedures than necessary.

d. Performance materiality is essentially the same posting materiality.

e. All of the above are true.

7-17 [LO 2] Which of the following statements represent the appropriate directional relationships between the concepts of inherent risk, control risk, audit risk, and detection risk?

a. As inherent risk goes up, audit risk goes up.

b. As inherent risk goes up, audit risk goes down.

c. As control risk goes up, detection risk goes up.

d. As control risk goes up, inherent risk goes down.

7-18 [LO 2] Which of the following statements is true regarding the concept of detection risk?

a. After assessing inherent and control risk and determining the level of acceptable audit risk, the auditor determines detection risk.

b. Detection risk is under the control of the auditor, and the level of audit effort that the auditor expends on the engagement depends on the level of detection risk.

c. When the risk of material misstatement is higher, detection risk is lower in order to reduce audit risk to an acceptable level.

d. The auditor controls detection risk through the nature, timing, and extent of substantive audit procedures.

e. All of the above are true.

7-19 [LO 3] Inherent risk is present in organizations at which of the following levels?

a. At the assertion level.

b. At the financial statement level in terms of business risk relating to operations.

c. At the financial statement level in terms of financial reporting.

d. All of the above.

7-20 [LO 3] Which of the following characteristics would lead the auditor to assess inherent risk relating to financial reporting at a higher level?

a. The account balance represents an asset that is relatively easily stolen.

b. The controls over the account balance are weak.

c. The company has a history of exactly meeting analyst estimates.

d. The company is in an industry that is mature and declining.

7-21 [LO 4] Which of the following statements is true regarding the concept of control risk?

a. When control risk is high, the auditor is concerned that a misstatement may not be prevented, or that if a misstatement exists in the organization's financial statements that it will not be detected, and therefore corrected by management.

b. Some organizations have zero control risk because they have made a significant commitment to the effective design and operation of controls.

c. Control risk relates to the susceptibility of an assertion to a misstatement, due to either error or fraud, before consideration of any related controls.

d. All of the above are true.

7-22 **LO 4** Which of the following characteristics would lead the auditor to assess control risk at a higher level?

a. It is difficult for the auditor to determine or gain access to the organization or individuals who own and/or control the entity.

b. The organization has inadequate accounting staff, or the staff lacks requisite expertise.

c. There exists a lack of supervision of accounting personnel.

d. The organization has inadequate information and communication systems.

e. All of the above.

7-23 **LO 5** Which of the following statements is true regarding analytical techniques?

a. Ratio analysis takes advantage of economic relationships between two or more accounts.

b. Ratio and trend analysis are generally carried out through a comparison of client data with expectations based on industry data, prior-period data, and expectations developed from industry trends, client budgets, and so on.

c. Developing expectations is the first step in performing analytical procedures.

d. All of the above are true.

7-24 **LO 5** Which of the following statements is false regarding brainstorming?

a. Brainstorming is a group discussion designed to encourage auditors to creatively assess client risks, particularly those relevant to the possible existence of fraud in an organization.

b. Brainstorming predominantly occurs during the early planning phases of the audit.

c. To facilitate the generation and evaluation of quality ideas during the brainstorming session, a typical practice during brainstorming is to invite criticism and value judgments about ideas generated.

d. Participants are encouraged to provide more ideas rather than fewer, with the intent to generate a variety of possible risk assessment scenarios that can be explored during the conduct of the audit.

e. All of the above are true.

7-25 **LO 6** Assume that the auditor sets audit risk at a low level, equal to 1%. What is the appropriate interpretation of this level of audit risk?

a. The auditor is willing to take only a 1% chance that audit procedures will not detect a material misstatement.

b. The auditor is 99% confident that the audit procedures will detect a material misstatement.

c. The auditor is willing to take only a 1% chance of expressing an audit opinion that the financial statements are fairly presented when they are materially misstated.

d. The auditor is 99% confident that the audit opinion is correct.

7-26 **LO 6** Assume for Client X that inherent risk is assessed at 30%, control risk is assessed at 100%, audit risk is 5%, and detection risk is therefore determined to be 17%. Assume for Client Z that inherent risk is assessed at 100%, control risk is assessed at 100%, audit risk is 1%, and detection risk is therefore determined to be 1%. What is true about the amount of audit work that will need to be conducted?

    a. Client X will require more audit work than Client Z.

    b. Client Z will require more audit work than Client X.

    c. Both clients will require a similar amount of audit work.

    d. The auditor will most likely resign from the Client Z audit because the inherent risk and control risk are so high.

7-27 `LO 7` When considering responses to risk at the individual assertion level, the auditor should do which of the following?

    a. Evaluate the reasons for the assessed risk of material misstatement.

    b. Estimate the likelihood of material misstatement due to the inherent risks of the client.

    c. Consider the role of internal controls, and determine whether control risk is relatively high or low, thereby determining whether the auditor should rely on controls or whether the auditor needs to conduct a more substantive audit.

    d. Obtain more relevant and reliable audit evidence as the auditor's assessment of the risk of material misstatement increases.

    e. All of the above.

7-28 `LO 7` Which of the following statements is false regarding the nature, timing, and extent of risk responses?

    a. The nature of risk response refers to the types of audit procedures applied given the nature of the account balance and the most relevant assertions regarding that account balance.

    b. The timing of risk response refers to when audit procedures are conducted and whether those procedures are conducted at announced or predictable times.

    c. When the risk of material misstatement is low, the auditor conducts the audit procedures closer to year end, on an unannounced basis, and includes some element of unpredictability in the timing of procedures.

    d. The extent of risk response refers to the sufficiency of evidence that is necessary given the client's assessed risks, materiality, and the acceptable level of audit risk.

REVIEW AND SHORT CASE QUESTIONS

7-29 `LO 1` Define the term *misstatement* and describe characteristics that would make a misstatement material.

7-30 `LO 1` Some audit firms develop very specific quantitative guidelines, either through quantitative measures or in tables, relating planning materiality to the size of sales or assets for a client. Other audit firms leave the materiality judgments up to the individual partner or manager in charge of the audit. What are the major advantages and disadvantages of each approach? Which approach do you favor? Explain.

7-31 `LO 1` Define the following terms: (a) *performance materiality*, (b) *tolerable misstatement*, (c) *clearly trivial*.

7-32 `LO 1` The SEC is very concerned that auditors recognize the qualitative aspect of materiality judgments. Explain what the qualitative aspect of materiality means. List some factors that would make a quantitatively small misstatement be judged as qualitatively material.

7-33 `LO 1` The SEC has criticized the auditing profession for not looking at significant changes in accounting estimates. For example, a reserve (liability estimate) may be estimated very high one year and then very low the next year. Explain how an accounting estimate might not be materially misstated for two consecutive years, but because of the

NOTE: Completing Review and Short Case Questions does not require the student to reference additional resources and materials.

NOTE: For the remaining problems, we make special note of those addressing fraud, international issues, professional skepticism, and ethics.

swing in the accounting estimate, net income could be misstated by a material amount.

PROFESSIONAL SKEPTICISM

7-34 LO 1 Auditors make materiality judgments during the planning phase of the audit in order to be sure they ultimately gather sufficient evidence during the audit to provide reasonable assurance that the financial statements are free of material misstatements. The lower the materiality threshold that an auditor has for an account balance, the more the evidence that the auditor must collect. Auditors often use quantitative benchmarks such as 1% of total assets or 5% of net income to determine whether misstatements materially affect the financial statements, but ultimately it is an auditor's individual professional judgment as to whether a given misstatement is or is not considered material.

a. What is the relationship between the level of riskiness of the client and the level of misstatement in an account balance that an auditor would consider material? For example, assume that Client A has weaker controls over accounts receivable compared to Client B (therefore, Client A is riskier than Client B). Assume that Client B is similar in size to Client A and that the auditor has concluded that a misstatement exceeding $5,000 would be material for Client B's accounts receivable account. Should the materiality threshold for Client A be the same as, more than, or less than that for Client B? Further, which client will require more audit evidence to be collected, Client A or Client B?

b. How might an auditor's individual characteristics affect his or her professional judgments about materiality?

c. Assume that one auditor is more professionally skeptical than another auditor, and that they are making the materiality judgment in part (a) of this problem. Compare the possible alternative monetary thresholds that a more versus less skeptical auditor might make for Client A.

7-35 LO 1 The audit report provides reasonable assurance that the financial statements are free from material misstatements. The auditor is put in a difficult situation because materiality is defined from a user's viewpoint, but the auditor must assess materiality in planning the audit to ensure that sufficient audit work is performed to detect material misstatements.

a. Define materiality as used in accounting and auditing, particularly emphasizing the differences that exist between the FASB and the U.S. Supreme Court materiality definitions.

b. Three major dimensions of materiality are (1) the dollar magnitude of the item, (2) the nature of the item under consideration, (3) the perspective of a particular user. Give an example of each.

c. Once the auditor develops an assessment of materiality, can it change during the course of the audit? Explain. If it does change, what is the implication of a change for audit work that has already been completed? Explain.

7-36 LO 2 Define the terms *inherent risk, control risk, audit risk,* and *detection risk.* Refer to Exhibit 7.1 and explain how these risks relate to each other.

7-37 LO 2 How are inherent risks of material misstatements related to internal controls? Why is it important to assess inherent risks of material misstatement prior to evaluating the quality of an organization's internal controls?

7-38 LO 2 What is the directional relationship between the risks of material misstatement (inherent and control risk) and both audit risk and detection risk? In other words, if the risks of material misstatement increase or decrease, how are audit risk and detection risk affected?

7-39 **LO 1,2** Explain how the concepts of audit risk and materiality are related. Must an auditor make a decision on materiality in order to determine the appropriate level of audit risk?

7-40 **LO 3** Describe factors that would lead the auditor to assess inherent risk at the assertion level at a higher level.

7-41 **LO 3** Inherent risk at the financial statement level relates to (a) business and operating-related risks and (b) financial reporting risks. *The Professional Judgment in Context* feature, "Risks Associated with Financial Statement Misstatements," summarizes various risks from ISA 315; that list is reproduced below. For each risk factor, categorize it as indicating (a) business and operating risk, (b) financial reporting risk, (c) other - describe.

- Operations in regions that are economically unstable, such as countries with significant currency devaluation or highly inflationary economies
- Operations exposed to volatile markets, such as futures trading
- Operations that are subject to a high degree of complex regulation
- Going concern and liquidity issues, including loss of significant customers or constraints on the availability of capital or credit
- Offering new products or moving into new lines of business
- Changes in the organization such as acquisitions or reorganizations
- Entities or business segments likely to be sold
- The existence of complex alliances and joint ventures
- Use of off-balance sheet financing, special-purpose entities, and other complex financing arrangements
- Significant transactions with related parties
- Lack of personnel with appropriate accounting and financial reporting skills
- Changes in key personnel, including departure of key executives
- Deficiencies in internal control, especially those not addressed by management
- Changes in the Information Technology (IT) system or environment and inconsistencies between the entity's IT strategy and its business strategies
- Inquiries into the entity's operations or financial results by regulatory bodies
- Past misstatements, history of errors, or significant adjustments at period end
- Significant amount of nonroutine or nonsystematic transactions, including intercompany transactions and large revenue transactions at period end
- Transactions that are recorded based on management's intent, such as debt refinancing, assets to be sold and classification of marketable securities
- Accounting measurements that involve complex processes
- Pending litigation and contingent liabilities, such as sales warranties, financial guarantees, and environmental remediation

7-42 **LO 3** Refer to the *Auditing in Practice* feature, "Pfizer Pharmaceuticals Risk Disclosures as an Example of Inherent Risk at the Financial Statement Level." Summarize the risks that Pfizer is disclosing. Comment on why these risks might be of concern to the auditor.

7-43 **LO 3** List the various resources that the auditor can access to learn about inherent risk relating to the operations of a company.

FRAUD

PROFESSIONAL SKEPTICISM

7-44 LO 3,7 The auditor needs to assess management integrity as a potential indicator of inherent risk, particularly as it relates to the potential for fraud. Although the assessment of management integrity takes place on every audit engagement, it is a difficult and subjective task. It requires professional skepticism on the part of the auditor because it is human nature to trust people whom we know and interact with.

a. Define management integrity and discuss its importance to the auditor in determining the type of evidence to be gathered on an audit and in evaluating the evidence.

b. Identify the types of evidence the auditor would gather in assessing the integrity of management. What are sources of each type of evidence?

c. For each of the following management scenarios, (1) indicate whether you believe the scenario reflects negatively on management integrity, and explain why; and (2) indicate how the assessment would affect the auditor's planning of the audit.

Management Scenarios

i. The owner/manager of a privately held company also owns three other companies. The entities could be run as one entity, but they engage extensively in related-party transactions to minimize the overall tax burden for the owner/ manager.

ii. The president of a publicly held company has a reputation for being stubborn with a violent temper. He fired a divisional manager on the spot when the manager did not achieve profit goals.

iii. The financial vice president of a publicly held company has worked her way to the top by gaining a reputation as a great accounting manipulator. She has earned the reputation by being very creative in finding ways to circumvent FASB pronouncements to keep debt off the balance sheet and in manipulating accounting to achieve short-term earnings. After each short-term success, she has moved on to another company to utilize her skills.

iv. The president of a small publicly held firm was indicted on tax evasion charges seven years ago. He settled with the IRS and served time doing community service. Since then, he has been considered a pillar of the community, making significant contributions to local charities. Inquiries of local bankers yield information that he is the partial or controlling owner of several corporations that may serve as "shell" organizations whose sole purpose is to assist the manager in moving income around to avoid taxes.

v. James J. James is the president of a privately held company that has been accused of illegally dumping waste and failing to meet government standards for worker safety. James responds that his attitude is to meet the minimum requirements of the law; if the government deems that he has not, he will clean up. "Besides," he asserts, "it is good business; it is less costly to clean up only when I have to, even if small fines are involved, than it is to take leadership positions and exceed government standards."

7-45 LO 4 List the factors that would lead auditors to assess control risk at a higher level. Discuss the techniques that the auditor uses to understand management's risk assessment and other internal control components.

7-46 LO 5 Explain how ratio analysis and industry comparisons can be useful to the auditor in identifying potential risk of material misstatement on an audit engagement. How can such analysis also help the auditor plan the audit?

7-47 `LO 5` Refer to Exhibit 7.3. What ratios would best indicate problems with potential inventory obsolescence or collectability of receivables? How are those ratios calculated?

7-48 `LO 5` Brainstorming is a group discussion designed to encourage auditors to creatively assess client risks, particularly those relevant to fraud.
a. When does brainstorming typically occur?
b. Who attends the brainstorming session? Who leads it?
c. Besides encouraging auditors to creatively assess client risks, what other purpose does brainstorming serve?
d. What are the guidelines that should be followed during a brainstorming session to maximize effectiveness?
e. What are the typical steps in the brainstorming process?

7-49 `LO 5,7` The following information shows the past two periods of results for a fictional company, Jones Manufacturing, and a comparison with industry data for the same period:

PROFESSIONAL SKEPTICISM

ANALYTICAL DATA FOR JONES MANUFACTURING

	Prior Period (000 omitted)	Percent of Sales	Current Period (000 omitted)	Percent of Sales	Percent Change	Industry Average as a Percent of Sales
Sales	$10,000	100	$11,000	100	10	100
Inventory	$2,000	20	$3,250	29.5	57.5	22.5
Cost of goods sold	$6,000	60	$6,050	55	0.83	59.5
Accounts payable	$1,200	12	$1,980	18	65	14.5
Sales commissions	$500	5	$550	5	10	Not available
Inventory turnover	6.3	—	4.2	—	(33)	5.85
Average number of days to collect	39	—	48	—	23	36
Employee turnover	5%	—	8%	—	60	4
Return on investment	14%	—	14.3%	—		13.8
Debt/Equity	35%	—	60%	—	71	30

a. From the preceding data, identify potential risk areas and explain why they represent potential risk. Briefly indicate how the risk analysis should affect the planning of the audit engagement.
b. Identify any of the above data that should cause the auditor to increase the level of professional skepticism.

7-50 `LO 5,7` The following table contains calculations of several key ratios for a fictional company, Indianola Pharmaceutical Company, a maker of proprietary and prescription drugs. The company is publicly held and is considered a small- to medium-size pharmaceutical company. Approximately 80% of its sales have been in prescription drugs; the remaining 20% are in medical supplies normally found in a drugstore. The primary purpose of the auditor's calculations is to identify potential risk areas for the upcoming audit. The auditor recognizes that some of the data might signal the need to gather other industry- or company-specific data. A number of the company's drugs are patented. Its best-selling drug, Anecillin, which will come off of patent in two years, has accounted for approximately 20% of the company's sales during the past five years. The auditor's expectation is that the company's own trends from the past few years should be relatively consistent this year, and that the company will not have significant deviations from industry norms.

INDIANOLA PHARMACEUTICAL RATIO ANALYSIS

Ratio	Current Year	One Year Previous	Two Years Previous	Three Years Previous	Current Industry
Current ratio	1.85	1.89	2.28	2.51	2.13
Quick ratio	0.85	0.93	1.32	1.76	1.40
Times interest earned	1.30	1.45	5.89	6.3	4.50
Days' sales in receivables	109	96	100	72	69
Inventory turnover	2.40	2.21	3.96	5.31	4.33
Days' sales in inventory	152	165	92	69	84
Research & development as % of sales	1.3	1.4	1.94	2.03	4.26
Cost of goods sold as % of sales	38.5	40.2	41.2	43.8	44.5
Debt/equity ratio	4.85	4.88	1.25	1.13	1.25
Earnings per share	$1.12	$2.50	$4.32	$4.26	n/a
Sales/tangible assets	0.68	0.64	0.89	0.87	0.99
Sales/total assets	0.33	0.35	0.89	0.87	0.78
Sales growth over past year	3%	15%	2%	4%	6%

a. What major conclusions regarding financial reporting risk can be drawn from the information shown in the table? Be specific in identifying specific account balances that have a high risk of material misstatement. State how that risk analysis will be used in planning the audit. You should identify a minimum of four financial reporting risks that should be addressed during the audit and how they should be addressed.

b. What other critical background information might you want to obtain as part of planning the audit? What information would you gather during the conduct of the audit? Briefly indicate the probable sources of that information.

c. Based on the information, what major actions did the company take during the immediately preceding year? Explain.

PROFESSIONAL SKEPTICISM

7-51 LO 5,7 The auditor for a fictional company, ABC Wholesaling, has just begun to perform preliminary analytical procedures as part of planning the audit for the coming year. ABC Wholesaling is in a competitive industry, selling products such as STP Brand products and Ortho Grow products to companies such as Wal-Mart, Kmart, and regional retail discount chains. The company is privately owned and has experienced financial difficulty this past year. The difficulty could lead to its major line of credit being pulled if the company does not make a profit in the current year. In performing the analytical procedures, the auditor notes the following changes in accounts related to accounts receivable:

	Current Year (000 omitted)	Previous Year (000 omitted)
Sales	$60,000	$59,000
Accounts receivable	$11,000	$7,200
Percent of accounts receivable current	72%	65%
No. of days' sales in accounts receivable	64	42
Gross margin	18.7%	15.9%
Industry gross margin	16.3%	16.3%
Increase in Nov.–Dec. sales over previous year	12%	3.1%

The auditor had expected the receivables balance to remain stable, but notes the large increase in receivables. After considering possible reasons for this increase, the auditor decides to make inquiries of management. Management explains that the change is due to two things: (1) a new computer system that has increased productivity, and (2) a new policy of rebilling items previously sold to customers, thereby extending the due dates from October to April. The rebilling is explained as follows: Many of the clients' products are seasonal—for example, lawn care products. To provide better service to ABC's customers, management instituted a new policy whereby management negotiated with a customer to determine the approximate amount of seasonal goods on hand at the end of the selling season (October). If the customer would continue to purchase from the client, management would rebill the existing inventory, thereby extending the due date from October until the following April, essentially giving an interest-free loan to the customer. The customer, in turn, agreed to keep the existing goods and store them on its site for next year's retail sales.

The key to planning analytical procedures is to identify areas of heightened risk of misstatement and then plan the audit to determine whether potential explanations satisfy all the unexpected changes that are observed in account balances. Further, it is important to be professionally skeptical of management-provided explanations. For example, does the explanation of a new computer system and the rebilling adequately explain all the changes? Whether the answer to that question is yes or no, are there other explanations that are equally viable? The auditor must be able to answer these questions to properly apply the risk-based approach to auditing. There are several factors that would indicate to a skeptical auditor that the explanations offered by ABC management might not hold:

- The company has a large increase in gross margin. This seems unlikely, because it is selling to large chains with considerable purchasing power. Further, other competitors are also likely to have effective computer systems.
- If the rebilling items are properly accounted for, there should not be a large increase in sales for the last two months of this year when the total sales for the previous year is practically the same as that of the preceding year.
- If the rebillings are for holding the inventory at customers' locations, the auditor should investigate to determine (a) if the items were properly recorded as a sale in the first place or if they should still be recorded as inventory, (b) what the client's

motivation is for extending credit to the customers indicated, and (c) whether it is a coincidence that all of the rebilled items were to large retailers who do not respond to accounts receivable confirmations received from auditors.

a. What potential hypotheses would likely explain the changes in the financial data given? Identify all that might explain the change in ratios, including those identified by management.

b. Of those identified, which hypothesis would best explain all the changes in the ratios and financial account balances? Explain the rationale for your answer.

c. Given the most likely hypothesis identified, what specific audit procedures do you recommend as highest priority? Why?

7-52 **LO 6** A staff auditor was listening to a conversation between two senior auditors regarding the audit risk model. The following are some statements made in that conversation regarding the audit risk model. State whether you agree or disagree with each of the statements, and explain why.

a. Setting audit risk at 5% is valid for controlling audit risk at a low level only if the auditor assumes that inherent risk is 100%, or significantly greater than the real level of inherent risk.

b. Inherent risk may be very small for some accounts (such as the recording of payroll transactions at Wal-Mart). In fact, some inherent risks may be close to 0.01%. In such cases, the auditor does not need to perform direct tests of account balances if he or she can be assured that inherent risk is indeed that low and that internal controls, as designed, are working appropriately.

c. Control risk refers to both (a) the design of controls and (b) the operation of controls. To assess control risk as low, the auditor must gather evidence on both the design and operation of controls.

d. Detection risk at 50% implies that the substantive tests of the account balance has a 50% chance of not detecting a material misstatement and that the auditor is relying on the client actions (assessment of inherent and control risk) to address the additional uncertainty regarding the possibility of a material misstatement.

e. Audit risk should vary inversely with both inherent risk and control risk; the higher the risk of material misstatement, the lower should be the audit risk taken.

f. In analyzing the audit risk model, it is important to understand that much of it is judgmental. For example, setting audit risk is judgmental, assessing inherent and control risk is judgmental, and setting detection risk is simply a matter of the individual risk preferences of the auditor.

7-53 **LO 6** Refer to Exhibit 7.3 and consider the audit risk model, whereby *Audit Risk = Inherent Risk × Control Risk × Detection Risk*. Complete the boxes in the table below. Describe generalizations about the relationships among the four components of the audit risk model that you gain from the completed table. In which case will the auditor conduct the greatest amount of audit work?

	Case 1	Case 2	Case 3	Case 4	Case 5	Case 6	Case 7	Case 8
Inherent Risk	30%	40%	50%	50%	70%	80%	90%	100%
Control Risk	50%	100%	60%	100%	70%	70%	80%	100%
Audit Risk	5%	5%	5%	5%	1%	1%	1%	1%
Detection Risk	?	?	?	?	?	?	?	?

7-54 **LO 7** Distinguish between a controls reliance audit and a substantive audit. Which approach should an auditor consider to be most effective?

7-55 **LO 7** What are examples of how an auditor might change (a) the nature of risk response, (b) the timing of risk response, and (c) the extent of risk response?

7-56 **LO 7** How can an auditor introduce unpredictability into audit procedures?

7-57 **LO 7** What audit procedures can be completed only at or after period end?

CONTEMPORARY AND HISTORICAL CASES

7-58 **KID CASTLE EDUCATIONAL CORPORATION AND BROCK, SCHECHTER & POLAKOFF LLP, PCAOB**
LO 3, 4, 5, 7, 8

PROFESSIONAL SKEPTICISM

INTERNATIONAL

ETHICS

General Background. On May 22, 2012, the audit firm of Brock, Schechter & Polakoff LLP (hereafter BSP) was censured and fined $20,000 by the PCAOB in relation to its audits of public companies located in Taiwan and the Chinese mainland. These public companies were listed on U.S. stock exchanges. James Waggoner, BSP's Director of Accounting and Auditing, was the BSP auditor responsible for the audits. The charges against BSP and Waggoner include the following:

- BSP failed to develop policies and procedures to assure that the firm undertook only audit engagements that it could expect to conduct with professional competence. Prior to undertaking the audits of companies from the Chinese mainland and Taiwan, the firm had no experience auditing public companies in general or companies based in these locations. Further, BSP personnel lacked the ability to communicate in Chinese.
- BSP failed to develop policies and procedures to assure that the personnel assigned to the audits had the requisite technical training and proficiency.
- BSP failed to monitor the audits during its annual internal review process.
- BSP failed to comply with PCAOB standards on the planning, performance, and supervision of the audits.
- BSP failed to gather sufficient evidence, failed to use due care, and failed to exercise professional skepticism on the audits.
- BSP allowed two other audit firms, which were located in Taiwan and the Chinese mainland, to plan and perform the audits. BSP had minimal contact with the foreign firms, and inadequately reviewed the working papers of the foreign firms. BSP also failed to obtain and review engagement completion documentation from the foreign firms prior to issuing the audit reports.
- Waggoner failed to comply with professional auditing standards. Further, he failed to cooperate with PCAOB inspectors, and he falsified documentation relating to the audits.

The Kid Castle Audits. Kid Castle is a company located in Taiwan that provides English-language instruction to Chinese-speaking children. Kid Castle was traded on the OTC Bulletin Board and Pink Sheets. A Taiwanese audit firm approached BSP in June 2006 concerning the Kid Castle audit, and BSP was hired as the auditor on July 26, 2006. BSP expressed unqualified audit opinions on the company's 2006–2008 financial statements.

In addition to the general criticisms detailed above, the PCAOB enforcement release provides detailed information on audit quality deficiencies on the Kid Castle audits, including the following:

- BSP failed to consider the nature, extent, and timing of audit work necessary to audit Kid Castle. Instead, BSP relied completely upon the Taiwan firm to make these considerations and to develop the audit program.
- BSP failed to adequately supervise the auditors of the Taiwan firm, including:
  - Failing to assess the technical competence of the Taiwan firm's auditors
  - Failing to assign the Taiwan auditors to tasks according to their abilities
  - Failing to instruct the Taiwan firm's auditors
  - Failing to inform the Taiwan firm's auditors about their responsibilities and the objectives of the audit
  - Failing to inform the Taiwan firm's auditors about matters that affected the nature, extent, and timing of audit procedures
  - Failing to direct the Taiwan firm's auditors to bring to BSP's attention significant accounting/auditing issues encountered during the audits
- BSP failed to adequately perform a review of the Taiwan firm's audit work, and such a review was the principal involvement required of BSP. In fact, Waggoner assigned the final responsibility for reviewing the audit to a BSP staff member.
- The reviewing staff member did find deficiencies in the audit procedures performed by the Taiwan auditor. Waggoner forwarded those deficiencies to the Taiwan firm's auditors, but they did not address those deficiencies or conduct additional audit work.
- For the 2007 audit, BSP did not receive or review any working papers from the Taiwan auditor, except for a set of worksheets showing consolidation work among Kid Castle's subsidiary accounts. For the 2008 audit, BSP did not receive or review *any* working papers.

Kid Castle Risk Factors and Financial Condition. In its December 31, 2008, Form 10K, Kid Castle management disclosed the following risk factors relating to its business:

- There is a history of operating losses and difficulty maintaining profitability.
- Demand for products and services is unpredictable.
- The company's operating results are dependent upon the success of its franchises.
- Market competition from established competitors could negatively affect the business.
- International expansion plans may not be successful.
- There exist risks relating to the company's potential inability to defend and protect its intellectual property.
- The company relies on loans from shareholders and bank loans, which may adversely affect liquidity.

- Because the company's officers and directors are not U.S. persons and because subsidiaries are Taiwanese or mainlander, judgments under the U.S. securities laws may not be able to be enforced.
- Internal controls are not effective in accordance with the requirements of Sarbanes-Oxley Act of 2002 (SOX).
- The company's assets and operations in the People's Republic of China are subject to political, regulatory, and economic uncertainties.

In addition, BSP issued a going-concern audit report, which indicates concern about the company's ability to remain operational. The financial statements of Kid Castle are as follows:

KID CASTLE EDUCATIONAL CORPORATION
CONSOLIDATED BALANCE SHEETS

	December 31, 2008	December 31, 2007
	(Expressed in U.S. Dollars)	
ASSETS		
Current assets		
Cash and bank balances	$1,985,818	$1,238,212
Bank fixed deposits–pledged (Note 12)	2,847	363,562
Notes and accounts receivable, net (Notes 3 and 20)	2,171,768	2,453,868
Inventories, net (Note 4)	1,933,153	2,008,739
Other receivables (Notes 5 and 20)	396,003	88,139
Prepayments and other current assets (Note 6)	475,617	542,794
Pledged notes receivable (Note 12)	416,238	557,983
Deferred income tax assets (Note 7)	45,617	42,335
Total current assets	7,427,061	7,295,632
Deferred income tax assets (Note 7)	49,528	50,481
Interest in associates (Note 8)	68,336	58,625
Property and equipment, net (Note 9)	2,775,663	2,312,065
Intangible assets, net of amortization (Note 10)	371,056	572,005
Long-term notes receivable	356,901	420,636
Pledged notes receivable (Note 12)	283,469	183,453
Other assets	255,288	268,388
Total assets	$11,587,302	$11,161,285

(continued)

	December 31, 2008	December 31, 2007
	(Expressed in U.S. Dollars)	
LIABILITIES AND SHAREHOLDERS' EQUITY		
Current liabilities		
Bank borrowings— short-term and maturing within one year (Note 12)	$ 242,879	$ 1,212,534
Notes and accounts payable (Note 19)	1,017,552	389,639
Accrued expenses (Note 11)	1,617,717	985,764
Amounts due to officers (Note 19)	—	—
Other payables	270,458	573,237
Deposits received (Note 13)	751,151	912,535
Receipts in advance (Note 14)	2,305,980	2,372,403
Income tax payable (Note 7)	$ 39,115	$ 124,418
Total current liabilities	6,244,852	6,570,530
Bank borrowings maturing after one year (Note 12)	1,583,968	1,752,776
Receipts in advance (Note 14)	1,001,801	1,034,260
Deposits received (Note 13)	839,295	680,694
Deferred liability	41,775	38,787
Accrued pension liabilities (Note 15)	446,038	401,893
Total liabilities	10,157,729	10,478,940
Commitments and contingencies (Note 16)		
Minority interest	216,754	162,343
Shareholders' equity		
Common stock, no par share (Note 17):		
60,000,000 shares authorized; 25,000,000 shares issued and outstanding at December 31, 2008 and 2007, respectively.	8,592,138	8,592,138
Additional paid-in capital	194,021	194,021
Legal reserve	65,320	65,320
Accumulated deficit (Note 18)	(6,340,449)	(7,179,418)
Accumulated other comprehensive loss	(1,026,713)	(932,027)
Net loss not recognized as pension cost	(271,498)	(220,032)
Total shareholders' equity	1,212,819	520,002
Total liabilities and shareholders' equity	$11,587,302	$11,161,285

KID CASTLE EDUCATIONAL CORPORATION
CONSOLIDATED STATEMENTS OF OPERATIONS

	Years Ended December 31		
	2008	**2007**	**2006**
	(Expressed in U.S. Dollars)		
Operating revenue (Note 21)			
Sales of goods	$ 7,905,949	$7,671,392	$6,774,260
Franchise income	2,380,930	2,205,668	2,080,551
Other operating revenue	2,558,232	1,359,552	856,772
Net operating revenue	12,845,111	11,236,612	9,711,583
Operating costs (Note 21)			
Cost of goods sold	(3,357,441)	(3,154,509)	(2,684,650)
Cost of franchising	(368,061)	(451,469)	(337,986)
Other operating costs	(1,777,862)	(491,869)	(616,102)
Total operating costs	(5,503,364)	(4,097,847)	(3,638,738)
Gross profit	7,341,747	7,138,765	6,072,845
Advertising costs	(22,735)	(29,241)	(21,833)
Other operating expenses	(6,272,753)	(5,342,216)	(5,526,318)
Profit from operations	1,046,259	1,767,308	524,694
Interest expense, net (Note 12)	(89,761)	(90,299)	(179,825)
Share of profit (loss) of investments	5,109	27,007	(39,489)
Other nonoperating income (loss), net	24,789	552,611	(153,803)
Profit before income taxes and minority interest income	986,396	2,256,627	151,577
Income taxes (expense) benefit (Note 7)	(106,215)	(278,191)	(173,325)
Income (loss) after income taxes	880,181	1,978,436	(21,748)
Minority interest income	(41,212)	(101,287)	(24,463)
Net income (loss)	$838,969	$1,877,149	$(46,211)
Income (loss) per share—basic and diluted	$ 0.034	$ 0.075	$ (0.002)

During 2010, Kid Castle stock was no longer trading in any U.S. markets. James Waggoner was censured by the PCAOB and cannot practice on any public company audits in the U.S. for at least three years.

a. Why would the inherent and control risks at Kid Castle be of concern to a potential auditor?

b. Review the financial statements and calculate the commonly used ratios from Exhibit 7.3 for the years ending 2008 and 2007. Assume that the auditor expected the 2008 financial results to be line with the 2007 financial results. Given this expectation, comment on the trends in the financial statements and ratios that would cause the auditor to assess heightened risk.

c. Based on your answers to (a) and (b), for what accounts would you recommend that the auditor plan to conduct more substantive audit procedures?

d. The 10-K discloses the fact that BSP earned total audit fees in 2007 and 2008 of $121,026 and $150,000, respectively. Comment on the motivations of BSP and Waggoner to accept the foreign audits and how those motivations might have affected Waggoner's lack of ethics and how those motivations might have affected his professional skepticism. Presumably, BSP had to pay the Taiwan and Chinese mainland audit firms a portion of the audit fee, and based on the allegations in the PCAOB enforcement release, BSP did virtually no audit work. Comment on your thoughts about the appropriateness of hiring a foreign audit firm to conduct the majority of audit work on an engagement and on BSP's actions (or lack thereof) in this regard.

e. Use the framework for making quality professional decisions from Chapter 4 to identify those steps in the framework where Waggoner went wrong and describe what he should have done differently.

f. Describe the risks that an audit firm faces when it attempts to audit a company in a foreign country.

For additional information on the PCAOB enforcement releases relating to this case, see PCAOB Release Nos. 105-2012-002 and 105-2012-003.

FRAUD **7-59** LINCOLN FEDERAL SAVINGS AND LOAN
LO **3, 4, 7** The following is a description of various factors that affected the operations of Lincoln Federal Savings and Loan, a California savings and loan (S&L). It was a subsidiary of American Continental Company, a real estate development company run by Charles Keating.

Lincoln Federal Savings & Loan

Savings and Loan industry background—The S&L industry was developed in the early part of the twentieth century in response to a perceived need to provide low-cost financing to encourage home ownership. As such, legislation by Congress made the S&L industry the primary financial group allowed to make low-cost home ownership loans (mortgages).

For many years, the industry operated by accepting relatively long-term deposits from customers and making 25- to 30-year loans at fixed rates on home mortgages. The industry was generally considered to be safe. Most of the S&Ls (also known as thrifts) were small, federally chartered institutions with deposits insured by the FSLIC. The motto of many S&L managers seemed to be, "Get your deposits in, make loans, sit back, and earn your returns. Get to work by 9 a.m. and out to the golf course by noon."

Changing economic environment—During the 1970s, two major economic events hit the S&L industry. First, the rate of inflation had reached an all-time high. Prime interest rates had gone as high as

19.5%. Second, deposits were being drawn away from the S&Ls by new competitors that offered short-term variable rates substantially higher than current passbook savings rates. The S&Ls responded by increasing the rates on certificates of deposit to extraordinary levels (15–16%) while servicing mortgages with 20- to 30-year maturities made at old rates of 7-8%. The S&Ls attempted to mitigate the problem by offering variable-rate mortgages or by selling off some of their mortgages (at substantial losses) to other firms.

However, following regulatory accounting principles, the S&Ls were not required to recognize market values of loans that were not sold. Thus, even if loan values were substantially less than the book value, they would continue to be carried at book value as long as the mortgage holder was not in default.

Changing regulatory environment—In the early 1980s, Congress moved to deregulate the S&L industry. During the first half of 1982, the S&L industry lost a record $3.3 billion (even without marking loans down to real value). In August 1982, President Reagan signed the Garn-St. Germain Depository Institutions Act of 1982, hailing it as the most important legislation for financial institutions in 50 years. The bill had several key elements:

- S&Ls would be allowed to offer money market funds free from withdrawal penalties or interest rate regulation.
- S&Ls could invest up to 40% of their assets in nonresidential real estate lending. Commercial lending was much riskier than home lending, but the potential returns were greater. In addition, the regulators helped the deregulatory fever by removing a regulation that had required a savings and loan institution to have 400 stockholders with no one owning more than 25%—allowing a single shareholder to own a savings and loan institution.
- The bill made it easier for an entrepreneur to purchase a savings and loan. Regulators allowed buyers to start (capitalize) their thrift with land or other noncash assets rather than money.
- The bill allowed thrifts to stop requiring traditional down payments and to provide 100% financing, with the borrower not required to invest a dime of personal money in the deal.
- The bill permitted thrifts to make real estate loans anywhere. They had previously been required to make loans on property located only in their own geographic area.

Accounting—In addition to these revolutionary changes, owners of troubled thrifts began stretching already liberal accounting rule (with regulators' blessings) to squeeze their balance sheets into (regulatory) compliance. For example, goodwill, defined as customer loyalty, market share, and other intangibles, accounted for over 40% of the thrift industry's net worth by 1986.

Lincoln Federal S&L—American Continental Corporation, a land development company run by Charles Keating and headquartered in Phoenix, purchased Lincoln Federal S&L in 1984. Immediately, Keating expanded the lending activity of Lincoln to assist in the development of American Continental projects, including the Phoenician Resort in Scottsdale.[1] Additionally, Keating sought higher returns by purchasing junk bonds marketed by Drexel Burnham and Michael Millken. Nine of Keating's relatives were on the Lincoln payroll at salaries ranging from over $500,000 to over $1 million.

Keating came up with novel ideas to raise capital. Rather than raising funds through deposits, he had commissioned agents working in the Lincoln offices who sold special bonds of American Continental Corporation. The investors were assured that their investments would be safe. Unfortunately, many elderly individuals put their life savings into these bonds, thinking they were backed by the FSLIC because they were sold at an S&L—but they were not. Keating continued investments in real estate deals, such as a planned megacommunity in the desert outside of Phoenix. He relied on appraisals, some obviously of dubious value, to serve as a basis for the loan valuation.

a. Discuss the risks identified and the implication of those risks for the conduct of the audit.

b. The auditor did review a few independent appraisals indicating the market value of the real estate in folders for loans. How convincing are such appraisals? In other words, what attributes are necessary in order for the appraisals to constitute appropriate (relevant and reliable) evidence?

Auditing the Revenue Cycle

CHAPTER OVERVIEW AND LEARNING OBJECTIVES

Accounts in the revenue cycle should be presumed to be high risk for most audits because these accounts are highly susceptible to misstatement. Auditors must carefully consider management's motivation to stretch accounting principles to achieve desired revenue reporting. Auditors need to understand the relationships present in the accounts and how to best approach the audit. In terms of the audit opinion formulation process, this chapter primarily involves Phases II, III, and IV—performing risk assessment procedures, tests of controls, and substantive procedures for the revenue cycle.

Through studying this chapter, you will be able to achieve these learning objectives:

通过本章的学习，你将能够实现以下学习目标：

1. Identify the significant accounts, disclosures, and relevant assertions in the revenue cycle.

   识别收入循环中重要的账户、披露和相关的认定。

2. Identify and assess inherent risks of material misstatement in the revenue cycle.

   识别和评估收入循环中重大错报的固有风险。

3. Identify and assess fraud risks of material misstatement in the revenue cycle.

   识别和评估收入循环中重大错报的舞弊风险。

4. Identify and assess control risks of material misstatement in the revenue cycle.

   识别和评估收入循环中重大错报的控制风险。

5. Describe how to use preliminary analytical procedures to identify possible material misstatements for revenue cycle accounts, disclosures, and assertions.

   描述如何运用初步的分析性程序识别与收入循环账户、披露和认定有关的可能的重大错报。

6. Determine appropriate responses to identified risks of material misstatement for revenue cycle accounts, disclosures, and assertions.

   明确对于识别的与收入循环账户、披露和认定有关的重大错报风险如何进行适当的反应。

7. Determine appropriate tests of controls and consider the results of tests of controls for revenue cycle accounts, disclosures, and assertions.

   确定适当的控制测试，并且考虑与收入循环账户、披露和认定有关的控制测试结果。

8. Determine and apply sufficient appropriate substantive audit procedures for testing revenue cycle accounts, disclosures, and assertions.

   确定和应用充分、适当的实质性审计程序以测试收入循环账户、披露和认定。

9. Apply the frameworks for professional decision making and ethical decision making to issues involving the audit of revenue cycle accounts, disclosures, and assertions.

   运用职业决策和职业道德决策框架解决与收入循环账户、披露和认定审计有关的问题。

THE AUDIT OPINION FORMULATION PROCESS

| I. Making Client Acceptance and Continuance Decisions
Chapter 14 | II. Performing Risk Assessment
Chapters 3, 7 and 9–13 | III. Obtaining Evidence about Internal Control Operating Effectiveness
Chapters 8–13 and 16 | IV. Obtaining Substantive Evidence about Accounts, Disclosures and Assertions
Chapters 8–13 and 16 | V. Completing the Audit and Making Reporting Decisions
Chapters 14 and 15 |

| The Auditing Profession, the Risk of Fraud and Mechanisms to Address Fraud: Regulation, Corporate Governance, and Audit Quality
Chapters 1 and 2 | Professional Liability and the Need for Quality Auditor Judgments and Ethical Decisions
Chapter 4 |

The Audit Opinion Formulation Process and A Framework for Obtaining Audit Evidence
Chapters 5 and 6

PROFESSIONAL JUDGMENT IN CONTEXT

How to Account for Virtual Sales at Zynga

Have you ever purchased a piece of virtual farm equipment while playing Zynga's popular game FarmVille? Maybe you have purchased a tractor that allows you to plow multiple plots of land at one time. You might have used FarmVille currency to make these purchases. Alternatively, you could have converted real dollars from a credit card or PayPal account into the FarmVille currency and then used that currency to buy a virtual tractor or other piece of equipment. For example, you could purchase a hot rod tractor for 55 in Farm Cash, which translates into $10 in real U.S. money. Sales of virtual goods, including goods from FarmVille and other games, accounted for nearly all of Zynga's $1.1 billion in 2011 revenues—and 12% of revenue for Zynga's distributor, Facebook.

How do the involved companies account for these sales? Consider, for example, that you buy and hold Facebook credits (used to buy virtual goods in games on Facebook). Facebook treats the purchase of these credits as deferred revenue. This approach works in the same way as a retailer would record the sale of a gift card. Now assume that you buy a FarmVille's hot rod tractor. To make this purchase, you could use your Facebook credits or charge $10 (which buys 100 Facebook credits that are

converted to 55 in Farm Cash). Facebook sends $7 to Zynga and keeps $3—30%—as a processing fee. At this point Facebook moves that $3 from deferred revenue into current revenue. Now the relevant question is: when does Zynga get to recognize its $7 in revenues? In general, revenue should not be recognized until it is realized or is realizable and earned. So even if a company has cash in hand, it cannot be counted as current revenue until the company has delivered the product or service it is being paid for. However, neither the Financial Accounting Standards Board (FASB) nor the Securities and Exchange Commission (SEC) has issued rules for sales of virtual harvesters or any other virtual products. Perhaps somewhat surprisingly, Zynga's audit firm, Ernst & Young (E&Y), has published a document that provides revenue recognition guidance in this area.

E&Y's guidance outlines three different revenue approaches: game-based, in which revenue is recognized very slowly, over the life of the game; user-based, a faster approach that lasts over the time a typical user sticks with the game; and speedy item-based, based on the properties of the individual virtual goods. Using the last method, Zynga recognizes revenues from consumable virtual items, like energy, immediately and revenues from durable ones, like tractors, over the time a player is projected to stick with a game. In many ways, these suggestions seem reasonable. The difficult part is that all of the methods are dependent on management estimates of the life of a game, a customer, or a virtual item. And, the estimates can make a big difference in Zynga's net income. For example, by estimating a shorter player life (from 19 months to 15 months), Zynga increased revenue for a six-month period ended June 30, 2011, by $27.3 million. This change came just before Zynga went public in mid-December at $10 a share.

From a bottom-line perspective, this change in player life allowed Zynga to change a net loss for the six-month period into net profit of $18.1 million.

As you read through this chapter, consider the following questions:

- What are the inherent risks associated with revenue transactions? (LO 2)
- What are management's incentives to misstate revenue transactions? (LO 3)
- What controls should management have in place to mitigate the risks associated with revenue transactions? (LO 4)
- How might auditors use preliminary analytical procedures to identify any potential concerns related to revenue? (LO 5)
- What is sufficient appropriate evidence when auditing revenue transactions and related accounts? (LO 6, 7, 8)

重要账户、披露和相关认定

LO 1 Identify the significant accounts, disclosures, and relevant assertions in the revenue cycle.

收入循环(revenue cycle)
所涉及的业务活动主要包括订单处理、核准赊销、发货、开具发票、会计记录、收款、坏账处理与销售调整。

Significant Accounts, Disclosures, and Relevant Assertions

The **revenue cycle** involves the process of receiving a customer's order, approving credit for a sale, determining whether the goods are available for shipment, shipping the goods, billing the customer, collecting cash, and recognizing the effect of this process on other related accounts such as accounts receivable, inventory, and sales commission expense. In the revenue cycle, the most significant accounts include revenue and accounts receivable. The auditor will likely obtain evidence related to each of the financial statement assertions discussed in Chapter 5 for both accounts. However, for specific accounts and specific clients, some assertions are more relevant than other assertions. For many clients, the existence assertion related to revenue may be one of the more relevant assertions, especially if the client has incentives to overstate revenues. For accounts receivable, the more relevant assertions are usually existence and valuation. The assertions that are determined to be more relevant are those for which the risk of material misstatement is higher and for which more and higher-quality audit evidence is needed.

The cycle approach recognizes the interrelationship of accounts. Audit evidence addressing the existence and valuation of accounts receivable also provides evidence on the existence and valuation of recorded revenue, and vice versa. When examining sales transactions and internal controls over revenue processing, the auditor also gathers evidence on credit authorization and valuation of the recorded transactions. Sales transactions often serve as a basis for computing commissions for sales staff. Sales information is used for strategic long-term decision-making and marketing analysis. Therefore, the accuracy of recording transactions in the revenue cycle is important for management decisions, as well as for the preparation of financial statements. The accounts typically affected by sales transactions are shown in Exhibit 9.1.

梳理收入交易

Processing Revenue Transactions

The revenue process may differ with each client, and each client may have more than one revenue process. For example, a sales transaction for a shirt in a department store differs from a sale of construction equipment, and both of these differ from a book sale on an Internet site. The Internet sale and the retail sale most likely require cash or credit card for payment. The construction equipment sale most likely involves an account receivable, or a loan may be arranged with a third party. Some sales transactions involve long-term contractual arrangements that affect when and how revenue will

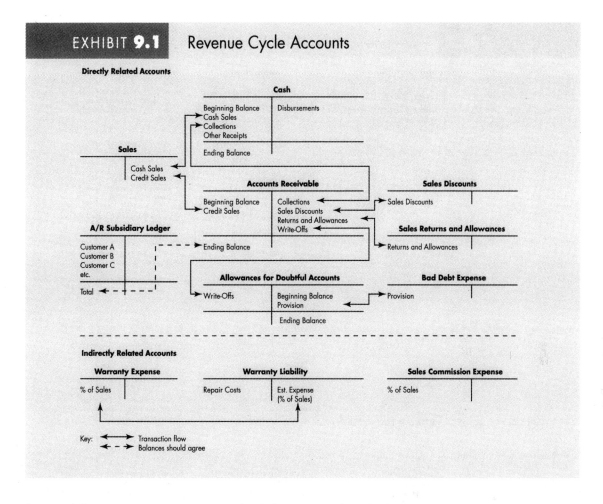

EXHIBIT **9.1** Revenue Cycle Accounts

be recorded. Some organizations generate detailed paper trails for sales documentation; others maintain an audit trail only in computerized form. Notwithstanding these differences, most sales transactions include the procedures and related documents shown in Exhibit 9.2, and discussed next.

1. Receive a Customer Purchase Order Processing begins with the receipt of a purchase order from a customer or the preparation of a sales order by a salesperson. The order might be taken by (1) a clerk at a checkout counter, (2) a salesperson making a call on a client, (3) a customer service agent of a catalog sales company answering a toll-free call, (4) a computer receiving purchase order information electronically from the customer's computer, or (5) the sales department directly receiving the purchase order. For example, consider a customer service agent for a catalog merchandiser taking an order over the phone. The information is keyed into a computer file, and each transaction is uniquely identified. The computer file (often referred to as a log of transactions) contains all the information for sales orders taken over a period of time and can be used for control and reconciliation purposes.

2. Check Inventory Stock Status Many organizations have computer systems capable of informing a customer of current inventory status and likely delivery date. The customer is informed of potential back-ordered items, as well as an expected delivery date.

EXHIBIT **9.2**   Overview of the Sales Process

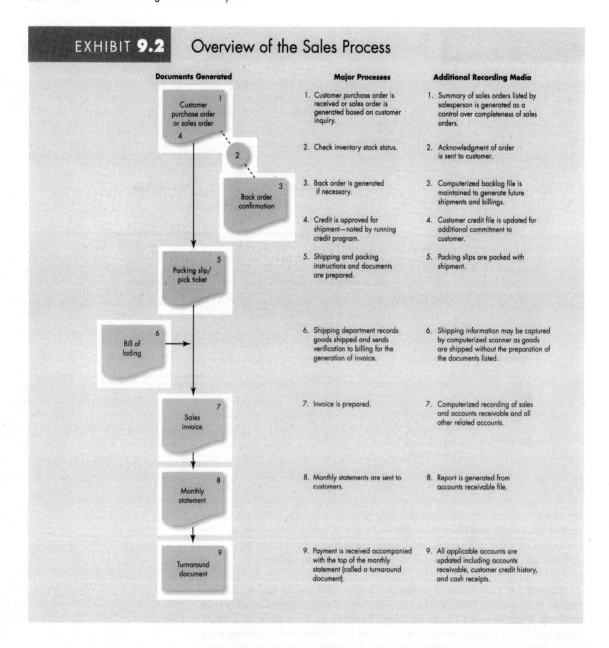

Documents Generated	Major Processes	Additional Recording Media
1, 4 Customer purchase order or sales order	1. Customer purchase order is received or sales order is generated based on customer inquiry.	1. Summary of sales orders listed by salesperson is generated as a control over completeness of sales orders.
2	2. Check inventory stock status.	2. Acknowledgment of order is sent to customer.
3 Back order confirmation	3. Back order is generated if necessary.	3. Computerized backlog file is maintained to generate future shipments and billings.
	4. Credit is approved for shipment—noted by running credit program.	4. Customer credit file is updated for additional commitment to customer.
5 Packing slip/ pick ticket	5. Shipping and packing instructions and documents are prepared.	5. Packing slips are packed with shipment.
6 Bill of lading	6. Shipping department records goods shipped and sends verification to billing for the generation of invoice.	6. Shipping information may be captured by computerized scanner as goods are shipped without the preparation of the documents listed.
7 Sales invoice	7. Invoice is prepared.	7. Computerized recording of sales and accounts receivable and all other related accounts.
8 Monthly statement	8. Monthly statements are sent to customers.	8. Report is generated from accounts receivable file.
9 Turnaround document	9. Payment is received accompanied with the top of the monthly statement (called a turnaround document).	9. All applicable accounts are updated including accounts receivable, customer credit history, and cash receipts.

3. Generate Back Order   If an item is to be back-ordered for later shipment to the customer, a confirmation of the back order is prepared and sent to the customer. If the back order is not filled within a specified time, the customer is often given the option of canceling the order. An accurate list of back-ordered items must be maintained to meet current customer demand and future inventory needs. Appending a separate field to the individual inventory records to show back-ordered items usually accomplishes this.

4. Obtain Credit Approval   Formal credit approval policies are implemented by organizations to minimize credit losses. Some organizations eliminate credit risk by requiring payment through a credit card. Others require that a check accompany the order, and generally they delay the shipment until the check clears through the banking system to assure that the payment is collectible.

Many industrial organizations issue credit to their customers because it is a more convenient way to transact business. However, the organization making the sale does accept some risk that it ultimately will not receive payment from the customer. Many reasons can be found for nonpayment, ranging from (a) dissatisfaction with, or return of, the goods received to (b) inability to make payments because of financial constraints. Therefore, organizations need to have a credit approval process that (a) evaluates the creditworthiness of new customers and (b) updates the creditworthiness (including timelines of payments) of existing customers. The credit approval might include a review of sales orders and customer credit information by a computer program that contains current account balance information and credit scoring information to determine whether credit should be extended to the customer. Most organizations set credit limits for customers and develop controls to assure that a pending sale will not push the customer over the credit limit.

5. Prepare Shipping and Packing Documents Many organizations have computerized the distribution process for shipping items from a warehouse. Picking tickets (documents that tell the warehouse personnel the most efficient sequence in which to pick items for shipment and the location of all items to be shipped) are generated from the sales order or from the customer's purchase order. Separate packing slips are prepared to insert with the shipment and to verify that all items have been shipped. Some organizations put a bar code on the shipping container that identifies the contents. The bar code can be scanned by the customer to record receipt of the order.

6. Ship and Verify Shipment of Goods Most goods are shipped to customers via common carriers such as independent trucking lines, railroads, or airfreight companies. The shipper prepares a bill of lading that describes the packages to be conveyed by the common carrier to the customer, the shipping terms, and the delivery address. The **bill of lading** is a formal legal document that conveys responsibility to the shipper. A representative of the common carrier signs the bill of lading, acknowledging receipt of the goods. The shipping department confirms the shipment by (1) completing the packing slip and returning it to the billing department, (2) electronically recording everything shipped and transmitting the shipping information to the billing department, or (3) preparing independent shipping documents, a copy of which is sent to the billing department.

7. Prepare and Send the Invoice Invoices are normally prepared when notice is received that goods were shipped. The invoice should include items such as the terms of sale, payment terms, and prices for merchandise shipped. The invoice will serve as an important document in terms of audit evidence.

8. Send Monthly Statements to Customers Many organizations prepare monthly statements of open items and mail these statements to customers. The monthly statement provides a detailed list of the customer's activity for the previous month and a statement of all open items.

9. Receive Payments The proper recording of all revenue receipts is crucial to the ultimate valuation of both cash and accounts receivable. This part of the revenue process is typically considered to be part of the cash transaction cycle, and is discussed in detail in Chapter 10.

在收入循环中实施风险评估程序

识别固有风险

在收入交易中，一个重要的固有风险是收入确认的时间。特别是当客户的产品和销售方式比较特殊时，固有风险更高。

Performing Risk Assessment Procedures in the Revenue Cycle

As part of performing risk assessment procedures, the auditor obtains information that is useful in assessing the risk of material misstatement. This includes information about inherent risks at the financial statement level (for example, client's business and operational risks, financial reporting risks) and at the account and assertion levels, fraud risks including feedback from audit team's brainstorming sessions, strengths and weaknesses in internal control, and results from preliminary analytical procedures. Once the risks of material misstatement have been identified, the auditor then determines how best to respond to them as part of the audit opinion formulation process.

Identifying Inherent Risks
Revenues: Identifying Inherent Risks

An important inherent risk related to revenue transactions is the timing of revenue recognition. Revenue may only be recognized when it is realized or is realizable and earned. Though these concepts seem simple, they are often difficult to apply in practice. Further, complex sales transactions often make it difficult to determine when a sale has actually taken place. For example, a transaction might be structured so that title passes only when some contingent situations are met, or the customer may have an extended period to return the goods. To audit the revenue cycle, the auditor must understand the following:

- The organization's principal business, that is, what is the organization in the business of selling?
- The earnings process and the nature of the obligations that extend beyond the normal shipment of goods. For example, after goods are shipped, does the seller have any ongoing service requirements to the purchaser?
- The impact of unusual terms, and when title has passed to the customer.
- The right of the customer to return a product, as well as the returns history.
- Contracts that are combinations of leases and sales.
- The proper treatment of sales transactions made with recourse or that have an abnormal or unpredictable amount of returns.

Exhibit 9.3 reports examples of sales transactions that have high inherent risk and have caused problems for auditors.

Criteria for Revenue Recognition When to recognize revenue and how much to recognize are often difficult decisions. Auditors should refer to authoritative guidance, such as that provided by the International Accounting Standards Board (IASB), SEC, Financial Accounting Standards Board (FASB), and American Institute of Certified Public Accountants (AICPA), to determine the appropriateness of their clients' methods of recognizing revenue. The basic concept for revenue recognition is that revenue should not be recognized until it is realized or is realizable and earned. The SEC staff has determined that the following criteria must be met in applying this concept:

- Persuasive evidence of an arrangement exists.
- Delivery has occurred, or services have been rendered.
- The seller's price to the buyer is fixed or determinable.
- Collectibility is reasonably assured.

These criteria are not as straightforward as they might seem. For example, the criterion of delivery seems simple enough. Consider, however, a situation in which the seller has delivered a product to a customer. The customer has the right to return the product, and the buyer's obligation to

| EXHIBIT **9.3** | Examples of Complex Sales Transactions |

DELIVERY

Company A receives purchase orders for products it manufactures. At the end of its fiscal quarters, customers may not yet be ready to take delivery of the products for various reasons. These reasons may include, but are not limited to, a lack of available space for inventory, having more than sufficient inventory in their distribution channel, or delays in customers' production schedules.

Question

May Company A recognize revenue for the sale of its products once it has completed manufacturing if it segregates the inventory of the products in its own warehouse from its own products? What if it ships the products to a third-party warehouse but (1) Company A retains title to the product and (2) payment by the customer is dependent upon ultimate delivery to a customer-specified site?

Answer

Generally, no. The SEC staff believes that delivery generally is not considered to have occurred unless the customer has taken title and assumed the risks and rewards of ownership. Typically this occurs when a product is delivered to the customer's delivery site (if the terms of the sale are FOB destination) or when a product is shipped to the customer (if the terms are FOB shipping point).

INTERNET SALES

Company B operates an Internet site from which it sells Company C's products. Customers place their orders for a product by selecting the product directly from the Internet site and providing a credit card number for the payment. Company B receives the order and authorization from the credit card company, and passes the order on to Company C. Company C ships the product directly to the customer. Company B does not take title to the product and has no risk of loss or other responsibility for the product. Company C is responsible for all product returns, defects, and disputed credit card charges. The product is typically sold for $200, of which Company B receives $30. If a credit card transaction is rejected, Company B loses its margin on the sale (i.e., the $30).

Question

Should Company B recognize revenue of $200 or $30?

Answer

The SEC's position is that Company B should recognize only $30. "In assessing whether revenue should be reported gross with separate display of cost of sales to arrive at gross profit or on a net basis, the staff considers whether the registrant:

1. Acts as principal in the transaction,
2. Takes title to the products,
3. Has risks and rewards of ownership, and
4. Acts as an agent or broker (including performing services, in substance, as an agent or broker) with compensation on a commission or fee basis."

Source: *SEC Staff Accounting Bulletin: No. 101–Revenue Recognition in Financial Statements*, December 3, 1999.

pay is contractually excused until the buyer resells the product. In this case, revenue should not be recognized until the buyer has the obligation to pay, that is, when the product is resold.

The SEC generally does not consider delivery to have occurred until the customer takes title and assumes the risks and rewards of ownership. Auditors may need to conduct research to determine when a client should recognize revenue and how to audit revenue. Some revenue recognition areas require special consideration. The following is a sample of some issues that have emerged in recent years:

• How much should be recognized as revenue when a company sells another company's product but does not take title until it is sold? For example, should Priceline.com (an Internet travel site) record the full sales price of airline tickets it sells or the net amount it earns on the sale (the sales commission)?

- Should shipment of magazines by a magazine distributor to retail stores result in revenue when delivered or await the sale to the ultimate consumers? What if the arrangement with convenience stores, such as 7-11, is that all magazines not sold can be returned to the distributor when the racks are filled with the next month's magazines?
- Should revenue be recognized in barter advertising in which two Web sites exchange advertising space?
- At what point in time should revenue be recognized when:
  - The right of return exists.
  - The product is being held awaiting the customer's instructions to ship (bill and hold).
  - A bundled product is sold. For example, assume that a software company sells software bundled with installation and service for a total of $5,000. Should the total revenue be $5,000, or should the service element be separately estimated and recognized along with an attendant liability to perform the service work? What if the software entitles the user to free updates for a period of three years?

The auditor is expected to know enough about the client's transactions to be able to exercise informed judgment in determining both the timing and extent of revenue recognition. Although the judgments may appear to be subjective, the SEC and other authoritative bodies have set forth objective criteria they expect both auditors and managers to use in determining revenue recognition. The *Auditing in Practice* feature "Channel Stuffing at ArthroCare—The Importance of Professional Skepticism" highlights the importance of professional skepticism when auditing revenue transactions.

Channel Stuffing at ArthroCare—The Importance of Professional Skepticism

AUDITING IN PRACTICE

Auditors need to be professionally skeptical and make judgments on whether and when sales should be recognized as revenue. The ArthroCare case highlights the material misstatements that can occur if a client chooses to improperly record revenue and the auditor fails to detect the misstatement.

ArthroCare is an Austin, Texas, based manufacturer of medical devices whose shares are traded on NASDAQ. From 2006 through the first quarter of 2008, two company sales executives, John Raffle and David Applegate, were alleged to have engaged in a channel stuffing scheme that improperly inflated company revenue and earnings. Specifically, the two salesmen shipped certain products to distributors even though the distributers often did not need them, or have the ability to pay for them. CEO Michael Baker and CFO Michael Gluck were also implicated

in the scheme. As a result, for 2006, 2007, and the first quarter of 2008, revenues were overstated by, respectively, 7.9%, 14.1% and 17.4%, totaling almost $72.3 million. For the same period, net income was overstated by 14.5% in 2006, 8,694% for 2007 and 315% for the first quarter of 2008, totaling about $53.7 million. The company eventually restated its financial statements.

In July 2010, a judge ultimately dismissed the charges against Raffle and Applegate, along with a lawsuit against the audit firm of Pricewaterhouse-Coopers (PwC). The charges against Baker and Gluck were maintained.

For further information on the progression of this case, refer to ArthroCare Corp. Securities Litigation, case number 1:08-cv-00574 in the U.S. District Court for the Western District of Texas.

Accounts Receivable: Identifying Inherent Risks

The primary inherent risk associated with receivables is that the net amount is not collectible, either because the receivables recorded do not represent genuine claims or an insufficient allowance exists for uncollectible accounts. If a valid sales transaction does not exist, a valid receivable does not exist. Alternatively, if the company has been shipping poor-quality goods, there is a high risk of return. Finally, some companies, in an attempt to increase sales, may have chosen to sell to new customers who have questionable credit-paying ability. The most relevant financial statement assertions for receivables are usually existence and valuation. Other important risks may be related to ownership due to the company selling or pledging receivables. For example, a company may desperately need cash and decide to sell the receivables to a bank, but the bank may have a right to seek assets from the company if the receivables are not collected.

Some of the inherent risks affecting receivables include the following:

- Receivables are pledged as collateral against specific loans with restricted use (disclosures of such restrictions are required).
- Receivables are incorrectly classified as current when the likelihood of collection during the next year is low.
- Collection of a receivable is contingent on specific events that cannot currently be estimated.
- Payment is not required until the purchaser sells the product to its end customers.
- Accounts receivable are aged incorrectly, and potentially uncollectible amounts are not recognized.
- Orders are accepted from customers with poor credit, but the allowance for doubtful accounts is not increased accordingly.

Performing Brainstorming Activities and Identifying Fraud Risk Factors

Auditing standards state that auditors should ordinarily presume there is a risk of material misstatement caused by fraud relating to revenue recognition. A recent research study sponsored by the Committee of Sponsoring Organizations (COSO), "Fraudulent Financial Reporting: 1998–2007—An Analysis of U.S. Public Companies," reviewed over 300 cases of fraudulent financial statements issued between 1988 and 2007 and documented that over 60% of the frauds involved inappropriate recording of revenue.

LO 3 Identify and assess fraud risks of material misstatement in the revenue cycle.

Fraud Schemes Fraud investigations undertaken by the SEC and Public Company Accounting Oversight Board (PCAOB) have uncovered a wide variety of methods used to misstate accounts in the revenue cycle, including:

- Recognition of revenue on shipments that never occurred
- Hidden side letters, agreements containing contract terms that are not part of the formal contract, giving customers an irrevocable right to return the product
- Recording consignment sales as final sales
- Early recognition of sales that occurred after the end of the fiscal period
- Shipment of unfinished product
- Shipment of product before customers wanted or agreed to delivery
- Creation of fictitious invoices
- Shipment of more product than the customer ordered
- Recording shipments to the company's own warehouse as sales
- Shipping goods that had been returned and recording the reshipment as a sale of new goods before issuing credit for the returned sale
- Incorrect aging of accounts receivable and not recording write-downs of potentially uncollectible amounts
- Recording purchase orders as completed sales

审计准则要求注册会计师应当假定收入确认存在由于舞弊导致的重大错报风险。假定收入确认存在由于舞弊导致的重大错报风险，并不意味着审计准则要求注册会计师无端地将与收入确认相关的所有认定都假定为存在舞弊风险。注册会计师需要结合对被审计单位及其环境的具体了解，考虑收入确认舞弊可能如何发生。

Exhibit 9.4 provides examples of the wide range of methods that have been used to inflate revenue. As discussed in Chapter 7, during the brainstorming session, the audit team should consider whether these schemes could be occurring at the audit client.

EXHIBIT **9.4**	Examples of Revenue Recognition and Accounts Receivable Schemes

Coca-Cola was charged with coercing its largest distributors to accept delivery of more syrup than they needed at the end of each quarter, thus inflating sales by about $10 million a year.

WorldCom's CEO, Bernard Ebbers, pressured the COO to find and record one-time revenue items that were fictitious and were hidden from the auditors by altering key documents and denying auditor access to the appropriate database.

HealthSouth understated its allowance for doubtful accounts when it was clear certain receivables would not be collected.

Gateway recorded revenue for each free subscription to AOL services that was given with each computer sale, thus overstating pretax income by over $450 million.

Royal Ahold (a Dutch company that was the world's second-biggest operator of grocery stores) booked higher promotional allowances, provided by suppliers to promote their goods, than they received in payment.

Kmart improperly included as revenue a $42.3 million payment from American Greetings Corp. that was subject to repayment under certain circumstances and therefore should not have been fully recognized booked by Kmart in that quarter.

Xerox improperly accelerated $6 billion of revenue from long-term leases of office equipment.

Qwest immediately recognized long-term contract revenue rather than over the 18-month to 2-year period of the contract, inflating revenue by $144 million.

Bristol-Myers inflated revenue by as much as $1 billion, using sales incentives to wholesalers who then packed their warehouses with extra inventory.

Lucent Technologies improperly booked $679 million in revenue. The bulk of this revenue, $452 million, reflected products sent to its distribution partners that were never actually sold to end customers.

Charter Communications, a cable company, added $17 million to revenue and cash flow in one year through a phony ad sales deal with an unnamed set-top decoder maker. They persuaded the set-top maker to add $20 onto the invoice price of each box. Charter held the cash and recorded it as an ad sale. Net income was not affected, but revenue was increased.

Nortel Networks, a telecommunications equipment company, fraudulently manipulated reserve accounts across two years to initially *decrease* profitability (so as to *not* return to profitability faster than analyst expectations) and to then increase profitability (so as to meet analyst expectations about the timing of a return to profitability and also to enable key executives to receive early return to profitability bonuses worth tens of millions of dollars). Nortel's board fired key executives, and the company restated its financial statements four times in four years, and remediated a key internal control material weakness associated with the fraud.

Diebold, Inc., an Ohio-based maker of ATMs, bank security systems, and electronic voting machines, agreed to pay $25 million to settle SEC charges related to accounting fraud. The alleged schemes included fraudulent use of bill-and-hold accounting and improper recognition of lease-agreement revenue. When company reports showed that the company was about to miss its analysts' earnings estimate, Diebold finance executives allegedly used these schemes to meet the earnings estimate.

General Electric (GE) paid $50 million to settle accounting fraud charges with the SEC for revenue recognition schemes. GE improperly booked revenues of $223 million and $158 million for six locomotives reportedly sold to

EXHIBIT **9.4**	Examples of Revenue Recognition and Accounts Receivable Schemes (*continued*)

financial institutions, "with the understanding that the financial institutions would resell the locomotives to GE's railroad customers in the first quarters of the subsequent fiscal years." The problem is that the six transactions were not true sales, and therefore did not qualify for revenue recognition under U.S. Generally Accepted Accounting Principles (GAAP). Most important, GE did not give up ownership of the trains to the financial institutions.

Motorola booked $275 million of earnings by keeping its third quarter books open after the quarter ended so that it could record the revenue, which represented 28% of the net income Motorola reported for that quarter.

Sources: *Atlanta Business Chronicle*, June 2, 2003; *The Wall Street Journal Online*, June 9, 2003; *Accountingweb.com*, July 14, 2003; *Accountingweb.com*, May 19, 2003; *The Wall Street Journal Online*, February 25, 2003; *The Wall Street Journal Online*, February 26, 2003; *The Wall Street Journal Online*, June 28, 2002; *St. Cloud Times*, p. 6A, February 26, 2003; *The Wall Street Journal Online*, July 11, 2002; *The Wall Street Journal Online*, February 9, 2001; *USA Today*, July 25, 2003; SEC Release 2007-217, September 12, 2007; cfo.com, Ex-Diebold CFOs Charged with Fraud, June 2, 2010; cfo.com, GE Settles Accounting Fraud Charges, August 4, 2009; *Bloomberg*, Dirty Secrets Fester in 50-Year Relationships, June 9, 2011.

Another scheme in this cycle involves **lapping**, which is a technique used to cover up the embezzlement of cash. This technique causes individual customer accounts receivable balances to be misstated. Lapping is most likely to occur when duties are inadequately segregated—an employee has access to cash or incoming checks *and* to the accounting records. To accomplish lapping, the employee first steals a payment from a customer. However, the employee does not give that customer credit for the payment. If no other action is taken, that customer will detect the absence of the credit for payment on the next monthly statement. To prevent detection, the employee then covers the fraud by posting another customer's payment to the first customer. Then the second customer's account is missing credit, which is covered up later when a subsequent collection from a third customer is posted to the second customer's account (hence the term lapping). At no time will any customer's account be very far behind in the posting of the credit. Of course, there will always be at least one customer whose balance is overstated, unless the employee repays the stolen cash. Lapping can occur even if all incoming receipts are in the form of checks. The employee can either restrictively endorse a check to another company or go to another bank and establish an account with a similar name. If the lapping scheme is sophisticated, very few accounts will be misstated at any one time.

Identifying Fraud Risk Factors There are many motivations to overstate revenue. For example, bankruptcy may be imminent because of operating losses, technology changes in the industry causing the company's products to become obsolete, or a general decline in the industry. Management bonuses or stock options may be dependent on reaching a certain earnings goal. Or, a merger may be pending, and management may want to negotiate the highest price possible. In other cases, management might make optimistic public announcements of the company's revenues, net income, and earnings per share before the auditor's work is completed. These earnings expectations put enormous pressure on management not to disappoint the market. The *Auditing in Practice* feature "The Importance of Professional Skepticism in Auditing Revenue at Tvia" provides an example of a case in which client personnel had significant financial motives to fraudulently overstate revenue.

The Importance of Professional Skepticism in Auditing Revenue at TVIA

AUDITING IN PRACTICE

In 2009, the SEC initiated enforcement actions involving executives at a Silicon Valley company named Tvia. The SEC alleges that Tvia's former vice president of worldwide sales, Benjamin Silva III, made side deals with customers and concealed this information from Tvia's executives and auditors. These side deals resulted in the company fraudulently reporting millions of dollars in revenue from 2005 to 2007. Importantly, SEC documents note that when Silva joined Tvia in September 2004, he received options on 250,000 shares of Tvia stock, with one quarter of the options vesting after one year and the remainder vesting monthly thereafter for the next three years. In May 2005, Silva received additional options grants. Silva received a 50,000-share options grant, again with one quarter of the options vesting after one year and the remainder vesting monthly thereafter for the next three years. Silva also received a 70,000-share performance-based options grant, which vested only if the company achieved $5 million in revenue in a fiscal quarter by June 30, 2006.

Auditors need to be alert to instances in which client personnel have significant financial motives to fraudulently overstate revenue. In these situations it is especially important to understand, and if appropriate, test the controls designed and implemented to prevent such behavior. If controls are ineffective, auditors need to exercise appropriate professional skepticism and extend substantive testing to obtain sufficient appropriate evidence.

The examples in Exhibit 9.4 are but a few of the revenue risk factors to which auditors should be alert. Identifying these risk factors involves the auditor:

- Assessing motivation to enhance revenue because of either internal or external pressures
- Reviewing the financial statements through preliminary analytical procedures to identify account balances that differ from expectations or general trends in the economy
- Recognizing that not all of the fraud will be instigated by management; for example, a CFO or accounting staff person may engage in misappropriating assets for his or her own use
- Becoming aware of representations made by management to analysts and the potential effect of those expectations on stock prices
- Determining whether the company's performance is significantly different from that of the rest of the industry or the economy
- Determining whether the company's accounting is being investigated by organizations such as the SEC
- Considering management compensation schemes, especially those that rely on stock options and therefore current stock prices
- Determining whether accounting functions are centralized, and if not centralized, assessing if the decentralization is appropriate (the *Auditing in Practice* feature "Risks Related to Decentralized Accounting Functions at WorldCom: The Case of WorldCom" provides a relevant example)
- Assessing whether the company engages in complex sales arrangements when simple transactions would suffice
- Assessing whether the company has a history of aggressive accounting interpretations
- Determining whether an uninterrupted history of continued growth in earnings per share or revenue might provide incentives to continue to show that growth
- Determining if the client has numerous manual journal entries affecting the revenue process (assuming that process is automated)

Risks Related to Decentralized Accounting Functions: The Case of WorldCom

WorldCom is a prime example of a company taking several actions that negatively affect the quality of its financial statements. WorldCom's transactions were complex, but they were made more difficult to understand and audit by means of several factors. First, many of the accounting personnel were not sufficiently qualified for their positions. Second, the accounting function was spread over at least three locations, without a good rationale for the decentralization. Third, the decentralization was by function. Many companies have decentralization with a full accounting unit at various locations, but WorldCom was not distributed that way; the property accounting function was located in Texas, while the revenue and line cost accounting were in Mississippi, and the equipment control was in Washington, D.C. Consequently, an accounting unit never saw the complete transaction. Only a few people at the very top were aware of the full accounting transactions. Auditors should exhibit appropriate professional skepticism when encountering such situations.

识别控制风险

LO 4 Identify and assess control risks of material misstatement in the revenue cycle.

当注册会计师了解了收入与应收账款账户中存在的重大错报固有风险和舞弊风险后，接下来注册会计师需要了解客户设计和执行的控制是否能够防止或者及时发现这些风险。

Identifying Control Risks

Once the auditor has obtained an understanding of the inherent and fraud risks of material misstatement in the revenue and accounts receivable accounts, the auditor needs to understand the controls that the client has designed and implemented to address those risks. Remember, the auditor is required to gain an overall understanding of internal controls for both integrated audits and financial statement only audits. Such understanding is normally gained by means of a walkthrough of the process, inquiry, observation, and review of the client's documentation. The auditor considers both entity-wide controls and transaction controls at the account and assertion levels. This understanding provides the auditor with a basis for making an initial control risk assessment.

At the entity-wide level, the auditor will consider the control environment, including such principles as commitment to financial accounting competencies and the independence of the board of directors. The auditor will also consider the remaining components of internal control that are typically entity-wide—risk assessment, information and communication, and monitoring controls. Although all the components of internal control need to be understood, the auditor typically finds it useful to focus on significant control activities in the revenue cycle. As part of this understanding, the auditor focuses on the relevant assertions for each account and identify the controls that relate to risks for these assertions. In an integrated audit or in a financial statement only audit where the auditor relies on controls, this understanding will be used to identify important controls that need to be tested.

Controls Related to Existence/Occurrence Controls for existence should provide reasonable assurance that a sale and accounts receivable are recorded only when shipment has occurred and the primary revenue-producing activity has been performed. Recall that sales transactions should be recorded only when title has passed and the company has received cash or a collectible receivable. A control to mitigate the risk that unearned revenues are recorded is to distribute monthly statements to customers. However, the control should be such that the statements are prepared and mailed by someone independent of the department who initially processed the transactions. Further, customer inquiries about their balances should be channeled to a department or individual that is independent of the original recording of the transactions.

Unusual transactions, either because of their size, complexity, or special terms, should require a high level of management review, with the review serving as a control. Upper levels of management—and maybe even the board—should be involved in approving highly complex and large transactions. For typical transactions, authorization should be part of an audit trail and should not be performed by the same person who records the transactions.

Controls Related to Completeness Controls related to completeness are intended to provide reasonable assurance that all valid sales transactions are recorded. For example, transactions may not be recorded because of sloppy procedures. In some cases, companies may choose to omit transactions because they want to minimize taxable income. Thus, the auditor needs to consider completeness controls, which might include the following:

- Use of prenumbered shipping documents and sales invoices and the subsequent accounting for all numbers
- Immediate online entry into the computer system and immediate assignment of unique identification number by the computer application
- Reconciliation of shipping records with billing records
- Supervisory review, such as review of transactions at a fast-food franchise
- Reconciliation of inventory with sales, such as the reconciliation of liquor at a bar at the end of the night with recorded sales

Controls Related to Valuation Implementing controls related to proper valuation of routine sales transactions should be relatively straightforward. Sales should be made from authorized price lists—for example, the price read by a scanner at Wal-Mart or the price accessed by a salesperson from a laptop. In these situations, the control procedures should provide reasonable assurance the correct input of authorized price changes into the computer files and limit access to those files, including the following:

- Limiting access to the files to authorized individuals
- Printing a list of changed prices for review by the department that authorized the changes
- Reconciling input with printed output reports to assure that all changes were made and no unauthorized ones were added
- Limiting authorization privileges to those individuals with the responsibility for pricing

Valuation issues most often arise in connection with unusual or uncertain sales terms. Examples include sales where the customer has recourse to the selling company, franchise sales, bundled sales, cost-plus contracts, or other contracts covering long periods with provisions for partial payments. If these complex transactions are common, the company should have established policies and processes for handling them that should be understood by the auditor.

Another issue affecting the valuation of sales is returns and allowances. Abnormal returns or allowances may be the first sign that a company has inappropriate recording of revenue. The *Auditing in Practice* feature "Risks Associated with Sales Returns: The Case of Medicis and Ernst & Young" notes the problems that can arise if controls related to returns and allowances are not designed and operating effectively, and the auditor does not appropriately respond to this control risk. Controls that the client should

Risks Associated with Sales Returns: The Case of Medicis and Ernst & Young

In 2012, the PCAOB settled a disciplinary order censuring Ernst & Young (E&Y), imposing a $2 million penalty against the firm, and sanctioning four of its current and former partners. In the audits of Medicis' December 31, 2005, 2006, and 2007 financial statements, the PCAOB found that E&Y and its partners failed to properly evaluate a material component of the company's financial statements—its sales returns reserve. E&Y did not properly evaluate Medicis' practice of reserving for most of its estimated product returns at replacement cost, instead of at gross sales price. It appears that E&Y accepted the company's basis for reserving at replacement cost, when the auditors should have known that this approach would not be supported by the audit evidence. By using replacement cost for the reserve, rather than gross sales price, Medicis' reported sales returns reserve were materially understated and its reported revenue was materially overstated.

Ultimately, E&Y concluded that Medicis' practice of reserving for its sales returns was not in conformity with GAAP. The company corrected its accounting for its sales returns reserve and had to file restated financial statements with the U.S. SEC.

For further details on this case, see PCAOB Release No. 105-2012-001.

implement for identifying and promptly recording returned goods include formal policies and procedures for:

- Clearly spelling out contractual return provisions in the sales contract
- Approving acceptance of returns
- Recording goods returned on prenumbered documents that are accounted for, to be sure they are all recorded promptly
- Identifying whether credit should be given or whether the goods will be reworked according to warranty provisions and returned to the customer
- Determining the potential obsolescence or defects in the goods
- Assuring proper classification of the goods and determining that the goods are not reshipped as if they were new goods
- Developing and implementing a sales returns reserve methodology, requiring reasonable and supportable assumptions

Valuation of accounts receivable also has important risks that need to be mitigated with appropriate controls. Formal credit policies are designed to provide reasonable assurance of the realization of the asset acquired in the sales transaction, that is, realization of the accounts receivable into cash. The following procedures should be used by a company in controlling its credit risk:

- A formal credit policy, which may be automated for most transactions but requires special approval for large and/or unusual transactions
- A periodic review of the credit policy by key executives to determine whether changes are dictated either by current economic events or by deterioration of the receivables
- Continuous monitoring of receivables for evidence of increased risk, such as increases in the number of days past due or an unusually high concentration in a few key customers whose financial prospects are declining
- Adequate segregation of duties in the credit department, with specific authorization to write off receivables segregated from individuals who handle cash transactions with the customer

An additional aspect of the valuation of net receivables is management's process for estimating the allowance account. Management should have a well-controlled process in place to develop a reasonable and supportable estimate for this allowance account.

Documenting Controls Auditors need to document their understanding of internal controls for both integrated audits and financial statement only audits. Exhibit 9.5 provides an example of an internal control questionnaire for sales and accounts receivable. The first part helps document the auditor's understanding of the process, and each negative answer in the second part of the questionnaire represents a potential internal control deficiency. Given a negative answer, the auditor should consider the effect of the response on the initial assessment of control risk. For example, a negative response to the question regarding the existence of a segregation of duties between those receiving cash and those authorizing write-offs or adjustments of accounts indicates that a risk exists that an individual could take cash receipts and cover up the fraud by writing off a customer's balance. Unless another control compensates for this deficiency, the auditor will likely have a control risk assessment of moderate or high in this area.

EXHIBIT 9.5 **Control Risk Assessment Questionnaire: Sales and Receivables**

SALES ORDERS

Sales authorized by: (Describe the source and scope of authority, and the documentation or other means of indicating authorizations. Include explicitly the authorization of prices for customers.)

Sales orders prepared by, or entered into the system by:

Individuals authorized to change price tables: (Indicate specific individuals and their authority to change prices on the system and the methods used to verify the correctness of changes.)

Existence of major contracts with customers that might merit special attention during the course of the audit: (Describe any major contracts and their terms.)

Restrictions on access to computer files for entering or changing orders: (Describe access control systems and indicate whether we have tested them in conjunction with our review of data processing general controls.)

EXHIBIT **9.5**	Control Risk Assessment Questionnaire: Sales and Receivables (*continued*)

	Check (x) one:	
	Yes	No
1. Are orders entered by individuals who do not have access to the goods being shipped?	____	____
2. Are orders authorized by individuals who do not have access to the goods being shipped?	____	____
3. Are batch and edit controls used effectively on this application? If so, describe the controls.	____	
4. Are sales invoices prenumbered? Is the sequence of prenumbered documents independently accounted for?	____	
5. Are control totals and reconciliations used effectively to ensure that all items are recorded and that subsidiary files are updated at the same time invoices are generated? If so, describe.	____	
6. Do procedures exist to ensure that the current credit status of a customer is checked before an order is shipped? If so, describe.	____	
7. Are price lists stored in the computer independently reconciled to authorized prices by the marketing manager or someone in the marketing manager's office?	____	
8. Are duties segregated such that the personnel receiving cash differ from the personnel authorized to make account write-offs or adjustments of accounts?	____	

EXHIBIT **9.6**	Partially Completed Controls Matrix for Contract Revenue

Control Description	Risk of Misstatement— Relevant Assertion(s)	Testing Approach (Nature of Testing)	Timing of Testing	Extent of Testing	Testing Results (Including Deficiencies)
A revenue recognition review is performed by the revenue accountant before revenue is recorded.	The risks are that revenue will be recorded before the criteria for recognizing revenue have been met or that revenue will be recorded at the incorrect amount. • Valuation • Existence	Reperformance of analyses performed by the revenue accountant.	Year end		

Note: The matrix is intended as a partial illustration. The matrix would typically be linked to a supporting flowchart that would detail the key controls related to contract review, and all key controls would be included in the matrix.

Although questionnaires have been used extensively in the past, they are currently being replaced by control matrices, flowcharts, and documented walkthroughs of processes. Exhibit 9.6 presents a partially completed control matrix for contract revenue that links the risk of misstatement to the client's control and provides a means for the auditor to document the testing approach and testing results.

实施初步的分析性程序

LO 5 Describe how to use preliminary analytical procedures to identify possible material misstatements for revenue cycle accounts, disclosures, and assertions.

初步的分析性程序可以帮助注册会计师识别潜在的错报领域。如果初步的分析性程序识别了不正常的或者非预期的关系，那么注册会计师需要调整计划的审计程序以发现这些潜在的重大错报。

Performing Preliminary Analytical Procedures

When planning the audit, the auditor is required to perform preliminary analytical procedures. These procedures can help auditors identify areas of potential misstatements. Auditors do not look at just the numbers when performing analytical procedures. Auditors need to go through the four-step process described in Chapter 7, which begins with developing expectations for account balances, ratios, and trends. Possible expected relationships in the revenue cycle include the following:

- There is no unusual year-end sales activity.
- Accounts receivable growth is consistent with revenue growth.
- Revenue growth, receivables growth, and gross margin are consistent with the activity in the industry.
- There is no unusual concentration of sales made to customers (in comparison with the prior year).
- The accounts receivable turnover is not significantly different from the prior year.
- The ratio of the allowance for doubtful accounts to total receivables or to credit sales is similar to the prior year.

If preliminary analytical procedures do not identify any unexpected relationships, the auditor would conclude that a heightened risk of material misstatements does not exist in these accounts. If there were unusual or unexpected relationships, the planned audit procedures (tests of controls, substantive procedures) would be adjusted to address the potential material misstatements. The auditor should be aware that if a revenue fraud is taking place, the financial statements usually will contain departures from industry norms, but may not differ from the expectations set by management. Thus, the auditor should compare the unaudited financial statements with both past results and industry trends. The following relationships might suggest a heightened risk of fraud:

- Revenue is increasing even though there is strong competition and a major competitor has introduced a new product.
- Revenue increases are not consistent with the industry or the economy.
- Gross margins are higher than average, or there is an unexpected change in gross margins.
- Large increases in revenue occur near the end of the quarter or year.
- Revenue has grown and net income has increased, but there is negative cash flow from operations.

Trend analyses of account balances and ratios are preliminary analytical procedures that are routinely used on revenue cycle accounts. Examples of ratios the auditor might consider for revenue cycle accounts are presented in Exhibit 9.7.

Trend Analysis When considering either ratios or account balances, the auditor may perform trend analysis, which considers the ratios or accounts over time. The auditor may have an expectation that current performance will continue in line with previous performance or industry trends unless something unusual is happening in the company. Unless a company has introduced significant new products or new ways of conducting its operations, it is reasonable to expect a company's performance to parallel industry trends. For example, it might have seemed unusual to some that WorldCom could report continuing increases in earnings when none of its major competitors could do so. Could it be because WorldCom had products the other companies did not have? Did WorldCom have superior

EXHIBIT **9.7**   Using Ratios in Preliminary Analytical Procedures in the Revenue Cycle

- Gross margin analysis
- Turnover of receivables (ratio of credit sales to average net receivables) or the number of days' sales in accounts receivable
- Average receivables balance per customer
- Receivables as a percentage of current assets
- Aging of receivables
- Allowance for uncollectible accounts as a percentage of accounts receivable
- Bad debt expense as a percentage of net credit sales
- Sales in the last month (or quarter) to total sales
- Sales discounts to credit sales
- Returns and allowances as a percentage of sales

management? Or could it be that the company should have merited greater professional skepticism and testing by the auditor?

Some basic trend analyses include the following:

- Monthly sales analysis compared with past years and budgets
- Identification of spikes in sales at the end of quarters or the end of the year
- Trends in discounts allowed to customers that exceed both past experience and the industry average

Ratio Analysis Example The following example demonstrates how ratio analysis may be helpful to the auditor. The company is a wholesaler selling to major retail chains in a competitive industry. The changes in ratios noted by the auditor include the following:

- The number of days' sales in accounts receivable increased in one year from 44 to 65.
- The gross margin increased from 16.7% to 18.3% (industry average was 16.3%).
- The amount of accounts receivable increased 35% from $9 million to $12 million, while sales remained virtually unchanged.

All of these ratios were substantially greater than the industry averages; the auditor's expectations were that the company should be somewhat similar to the industry averages. An auditor comparing the client's ratios with the auditor's expectations should carefully consider the business reasons for the changes: (1) Is there a business reason why these ratios changed? (2) What alternatives could potentially explain these changes? and (3) What corroborating evidence is available for potential explanations?

The auditor should develop a potential set of explanations that could account for the changes in all three ratios and design audit procedures to gather independent corroborating evidence that either supports or contradicts that explanation. In this example, the company was engaged in a complicated scheme of recording fictitious sales. A number of other explanations were offered by management—increased efficiency, better computer system, better customer service, and so forth. However, only fictitious sales could account for the change in the gross margin, the increase in the number of days' sales in accounts receivable, and the increase in the total balance of accounts receivable that occurred when sales were not increasing.

对识别的重大错报风险的反应

 Determine appropriate responses to identified risks of material misstatement for revenue cycle accounts, disclosures, and assertions.

Responding to Identified Risks of Material Misstatement

Once the auditor understands the risks of material misstatement, the auditor is in a position to determine the appropriate audit procedures to perform. Audit procedures should be proportional to the assessed risks, with areas of higher risk receiving more audit attention and effort. Responding to identified risks typically involves developing an audit approach that contains substantive procedures (for example, tests of details and, when appropriate, substantive analytical procedures) and tests of controls, when applicable. The sufficiency and appropriateness of selected procedures will vary to achieve the desired level of assurance for each relevant assertion. While audit firms may have a standardized audit program for the revenue cycle, the auditor should customize the audit program based on the assessment of risk of material misstatement.

Consider a client where the auditor has assessed the risk of material misstatement related to the completeness of revenue at slightly below the maximum. This client has incentives to understate revenue in an effort to smooth earnings, and has implemented somewhat effective controls in this area. The auditor may develop an audit program that consists of first performing limited tests of operating effectiveness of controls, then performing limited substantive analytical procedures, and finally performing substantive tests of details. Because of the high risk, the auditor will want to obtain a great deal of evidence directly from tests of details. In contrast, consider a client where the auditor has assessed the risk of material misstatement related to the completeness of revenues as low, and believes that the client has implemented effective controls in this area. For this client, the auditor can likely perform tests of controls, gain a high level of assurance from substantive analytical procedures such as a reasonableness test, and then complete the substantive procedures by performing tests of details at a limited level.

Panel A of Exhibit 9.8 makes the point that because of differences in risk, the box of evidence to be filled for testing the completeness of revenue at the low-risk client is smaller than that at the high-risk client. Panel B of Exhibit 9.8 illustrates the different levels of assurance that the auditor will obtain from tests of controls and substantive procedures for the two assertions. Panel B makes the point that because of the higher risk associated with the completeness of revenue at Client B, the auditor will want to design the audit so that more of the assurance or evidence is coming from direct tests of account balances. Note that the relative percentages are judgmental in nature; the examples are simply intended to give you a sense of how an auditor might select an appropriate mix of procedures.

在收入循环中获取内部控制运行有效性的证据

 Determine appropriate tests of controls and consider the results of tests of controls for revenue cycle accounts, disclosures, and assertions.

选择测试的控制和实施控制测试

Obtaining Evidence about Internal Control Operating Effectiveness in the Revenue Cycle

For integrated audits, the auditor will test the operating effectiveness of important controls as of the client's year end. If the auditor wants to rely on controls for the financial statement audit, the auditor will test the operating effectiveness of those controls throughout the year.

Selecting Controls to Test and Performing Tests of Controls

The auditor selects controls that are important to the auditor's conclusion about whether the organization's controls adequately address the assessed risk of material misstatement in the revenue cycle. The auditor will select both entity-wide and transaction controls for testing. Typical tests of transaction controls include inquiry of personnel performing the control, observation of the control being performed, inspection of documentation confirming that the control has been performed, and reperformance of the control by the individual testing the control.

| EXHIBIT **9.8** | Panel A: Sufficiency of Evidence for Completeness of Revenue |

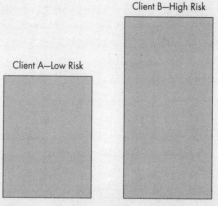

Panel B: Approaches to Obtaining Audit Evidence for Completeness of Revenue

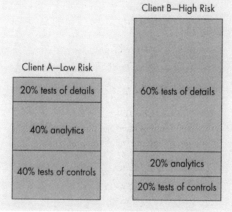

For example, a control may include reconciliation between the sales sub-ledger and the general ledger. The approaches to testing the reconciliation control could involve one or more of the following:

- *Inquiry*—Talk with the personnel who perform the control about the procedures and processes involved in the reconciliation.
- *Observation*—Observe the entity personnel performing the reconciliation.
- *Inspection*—Review the documentation supporting completion of the reconciliation.
- *Reperformance*—Perform the reconciliation and agree to the reconciliation completed by the entity personnel.

The auditor uses professional judgment to determine the appropriate types of tests of controls to perform. However, inquiry alone is generally not sufficient evidence and would typically be supplemented with observation, examination, and/or reperformance.

Exhibit 9.9 presents an overview of various transaction controls that might be used to mitigate risks in the revenue cycle and how the controls might be tested. Note that the tests of controls include selecting samples of transactions and obtaining supporting documents, reviewing monitoring

EXHIBIT **9.9** Control Examples and Tests

Objective	Examples of Controls	How Control Would Be Tested	Implications if Control Not Working
1. Recorded transactions are authorized and actually occurred.	a. Sales recorded only with valid customer order and shipping document. b. Credit is approved before shipment.	a. Sample recorded sales transactions and vouch back to source documents. Use generalized audit software to match sales with electronic shipping document or customer order. b. Use ACL to determine each customer's balance and compare with its credit limit.	a. Recorded sales may not have occurred. Extend accounts receivable confirmation work and review of subsequent collections. b. Receivables may not be collectible. Expand confirmation work and review of subsequent collections.
2. Sales are recorded in the correct accounting period.	a. Computer records sale upon entry of customer order and shipping information. Transactions entered, but not yet processed, are identified for an exception report and followed up. b. Monthly statements are sent to customers. A group independent of those recording the transactions receives and follows up complaints.	a. Review monitoring controls (for example management's review of transactions entered into the system and not shipped and billed). b. Review nature of complaints received. Investigate to determine if there is a pattern.	a. Company may have unrecorded sales transactions. Discuss with management to determine if it has plans to bill the sales. b. Sales may be recorded in the wrong year. Expand sales cutoff testing.
3. All sales are recorded.	a. Prenumbered shipping documents and invoices which are periodically accounted for. b. Online input of transactions and independent logging are done. c. Monitoring: Transactions are reviewed and compared with budgets, and differences are investigated.	a. Review reconciliations to determine that control is working. b. Use generalized audit software to verify transaction trails. c. Review management reports and evidence of actions taken.	a–c. Expand cutoff tests at year end to determine that all transactions are recorded in the correct period.
4. Sales are accurately recorded.	a. Sales price comes from authorized sales price list maintained on the computer.	a. Test access controls. Take a sample of recorded sales invoices and trace price back to authorized list.	a. Accounts receivable may be overstated or understated due to pricing errors. Expand confirmation and subsequent collection procedures.
5. Sales are correctly classified.	a. Chart of accounts is up to date and used. b. Computer program is tested before implementation.	a. Take a sample of transactions and trace to general ledger to see if they are properly classified. b. When testing general controls, determine that controls over program changes are working.	a. Expand test of sales and receivables to determine that all items represent bona fide contracts and not consignment sales or sale of operating assets. b. Expand confirmations to customers.

controls, testing computer access controls, using generalized audit software (GAS) to match documents and look for gaps or duplicate document numbers, reviewing customer complaints, reviewing documents such as reconciliations and management reports noting timely action taken, and reviewing sales contracts.

Considering the Results of Tests of Controls

考虑控制测试的结果

The auditor will analyze the results of the tests of controls to determine additional appropriate procedures. There are two potential outcomes:

1. If control deficiencies are identified, the auditor will assess those deficiencies to determine their severity (are they significant deficiencies or material weaknesses?). The auditor would then modify the preliminary control risk assessment (possibly from low to moderate or high) and document the implications of the control deficiencies. The last column in Exhibit 9.9 provides examples of implications of control deficiencies for substantive testing. Appropriate modifications to planned substantive audit procedures will be determined by the types of misstatements that are most likely to occur because of the control deficiency.

如果识别了控制缺陷，注册会计师会评估这些缺陷以确定它们的严重程度。进而，注册会计师会对初步的控制风险评估进行修正，同时记录控制缺陷的潜在影响。

2. If no control deficiencies are identified, the auditor will likely determine that the preliminary assessment of control risk as low is still appropriate. The auditor will then determine the extent that controls can provide evidence on the correctness of account balances, and determine planned substantive audit procedures. The level of substantive testing in this situation will be less than what is required in circumstances where deficiencies in internal control were identified. From the audit risk model, we know that companies with effective internal controls should require less substantive testing of account balances.

Obtaining Substantive Evidence about Accounts, Disclosures, and Assertions in the Revenue Cycle

在收入循环中获取账户、披露和认定的实质性证据

LO 8 Determine and apply sufficient appropriate substantive audit procedures for testing revenue cycle accounts, disclosures, and assertions.

In performing substantive procedures, the auditor wants reasonable assurance that the client's revenue recognition approaches are appropriate, and that revenue transactions are in accordance with GAAP. Substantive procedures (substantive analytical procedures, tests of details, or both) should be performed for all relevant assertions related to significant revenue cycle accounts and disclosures. Even if the auditor has evidence indicating that controls are operating effectively, the auditor cannot rely solely on control testing to provide evidence on the reliability of these accounts and assertions. Substantive tests in the revenue cycle are typically performed to provide evidence that:

- Sales transactions do exist and are properly valued.
- Accounts receivable exist.
- The balance in the allowance account is reasonable.
- Fraudulent transactions are not included in the financial statements.

Typical substantive procedures for sales and accounts receivable are shown in Exhibit 9.10. The extent to which substantive analytical procedures and tests of details are performed depends on a number of factors, including the risk of material misstatement and the effectiveness of controls. The *Auditing in Practice* feature "Performing Appropriate Substantive Audit Procedures in the Revenue Cycle: The Case of Kyoto Audit Corporation" highlights the importance of performing and documenting sufficient appropriate substantive procedures in the revenue cycle.

EXHIBIT **9.10**	Management Assertions and Substantive Procedures in the Revenue Cycle

Management Assertion	**Substantive Procedure**
Existence or occurrence—Recorded sales and accounts receivable are valid.	1. Perform substantive analytical procedures. 2. Trace sales invoices to customer orders and bills of lading. 3. Confirm balances or unpaid invoices with customers. 4. Examine subsequent collections as evidence that the sale existed. 5. Scan sales journal for duplicate entries.
Completeness—All sales are recorded.	1. Perform substantive analytical procedures. 2. Trace bills of lading to sales invoice and sales journal. 3. Account for sequence of sales invoices in sales journal.
Rights and obligations—Pledged, discounted, assigned, and related-party accounts receivable are properly accounted for in accordance with GAAP.	1. Inquire of management. 2. Review trial balance of accounts receivable for related parties. 3. Review loan agreements and minutes of board meetings.
Valuation or allocation—Sales and accounts receivable are properly valued and recorded in the correct period. Revenue has been recognized in accordance with GAAP.	1. Verify clerical accuracy of sales invoices and agreement of sales invoices with supporting documents. 2. Trace sales invoices to sales journal and customer's ledger. 3. Confirm balances or unpaid invoices with customers. 4. Foot sales journal and accounts receivable trial balance and reconcile accounts receivable trial balance with control account. 5. Review adequacy of the allowance for doubtful accounts. 6. Perform sales cutoff test.
Presentation and disclosure—Pledged, discounted, assigned, and related-party accounts receivable are properly disclosed. Revenue recognition policies have been properly disclosed.	1. Obtain confirmations from banks and other financial institutions. 2. Inquire of management. 3. Review work performed in other audit areas. 4. Review revenue recognition policies for appropriateness and consistency.

收入：实质性分析程序

Revenue: Substantive Analytical Procedures

Before performing tests of details, the auditor may perform substantive analytical procedures such as a reasonableness test or regression analysis. An example of a reasonableness test would be estimating room revenue for a hotel using the number of rooms, the average room rate, and average occupancy rate. Alternatively, the revenue from an electrical utility company should be related to revenue rates approved by a Public Service Commission (where applicable) and demographic information about growth in households and industry in the service area the company serves. If the auditor's expectations are significantly different from what the client has recorded, the auditor will need to follow up with sufficient appropriate tests of details. If the auditor's expectations are not significantly different from what the client has recorded, the auditor may be able reduce tests of details.

The auditor could also use regression analysis. Often, regression analysis is performed as a time-series analysis by examining trends in relationship with previous results. For example, it might be used to estimate monthly sales by product line based on the historical relationship of sales and independent variables such as cost of sales, selected selling expenses, or growth in total sales for the industry. Another form of regression analysis is referred to as cross-sectional analysis. Rather than comparing relationships over a period of time, cross-sectional analysis is designed to compare results across a number of locations. For example, Home Depot and Lowe's might have

AUDITING IN PRACTICE

Performing Appropriate Substantive Audit Procedures in the Revenue Cycle: The Case of Kyoto Audit Corporation

In February 2012, the PCAOB released its first inspection report on Kyoto Audit Corporation (Kyoto), a Japanese affiliate of the Big 4 audit firm PricewaterhouseCoopers (PwC). PwC describes Kyoto as a cooperating firm. While Kyoto is not a full member of PwC's global network, it appears that Kyoto has the right to use PwC's audit methodology and has access to the expertise of the PwC network.

In December 2010 and January 2011, the PCAOB's staff reviewed Kyoto's audits for two companies and found audit deficiencies in both audits. The deficiencies were so severe it appeared that "the firm at the time it issued its audit report had not obtained sufficient competent evidential matter to support its opinion on the issuer's financial statements." The deficiencies they found included "the failure, in both audits, to perform adequate substantive analytical audit procedures to test revenue." The report also cited Kyoto's failures to

perform sufficient procedures "to test the allowance for doubtful accounts." It appears that the audit firm had not gathered sufficient appropriate evidence to determine whether recorded revenue was accurate or whether customers could pay their bills.

While most audits are quality audits, this inspection report serves to illustrate the importance of complying with professional standards in performing and documenting sufficient appropriate substantive procedures in the revenue cycle. Kyoto ultimately performed additional audit procedures in response to the PCAOB inspection report, but did not change the audit reports issued. The companies with the audit deficiencies did not change their financial statements. Therefore, it appears that while the procedures performed by Kyoto were insufficient, the underlying financial accounts and assertions were not materially misstated.

For further details on this case, see PCAOB Release No. 104-2012-053.

---

hundreds of stores—each with a basic store layout and size. Cross-sectional analysis allows the auditor to identify any unusual store performance. For example, the auditor may identify potential problems by comparing sales per square foot of retail space among the stores, looking for those with significantly more sales per square foot than the other stores. More substantive tests of details should be performed at those suspect stores.

In general, if substantive analytical procedures do not result in unresolved issues, direct testing of account balances can be reduced. However, in the revenue cycle it is unlikely that audit evidence obtained from substantive analytical procedures alone will be sufficient evidence for the auditor.

Revenue: Substantive Tests of Details   收入：实质性细节测试

Substantive tests of details for revenue transactions would primarily involve inspection of relevant client documentation. These tests would be focused on the existence and valuation assertions, although the auditor might also perform tests of details related to completeness.

Revenue: Existence and Valuation Assertions

The existence and valuation assertions are usually the most relevant·for revenue accounts. Vouching a sample of recorded sales transactions back to customer orders and shipping documents provides support for the existence assertion. The auditor should compare the quantities billed and shipped with customer orders and verify the clerical accuracy of the sales invoices to provide assurance on valuation. These procedures will also provide evidence on the existence and valuation of accounts receivable.

As discussed in Chapter 8, computerized audit techniques can also be useful. Audit software can be used to identify duplicate sales. GAS can also select a sample of recorded sales transactions for vouching. Further, such software may be able to compare the transactions detail with the supporting electronic documents. GAS can also be used to verify the clerical accuracy of the invoices and foot the sales journal.

Revenue: Completeness Assertion

An important control to assure completeness is prenumbered shipping and billing documents. The auditor would select a sample of shipping documents and trace them into the sales journal to obtain evidence on whether all shipments have been recorded as sales transactions. The auditor can use audit software to look for gaps in the recorded sales invoice numbers and verify that the missing numbers are appropriate and do not represent unrecorded sales. For example, the gaps may be caused by voided documents or by using different numbers at different locations. These procedures will also provide evidence on the completeness of accounts receivable.

Revenue: Cutoff Issues

注册会计师需要特别注意资产负债表日前后销售业务的入账时间是否合理，防止客户提前或者推迟确认收入。

Additional audit attention should be given to sales transactions recorded just before and after year end. A specific concern related to existence is whether a recorded revenue transaction actually occurred before the end of the accounting period. For an example, refer back to Exhibit 9.4, which describes Motorola as keeping its third quarter books open after the quarter ended so that it could record revenues. Additionally, the auditor is also concerned with whether transactions recorded in the subsequent year actually relate to the year being audited. Performing cutoff tests with sales transactions recorded several days before and after year end is important to assuring both the existence and completeness of the revenue transactions.

The following items can be examined to determine whether a proper cutoff of sales and sales returns has been achieved:

Cutoff Test	Items to Examine
Sales	Shipping documents and related recorded sales
Sales returns	Receiving reports and related credits to customer accounts

Sales cutoff can be tested in alternative ways. For example, the auditor can select a sample of sales transactions from the cutoff period to determine when the transaction occurred. The auditor will look at the shipping terms and shipment dates to determine whether there was an appropriate cutoff. The auditor may also want to inspect the sales contracts for terms indicating that the recording of the sale should be postponed; for example, the customer's right of return (and a high probability of return), the existence of additional performance by the seller, the probability of collection based on some future event (contingency), or the existence of an unusually low probability of collection.

As a second approach to cutoff testing, if reliable shipping dates are stored electronically, GAS can be used to identify any sales recorded in the wrong period.

应收账款：基于账龄分析表的实质性程序

Accounts Receivable: Substantive Procedures Based on the Aged Trial Balance

A starting point for accounts receivable substantive procedures is obtaining a detailed aged accounts receivable trial balance from the client, manually preparing a trial balance, or using GAS to develop aging information. Exhibit 9.11 provides an example of an aged trial balance. A detailed trial

EXHIBIT **9.11**		Accounts Receivable Aging				
Name	**Balance**	**Current**	**30–60**	**61–90**	**91–120**	**Over 120**
Alvies	154,931	154,931				
Basch	71,812		71,812			
Carlson	115,539	115,539				
Draper	106,682	106,682				
Ernst	60,003			60,003		
Faust	90,907	90,907				
Gerber	241,129	211,643	29,486			
Hal	51,516	51,516				
Harv	237,881	237,881				
Kaas	18,504				18,504	
Kruze	44,765	44,765				
Lere	28,937	28,937				
Misty	210,334	210,334				
Mooney	216,961	216,961				
Otto	273,913	273,913				
Paggen	209,638	209,638				
Quast	88,038					88,038
Rauch	279,937	279,937				
Sundby	97,898	97,898				
Towler	96,408	85,908		10,500		
Zook	31,886	31,886				
	...	...				
Zough	245,927	245,927				
Totals	2,973,546	2,695,203	101,298	70,503	18,504	88,038

balance lists each customer's balance or unpaid invoices, with columns to show those that are current, 30 days overdue, 60 days, and so on.

If the client prepared the trial balance, the mathematical and aging accuracy should be recalculated by the auditor and it should be agreed to the general ledger. Credit balances can also be identified and, if significant, reclassified as liabilities. The aged trial balance is used by the auditor to:

- Agree the detail to the balance in the control account
- Select customer balances for confirmation
- Identify amounts due from officers, employees, or other related parties or any nontrade receivables that need to be separately disclosed in the financial statements
- Help determine the reasonableness of the allowance for doubtful accounts by identifying past-due balances

Accounts Receivable: Substantive Tests of Details—Confirmations

应收账款：实质性细节测试——函证

A widely used auditing procedure is to ask the client's customers to confirm the existence and the amount they owe to the client. Existence is necessary for correct valuation. However, existence does not necessarily assure correct

A PCAOB Proposed Auditing Standard on Confirmations

The PCAOB adopted AU Section 330 as an interim standard in 2003. However, in July 2010 the PCAOB issued an Exposure Draft, *Confirmation*, which would supersede AU Section 330 for public company audits. The comment period ended on September 13, 2010. The PCAOB staff has analyzed the comments received and is drafting revisions for the board's consideration.

Based on the Exposure Draft, changes from the current standard (AU Section 330) would limit the internal auditors' involvement in the confirmation process, clarify that the receipt of an oral response to a confirmation request does not meet the definition of an external confirmation, not include exceptions for not confirming receivables, require the auditor to communicate with those charged with governance if the auditor concludes that management's refusal to allow confirmations is unreasonable, limit instances in which negative confirmation requests are the only form of confirmation request to address the assessed risk of material misstatement at the assertion level, and allow auditors to use electronic media to send confirmation requests and receive confirmation responses.

valuation; for example, a customer might acknowledge the existence of the debt, but might not have sufficient resources to pay it. Confirmations are generally considered to provide quality evidence about the existence of receivables and the completeness of collections, sales discounts, and sales returns and allowances. For example, if a payment had been made but was not recorded by the client, or an invoice was recorded but no shipment occurred, the customer would likely report the discrepancy on the confirmation. A confirmation can be very effective in addressing the existence of fictitious sales. The presumption is that if fictitious sales are recorded to the account of a valid customer, the customer will note that some of the recorded sales are not correct.

审计准则要求注册会计师对应收账款实施函证程序，除非应收账款是不重要的，或者预期使用函证程序是无效的，或者注册会计师对应收账款重大错报风险评估为低水平且评估是充分的。

Auditing standards in the United States generally require the use of confirmations unless one of the following conditions exists:

- Accounts receivable are not material.
- The use of confirmations would be ineffective. An auditor might determine that confirmations are ineffective if customers have previously refused to confirm balances or customers do not have a good basis on which to respond to the confirmation.
- The auditor's assessment of the risk of material misstatement is low, and that assessment, in conjunction with the evidence provided by other substantive tests, is sufficient.

While U.S. standards generally require the use of confirmations, the international auditing standards do not include this requirement.

The *Auditing in Practice* feature "A PCAOB Proposed Auditing Standard on Confirmations" provides details on the PCAOB's efforts in developing a new standard related to confirmations for U.S. public companies.

Types of Confirmations

There are two types of accounts receivable confirmations: positive confirmations and negative confirmations.

Positive Confirmations **Positive confirmations** are letters sent to a sample of customers, asking them to review the current balance or unpaid invoice(s) due to the client and return the letters directly to the auditor indicating whether they agree with the balance. If the customer does not return a signed confirmation, the auditor needs to use follow-up audit procedures to verify the existence of the customer's balance. An example of a positive confirmation is shown in Exhibit 9.12. Notice that it is printed on the client's letterhead, is addressed to the customer, is signed by the client, indicates the balance or unpaid invoice amount as of a particular date—referred to as the confirmation date—and tells the customer to respond directly to the auditor in an enclosed self-addressed, postage-paid envelope.

Auditors may choose to confirm the terms of unusual or complex agreements or transactions in conjunction with or separately from the confirmation of account balances. The confirmation may need to be addressed to customer personnel who would be familiar with the details rather than to their accounts payable personnel. Auditors should also specifically inquire during the

---

EXHIBIT 9.12 Positive Confirmation

NSG Manufacturing Company

200 Pine Way, Kirkville, WI 53800
January 10, 2014

A.J. Draper Co.
215 Kilian Avenue
Justice, WI 53622

Our auditors, Johnstone, & Gramling, CPAs, are making an annual audit of our financial statements. Please confirm the balance due our company as of December 31, 2013, which is shown in our records as $32,012.38.

Please indicate in the space provided below if the amount is in agreement with your records. If there are differences, please provide any information that will assist our auditors in reconciling the difference.

Please mail your reply directly to Johnstone, & Gramling, CPAs, 5823 Monticello Business Park, Madison, WI 53711, in the enclosed return envelope. PLEASE DO NOT MAIL PAYMENTS ON THIS BALANCE TO OUR AUDITORS.

Very truly yours,

Joleen Soyka

Joleen Soyka
Controller
NSG Manufacturing Company
To: Johnstone, & Gramling, CPAs
The balance due NSG Manufacturing Company of $32,012.38 as of 12/31/13 is correct with the following exceptions, (if any):

Signature:_____
Title:_____
Date:_____

confirmation process about the possibility of bill-and-hold transactions (such as transactions in which the seller recognizes the sale and bills the customer but does not actually deliver the goods/services), extended payment terms or nonstandard installment receivables, or an unusual volume of sales to distributors/retailers (possible channel stuffing). Further, the auditor should confirm not only the terms of the transactions, but also the potential existence and content of side letters. A side letter is an agreement containing contract terms that are not part of the formal contract (often involving rights of return), thereby increasing audit risk because it enables key contract terms affecting revenue recognition to be hidden from the auditor as part of a revenue recognition fraud. Side letters are often associated with material revenue misstatements.

Negative Confirmations A negative confirmation asks the customer to review the balance owed to the client, but requests the customer to respond directly to the auditor only if the customer disagrees with the indicated balance. Exhibit 9.13 provides an example of a negative confirmation.

EXHIBIT **9.13** Negative Confirmation

NSG Manufacturing Company

200 Pine Way, Kirkville, WI 53800
January 10, 2014

B.D. Kruze
8163 Pleasant Way
Lucas, TX 77677

Our auditors are making an annual audit of our financial statements. Our records show an amount of $1,255.78 due from you as of 12/31/13. If the amount is not correct, please report any differences directly to our auditors, Johnstone, & Gramling, CPAs, using the space below and the enclosed return envelope. NO REPLY IS NECESSARY IF THIS AMOUNT AGREES WITH YOUR RECORDS. PLEASE DO NOT MAIL PAYMENTS ON ACCOUNT TO OUR AUDITORS.

Very truly yours,

Joleen Soyka

Joleen Soyka
Controller
NSG Manufacturing Company

Differences Noted (If Any)

The balance due NSG Manufacturing Company of $1,255.78 at 12/31/13 does not agree with our records because (No reply is necessary if your records agree):

Signature:_____
Title:_____
Date:_____

A negative confirmation is less expensive to administer than a positive confirmation because it does not require follow-up procedures when a customer does not return the confirmation. The auditor assumes that a nonresponse means that the customer agrees with the stated balance.

Negative confirmations would be used if the following conditions exist:

1. There are a large number of relatively small customer balances.
2. The assessed level of the risk of material misstatement for receivables and related revenue transactions is low.
3. The auditor has a reason to believe that the customers are likely to give proper attention to the requests; for example, the customers have independent records from which to make an evaluation, will take the time to do so, and will return the confirmation to the auditor if significant discrepancies exist.

Comparing Positive and Negative Confirmations Positive confirmations are considered to provide higher-quality evidence than negative confirmations because they result in either (1) the receipt of a response from the customer or (2) the use of alternative procedures to verify the existence of the receivable. Auditors may choose to use positive confirmations for large receivable balances and negative confirmations for smaller balances.

Regardless of the type of confirmation used, auditors need to take care that the confirmation process used adheres to professional auditing standards. The *Auditing in Practice* feature "PCAOB Enforcement Actions Related to Confirming Accounts Receivable" highlights some problems auditors have had related to adhering to the professional standards in this area.

The Confirmation Process

Confirmations may be prepared manually, but are typically prepared using GAS. The auditor should assure that the information in each confirmation is correct and should control the mailing of the confirmation requests so that the client cannot modify them. Customers are requested to return confirmations directly to the auditor's office in an enclosed self-addressed, postage-paid envelope. Similarly, the mailing should show the auditor's address as the return address if the confirmation is not deliverable. Undeliverable confirmations should raise the auditor's suspicion regarding the existence of the recorded receivable. To avoid receiving confirmation responses for fictitious receivables, the auditor must take care to assure that the confirmation will not be delivered to a location where the client can act as a surrogate and confirm an inappropriate receivable.

在询证函中应指明直接向接受委托的会计师事务所回函，而且询证函经被审计单位盖章后由注册会计师直接发出。

Sample Selection There are several approaches to selecting the specific receivables that will be confirmed. The auditor can confirm all of the large balances and randomly or haphazardly select some of the smaller balances using either nonstatistical or monetary unit sampling (MUS). The auditor may decide to include in the sample those accounts that have credit balances, are significant and past due, and/or have unusual customer names that are unfamiliar to the auditor.

Sampling Unit The sampling unit can be a customer's entire account balance or one or more of the unpaid invoices that make up that balance. When a balance is composed of several unpaid invoices, it will help the customer if a list of those invoices is attached to the confirmation.

Undeliverable Confirmations If some confirmations are returned as undeliverable, the auditor should determine why this occurred. If the wrong

PCAOB Enforcement Actions Related To Confirming Accounts Receivable

Regulatory enforcement actions provide many examples of auditors not adhering to professional standards related to confirming accounts receivable. Two enforcement actions that illustrate this point are summarized here.

In a PCAOB enforcement action against Moore & Associates, the PCAOB notes that the audit firm's staff often did not do any work to confirm either the existence or the valuation of clients' receivables. At one client, the audit team documented that confirmation procedures were not applicable without documenting how they came to that unusual conclusion. Further, for another client, the firm's staff considered confirmation responses from management as acceptable, when in fact confirmations should have come directly to the auditors from the clients' customers.

In a PCAOB enforcement action involving the audits of Satyam, the PCAOB notes the failure of the auditors to audit Satyam's accounts receivable balances in accordance with PCAOB standards. Specifically, the enforcement action indicates that the

engagement team relied on Satyam's management to send confirmation requests associated with accounts receivable balances. Further, the auditors received no responses to these confirmation requests, but made no attempt to follow up on the nonresponses with second confirmation requests. The auditors did perform alternative procedures to test receivables through the verification of subsequent receipts. However, no audit procedures were performed to ensure that the subsequent receipts were reconciled to individual invoices outstanding at fiscal year end.

Thus, while U.S. professional auditing standards are quite clear on the need to confirm accounts receivable, there exist examples in which auditors inexplicably do not adhere to those standards. While most audits are performed in a quality manner, these examples serve to illustrate that problems do occur and that you should be aware of such a possibility as you enter the profession.

For further details on these cases, see PCAOB Release No. 105-2009-006 and PCAOB Release No. 105-2011-002.

address was used, the correct address should be obtained and another request should be sent. It is also possible that the customer does not exist. Every effort should be made to determine the customer's existence. For example, the customer's name and address could be located in the telephone directory, in the publication of a credit rating service, or on the Internet. If a valid address cannot be located, the auditor should presume that the account does not exist or might be fictitious.

Follow-Up to Nonresponses for Positive Confirmations Follow-up procedures are required for positive confirmations that are not returned within a reasonable time after being mailed, such as two weeks. Second, and sometimes third, requests are mailed. If the amount being confirmed is relatively large, the auditor may consider calling the customer to encourage a written reply. When customers do not respond to the positive confirmation requests, the auditor should perform other procedures, referred to as **alternative procedures**, to verify the existence of the receivable. Remember that mailed confirmations represent only a sample of the many account balances shown in the client's records. The results of the sample are intended to represent the total population; therefore, it is important that the auditor develop sufficient follow-up procedures to gain satisfaction about each of the balances selected for confirmation. Alternative procedures that can be considered include the following:

- *Subsequent collection of the balance after year end*—Care should be taken to assure that these subsequent receipts relate to the balance as of the confirmation date, not to subsequent sales. Evidence obtained from testing subsequent collections is often believed to be a stronger indicator of the validity of the customer's balance than that obtained from confirmations. If a significant amount of the year-end receivables balance is normally collected before the end of the audit, the auditor may choose to emphasize tests of subsequent collections and minimize confirmation work. Testing subsequent collections provides strong evidence about both the existence and valuation of the related receivables.

- *Examination of supporting documents*—If all, or a portion, of the balance has not been collected at the time alternative procedures are being performed, documents supporting the uncollected invoices should be inspected. These documents include customer orders, sales orders, bills of lading or internal shipping documents, and sales invoices. The auditor must consider that evidence obtained from internal copies of customer orders, internal shipping documents, and sales invoices is not as persuasive as that obtained from subsequent cash receipts. Bills of lading are usually external and provide independent verification of shipments.

Follow-Up Procedures for Exceptions Noted on Positive Confirmations Customers are asked to provide details of any differences between their records and the amount shown on the confirmation. Differences are referred to as **exceptions**. The auditor investigates exceptions to determine whether the difference is a customer error, an item in dispute, a client misstatement, or a timing difference. **Timing differences** are due to transactions that are in process at the confirmation date, such as in-transit shipments or payments. If the auditor can determine that the timing difference did not result in recording the receivable in the wrong period, the differences do not represent misstatements in the account balance. Examples of exceptions include the following:

- *Payment has already been made*—This exception occurs when the customer has made a payment before the confirmation date, but the client has not received the payment before the confirmation date.
- *Merchandise has not been received*—This exception occurs when the client records the sale at the date of shipment and the customer records the purchase when the goods are received. The time the goods are in transit is typically the cause of this type of exception.
- *The goods have been returned*—This exception might be due to the client's failure to record a credit memo. Such a failure could result from timing differences or from the improper recording of sales returns and allowances.
- *Clerical errors and disputed amounts exist*—Some exceptions occur because the customer states that there is an error in the price charged for the goods, the goods are damaged, the proper quantity of goods was not received, or there is some other type of customer issue. These exceptions should be investigated to determine whether the client's records are in error and, if so, the amount of the error. Such differences might have implications for the valuation of the receivables account. However, what may initially appear to be a timing difference may actually be the result of lapping, which was discussed earlier in the chapter.

Because the auditor selects only a sample of accounts receivable for confirmation purposes, investigation of all exceptions and determination of the cause for any exceptions, rather than rationalizing the exception away as an isolated instance, are important. As discussed in Chapter 8, misstatements must be projected to the entire population of receivables to determine whether there is a material misstatement in the account balance. If the projected amount of misstatement appears to have a material effect on the financial statements, the magnitude and cause of such misstatement should be discussed with the client to decide the appropriate response. If subsequent work supports the conclusion of a material misstatement, a client adjustment will be required.

Follow-Up for Negative Confirmations The basic premise underlying negative confirmations is that if no response is received, the auditor assumes that the customer agrees with the balance. This is not always the correct assumption. The customer may not respond even though the balance is wrong because (1) the letter was lost, misplaced, or sent to the wrong address; (2) the customer did not understand the request; or (3) the request was simply ignored and thrown away. The auditor must have some assurance that the reliability of the negative confirmation process is not compromised because of any of the factors just described. The auditor does not expect that a large number of negative confirmations will be returned. However, when they are returned, reasons for their return include the following:

- The customer did not understand the request.
- The customer confirms an incorrect amount because payments or shipments are in transit.
- The amount recorded by the client is in error.

The auditor must perform follow-up work to determine whether the confirmed amount really represents a misstatement. The auditor might look at subsequent cash receipts or vouch back to the customer's order and evidence of shipment to help make this assessment. If errors are detected, the auditor should use expanded procedures to (1) find the underlying cause of the errors and (2) estimate the amount of misstatement in the account balance.

Additional Procedures When Accounts Are Confirmed at an Interim Date If the auditor confirms receivables at an interim date, the auditor must gather additional evidence during the roll-forward period. Roll-forward procedures in the revenue cycle include:

- Comparing individual customer balances at the interim confirmation date with year-end balances and confirming any that have substantially increased
- Comparing monthly sales, collections, sales discounts, and sales returns and allowances during the roll-forward period with those for prior months and prior years to see whether they appear out of line; if they do, obtaining an explanation from management and acquiring corroborative evidence to determine whether that explanation is valid
- Reconciling receivable subsidiary records to the general ledger at both the confirmation date and year end
- Testing the cutoff of sales, cash collections, and credit memos for returns and allowances at year end
- Scanning journals to identify receivables postings from unusual sources and investigate unusual items
- Computing the number of days' sales in receivables at both the confirmation date and year end, and comparing these data and data from prior periods
- Computing the gross profit percentage during the roll-forward period, and comparing that to the percentage for the year and for prior periods

应收账款：备抵账户的实质性程序

Accounts Receivable: Substantive Procedures for the Allowance Account

Substantive procedures related to the allowance account are relevant to the valuation of accounts receivable. Tests of details for the revenue account will provide evidence as to whether receivables transactions are initially recorded at their correct value (gross value). However, the auditor is also concerned as to whether it is likely that the client will collect the outstanding receivables (net realizable value). This concern relates to determining the reasonableness of the client's allowance for doubtful accounts. Accounts receivable should be valued at its net realizable value; that is, the gross amount customers owe less the allowance for doubtful accounts.

Determining the reasonableness of the client's estimate of the allowance for doubtful accounts is one of the more difficult audit tasks because, at the time of the audit, a single correct answer is not available. Recording the allowance for doubtful accounts and determining bad-debt expense for the year is the result of an accounting estimate. The allowance should reflect management's best estimate of accounts receivable that will not be collected at year end. The client's estimate must reflect the economic status of the client's customers, current economic conditions, and an informed expectation about potential default on payment. For many companies, determining the allowance will have a substantial effect on the company's profitability.

After reviewing and testing the process used by management, including the controls over the process, auditors generally use one or a combination of the following approaches to obtain evidence about the reasonableness of the client's estimate:

- Inquire of management about the collectibility of customer balances, particularly those that are large and long overdue
- Develop an independent model to estimate the accounts
- Review credit reports from outside credit bureaus, such as Dun & Bradstreet (*www.dnbisolutions.com*), to help determine the likelihood of collection of specific accounts
- Review customer correspondence files to gain additional insight into the collectibility of specific accounts
- For accounts that are unusually large or past due, review the customer's latest financial statements to perform an independent analysis of collectibility
- Inquire about the client's procedures for deciding when to write off an account

Accounts Receivable: Other Substantive Procedures
Accounts Receivable: Rights and Obligations

应收账款：其他的实质性程序

Some companies sell their receivables to banks or other financial institutions but may retain responsibility for collecting the receivables, and may be liable if the percentage of collection falls below a specified minimum. Receivables that have been sold with recourse, discounted, or pledged as collateral on loans should be disclosed in the notes to the financial statements. Substantive audit procedures that would reveal these ownership and related disclosure issues include:

- Reviewing all such arrangements and obtaining confirmations from the client's banks about any contingent liabilities
- Inquiring of management about any activities related to the receivables
- Scanning the cash receipts journal for relatively large inflows of cash that are posted from unusual sources
- Obtaining bank confirmations, which includes information on obligations to the bank and loan collateral
- Reviewing the board of directors' minutes, which generally contain approval for these items

Accounts Receivable: Presentation and Disclosure

Accounting standards require that trade accounts receivable be presented separately from other receivables. For example, material receivables from related parties, including officers, directors, stockholders, and employees, should be shown separately in the financial statements, with appropriate disclosures being provided. Audit procedures directed toward identifying related-party transactions such as these include the following:

- Reviewing SEC filings
- Reviewing the accounts receivable trial balance
- Inquiring of management and the audit committee about receivables from related parties

Material debit balances in accounts payable for amounts due from vendors should be reclassified as accounts receivable. Material credit balances in accounts receivable should be reclassified as accounts payable. Receivables that are not due within the normal operating cycle or one year should be listed as noncurrent assets. Audit procedures to identify misclassified receivables include making inquiries of management, reviewing the aged trial balance for large or old outstanding balances, reading the board of directors' minutes, and scanning the subsidiary ledger to identify unusually large receivable balances (particularly those that resulted from a single transaction or that were posted from an unusual source).

实施与舞弊相关的实质性 ## Performing Substantive Fraud-Related Procedures
程序

Substantive procedures are adjusted when specific fraud risk factors are present. Potential fraud risk factors in the revenue cycle include:

- Excessive credit memos or other credit adjustments to accounts receivable after the end of the fiscal year
- Customer complaints and discrepancies in accounts receivable confirmations (for example, disputes over terms, prices, or amounts)
- Unusual entries to the accounts receivable subsidiary ledger or sales journal
- Missing or altered source documents or the inability of the client to produce original documents in a reasonable period of time
- A lack of cash flow from operating activities when income from operating activities has been reported
- Unusual reconciling differences between the accounts receivable subsidiary ledger and control account
- Sales to customers in the last month of the fiscal period at terms more favorable than previous months
- Predated or postdated transactions
- Large or unusual adjustments to sales accounts just prior to or just after the fiscal year end

The following fraud-related audit procedures can be used to respond to these fraud risk factors:

- Perform a thorough review of original source documents, including invoices, shipping documents, customer purchase orders, cash receipts, and written correspondence between the client and the customer
- Analyze and review credit memos and other accounts receivable adjustments for the period subsequent to the balance sheet date
- Analyze all large or unusual sales made near year end and vouch to original source documents
- Confirm terms of the transaction directly with the customer, such as the absence of side agreements, acceptance criteria, delivery and payment terms, the right to return the product, and refund policies

- Compare the number of weeks of inventory in distribution channels with prior periods for unusual changes that may indicate channel stuffing
- Scan the general ledger, accounts receivable subsidiary ledger, and sales journal for unusual activity
- Perform analytical reviews of credit memo and write-off activity by comparing to prior periods. Look for unusual trends or patterns, such as large numbers of credit memos pertaining to one customer or salesperson, or those processed shortly after the close of the accounting period.
- Analyze recoveries of written-off accounts
- Inquire of the company's non-accounting personnel (e.g., sales and marketing personnel or even in-house legal counsel) about sales or shipments near year end and whether they are aware of any unusual terms or conditions in connection with these sales

If any of these procedures were part of the original audit program, the auditor should consider expanding the extent of testing, or in some way modifying the timing or nature of testing, if significant fraud risk factors are identified.

Documenting Substantive Procedures

记录实质性程序

A number of important items should be documented for this cycle. Documentation of confirmation procedures should detail the extent of dollars and items confirmed, the confirmation response rate, the number and dollar amount of exceptions that were not misstatements, the number and amount of exceptions that were misstatements (cross-referenced to the working paper B-4 that includes an explanation and conclusion), and a projection of the sample misstatements to the population. The following is an example of such a summary:

	Items	Amount
Population	3,810	5,643,200.00
Positive confirmations	29	193,038.71
Percent confirmed	0.76%	3.42%
Responses	27	180,100.11
Percent responding	93.1%	93.3%
Exceptions	5	32,061.50
Cleared	4	19,105.82
Misstatements—B-4	1	971.68
Projected to the population		30,446.31

Other documentation requirements for accounts receivable include:

- Tests of the adequacy of the allowance for doubtful accounts
- Details on inquires made regarding whether receivables are sold, pledged, or assigned
- Cutoff tests
- Evidence of roll-forward procedures if confirmations were sent at an interim date

Documentation related to the revenue substantive procedures would typically include:

- Substantive analytical procedures performed
- Unusual sales transactions

- Information indicating an understanding of the client's revenue recognition policies
- Identification of specific items tests (for example, all sales transactions in excess of $100,000)
- Relevant information on tests of details

SUMMARY AND NEXT STEPS

The revenue cycle presents a number of challenges for the auditor. First, revenue is typically considered to be a high-risk account because of management incentives for misstatement. Second, management needs to make a number of estimates, most notably the allowance for doubtful accounts, which are subject to manipulation. Notwithstanding these challenges, the auditor needs to determine if accounts receivable and revenue are fairly presented in the context of the financial statements as a whole. After identifying the risks of material misstatement through appropriate risk assessment procedures, the auditor will determine the appropriate audit approach and then carry out the planned procedures. One substantive procedure typically performed in this cycle is the confirmation of accounts receivable. And because the revenue account is closely related to accounts receivable, evidence about accounts receivable also provides evidence about revenues. For example, having confirmation evidence that an accounts receivable does exist also provides evidence about the existence of the related revenue transaction. Now that you understand how to audit the revenue cycle, in the next chapter we turn to auditing cash and marketable securities accounts.

SIGNIFICANT TERMS

Alternative procedures Procedures used to obtain evidence about the existence and valuation of accounts receivable when a positive confirmation is not returned, including examining cash collected after the confirmation date and vouching unpaid invoices to customers' orders, sales orders, shipping documents, and sales invoices.

Bill of lading A shipping document that describes items being shipped, the shipping terms, and delivery address; a formal legal document that conveys responsibility for the safety and shipment of items to the shipper.

Exceptions Differences between a customer's records and the client's records reported on positive or negative confirmations.

Lapping A technique used to cover up the embezzlement of cash whereby a cash collection from one customer is stolen by an employee who takes another customer's payment and credits the first customer. This process continues, and at any point in time at least one customer's account is overstated.

Negative confirmation A request to customers asking them to respond directly to the auditor only if they disagree with the indicated balance.

Positive confirmation A request to customers asking them to respond directly to the auditor if they agree or disagree with the indicated balance.

Revenue cycle The process of receiving a customer's order, approving credit for a sale, determining whether the goods are available for shipment, shipping the goods, billing the customers, collecting cash, and recognizing the effect of this process on other related accounts.

Side letter An agreement containing contract terms that are not part of the formal contract (often involving rights of return). Side letters increase audit risk because they enable key contract terms affecting revenue recognition to be hidden from the auditor as part of a revenue recognition fraud.

Timing difference Confirmation exceptions caused by transactions that are in process at the confirmation date, such as in-transit shipments or payments. These are not misstatements.

TRUE-FALSE QUESTIONS

9-1 [LO 1] Auditors should expect clients to have only one revenue process in place.

9-2 [LO 1] The revenue cycle begins when the goods are shipped to a customer.

9-3 [LO 2] An important inherent risk in the revenue cycle is that revenue will be recorded prior to when it has been earned.

9-4 [LO 2] Determining whether revenue has been earned is a very straightforward process that is not subject to inherent risk.

9-5 [LO 3] Recent research by COSO indicates that the majority of fraudulent financial statements involved inappropriate recording of revenue.

9-6 [LO 3] When assessing fraud risk factors, the auditor should consider the client's motivation to increase revenue because of either internal or external pressures.

9-7 [LO 4] It is not possible for internal controls to mitigate risks associated with the valuation of accounts receivable.

9-8 [LO 4] Using prenumbered shipping documents is a control that can provide reasonable assurance that all sales are recorded.

9-9 [LO 5] The auditor might believe a heightened risk of fraud exists if the preliminary analytical procedures indicate increases in revenue and net income, but negative cash flow from operations.

9-10 [LO 5] When performing preliminary analytical procedures, the auditor could perform trend analysis with ratios, but not with account balances.

9-11 [LO 6] In responding to identified risks of material misstatement in the revenue cycle, the auditor would never perform tests of controls, as only substantive procedures would be required.

9-12 [LO 6] In responding to identified risks of material misstatement related to the completeness of revenue cycle, the auditor will always perform a significant amount of tests of details.

9-13 [LO 7] In testing controls over whether sales are properly valued, the auditor could take a sample of recorded sales invoices and agree the price on the invoice to an authorized price list.

9-14 [LO 7] When testing a client's reconciliation between the sales subledger and the general ledger, the auditor is required to reperform the control.

9-15 [LO 8] The quality of evidence obtained from positive and negative confirmations is about the same.

9-16 [LO 8] To obtain evidence on the completeness assertion for revenue, the auditor would select a sample of shipping documents and trace them to the sales journal.

MULTIPLE-CHOICE QUESTIONS

9-17 [LO 1] Which of the following statements is true regarding assertions in the revenue cycle?

a. It is typical that all five assertions for revenue are equally important.

b. If a client has an incentive to overstate revenues, the existence assertion would be more relevant than the completeness assertion.

c. Audit evidence about the existence of revenues is also appropriate evidence about the valuation of receivables.

d. The allowance for doubtful accounts has important implications for the ownership assertion of accounts receivable.

9-18 [LO 1] Which of the following statements is true regarding the processing and recording of revenue transactions?

a. The accurate recording of revenue transactions is important for preparing financial statements, but not important for the client's management decisions.

b. Invoices should be prepared once the client determines that the goods ordered by a customer are available.

c. A bill of lading provides documentation that the customer has received the goods.

d. Sales transactions typically begin with the receipt of a purchase order from a customer.

9-19 [LO 2] Which of the following would *not* represent a factor the auditor would consider when assessing the inherent risk associated with a sales transaction?

a. The existence of terms that specify the right of return or the right to modify the purchase agreement.

b. Contracts that are a combination of leases and sales.

c. Goods billed according to a percentage-of-completion methodology.

d. The nature of the credit authorization process.

9-20 [LO 2] Which of the following statements is false regarding inherent risks associated with accounts receivable?

a. The rights and obligations assertion for accounts receivable may have a high level of inherent risk if the company sells or pledges accounts receivable.

b. If accounts receivable are improperly aged, the allowance for doubtful accounts may be misstated.

c. If the client accepts orders from customers with poor credit, the risk associated with the valuation of net accounts receivable is not affected since the customer did indeed place the order.

d. Having the collection of a receivable be contingent on specific events that cannot be easily estimated increases the inherent risk of misstatement of the accounts receivable account.

9-21 [LO 3] Which of the following factors is not a motivation for clients to fraudulently misstate revenue?

a. Bankruptcy may be imminent.

b. Management bonuses are contingent on a certain revenue goal.

c. Controls over revenue process are ineffective.

d. Management wants to meet publicly announced earnings expectations.

9-22 `LO 3` Which of the following explanations best describes the purpose of lapping?

a. Lapping is a technique used by client personnel to cover up the embezzlement of cash.

b. Lapping is an approach used by client personnel to eliminate differences between a customer's records and the client's records reported on confirmations.

c. Lapping is a procedure used by the auditor to obtain evidence when a positive confirmation is not returned by the client's customer.

d. Lapping is an agreement containing contract terms that are not part of a formal sales contract.

9-23 `LO 4` Which of the following should an auditor gain an understanding of as part of the risk assessment procedures?

a. Internal controls related to revenue recognition.

b. Revenue-related computer applications.

c. Key revenue-related documents.

d. All of the above.

9-24 `LO 4` Consider an organization that sells products through a catalog and takes orders over the phone. All orders are entered online, and the organization's objective is to ship all orders within 24 hours. The audit trail is kept in machine-readable form. The only papers generated are the packing slip and the invoice sent to the customer. Revenue is recorded upon shipment of the goods. The organization maintains a detailed customer database that allows the customer to return goods for credit at any time. The company maintains a product database containing all the authorized prices. Only the marketing manager has authorization to make changes in the price database. The marketing manager either makes the changes or authorizes the changes by signing an authorization form, and his assistant implements the changes. Which of the following controls would be *least* effective in assuring that the correct product is shipped and that it is billed at the approved price?

a. Self-checking digits are used on all product numbers, and customers must order from a catalog with product numbers.

b. The sales order taker verbally verifies both the product description and price with the customer before the order is closed for processing.

c. The sales order taker prepares batch totals of the number of items ordered and the total dollar amount for all items processed during a specified period of time (e.g., one hour).

d. The product price table is restricted to the director of marketing, who alone can approve changes to the price file.

9-25 `LO 5` Which of the following statements is false regarding preliminary analytical procedures in the revenue cycle?

a. Since revenue is typically regarded as a high-risk account, preliminary analytical procedures related to revenue are not required.

b. Auditors completing preliminary analytical procedures do not need to use the four-step process that would be required for substantive analytical procedures.

    c. Trend analysis would not be appropriate as a preliminary analytical procedure in the revenue cycle.

    d. All of the above statements are false.

9-26 `LO 5` Assume that an auditor expected that the client's activities related to sales and accounts receivable would be similar to industry averages. Which of the following relationships detected as part of preliminary analytical procedures would suggest a heighted risk of misstatement in the revenue cycle?

    a. The number of days' sales in accounts receivable increased from 44 days in the prior year to 65 days in the year being audited. The industry average increased from 45 to 47 days.

    b. The gross margin increased from 16.7% to 18.3%, while the industry average changed from 16.7% to 16.3%.

    c. Accounts receivable increased 35% over the prior year, while sales stayed relatively stable.

    d. All of the above.

9-27 `LO 6` After identifying the risks of material misstatement, the auditor develops an audit plan in response to those risks. Which of the following plans for testing revenue would be most likely when the auditor believes that control risk is high?

    a. The only evidence the auditor plans to obtain is from tests of details.

    b. The auditor plans to obtain 40% of the necessary audit evidence from tests of controls, and the remaining 60% from substantive analytical procedures.

    c. The auditor plans to obtain the majority of the necessary audit evidence from tests of controls.

    d. Any of the above would be an appropriate audit plan if the auditor believes that control risk is high.

9-28 `LO 6` Responding to identified risks involves developing an audit approach that addresses those risks. Which of the following statements about the planned audit approach is true?

    a. The audit approach needs to include tests of controls, substantive analytical procedures, and tests of details.

    b. The audit approach will typically require more evidence for higher-risk areas than lower-risk areas.

    c. The audit approach should follow the audit firm's standardized audit program.

    d. The sufficiency and appropriateness of selected procedures will not vary across assertions.

9-29 `LO 7` When auditing a nonpublic company, the auditor would generally make a decision not to test the operating effectiveness of controls in which of the following situations?

    a. The preliminary assessment of control risk is at the maximum.

    b. It is more cost efficient to directly test ending account balances than to test controls.

    c. The auditor believes that controls are designed effectively, but are not operating as described.

    d. All of the above are situations when the auditor would likely not test the operating effectiveness of controls.

9-30 `LO 7` An auditor performs tests of controls in the sales cycle. First, the auditor makes inquiries of company personnel about credit-granting policies. The auditor then selects a sample of sales transactions and examines documentary evidence of credit approval. This test of controls most likely supports which of the financial statement assertion(s)?

Completeness	Valuation or Allocation
a. Yes	Yes
b. No	Yes
c. Yes	No
d. No	No

9-31 `LO 8` To test the completeness of sales, the auditor would select a sample of transactions from which of the following populations?
a. Customer order file.
b. Open invoice file.
c. Bill of lading file.
d. Sales invoice file.

9-32 `LO 8` The auditor is concerned that fictitious sales have been recorded. The best audit procedure to identify the existence of the fictitious sales would be to perform which of the following?
a. Select a sample of recorded sales invoices and trace to shipping documents (bills of lading and packing slips) to verify shipment of goods.
b. Select a random sample of shipping documents (bills of lading) and trace to the sales invoice to determine whether the invoice was properly recorded.
c. Select a sample of customer purchase orders and trace through to the generation of a sales invoice.
d. Select a sample of customer purchase orders to determine whether a valid customer actually exists.

REVIEW AND SHORT CASE QUESTIONS

9-33 `LO 1` Refer to Exhibit 9.1. Which accounts are typically affected by transactions in the revenue cycle? Identify the relationships among them.

9-34 `LO 1` For accounts receivable, what are the more relevant assertions? Why should an auditor identify which assertions are more relevant?

9-35 `LO 1` Refer to Exhibit 9.2. What are the major activities involved in generating and recording a sales transaction? What are the major documents generated as a part of each activity?

9-36 `LO 2` An important task in the audit of the revenue cycle is determining whether a client has appropriately recognized revenue.
a. In assessing the risks associated with revenue recognition, the auditor of U.S. companies will likely consult criteria provided by the SEC. What general criteria has the SEC used to help determine if revenue can be recognized? Why might the auditor need to do additional research and consider additional criteria on revenue recognition?
b. The following are situations in which the auditor will be required to make decisions about the amount of revenue to be recognized. For each of the following scenarios (labeled 1–6 below):
   • Identify the key issues to address in determining whether or not revenue should be recognized.
   • Identify additional information the auditor may want to gather in making a decision on revenue recognition.

NOTE: Completing Review and Short Case Questions does not require the student to reference additional resources and materials.

NOTE: For the remaining problems, we make special note of those addressing fraud, international issues, professional skepticism, and ethics.

- Based only on the information presented, develop a rationale for either the recognition or nonrecognition of revenue.

1. AOL sells software that is unique as a provider of Internet services. The software contract includes a service fee of $19.95 for up to 500 hours of Internet service each month. The minimum requirement is a one-year contract. The company proposes to immediately recognize 30% of the first-year's contract as revenue from the sale of software and 70% as Internet services on a monthly basis as fees are collected from the customer.

2. Modis Manufacturing builds specialty packaging machinery for other manufacturers. All of the products are high end and range in sales price from $5 million to $25 million.
A major customer is rebuilding one of its factories and has ordered three machines with total revenue for Modis of $45 million. The contracted date to complete the production was November, and the company met the contract date. The customer acknowledges the contract and confirms the amount. However, because the factory is not yet complete, it has asked Modis to hold the products in the warehouse as a courtesy until its building is complete.

3. Standish Stoneware has developed a new low-end line of baking products that will be sold directly to consumers and to low-end discount retailers. The company had previously sold high-end silverware products to specialty stores and has a track record of returned items for the high-end stores. The new products tend to have more defects, but the defects are not necessarily recognizable in production. For example, they are more likely to crack when first used in baking. The company does not have a history of returns from these products, but because the products are new it grants each customer the right to return the merchandise for a full refund or replacement within one year of purchase.

4. Omer Technologies is a high-growth company that sells electronic products to the custom copying business. It is an industry with high innovation, but Omer's technology is basic. In order to achieve growth, management has empowered the sales staff to make special deals to increase sales in the fourth quarter of the year. The sales deals include a price break and an increased salesperson commission but not an extension of either the product warranty or the customer's right to return the product.

5. Electric City is a new company in the Chicago area that has the exclusive right to a new technology that saves municipalities a substantial amount of energy for large-scale lighting purposes (for example, for ball fields, parking lots, and shopping centers). The technology has been shown to be very cost-effective in Europe. In order to get new customers to try the product, the sales force allows customers to try the product for up to six months to prove the amount of energy savings they will realize. The company is so confident that customers will buy the product that it allows this pilot-testing period. Revenue is recognized at the time the product is installed at the customer location, with a small provision made for potential returns.

6. Jackson Products decided to quit manufacturing a line of its products and outsourced the production. However, much of its

manufacturing equipment could be used by other companies. In addition, it had over $5 million of new manufacturing equipment on order in a noncancelable deal. The company decided to become a sales representative to sell the new equipment ordered and its existing equipment. All of the sales were recorded as revenue.

9-37 [LO 2] Refer to Exhibit 9.3. What are some examples of sales transactions that involve product delivery that might have a high level of inherent risk?

9-38 [LO 3] Why should auditors ordinarily consider revenue recognition to be a fraud risk factor? What are some reasons that management might want to fraudulently overstate revenue? `FRAUD`

9-39 [LO 3] Refer to Exhibit 9.4 and to the *Auditing in Practice* features "Channel Stuffing at ArthroCare—The Importance of Professional Skepticism" and "The Importance of Professional Skepticism in Auditing Revenue at Tvia." What methods have been used to fraudulently inflate revenue? How can auditors use professional skepticism to help identify these fraud schemes? `FRAUD` `PROFESSIONAL SKEPTICISM`

9-40 [LO 3] What steps should an auditor take to help identify fraud risk factors? `FRAUD`

9-41 [LO 4] Refer to Exhibits 9.5 and 9.6. What are a control risk assessment questionnaire and a controls matrix? How are these documents used by the auditor?

9-42 [LO 4] Why are monthly customer statements considered a control? Why is it important to separate the duties of responding to customer complaints from the accounts receivable and cash collection functions?

9-43 [LO 4] Refer to the *Auditing in Practice* feature "Risks Associated with Sales Returns: The Case of Medicis and Ernst & Young." What problems can occur if controls related to sales returns and allowances are not designed and operating effectively?

9-44 [LO 4] Field, CPA, is auditing the financial statements of Miller Mailorder, Inc. (MMI). Field has compiled a list of possible inherent and fraud risks in the revenue cycle that may result in the misstatement of MMI's financial statements and a corresponding list of internal controls, which, if properly designed and implemented, could assist MMI in preventing or detecting material misstatements. For each risk numbered 1 through 15 in column 1, select one internal control from column 2 (labeled a. through t.), which, if properly designed and implemented, most likely could assist MMI in preventing or detecting material misstatements. Internal controls can be selected for more than one risk. `FRAUD`

Inherent and Fraud Risks	Internal Controls
1. Invoices for goods sold are posted to incorrect customer accounts.	a. Shipping clerks compare goods received from the warehouse with the details on the shipping documents.
2. Goods ordered by customers are shipped but are not billed to anyone.	b. Approved sales orders are required for goods to be released from the warehouse.
3. Invoices are sent for shipped goods but are not recorded in the sales journal.	c. Monthly statements are mailed to all customers with outstanding balances.
4. Invoices are sent for shipped goods and are recorded in the	

(continued)

Inherent and Fraud Risks	Internal Controls
sales journal but are not posted to any customer account.	d. Shipping clerks compare goods received from the warehouse with approved sales orders.
5. Credit sales are made to individuals with unsatisfactory credit ratings.	e. Customer orders are compared with the inventory master file to determine whether items ordered are in stock.
6. Goods are removed from inventory for unauthorized orders.	
7. Goods shipped to customers do not agree with goods ordered by customers.	f. Daily sales summaries are compared with control totals of invoices.
8. Invoices are sent to allies in a fraudulent scheme, and sales are recorded for fictitious transactions.	g. Shipping documents are compared with sales invoices when goods are shipped.
9. Customers' checks are received for less than the customers' full account balances, but the customers' full account balances are credited.	h. Sales invoices are compared with the master price file.
	i. Customer orders are compared with an approved customer list.
	j. Sales orders are prepared for each customer order.
10. Customers' checks are misappropriated before they are forwarded to the cashier for deposit.	k. Control amounts posted to the accounts receivable ledger are compared with control totals of invoices.
11. Customers' checks are credited to incorrect customer accounts.	
12. Different customer accounts are each credited for the same cash receipt.	l. Sales invoices are compared with shipping documents and approved customer orders before invoices are mailed.
13. Customers' checks are properly credited to customer accounts and are properly deposited, but errors are made in recording receipts in the cash receipts journal.	m. Prenumbered credit memos are used for granting credit for goods returned.
14. Customers' checks are misappropriated after they are forwarded to the cashier for deposit.	n. Goods returned for credit are approved by the supervisor of the sales department.
15. Invalid transactions granting credit for sales returns are recorded.	o. Remittance advices are separated from the checks in the mailroom and forwarded to the accounting department.
	p. Total amounts posted to the accounts receivable ledger from remittance advices are compared with the validated bank deposit slip.
	q. The cashier examines each check for proper endorsement.
	r. Validated deposit slips are compared with the cashier's daily cash summaries.
	s. An employee, other than the bookkeeper, periodically prepares a bank reconciliation.
	t. The same employee who issues receiving reports evidencing actual return of goods approves sales returns.

9-45 LO 5 Refer to Exhibit 9.7. Identify preliminary analytical procedures that can help auditors identify areas of potential material misstatements in the revenue cycle.

9-46 LO 5 Consider an audit client that manufactures fishing boats and sells them all over the country. Boats are sold to dealers who finance their purchases with their banks. The banks usually pay your client within two weeks of shipment. The company's profits have been increasing over the past several years. To perform preliminary analytical procedures you have obtained the following information related to your 2014 audit ($ in millions):

	2014**	2013*	2012*	2011*	2010*	Major Competitor (2014)
Accounts receivable	6.8	3.3	2.3	1.8	1.7	4.2
Inventory	16.0	10.0	7.2	5.5	5.1	13.9
Accounts payable	3.1	2.6	1.9	1.5	1.4	3.2
Sales	84.7	77.9	56.8	43.6	39.8	110.3
Gross profit (%)	19	17	18	17	18	21
Number of days' sales in receivables	29	16	15	16	16	14
Number of Days' Sales in ending inventory	69	47	46	46	47	46

*Audited
**Unaudited

a. Assume that you had expected that your client's performance would be similar to that of the client's major competitor. Based on these expectations, identify potential risk areas and explain why they represent potential risks.
b. Suggest possible explanations for any unexpected results.
c. What inquiries and follow-up audit procedures might be performed to determine the accuracy of the client's data?
d. As part of the brainstorming session, be prepared to discuss how the CFO might use accounts receivable and inventory to conceal the embezzlement of cash.
e. Discuss the importance of professional skepticism when performing preliminary analytical procedures.

9-47 LO 5 Stainless Steel Specialties (SSS) is a manufacturer of hot water–based heating systems for homes and commercial businesses. The company has grown about 10% in each of the past five years.

The company has not made any acquisitions. Following are some of the statistics for the company:

Overview of Operational Data Stainless Steel Specialties (SSS)
(Sales and Net Income Reported in $ Millions)

	2010	2011	2012	2013	2014 (unaudited)
Sales	$800	$880	$950	$1,050	$1,300
Net income	$28	$38	$42	$52	$68
Stock price	$17	$24	$19	$28	$47
Economic growth in areas served (index with 1.00 for 20 × 1)	1.00	1.04	1.09	1.13	1.14
Percent of heating market by SSS	8.9	9.4	9.6	10.8	14.0
Accounts receivable	$180	$170	$196	$210	$297
Percent of sales made in last quarter	38	36	40	38	43
Gross margin (%)	28.0	28.3	28.8	29.2	33.6

Additional information available to the auditor includes the following:

- The company has touted its new and improved technology for the increase both in sales and in gross margin.
- The company claims to have decreased administrative expense, thus increasing net profits.
- The company has reorganized its sales process to a more centralized approach and has empowered individual sales managers to negotiate better prices to drive sales as long as the amounts are within corporate guidelines.
- The company has changed its salesperson compensation by increasing the commission on sales to new customers.
- Sales commissions are no longer affected by returned goods if the goods are returned more than 90 days after sale and/or by not collecting the receivables. SSS has justified the changes in sales commissions on the following grounds:
- The salesperson is not responsible for quality issues—the main reason that products are returned.
- The salesperson is not responsible for approving credit; rather credit approval is under the direction of the global sales manager.
  a. What is the importance of the information about salesperson compensation to the audit of receivables and revenue? Explain how the information would be used in performing preliminary analytical procedures.
  b. Perform preliminary analytical review procedures using the data included in the table and the information about the change in performance. What are the important insights that the auditor should gain from performing the analytical review?

    c. Why should the auditor be interested in a company's stock price when performing an audit, since stock price is dependent, at least in part, on audited financial reports?

    d. What information about SSS might be considered as fraud risk factors?

    e. Identify specific substantive audit procedures that should be performed as a result of the preliminary analytical procedures performed by the auditor.

9-48 `LO 6` How do auditors use their knowledge about the risk of material misstatement, including their knowledge of the design effectiveness of controls, in developing an audit approach? Comment on extensiveness of testing, types of audit procedures, and the rigor of audit procedures in higher- versus lower-risk settings.

9-49 `LO 6` Refer to Exhibit 9.8. Describe the differences in the planned audit approaches for Clients A and B and the reasons for such differences.

9-50 `LO 6` Read the following description of Drea Tech Company and identify the elements of inherent risk associated with the revenue cycle. Determine the appropriate audit response (audit procedure) to address the risks.

    Drea Tech Company has been growing rapidly and has recently engaged your firm as its auditor. It is actively traded over the counter and management believes it has outgrown the service capabilities of its previous auditor. However, on contacting the previous auditor, you learn that a dispute led to the firm's dismissal. The client wanted to recognize income on contracts for items produced but not shipped. The client believed the contracts were firm and that all the principal revenue-producing activities were performed. The change in accounting principle would have increased net income by 33% during the last year.

    Drea is 32% owned by Anthony Dreason, who has a reputation as a turnaround artist. He bought out the previous owner of Drea Tech three years ago. The company's primary products are in the materials handling business, such as automated conveyors for warehouses and production lines. Dreason has increased profits by slashing operating expenses, most notably personnel and research and development. In addition, he has outsourced a significant portion of component part production. Approximately 10% of the company's product is now obtained from Materials Movement, Inc., a privately held company 50% owned by Dreason and his brother.

    A brief analysis of previous financial statements shows that sales have been increasing by approximately 20% per year since Dreason assumed control. Profitability has increased even more. However, a tour of the plant gives the impression that it is somewhat old and not kept up to date. Additionally, a large amount of inventory is sitting near the receiving dock awaiting final disposition.

9-51 `LO 7` What is the effect on the substantive tests of accounts receivable when the risk of material misstatement is assessed as low rather than high because a client has effective internal controls? Provide specific examples.

9-52 `LO 7` When assessing whether the controls are operating effectively, does the auditor need to reperform the control? For example, if personnel check the correctness of computations on an invoice and initial the bottom of a document to indicate that the control has been performed, does the auditor need to reperform the procedure? Explain the rationale for your response.

9-53 [LO 7] The following is a list of controls (numbered 1 through 7 below) typically implemented in the revenue cycle.

a. For each control identified, briefly indicate the financial misstatement that could occur if the control is not implemented effectively.

b. Identify a test of control that the auditor can perform to determine the operating effectiveness of the control.

1. All transactions under $10,000 may be approved by the computer authorization program. The credit manager must approve all transactions over $10,000.

2. All invoices are priced according to the authorized price list maintained on the computer. Either the regional or divisional sales manager must approve any exceptions.

3. All shipping documents are prenumbered and periodically accounted for. Shipping document references are noted on all sales invoices.

4. Customer complaints regarding receipt of goods are routed to a customer service representative. Any discrepancies are immediately followed up to determine the cause of the discrepancy.

5. All merchandise returns must be received by the receiving department and recorded on prenumbered documents for receipts. A document is created for each item (or batches of like items). Returns are sent to quality control for testing, and a recommendation for ultimate disposition is made (scrap, rework and sell as a second, or close out as is), noted, and sent to accounting for proper inventorying.

6. The quantity of items invoiced is reconciled with the packing document developed on receipt of the order and the shipping notice by a computer program as the goods are marked for shipment. If discrepancies appear, the shipping document prevails. A discrepancy report is prepared daily and sent to the warehouse manager for follow-up.

7. The company pays all freight charges, but the customer is charged a freight fee based on a minimum amount and a sliding scale as a percentage of the total invoice. The policy is documented, and the computer automatically adds the charge.

9-54 [LO 7] Most accounting systems have the ability to generate exception reports that immediately identify control procedure failures or transactions that are out of the norm so that management can determine whether any special action is needed.

a. Identify how the auditor might use each of the following four types of exception reports (labeled 1. through 4. below) in assessing the effectiveness of controls.

b. For each type of exception report address the following question. If the exceptions are properly followed up and corrected, would the fact that many exceptions occurred affect the auditor's judgment of the effectiveness of controls and the auditor's assessment of control risk? Explain.

1. A list of all invoices over $5,000 for which credit was not preauthorized by the credit manager (the computer program is designed so that if the authorization is not provided within 24 hours of the original notice to the credit manager, the shipment is made as if it were authorized). This exception report goes to the credit manager.

2. A report of any sales volume to one customer exceeding $2 million in a month sent to the sales manager with a copy to the credit manager.

3. A report of exceptions for which shipping documents and packing slips did not reconcile.

4. A report noting that goods ordered were not shipped (or back-ordered) within five days of receipt of the order as is required per company policy.

9-55 `LO 7` The audit of the revenue cycle accounts of Acco, Inc. has been planned with a low preliminary assessment of control risk related to each of the relevant assertions. A sample of sales transactions was selected for testing. Each of the following types of control or transaction processing deficiencies uncovered in the sample was significant enough to cause the auditor to increase control risk assessment from low to moderate. For each deficiency (labeled as a. though i. below) discuss the type of financial statement misstatement that may result, the assertion(s) affected, and the effect on the nature, timing, and/or extent of related substantive tests. Each type of deficiency should be considered independently from the others.

a. No evidence that price and quantity on the invoice were compared with the supporting documents

b. Failure to approve customer credit before shipping the merchandise on open account

c. Recording sales before they were shipped

d. Recording sales several days after they should have been recorded

e. Recording sales several days before and several days after they should have been recorded

f. Lack of customer orders; items were shipped

g. Lack of shipping documents; customer order was found

h. Incorrect invoice price

i. Quantity shipped differed from the quantity billed

9-56 `LO 7` Assume the auditor wishes to test controls over the shipment and recording of sales transactions. Identify the controls that the auditor would expect to find to achieve the objective that all transactions are recorded correctly, and in the correct time period. For each control identified, indicate how the auditor would test whether the control operated effectively.

9-57 `LO 8` Refer to the *Auditing in Practice* feature "Performing Appropriate Substantive Procedures in the Revenue Cycle: The Case of Kyoto Audit Corporation." What substantive procedures did Kyoto not perform appropriately? If such procedures are not performed appropriately, will the client's financial statements be misstated? Explain your answer.

9-58 `LO 8` When might it be advisable to send the confirmation to the customer's personnel who are familiar with the details of sales contracts rather than to the accounts payable department?

9-59 `LO 8`

a. Refer to Exhibit 9.10. What are typical substantive procedures in the revenue cycle, and how are these procedures related to management assertions?

b. For the following procedures (numbered 1 through 6), indicate the assertion that is being tested.

1. Take a block of shipping orders and account for the invoicing of all items in the block and account for the prenumbering of the documents.

2. Review the general access controls to the computer application and the authorized ability to make changes to computer price files.

3. Recompute the invoice total and individual line items on a sample of sales invoices.
4. Review client documentation to determine policy for credit authorization.
5. Select a sample of shipping notices and trace to invoices.
6. Randomly sample entries into the sales journal and trace back to sales orders and shipping documents.

9-60 LO 8   Refer to Exhibit 9.11. What is an aged trial balance of accounts receivable? How does an auditor use it? How does an auditor determine that it is correctly aged?

9-61 LO 8   Refer to Exhibits 9.12 and 9.13. Distinguish between the positive and negative forms of accounts receivable confirmations. Which confirmation type, positive or negative, is considered the more reliable? Why?

9-62 LO 8   If a confirmation is not returned by a customer, what follow-up work should the auditor perform for (a) positive confirmations and (b) negative confirmations?

FRAUD   **9-63** LO 8   Identify potential fraud risk factors in the revenue cycle. What substantive audit procedures could be used to help determine if fraud has occurred in the revenue cycle?

9-64 LO 8   Address the following questions about the confirmation of customers' accounts receivable.
a. Why do confirmations not typically provide reliable evidence about the completeness assertion?
b. What is a confirmation exception, and why is it important to investigate a confirmation exception?
c. When should an auditor perform alternative procedures to substantiate the existence of accounts receivable?
d. Under what condition would substantive testing of accounts receivable before the balance sheet date be appropriate?

9-65 LO 8   During a discussion, one auditor noted that her approach to testing sales transactions was to select a random sample of recorded sales and trace back through the system to supporting documents, noting that all items billed were shipped and were invoiced at correct prices. She stated that she then had good confidence about the correctness of the sales account, and, therefore, having performed a dual-purpose test, the remaining work on sales (assuming the procedures also evidenced the working of control procedures) could be limited.

A second auditor disagreed. Her approach was to select evidence of shipments, such as prenumbered shipping documents, and then trace forward through the system to the actual invoice, noting the existence of control procedures and the correctness of the invoice processing. If no exceptions were noted, however, she agreed with the first auditor that the remaining audit work on the sales account could be limited.
a. Which auditor is right, or are both right? Explain.
b. What assertion is tested by the second auditor?
c. What is a dual-purpose test? Explain whether the tests performed by both of the auditors would be considered dual-purpose tests.

9-66 LO 8   Bert Finney, CPA, was engaged to conduct an audit of the financial statements of Clayton Realty Corporation for the month ending January 31, 2014. Examining documentation of the monthly rent reconciliation is an important part of the audit engagement.

The following rent reconciliation was prepared by the controller of Clayton Realty Corporation and was presented to Finney, who subjected it to various audit procedures:

Clayton Realty Corporation
Rent Reconciliation
For the Month Ended January 31, 2014

Gross apartment rents (Schedule A)	$1,600,800†
Less vacancies (Schedule B)	20,500†
Net apartment rentals	1,580,300
Less unpaid January rents (Schedule C)	7,800†
Total	1,572,500
Add prepaid rent collected (Apartment 116)	500†
Total cash collected	$1,573,000†

Schedules A, B, and C are available to Finney but are not presented here. Finney evaluated and tested internal controls and found that they could be relied on to produce reliable accounting information. Cash receipts from rental operations are deposited in a special bank account.

What substantive audit procedures should Finney use during the audit to obtain evidence of each of the dollar amounts marked by the dagger (†)?

9-67 **LO 8** You are auditing the revenue from membership fees of your local chapter of the Institute of Management Accountants, of which you are not a member. The local chapter receives an allocation of national dues. The remainder of the dues comes from chapter members. The chapter maintains a detailed list of membership. Describe some substantive analytical procedures you could use to provide assurance that fee revenue is fairly stated.

9-68 **LO 8** As part of the audit of KC Enterprises, the auditor assessed control risk for the existence and valuation assertions related to accounts receivable at the maximum level. Katie, the staff person assigned to the engagement, sent positive confirmation requests to a sample of the company customers based on their balances as of December 31, 2013. For each of the three customers described here, review the relevant confirmation letter and Katie's comments at the bottom of each. Select the procedure that should be followed to clear the exception, if one exists. Choose only one procedure per confirmation. A procedure may be used once, more than once, or not at all.
a.

February 1, 2014

Meehan Marine Sales, Inc.
1284 River Road
Louisville, Kentucky 40059

Re: Balance at December 31, 2013—$267,000

As of December 31, 2013, our records indicate your balance with our company as the amount listed above. Please complete and sign the

(continued)

bottom portion of this letter and return the entire letter to our auditors, GJ LLP, P.O. Box 100, Orlando, Florida 32806.

A stamped, self-addressed envelope is enclosed for your convenience.

Sincerely,

_____

KC Enterprises

· ·

The above balance is   Correct

                     X   Incorrect (show amount)   *$325,000*

If incorrect, please provide information that could help to reconcile your account.

Response: We placed an order for $58,000 on December 26, 2013.

Signature:_____
Title:_____
Date:_____

_____

Katie's note to file:
    Per discussion with the controller and review of relevant documentation, the order for $58,000 was shipped f.o.b. shipping point on December 30, 2013, and was received by the customer on January 3, 2014. Therefore, the client has made no entry to record the sale in 2013.

b.

February 1, 2014

West Coast Ski Center, Inc.
163 Tide Avenue
Monterey, California 93940

Re: Balance at December 31, 2013—$414,000

As of December 31, 2013, our records indicate your balance with our company as the amount listed above. Please complete and sign the bottom portion of this letter and return the entire letter to our auditors, GJ LLP, P.O. Box 100, Orlando, Florida 32806.

A stamped, self-addressed envelope is enclosed for your convenience.

Sincerely,

_____

(continued)

KC Enterprises

· ·

The above balance is   Correct

                     X   Incorrect (show amount)   _$508,000_

If incorrect, please provide information that could help to reconcile your account.

Response: We made a payment of $94,000 on December 12, 2013.

Signature:_____
Title:_____
Date:_____

_____

Katie's note to file:
  Per discussion with the controller and review of relevant documentation, the company received the payment of $94,000 on December 15, 2013, and posted it to "Other Income."

c.

February 1, 2014

Fish & Ski World, Inc.
5660 Ocean Blvd
Port Arkansas, Texas 78373

Re: Balance at December 31, 2013—$72,000

As of December 31, 2013, our records indicate your balance with our company as the amount listed above. Please complete and sign the bottom portion of this letter and return the entire letter to our auditors, GJ LLP, P.O. Box 100, Orlando, Florida 32806.

A stamped, self-addressed envelope is enclosed for your convenience.

Sincerely,

_____

KC Enterprises

· ·

The above balance is   Correct

                     X   Incorrect (show amount)   _$163,000_

If incorrect, please provide information that could help to reconcile your account.

(continued)

Response: Per our records, the following invoices are outstanding:
  Invoice #4212 $72,000
  Invoice #4593 $66,000
  Invoice #4738 $25,000

Signature:_____
 Title:_____
Date:_____

_____

Katie's note to file:
  Per review of the A/R aging report, invoices #4593 and 4738 are not
  on the A/R aging report at December 31, 2013.

Possible procedures:
1. Not an exception, no adjustment necessary. Determine the sufficiency of allowance for doubtful accounts.
2. Exception noted; propose adjustment and request that the controller post it to the accounting records.
3. Verify by examining subsequent cash collections and/or shipping documents.
4. Review appropriate documentation to verify that additional invoices noted on confirmation pertain to the subsequent year.

9-69 **LO 8** Read the following scenario about Strang Corporation and identify the substantive procedures that the CPA (Stanley) should perform to determine whether lapping exists. Do not discuss deficiencies in the system of internal control.

During the year, Strang Corporation began to encounter cash flow difficulties, and a cursory review by management revealed receivable collection problems. Strang's management engaged Elaine Stanley, CPA, to perform a special investigation. Stanley studied the billing and collection cycle and noted the following:

The accounting department employs one bookkeeper who receives and opens all incoming mail. This bookkeeper is also responsible for depositing receipts, filing daily remittance advices, recording receipts in the cash receipts journal, and posting receipts in the individual customer accounts and the general ledger accounts. There are no cash sales. The bookkeeper prepares and controls the mailing of monthly statements to customers.

The concentration of functions and the receivable collection problems caused Stanley to suspect that a systematic defalcation of customers' payments through a delayed posting of remittances (lapping of accounts receivable) is present. Stanley was surprised to find that no customers complained about receiving erroneous monthly statements.

9-70 **LO 8** Your audit client, Madison, Inc., has a computerized accounts receivable system. There are two master files, a customer data file and an unpaid invoice file. The customer data file contains the customer's name, billing address, shipping address, identification number, phone number, purchase and cash payment history, and credit limit. For each unpaid invoice, the second file contains the customer's identification number, invoice number and date, date of shipment, method of shipment, credit terms, and gross invoice amount. Discuss how GAS could be used to aid in the audit of Madison's accounts receivable.

9-71 ▮LO 8▮ You have sent confirmations to 40 customers of Berg-Shovick Express, a long-time audit client experiencing some financial difficulty. The company sells specialized high-technology goods. You have received confirmations from 32 of the 40 positive confirmations sent. A few minor errors were noted on these accounts, but the projected amount of errors on the confirmations returned is just below tolerable error. The following information is available to you:

Book value of receivables	$7,782,292
Book value of items selected for confirmations	$3,100,110
Book value of items confirmed	$1,464,000
Audit value of items confirmed	$1,335,000

Summary of items selected but confirmations not returned:

Name	Outstanding Amount	Management Comments on Account Balance
Yunkel Specialty Mfg.	$432,000	Regular sales, but extended credit terms were given on $200,000 of goods. Yunkel has responded that it does not respond to confirmations.
Hi-Tech Combonitics	$300,000	No response to either confirmation request. Management indicates the sale was a special-term sale, and the goods are being held for the convenience of this company. The company is located in Albuquerque, New Mexico, and recently had a fire in its main production plant but expects to resume production early next month. The goods will be shipped as soon as production begins, but the sale has legally been completed.
Beaver Dam Electronics	$275,000	Account balance represents sales of specialty products made in late December. The president of Berg-Shovick has orally confirmed the receivable because Beaver Dam Electronics is 50% owned by him.
California Hi-Fi	$200,000	Regular sales, but company has renegotiated its account balance due because of defective merchandise. Management has indicated it has issued a credit to the company, but because management had inspected the goods on the customer's property, it did not require the return of the merchandise. It expects the company to pay the $200,000.
Brenner Specialties	$175,000	Regular sales. This is a new company. Most of the sales ($100,000) were made in December.

(continues)

Name	Outstanding Amount	Management Comments on Account Balance
Sprague Electronics	$100,000	Regular sales. Customer is negotiating a potential return of defective items.
Williams Pipeline	$100,000	Williams is a large company. Prior experience indicates that it does not respond to confirmations.
Long Tom Towers	$54,110	Customer is new this year and is located in Medicine Hat. Saskatchewan.

a. Indicate the audit procedures (and be specific as to what those procedures will accomplish) to complete the work on accounts receivable related to the confirmation process. In other words, identify the specific alternative audit procedures that should be performed.

b. Assuming that all items could not be cleared to the auditor's satisfaction, identify the audit procedures that should be implemented to finish auditing the valuation and existence assertions for accounts receivable.

10

Auditing Cash and Marketable Securities

CHAPTER OVERVIEW AND LEARNING OBJECTIVES

A high volume of transactions flows through cash accounts. Because of the vulnerability to error or fraud, organizations and auditors usually emphasize the quality of controls over the cash transactions. In this chapter, we examine approaches that auditors take to assess risks associated with cash and to evaluate controls over cash accounts. We also address issues concerning the audit of marketable securities. In terms of the audit opinion formulation process, this chapter primarily involves Phases II, III, and IV—performing risk assessment procedures, tests of controls, and substantive procedures for cash and marketable securities.

Through studying this chapter, you will be able to achieve these learning objectives:

通过本章的学习，你将能够实现以下学习目标：

1. Identify the significant accounts, disclosures, and relevant assertions in auditing cash accounts.
   在审计现金账户时识别重要的账户、披露和相关的认定。

2. Identify and assess inherent risks of material misstatement in cash accounts.
   识别和评估现金账户重大错报的固有风险。

3. Identify and assess fraud risks of material misstatement in cash accounts.
   识别和评估现金账户重大错报的舞弊风险。

4. Identify and assess control risks of material misstatement in cash accounts.
   识别和评估现金账户重大错报的控制风险。

5. Describe how to use preliminary analytical procedures to identify possible material misstatements for cash accounts, disclosures, and assertions.
   描述如何运用初步的分析性程序识别与现金账户、披露和认定有关的可能的重大错报。

6. Determine appropriate responses to identified risks of material misstatement for cash accounts, disclosures, and assertions.
   明确对于识别的与现金账户、披露和认定有关的重大错报风险如何进行适当的反应。

7. Determine appropriate tests of controls and consider the results of tests of controls for cash accounts, disclosures, and assertions.
   确定适当的控制测试，并且考虑与现金账户、披露和认定有关的控制测试结果。

8. Determine and apply sufficient appropriate substantive audit procedures for testing cash accounts, disclosures, and assertions.
   确定和应用充分、适当的实质性审计程序以测试现金账户、披露和认定。

9. Identify types of marketable securities, articulate the risks and controls typically associated with these accounts, and outline an audit approach for testing these accounts.
   识别有价证券的类型，描述与这些账户典型相关的风险和控制，列出测试这些账户的审计方法。

10. Apply the frameworks for professional decision making and ethical decision making to issues involving the audit of cash accounts, disclosures, and assertions.
    运用职业决策和职业道德决策框架解决与现金账户、披露和认定审计有关的问题。

THE AUDIT OPINION FORMULATION PROCESS

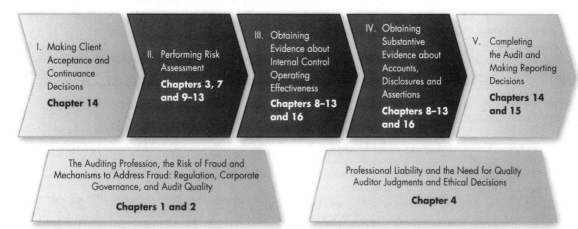

I. Making Client Acceptance and Continuance Decisions
Chapter 14

II. Performing Risk Assessment
Chapters 3, 7 and 9–13

III. Obtaining Evidence about Internal Control Operating Effectiveness
Chapters 8–13 and 16

IV. Obtaining Substantive Evidence about Accounts, Disclosures and Assertions
Chapters 8–13 and 16

V. Completing the Audit and Making Reporting Decisions
Chapters 14 and 15

The Auditing Profession, the Risk of Fraud and Mechanisms to Address Fraud: Regulation, Corporate Governance, and Audit Quality
Chapters 1 and 2

Professional Liability and the Need for Quality Auditor Judgments and Ethical Decisions
Chapter 4

The Audit Opinion Formulation Process and A Framework for Obtaining Audit Evidence
Chapters 5 and 6

PROFESSIONAL JUDGMENT IN CONTEXT

Fraudulent Petty Cash Transactions at Koss Corporation and the Fraud at Peregrine Financial Group, Inc.

This *Professional Judgment in Context* feature provides details on two high-profile frauds involving cash. The first, introduced in Chapter 2, involves Sue Sachdeva, former vice president of finance for Koss Corporation. Sachdeva orchestrated a $31 million embezzlement at Koss Corporation. In addition to expenditures at upscale clothing retailers, she used Koss funds on various luxury items such as a personal trainer, limousine rides, vacations, and items for her personal home. Astonishingly, more than 22,000 items—some with price tags still attached—were taken by federal authorities in connection with the investigation. The seized items included fur coats, designer clothing, jewelry, art items, and hundreds of pairs of shoes. As part of the embezzlement scheme, Sachdeva took more than $145,000 from petty cash, in increments ranging from $482 to $9,049. While that is a lot of disbursements coming out of petty cash, it is often true that petty cash doesn't get a lot of attention. Following this embezzlement, Koss took various remediation actions, which included eliminating the petty cash fund so that all

reimbursements are processed through standard controlled accounts payable processes.

The second fraud involves Russell Wasendorf, Sr., who attempted to commit suicide after embezzling over $200 million from Peregrine Financial Group's (PFG) brokerage clients over a 20-year period. His son, Russell Wasendorf, Jr., ran the operations of PFG and was the president and chief operating officer of the company, but did not have detailed access to important financial records of the company. Instead, Russell Wasendorf, Sr. had sole control of the company's bank accounts. Wasendorf, Sr. left a detailed suicide note in which he explained his actions and described how he committed the fraud. One part of the suicide note reads as follows: "I was able to conceal my crime of forgery by being the sole individual with access to the US Bank accounts held by PFG. No one else in the company ever saw an actual US Bank statement. I made counterfeit statements within a few hours of receiving the actual statements and gave the forgeries to the accounting department." He also stated:

"With careful concealment and blunt authority I was able to hide my fraud from others at PFG. If anyone questioned my authority I would simply point out that I was the sole shareholder. I ordered that US Bank statements were to be delivered directly to me unopened, to make sure no one was able to examine an actual US Bank Statement. On US Bank side, I told representatives at the Bank that I was the only person they should interface with at PFG."

The December 31, 2011, financial statements showed that PFG had over $220 million in its bank account, but in reality the bank account contained only about $6 million. What likely prompted the timing of Wasendorf's attempted suicide was the fact that the National Futures Association (NFA) had just implemented a change to its online system whereby bank statement information would be sent electronically from the banks directly to the NFA

(see *www.confirmation.com*). The NFA started receiving confirmations through that system one day before Wasendorf's attempted suicide. PFG filed for bankruptcy almost immediately after Wasendorf's attempted suicide and subsequent arrest. (See Problem 10-70 in the Contemporary and Historical Cases section for more details on the Wasendorf case.)

As you read through this chapter, consider the following questions:

- Why is cash an inherently risky account? (LO 2, 3)
- What controls should be in place to help ensure that cash accounts are not misappropriated? (LO 4)
- What are the audit implications of poor controls over cash accounts? (LO 6)
- What types of audit procedures would auditors employ when auditing cash? (LO 7, 8)

重要账户和相关认定

现金账户概述

 Identify the significant accounts, disclosures, and relevant assertions in auditing cash accounts.

Significant Accounts and Relevant Assertions

Overview of Cash Accounts

An organization may have many different kinds of cash accounts. Major types of cash accounts include general checking accounts, cash management accounts, petty cash, and imprest payroll accounts. In addition to these accounts, many organizations have **marketable security** accounts.

General Checking Accounts A general checking account is used for most cash transactions. The organization's regular cash receipts and disbursements are processed through this account. In some cases, the receipts are received directly by the bank through a lockbox or electronic funds transfers (EFT) and are directly deposited in the client's account by the bank. Most organizations have cash budgets to assist in planning disbursements, and they have cash management arrangements with the bank to temporarily invest excess funds in interest-bearing securities.

Cash Management Accounts Good cash management requires the organization to earn the greatest possible return on idle cash balances. Most organizations have developed relationships with their financial institutions to move excess cash into and out of short-term savings accounts to generate extra returns.

Imprest Payroll Accounts Some organizations disburse their payroll through an **imprest bank account**, into which cash is deposited as needed to cover payroll checks when they are issued. If the employees cash all payroll checks, the bank balance returns to zero. The need for an imprest payroll account is disappearing as most organizations now directly deposit employees' earnings into their respective bank accounts.

Petty Cash Accounts Almost all organizations use one or more petty cash accounts to disburse funds to employees who are authorized to make various purchases on behalf of the organization. The petty cash fund should have a sufficient amount of money to pay for routine expenses. While most petty cash funds involve only a small amount of money, a risk of fraud is associated with this fund, as illustrated in the *Professional Judgment in Context* feature (the first fraud that was discussed). As that example illustrates, the cumulative disbursements made through petty cash funds can become significant.

Cash Management Techniques

现金管理方法

Cash management techniques have been developed to (1) speed the collection and deposit of cash while minimizing the possibility of error or fraud in the process, (2) reduce the amount of paperwork, and (3) automate the cash management process. Most cash management is computerized and tied to electronic commerce agreements with vendors and customers. Four of the more important cash management techniques are the use of lockboxes, electronic data interchange and automated transfers, cash management agreements with financial institutions, and compensating balances.

Lockboxes The collection of cash and reduction of the possibility of fraud can be facilitated by the use of **lockboxes**. Customers are instructed to send payments directly to the company at a specific post office box number, which is a depository (lockbox) at the organization's banking institution. The bank receives and opens the remittances, prepares a list of cash receipts by customer, credits the client's general cash account, and notifies the client about details of the transactions. Notification can be either a document listing customer receipts or an electronic list of the same information. The financial institution performs this processing for a fee. The client's personnel use the data sent by the bank to update cash and accounts receivable.

银行存款箱(lockboxes)
是加快收取汇款的一个重要工具。公司在当地邮局租赁一个邮箱，并授权自己的开户银行用该邮箱收取汇款。客户收到发票并被告知将款项汇到该存款箱。公司的开户银行及时收取邮件，并将支票直接存入该公司的银行存款账户。

Lockbox arrangements have these distinct advantages for the audit client:

- Cash is deposited directly at the bank. There is no delay, and the client immediately earns interest on the deposited funds.
- The manual processing associated with opening remittances, maintaining control of receipts, and developing detail for posting accounts receivable is shifted to the bank.
- The client usually establishes several lockboxes in different geographic locations to minimize the delay between the time the check leaves the customer's premises and the time the client receives the cash. This arrangement speeds the receipt of cash and allows the organization to use the cash to earn a return.

Electronic Funds Transfers Many organizations have adopted EFT as an integral part of their business. Cash transfers are made automatically and instantaneously; checks are not used.

Cash Management Agreements with Financial Institutions Financial institutions provide automated services such as cash management programs for many of their clients.

Compensating Balances Most companies have short-term loans and lines of credit with their primary financial institution. The line of credit provides the company with a prenegotiated loan, available for use when the company needs it. The financial institutions usually require the company to maintain a specified balance in a non-interest-bearing account. The amount available for the loan is the credit line minus the compensating balance. If the amounts are material, the company is required to disclose the compensating balance arrangement and its effect on the effective rate of interest.

相关的财务报表认定

Relevant Financial Statement Assertions

The five management assertions relevant to cash are as follows:

1. *Existence or occurrence*—Cash balances exist at the balance sheet date.
2. *Completeness*—Cash balances include all cash transactions that have taken place during the period.
3. *Rights and obligations*—The company has title to the cash accounts as of the balance sheet date.
4. *Valuation or allocation*—The recorded balances reflect the true underlying economic value of those assets.
5. *Presentation and disclosure*—Cash is properly classified on the balance sheet and disclosed in the notes to the financial statements.

The existence/occurrence and completeness assertions are usually the most relevant for auditing cash because the auditor is concerned that cash does, in fact, actually exist and that all cash transactions have been recorded.

对现金账户实施风险评估程序

Performing Risk Assessment Procedures for Cash Accounts

As part of performing risk assessment procedures, the auditor obtains information that is useful in assessing the risk of material misstatement. This includes information about inherent risks at the financial statement level (for example, the client's business and operational risks, financial reporting risks) and, at the account and assertion levels, fraud risks including feedback from audit team brainstorming sessions, strengths and weaknesses in internal control, and results from preliminary analytical procedures. Once the risks of material misstatement have been identified, the auditor then determines how best to respond to them as part of the audit opinion formulation process.

识别固有风险

LO 2 Identify and assess inherent risks of material misstatement in cash accounts.

货币资产的固有风险很高。货币资金可能用于非授权的目的，转到错误的客户账户或者不及时的记录。

Identifying Inherent Risks

Cash is an inherently risky asset. Cash may be used for unauthorized purposes, posted to the wrong customer's account, or not recorded on a timely basis. Inherent risk for cash is usually assessed as high because of the following reasons:

- *Volume of activity*—The volume of transactions flowing through the account during the year makes the account more susceptible to error than most other accounts.
- *Liquidity*—The cash account is more susceptible to fraud than most other accounts because cash is liquid and easily transferable.
- *Automated systems*—The electronic transfer of cash and the automated controls over cash are such that if errors are built into computer programs, they will be repeated on a large volume of transactions.
- *Importance in meeting debt covenants*—Many debt covenants may be tied to cash balances or to maintaining minimum levels of working capital. Debt covenants specify restrictions on the organization to protect the lender. Typical covenants restrict cash balances, specify the maintenance of minimum working capital, and may restrict the company's ability to pay dividends. The covenants may affect management's actions in its endeavor to present financial statements that do not violate the debt covenants.
- *Can be easily manipulated*—As the Koss fraud described in the *Professional Judgment in Context* feature illustrates, cash can be manipulated or stolen by a CFO or other personnel with power over the account balances if there exists a lack of oversight.

Examples of questions used in assessing inherent risk in cash accounts are shown in Exhibit 10.1.

EXHIBIT **10.1**	Inherent Risk Analysis Questionnaire: Cash

1. Does the company have significant cash flow problems in meeting its current obligations on a timely basis?
2. Does the company use cash budgeting techniques? How effective are the company's cash management budgeting techniques?
3. Does the company use the cash management services offered by its banker? What is the nature of these arrangements?
4. Has the company made significant changes in its cash processing during the past year? Have any major changes taken place in the company's computerized cash management applications during the year?
5. Does the company have loan or bond covenants that influence the use of cash or the maintenance of working-capital ratios?
6. Is there any reason to suspect that management may desire to misstate the cash balance?

Performing Brainstorming Activities and Identifying Fraud Risk Factors

In assessing inherent risk relating to fraud, auditors brainstorm about potential fraud risks. Questions to ask in a brainstorming session can be categorized as relating to incentives, opportunities to commit fraud, and rationalization:

LO 3 Identify and assess fraud risks of material misstatement in cash accounts.

Incentives
*   Is an individual with access to cash or its recording experiencing financial or personal distress?
*   Is an individual with access to cash or its recording being paid an amount that he or she might consider too low?
*   Is the company in potential violation of its debt covenants?
*   Does the company have sufficient cash flow to support continuing operations?

Opportunities
*   Does the company conduct background checks and credit checks on employees with access to cash? Are these checks completed on a routine basis thereafter?
*   Can employees easily convert the company's assets to their own use?
*   Is cash physically available to employees?
*   Is there insufficient segregation of duties related to cash?
*   Are the company's records for cash inadequate?
*   Is there lack of oversight and review of cash or cash-related transactions?
*   Does the company have an anonymous way for employees to report on suspicions of fraud related to cash?
*   Does the company have a policy of job or assignment rotation for employees with access to cash?

Rationalization
*   Is top management setting a poor tone by taking cash without recording those transactions?
*   Is the organization and/or management ostentatious with displays of wealth, thereby inciting jealousy in its employees?
*   Has top management ignored past instances of misappropriations of cash, thereby inciting a sense of entitlement in the organization's employees?

The auditor should consider the answers to these types of questions in determining whether to assess fraud risk at a higher level. The *Auditing in*

Common Fraud Schemes Relating to Cash

The theft of cash is as old as time itself. The following is a list of common schemes relating to cash receipts:

- Inventory is sold, but the employee making the sale does not record the sale and steals the cash.
- An employee receives a check and deposits it, but does not record the sale; then the employee writes a check out to himself and does not record the disbursement.
- The employee collects a customer payment, steals the cash, and writes off the accounts receivable as uncollectible.
- The employee steals a payment from Customer X. To cover the theft, the employee applies a payment from Customer Y to Customer X's account. Before Customer Y has time to notice that its account has not been appropriately credited, the employee applies a payment from Customer Z to Customer Y's account. This type of conduct is known as **lapping**.

- The employee makes a sale but does not record it, and steals the cash. This type of conduct is known as **skimming**.

The following is a list of common schemes relating to cash payments:

- The employee purchases merchandise and records the sale at an unauthorized discounted amount.
- The employee sells merchandise to a friend at a discounted price; the friend returns the merchandise for a refund at the undiscounted price; the two split the profits.
- The employee steals cash and conceals it by recording a fictitious discount.
- The employee writes a check to a fictitious vendor and deposits the check into an account that he or she controls that has been set up in the name of the fictitious vendor.

Practice feature "Common Fraud Schemes Relating to Cash" provides examples of common cash-related frauds.

识别控制风险

LO 4 Identify and assess control risks of material misstatement in cash accounts.

Identifying Control Risks

Once the auditor understands the inherent and fraud risks of material misstatement in cash accounts, the auditor needs to understand the controls that the client has designed and implemented to address those risks.

Typical Controls Over Cash

The following are the types of common controls over cash:

- Segregation of duties
- Restrictive endorsements of customer checks
- Independent bank reconciliations by employees who do not handle cash
- Computerized control totals and edit tests
- Authorization of transactions
- Prenumbered cash receipt documents and turnaround documents
- Periodic internal audits
- Competent, well-trained employees

职责分离(segregation of duties)
是指遵循不相容职责相分离的原则，实现合理的组织分工。例如，货币资金支出的审批人员与出纳人员、支票保管人员和银行存款账目、现金账目的记录人员应当相互分离。

Segregation of Duties The general concept of segregation of duties does not change as processing systems become more automated and integrated. Automation can enhance control, yet there is a risk of errors or fraud occurring on a larger scale. Companies have controls to make sure that incoming customer cash and checks are segregated upon receipt and are processed by different people. Postings to accounts receivable should be reconciled to the postings to cash and checks received. Segregation of duties is further enhanced if inquiries by customers concerning their account balances are referred to an independent group, such as a customer relations department, for investigation. Finally, the individuals who reconcile the bank accounts should not handle cash or record cash transactions.

Restrictive Endorsements Customer checks should be restrictively endorsed for deposit when received. The restrictive endorsement helps prevent modifications and theft of customer payments.

Independent Bank Reconciliations Two types of reconciliations should occur:

1. *Reconciliation of items received with items recorded (control totals)*— Reconciliation is made more effective when control procedures exist to establish the initial integrity of the population. In an electronic environment, the client may have a procedure by which the bank sends details of each remittance directly to the client for posting to cash and accounts receivable. These control totals should be reconciled daily with the amount shown as direct deposits by the bank.
2. *Periodic reconciliation of the bank accounts*—Independent reconciliation of the balance on the bank statement with the balance on the books should identify misstatements and unusual banking activity that may have occurred.

The auditor can test the reconciliation controls by reviewing the client's reconciliations to determine that they were independently performed.

Computerized Control Totals and Edit Tests Computerized controls should be designed to assure that all items are uniquely identified and that an adequate audit trail exists for transactions. Controls include the following:

- *A unique identifier assigned to each item*—The unique identifier establishes the integrity of the total population and provides a basis for assuring that no items are added to or dropped from the population.
- *Control totals to assure the completeness of processing*—Control totals should be established and reconciled with the computer-generated totals. A control total would also be established to reconcile the debits to cash and the credits to accounts receivable.
- *Edit tests to identify unusual or incorrect items*—Standard edit tests such as reasonableness tests, field checks, self-checking digits on account numbers, and alphanumeric tests should be implemented as deemed practical for the particular application.

Authorization of Transactions Individuals with proper authorization are able to electronically transfer very material sums of money each day. As a result, opportunities for abuse abound. The following authorization and authentication controls should be implemented:

- Authorization privileges should be assigned to individuals based on unique activities associated with the individual and position. Authorization should follow the principles of *need to know* and *right to know*. Authorizations should be reviewed periodically by senior management.
- Authentication procedures should assure that only authorized personnel execute transactions. The authentication process may be implemented through electronic verification by using elements such as passwords, physical characteristics, cards, encryption, or terminals that are hardwired to the computer. In a manual system, the authorization controls may involve limiting access to the area where checks are signed and to the prenumbered checks.
- Any changes to existing bank accounts or the opening of a new bank account must be authorized and reviewed by senior management.

- Monitoring should be established so that a detailed, daily review of transactions occurs and is compared with cash budgets, authorization limits by individuals, and riskiness of transactions.

Prenumbered Documents and Turnaround Documents Prenumbered documents are important in establishing the completeness of a population. The numbering may occur after the receipt where each payment is assigned a unique identifier when it is received by the company. Another option is to use turnaround documents that customers return with their cash payment. A clerk can quickly review the turnaround document and compare the amount indicated paid with the actual cash remittance. The turnaround document contains other information useful for further processing, such as account number, invoice number, date billed, and date received (entered by clerk). Of course, turnaround documents are unnecessary in an electronic payment environment.

Periodic Internal Audits Internal audit departments are effective deterrents when they periodically conduct detailed audits of cash controls and cash management. Internal auditors may also review the development of new systems to determine whether adequate controls have been built into the new systems.

Competent, Well-Trained Employees To better ensure that cash is handled appropriately, the organization should have competent, well-trained employees. Such employees are in a better position to carry out their assigned responsibilities, including their control-related responsibilities.

Implications of Weak Controls Related to Existence/Occurrence Controls for existence should provide reasonable assurance that the cash balances actually do exist, for example, computerized control totals. The *Auditing in Practice* feature "The Parmalat Fraud and Its Many Victims" provides

The Parmalat Fraud and its Many Victims   AUDITING IN PRACTICE

Parmalat is an international company based in Italy that produces milk, dairy, and fruit-based beverages. The financial fraud involving Parmalat evolved over a 10-year period and ultimately included the invention of over $11 billion in fictitious cash in offshore front companies to offset liabilities at the parent company. The fraud was led by Chairman Calisto Tanzi and his son, Stefano Tanzi, and was orchestrated by the company's Chief Financial Officer Fausto Tonna. In one of the telling moments of the unraveling of the fraud, representatives of a New York–based private equity firm raised questions about Parmalat's financial statements during meetings regarding a possible leveraged buyout of the company. During the meeting, the representative commented on liquidity problems at Parmalat, which contrasted with Parmalat's issued financial statements showing that the company had a large amount of cash. Stefano Tanzi admitted that the cash was not accounted for and that Parmalat actually had only about 500 million euros in cash.

Approximately 35,000 shareholders lost money in Parmalat's collapse, and shareholders were not the only ones affected by the fraud. Alessandro Bassi, a 32-year-old accountant, who worked in the financial director's office at Parmalat, killed himself by jumping off a bridge near the company's Italian headquarters. Mr. Bassi worked for the company's CFO and had been questioned by a prosecutor in the case earlier on the day of his suicide. Ultimately, Mr. Tanzi admitted to moving over $630 million from the company to family-owned related entities. One of the most shocking features of the fraud was that it involved a large number of individuals acting collusively in various ways. In the end, 29 former Parmalat executives, along with bankers, auditors, and various financial institutions, were implicated in the fraud.

an example in which the company showed a material amount of fictitious cash on its financial statements, thereby violating the existence assertion.

Implications of Weak Controls Related to Completeness Controls related to completeness are intended to provide reasonable assurance that all valid cash transactions are recorded, for example, prenumbered cash receipts documents, competent and well-trained employees. The main concern related to the completeness assertion for cash accounts is that an employee who should be recording a cash receipt simply does not record the transaction, thereby not reflecting the fact that cash was received, a sale was made, or accounts receivable was reduced. Therefore, there is no accounting record for the transaction. The *Auditing in Practice* feature "Skimming and the

Skimming and the Completeness Assertion

In the restaurant and bar business, shrinkage due to thefts of inventory and thefts of cash are a significant source of losses. Industry estimates show that about 2% to 4% of sales are lost to such shrinkage at the overall restaurant level, and that about 20% is lost to shrinkage in terms of liquor and draft beer. So, how do bartenders accomplish this type of fraud? Consider the elements of the fraud triangle:

- They are usually compensated with a low hourly wage, and therefore depend upon cash tips as their primary source of income. This provides bartenders with an incentive to steal cash from their employer, and a rationalization afterward.
- They operate in an environment where they are typically unsupervised, and have weak or non-existent physical controls. This provides an opportunity for theft.

To actually accomplish the theft of inventory, the bartender can simply give out free drinks. To accomplish the theft of cash, the bartender engages in skimming. Skimming is accomplished in the following manner:

- The customer orders a drink for $4 and gives the bartender $20 in cash.
- The bartender hits the *No Sale* button on the cash register to open the drawer. The bartender deposits the $20 and gives the customer the correct change of $16. So, the customer is satisfied. But the bartender did not record the sale, thereby violating the completeness assertion. An important and necessary control implied in this part of the example is that the cash register should have controls to ensure that it opens only upon the recording of a sale.

- The cash register now has $4 in it that should not be there according to the accounting records. So, the bartender somehow has to get the $4 out of the register without detection.
- The next customer orders a drink for $7 and gives the bartender $20 in cash. This time, the bartender records the sale, thereby opening the register. The bartender deposits the $20 and gives the customer the correct change of $13, but the bartender also takes $4 out and puts it in his or her tip jar. Theft accomplished! And there is no record of it in the accounting records, making it very difficult to detect via the audit. An important and necessary control implied in this part of the example is that video camera surveillance of the cash register area, and the bar in general, should occur.
- This example is a simplification. Usually, bartenders accomplishing fraud of this type keep track of the extra money in the cash register and do not remove it until it reaches a threshold, for example, $100. Therefore, surprise counts of cash registers are a method used to detect this type of behavior. If the surprise count reveals more cash than has been recorded, there is evidence consistent with fraud.
- Obviously, this type of theft is as old as the business itself, and sophisticated restaurant and bar owners have controls in place to prevent and detect such fraud. If they do not, they will likely be victims of a skimming fraud.

While this example is taken from the restaurant and bar business, it applies to any business where customers pay cash directly to an employee, thus providing an opportunity for skimming. When a transaction is not immediately recorded, the completeness assertion is violated.

Completeness Assertion" provides an example of fraud involving theft of cash where the transaction is never recorded, and cash is simply pocketed by the employee.

Controls for Petty Cash

Companies should have policies and procedures related to petty cash funds. These controls could include the following:

- Limiting access to petty cash funds by keeping funds in a locked box and restricting the number of employees who have access
- Requiring receipts for all petty cash disbursements with the date, amount received, purpose or use for the funds, and name of the employee receiving the funds listed on the receipt
- Reconciling the petty cash fund before replenishing it
- Keeping customer receipts separate from petty cash funds

Controls for Cash Management Techniques

Cash management techniques require controls specific to the risks associated with those techniques.

Lockboxes Sufficient controls must be established to make sure that all customer payments received by the bank are posted. For example, evidence of payments should be sent to the client to facilitate follow-up should the customer have any questions about the posting of accounts. The client should also reconcile the total of the customer payments with the cash deposit recorded by the bank.

Electronic Funds Transfers The client should have EFT agreements with vendors, customers, and banks that have adequate controls built into the process. For example, notification of the payment should be made directly to the client and the bank, automated or manual reconciliation procedures between the client and the bank should be in place, and a complete audit trail should be maintained to answer questions about the completeness of payments and disputed items.

Cash Management Agreements with Financial Institutions The client needs to take care regarding the amount of control given to the financial institution regarding the investment of cash. For example, if the client invests most of its cash in high-risk securities or nonliquid securities, the client should have a risk assessment process in place related to understanding the risks associated with the investments.

Assessing Control Risk for Cash

Once the auditor identifies the potential risks to the cash accounts, the auditor will assess the controls the client has in place to minimize those risks. The auditor is required to gain an overall understanding of the internal controls for both integrated audits and financial statement only audits. Such understanding is normally gained by means of a walkthrough of the process, inquiry, observation, and review of the client's documentation. The auditor considers both entity-wide controls and transaction controls at the account and assertion levels. This understanding provides the auditor with a basis for making an initial control risk assessment. Examples of questions used in assessing control risk in cash accounts are shown in Exhibit 10.2.

EXHIBIT 10.2 Control Risk Questionnaire: Cash

1. Have cash management service arrangements been reviewed by management and the board of directors? Are the arrangements monitored on a current basis?
2. Do management and the board periodically review the cash management process? Does the cash management organization provide for effective segregation of duties, review, and supervision?
3. Are cash transactions, including electronic cash transfers, properly authorized? What authorization is required to make electronic cash transfers?
4. Are bank reconciliations performed on a timely basis by personnel independent of processing? Is follow-up action taken promptly on all reconciling items?
5. Does the internal audit department conduct timely reviews of the cash management and cash handling process? If yes, review recent internal audit reports.
6. Does the company use a lockbox to collect cash receipts? What is the agreement with the financial institution? What are the company's controls associated with the lockbox agreement?
7. Who is authorized to make cash transfers, including electronic fund transfers, and what are the procedures by which that authorization is verified before the transfers take place? What procedures does management use to assure that the authorization process is monitored?
8. Are there any restrictions in getting access to cash? For example, does the company have cash in sweep accounts, or other accounts with financial institutions that may be in trouble, and that may restrict access to cash?

At the entity-wide level, the auditor considers the control environment, including such principles as a commitment to financial accounting competencies and the independence of the board of directors. The auditor also considers the remaining components of internal control that are typically entity-wide—risk assessment, information and communication, and monitoring controls. As part of this understanding, the auditor focuses on the relevant assertions for each account and identifies the controls, including control activities, that relate to risks for these assertions. In an integrated audit or in a financial statement only audit where the auditor intends to rely on controls, the auditor uses this understanding to identify important controls that need to be tested.

The integrated audit of cash involves evaluating the design of internal controls as well as the operation of controls throughout the year. In some smaller organizations, audit effort will be concentrated on substantive testing of these accounts at year end, and therefore testing of the operating effectiveness of the controls is not part of the audit. Audits of larger organizations more often focus on evaluating and testing internal controls via an integrated audit. In making an initial assessment of control risk, the auditor is concerned with the design effectiveness of the controls and their effects on cash management.

Documenting Controls Auditors need to document their understanding of internal controls for both integrated audits and financial statement only audits. A questionnaire, such as the one shown in Exhibit 10.3, is often used to guide auditors in documenting the understanding of internal controls. The questionnaire is designed to elicit information about specific controls performed. Usually, the questionnaire identifies the specific individual responsible for performing each procedure, which assists the auditor in evaluating the segregation of duties. As you review Exhibit 10.3, note the heavy emphasis on management reports that signal departure from what is expected and indicate a need for follow-up action. Note that a negative answer in the questionnaire

EXHIBIT **10.3**	Control Activities Questionnaire: Cash Receipts (Partial Example)

	Yes	No	N/A

OBJECTIVE OF CONTROLS: Are all payments received deposited intact on a timely basis? Consider:

Procedures for Cash Remittances Received In-House

1. Key control activities

a. A list of incoming receipts is prepared by the person who opens the remittances and who delivers the list to a person independent of the deposit function.

b. A duplicate deposit slip is prepared by someone other than the person opening the mail.

c. Deposits are made daily.

d. An authorized person compares the deposit slip with the listing prepared in step 1(a), noting agreement and completeness of deposit.

2. Documented evidence of performance

a. The listing prepared in step 1(a) is initialed by its preparer.

b. The listing is attached to the deposit slip and is initialed by the person in step 1(d).

c. Bank accounts are independently reconciled.

Procedures for Cash Remittances Received Electronically by Bank on Behalf of Client

1. Key control activities

a. An agreement exists between the bank and the company on cash-handling activities, including when the remittances are added to the client's account.

b. Procedures and responsibilities exist for forwarding detailed remittance advices to client on a daily basis.

c. An independent reconciliation of cash received is reported by bank, with remittance advices forwarded to company and posted to accounts receivable.

d. Management monitors controls to follow up on discrepancies in accounts receivable postings reported by customers.

e. Access to cash is limited through computerized access controls, including passwords and biometrics to those individuals with a need to know or to engage in transactions.

2. Documented evidence of performance

a. Reports of daily reconciliations and follow-up are done by treasury personnel.

b. Periodic reviews by internal audit or the treasury function are conducted.

c. A periodic comparison is made by the treasury function to contrast cash budgets with projections.

EXHIBIT **10.3**	Control Activities Questionnaire: Cash Receipts (Partial Example) (*continued*)		

	Yes	No	N/A
OBJECTIVE OF CONTROLS: Are payments received completely credited to the correct customer accounts? Consider:			
1. Controls			
a. When the posting process is a function of a computerized application, assurance is gained by the following ways:			
(1) Prenumbered batch control tickets include control totals of number of remittances to be processed and total dollars to be applied.	_____	_____	_____
(2) Edit reports or online edit routines are used to identify invalid customer numbers, invoice numbers, and invoice amounts.	_____	_____	_____
(3) Online entry includes the input of a control total and/or hash total for each payment.	_____	_____	_____
2. Documented evidence of performance			
a. Edit reports and/or processing transmittals exist, which are saved and signed by the person clearing the exceptions.	_____	_____	_____
b. The person performing the independent check initials the remittance, noting agreement of the posting operation.	_____	_____	_____
c. Online entry control totals and/or hash totals are noted on the face of the appropriate documents.	_____	_____	_____
d. Batch control tickets are agreed to the edit reports and initialed to indicate agreement.	_____	_____	_____
OBJECTIVE OF CONTROLS: Are all overdue accounts followed up? Consider:			
1. Controls			
a. An authorized individual makes regular collection calls on past-due accounts.	_____	_____	_____
b. The company systematically sends past-due notices to delinquent customers.	_____	_____	_____
c. Past-due accounts are periodically reviewed by senior collection officials to determine alternative collection procedures.	_____	_____	_____
2. Documented evidence of performance			
a. Review procedures and discuss past-due accounts with the credit manager.	_____	_____	_____

Conclusion

Controls appear adequate to justify a preliminary control risk assessment as:

_____ Low control risk

_____ Moderate control risk

_____ High control risk

represents a potential internal control deficiency. Given a negative answer, the auditor should consider the effect of the response on the initial assessment of control risk. Unless another control compensates for this deficiency, the auditor will likely have a control risk assessment of moderate or high in this area.

实施初步的分析性程序

LO 5 Describe how to use preliminary analytical procedures to identify possible material misstatements for cash accounts, disclosures, and assertions.

Performing Preliminary Analytical Procedures

When planning the audit, the auditor is required to perform preliminary analytical procedures. These procedures can help auditors identify areas of potential misstatements. Auditors need to go through the four-step process described in Chapter 7, which begins with developing expectations for account balances, ratios, and trends. Analytical procedures for cash balances often do not reveal a stable relationship with past cash levels because cash usually has a relatively small ending balance. However, auditors may examine cash in relation to operational data and budgetary forecasts. Further, auditors should be aware of the importance of cash balances to debt covenants. For example, the auditor can read the debt covenants, determine the relevant thresholds for cash or other liquid assets contained in those covenants, and then track how close the company is to violating those covenants over time.

The following are examples of possible expected relationships for cash accounts:

- No unusual large cash transactions
- Operating cash flow consistent with sales and net income
- Operating cash flow not significantly different from the prior year
- Investment income consistent with the level of and returns expected from the investments

If preliminary analytical procedures do not identify any unexpected relationships, the auditor would conclude that there is not a heightened risk of material misstatements in these accounts. If preliminary analytical procedures do identify unusual or unexpected relationships, the auditor would adjust the planned audit procedures (tests of controls, substantive procedures) to address the potential material misstatements. The auditor should compare the unaudited financial statements with both past results and industry trends. The following relationships might suggest a heightened risk of fraud in cash:

表明货币资金可能具有较高舞弊风险的关系还有很多。例如，库存现金规模明显超过业务周转所需资金；银行账户开立数量与企业实际的业务规模不匹配；存在大额自有资金的同时向银行高额举债等。

- Consistent profits over several years, but cash flows are declining
- Unexpected reductions in accounts receivable collections, or the timeliness of collections
- Unexpected declines in the petty cash account

Trend Analysis Trend analysis of account balances and ratios are preliminary analytical procedures that are routinely used on cash accounts. The auditor should consider the observed trends in relation to the expectations developed at the outset of performing preliminary analytical procedures. Examples of trend analysis of accounts and ratios the auditor might consider for cash accounts are presented in Exhibit 10.4.

对识别的重大错报风险的反应

LO 6 Determine appropriate responses to identified risks of material misstatement for cash accounts, disclosures, and assertions.

Responding to Identified Risks of Material Misstatement

Once the auditor understands the risks of material misstatement, the auditor can determine the appropriate audit procedures to perform. Audit procedures should be proportional to the assessed risks, with areas of higher risk receiving more audit attention and effort. Responding to identified risks typically involves developing an audit approach that contains substantive procedures (for example, tests of details and, when appropriate, substantive analytical procedures) and tests of controls, when applicable. The sufficiency and appropriateness of selected procedures vary to achieve the desired level of

EXHIBIT **10.4**	Using Trend Analysis of Account Balances and Ratios in Preliminary Analytical Procedures for Cash Accounts

- Compare monthly cash balances with past years and budgets.
- Identify unexpected spikes or lows in cash during the year.
- Compute trends in interest returns on investments.
- Analyze cash balances, and changes therein, in relation to new or retiring debt obligations.
- Compare cash ending account balances with those of preceding years, possibly on a month-by-month basis if there are anticipated collection patterns.
- Compute typical short-term liquidity ratios, including the current ratio (current assets/current liabilities) and the quick ratio (cash + cash equivalents + net receivables/current liabilities).
- Compare cash flow to sales (operating cash flow/sales) and profitability (operating cash flow/net income).

assurance for each relevant assertion. While audit firms may have a standardized audit program for auditing cash accounts, the auditor should customize the audit program based on the assessment of risk of material misstatement.

Consider a client where the auditor has assessed the risk of material misstatement related to the existence and completeness of cash at the maximum level. This client has incentives to overstate cash in order to meet debt covenants. Further, the client has relatively weak controls to prevent theft of cash, with a few controls being somewhat effective. The auditor may develop an audit program that consists of first performing limited tests of operating effectiveness of controls, then performing limited substantive analytical procedures, and finally performing significant substantive tests of details. Because of the high risk, the auditor will want to obtain a great deal of evidence directly from tests of details. In contrast, consider a client where the auditor has assessed the risk of material misstatement related to the existence and completeness of cash as low, and believes that the client has implemented effective controls in this area. Because substantive analytical procedures are relatively ineffective for cash accounts, the auditor will still perform only limited substantive analytical procedures. But the auditor will likely perform tests of controls and then complete the substantive procedures by performing tests of details at a more limited level.

Panel A of Exhibit 10.5 shows that because of differences in risk, the box of evidence to be filled for testing the existence and completeness of cash at the low-risk client is smaller than that at a high-risk client. Panel B of Exhibit 10.5 illustrates the different levels of assurance that the auditor will obtain from tests of controls and substantive procedures for the two clients. Panel B makes the point that because of the higher risk associated with the existence and completeness of cash at Client B, the auditor will want to design the audit so that more of the assurance is coming from direct tests of account balances. Note that the relative percentages are judgmental in nature; the examples are simply intended to give you a sense of how an auditor might select an appropriate mix of procedures.

Obtaining Evidence about Internal Control Operating Effectiveness for Cash

For integrated audits, the auditor will test the operating effectiveness of important controls as of the client's year end. If the auditor wants to rely on controls for the financial statement audit, the auditor will test the operating effectiveness of those controls throughout the year.

获取与现金相关的内部控制运行有效性的证据

LO 7 Determine appropriate tests of controls and consider the results of tests of controls for cash accounts, disclosures, and assertions.

EXHIBIT 10.5 Panel A: Sufficiency of Evidence for Existence and Completeness of Cash

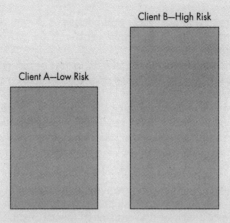

Panel B: Approaches to Obtaining Audit Evidence for Existence and Completeness of Cash

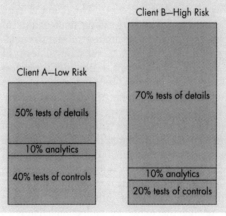

选择测试的控制和实施控制测试

Selecting Controls to Test and Performing Tests of Controls

Once the auditor understands the various types of controls in place, the auditor makes the decision about which controls to test for formulating an opinion on the entity's internal controls and/or for deciding whether the level of control risk warrants reduction of substantive testing. Each audit will be different in this regard because each client will have unique controls in place. The auditor should be aware that to simply replicate control testing from prior years is inappropriate. Rather, some effort should be made to rotate control testing over time so that different controls are tested on a rotating and somewhat unpredictable basis. Doing so will help prevent frauds in cash since employees may be deterred from committing a fraud out of fear they will be discovered by the auditor via rotations in control testing.

The auditor selects controls that are important to the auditor's conclusion about whether the organization's controls adequately address the assessed risk of material misstatement for cash accounts. The auditor will select both entity-wide and transaction controls for testing. Typical tests of transactions controls include inquiry of personnel performing the control, observation of the control being performed, inspection of documentation confirming that the control has been performed, and reperformance of the control by the individual testing the control.

Exhibit 10.6 shows an example of an audit program for testing the controls. The first part of the program focuses on gaining an understanding of the internal controls; the remaining parts identify tests of controls.

| EXHIBIT **10.6** | Audit Program for Cash Receipts and Cash Management Controls |

Procedures	By	Ref.

Understanding Controls

1. Inquire of management about the existence of lines of credit, special cash management programs, and related fees with the company's primary banking institution. Analyze the arrangements for the existence of special risks and for obligations of the client that should be considered in the audit.   _____   _____

2. Review the company risk analysis and assess the motivation to misstate or manage cash. Consider such items as: _____   _____

   a. Financial condition of the company

   b. Past problems with cash

   c. Control environment

   d. Financial needs and liquidity problems

   e. Nonexistence of effective monitoring controls

Based on the risk assessment, determine the risk that material misstatements could be occurring and would not be detected by the control system. Based on the risk assessment, make a preliminary determination as to whether satisfaction regarding controls can be determined by reviewing important monitoring controls, or if it is likely that detailed tests of cash transactions need to be performed.   _____   _____

3. Document internal controls over cash by completing the internal control questionnaire or by flowcharting the process.   _____   _____

4. Document the monitoring controls management has developed to determine whether other controls are working effectively. Determine whether:

   a. Monitoring activities are sufficient to alert management to breakdowns in other controls.   _____   _____

   b. Monitoring reports are prepared on a timely basis and are reviewed by the proper levels of management.   _____   _____

   c. Corrective action is taken on a timely basis, any control breakdowns are identified, and corrective action is taken.   _____   _____

Examples of monitoring controls include the following:

• Reconciliations of reported cash receipts with remittances prepared by independent parties

• Daily review of cash budgets and comparison with actual cash balances.

• Reviews of discrepancies in cash balances

• Weekly reporting of customer complaints regarding posting of cash balances and prompt investigation to follow up on the cause of complaints

• Reports on all unauthorized attempts to gain access to cash

• Daily reports on any unusual cash activities by location or personnel

5. Prepare and document a preliminary assessment of control risk. Identify specific controls to be tested if control risk is assessed at less than the maximum   _____   _____

(The following audit steps assume that effective controls are present in the system.)

(continued)

EXHIBIT **10.6**	Audit Program for Cash Receipts and Cash Management Controls (*continued*)		
Procedures		**By**	**Ref.**

General Tests of Controls

6. Review the frequency of monitoring activities; determine their effectiveness through reviews of the reports, indications of management actions, descriptions of corrective actions taken, and interviews with key personnel. Determine if evidence is persuasive that the monitoring controls are sufficient. _____ _____

   Note: If monitoring controls are effective, the auditor may determine that control risk is low and performing any of the following audit procedures is not necessary. If some monitoring controls are not effective, then the auditor should test the part of the system that would have been affected by the monitoring controls.

Testing of Controls over Cash Receipts If Monitoring Controls Are Not Effective

7. Perform a walkthrough of the processing of cash collections, starting with their receipt through the preparation of documents for processing. Note how conscientiously and efficiently the work is done, and the procedures used in developing batches and performing reconciliations. Interview supervisory personnel regarding potential problem areas. Identify any concerns regarding employee conscientiousness that would affect the risk assessment. _____ _____

Testing of Specific Control Activities

8. Select *x* number of cash receipts and determine that the following procedure takes place:

   a. Each payment is given a unique identifier, which is subsequently entered into the system. _____ _____

   b. The payments received are the same as the amount applied to the update of accounts receivable. Determine how differences (if any) are handled. _____ _____

   c. Payments are segregated into batches for processing. _____ _____

   d. Batches are prepared according to company standards. Review the reconciliation of batch controls to determine their accuracy and timeliness. _____ _____

   e. Exception reports contain all items rejected by the edit controls. The rejected items are properly followed up and recorded correctly. _____ _____

9. Determine who has the authorization to:

   a. Make changes in documents or adjustments when cash amounts differ from invoiced amounts. _____ _____

   b. Make deposits. _____ _____

   c. Make withdrawals. _____ _____

   d. Make transfers among the organization's accounts or between the organization and other entities. _____ _____

10. Review reports for unusual cash transactions such as transfer of funds to other accounts, deposits other than through the normal cash receipts process, and disbursements not processed through the regular cash disbursements process. Select a sample of the transactions and review for proper authorization and completeness and correctness of processing. _____ _____

EXHIBIT **10.6**	Audit Program for Cash Receipts and Cash Management Controls (*continued*)		
	Procedures	**By**	**Ref.**

11. Review the procedures for authorizing passwords or other access codes for individuals who are authorized to initiate electronic transfers of cash. Select a limited number of transactions and trace back to the authorization. (As part of the general controls review of data processing, determine the procedures for ensuring that passwords are provided only to those properly authorized and that the passwords are kept secure. Determine through testing and observation that such controls continue to exist.)

12. Review bank reconciliations for completeness, and trace selected items on the reconciliation to the bank statement. Determine that reconciliations are performed by someone independent of the processing. If there is evidence that bank reconciliations are performed regularly and that the auditor has assessed overall risk as low, there may be less need to test the reconciliations or other procedures.

Documenting Work Performed

13. Document the control risk assessment, including the types of misstatements that might occur because of any deficiencies in controls. Write a brief memo citing implications for the remainder of the audit.

Considering the Results of Tests of Controls 考虑控制测试的结果

The auditor will analyze the results of the tests of controls to determine additional appropriate procedures. There are two potential outcomes:

1. If control deficiencies are identified, the auditor will assess those deficiencies to determine their severity (are they significant deficiencies or material weaknesses?). The auditor would then need to modify the preliminary control risk assessment (possibly from low to moderate or high) and document the implications of the control deficiencies. Appropriate modifications to planned substantive audit procedures will be determined by the types of misstatements that are most likely to occur because of the control deficiency.

2. If no control deficiencies are identified, the auditor will likely determine that the preliminary assessment of control risk as low is still appropriate. The auditor will then determine the extent that controls can provide evidence on the correctness of account balances, and determine planned substantive audit procedures. The level of substantive testing in this situation will be less than what is required in circumstances where deficiencies in internal control were identified. From the audit risk model, we know that organizations with effective internal controls should require less substantive testing of account balances.

Obtaining Substantive Evidence about Cash Accounts, Disclosures, and Assertions 获取现金账户、披露和认定的实质性证据

In performing substantive procedures, the auditor wants reasonable assurance that the client's cash transactions are in accordance with generally accepted accounting principles (GAAP). The *Auditing in Practice* feature "Weaknesses in Substantive Procedures Related to Cash: Evidence from

Weaknesses in Substantive Procedures Related to Cash: Evidence from PCAOB Disciplinary Proceedings

Two PCAOB disciplinary proceedings against audit firms provide insight on weaknesses in cash-related audit procedures. The first example involves Jaspers + Hall PC (hereafter J + H) and its two audit partners. In one audit, they failed to perform sufficient procedures to verify the existence of approximately $155 million of cash, which represented 57% of the client's assets. J + H's workpapers included copies of the client's bank statements, accounting for approximately two-thirds of the reported cash, but when J + H received no reply to a confirmation request sent to the bank, the auditors failed to perform alternative procedures to verify that the client actually had the cash. They also failed to perform any procedures or obtain any audit evidence concerning the other one-third of the reported cash. *For further details, see PCAOB Release No. 105-2008-002.*

The second example involves Armando C. Ibarra, P.C. and its two audit partners. In one of their audits they failed to audit a client's cash balance of $687,971, which represented approximately 95% of total assets. Basically, they failed to test the cash balance. *For further details, see PCAOB Release No. 105-2006-001.*

The auditor needs to consider the types of substantive procedures for cash that should be performed and then make sure that the engagement team does perform these procedures. This is especially true when the cash balance represents a significant portion of the client's assets.

LO 8 Determine and apply sufficient appropriate substantive audit procedures for testing cash accounts, disclosures, and assertions.

现金账户的实质性分析程序

现金账户的实质性细节测试

PCAOB Disciplinary Proceedings" provides evidence of the types of substantive audit procedures related to cash that should be performed, and illustrates examples where such procedures were not performed.

Substantive Analytics for Cash Accounts

The auditor usually performs relatively limited substantive analytics for cash accounts and instead focuses on substantive tests of details. The minimal substantive analytics that would be performed include identifying significant fluctuations in cash balances or significant differences between budgeted and actual levels of cash.

Substantive Tests of Details for Cash Accounts

Substantive tests of details for cash accounts include the following:

- Preparing independent bank reconciliations
- Obtaining bank confirmations and obtaining bank cutoff statements
- Preparing bank transfer schedules

Preparing Independent Bank Reconciliations

The auditor's performance of an independent reconciliation of the client's bank accounts provides evidence as to the accuracy of the year-end cash balance. The process reconciles the balance per the bank statements with the balance per the books. An independent test of the bank reconciliation is quite effective in detecting signficiant misstatements, such as those that might be covered up by omitting or underfooting outstanding checks. When testing the client's bank reconciliation, the auditor should independently verify all material items such as the balance per the bank statement, deposits in transit, outstanding checks, and other adjustments. The auditor should also foot all totals. An example of bank reconciliation documentation is shown in Exhibit 10.7.

EXHIBIT **10.7**	Tests of Client's Bank Reconciliation

ABC Client	Prepared by _KMJ_
December Bank Reconciliation	Reviewed by _____
Year Ended December 31, 2013	Date _____

Balance per bank statement		$1,073,852.65*
Add: Deposits in transit:		
12/28 Deposit	$287,000.00†	
12/31 Deposit	300,000.00†	587,000.00 F
Less: Outstanding checks:		
2809	$ 435.56#	
3678	67,892.09#	
3679	75,000.00#	
3899	700.00**	
3901	12,500.00#	
3903	50,000.00#	(206,527.65) F
Adjusted balance		$1,454,325.00 F
Balance per books		**$1,481,350.00** TB
Bank charges not recorded		(25.00)‡
NSF checks:		
Bailey's Main	$ 12,000.00§	
Crazy Eddie's	15,000.00!	(27,000.00) F
Adjusted balance		$1,454,325.00 F

Note: Legend of Audit Work Performed:

*Confirmed per bank. See WP reference C–1.

†Traced to deposits shown on bank statement on 1/3 and 1/4 contained in bank cutoff statement. The 12/31 deposit was traced to bank transfer WP C–12 and was listed as an outstanding check on the subsidiary account.

‡Traced to bank cutoff statement. Charge was for service fees, which should have been recorded by the client. Amount is not material, and no adjustment is proposed.

§NSF check was returned with 12/31 bank statement. Examined support showing client redeposited the checks. Traced to deposit in cutoff bank statement and determined that it had not been returned in subsequent statement.

!Examined NSF check returned with 12/31 bank statement. Crazy Eddie's is a retail company that has gone bankrupt. The likelihood of ultimate collection is low. Based on discussion with the client, the amount should be written off. See AJE 35.

#Outstanding checks were traced to checks returned on 1/20/14 bank cutoff statements. Checks were examined, and all were dated 12/31 or earlier and were canceled by the bank subsequent to 12/31.

**Check had not cleared as of 1/20/14. Examined supporting document for the check. All appeared proper, and no exceptions were noted.

TB Traced to general ledger.

F Footed, no exceptions noted.

Obtaining Bank Confirmations

The auditor usually sends a standard **bank confirmation** to each bank with which the company has transacted business during the year. The confirmations have two parts. The first part, shown in Exhibit 10.8, seeks information on the client's deposit balances, the existence of loans, due dates of the loans, interest rates, dates through which interest has been paid, and **collateral** for all loans

通过向往来银行函证，注册会计师不仅可以了解客户资产的存在，还可以了解客户账面反映所欠银行债务的情况，并有助于发现客户未入账的银行借款和未披露的或有负债。

| EXHIBIT **10.8** | Standard Bank Confirmation—Account Balances |

Financial
Institution's
Name and
Address

[   ]

[   ]

CUSTOMER NAME

We have provided to our accountants the following information as of the close of business on ——, 20—, regarding our deposit and loan balances. Please confirm the accuracy of the information, noting any exceptions to the information provided. If the balances have been left blank, please complete this form by furnishing the balance in the appropriate space below. Although we do not request nor expect you to conduct a comprehensive, detailed search of your records, if during the process of completing this confirmation additional information about other deposit and loan accounts we may have with you comes to your attention, please include such information below. Please use the enclosed envelope to return the form directly to our accountants.

1. At the close of business on the date listed above, our records indicated the following deposit balance(s):

ACCOUNT NAME	ACCOUNT NO.	INTEREST RATE	BALANCE*

2. We were directly liable to the financial institution for loans at the close of business on the date listed above as follows:

ACCOUNT NO./ DESCRIPTION	BALANCE**	DATE DUE	INTEREST RATE	DATE THROUGH WHICH INTEREST IS PAID	DESCRIPTION OF COLLATERAL

_____   _____
(Customer's Authorized Signature)   (Date)

The information presented above by the customer is in agreement with our records. Although we have not conducted a comprehensive, detailed search of our records, no other deposit or loan accounts have come to our attention except as noted below.

_____   _____
(Financial Institution Authorized Signature)   (Date)

_____
(Title)

EXCEPTIONS AND/OR COMMENTS

Please return this form directly to our accountants:

[   ]

*Ordinarily, balances are intentionally left blank if they are not available at the time the form is prepared.

Approved 1990 by American Bankers Association, American Institute of Certified Public Accountants, and Bank Administration Institute. Additional forms available from: AICPA—Order Department, P.O. Box 1003, NY, NY 10108-1003.   D 451 5851

Confirmations With Financial Institutions: Possible New PCAOB Guidance

Auditors typically send confirmations to financial institutions where their clients have cash accounts or other relationships. However, a PCAOB-proposed Auditing Standard (AS) would require the auditor to perform confirmation procedures for cash and other relationships with financial institutions. Specifically, the proposed standard requires the auditor to perform confirmation procedures for cash with financial institutions, such as banks, brokerage firms, trust companies, and other similar entities. The other PCAOB-proposed items that should be confirmed include the following:

(a) Other relationships, such as lines of credit, other indebtedness, compensating balance arrangements, and contingent liabilities, including guarantees

(b) Any additional information about other deposit or loan accounts that has come to the attention of the financial institution during the process of completing the confirmation response

Ultimately, auditors need to stay alert to changes in required procedures and be aware when required procedures may differ between U.S. public companies and other types of organizations.

---

outstanding with the bank at year end. The *Auditing in Practice* feature "Confirmations with Financial Institutions: Possible New PCAOB Guidance" describes potential emerging guidance with regard to confirmations.

The second part of the bank confirmation, shown in Exhibit 10.9, seeks information about any loan guarantees. If loans are outstanding, the auditor usually asks for copies of the loan agreements to identify restrictions on the ability of the organization to pay dividends or to determine whether the organization will have to maintain specific working-capital or debt ratios. These requirements are generally referred to as *covenants*, a violation of which will make the loans immediately due and payable unless the financial institution temporarily waives the violation. If covenants are violated and the financial institution will not waive them, the auditor will have to consider whether the client will be able to continue to operate as a going concern and, if it is a long-term debt, reclassify it as a current liability. Additionally, the auditor normally inquires about the existence of cash management or other programs that the client has with the financial institution.

Obtaining Year-End Cutoff Information as Part of the Bank Confirmation Process In many instances of fraud, management has either held open the cash receipts book to record the next period's sales collections as part of the current period or has mailed checks to vendors but did not record the cash disbursements until the subsequent period. Sometimes these problems occur because a company is in dire financial straits and needs an improved balance sheet to avoid violation of loan covenants. If the auditor assesses the risk of such misstatements to be high, the following substantive procedures should be considered:

客户可能将应该下一期确认的货币资金收入提前确认在本期，也可能将本期应该确认的货币资金支出推迟到下一期确认。所以，注册会计师应特别关注截止信息。

- Obtain information on the last checks issued by the fiscal year end, such as the last check number, and observe that all previous checks had been mailed. The mailing of the checks can be corroborated by observing whether the checks clear the bank in a timely fashion, as evidenced in the bank cutoff statement.
- Obtain information on the last cash receipts. The auditor usually notes the last few receipts as a basis for determining the recording in the

| EXHIBIT **10.9** | Standard Bank Confirmation—Loan Guarantees |

(*Date*)
Financial Institution Official*
First United Bank
Anytown, USA

Dear Financial Institution Official:

In connection with an audit of the financial statements of (name of customer) as of (balance-sheet date) and for the (period) then ended, we have advised our independent auditors of the information listed below, which we believe is a complete and accurate description of our contingent liabilities, including oral and written guarantees, with your financial institution. Although we do not request nor expect you to conduct a comprehensive, detailed search of your records, if during the process of completing this confirmation, additional information about other contingent liabilities, including oral and written guarantees, between (name of customer) and your financial institution comes to your attention, please include such information below.

Name of Maker	Date of Note	Due Date	Current Balance	Interest Rate	Date Through Which Interest Is Paid	Description of Collateral	Description of Purpose of Note

Information related to oral and written guarantees is as follows:
_____
_____
_____

Please confirm whether the information about contingent liabilities presented above is correct by signing below and returning this directly to our independent auditors (name and address of audit firm).

Sincerely,

(*Name of Customer*)
_____

By: _____
(*Authorized Signature*)

Dear Audit Firm:

The above information listing contingent liabilities, including oral and written guarantees, agrees with the records of this financial institution.** Although we have not conducted a comprehensive, detailed search of our records, no information about other contingent liabilities, including oral and written guarantees, came to our attention. (Note exceptions below or in an attached letter.)
_____
_____
_____
_____

                                                            _____
                                                            (*Name of Financial Institution*)

                                                            _____
                                                            (*Officer and Title*)   (*Date*)

*This letter should be addressed to a financial institution official who is responsible for the financial institution's relationship with the client or is knowledgeable about the transactions or arrangements. Some financial institutions centralize this function by assigning responsibility for responding to confirmation requests to a separate function. Independent auditors should ascertain the appropriate recipient.

**If applicable, comments similar to the following may be added to the confirmation reply by the financial institution. This confirmation does not relate to arrangements, if any, with other branches or affiliates of this financial institution. Information should be sought separately from such branches or affiliates with which any such arrangements might exist.

correct period. The information is traced to the company's bank reconciliation and bank accounts to determine if items were recorded in the proper period.

These procedures are more likely to be used on smaller businesses that still handle checks manually.

Obtaining Cutoff Bank Statements

A normal bank statement prepared at an interim agreed-upon date that is sent directly to the auditor is called a **cutoff bank statement**. The auditor asks the client to arrange for the bank to send a cutoff bank statement directly to the auditor for some period after year end, usually two weeks. For example, if the client's year end is December 31, the client may arrange for the bank to send a cutoff bank statement as of January 14 directly to the auditor. The auditor can examine canceled checks returned with the bank statement to determine that the checks dated prior to year end were included as outstanding checks on the reconciliation and can trace deposits in transit into the statement to determine if they were deposited in a timely fashion. The auditor should be alert for groups of checks that do not clear for an unusually long time after year end. The delay in clearing the bank may indicate the recording of checks but not mailing them until after year end in an effort to improve the appearance of the balance sheet.

Preparing Bank Transfer Schedules

A company with many divisions frequently transfers cash from one division to another. The auditor should be alert to the fact that companies wanting to overstate cash may use a technique called **kiting** to record the same cash twice. Kiting is done by making transfers near year end from one bank account to another bank account, recording the deposit in the second division's account but not recording the disbursement on the first division's account until the next fiscal period. For example, a December 31 transfer would show the receipt on one account but not the disbursement on the other, resulting in the recording of the transferred amount twice. Exhibit 10.10 shows the elements of a classic kiting scheme.

The most effective and efficient way to test for the existence of kiting is to prepare a **bank transfer schedule** like the one shown in Exhibit 10.11. The bank transfer schedule lists all transfers between the company's bank accounts for a short period of time before and after year end. All transfers are accounted for to determine that they are recorded in the

客户可能通过腾挪的方法重复确认货币资金，以实现高估资产的目的。例如，在年末，客户将货币资金从一个银行账户转到另外一个银行账户，转入的银行账户记录货币资金的增加，而转出的账户不记录货币资金的减少。

EXHIBIT **10.10** Example of Kiting—All Within One Company

Division A

- Transfers $1,000,000 to Division B near the end of the year but records the transaction in the following year.
- Transfer does not clear the bank in the current year.
- Transfer does not decrease the year-end cash balance because it has not been recorded in the current year.

Division B

- Receives $1,000,000 before year end and records the deposit in the current year.
- Deposit may or may not be deposited by year end. If not, the deposit will be shown as a deposit in transit in the division's bank reconciliation.
- Transfer increases the year-end cash balance by the amount of the transfer. The net effect is to overstate cash on the consolidated financial statements by the amount of the transfer.

Cash is recorded in both divisions at year end, resulting in the double counting.

EXHIBIT **10.11**	Bank Transfer Schedule—XYZ Company for the Year Ended December 31, 2013

| | | | DATE DEPOSITED | | DATE WITHDRAWN | |
Transferred from Branch	Check Number	Amount	Per Books	Per Bank	Per Branch Books	Per Bank
Cleveland	15910	$ 45,000	12/26*	12/27†	12/26*	12/30†
Cleveland	15980	100,000	12/28*	12/29†	12/27*	12/31†
Rockford	8702	87,000	12/30*	12/31†	1/2‡	1/3†
Cleveland	16110	25,000	1/3*	1/4†	1/2*	1/5†
Rockford	8725	65,000	1/5*	1/7*	1/4*	1/8†

*Traced to cash receipts/disbursements records.

†Traced to bank statement.

‡Withdrawal recorded in wrong period. See AJE C–11.

correct period and the client is not overstating the year-end cash account. Note the transfer of check number 8702, recorded as a deposit on December 30—an example of kiting. The check was recorded as a deposit in the Cleveland account on December 31 but was not recorded as a disbursement in the Rockford account until after year end.

Fraud-Related Substantive Procedures for Cash Accounts

The following are examples of substantive procedures for cash accounts that address the risk of fraud:

- Confirm with financial institutions those individuals that are authorized to access cash accounts, along with those authorized to start a new account or eliminate an existing account
- Scrutinize checks that are payable to cash
- Scrutinize checks with unusual vendor names
- Scrutinize checks made out to employees outside of the normal payroll processing system
- Compare the timing of deposits into bank accounts with the timing of cash receipts, noting any unusual time lags
- Compare time lags between the date a check was issued for payment and the date that it clears the bank, noting any unusual time lags
- Investigate voided checks and analyze voided transactions

Documenting Substantive Procedures

The auditor would normally include the following types of documentation related to the substantive procedures for cash accounts:

- Copies of independent bank reconciliations
- Copies of bank confirmations
- Documentation of oral confirmations, if applicable
- Copies of bank cutoff statements
- Copies of bank transfer schedules
- Evidence of any restrictions on the use of cash balances or bank compensating balances

Auditing Marketable Securities

Significant Accounts and Relevant Assertions

Marketable securities include a wide variety of financial instruments, including the following:

- Marketable securities (held as temporary investments, either equity or debt securities)
- Short-term cash management securities, such as U.S. Treasury bills, certificates of deposit (CDs), and **commercial paper**
- Other short-term hybrid-type securities intended to improve return on temporary investments (often referred to as financial derivatives, which we discuss in detail in Chapter 16)

Two points about marketable securities and financial instruments directly affect the proper accounting for those securities. First, there is an obvious implication about whether the security is, indeed, marketable, that is, able to be purchased and/or sold in a functioning market. Second, securities may carry various levels of risk, including the risk that they may not be tradable at all if the market turns down. Ultimately, it will be very important that the auditor understand the economic purpose of major marketable securities transactions in relation to the risk undertaken by management in making the investment.

The investments in securities are classified as:

1. Held-to-maturity securities
2. Trading securities
3. Available-for-sale securities

There are important financial reporting and audit implications for the classification chosen by the company. The held-to-maturity securities are valued at amortized cost, subject to an impairment test. Both the trading securities and the available-for-sale securities are carried at fair market value. Thus, the auditor has a major judgmental challenge in:

- Corroborating management's intent in classifying the assets, including gathering information about management's trades in the investments, the importance of market value to management compensation
- Determining fair market value

The market value of regularly traded securities (for example, stocks listed on the NYSE or NASDAQ) is easy to assess because trading data is regularly available. However, for more thinly traded securities, the market does not have many participants and a financial crisis can cause the market to dry up. In such cases, the financial institutions that hold many of the securities have been very reluctant to mark the values to fair market value.

Relevant Financial Statement Assertions

The five management assertions relevant to marketable securities are as follows:

1. *Existence or occurrence*—The marketable securities exist at the balance sheet date.
2. *Completeness*—The marketable securities balances include all securities transactions that have taken place during the period.
3. *Rights and obligations*—The company has title to marketable securities accounts as of the balance sheet date.
4. *Valuation or allocation*—The recorded balances reflect the true underlying economic value of those assets.

有价证券审计
重要的账户和相关认定

LO 9 Identify types of marketable securities, articulate the risks and controls typically associated with these accounts, and outline an audit approach for testing these accounts.

在确认和计量有价证券时应特别关注是否存在活跃的市场。存在活跃市场时，活跃市场中的报价能很好地用于确定其公允价值。不存在活跃市场的，应当采用估值技术确定其公允价值，此时主观判断的因素较多。

5. *Presentation and disclosure*—Marketable securities are properly classified on the balance sheet and disclosed in the notes to the financial statements.

The valuation assertion is usually the most relevant for auditing marketable securities because of the difficulties sometimes experienced when securities are thinly traded and management reluctance in writing down the value of securities.

识别和评估与有价证券相关的固有风险、舞弊风险和控制风险

Identify and Assess Inherent, Fraud, and Control Risks Relevant to Marketable Securities

A company may invest in many types of marketable securities. Some are more marketable than others, and some carry promises of greater return (but at much greater risk) than others. Traditional marketable securities are straightforward and do not present much in the way of inherent risk. Traditional marketable securities are readily traded, and management usually intends to hold them for a short period of time. Because they are held for trading, or available for sale, they are valued at market value. In normal market situations, these short-term investments turn over and are not complex to audit. However, some inherent and control risks relating to marketable securities still exist.

Inherent and Fraud Risks

- Risk of sudden market declines, which would adversely affect the valuation of securities
- Management manipulation of the classification of securities to achieve preferable valuation treatment, that is, market value versus amortized cost
- Management manipulation of the valuation of fair market value if the securities are thinly traded

Control Risks

- Risk of theft of securities if they are not physically controlled, or if authorization and monitoring over their purchase or sale is not effective
- Lack of policies over purchase or sale of securities
- Lack of monitoring of changes in securities balances
- Lack of policies over valuation or classification of securities
- Lack of segregation of duties between individuals responsible for making investment decisions and those responsible for the custody of securities
- Lack of involvement or oversight by internal audit in relation to securities

To help auditors assess inherent and control risks relating to marketable securities, they complete an inherent risk analysis questionnaire (see Exhibit 10.12) and a control risk analysis questionnaire (see Exhibit 10.13). Also, see the *Auditing in Practice* feature "Common Fraud Schemes Relating to Investments" for a discussion of fraud risks.

EXHIBIT **10.12** Inherent Risk Analysis Questionnaire: Marketable Securities

1. Does the company regularly invest in marketable securities? How material are the balances in marketable securities accounts?
2. Has management changed the classification of securities during the year from either trading securities or available-for-sale securities to held-to-maturity securities? If yes, what is the reason for the change?
3. Is there a ready market for the securities?

Common Fraud Schemes Relating to Investments

The following are common fraud schemes relating to investments:

- Securities are purchased, but those purchases are not authorized.
- Securities are purchased, but are not recorded as purchased. Or securities are recorded as purchased, but they are not actually purchased.
- Securities are sold, but are not recorded as sold. Or securities are recorded as sold, but they are not actually sold.

- Investment income (for example, dividends or interest) is stolen.
- Investments are purposely valued inaccurately, that is, by making inaccurate fair value judgments.
- Investment classifications are purposely inaccurate.

Analytical Procedures for Marketable Securities

对有价证券实施的分析性程序

The following are examples of common analytical procedures that may be conducted for marketable securities accounts, either at the preliminary planning phase or as a substantive procedure:

- Develop expectations about the level of amounts in ending balances of marketable securities accounts based on purchase or sales activity reported by management during the year
- Develop expectations about the relationship between the balances in marketable securities accounts, the rates anticipated to be earned on those accounts, and any changes therein, and associated interest and dividend revenues
- Review changes in the balances, risk composition, and classification types of marketable securities in relation to stated investment policies and plans

---

EXHIBIT 10.13 Control Risk Analysis Questionnaire: Marketable Securities

1. Does the company have written policies and guidelines regarding investments in marketable securities? Are the policies approved by the board of directors? What process is used to authorize investments in marketable securities?
2. Does the company have a clear policy as to whether marketable securities are properly classified as trading securities, available-for-sale securities, or held-to-maturity securities? Is there evidence that the company follows the policy?
3. If management has changed the classification of securities during the year from either trading securities or available-for-sale securities to held-to-maturity securities, are the amounts significant? Were they reviewed by the audit committee? Do the audit committee and the board concur with the change?
4. If a liquid market does not exist for the marketable securities, how does management estimate the value of the securities that need to be marked to current market value?
5. Does the company provide for effective segregation of duties among individuals responsible for making investment decisions and those responsible for the custody of securities?
6. Does the internal audit department conduct regular audits of the controls over marketable securities? If yes, review recent reports.

**对有价证券实施的控制测
试和实质性细节测试**

Tests of Controls and Substantive Tests of Details for Marketable Securities

Tests of Controls

The following are common tests of controls for marketable securities:

- Review policies for authorization to purchase, sell, and manage marketable securities
- Inquire of the board of directors about the board's oversight of the marketable securities process and examine related documentation
- Examine documentation of authorization for selected purchases and sales of marketable securities during the year
- Review the minutes of the board meetings for reference to investment policies and associated oversight
- Examine evidence of authorization controls for changes in classification of marketable securities
- Inquire of management about its process for establishing valuation of marketable securities and review related documentation
- Inquire of management about their process for reclassifications and review related documentation
- Examine documentation for selected marketable securities transactions to determine whether segregation of duties is maintained
- Review reports of internal audit in relation to their activities involving monitoring of marketable securities

Substantive Tests of Details

Exhibit 10.14 contains an example of various substantive tests of detail applicable to marketable securities, along with their relationship to relevant assertions. Exhibit 10.15 contains an example of an audit workpaper for testing marketable equity securities.

EXHIBIT **10.14**   Assertions and Related Substantive Tests of Details: Marketable Securities

Assertion		Substantive Tests of Details
Existence/occurrence	1.	Request that the client prepare a schedule of all marketable securities held by the company at year end. Verify the existence of securities by either (a) counting and examining selected securities or (b) confirming the existence with trustees holding them. Reconcile the amounts with the general ledger.
Completeness	2.	Foot the schedule of marketable securities and examine the securities (step 1). Examine selected transactions and brokers' advices near year end to determine that the transactions are recorded in the correct period.
Rights	3.	Examine selected documents to determine if there are any restrictions on the marketability of securities. Inquire of management as to existence of any restrictions.
Valuation/allocation	4.	Determine current market value through reference to a financial reporting service or a similar electronic source.
	5.	Recompute interest and determine that accrued interest is properly recorded at year end.
Presentation and disclosure	6.	Determine management's intent to hold securities and review classification. Document that intention in a management representation letter.
	7.	Determine whether the securities are properly classified, and that any restrictions on their use are appropriately disclosed in the notes to the financial statements.

EXHIBIT 10.15

Nature Sporting Goods Manufacturing Company
Marketable Securities
for the Year Ended December 31, 2013

Prepared by _AMD_
Date _1/28/14_
Reviewed by _____
Date _____

Marketable Investments	Beginning Balance	PURCHASES Date	PURCHASES Amount	DISPOSALS Date	DISPOSALS Amount	Gain/Loss Disposal	Ending Balance	Market Value (12/31)	INCOME ACCOUNTS Interest	INCOME ACCOUNTS Dividends	Total
Gen. Motors 8% comm. paper	$45,000.00	10/31/11		4/30/13	$45,000.00*	$0.00	$0.00	$0.00	$1,800.00ᴿ		$1,800.00
Ford Motor 8.25% comm. paper	100,000.00	12/1/12					100,000.00ᶜ	$100,000.00†	8,937.50ᴿ		8,937.50
1000 Sh Sears' common stk	22,367.00	10/31/12					22,367.00ᶜ	16,375.00†		$1,000.00ᴿ	1,000.00
1000 Sh AMOCO	48,375.00	12/31/09		7/13/13	62,375.00*	14,000.00ᴿ	0.00	0.00		1,000.00ᴿ	1,000.00
1000 Sh Consolidated paper	0.00	7/31/11	$41,250.00*				41,250.00ᶜ	44,500.00†		500.00‡	500.00
2010 Bank America Zero Cpn Bond	1,378.00	6/30/12					1,378.00ᶜ	1,587.00†	209.00ᴿ		209.00
Totals	$217,120.00 T/B		$41,250.00 F		$107,375.00 F	$14,000.00 F	$164,995.00 CF F	$162,462.00 F	$10,946.50 F	$2,500.00 F	$13,446.50 F

Market value $162,462.00
Excess cost >   #
Mkt. Value $2,533.00§
   F

* Correct, per examination of broker's invoice.

C Securities held in broker's account, confirmed "with broker.

R Recomputed, no exceptions.

† Per December 31 stock transaction listing in the *Wall Street Journal.*

‡ Amount should be $1,000. Company failed to accrue dividend declared.

T/B Per December 31, 2012 trial balance and 12/31 "working papers, schedule M-2.

F Footed.

CF Cross-footed.

§ Loss not recorded. Trace to AJE 31.

|| Traced to year-end trial balance.

Interest and dividend payments verified through examination of Standard & Poor's *Dividend and Interest Digest* for year end December 31, 2013.

You should note the following about the audit workpaper in Exhibit 10.15:

1. The client prepares a schedule of all marketable securities it owns at year end. The schedule includes the accrued interest and dividends associated with each security for the period of time held. The auditor is testing both the balance sheet and the related income accounts at the same time.
2. If the risk of material misstatement is low, the auditor will test only a small sample of the items. If risk is high, the auditor may verify all the material items on the worksheet.
3. The document shows three items related to the value of the security:
   • Cost
   • Year-end market value
   • Carrying value for debt instruments
4. Disposals and resulting gains/losses are shown for all accounts during the year.
5. The auditor verifies the cost or sales price of the assets by examining broker's advices evidencing either the purchase or sale of the security. If control risk is low, the verification can be performed on a sample of the transactions.
6. The schedule is an abbreviated worksheet. For most audits, the auditor will have to determine whether securities are properly classified either as intent to hold to maturity or trading. That determination must be corroborated by, and consistent with, management's actions. The appropriate classification determines the accounting valuation.
7. For most investments, the current market value is determined by referring to the year-end closing price in the *Wall Street Journal* or by collecting this data electronically on the audit firm's own database. For securities that are in illiquid markets, the auditor will have to do substantially more work to determine market value.
8. Income is recomputed on a selected basis for interest, dividends, and realized and unrealized gains and losses.
9. The schedule is footed to determine the mechanical accuracy and the correct valuation of the account.
10. The audit tests address all of the audit assertions except presentation and disclosure. That assertion is verified directly with management and documented separately.
11. Document the conclusion regarding the fairness of presentation of the account balance as adjusted.

The *Auditing in Practice* feature "Audit Procedures Used to Address Risk Related to Common Fraud Schemes for Investments" provides

Audit Procedures Used to Address Risk Related to Common Fraud Schemes for Investments

AUDITING IN PRACTICE

The following substantive procedures are often used to address the risks relating to fraud in investments:

• Employ a specialist to assist in fair value measurements
• Conduct background checks on and credit ratings of employees who have access to investment accounts, or the authorization to purchase or sell securities

• Require that the client produce original documentation of securities, not copies or faxes
• Trace dividend payments, interest payments, and sales of securities to cash deposits recorded on the bank statement
• Trace purchases of securities to cash disbursements on the bank statement
• Review any unusual journal entries in investment accounts

examples of other substantive procedures that auditors may apply as necessary given the assessed level of fraud risk.

Documenting Substantive Procedures

The auditor would normally include the following types of documentation related to the substantive procedures for marketable securities:

- Schedule of marketable securities as prepared by the client, and as reviewed by the auditor, including purchases, sales, dates, market values, interest income, and gains or losses on sale
- Documentation of any confirmation of securities
- Documentation of marketable securities transactions that were scrutinized, for example, those exceeding a certain dollar value
- Memo containing rationalization for judgments made about management's classification of securities
- Memo containing rationalization for judgments made about management's valuation of securities
- Reports of any outside valuation experts
- Documentation of calculation of any potential impairments

SUMMARY AND NEXT STEPS

Cash is an inherently risky asset due to the volume of activity in the account, its liquidity, and the fact that it can be easily manipulated if controls are weak. Fraud is therefore an important consideration in the audit of cash, even though the ending balance of cash at the end of the year is usually low. Major substantive procedures that the auditor will perform for cash accounts include preparing independent bank reconciliations, obtaining bank confirmations, obtaining bank cutoff statements, and preparing bank transfer schedules. Marketable securities also present unique risks, particularly in terms of valuation. In auditing marketable securities, the auditor will obtain assurance on purchases, sales, interest revenue, and any gains or losses on disposals. Looking forward, in Chapter 11 we discuss risk assessment procedures, tests of controls, and substantive procedures for auditing the purchases of goods, services and inventory, that is, the acquisition and payment cycle.

SIGNIFICANT TERMS

Bank confirmation A standard confirmation sent to all banks with which the client had business during the year to obtain information about the year-end cash balance and additional information about loans outstanding.

Bank transfer schedule An audit document that lists all transfers between client bank accounts starting a short period before year end and continuing for a short period after year end; its purpose is to assure that cash in transit is not recorded twice.

Collateral An asset or a claim on an asset usually held by a borrower or an issuer of a debt instrument to serve as a guarantee for the value of a loan or security. If the borrower fails to pay interest or principal, the collateral is available to the lender as a basis to recover the principal amount of the loan or debt instrument.

Commercial paper Notes issued by major corporations, usually for short periods of time and at rates approximating prime lending rates, usually with high credit rating; their quality may change if the financial strength of the issuer declines.

Cutoff bank statement A bank statement for a period of time determined by the client and the auditor that is shorter than that of the regular month-end statements; sent directly to the auditor, who uses it to verify reconciling items on the client's year-end bank reconciliation.

Imprest bank account A bank account that normally carries a zero balance and is replenished by the company when checks are to be written against the account; provides additional control over cash. The most widely used imprest bank account is the payroll account, to which the company makes a deposit equal to the amount of payroll checks issued.

Kiting A fraudulent cash scheme to overstate cash assets at year end by showing the same cash in two different bank accounts using an interbank transfer.

Lapping This type of fraud occurs when an employee steals a payment from one customer, and covers it up by using payments from another customer to disguise the theft. For example, the employee steals a payment from Customer X. To cover the theft, the employee applies a payment from Customer Y to Customer X's account. Before Customer Y has time to notice that its account has not been appropriately credited, the employee applies a payment from Customer Z to Customer Y's account.

Lockbox A cash management arrangement with a bank whereby an organization's customers send payments directly to a post office box number accessible to the client's bank; the bank opens the cash remittances and directly deposits the money in the client's account.

Marketable security A security that is readily marketable and held by the company as an investment.

Skimming This type of fraud occurs when an employee makes a sale but does not record it, and steals the cash.

Turnaround document A document sent to the customer to be returned with the customer's remittance; may be machine-readable and may contain information to improve the efficiency of receipt processing.

TRUE-FALSE QUESTIONS

10-1 [LO 1] The existence/occurrence assertion with respect to cash implies that recorded balances reflect the true underlying economic value of those assets.

10-2 [LO 1] Common cash accounts include lockboxes, electronic funds transfers, cash management agreements, and compensating balances.

10-3 ☐2 Inherent risk for cash is usually assessed as high because cash may be used for unauthorized purposes, posted to the wrong customer's account, or not recorded on a timely basis.

10-4 ☐2 The volume of transactions flowing through cash accounts throughout the year makes the account highly susceptible to error.

10-5 ☐3 Lapping occurs when an employee steals a payment from one customer, and covers it up by using payments from another customer to disguise the theft.

10-6 ☐3 Skimming occurs when an employee purchases merchandise and records the sale at an unauthorized discounted price.

10-7 ☐4 Controls for completeness of cash are important because they help to provide reasonable assurance that the cash actually does exist.

10-8 ☐4 Because the primary concern is that cash will be stolen and is thus understated, the auditor is not usually concerned about overstatements of cash.

10-9 ☐5 Analytical procedures are particularly useful to the auditor in gaining assurance about the cash account because the usually small ending balances in cash tend to be stable over time.

10-10 ☐5 If the auditor observes that the company reports consistent profits over several years while cash flows are decreasing, then the auditor should assess heightened risk of fraud in cash.

10-11 ☐6 The relative percentage of substantive analytics that will be used by the auditor as evidence in the audit of cash will be somewhat limited regardless of the riskiness of the client.

10-12 ☐6 When auditing cash, the auditor will perform a relatively larger percentage of tests of details for a high-risk client compared to a low-risk client.

10-13 ☐7 An example of a monitoring control in cash would include a daily review of cash budgets and a comparison of them with actual cash balances, with appropriate follow-up.

10-14 ☐7 If monitoring controls are effective, then the auditor will be required to perform a walkthrough of the processing of cash collections, starting with their receipt through the preparation of documents for processing.

10-15 ☐8 Because cash balances are usually relatively low at year end, auditing standards encourage auditors to send bank confirmations on a sample basis.

10-16 ☐8 A normal bank statement prepared at an interim agreed-upon date that is sent directly to the auditor is called a bank transfer statement.

10-17 ☐9 The major judgmental challenges that auditors face in auditing marketable securities include corroborating management's intent in classifying these assets into the proper categories and determining fair market value.

10-18 ☐9 An appropriate audit procedure to test the valuation assertion for marketable securities involves reviewing the client's schedule of marketable securities and confirming with trustees that those securities do, indeed, belong to the company.

MULTIPLE-CHOICE QUESTIONS

10-19 `LO 1` Which of the following assertions is relevant to whether the company has title to the cash accounts as of the balance sheet date?
a. Existence or occurrence.
b. Completeness.
c. Rights and obligations.
d. Valuation or allocation.
e. All of the above.

10-20 `LO 1` Which of the following assertions is relevant to whether the cash balances reflect the true underlying economic value of those assets?
a. Existence or occurrence.
b. Completeness.
c. Rights and obligations.
d. Valuation or allocation.
e. All of the above.

10-21 `LO 2` Inherent risk for cash is usually assessed as high for which of the following reasons?
a. The volume of transactions flowing through cash accounts throughout the year makes the account more susceptible to error.
b. The cash account is more susceptible to fraud because cash is liquid and easily transferable.
c. The electronic transfer of cash and the automated controls over cash are such that if errors are built into computer programs, they will be repeated on a large volume of transactions.
d. Cash can be easily manipulated.
e. All of the above.

10-22 `LO 2` Which of the following questions would be relevant for an inherent risk analysis questionnaire related to cash?
a. Does the company have significant cash flow problems in meeting its current obligations on a timely basis?
b. Are cash transactions properly authorized?
c. Are bank reconciliations performed on a timely basis by personnel independent of processing?
d. Does the internal audit department conduct timely reviews of the cash management and cash handling process?
e. All of the above.

10-23 `LO 3` Affirmative answers to which of the following questions would lead the auditor to assess fraud risk at a higher level for cash or other liquid assets?
a. Is an individual with access to cash or its recording experiencing financial or personal distress?
b. Is an individual with access to cash or its recording being compensated at an amount that he or she might consider low?
c. Is the company in potential violation of its debt covenants?
d. Is cash physically available to employees?
e. All of the above.

10-24 ᴸᴼ **3** Which of the following terms best defines this scenario? The employee steals a payment from Customer X. To cover the theft, the employee applies a payment from Customer Y to Customer X's account. Before Customer Y has time to notice that its account has not been appropriately credited, the employee applies a payment from Customer Z to Customer Y's account.
a. Skimming.
b. Kiting.
c. Collateralizing.
d. Lapping.

10-25 ᴸᴼ **4** Which of the following controls represents a control over cash that is unique to cash accounts?
a. Separation of duties.
b. Restrictive endorsements of customer checks.
c. Periodic internal audits.
d. Competent, well-trained employees.

10-26 ᴸᴼ **4** Which of the following controls represents a computerized control used in the audit of cash or other liquid asset accounts?
a. A unique identifier is assigned to each item.
b. Control totals are used to assure the completeness of processing.
c. Edit tests are used to identify unusual or incorrect items.
d. All of the above.

10-27 ᴸᴼ **5** The first step in performing preliminary analytical procedures is to develop an expectation of the account balance. Which of the following does *not* typically represent a likely expected relationship for cash accounts?
a. The company reports consistent profits over several years, but operating cash flows are declining.
b. No unusual large cash or other liquid asset transactions are found.
c. Operating cash flow is not significantly different from that of the prior year.
d. Investment income is consistent with the level of and returns expected from the investments.
e. All of the above represent likely expected relationships.

10-28 ᴸᴼ **5** Which of the following is a common example of trend analysis of accounts and ratios that the auditor might consider for cash accounts?
a. Compare monthly cash balances with past years and budgets.
b. Identify unexpected spikes or lows in cash during the year.
c. Compute trends in interest returns on investments.
d. Analyze cash balances, and changes therein, in relation to new or retiring debt obligations.
e. All of the above.

10-29 ᴸᴼ **6** Which mix of evidence would be most appropriate for the following scenario? This is a client where the auditor has assessed the risk of material misstatement related to the existence and completeness of cash at the maximum level. This client has incentives to overstate cash in order to meet debt covenants. Further, the client has relatively weak controls to prevent theft of cash, with a few controls being somewhat effective.
a. 100% tests of details.
b. 70% tests of details, 10% analytics, 20% tests of controls.
c. 50% tests of details, 10% analytics, 40% tests of controls.
d. 20% tests of details, 40% analytics, 40% tests of controls.

10-30 [L0 6] Which mix of evidence would be most appropriate for the following scenario? This is a client where the auditor has assessed the risk of material misstatement related to the existence and completeness of cash as low, and believes that the client has implemented effective controls in this area.
   a. 100% tests of details.
   b. 70% tests of details, 10% analytics, 20% tests of controls.
   c. 50% tests of details, 10% analytics, 40% tests of controls.
   d. 20% tests of details, 40% analytics, 40% tests of controls.

10-31 [L0 7] Refer to Exhibit 10.6. Which of the following represents a reasonable test of controls for cash receipts and cash management controls?
   a. Document internal controls over cash by completing the internal control questionnaire or by flowcharting the process.
   b. Prepare an independent bank reconciliation.
   c. Obtain a bank confirmation.
   d. Obtain a bank cutoff statement.
   e. All of the above.

10-32 [L0 7] Refer to Exhibit 10.6. Which of the following represents a monitoring control in the audit program for cash receipts and cash management controls?
   a. Reconciliations of reported cash receipts with remittances prepared by independent parties.
   b. Daily review of cash budgets and comparison of them with actual cash balances.
   c. Reviews of discrepancies in cash balances.
   d. Weekly reporting of customer complaints regarding posting of cash balances and prompt investigation to follow up on cause of complaints.
   e. All of the above.

10-33 [L0 8] Which of the following statements regarding independent bank reconciliations is true?
   a. The auditor's performance of an independent reconciliation of the client's bank accounts provides evidence as to the accuracy of the year-end cash balance.
   b. The process reconciles the balance per the bank statements with the balance per the books.
   c. An independent test of the bank reconciliation is quite effective in detecting major errors, such as those that might be covered up by omitting or underfooting outstanding checks.
   d. When testing the client's bank reconciliation, the auditor should independently verify all material items, such as the balance per the bank statement, deposits in transit, outstanding checks, and other adjustments.
   e. All of the above are true.

10-34 [L0 8] A bank confirmation contains which of the following two parts?
   1. A part that seeks information on the client's deposit balances, the existence of loans, due dates of the loans, interest rates, dates through which interest has been paid, and collateral for loans outstanding
   2. A part that contains a listing of the last checks issued near year end
   3. A part that seeks information about any loan guarantees

4. A part that lists all transfers between the company's bank accounts for a short period of time before and after year end
   a. 1 & 2.
   b. 1 & 3.
   c. 2 & 3.
   d. 2 & 4.
   e. 3 & 4.

10-35 `LO 9` Which of the following assertions is relevant to whether the marketable securities balances include all securities transactions that have taken place during the period?
a. Existence or occurrence.
b. Completeness.
c. Rights and obligations.
d. Valuation or allocation.
e. All of the above.

10-36 `LO 9` Refer to Exhibit 10.14. Which of the following assertions is relevant to the audit procedure for marketable securities that requires the auditor to examine selected documents to identify any restrictions on the marketability of securities?
a. Existence or occurrence.
b. Completeness.
c. Rights and obligations.
d. Valuation or allocation.
e. All of the above.

REVIEW AND SHORT CASE QUESTIONS

10-37 `LO 1` Describe the following types of cash accounts: (a) general checking accounts, (b) cash management accounts, (c) imprest payroll accounts, and (d) petty cash accounts.

10-38 `LO 1` Describe the following types of cash management techniques: (a) lockboxes, (b) electronic funds transfers, (c) cash management agreements, (d) compensating balances.

10-39 `LO 1` Match the following assertions with their associated description: (a) existence or occurrence, (b) completeness, (c) rights and obligations, (d) valuation or allocation, (e) presentation and disclosure.
1. Cash accounts are properly classified on the balance sheet and disclosed in the notes to the financial statements.
2. Cash balances exist at the balance sheet date.
3. The recorded balances reflect the true underlying economic value of those assets.
4. The company has title to the cash accounts as of the balance sheet date.
5. Cash balances include all cash transactions that have taken place during the period.

10-40 `LO 2` Refer to the *Professional Judgment in Context* feature at the beginning of the chapter. Why is cash in general a risky asset, and why was the petty cash account at Koss Corporation inherently risky?

`FRAUD`

10-41 `LO 2` Evaluate the following statement made by a third-year auditor: "In comparison with other accounts, such as accounts receivable or property, plant, and equipment, it is my assessment that cash contains less inherent risk. There are no significant valuation

NOTE: Completing Review and Short Case Questions does not require the student to reference additional resources and materials.

NOTE: For the remaining problems, we make special note of those addressing fraud, international issues, professional skepticism, and ethics.

problems with cash." Do you agree or disagree with the auditor's assessment of inherent risk? Explain.

10-42 `LO 2, 4` The following are items on the inherent risk and control risk questionnaires contained in Exhibits 10.1 and 10.2. Categorize each item as belonging on (a) the inherent risk analysis questionnaire or the (b) control risk analysis questionnaire.

1. Does the company have significant cash flow problems in meeting its current obligations on a timely basis?
2. Are there any restrictions in getting access to cash? For example, does the company have cash in sweep accounts, or other accounts with financial institutions that may be in trouble, and that may restrict access to cash?
3. Does the internal audit department conduct timely reviews of the cash management and cash handling process? If yes, review recent internal audit reports.
4. Does the company use cash budgeting techniques? How effective are the company's cash management budgeting techniques?
5. Are bank reconciliations performed on a timely basis by personnel independent of processing? Is follow-up action taken promptly on all reconciling items?
6. Does the company use the cash management services offered by its banker? What is the nature of these arrangements?
7. Has the company made significant changes in its cash processing during the past year? Have any major changes taken place in the company's computerized cash management applications during the year?
8. Have cash management service arrangements been reviewed by management and the board of directors? Are the arrangements monitored on a current basis?
9. Does the company have loan or bond covenants that influence the use of cash or the maintenance of working-capital ratios?
10. Are cash transactions, including electronic cash transfers, properly authorized? What authorization is required to make electronic cash transfers?
11. Does the company use a lockbox to collect cash receipts? What is the agreement with the financial institution? What are the company's controls associated with the lockbox agreement?
12. Is there any reason to suspect that management may desire to misstate the cash balance?
13. Do management and the board periodically review the cash management process? Does the cash management organization provide for effective segregation of duties, review, and supervision?
14. Who is authorized to make cash transfers, including electronic fund transfers, and what are the procedures by which that authorization is verified before the transfers take place? What procedures does management use to assure that the authorization process is monitored?

FRAUD **10-43** `LO 3` Refer to the *Auditing in Practice* feature "Common Fraud Schemes Relating to Cash" and describe at least three such schemes. Be prepared to discuss fraud schemes that you have learned about in your local community.

FRAUD **10-44** `LO 3` Describe the fraudulent conduct that is known as (a) lapping and (b) skimming.

10-45 [LO 4] Using the following categories, define the purpose of each of the common controls over cash listed below. You may use multiple categories for each control. [FRAUD]

Categories of Purposes of Each Common Control
1. To prevent theft of cash.
2. To ensure complete recording of cash.
3. To prevent modification of the recording of cash.
4. To detect inaccuracy of ending cash balance or misstatements therein.
5. To ensure that all items are uniquely identified and that an adequate audit trail exists for transactions.
6. To serve as a deterrent for fraud.

Common Controls Over Cash
a. Segregation of duties.
b. Restrictive endorsements of customer checks.
c. Independent bank reconciliations by employees who do not handle cash.
d. Computerized control totals and edit tests.
e. Authorization of transactions.
f. Prenumbered cash receipt documents and turnaround documents.
g. Periodic internal audits.
h. Competent, well-trained employees.

10-46 [LO 4] List at least three common controls for petty cash.

10-47 [LO 4] Refer to Exhibit 10.3. Match each of the following objectives to the relevant control activities.

Objectives That Controls Are Trying to Achieve
a. Payments received are deposited intact on a timely basis.
b. Payments received are completely credited to the correct customer accounts.
c. Overdue accounts are followed up.

Control Activities
1. A list of incoming receipts is prepared by the person who opens the remittances and who delivers the list to a person independent of the deposit function.
2. An authorized individual makes regular collection calls on past-due accounts.
3. Online entry that includes the input of a control total and/or hash total is used for each payment.
4. A duplicate deposit slip is prepared by someone other than the person opening the mail.
5. The company systematically sends past-due notices to delinquent customers.
6. Deposits are made daily.
7. Prenumbered batch control tickets include control totals of the number of remittances to be processed and total dollars to be applied.
8. Past-due accounts are periodically reviewed by senior collection officials to determine alternative collection procedures.
9. An agreement exists between the bank and the company on cash-handling activities, including when the remittances are added to the company's account.
10. Management monitors controls to follow up on discrepancies in accounts receivable postings.

INTERNATIONAL **10-48** [LO 4,7,8] This problem is designed to get you to think creatively about controls that would be effective in a real-world setting. The Canada Border Services Agency (CBSA) receives cash payments for services, fees, and taxes (for example, customs duties, excise taxes, taxes on goods and services) at various ports of entry around Canada. Cash is defined as payments made in liquid cash, by debit or credit cards, and by checks.

a. What types of controls should the CBSA have over its cash receipts?

b. Given the controls that you identified in part (a), what types of tests of controls or substantive audit procedures should be performed?

FRAUD **10-49** [LO 5] Categorize each of the following trends or relationships as suggesting either (a) a normal trend or relationship or (b) a fraud-related trend or relationship:

1. The company reports consistent profits over several years, but cash flows are declining.
2. Operating cash flow is consistent with sales and net income.
3. The timeliness of accounts receivable collections declines, but credit policies are unchanged.
4. Operating cash flow is not significantly different from that of the prior year, and operations have been consistent across the two years.
5. Investment income is consistent with the level of and returns expected from investments.
6. There are unexpected declines in the petty cash account.

10-50 [LO 7] Refer to Exhibit 10.3. Describe the major components of an audit program for cash receipts and cash management controls. Provide examples of each component.

PROFESSIONAL SKEPTICISM **10-51** [LO 8] What is the impact on the audit if the client does not perform independent periodic reconciliations of its cash accounts? What substantive audit procedures would be dictated by the lack of the client's independent reconciliations? How would the fact that the client does not perform this important control affect the auditor's professional skepticism?

10-52 [LO 8] Explain the purpose of the following audit procedures:

a. Sending a bank confirmation to all the banks with which the company does business.

b. Obtaining a bank cutoff statement.

c. Preparing a bank transfer statement.

FRAUD **10-53** [LO 8] Define and illustrate *kiting*. What controls should the client institute to prevent it? What audit procedures should the auditor use to detect kiting?

FRAUD **10-54** [LO 8] The following information was taken from the bank transfer schedule prepared during the audit of Fox Co.'s financial statements for the year ended December 31, 2013. Assume all checks are dated and issued on December 30, 2013.

	Bank Accounts		Disbursement Date		Receipt Date	
Check No.	From	To	Per Books	Per Bank	Per Books	Per Bank
101	National	Federal	Dec. 30	Jan. 4	Dec. 30	Jan. 3
202	County	State	Jan. 3	Jan. 2	Dec. 30	Dec. 31
303	Federal	State	Dec. 31	Jan. 3	Jan. 2	Jan. 2
404	State	County	Jan. 2	Jan. 2	Jan. 2	Dec. 31

a. Which of the checks might indicate kiting?

b. Which of the checks illustrates deposits/transfers in transit on December 31, 2013?

10-55 `LO 8` The following items were discovered during the audit of a cash account. For each item identified, indicate the substantive audit procedure that most likely would have led to the discovery of the misstatement.   `FRAUD`

1. The company had overstated cash by transferring funds at year end to another account but failed to record the withdrawal until after year end.

2. On occasion, customers with smaller balances send in checks without specific identification of the customer except the name printed on the check. The client has an automated cash receipts process, but the employee opening the envelopes pocketed the cash and destroyed other supporting documentation.

3. Same as finding (2), but the employee prepared a turnaround document that showed either an additional discount for the customer or a credit to the customer's account.

4. The controller was temporarily taking cash for personal purposes but intended to repay the company (although the repayment never occurred). The cover-up was executed by understating outstanding checks in the monthly bank reconciliation.

5. The company had temporary investments in six-month CDs at the bank. The CDs were supposed to yield an annual interest rate of 12% but apparently are yielding only 6%.

6. Cash remittances are not deposited in a timely fashion and are sometimes lost.

7. Substantial bank service charges have not been recorded by the client prior to year end.

8. A loan has been negotiated with the bank to provide funds for a subsidiary company. The loan was negotiated by the controller of the division, who apparently was not authorized to negotiate the loan.

9. A check written to a vendor had been recorded twice in the cash disbursements journal to cover a cash shortage.

10-56 `LO 8` Pembrook Company had poor internal control over its cash transactions. The following are facts about its cash position on November 30:   `FRAUD`

- The cash books showed a balance of $18,901.62, which included undeposited receipts.
- A credit of $100 on the bank statement did not appear on the company's books.
- The balance, according to the bank statement, was $15,550.
- Outstanding checks were:
  - no. 62 for $116.25
  - no. 183 for $150.00
  - no. 284 for $253.25
  - no. 8621 for $190.71
  - no. 8623 for $206.80
  - no. 8632 for $145.28.

The only deposit was in the amount of $3,794.41 on December 7. The cashier handles all incoming cash and makes the bank deposits personally. He also reconciles the monthly bank statement. His November 30 reconciliation follows:

Balance, per books, November 30		$18,901.62
Add: Outstanding checks:		
8621	$190.71	
8623	206.80	
8632	45.28	442.79
		$19,344.41
Less: Undeposited receipts		3,794.41
Balance per bank, November 30		$15,550.00
Deduct: Unrecorded credit		100.00
True cash, November 30		$15,450.00

a. You suspect that the cashier may have misappropriated some money and are concerned specifically that some of the undeposited receipts of $3,794.41 may have been taken. Prepare a schedule showing your estimate of the loss.

b. How did the cashier attempt to conceal the theft?

c. On the basis of this information only, name two specific features of internal control that were apparently missing.

d. If the cashier's October 31 reconciliation is known to be proper and you start your audit on December 10, what specific substantive audit procedures would help you discover the theft?

10-57 **LO 8** Toyco, a retail toy chain, honors two bank credit cards and makes daily deposits of credit card sales in two credit card bank accounts (Bank A and Bank B). Each day, Toyco batches its credit card sales slips, bank deposit slips, and authorized sales return documents, and sends them to data processing for data entry. Each week, detailed computer printouts of the general ledger credit card cash accounts are prepared. Credit card banks have been instructed to make an automatic weekly transfer of cash to Toyco's general bank account. The credit card banks charge back deposits that include sales to holders of stolen or expired cards. The auditor examining the Toyco financial statements has obtained copies of the detailed general ledger cash account printouts, a summary of the bank statements, and the manually prepared bank reconciliations, all for the week ended December 31, as shown here.

Review the December 31 bank reconciliation and the related information contained in the following schedules and describe what actions the auditor should take to obtain evidence for each item on the bank reconciliation. Assume that all amounts are material and that all computations are accurate. Organize your answer sheet as follows, using the code contained on the bank reconciliation.

Code Number	Actions to Be Taken by the Auditor to Obtain Evidence
1.	
2.	
3.	
etc.	

Toyco

Bank Reconciliation
for December 31, 2013

	Bank A	Bank B
Code No.	Add or (Deduct)	
1. Balance per bank statement, December 31	$8,600	$-0-
2. Deposits in transit, December 31	2,200	6,000
3. Redeposit of invalid deposits (deposited in wrong account)	1,000	1,400
4. Difference in deposits of December 29	(2,000)	(100)
5. Unexplained bank charge	400	
6. Bank cash transfer not yet recorded	-0-	22,600
7. Bank service charges	-0-	500
8. Chargebacks not recorded—stolen cards	100	-0-
9. Sales returns recorded but not reported to the bank	(600)	(1,200)
10. Balance per general ledger, December 31	$9,700	$29,200

Toyco

Detailed General Ledger Credit Card Cash Accounts Printouts
for the Week Ended December 31, 2013

	Bank A	Bank B
	Dr. or (Cr.)	
Beginning balance, December 24	$12,100	$4,200
Deposits: December 27	2,500	5,000
December 28	3,000	7,000
December 29	0	5,400
December 30	1,900	4,000
December 31	2,200	6,000
Cash transfer, December 17	(10,700)	-0-
Chargebacks—expired cards	(300)	(1,600)
Invalid deposits (deposited in wrong account)	(1,400)	(1,000)
Redeposit of invalid deposits	1,000	1,400
Sales returns for week ended December 31	(600)	(1,200)
Ending balance	$9,700	$29,200

Toyco

Summary of the Bank Statements
for the Week Ended December 31, 2013

	Bank A	Bank B
	(Charges) or Credits	
Beginning balance, December 24	$10,000	$-0-
Deposits dated: December 24	2,100	4,200
December 27	2,500	5,000
December 28	3,000	7,000
December 29	2,000	5,500
December 30	1,900	4,000
Cash transfers to general bank account:		
December 27	(10,700)	-0-
December 31	-0-	(22,600)
Chargebacks:		
Stolen cards	(100)	-0-
Expired cards	(300)	(1,600)
Invalid deposits	(1,400)	(1,000)
Bank service charges	-0-	(500)
Bank charge (unexplained)	(400)	(-0-)
Ending balance	$8,600	$-0-

10-58 **LO 8** The AICPA has developed a standard bank confirmation form to assure consistent communication with the banking community.

a. Is the auditor required to send a bank confirmation to banks from which the client receives a bank cutoff statement shortly after year end? Explain.

b. What additional information is gathered through a bank confirmation? Explain how the other information gathered is used on the audit.

c. For each scenario in the following list (labeled 1.–3. below), recommend a substantive audit procedure or additional audit work that should be performed:

1. The client has one major bank account located in a distant city, and the auditor is not familiar with the bank. The auditor has assessed control risk as high on this engagement. The mailing address of the bank is simply a post office box number, but such a number is not considered unusual.

2. The client has three accounts with its major bank. For two of the three accounts, the confirmation returned by the bank shows different balances from what the client shows. The balance per the client for one of the accounts is the same as the bank shows in the cutoff statement received from the bank shortly after year end. The auditor did not request a cutoff statement on the other account for which the confirmation differs.

3. The returned confirmation shows a loan that the client does not list as a liability.

10-59 `LO 8` The following client-prepared bank reconciliation is being examined by Kautz, CPA, during an examination of the financial statements of Concrete Products, Inc.:

Concrete Products, Inc.
Bank Reconciliation
December 31, 2013

Balance per bank (a)		$18,375.91
Deposits in transit (b):		
December 30	1,471.10	
December 31	2,840.69	4,311.79
Outstanding checks (c):		
837	6,000.00	
1941	671.80	
1966	320.00	
1984	1,855.42	
1985	3,621.22	
1986	2,576.89	
1991	4,420.88	(19,466.21)
Subtotal		3,221.49
NSF check returned Dec. 29 (d)		200.00
Bank charges		5.50
Error check no. 1932		148.10
Customer note collected by the bank		
($2,750 plus $275 interest) (e)		(3,025.00)
Balance per books (f)		$ 550.09

Identify one or more substantive audit procedures that should be performed by Kautz in gathering evidence in support of each of the items (a) through (f) in this bank reconciliation.

10-60 `LO 8` Eagle River Plastics Company has a major branch located in Phoenix. The branch deposits cash receipts daily and periodically transfers the receipts to the company's home office in Eagle River. The transfers are accounted for as intercompany entries into the home office and branch office accounts. All accounting, however, is performed at the home office under the direction of the assistant controller. The assistant controller is also responsible for the transfers. The controller, however, independently reconciles the bank account each month or assigns the reconciliation to someone in the department (in some cases, could be the assistant controller). The company is relatively small; therefore, the controller is also the financial planner and treasurer for the company. As part of the year-end audit, you are assigned the task of conducting an audit of bank transfers. As part of the process, you prepare the following schedule of transfers:

Information from Client's Records			Information per Bank Statements	
			Date Cleared	
Date per Branch	Date per Amount	Date Deposited Home Office	per Home Bank	per Branch Bank
12-27	$23,000	12-31	12-31	1-3
12-29	$40,000	12-31	12-31	1-7
12-31	$45,000	1-2	1-3	1-8
1-2	$14,000	12-31	12-31	1-5
1-5	$28,000	1-3	1-7	1-12
1-3	$10,000	1-3	12-31	1-5

a. Identify the substantive audit procedures that would be used to test the correctness of the client's bank transfers.
b. Identify any adjusting journal entries that would be needed on either the home or branch office accounting records as a result of the preceding transactions.

PROFESSIONAL SKEPTICISM **10-61** **LO 8** The following are weaknesses in internal controls over cash. For each weakness, indicate what substantive audit procedure(s) should be performed to determine whether any material misstatements have occurred. Consider each weakness independently of the others. While each weakness poses potential problems, identify two that would heighten your professional skepticism the most and explain your rationale.
a. The person who opens the mail prepares the deposit when the cashier is not available.
b. If a customer does not submit a remittance advice with a payment, the mail clerk sometimes does not prepare one for the accounts receivable department.
c. Occasionally, the treasurer's department does not cancel the supporting documents for cash disbursements.
d. Customer correspondence concerning monthly statements is handled by the person who makes the bank deposits.
e. Bank reconciliations are not prepared on a timely basis. When prepared, they are prepared by the person who handles incoming mail.

10-62 **LO 8, 10** One of the procedures that you have been assigned to perform on the audit of Reengage Corporation is sending bank confirmations. Your audit firm has a policy of sending confirmations to all financial institutions where a banking relationship exists, although the policy acknowledges that various instances may not require sending confirmations (for example, accounts with no activity for the period under audit, petty cash accounts at branch locations). You note several accounts in which the cash balances are relatively small. You believe that sending confirmations will not be necessary to the financial institutions where Reengage Corporation has an account with a small balance.
a. What type of evidence is obtained through bank confirmations?
b. Use the framework for professional decision making from Chapter 4 to determine the appropriate steps to take in

deciding on to which financial institutions a confirmation should be sent. Recall that the framework is as follows:

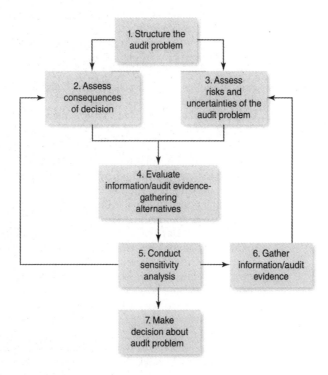

Source: Adapted from *Judgment and Choice*, by Robin Hogarth.

10-63 LO 9 What are the three major categories of marketable securities? What is the GAAP classification for such securities? What judgmental challenges do auditors face in auditing marketable securities?

10-64 LO 9 Match the following assertions related to marketable securities with their associated description: (a) existence or occurrence, (b) completeness, (c) rights and obligations, (d) valuation or allocation, (e) presentation and disclosure.
1. The marketable securities balances include all securities transactions that have taken place during the period.
2. The company has title to marketable securities accounts as of the balance sheet date.
3. The recorded balances reflect the true underlying economic value of those assets.
4. Marketable securities are properly classified on the balance sheet and disclosed in the notes to the financial statements.
5. Marketable securities exist at the balance sheet date.

10-65 LO 9 The following are risks relating to marketable securities. FRAUD Categorize each risk as relating to either (a) inherent or fraud risk or (b) control risk.
1. Management manipulation of the classification of securities to achieve preferable valuation treatment, for example, market value versus amortized cost.
2. Lack of policies over valuation or classification of securities.
3. Management manipulation of the valuation of market value if the securities are thinly traded.

4. Lack of policies over purchase or sale of securities.

5. Lack of monitoring of changes in securities balances.

6. Lack of segregation of duties between individuals responsible for making investment decisions and those responsible for the custody of securities.

7. Risk of theft of securities if they are not physically controlled, or if authorization and monitoring over their purchase or sale is not adequate.

8. Risk of sudden market declines, which would adversely affect the valuation of securities.

9. Lack of involvement or oversight by internal audit in relation to securities.

10-66 [LO 9] Refer to Exhibits 10.12 and 10.13. Categorize each of the following questions relating to marketable securities as being appropriate for use in (a) an inherent risk questionnaire or a (b) control risk questionnaire.

1. Does the internal audit department conduct regular audits of the controls over marketable securities? If yes, review recent reports.

2. If management has changed the classification of securities during the year from either trading securities or available-for-sale securities to held-to-maturity securities, are the amounts significant? Were they reviewed by the audit committee? Do the audit committee and the board concur with the change?

3. Does the company regularly invest in marketable securities? How material are the balances in marketable securities accounts?

4. Does the company have written policies and guidelines regarding investments in marketable securities? Are the policies approved by the board of directors? What process is used to authorize investments in marketable securities?

5. Does the company have a clear policy as to properly classifying marketable securities as trading securities, available-for-sale securities, or held-to-maturity securities? Is there evidence that the company follows the policy?

6. Has management changed the classification of securities during the year from either trading securities or available-for-sale securities to held-to-maturity securities? If yes, what is the reason for the change?

7. If a liquid market does not exist for marketable securities, how does management estimate the value of the securities that need to be marked to current market value?

8. Does the company provide for effective segregation of duties among individuals responsible for making investment decisions and those responsible for the custody of securities?

9. Is there a ready market for the securities?

10-67 [LO 9] How would the following factors affect the auditor's assessment of the internal control effectiveness for marketable securities? Assume that the company's investment in marketable securities is material to the financial statements.

a. The board of directors is not actively involved in monitoring the company's policies regarding marketable securities.

b. The company has an internal audit department, but it does not have any computer audit expertise and has not conducted audits of the cash or marketable securities account during the past three years.

c. Management does not have written guidelines for investments in marketable securities. The CFO has been successful in procuring good returns on investments in the past, and management does not want to tamper with success.

10-68 LO 9 A client prepared the following worksheet listing all activities in the marketable securities accounts for the year under audit. For the purpose of this question, assume that no unusual securities exist except the note from XYNO Corporation (a related party) and a note from Allis-Chalmers Corporation (a customer). Assume also that control risk was assessed as moderate to high and that the auditor decides to concentrate on substantive tests of details for the account balance. The account balances at the beginning and end of the year per the company's trial balance are as follows:

	Beginning Balance	Ending Balance
Investment in marketable securities	$400,000	$675,000
Allowance to reduce securities to market	$ 35,000	$ 35,000
Balance per general ledger	$365,000	$640,000
Interest income		$ 25,000
Dividend income		$ 18,000
Net gain on the disposal of securities		$ 32,000

Identify the audit procedures needed to complete the audit of marketable securities for year end. You may assume that the client was audited by the same firm last year. Be sure to cover the steps the auditor would use to determine that the securities are properly classified.

10-69 LO 9 Justin Company, a medium-size manufacturing client located in the Southwest, produces supplies for the automobile industry. The company is publicly traded on the American Stock Exchange. Joann Sielig took over as chief executive officer (CEO) three years ago after a successful career with a New York investment-banking firm. The company had been earning minimal returns, and Sielig is intent on turning the company around. She has analyzed the situation and determined that the company's main manufacturing arm could be treated as a cash cow. In other words, although the operations do not generate a lot of profit, they do generate cash flow that could be used for investment purposes.

FRAUD

Sielig has decided that the best opportunities for superior returns lie in investments in high-risk marketable securities. When questioned on this strategy during a board meeting, she cited finance literature that, she asserted, shows greater returns are consistent only with greater risk. However, the risk can be minimized by appropriately diversifying the investment portfolio. Given Sielig's knowledge of the subject and quick grasp of the company's situation, the board gave her complete control over all aspects of management. She personally manages the investment portfolio. Moreover, the board was so impressed with her analysis that she was given an incentive pay contract with an annual bonus based on a percentage of profits in excess of the previous year's profits. In addition, she received stock options.

The company has an internal audit department that reports directly to the CEO (Sielig). Although there is an audit committee, it exists more in form than in substance and meets with the director of internal audit only occasionally. The internal audit program for the year is determined by the director of internal audit in conjunction with Sielig and is strongly influenced by two factors: (1) Sielig's perception of areas needing review and (2) areas of potential cost savings.

Sielig has let it be known that all units of the company must justify their existence, and if the internal audit department expected future budget increases, it must generate recommended cost savings in excess of the current internal audit budget.

Your firm audits Justin Company. During the planning and risk assessment for the audit, you note the following:

1. The investment account has grown from approximately 7% of total assets to approximately 30% of total assets.
2. The investment portfolio includes some long-term investments in company stocks; however, many of the stocks held in the portfolio are high-risk stocks (with hopes of greater returns).
3. The remainder of the investment portfolio consists of a wide variety of complex financial instruments, including derivative securities.
4. Broker fees have increased dramatically. There is also a new line item for investment consulting fees. It appears that most of these fees are owed to a company that might be somehow related to Sielig.
5. Most of the securities are held by the brokerage firm, but a few are held by the investment consulting company, and a few others are held directly by the company.
6. The company has shown a 25% increase in reported net income during the past year.
7. The company's stock value has appreciated more than 20% during the past year.
   a. Identify the elements of inherent risk (including fraud risk) and control risk in the preceding scenario that should be considered in planning the audit, and indicate potential audit implications.
   b. Outline an audit program that could be used for auditing the marketable securities account.
   c. Given only the information presented in the scenario, identify the specific factors the auditor would evaluate in formulating an opinion on the required public reporting of internal control over financial reporting.

CONTEMPORARY AND HISTORICAL CASES

FRAUD

ETHICS

PROFESSIONAL SKEPTICISM

10-70 **PEREGRINE FINANCIAL GROUP (PFG), INC., AND RUSSELL WASENDORF SR.**
LO 2, 3, 4, 8, 10

Refer to the *Professional Judgment in Context* feature at the beginning of the chapter. Additional details on PFG and Wasendorf are presented below. On July 14, 2012, Russell Wasendorf, Sr. attempted to commit suicide inside his vehicle in the parking lot of Peregrine Financial Group, Inc.'s (PFG) corporate offices, leaving a remarkable suicide note in his vehicle detailing a fraud scheme in which he embezzled over $200 million from PFG's brokerage clients over a 20-year period. Wasendorf led a very interesting and affluent lifestyle and ran the business in some unusual ways. Examples include the following:

- In addition to owning PFG, he also owned an Italian restaurant My Verona in Cedar Rapids, Iowa, along with publishing companies (SFO Magazine and W&A Publishing/Trader's Press) and a real estate operation in Bucharest, Romania.
- He married his fiancée, who works at My Verona, in the Bellagio Hotel in Las Vegas on June 30, 2012.
- His son, Russell Wasendorf, Jr., ran the operations of PFG and was the president and chief operating officer of the company, but did not have detailed access to important financial records of the company. Instead, Russell Wasendorf, Sr., had sole control of the company's bank accounts.
- He flew his private jet to Chicago often for business, but was also known to take the jet all around the world to attend Lady Gaga concerts.
- He recently pledged a $2 million donation to the Athletic Department at the University of Northern Iowa.
- He attempted, but failed, to commit suicide by hooking up a tube to his car's tailpipe when suspicions of the fraud were revealed. An empty bottle of vodka was found next to his body. He was subsequently hospitalized at the University of Iowa Hospitals and Clinics in Iowa City, and was removed from his hospital bed by FBI agents while simultaneously speaking to his Chicago-based lawyer, Thomas Breen. Later that day, he appeared in federal court related to charges of lying to federal regulators and was considered a flight risk.

Below are quotes from Wasendorf's suicide note:

I have committed fraud. For this I feel constant and intense guilt. I am remorseful that my greatest transgressions have been to my fellow man. Through a scheme of using false bank statements I have been able to embezzle millions of dollars from customer accounts at Peregrine Financial Group, Inc. The forgeries started nearly twenty years ago and have gone undetected until now. I was able to conceal my crime of forgery by being the sole individual with access to the US Bank accounts held by PFG. No one else in the company ever saw an actual US Bank statement. The Bank statements were always delivered directly to me when they arrived in the mail. I made counterfeit statements within a few hours of receiving the actual statements and gave the forgeries to the accounting department.

I had no access to additional capital and I was forced into a difficult decision: Should I go out of business or cheat? I guess my ego was too big to admit failure. So I cheated, I falsified the very core of the financial documents of PFG, the Bank Statements. At first I had to make forgeries of both the Firstar Bank Statements and the Harris Bank Statements. When I chose to close the Harris Account I only had to falsify the Firstar statements. [Note: Firstar eventually became U.S. Bank.] I also made forgeries of official letters and correspondence from the bank, as well as transaction confirmation statements.

Using a combination of PhotoShop, Excel, scanners, and both laser and ink jet printers I was able to make very convincing forgeries of nearly every document that came from the Bank. I could create forgeries very quickly so no one suspected that my forgeries were not the real thing that had just arrived in the mail.

With careful concealment and blunt authority I was able to hide my fraud from others at PFG. PFG grew out of a one man shop, a business I started in the basement of my home. As I added people to the company everyone knew I was the guy in charge. If anyone questioned my authority I would simply point out that I was the sole shareholder. I established rules and procedures as each new situation arose. I ordered that US Bank statements were to be delivered directly to me unopened, to make sure no one was able to examine an actual US Bank Statement. I was also the only person with online access to PFG's account using US Bank's online portal. On US Bank side, I told representatives at the Bank that I was the only person they should interface with at PFG.

When it became common practice for Certified Auditors and the Field Auditors of the Regulators to mail Balance Confirmation Forms to Banks and other entities holding customer funds I opened a post office box. The box was originally in the name of Firstar Bank but was eventually changed to US Bank. I put the address "PO Box 706, Cedar Falls, IA 50613-0030" on the counterfeit Bank Statements. When the auditors mailed the Confirmation Forms to the Bank's false address, I would intercept the Form, type in the amount I needed to show, forge a Bank Officer's signature and mail it back to the Regulator or Certified Auditor. When online Banking became prevalent I learned how to falsify online Bank Statements and the Regulators accepted them without question.

At about the same time that emergency officials responded to the 911 call in the parking lot of PFG's offices, Russell Wasendorf, Jr. arrived at his office inside the building and found an exact copy of the suicide note. Immediately thereafter, he contacted U.S. Bank and obtained a bank statement with an ending balance as of December 31, 2011, equaling $6,337,628.14. The ending balance reported by his father on the falsified bank statement was $221,770,946.18.

PFG is a futures trading firm. Futures trading firms match buyers and sellers of contracts for commodities like wheat, oil, and aluminum and charge a commission for the service. Companies use futures contracts to protect themselves from price fluctuations. PFG is a privately held entity, so it is not subject to oversight by the SEC or PCAOB. Instead, the U.S. Commodities Futures Trading Commission (CFTC) is the regulatory agency responsible for the oversight of the industry, and the NFA is the industry association that operates under the supervision of the CFTC. The NFA is responsible for monitoring and auditing PFG for compliance with financial reporting requirements of the domestic exchanges, of which PFG was a member. The NFA never required electronic verification of PFG's bank statements.

In 2004, a PFG client complained to the NFA that PFG was misusing customer funds. In 2009, an anonymous complaint was filed with the NFA asking for a review of PFG's bank account information. What, if anything, the NFA did about the complaint was not known. Interestingly, Wasendorf, Sr. serves on an advisory committee of the NFA. Veraja-Snelling Co. is PFG's audit firm. The firm is operated out of a home in Glendale Heights, Illinois. Jeannie Veraja-Snelling is the sole practitioner and has never performed any public company audits, even though she did register her audit firm with the PCAOB in 2010. On the December 31, 2010, financial statements, Veraja-Snelling certified that PFG was in compliance with federal commodities regulations governing the segregation of customer money.

What likely prompted the timing of Wasendorf's attempted suicide was the fact that the NFA had just implemented a change to its online system whereby bank statement information would be directed electronically from the banks directly to the NFA (the system can be viewed at *www.confirmation.com*). The NFA started receiving confirmations through that system one day before Wasendorf's attempted suicide.

PFG filed for bankruptcy almost immediately after Wasendorf's attempted suicide and subsequent arrest. In addition, all the other businesses that Wasendorf ran immediately ceased operations, firing all employees. These businesses began the process of immediate liquidation. All customer accounts at PFG have been frozen, so investors have no access to their assets. Because PFG is a futures trading firm, not a traditional brokerage firm, investors do not have access to the protections normally provided by the Securities Investor Protection Corporation, which returns assets held in accounts of traditional brokerage firms that fail.

a. Describe any inherent, fraud, or control risks that are evident from the facts in the case.

b. Comment on your perceptions of the quality of the NFA's oversight of PFG.

c. Do you think it is ethically problematic that Wasendorf served on an advisory committee of the NFA? Why might NFA wanted Wasendorf to serve on its advisory committee? What conflict might that have caused?

d. Comment on your perceptions of the quality of Veraja-Snelling's certification of PFG's compliance status. Is a sole practitioner likely capable of sufficiently overseeing a large, complex entity like PFG? Was it acceptable for Veraja-Snelling to accept a paper copy of the bank confirmation, which she would have believed came directly from U.S. Bank? Why might Veraja-Snelling have lacked professional skepticism for this engagement?

e. Having the CEO personally involved in receiving bank statements and in limiting the bank's access to other individuals within the company would be very unusual for a large company such as PFG. Further, U.S. Bank should have expected to receive an auditor's confirmation request annually, but did not because Wasendorf circumvented the process. Using the ethical decision making framework from Chapter 4, comment on whether you think that U.S. Bank is responsible in any way for this fraud. Explain. Recall that the steps are as follows: (1) identify the ethical issue, (2) determine the affected parties and identify their rights, (3) determine the most important rights for each affected party, (4) develop alternative courses of action, (5) determine the likely consequences of each proposed course of action on each affected party, (6) assess the possible consequences, and (7) decide on an appropriate course of action.

10-71 **PCAOB, SEC, SATYAM COMPUTER SERVICES AND RAMALINGA RAJU**

LO 1, 2, 3, 4, 7, 8, 10

FRAUD

ETHICS

PROFESSIONAL SKEPTICISM

INTERNATIONAL

In the late 1990s, Satyam Computer Services (Satyam) was a relatively unknown, family-owned information technology (IT) company located in Hyderabad, India. All that changed when Satyam was awarded a contract to establish IT architecture at the World Bank. The selection of Satyam was, at the time, quite surprising given Satyam's relative size and obscure reputation. But the company's business continued to thrive as demand grew for IT outsourcing from Indian companies like Satyam. At the height of its success, Satyam employed about 50,000 employees and operated in 67 countries around the world. As it turns out, the reason for selecting

Satyam for the World Bank contract was that Mohamed Muhsin, the chief information officer for the World Bank, was financially involved in Satyam. After suspicions of this became known in 2006, Muhsin retired and was subsequently banned from any further relationship with the World Bank. According to World Bank officials, they alerted the U.S. Department of Justice that Satyam top management engaged in fraudulent and corrupt business practices.

In October 2008 the World Bank fired Satyam, accusing the company of installing spy systems on its computers and of stealing assets from the World Bank. Also during October 2008, a stock analyst questioned Satyam's large cash balances during an earnings conference call. The stock analyst's questions were largely ignored, and the company's stock price continued to rise. Satyam continued to report record profits despite the worldwide economic downturn. In December 2008, Satyam's board of directors approved the purchase of two companies owned by Raju's family, Maytas Properties and Maytas Infrastructure. Investors were outraged by the proposed transaction because of the relationship between Raju and the two companies. As a result of the outcry, the transaction was not finalized. However, the resulting bad press coverage caused analysts to put sell recommendations on Satyam's stock, sending share prices down 10% and resulting in four of five independent board members resigning.

Responding to the resulting pressure, on January 7, 2009, Raju made a shocking revelation admitting to a massive fraud, in a letter addressed to Satyam's remaining board members. Portions of the letter are reproduced below (*note that original typos are retained for accuracy*):

It is with deep regret, and tremendous burden that I am carrying on my conscience, that I would like to bring the following facts to your notice:

1. The Balance Sheet carries as of September 30 2008
    1. Inflated (non-existent) cash and bank balances of Rs. 5,040 crore (as against Rs. 5361 crore reflected in the books)
    2. An accrued interest of Rs. 376 crore which is non-existent
    3. An understated liability of Rs. 1,230 crore on account of funds arranged by me
    4. An over stated debtors position of Rs. 490 crore (as against Rs. 2651 in the books)
2. For the September quarter (Q2) we reported a revenue of Rs. 2,700 crore and an operating margin of Rs. 649 crore (24% Of revenues) as against the actual revenues of Rs. 2,112 crore and an actual operating margin of Rs. 61 Crore (3% of revenues). This has resulted in artificial cash and bank balances going up by Rs. 588 crore in Q2 alone.

This gap in the Balance Sheet has arisen on account of inflated profits over a period of last several years (limited only to Satyam standalone, books of subsidiaries reflecting true performance). What started as a marginal gap between actual operating profit and the one reflected in the books of accounts continued to grow over the years. It has attained unmanageable proportions as the size of company operations grew significantly.... Every attempt made to eliminate the gap failed. As the promoters held a small percentage of equity, the concern was that poor performance would result in a take-over, thereby exposing the gap. It was like riding a tiger, not knowing how to get off without being eaten.

Under the circumstances, I am tendering my resignation as the chairman of Satyam and shall continue in this position only till such time the current board is expanded. My continuance is just to ensure enhancement of the board over the next several days or as early as possible. I am now prepared to subject myself to the laws of the land and face consequences thereof.

(B. Ramalinga Raju)

Copies marked to:

1. Chairman SEBI
2. Stock Exchanges

Ultimately, it was revealed that assets on Satyam's balance sheet were overstated by about $1.5 billion, and that over $1 billion in bank loans and cash that the company claimed to own were non-existent. The fictitious assets accounted for 50% of the company's total assets. To accomplish the fraud, Raju and other individuals in top management (including the CFO, the head of internal audit, and Raju's brother) took the following actions:

- Created fictitious bank statements to inflate cash
- Reported fictitious interest income from the fictitious bank accounts
- Created 6,000 fake salary accounts and stole the money after Satyam deposited it
- Created fictitious customer identities and generated fictitious invoices against their names to inflate revenue
- Forged board of director resolutions to obtain loans for Satyam

PricewaterhouseCoopers (PwC) was Satyam's auditor from 2000 to the time the fraud was revealed. PwC was criticized for failing to exercise professional skepticism regarding the $1.04 billion cash balance of non-interest-bearing deposits. Normally, companies would either invest that money in an interest-bearing account or disburse the money through dividends to shareholders. As such, the large amount of cash should have been a red flag to the auditors that verification of the account balances was necessary. It was later revealed that PwC did not independently confirm the cash accounts with the banks in which Satyam claimed to have accounts. Subsequent PCAOB and SEC investigations revealed that PwC allowed their audit clients to control the cash confirmation process and did not challenge management regarding the validity of confirmations. In fact, some banks sent PwC confirmations directly, and those confirmations contradicted the statements that management had provided. For example, one bank told PwC that the Satyam account had a balance of $11.2 million, but management reported a balance of $108.6 million. Another bank reported $330,172 in the Satyam account, but management reported a balance of $152.9 million. Further complicating matters, the PwC network firm partner reviewed the working papers for the 2008 audit one month before the audit report was issued. During the review, the partner noted the deficiencies in the confirmation process and advised the engagement team not to rely on confirmations that were not received directly from the banks. The engagement team ignored the review comment, taking no actions to address the confirmation process weaknesses. It is unclear whether the reviewing partner knew that the comments were left unaddressed, but in any case the partner should have followed up to make sure that the audit opinion was not issued until the confirmation process weaknesses were resolved.

Raju, his brother, the former managing director of the board, the head of internal audit, and the CFO were all arrested by Indian officials on charges of fraud. Indian officials also arrested two of the PwC auditors on charges of fraud. On April 5, 2011, the SEC settled a civil action with Satyam Computer Services, in which the company paid a penalty of $10 million (see Accounting and Auditing Enforcement Release No. 3258). On May 6, 2011, PwC and its Indian affiliates agreed to a $25.5 million settlement in a class action lawsuit. On October 12, 2011, the two PwC auditors were granted bail and left jail.

a. Aside from the shocking disclosure of the fraud and its magnitude, one of the most interesting comments in Raju's statement to the board of directors was "It was like riding a tiger, not knowing how to get off without being eaten." Speculate on why he may have stated that.

b. Describe why PwC's cash confirmation process was flawed. Comment on why PwC may have had an incentive to not exercise professional skepticism in this situation.

c. Which management assertion did Raju's fraud violate?

d. What internal controls over cash appear to have been missing or violated based on the facts in this case?

e. Consider the situation of the PwC network firm partner. That individual correctly reviewed the workpapers and suggested that the engagement team should not have relied on the cash confirmations from management. Using the ethical decision making framework from Chapter 4, determine what next steps the audit partner should have taken upon making the review suggestions. Recall that the steps are as follows: (1) identify the ethical issue; in this case the ethical issue is how to properly ensure that the review comments are taken seriously and addressed; (2) determine the affected parties and identify their rights; (3) determine the most important rights for each affected party; (4) develop alternative courses of action; (5) determine the likely consequences of each proposed course of action on each affected party; (6) assess the possible consequences; and (7) decide on an appropriate course of action.

10-72 **PARMALAT**

FRAUD

PROFESSIONAL SKEPTICISM

INTERNATIONAL

LO 8 As an example of difficulties that auditors experience in collecting confirmations of cash balances, consider the Parmalat fraud that was exposed in 2003. In that case, the company overstated cash by about $5 billion, which reflected a fictitious amount in a Bank of America account in the Cayman Islands. The Italian segment of the audit firm, Grant Thornton, received a cash confirmation that noted no exceptions to the confirmation the audit firm had sent. Parmalat accomplished the deception, in part, by providing the audit firm with a fictitious bank mailing address.

a. What role does the concept of materiality play in the substantive testing of cash balances?

b. How might the Internet and associated electronic confirmation processes help to avoid fraud associated with cash confirmations?

c. What are two or three key factors the auditor might consider that could have indicated that the cash account was a high-risk account for this client and would require more skeptical audit work?

11

Auditing Inventory, Goods and Services, and Accounts Payable: The Acquisition and Payment Cycle

CHAPTER OVERVIEW AND LEARNING OBJECTIVES

The acquisition and payment cycle includes processes for identifying products or services to be acquired, purchasing goods and services, receiving the goods, approving payments, and paying for goods and services received. In terms of the audit opinion formulation process, this chapter primarily involves Phases II, III, and IV, that is, performing risk assessment procedures, tests of controls, and substantive procedures for the acquisition and payment cycle.

Through studying this chapter, you will be able to achieve these learning objectives:

通过本章的学习，你将能够实现以下学习目标：

1. Identify the significant accounts, disclosures, and relevant assertions in the acquisition and payment cycle.

   识别采购与付款循环中重要的账户、披露和相关的认定。

2. Identify and assess inherent risks of material misstatement in the acquisition and payment cycle.

   识别和评估采购与付款循环中重大错报的固有风险。

3. Identify and assess fraud risks of material misstatement in the acquisition and payment cycle.

   识别和评估采购与付款循环中重大错报的舞弊风险。

4. Identify and assess control risks of material misstatement in the acquisition and payment cycle.

   识别和评估采购与付款循环中重大错报的控制风险。

5. Describe how to use preliminary analytical procedures to identify possible material misstatements in acquisition and payment cycle accounts, disclosures, and assertions.

   描述如何运用初步的分析性程序识别与采购与付款循环账户、披露和认定有关的可能的重大错报。

6. Determine appropriate responses to identified risks of material misstatement for acquisition and payment cycle accounts, disclosures, and assertions.

   明确对于识别的与采购与付款循环账户、披露和认定有关的重大错报风险如何进行适当的反应。

7. Determine appropriate tests of controls and consider the results of tests of controls for acquisition and payment cycle accounts, disclosures, and assertions.

   确定适当的控制测试，并且考虑和采购与付款循环账户、披露和认定有关的控制测试结果。

8. Determine and apply sufficient appropriate substantive audit procedures for testing acquisition and payment cycle accounts, disclosures, and assertions.

   确定和应用充分、适当的实质性审计程序以测试采购与付款循环账户、披露和认定。

9. Apply the frameworks for professional decision making and ethical decision making to issues involving conducting the audit of acquisition and payment cycle accounts, disclosures, and assertions.

   运用职业决策和职业道德决策框架解决与采购与付款循环账户、披露和认定审计有关的问题。

THE AUDIT OPINION FORMULATION PROCESS

I. Making Client Acceptance and Continuance Decisions
Chapter 14

II. Performing Risk Assessment
Chapters 3, 7 and 9–13

III. Obtaining Evidence about Internal Control Operating Effectiveness
Chapters 8–13 and 16

IV. Obtaining Substantive Evidence about Accounts, Disclosures and Assertions
Chapters 8–13 and 16

V. Completing the Audit and Making Reporting Decisions
Chapters 14 and 15

The Auditing Profession, the Risk of Fraud and Mechanisms to Address Fraud: Regulation, Corporate Governance, and Audit Quality
Chapters 1 and 2

Professional Liability and the Need for Quality Auditor Judgments and Ethical Decisions
Chapter 4

The Audit Opinion Formulation Process and A Framework for Obtaining Audit Evidence
Chapters 5 and 6

PROFESSIONAL JUDGMENT IN CONTEXT

Thor Industries, Inc. and Mark Schwartzhoff: Fraudulent Reductions in Cost of Goods Sold Through Manipulation of Inventory Accounts

On May 13, 2011, the Securities and Exchange Commission (SEC) filed settled enforcement actions against Thor Industries, Inc. and Mark Schwartzhoff, the former vice president of finance at Thor's Dutchmen Manufacturing subsidiary. Thor produces and sells recreational vehicles, and Dutchmen is one of Thor's 15 subsidiaries. During the period of the fraud, Schwartzhoff served as an internal auditor, controller, and ultimately vice president of finance, which was Dutchmen's most senior financial officer position.

From 2002 to January 2007, Schwartzhoff engaged in a fraudulent accounting scheme to understate Dutchmen's cost of goods sold in order to avoid recognizing rising inventory costs during the period. Schwartzhoff had access to all of Dutchmen's accounting systems and could make manual journal entries without authorization or meaningful review by anyone at either Dutchmen or Thor headquarters. Schwartzhoff perpetrated the fraud by making fictitious journal entries, understating the cost of inventory purchases, thereby achieving lower cost of goods sold and higher net income. Schwartzhoff credited inventory purchases accounts and made offsetting debits to increase other assets or decrease liabilities. To hide the

fraud, Schwartzhoff created fictitious documentation and reconciliations and submitted them to Thor's external auditor. He falsified inventory records to make it appear that ending inventory had increased when, in fact, it had not. Schwartzhoff also concealed the fraud by delaying the recruiting and hiring of the controller position at Dutchmen, and he assigned the duties of his subordinates so that he would retain the ability to continue perpetrating the fraud without detection. Thor headquarters did not supervise Schwartzhoff, and did not conduct internal audits of Dutchmen.

The magnitude of the fraud grew from less than $1 million in 2003 to $14 million by 2006. Throughout the entire period of the fraud, pretax income was overstated by about $27 million. Despite this manipulation, Thor's auditor, Deloitte, issued unqualified audit opinions and agreed with management's assessment that internal controls were effective. Schwartzhoff perpetrated the fraud because it resulted in increased bonuses from his incentive compensation plan. His bonus was calculated as a percentage of pretax income, so by understating cost of goods sold he was able to show higher income, and thereby earn a larger bonus. Ultimately, he earned about $300,000 in excess, fraudulently derived, bonus compensation. Once the fraud was uncovered, Thor fired Schwartzhoff and had to restate its financial statements from 2004 to 2007. Following the discovery of the fraud, Thor also reported a material weakness in its internal controls relating to the conduct of Schwartzhoff.

Thor was fined $1 million. Schwartzhoff was permanently barred from serving as an officer or director of a public company, and was fined $394,830 by the SEC. He was also convicted of one count of wire fraud and had to pay restitution to the U.S. Attorney's Office for the Northern District of Indiana for $1.9 million.

For further details on this case, see SEC Litigation Release No. 21966 (May 13, 2011).

As you read through this chapter, consider the following questions:

- What types of accounts are included in the audit of the acquisition and payment cycle? (LO 1)
- What are the inherent, fraud, and control risks that exist in this cycle? (LO 2, 3, 4)
- The Thor and Schwartzhoff case illustrates control deficiencies that enabled the fraud to go undetected. What do these types of control deficiencies imply about the approach the auditor will need to use to audit the inventory-related accounts and assertions? (LO 4, 6, 7)
- What controls can mitigate the risks associated with accounts in the acquisition and payment cycle? (LO 4)
- What substantive audit procedures could have detected this type of fraud earlier? (LO 6, 8)

重要账户和相关认定　Significant Accounts and Relevant Assertions

LO 1 Identify the significant accounts, disclosures, and relevant assertions in the acquisition and payment cycle.

The major accounts in the acquisition and payment cycle are inventory, cost of goods sold, accounts payable, and other expense accounts. An overview of the significant and relevant accounts typically included in this cycle is shown in Exhibit 11.1.

Accounting for inventories is a major consideration for many companies because of its significance to both the balance sheet and the income statement. Inventories are defined as items of tangible personal property that are held for sale in the ordinary course of business, that are in the process of production for such sale, or that are to be currently consumed in the production of goods or services to be available for sale. For example, inventory includes such items as steel held for future production of an automobile, electronic goods in a retail store, drugs on shelves in hospitals or pharmaceutical companies, and petroleum products at an oil-refining company. While the focus of this chapter concerns the purchase of inventory, organizations also purchase a variety of services (for example, consulting and legal) and other goods (for example, supplies). The purchases of inventory, services, and other goods differ somewhat from those of long-term assets, such as equipment and buildings. We discuss the purchases of these long-term assets in the next chapter.

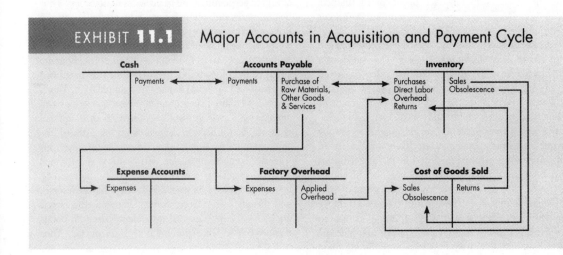

EXHIBIT **11.1**　Major Accounts in Acquisition and Payment Cycle

Activities Involved in the Acquisition and Payment Cycle

The acquisition and payment cycle consists of five distinct activities.

1. Requisition (request) for goods or services
2. Purchase of goods and services
3. Receipt of, and accounting for, goods and services
4. Approval of items for payment
5. Cash disbursements

采购与付款循环涉及的主要活动

采购与付款循环所涉及的业务活动主要包括请购、采购、开具发票、会计记录、付款的审批和支付款项。

The acquisition process begins with a **requisition** (formal request) for goods and services. An approved requisition will result in a purchase. The receipt of goods or services should cause the recognition of accounts payable with debits to an expense account (for example, legal expense) or an inventory account. Most companies will have specific procedures for approving the payments for these purchases. When the approved payment for goods or services received is made, the payment is reflected as a cash disbursement.

Many companies have an **automated purchasing system**—a networked software system linking to vendors whose offerings and prices have been preapproved by appropriate management. The technology enables purchasers to negotiate favorable prices with vendors while streamlining the buying process. Best practice for an automated system consolidates all the different functions or activities involved, assuring timely and accurate orders. An automated purchasing system will perform the following beneficial tasks:

- Apply preloaded specifications and materials lists to the system to start the process
- Automatically flag invoices that do not reconcile with purchase orders
- Create change orders and analyze variances from purchase orders

For many companies, the acquisition and payment cycle is a computerized process that is integrated with **supply chain management**. Supply chain management is the management and control of materials in the logistics process from the acquisition of raw materials to the delivery of finished products to the end user (customer). A number of companies have specific contracts with vendors that specify price and delivery terms to meet the client's production or sales needs. Companies such as Wal-Mart and JCPenney have arrangements with some vendors whereby title to the goods does not pass until a consumer purchases them at the checkout counter. Many companies using such approaches have been successful in reducing inventory levels and associated carrying costs.

Relevant Financial Statement Assertions
Assertions Relevant to Inventory

相关的财务报表认定

The five management assertions relevant to inventory are as follows:

1. *Existence or occurrence*—Inventory balances exist at the balance sheet date.
2. *Completeness*—Inventory balances include all inventory transactions that have taken place during the period.
3. *Rights and obligations*—The company has title to the inventory as of the balance sheet date.
4. *Valuation or allocation*—The recorded balances reflect the true underlying economic value of those assets.
5. *Presentation and disclosure*—Inventory is properly classified on the balance sheet and disclosed in the notes to the financial statements.

The existence and valuation assertions are usually the most relevant for inventory. Existence is a concern because, as the Thor Industries, Inc., and Schwartzhoff example from the *Professional Judgment in Context* feature illustrates, managers can manipulate the inventory account to manipulate cost of goods sold and net income. We do not separately discuss assertions for cost of goods sold. Recall that cost of goods sold is simply the result of the following calculation: *beginning inventory + purchases − ending inventory = cost of goods sold*. The most common concerns for inventory are that purchases are understated or ending inventory is overstated, which will result in both lower cost of goods sold and higher net income. Valuation is a concern because inventory may fluctuate in value, and there may be complexities in assessing an accurate value. Rights and obligations can also be a concern because the fact that a company has possession of inventory does not necessarily imply that the company actually owns it.

Assertions Relevant to Accounts Payable

The five management assertions relevant to accounts payable are as follows:

1. *Existence or occurrence*—Accounts payable balances exist at the balance sheet date.
2. *Completeness*—Accounts payable balances include all accounts payable transactions that have taken place during the period.
3. *Rights and obligations*—The company actually owes a liability for the accounts payable as of the balance sheet date.
4. *Valuation or allocation*—The recorded balances reflect the true underlying economic value of those liabilities.
5. *Presentation and disclosure*—Accounts payable is properly classified on the balance sheet and disclosed in the notes to the financial statements.

Completeness is usually the most relevant assertion for accounts payable. The primary concern regarding completeness is that the account is understated; managers may not record accounts payable transactions because they do not want to record the associated liability and expense.

**对采购与付款循环实施
风险评估程序**

Performing Risk Assessment Procedures in the Acquisition and Payment Cycle

LO 2 Identify and assess inherent risks of material misstatement in the acquisition and payment cycle.

As part of performing risk assessment procedures, the auditor obtains information that is useful in assessing the risk of material misstatement. This includes information about inherent risks at the financial statement level (for example, the client's business and operational risks, financial reporting risks) and at the account and assertion levels, fraud risks including feedback from audit team brainstorming sessions, strengths and weaknesses in internal control, and results from preliminary analytical procedures. Once the risks of material misstatement have been identified, the auditor then determines how best to respond to them as part of the audit opinion formulation process.

识别固有风险

Identifying Inherent Risks

Inventory is usually material, complex, and subject to manipulation. Given the large number of inventory-related frauds that have been perpetrated, auditors should exercise particularly high levels of professional skepticism in audits of inventory and cost of goods sold accounts. Inventory is a complex accounting and auditing area because of the following:

- A great variety (diversity) of items exists in inventory.
- Inventory accounts typically experience a high volume of activity.
- Inventory accounts may be valued according to various accounting valuation methods.
- Identifying obsolete inventory and applying the lower of cost or market principle to determine valuation are difficult tasks.
- Inventory is easily transportable.

- Inventory often exists at multiple locations, with some locations being remote from the company's headquarters.
- Inventory may become obsolete because of technological advances even though there are no visible signs of wear.
- Inventory is often returned by customers, so care must be taken to separately identify returned merchandise, check it for quality, and record it at net realizable value.
- Because inventory often includes a variety of types of products, the auditor must possess and apply significant knowledge about the business in order to address obsolescence and valuation questions.
- Individuals involved with the purchase of inventory may have incentives to exploit weaknesses in the control system to their economic advantage.

Identifying Fraud Risk Factors

Because of the volume of transactions, as well as the ability to physically move inventory, the acquisition and payment cycle is often the subject of fraud. Most of the frauds in this cycle involve overstatement of inventory or assets and understatement of expenses. Many disbursement frauds involve fictitious purchases or, in some cases, kickbacks to the purchasing agent. Examples of fraud in the acquisition and payment cycle include:

LO 3 Identify and assess fraud risks of material misstatement in the acquisition and payment cycle.

- Theft of inventory by the employee
- **Inventory shrinkage**, which is a reduction in inventory presumed to be due to physical loss or theft
- Employee schemes involving fictitious vendors as means to transfer payments to themselves
- Executives recording fictious inventory or inappropriately recording higher values for existing inventory by creating false records for items that do not exist (for example, inflated inventory count sheets and bogus receiving reports or purchase orders)

通过伪造虚假的会计记录，管理层记录不存在的存货或者不恰当地高估已有存货的价值。

- Large manual adjustments to inventory accounts
- Schemes to classify expenses as assets (for example, inappropriately capitalizing items that are truly current-period expenses)
- Executives misusing travel and entertainment accounts and charging them as company expenses

Exhibit 11.2 identifies some of the possible fraudulent schemes for manipulating inventory and cost of goods sold.

EXHIBIT **11.2**	Approaches for Manipulating Inventory and Cost of Goods Sold	
Event	**Affected Accounts**	**Possible Manipulations**
1. Purchase inventory	Inventory, accounts payable	Under-record purchases Record purchases in a later period Not record purchases
2. Return inventory to supplier	Accounts payable, inventory	Overstate returns Record returns in an earlier period
3. Inventory is sold	Cost of goods sold, inventory	Record at too low an amount Not record cost of goods sold nor reduce inventory
4. Inventory becomes obsolete	Loss on write-down of inventory, inventory	Not write off or write down obsolete inventory
5. Periodic count of inventory quantities	Inventory shrinkage, inventory	Overcount inventory (double counting, etc.)

Fraud in the Acquisition and Payment Cycle at WorldCom and Phar-Mor

WorldCom

WorldCom management recorded billions of line rental expenses as fixed assets. In other words, managers inappropriately debited fixed assets rather than debiting expenses, thereby bolstering their current period income. Managers were motivated to engage in the fraud to meet earnings expectations and to show that they were able to manage their line expenses better than the rest of the industry. Because the expenses were consistent with previous years, their relatively low level did not raise auditor suspicion. In this case, the auditors should have been skeptical that WorldCom was able to achieve what other companies in its industry could not.

Phar-Mor

Phar-Mor, a major discount retailer, had over 300 stores in the 1990s with great operating results and a concept that captured the imagination of Wall Street. Typical of many frauds, the company was dominated by an officer who viewed the company as his own and diverted more than $10 million to support a now failed minor-league basketball league. To cover up this misuse of company money, the officers directed the managers of each store to inflate their inventory costs. For example, if a carton of Coca-Cola cost $1.99, they were to value it at $2.99. The overstatements were needed to balance the cash outflow to the creation of an asset. Company management was emboldened to commit the fraud because it knew that the auditor would not visit all 300 stores to test inventory valuation.

The *Auditing in Practice* feature "Fraud in the Acquisition and Payment Cycle at WorldCom and Phar-Mor" provides details on two well-known frauds in this area.

识别控制风险

LO 4 Identify and assess control risks of material misstatement in the acquisition and payment cycle.

Identifying Control Risks

Once the auditor has obtained an understanding of the inherent and fraud risks of material misstatement in the acquisition and payment cycle accounts, the auditor needs to understand the controls that the client has designed and implemented to address those risks. Remember, the auditor is required to gain an overall understanding of internal controls for both integrated audits and financial statement only audits. Such understanding is normally gained by means of a walkthrough of the process, inquiry, observation, and review of the client's documentation. The auditor considers both entity-wide controls and transaction controls at the account and assertion levels. This understanding provides the auditor with a basis for making an initial control risk assessment.

At the entity-wide level, the auditor considers the control environment, including such principles as a commitment to integrity and ethical values and holding individuals accountable for their internal control responsibilities. The auditor also considers the remaining components of internal control that are typically entity-wide—risk assessment, information and communication, and monitoring controls. Although all the components of internal control need to be understood, the auditor typically finds it useful to focus on significant control activities in the acquisition and payment cycle. As part of this understanding, the auditor focuses on the relevant assertions for each account and identifies the controls that relate to risks for these assertions. In an integrated audit or in a controls reliance audit of the financial statements, the auditor uses this understanding to identify important controls that need to be tested.

Overview of Internal Controls for Accounts in the Acquisition and Payment Cycle

The auditor usually begins by developing an understanding of the cost components of inventory and how inventory valuation is affected by current market prices. We concentrate on the inventories of a manufacturing client because that setting is the most complex and normally presents the most difficult audit problems. A well-conceived inventory control system should provide reasonable assurance of the following:

- All purchases are authorized.
- There exists a timely, accurate, and complete recording of inventory transactions.
- Receipt of inventory is properly accounted for and independently tested to verify quality in adherence to company standards.
- The cost accounting system is up-to-date; costs are properly identified and assigned to products; and variances are analyzed, investigated, and properly allocated to inventory and cost of goods sold.
- A **periodic inventory system** may serve as a basis for management reports and to assist in managing inventory. A periodic inventory system is a system of inventory recordkeeping in which no continuous record of changes in inventory (receipts and issues of inventory items) is kept. At the end of an accounting period, the ending inventory is determined by an actual physical count of every item, and its cost is computed using a suitable method.
- A **perpetual inventory system** may serve as a basis for management reports and to assist in managing inventory. A perpetual inventory system is a system of inventory recordkeeping where book inventory is continuously in agreement with inventory on hand within specified time periods. In some cases, book inventory and inventory on hand may be reconciled with each transaction; in other systems, these two numbers may be reconciled less often. This process is useful in keeping track of actual availability of goods and determining what the correct time to reorder from suppliers might be.
- **Cycle counts** are taken as part of the perpetual inventory system. Cycle counts involve periodic testing of the accuracy of the perpetual inventory record by counting all inventories on a cyclical, or periodic, basis.
- All products are systematically reviewed for obsolescence, and appropriate accounting action is taken.
- Management periodically reviews inventory, takes action on excessive inventory, and manages inventory to minimize losses caused by technological obsolescence.
- New products are introduced only after market studies and quality-control tests are made.
- Long-term contracts are closely monitored. Excess purchase requirements are monitored, and potential losses are recognized.

永续盘存制
(perpetual inventory system)
是对存货项目设置动态的库存记录，按品名、规格设置存货明细账，逐笔或者逐日登记存货的收入和发出，并随时计列结存数。

The specific controls implemented by the client will vary with the amount of automation of the process. The following discussion highlights typical controls for each of the five activities of the acquisition and payment cycle.

1. Requisition (Request) for Goods and Services The acquisition process for inventory begins with the company's production or sales plan. Some companies will have long-term production plans. For example, in the automotive industry a manufacturer might schedule production for a month in advance and notify its suppliers of the production plan. In other situations (for example, Dell Computer), the production process begins when Dell receives an order for the computer. The auditor must thoroughly understand the company's relationships with its suppliers and should examine major contracts that specify delivery, quantity, timing, and quality conditions. The traditional acquisition process begins with recognizing the need for the purchase—either by an individual or by an automated process that monitors inventory or production.

Embedded in the requisition process are a number of controls to help assure that all purchases are properly approved. Normally, a requisition form is forwarded to the purchasing department by a supervisor, although some departments may have authority for individual purchases up to a specific dollar limit. Computer-generated purchase orders are often reviewed by the purchasing department, but in some automated systems the purchase order may be electronically communicated to the vendor with no additional review. Important controls in requisition include a production plan and authorization of a requisition form that is sent to an approved vendor by a purchasing agent or that is sent through the computer system according to preexisting contracts. Many companies use an automated purchasing system, which is a networked software system that links a company's Web site to other vendors whose offerings and prices have been preapproved by appropriate management, to control the process.

The organization may also purchase supplies, which will go through a similar process as inventory requisitions. Purchases of services, such as legal or consulting services, will be accomplished through ongoing contractual arrangements with the law firm or consulting firm.

An overview of controls over the requisition process at different types of organizations and for different types of purchases is shown in Exhibit 11.3.

Many companies partner with major suppliers to improve their supply-chain management process. For example, General Motors partnered with Eaton Corporation to furnish already-assembled subassemblies that are loaded

---

EXHIBIT 11.3 Overview of Common Controls in the Requisition Process

Inventory Purchases: Manufacturing Organization
- Written requisitions are made for specific products by the production manager or stockroom manager.
- Computer-generated requisitions are generated based on current inventory levels and production plans.

Inventory Purchases: Retail Organization
- Overall authorization to purchase product lines is delegated to individual buyers by the marketing manager. The authorization is built into the computer as a control. The limits for individual goods can be exceeded only on specific approval by the marketing manager.
- Store managers may be granted authority to purchase a limited number of goods. The store manager's ability to issue a purchase order may be subject to overall corporate limits, usually specified in dollars.
- The supplier may have access to the retailer's inventory database and, by contract, ship replacement merchandise based on sales activity and reorder points.

Inventory Purchases: Just-in-Time Manufacturing Process
- An agreement is signed with the supplier whereby the supplier agrees to ship merchandise (just in time) according to the production schedule set by the manufacturer. A long-term supply contract is negotiated specifying price, quality of products, estimated quantities, penalties for product shortages or quality problems, and so forth. Specific purchase orders are not issued; rather, the production plan is communicated to the supplier with the specified delivery dates. The production plan serves as the requisition.

Supplies Purchases
- Requisitions are issued by individual departments and sent to the appropriate department manager for approval.
- Each department may be given a budget for supplies and may have the ability to issue purchase orders directly for the needed items or may be able to purchase a limited number of items without a purchase order.

directly into the production line. This kind of relationship requires close coordination and may never involve a requisition form. It may involve only the development of a long-term contract and the sharing of production schedules with the supplier. Goods are delivered and moved directly into production. There is no formal receiving department, and Eaton Corporation is paid upon the production of an automobile. Since the requisition process is automated, the company will likely implement automated controls in this process.

2. Purchase of Goods and Services Many companies centralize the purchasing function in a purchasing department. The rationale for a separate purchasing function is that it:

- Promotes efficiency and effectiveness
- Eliminates potential favoritism that could take place if individual department heads were allowed to place orders
- Reduces the opportunity for fraud by segregating the authorization to purchase from the custody and recording functions
- Centralizes control in one function

Important purchasing controls include the approval of a contract with suppliers, restricted access to the computer program, and monitoring of inventory and purchase levels by management. The *Auditing in Practice* feature "Weak Internal Controls, Unethical Decisions, and a Fictitious Vendor at Baird Products" provides an example in which weak controls led to a fraud in the automotive parts production industry. Some services that are purchased, such as auditing services, will have additional controls, including review and approval by the audit committee.

重要的采购控制包括采购合同的审批、限制接触计算机程序以及管理者对存货和采购水平的监督。

Although there are advantages to centralized purchasing, there is a risk that purchasing agents may enter into kickback arrangements with vendors. Controls include requiring competitive bids for large purchases and rotating purchase agents across product lines. Perhaps the most important control is an authorized vendor database. Company employees cannot purchase from vendors other than those in the database, thereby making it difficult to set up fictitious vendors.

In traditional purchasing situations, prenumbered forms are used to establish the uniqueness of each order and the completeness of the purchase order population. The purchase order identifies the quantity and prices of goods ordered, quality specifications, and the delivery date. The receiving department uses the purchase order to determine whether a shipment of goods should be accepted. The accounting department uses the purchase order to determine whether a purchase was authorized and whether the vendor's invoice is correct.

Two variations of the traditional purchase order are becoming more common: the automated system-generated purchase order and the supply-chain delivery contract. Good inventory management identifies levels for inventory reorders. When inventory drops below a specified level, or in response to production plans, the company's information system generates a purchase order that is sent directly to a prespecified vendor. Companies may consider additional controls, such as (1) a maximum quantity that can be ordered within a given time period, (2) a minimum amount of previous usage during a specified time period, and (3) a required review by a purchasing agent for some accounts or for high-dollar levels. A variation of the system-generated purchase order is the electronic consignment system used by some retailers. For example, Wal-Mart encourages its partners to monitor store activities, inventory levels, and current trends in sales and authorizes the vendor to ship additional goods to stores when inventory levels decrease. However, the trade-off is that the partner—for example, Levi Strauss—maintains ownership of its product until a consumer

Weak Internal Controls, Unethical Decisions, and a Fictitious Vendor at Baird Products

AUDITING IN PRACTICE

Baird Products manufactures metal parts for the automotive parts products industry. Robert Grant was the manager in charge of the metal casting department, and he reported to Linda Thompson, the facility manager. Thompson trusted Grant and relied on his judgment and honesty. However, Grant developed a fairly lavish lifestyle that included gambling, and he also had three college-age children to support. The purchasing process and controls at Baird were uncomplicated. All purchase requests were to be approved by the department manager and then sent to the accounting department for issuance of the purchase order. The accounting department would then determine whether the purchase is within the budget and whether the vendor is on an approved list. Although the accounting department required that approved vendors provide a company name, address, telephone number, and principal contact, it did no actual verification of the vendors, a control weakness that Grant learned about and ultimately exploited.

Grant's fraud began with suppliers for products in his department. He began requiring vendors to provide him with money and gifts in order to maintain their sales volume at Baird, and vendors that refused risked being shut out of business with Baird. Later, the fraud grew larger when he required all the vendors that he dealt with to pay him a commission on their sales to Baird that essentially amounted to a bribe. Vendors feared losing sales if they did not comply, so they did not report this practice to Thompson or other members of management. The fraud grew still larger when Grant set up a fictitious

vendor (RGWB, Inc.), and embezzled nearly $200,000 over about 18 months. The fraud was finally discovered when Grant became ill and another employee took over his job during his absence. Baird fired Grant and brought criminal charges against him, but Grant fled and never faced justice. Baird learned the following lessons from this fraud:

- Even though controls are in place, they are sometimes not followed or they are followed incompletely, and if employees understand this control weakness they may exploit it.
- Companies need to have fraud hotlines where employees, vendors, and third parties can report inappropriate activity without fear of retaliation.
- Employees who seem honest and trustworthy sometimes violate that trust. Anyone in a position of trust with control over monetary resources needs to be treated with professional skepticism, both by the company itself and by its external auditors.
- Controls must be strong in the purchasing area, and there should be adequate segregation of duties of individuals who place orders versus individuals who select vendors, compare prices, and make the actual orders. Further, adequate supervision and knowledge of vendors is a vital job for top management.
- For ongoing frauds to be successful, it is often necessary for the employee(s) involved to be in a position to continue the fraud on a daily basis. Mandating vacations for all employees can be a useful control in trying to prevent and detect fraud.

purchases it. When the consumer brings the jeans to the checkout counter, the ownership transfers to Wal-Mart and then immediately to the consumer. The sales information is captured, and the accounting system records the sale as well as the cost of goods sold and a payable to Levi Strauss. The contract between the trading partners also specifies controls to assure that Wal-Mart acknowledges receipt of goods and takes steps to assure that the goods are not subject to damage, theft, or loss.

3. Receipt of, and Accounting for, Goods and Services Receiving departments should make sure that only authorized goods are received, the goods meet order specifications, an accurate count of the goods received is taken, and that accountability is established to assure that all receipts are recorded. Several alternative methods of recording the receipt of goods include the following:

- The receiving department prepares prenumbered receiving documents to record all receipts.

- The receiving department electronically scans bar codes on the goods received to record quantity and vendor and then visually inspects the goods for quality. The information system prepares a sequentially numbered receiving record for goods scanned in.
- Departments may receive goods directly, such as office supplies, and must approve payment for the merchandise.
- Goods are received directly into the production process. The vendor is paid according to the long-term contract based on the purchaser's actual production, and the vendor is penalized for production delays that are due to failures to deliver the goods.

The traditional receiving process creates a prenumbered receiving document based on a count of the merchandise received. A copy of the purchase order (usually with quantities blanked out to help assure an independent count) is reviewed to determine whether a shipment is authorized. Prenumbered receiving documents establish the completeness of the population and are useful in determining that all goods are recorded in the correct period.

Automated scanning can improve both control and efficiency of the receiving process. Products shipped with bar codes can be directly scanned into the system. Actual receipts can be automatically matched with purchase orders to determine if the shipment contains errors. Goods received into production must match the production process. If they do not, then there is a potential problem of the production line either shutting down or producing the wrong subcomponents. For example, if Eaton fails to deliver the correct subassembly to General Motors, the production line will shut down and General Motors will know the cause. Although this is not a traditional accounting control, it is very effective because any failure immediately gets the attention of management and the vendor. Therefore, there is strong motivation to avoid any mistakes.

As auditors increasingly encounter these integrated order, delivery, and payment supply-chain management systems, they have to consider the types of controls that should be present. Exhibit 11.4 provides an overview of controls that are found in traditional receiving systems and in more automated systems. Regardless of the approach taken to the receiving function, the auditor must gain reasonable assurance that management has effective controls related to receiving.

4. Approval of Items for Payment Approval typically involves a **three-way match** among the vendor invoice, the purchase order, and the receiving report. This match can occur either manually or through an automated process. The traditional, document-based acquisition and payment system requires personnel in accounts payable to match the vendor invoice, the purchase order, and the receiving report to determine the validity of the requested payment. If all items on the three documents properly match, the vendor's invoice is set up as an account payable with a scheduled payment date. Discrepancies are reviewed with the purchasing agent. The supporting documentation and authorization are then presented to the accounts payable department for payment. Internal controls should assure that all items are recorded in a timely manner, that the authorization process includes a review of documents, and that supporting documentation is canceled on payment to avoid duplicate payments.

审批通常包括三方的核对相符，这三方包括供应商发票、采购订单和验收报告。

The traditional approach to controlling the receipt of, and payment for, purchases is labor-intensive and error-prone. The automated matching process represents an efficient alternative. Purchase orders are entered into a purchase order database that is accessed by the receiving department to determine whether an incoming shipment of goods should be accepted. The receiving department electronically records the receipt of goods through

EXHIBIT **11.4** Comparison of Controls in Traditional and Automated Systems

Traditional Receiving System	Automated Integrated Receiving System
Purchase orders are prepared and sent to vendors.	Long-term contract is signed with vendor specifying: • Quality • Shipping and delivery requirements • Payment terms • Penalties for performance failures • Reconciliations between trading partners for goods shipped/received
Purchase orders are based on projected sales or production, or current inventory levels.	Quantities are based on production plans or sales programs. Quantities and delivery times are updated monthly or more frequently depending on scheduling and shipping constraints.
Price is either negotiated or competitively bid among a number of vendors.	Price is locked in with a preferred vendor.
Independent receiving function exists.	Goods are delivered to production line.
Independent, sequentially numbered receiving documents are prepared to provide evidence that the goods are received.	Disruptions of production provide evidence that goods were not delivered.
Accounts payable department matches purchase order, receiving document, and invoice and accrues accounts payable.	Accruals are set up based on contract (production, sales of goods, etc.).
Payments are made via check or by electronic transfer once or twice a month.	Payments are electronically transferred to vendor based on contractual terms.
Differences between goods received and goods ordered are identified before payments are made.	Processes are described in the contract to resolve difference between goods received and goods that were shipped by vendor.

scanning the bar code or other means and cross-references the receipt to the purchase order. The computerized application matches the three documents (purchase order, receiving document, and vendor invoice), and if the three-way match is within a prespecified tolerance limit, the invoice is approved for payment. A payment date is scheduled, and a check is automatically generated on the scheduled date and is signed using an authorized signature plate. The complete payment process occurs without any apparent human intervention. There is no authorized reviewer, no physical matching, and no individual physically signing the checks. In some systems, the payment may be transferred electronically to the vendor.

The lack of human intervention is compensated for by control procedures and authorization concepts built into the system such as the following:

• *Authorized vendors*—Purchases can be made only from authorized vendors.
• *Restricted access*—Access is restricted to databases, in particular to the vendor database and the purchasing database. Anyone with the ability to add a vendor or make unauthorized purchase orders is in a position to set up fictitious vendors and purchases. Therefore, someone outside the purchasing department should maintain the vendor database (a list of authorized vendors).

- *Automatic processes*—Although the receiving department has access to the purchase order (read-only), the use of automatic scanners and other counting devices decreases counting and identification errors.
- *Reconciliations inherent in the process*—Most retailers mark retail prices on the goods at the distribution center when they are received. The retail price tickets for an order can be generated from the purchase order. The actual number of tickets used should be reconciled with the goods received, and any leftover tickets should be an adjustment made to the receiving report.
- *Automation of error-prone activities*—Vendor invoices are traditionally entered into the system by accounts payable personnel, thereby segregating this process from the other two functions. An alternative is to receive invoices electronically. It is still important that purchasing and receiving not have the ability to enter vendor invoice data or access the vendor invoice file.
- *Restricted access to transferring funds*—Access to physical checks, or authorization of electronic cash transfers, is limited to the appropriate, designated individuals.
- *Monitoring*—Activity reports are prepared on a regular basis for management review.

Because most of the control procedures are developed during the system design process, it is important that users and internal auditors actively participate in reviewing the effectiveness of controls designed into the computer application.

5. Cash Disbursements In a manual system, an individual in a position of authority reviews the completeness of the documentation supporting a request for cash disbursement and signs a check for payment of goods or services. In most automated systems, the checks, or electronic transfers, are generated automatically according to the scheduled payment date and the supporting documents are canceled when the invoice is set up for payment. The most important controls in these systems are (1) review of transactions, by which someone reviews the expenditures and compares them to other key data (for example, production, budgets, other measures of volume) and (2) the direction of vendor disputes to someone outside the process. Other controls include the periodic review of the system by the internal audit department and periodic reconciliation of inventory on hand with inventory per the books.

Documenting Controls Auditors need to document their understanding of internal controls for both integrated audits and financial statement only audits. Exhibit 11.5 provides an example of a partial internal control questionnaire for the acquisition and payment cycle. Each negative answer in the questionnaire represents a potential internal control deficiency. Given a negative answer, the auditor should consider the effect of the response on the initial assessment of control risk. Unless another control compensates for a control weakness, the auditor will likely have a control risk assessment of moderate or high in this area.

Performing Preliminary Analytical Procedures

When planning the audit, the auditor is required to perform preliminary analytical procedures. These procedures can help auditors identify areas of potential misstatements. Auditors need to go through the four-step process described in Chapter 7, which begins with developing expectations for account balances, ratios, and trends. The following are examples of possible expected relationships in the acquisition and payment cycle:

- Assume that the company's production and pricing strategies have remained the same during the past year. Gross margin is expected to be stable and consistent with the industry average.

实施初步的分析性程序

LO 5 Describe how to use preliminary analytical procedures to identify possible material misstatements in acquisition and payment cycle accounts, disclosures, and assertions.

EXHIBIT **11.5**	Control Risk Assessment Questionnaire: Acquisition and Payment Cycle		
		Check (x) one:	
		Yes	No
1. Are purchases of inventory approved at the proper level?		_____	_____
2. Is there adequate documentation of approvals?		_____	_____
3. Are purchase orders prenumbered and accounted for?		_____	_____
4. Are purchases of inventory made from an approved vendor list?		_____	_____
5. Are changes to the approved vendor list approved at the proper level?		_____	_____
6. Does the company have a formal policy and appropriate oversight about the nature of appropriate vendor relationships and gifts?		_____	_____
7. Are controls over the process of handling returned goods adequate?		_____	_____
8. Is the recording of purchases made in a timely manner?		_____	_____
9. Is the recording of returns made in a timely manner?		_____	_____

- Assume that the company has introduced a new product with a low price point and significant customer demand. Inventory turnover is expected to increase, and days' sales in inventory are expected to decrease.
- Assume that the company has invested in a new manufacturing process that results in significantly less waste and overall increases in efficiency during the production process. Cost of goods sold is expected to decline, and gross margin is expected to increase.

Certain analytical procedures may help the auditor identify potential misstatements in acquisition and payment cycle accounts. Calculating and analyzing the dollar and percent change in inventory, cost of goods sold, and expense account balances relative to both past performance and industry performance may identify unexpected results. Further, several ratios that are presented in Exhibit 11.6 can provide useful insights. The analysis can

EXHIBIT **11.6**	Using Ratios in Preliminary Analytical Procedures in the Acquisition and Payment Cycle

Inventory Ratios
- Gross margin analysis
- Inventory turnover (cost of goods sold/ending inventory)
- Number of days' sales in inventory (365/inventory turnover)
- Shrinkage ratio (inventory write-down/ending inventory)
- Inventory per square foot of retail space (for retail clients; and comparisons should be made across locations in stores of comparable size and product mix to test for unexpected differences)
- Inventory overhead application. Analyze the relationship between materials, labor, and overhead to total product costing; compare over time and across product categories.

Accounts Payable Ratios
- Accounts payable turnover (purchases/average accounts payable)
- Days outstanding in accounts payable (365/accounts payable turnover)
- Accounts payable/current liabilities
- Purchase returns and allowances/purchases

be disaggregated by product line or location. A common-sized income statement can help identify cost of goods sold or expense accounts that are out of line with the auditor's expectations, which should be based on prior years, industry information, and the auditor's knowledge of the business.

If preliminary analytical procedures do not identify any unexpected relationships, the auditor would conclude that there is not a heightened risk of material misstatements in these accounts. If unusual or unexpected relationships exist, the planned audit procedures (tests of controls, substantive procedures) would be adjusted to address the potential material misstatements. The auditor should be aware that if a fraud is taking place in the acquisition and payment cycle, the financial statements usually will contain departures from industry norms, but may not differ from the expectations set by management. Therefore, the auditor should compare the unaudited financial statements with both past results and industry trends. The following relationships might suggest a heightened risk of fraud in the acquisition or payment cycle:

可能表明较高舞弊风险的关系包括毛利率的非预期增加、存货的增长速度高于收入的增长速度、费用显著地高于或者低于行业水平、供应商数量的非预期增加等。

- Unexpected increases in gross margin
- Inventory that is growing at a rate greater than sales
- Expenses that are either significantly above or below industry norms
- Unexpected increases in the number of suppliers
- Capital assets that seem to be growing faster than the business and for which there are no strategic plans
- Expense accounts that have significant credit entries
- Travel and entertainment expense accounts, but no documentation or approval of expenditures
- Inadequate follow-up to the auditor's recommendations on needed controls

Responding to Identified Risks of Material Misstatement

Once the auditor has developed an understanding of the risks of material misstatement, the auditor can determine the appropriate audit procedures to perform. Audit procedures should be proportional to the assessed risks, with areas of higher risk receiving more audit attention and effort. Responding to identified risks typically involves developing an audit approach that contains substantive procedures (for example, tests of details and, when appropriate, substantive analytical procedures) and tests of controls, when applicable. The appropriateness and sufficiency of selected procedures vary to achieve the desired level of assurance for each relevant assertion. While audit firms may have a standardized audit program for auditing the acquisition and payment cycle, the auditor should customize the audit program based on the assessment of risk of material misstatement.

Consider a client where the auditor has assessed the risk of material misstatement related to the existence of inventory at slightly below the maximum. Similar to the Thor Industries, Inc. and Schwartzhoff example from the *Professional Judgment in Context* feature, assume that incentives exist to overstate income to achieve profit targets that affect management bonuses, and oversight of the vice president of finance is relatively weak because of a lack of supervision by top management. The auditor may develop an audit program that consists of first performing limited tests of operating effectiveness of controls, then performing limited to moderate substantive analytical procedures, and finally performing extensive substantive tests of details. Because of the high risk, the auditor will want to obtain a great deal of evidence directly from tests of details. In contrast, consider a client where the auditor has assessed the risk of material

对识别的重大错报风险的反应

LO 6 Determine appropriate responses to identified risks of material misstatement for acquisition and payment cycle accounts, disclosures, and assertions.

EXHIBIT **11.7**   Panel A: Sufficiency of Evidence for Existence of Inventory

Client B—High Risk

Client A—Low Risk

Panel B: Approaches to Obtaining Audit Evidence for Existence of Inventory

Client B—High Risk

Client A—Low Risk

30% tests of details	50% tests of details
40% analytics	30% analytics
30% tests of controls	20% tests of controls

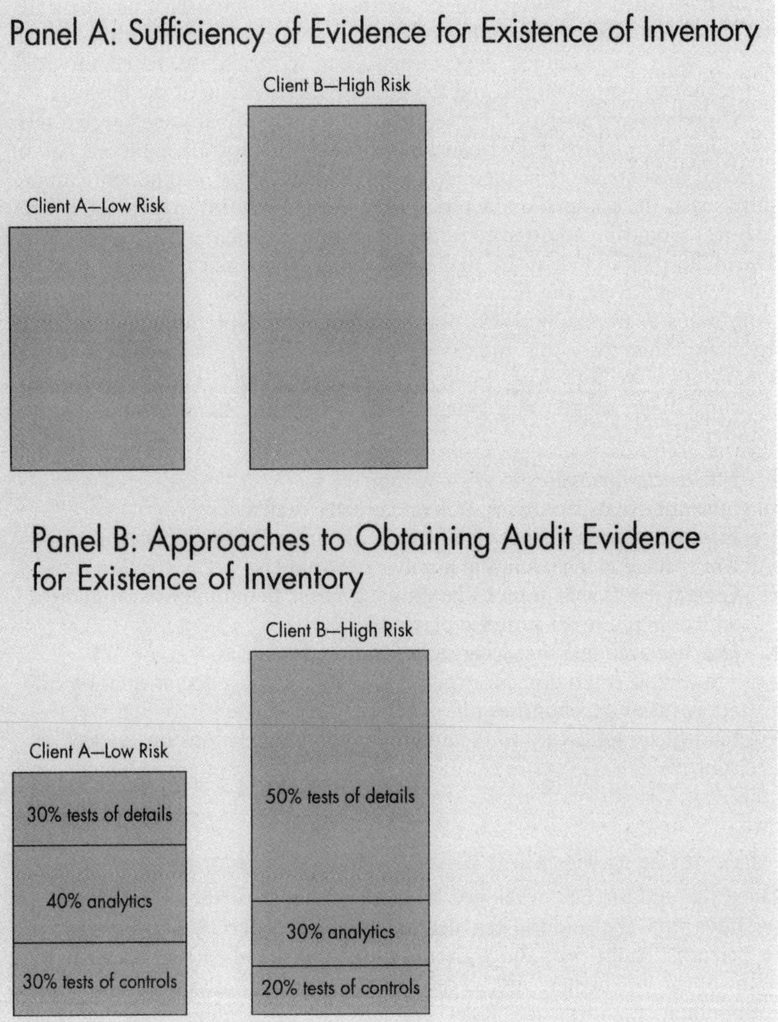

misstatement related to the existence of inventory as low, and believes that the client has implemented effective controls in this area. For this client, the auditor will likely perform tests of controls, gain a high level of assurance from substantive analytical procedures such as a reasonableness test, and then complete the substantive procedures by performing tests of details at a limited level.

Panel A of Exhibit 11.7 shows that because of differences in risk, the box of evidence to be filled for testing the existence of inventory at the low risk client is smaller than that at a high risk client. Panel B of Exhibit 11.7 illustrates the different levels of assurance that the auditor will obtain from tests of controls and substantive procedures for the two assertions. Panel B makes the point that because of the higher risk associated with the existence of inventory at Client B, the auditor will want to design the audit so that more of the assurance is coming from tests of details. Note that the relative percentages are judgmental in nature; the examples are simply intended to give you a sense of how an auditor might select an appropriate mix of procedures.

Obtaining Evidence about Internal Control Operating Effectiveness in the Acquisition and Payment Cycle

For integrated audits, the auditor will test the operating effectiveness of important controls as of the client's year end. If the auditor wants to rely on controls for the financial statement audit, the auditor will test the operating effectiveness of those controls throughout the year.

Selecting Controls to Test and Performing Tests of Controls

The auditor selects controls that are important to the auditor's conclusion about whether the organization's controls adequately address the assessed risk of material misstatement in the acquisition and payment cycle. The auditor selects both entity-wide and transaction controls for testing. The internal controls to be tested are those that help to assure that all purchases are authorized and all payments are for goods received, are made at the appropriate amount and in the correct time period, and are paid only once to the authorized vendor. Typical tests of controls include inquiry of relevant personnel, observation of the control being performed, examination of documentation corroborating that the control has been performed, and reperformance of the control by the auditor testing the control. However, all types of tests of controls are not necessarily relevant to every control. Furthermore, many tests of controls involve computerized controls, for example, an automated three-way match.

For manual controls, the auditor may test whether the three-way matching control was operating effectively by taking a sample of payments and tracing them to the documentation corroborating that the control has been performed. Attribute sampling, which is discussed in Chapter 8, would likely be used to determine and select the sample. In addition, the auditor might take a sample of receiving reports and trace through the system to test controls related to the completeness assertion for inventory and accounts payable. Significant lags in recording the liability indicate potential problems that should be addressed during substantive testing of accounts payable at year end.

Evidence of proper authorization should be available for each purchase and payment. Paper-based systems provide evidence of authorization through signatures. To test these types of controls, the auditor usually checks if signatures are present on the appropriate documentation, and if not, follows up with responsible personnel. Computerized systems are controlled through access controls and exception reports that are tested by the auditor using computerized audit techniques, as well as inquiry and examination of documentation.

Considering the Results of Tests of Controls

The auditor will analyze the results of the tests of controls to determine additional appropriate procedures. There are two potential outcomes:

1. If control deficiencies are identified, the auditor will assess those deficiencies to determine their severity (are they significant deficiencies or material weaknesses?). The auditor would then need to modify the preliminary control risk assessment (possibly from low to moderate or high) and document the implications of the control deficiencies. Appropriate modifications to planned substantive audit procedures will be determined by the types of misstatements that are most likely to occur because of the control deficiency.
2. If no control deficiencies are identified, the auditor will likely determine that the preliminary assessment of control risk as low is still appropriate. The auditor will then determine the extent that controls can provide

在采购与付款循环获取内部控制运行有效性的证据

LO 7 Determine appropriate tests of controls and consider the results of tests of controls for acquisition and payment cycle accounts, disclosures, and assertions.

选择要测试的控制和实施控制测试

考虑控制测试的结果

Inventory Controls at CSK Auto Corporation

The following is an excerpt from CSK's Management Report on Internal Controls over Financial Reporting for the year ended February 3, 2008.

> The Company did not maintain effective controls over the completeness, accuracy, existence and valuation of its inventory. Specifically, effective controls, including monitoring, were not maintained to ensure that the Company's inventory systems completely and accurately processed and accounted for inventory movements within the Company's distribution network, particularly the disposition of inventory returns from customers. Additionally, the Company did not maintain effective monitoring and review over in-transit inventory, defective product warranty costs, core inventory and related core return liability accounts and shrink expense and shrink accruals. Furthermore, reconciliations of distribution center and warehouse physical inventory counts to the general ledger balances were not performed accurately, resulting in adjustments to year-end inventory balances.

These material weaknesses in inventory-related controls would significantly influence the approach the auditor should use to audit the inventory-related accounts, assertions, and dislcosures.

evidence on the correctness of account balances, and determine planned substantive audit procedures. The level of substantive testing in this situation will be less than what is required in circumstances where deficiencies in internal control were identified. From the audit risk model, we know that companies with effective internal controls should require less substantive testing of account balances.

The relative strengths of the client's internal controls have a significant impact on the audit of the accounts and assertions in the acquisition and payment cycle. The *Auditing in Practice* feature "Inventory Controls at CSK Auto Corporation" highlights the implications of ineffective controls over inventory. These control deficiencies were assessed to be material weaknesses and likely meant that CSK's auditors would have had to rely heavily on substantive tests of details to obtain sufficient appropriate evidence related to inventory.

在采购与付款循环获取账户、披露和认定的实质性证据

Obtaining Substantive Evidence about Accounts, Disclosures, and Assertions in the Acquisition and Payment Cycle

存货与已售商品成本的实质性测试

Substantive Tests of Inventory and Cost of Goods Sold

LO 8 Determine and apply sufficient appropriate substantive audit procedures for testing acquisition and payment cycle accounts, disclosures, and assertions.

In performing substantive procedures for inventory and cost of goods sold, the auditor wants reasonable assurance that inventory exists, that it is actually owned by the company, and that the value of inventory is accurate. Substantive procedures (substantive analytical procedures, tests of details, or both) should be performed for all relevant assertions related to significant acquisition and payment cycle accounts and disclosures. Even if the auditor has evidence indicating that controls are operating effectively, the auditor cannot rely solely on control testing to provide evidence on the reliability of these accounts and assertions. Exhibit 11.8 presents the assertions and substantive audit procedures that would be used to gather evidence regarding inventory and cost of goods sold.

EXHIBIT **11.8**	Assertions and Substantive Audit Procedures for Inventory and Cost of Goods Sold

Assertions	Substantive Audit Procedures
Existence/ occurrence	1. Review the client's proposed physical inventory procedures to determine whether they are likely to result in a complete and correct physical inventory. 2. Observe the client's count of the annual physical inventory. Randomly select items from the client's perpetual inventory record and observe (count) the items on hand. Sample should emphasize high-dollar-value items.
Completeness	1. Perform year-end cutoff tests by noting the last shipping and receiving document numbers used before physical inventory is taken. Review the purchase and sales journal for a period of time shortly before and after year end, noting the shipping and receiving document numbers to determine whether the goods are recorded in the proper time period. 2. Make inquiries of the client regarding the potential existence of goods on consignment or located in outside warehouses. For material items, either visit the locations or send a confirmation to the outside warehouse management. 3. Make inquiries of the client regarding allowances made for expected returns. Determine client policy for accounting for returned items. Review receipt of transactions for a selected period of time to determine whether significant returns are received and appropriately accounted for.
Rights and obligations	1. Review vendor invoices when testing disbursements to determine that proper title is conveyed. 2. Review purchase contracts to assess rights to return merchandise.
Valuation/ allocation	1. Determine whether the valuation method is appropriate for the client. 2. Inquire of production and warehouse personnel about the existence of obsolete inventory. 3. Note potentially obsolete inventory while observing the physical inventory counts. Trace the potentially obsolete items to the client's inventory compilation, and determine whether they are properly labeled as obsolete items. 4. Test inventory cost by taking a sample of recorded inventory, and trace to source documents, including: • Tracing raw material purchases to vendor invoices • Testing standard costs as built up through the standard cost system 5. Test for the possibility of obsolete inventory that should be written down to market value: • Review trade journals for changes in product technology. • Follow-up potentially obsolete items noted during the observation of the client's physical inventory counts. • Use audit software to read the inventory file and age the inventory items and compute inventory turnover. Investigate products with unusually low turnover or items that have not been used or sold for an extended period of time. • Inquire of the client about sales adjustments (markdowns) that have been offered to sell any products. • Verify sales price by reviewing recent invoices to determine whether the sales price is the same as that included on the computer file. Use generalized audit software (GAS) to compute net realizable value for inventory items, and prepare an inventory printout for all items where net realizable value is less than cost. • Analyze sales by product line, noting any significant decreases in product-line sales. • Review purchase commitments for potential loss exposures. Determine whether contingent losses are properly disclosed or recorded. • Use audit software to test extensions and prepare a printout of differences. • Use audit software to foot the inventory compilation. Trace the total to the trial balance.

(continued)

EXHIBIT **11.8**	Assertions and Substantive Audit Procedures for Inventory and Cost of Goods Sold (*continued*)
Assertions	**Substantive Audit Procedures**

Presentation and disclosure	1. Review client's financial statement disclosure of:
	  • Inventory valuation methods used
	  • FIFO cost figures and LIFO liquidation effects if LIFO is used
	  • The percentage of inventory valued by each different valuation method
	  • The classification of inventory as raw material, work in process, and finished goods
	  • The existence of contingent losses associated with long-term contracts or purchase commitments
	  • Inventory policy regarding returns and allowances, if expected to be material, for merchandise expected to be returned

Inventory and Cost of Goods Sold: Substantive Analytical Procedures

Before performing tests of details, the auditor may perform substantive analytical procedures, such as a reasonableness test or regression analysis. An example of a reasonableness test would be to estimate the account balance and to determine whether that amount is close to what the client has recorded. For example, if purchases and sales volume are relatively stable from year to year, the auditor might compare ending inventory balances by location to prior year balances to see if they are similar, or if they are materially different to consider why that would be the case. If the auditor's expectations are significantly different from what the client has recorded, the auditor needs to follow up with sufficient appropriate tests of details. If the auditor's expectations are not significantly different from what the client has recorded, the auditor may be able reduce tests of details.

In general, if substantive analytical procedures do not result in unresolved issues, direct testing of account balances can be reduced. However, in the acquisition and payment cycle it is unlikely that audit evidence obtained from substantive analytical procedures alone will be sufficient evidence for the auditor. The *Auditing in Practice* feature "Weaknesses in Performing Substantive Analytical Procedures: The Case of Deloitte's PCAOB Inspection Report" provides an example of the inappropriate use of substantive analytical procedures.

Inventory and Cost of Goods Sold: Existence or Occurrence Assertion

审计准则要求注册会计师对客户的存货项目实施监盘程序。监盘程序可以在年末一起实施，也可以在全年中循环实施。

Auditing standards require auditors to observe the client taking physical inventory in order to ensure existence of inventory. This may be done in its entirety at year end or on a cycle basis throughout the year. It is important to note that the audit of cost of goods sold can be directly tied to the audit of inventories. If beginning and ending inventory have been verified and acquisitions have been tested, cost of goods sold can be directly calculated. So, while observing physical inventory to ensure that its existence relates to the inventory existence assertion, the resulting calculation of cost of goods sold relates to the completeness assertion; in other words, if inventory exists then the recording of cost of goods sold is complete. The auditor should apply analytical techniques to cost of goods sold, however, to determine if any unexpected significant variations—either overall or by product line—occur. Significant variations, especially those that cannot be easily explained, might indicate a need for further inventory work.

Weaknesses in Performing Substantive Analytical Procedures: The Case of Deloitte's PCAOB Inspection Report

AUDITING IN PRACTICE

The inappropriate use of substantive analytical procedures was revealed in the 2010 Public Company Accounting Oversight Board (PCAOB) inspection of Deloitte &Touche LLP.

> The Firm failed to perform sufficient procedures to test the existence of the issuer's inventory. The Firm performed physical inventory observations at approximately one-half of one percent of the issuer's locations during the first half of the year, and used a substantive analytical procedure to test the year-end inventory balance. To develop its expectation of the year-end inventory balance, the Firm used the inventory balances from the small number of locations at which it had performed inventory observations during the first

half of the year to predict the inventory balances for all the locations at the end of the year. The Firm, however, did not obtain evidence that the inventory balances at the issuer's retail locations were similar. In fact, there was considerable variation, approximately 15 percent, in the inventory balances at the three retail stores where physical inventories were observed. In addition, the Firm did not have evidence that the inventory balances in the first half of the year could be expected to be predictive of the balances at year end.

For further details, see PCAOB Release Number 104-2011-290.

Complete Year-End Physical Inventory Not many years ago, standard procedure for most organizations was to shut down operations at year end or near year end to take a complete physical count of inventory (often referred to as the *physical*). The client's book inventory was adjusted to this physical inventory (often referred to as the *book to physical adjustment*). These procedures are still followed by many small companies that use a periodic inventory system, or where the perpetual records are not sufficiently reliable, or where fraud risk indicators exist.

If a year-end inventory is taken, the auditor should (1) observe the client taking inventory to determine the accuracy of the procedures, (2) make selected test counts that can later be traced into the client's inventory compilation, (3) test the client's inventory compilation by tracing test counts to the compilation and independently test the client's computation of extended cost, and (4) look for evidence of slow-moving, obsolete, or damaged inventory that may need to be written down to lower of cost or market. An auditor can use GAS to gather the following types of evidence:

- The mathematical accuracy of inventory records
- Reports of recent shipments to be used for cutoff testing
- Items to be counted during the physical inventory observation
- Evaluations of gross margin amounts by product line
- Analyses of inventory whose cost exceeds the market value
- Comparisons of inventory quantities to budgetary plans
- Lists of inventory items with unusual prices, units, or descriptions

The auditor should review the client's plan to count inventory and plan to observe the client's count. The overall procedures for observing the conduct of the client's physical inventory are shown in Exhibit 11.9. The process assumes that the client systematically arranges the inventory for ease of counting and attaches prenumbered tags (paper or electronic) to each group

EXHIBIT **11.9**   Procedures for Observing a Client's Physical Inventory

1. Meet with the client to discuss the procedures, timing, location, and personnel involved in taking the annual physical inventory.
2. Review the client's plans for counting and tagging inventory items.
3. Review the inventory-taking procedures with all audit personnel. Familiarize them with the nature of the client's inventory, potential problems with the inventory, and any other information that will ensure that the client and audit personnel will properly recognize inventory items, high-dollar-value items, and obsolete items, and understand potential problems that might occur in counting the inventory.
4. Determine whether specialists are needed to test or assist in correctly identifying inventory items.
5. Upon arriving at each site:
   a. Meet with client personnel, obtain a map of the area, and obtain a schedule of inventory counts to be made for each area.
   b. Obtain a list of sequential tag numbers to be used in each area.
   c. Observe the procedures the client has implemented to shut down receipt or shipment of goods.
   d. Observe that the client has shut down production.
   e. Obtain document numbers for the last shipment and receipt of goods before the physical inventory is taken. Use the information to perform cutoff tests.
6. Observe the counting of inventory and note the following on inventory count working papers:
   a. The first and last tag number used in the section.
   b. All tag numbers and the disposition of all tag numbers in the sequence.
   c. The product identification, product description, units of measure, and number of items on a count sheet.
   d. Items that appear to be obsolete or of questionable value.
   e. All high-dollar-value items included in inventory.
   f. Movement of goods into or out of the company during the process of inventory taking. Determine if goods are properly counted or excluded from inventory.
7. Document your conclusion as to the quality of the client's inventory-taking process, noting any problems that could be of audit significance. Determine whether a sufficient inventory count has been taken to properly reflect the goods on hand at year end.

of products. Supervisory personnel (usually from the accounting department) and the auditors review the counts. The count tags are then used to compile the year-end physical inventory. During the counting process, the client arranges not to ship or receive goods or segregates all goods received during the process to be labeled and counted as *after inventory*.

The auditor walks through the inventory areas, documenting the first and last tag numbers used as well as the tag numbers not used. The auditor also performs the following tasks:

- Makes test counts of selected items and records the test counts for subsequent tracing into the client's inventory compilation
- Takes notations of all items that appear to be obsolete or are in questionable condition; the auditor follows up on these items with inquiries of client personnel and retains the data to determine how they are accounted for in the inventory compilation
- Observes the handling of scrap and other material
- Observes whether any physical movement of goods occurs during the counting of inventory
- Records all high-dollar-value items for subsequent tracing into the client's records

The notation of high-dollar-value items is a check against potential client manipulation of inventory by adding new items or adjusting the cost or quantities of existing items after the physical inventory is completed. Because high-dollar-value items are noted, the auditor can systematically review documentary support for major items included on the final inventory compilation that were not noted during the physical inventory observation.

After the inventory count is taken, the auditor's observations and test counts provide an independent source of evidence on the correctness of the client's inventory compilation. Noting the unused tag numbers prohibits the insertion of additional inventory items.

Many organizations have multiple locations, therefore making it difficult to take an annual inventory. For example, one major company that perpetrated a famous fraud was Phar-Mor, Inc. The company had more than 300 stores scattered across the country. The auditors insisted that a year-end physical count be taken, but notified the client that they would observe the taking of inventory at only a few select locations. To expedite the observation of inventory, the auditor worked with the client to identify the locations that would be observed. Although there was a massive overstatement of inventory by Phar-Mor, Inc., the misstatement was not discovered by the auditors because the company made sure that no material misstatements occurred at the locations visited by the auditors.

When multiple locations contain inventory, the auditor should review a variety of locations to determine that they are comparable and should use analytical procedures to see if the locations not visited seem to have inventory levels that are significantly different from those observed. If there are significant differences, the auditor may need to observe more locations, or at least follow up with other procedures. The auditor may also want to plan to visit some locations on an unannounced or surprise basis to avoid the type of fraudulent activity that occurred at Phar-Mor.

Many organizations that take an annual physical inventory find that year end is not the most convenient time to do it. For example, the company may have a natural model changeover and shut down operations during that time, or it may want to take the physical inventory shortly before or after year end to expedite the preparation of year-end financial statements. It is acceptable to have the client take the physical inventory before year end provided that:

- Internal control is effective.
- There are no red flags that might indicate both opportunity and motivation to misstate inventory.
- The auditor can effectively test the year-end balance through a combination of analytical procedures and selective testing of transactions between the physical count and year end.
- The auditor reviews transactions in the roll-forward period for evidence of any manipulation or unusual activity.

在期末之前对存货进行实物盘点必须满足的条件包括：内部控制有效；没有明显的迹象表明有存货舞弊的动机和机会；注册会计师能够通过分析性程序和剩余期间选择性的交易测试有效地测试期末余额；注册会计师复核剩余期间的交易以发现任何操纵或者不正常活动的证据。

As companies move toward innovative partnerships with their suppliers and customers, more agreements will take place where a supplier's goods will be at a retailer such as Wal-Mart, but title will not change until the sale to the customer is made. In these situations, the auditor will need to determine that the client has a sound methodology for determining the amount of inventory that is physically stored at a customer's location. Many times, the client will have monitoring controls with which it examines existing inventory at the customer's locations and compares it to the perpetual records. If such controls do not exist, the auditor will need to consider complementary testing methodologies, which might include (a) confirming inventory amounts with the trading partner, (b) examining subsequent payments from the trading partner, or (c) visiting selected trading partners to inspect inventory.

It is not sufficient for a client to just assert that its inventory is held by its trading partner. The auditor must examine the contract, determine the existence and effectiveness of controls, and examine documentation of reconciliations between trading partners, cash remittances, and client accounting records. If red flags are present, the auditor must go beyond these procedures and talk with the trading partner to obtain information on the amount of the client's inventory the trading partner shows on hand. Finally, the auditor needs to develop assurance that the trading partner is a real company.

There may be rare cases in which it is difficult or impractical for the auditor to attend the physical inventory count. For example, the nature and location of the inventory, or where it is held, may pose safety threats for the auditor. In these situations, the auditor must conduct alternative audit procedures. Such procedures could include inspecting documents related to the subsequent sale of specific inventory items to validate their existence and valuation as of the balance sheet date.

If, however, it is simply inconvenient for the auditor to attend the physical inventory count, then the auditor has an obligation to find a way to be present. If it is truly impossible for the auditor to attend the physical inventory counting, and the auditor is unable to conduct alternative procedures, then the auditor's report would have to be modified as a result of this scope limitation (assuming that inventory is a material amount to the financial statements as a whole). Scope limitations to the standard audit report are discussed in Chapter 15.

Inventory and Cost of Goods Sold: Completeness Assertion

The auditor normally performs a cutoff test of receipts and shipments of inventory at year end to determine that all items are recorded in the correct time period. The cutoff test is usually accomplished by capturing information on the last items shipped and received at year end and examining samples of transactions recorded in the sales and purchases journals near year end. In addition, audit software can be used to match shipping dates and billing dates if the files containing that information have been tested for accuracy. The auditor should also inquire about any inventory out on consignment or stored in a public warehouse and consider confirming its existence.

> *Cutoff example*—A sale of $100 is recorded on December 30 for a product costing $80 that is not shipped until the next month. If a physical count of inventory is taken on December 31, this product will be included in the physical count, which will exceed the quantity shown in the perpetual records. The perpetual inventory record is always adjusted to the actual count (in this case by debiting inventory and crediting cost of goods sold). Unless corrected, sales, gross profit, and pretax income are overstated by the full $100. The client can correct this misstatement by reversing the sales entry, including the entry to accounts receivable. Because the perpetual inventory is adjusted to the physical count, that part of the original entry (debiting inventory, crediting cost of goods sold) is already made.

Allowance for Returns In most situations, the expected amount of returns is not material. However, some companies (for example, mail-order companies like Lands' End or L.L. Bean) provide return guarantees and expect significant returns—especially after year-end holiday sales. They use previous experience, updated for current economic conditions, to develop estimates of returns. When such returns are material to the overall financial presentation, allowances for returns should be established and the gross profit on the original sale reversed. The allowance is not restricted to mail-order companies; it should be considered when a company is experiencing a large volume of returns. As with other accounting estimates, the auditor needs to understand management's process for determining the estimate and then test the reasonable of that process.

Inventory and Cost of Goods Sold: Rights and Obligations Assertion

Most of the audit work regarding rights to and ownership of inventory is addressed during the auditor's test of the initial recording of purchases. The auditor should also review long-term contracts to determine obligations to take delivery of merchandise, customer rights to return merchandise, or buy-back obligations. Inquiries should be made concerning any inventory held on consignment.

Inventory and Cost of Goods Sold: Valuation or Allocation Assertion

Valuation is the most complex assertion related to inventory because of the volume of transactions, diversity of products, variety of costing methods, and difficulty in estimating net realizable value of products. A combination of tests of details and substantive analytical procedures is used to determine inventory valuation. The auditor should verify the correct cost of inventory and then test for lower of cost or market valuation. Usually, the cost part of the valuation assertion is tested by looking at underlying invoices and/or supporting cost records. The auditor usually examines current market data and other information that might indicate a drop in sales price or potential inventory obsolescence.

Direct Tests of Product Costs Statistical sampling techniques, as discussed in Chapter 8, should be used to select items for testing. Then, the auditor should examine underlying supporting documentation—for example, invoices—to determine that the cost is recorded correctly. As an example, assume that the auditor selected product YG350 to test the cost of inventory recorded on the FIFO basis as part of a perpetual inventory system:

Product YG350

Transaction	Total		Balance	
	Quantity	Cost	Quantity	Dollars
Beginning balance			100	$1,000
3/1 Purchase	50	550	150	1,550
6/1 Purchase	100	1,200	250	2,750
6/1 Sale	150	1,550	100	1,200
9/1 Purchase	50	500	150	1,700
10/1 Sale	25	275	125	1,425
12/1 Sale	50	600	75	825
12/1 Purchase	75	975	150	1,800

Vendor invoices would be examined for the purchases of the last 150 items (12/1, 9/1, and 6/1) to determine whether $1,800 was the correct cost. (*Note:* You should verify that the recorded cost should have been $1,775. The calculation is as follows: 12/1 is $975, 9/1 is $500, and the remaining 25 units are from 6/1 at a cost of $25 × $12/unit, for a total of $1,775.)

Any differences noted between vendor invoices and recorded amounts should be identified as an error and should be projected to the population as a whole using statistical sampling to determine whether they might be material. Similar tests should be performed if the company uses other valuation methods, such as average cost or LIFO. If the company uses a standard cost system, the costs are verified by tests of the cost system and by tracing the selected items to standard costs. Significant variances should be allocated between cost of goods sold and inventory.

Tests for Obsolete Inventory (Net Realizable Value Tests) Determining the amount that should be written off because of obsolescence is a difficult and challenging audit task because (1) the client will usually state that most of the goods are still salable at current selling prices and (2) net realizable value is only an estimate (for example, there is no specific, correct price at which inventory should be valued). The auditor should understand management's process for determining the value of its inventory. And the auditor attempts to gather evidence on potential inventory obsolescence from a number of corroborating sources, including the following:

- Noting potential obsolete inventory when observing the client's physical inventory
- Calculating inventory turnover, number of days' sales in inventory, date of last sale or purchase, and other similar analytic techniques to identify potential obsolescence
- Calculating net realizable value for products by referring to current selling prices, cost of disposal, and sales commissions
- Monitoring trade journals and the Internet for information regarding the introduction of competitive products
- Inquiring of management about its approach to identifying and classifying obsolete items
- Monitoring turnover or age of products individually or by product lines and comparing the turnover with past performance and expectations for the current period
- Comparing current sales with budgeted sales
- Periodically reviewing, by product line, the number of days of sales currently in inventory
- Adjusting for poor condition of inventory, reported as part of periodic cycle counts
- Monitoring sales for amount of product markdown and periodic comparison of net realizable value with inventoried costs
- Reviewing current inventory in light of planned new-product introductions

Auditors often investigate items that appear to be obsolete by reviewing sales subsequent to year end and discussing future sales prospects with management. The *Auditing in Practice* feature "The Importance of Professional Skepticism in Testing the Valuation of Inventory: The PCAOB Disciplines Ibarra" provides an example of difficulties that the auditors encountered in testing the valuation of inventory.

The Importance of Professional Skepticism in Testing the Valuation of Inventory: The PCAOB Disciplines Ibarra

AUDITING IN PRACTICE

The PCAOB disciplined the Ibarra audit firm because the auditors failed to identify and address a departure from GAAP relating to their client's valuation of inventory. GAAP requires inventory to be valued at the lower of cost or market value. The inspection report notes that the client's consolidated balance sheet reported inventory of $356,973, or approximately 95% of total assets. However, based on cost of goods actually sold during that fiscal year, the client's inventory balance represented approximately 22 years' worth of sales. This fact alone should have increased the auditors' skepticism about the inventory's stated value. Instead, the auditors relied solely on management's representation regarding the valuation of inventory and mechanical tests of inventory costs, and they missed the big picture. Auditing standards require auditors to look at evidence from multiple sources in reaching a conclusion about an account balance.

For further details on this case, see PCAOB Release No. 2006-009.

Testing a Standard Costing System Most manufacturing companies use standard cost systems to assist in controlling costs, streamlining accounting, and costing inventory. Valuation of ending inventory is directly affected by the quality of the client's cost system. The auditor should make inquiries about the following:

- The method for developing standard costs
- How recently the standards have been updated
- The method for identifying components of overhead and of allocating overhead to products
- The methods for identifying variances, following up on their causes, and allocating them to inventory and cost of goods sold

The auditor also tests the procedures for assigning raw material costs to products or cost centers. The auditor should be conversant with activity-based costing systems to determine their appropriateness for allocating costs to products.

An audit program to test the standard cost system is shown in Exhibit 11.10. The program is intended to determine the accuracy and reliability of the standard cost system as a basis for valuing a client's year-end inventory. The audit program assumes a standard cost system, but the concepts implicit in the program could be modified for other systems, such as a job cost system. Note that the program requires the auditor to understand the client's business process as well as its standard cost system (including methods of estimating costs). The program also requires analyses of both variances and individual cost assignments.

Testing a Perpetual Inventory System Most organizations use a perpetual inventory system to help manage inventory. If there is a low risk that the perpetual inventory records are inaccurate, the client may save the time and cost associated with a complete year-end count of inventory. The auditor will normally test perpetual inventory records to determine that (1) authorized receipts and sales of inventory are recorded accurately and promptly and (2) only authorized receipts and sales of inventory have been recorded. The auditor selects transactions from the perpetual records and traces them back to source documents to determine that only authorized transactions have been recorded and that unit costs are accurate. The auditor also selects items from the source documents and traces them to the perpetual records to determine that all receipts and sales are recorded accurately and on a timely basis. Finally, the auditor examines support for any material adjustments made to the perpetual records based on physical counts.

Using the Work of a Specialist or Expert When Auditing Inventory The nature of inventory at some clients may require the auditor to rely on the work of a specialist in determining quantities and valuation of inventory. For example, a specialist might be needed to determine the physical characteristics relating to inventory on hand or condition of minerals, mineral reserves, or materials stored in stockpiles.

Inventory and Cost of Goods Sold: Presentation and Disclosure Assertion

The auditor reviews the client's proposed disclosure for compliance with the guidelines established by the relevant accounting literature. In addition to the normally required inventory disclosures, the auditor must identify any unusual circumstances regarding sales or purchase contracts that would merit additional disclosure. A number of financial disclosures are required for inventory:

除了正常要求的存货披露外，注册会计师必须识别需要增加披露的销售或者采购合同的非正常情况。

- Inventory valuation method used (FIFO, LIFO, moving average) and the percentage of inventory valued under each method
- Changes made in the method of valuing inventory
- FIFO or current cost if the inventory is valued using LIFO

- Composition of inventory as to raw materials, work-in-process, and finished goods
- Purchase commitments that could have an adverse affect on future financial results

---

EXHIBIT **11.10** Audit Program for Standard Cost System

AUDIT OF STANDARD COST SYSTEM

Prepared by _____

Reviewed by _____

	Performed by:	W/P Ref:
1. Review prior-year audit documentation for a description of the standard cost system. Inquire about any major changes made in the system during the current year.	_____	_____
2. Tour the production facilities and make note of cost centers, general layout of the plant, storage of inventory, functioning of the quality control department, and process for identifying and accounting for scrap or defective items.	_____	_____
3. Examine prior-year audit documentation and current-year variance accounts as a basis for determining the amount of variances identified by the standard cost accounting system. Determine whether the variances imply the need for significant revisions in the standard cost system.	_____	_____
4. Inquire of the process used to update standard costs. Determine the extent to which revisions have been made during the current year.	_____	_____
5. Inquire whether significant changes have been made in the production process during the current year, whether major manufacturing renovations have taken place, and whether new products have been added.	_____	_____
6. Randomly select X number of standard cost buildups for products, and for each product buildup selected:	_____	_____
• Review engineering studies on the cost buildup, noting the items used, amount of product used, and standard cost of the product used.	_____	_____
• Test the reasonableness of the client's costs by randomly sampling components of product cost and tracing back to purchases or contracts with suppliers.	_____	_____
• Review payroll records to determine that labor costs are specifically identified byproduct or cost center and used in calculating variances.	_____	_____
• Review the reasonableness of the method for allocating overhead to products. Determine whether any significant changes have been made in the method of allocation.	_____	_____
7. Select a representative sample of products requisitioned into work in process, and determine that all entries are properly recorded.	_____	_____
8. Review the method for identifying overhead costs. Select a representative sample of expenditure charged to overhead, and trace to underlying support to determine that the costs are properly classified.	_____	_____
9. Review variance reports. Determine the extent to which the client has investigated and determined the causes of the variances. Determine whether the causes of the variances signal a need to revise the standard cost system.	_____	_____
10. Inquire about the method used by the client to allocate variances to inventory and cost of goods sold at year end. Determine the reasonableness of the method and its consistency with prior years.	_____	_____
11. Document your conclusion on the accuracy and completeness of the standard cost system used by the client. Indicate whether the standard costs can be relied on in assigning costs to year-end inventory.	_____	_____

| EXHIBIT **11.11** | Ford Motor Company Inventory Footnote from the 2011 Annual Report |

NOTE 10. INVENTORIES

All inventories are stated at the lower of cost or market. Cost for a substantial portion of U.S. inventories is determined on a last-in, first-out ("LIFO") basis. LIFO was used for approximately 32% of total inventories at December 31, 2011 and 2010. Cost of other inventories is determined by costing methods that approximate a first-in, first-out ("FIFO") basis.

Inventories at December 31 were as follows (in millions):

	2011	2010
Raw materials, work-in-process and supplies	$ 2,847	$ 2,812
Finished products	3,982	3,970
Total inventories under FIFO	6,829	6,782
Less: LIFO adjustment	(928)	(865)
Total inventories	$ 5,901	$ 5,917

The auditor reviews the client's inventory footnote for completeness and accuracy. Most of the information described in the notes will be independently verified by the auditor in the process of completing the audit and the data will be contained in the audit documentation. An example of a typical inventory disclosure for Ford Motor Company is shown in Exhibit 11.11.

Fraud-Related Substantive Procedures for Inventory and Cost of Goods Sold

In those audits where there is a heightened risk of fraud related to inventory and cost of goods sold, the auditor will want to consider performing the following procedures or, if the procedures are already being performed, altering the timing and extent of the procedures:

- Observe all inventory locations simultaneously
- Confirm inventories at locations that are outside the entity
- Compare carrying inventory amounts to recent sales amounts
- Examine consignment agreements and determine that consignments are properly accounted for
- Send confirmations to vendors confirming invoices and unusual terms
- Determine if there are bulk sales at steep discounts, as these sales could indicate decreasing values for the company's products

The *Auditing in Practice* feature "Examples of Fraud in the Physical Observation of Inventory" outlines common inventory-related frauds.

Substantive Tests of Accounts Payable and Related Expense Accounts

应付账款和相关费用账户的实质性测试

The auditor's major concern with accounts payable is that the account (and related expense accounts) will be understated. Therefore, the most relevant assertion is the completeness assertion. The testing to be performed depends on the risk of an understatement of accounts payable. If there is little risk, the testing might be limited to substantive analytical procedures, such as a comparison of underlying expenses with that of the prior year and related

Examples of Fraud in the Physical Observation of Inventory

AICPA Practice Alert No. 94-2, *Auditing Inventories —Physical Observations,* provides examples of how clients fraudulently manipulate inventory amounts. Auditors should be on the alert for the following:

- Empty boxes or hollow squares in stacked goods
- Mislabeled boxes containing scrap, obsolete items, or lower-value materials
- Consigned inventory, inventory that is rented, or traded-in items for which credits have not been issued
- Inventory diluted so it is less valuable (for example, adding water to liquid substances)
- Altering the inventory counts for those items the auditor did not test count
- Programming the computer to produce fraudulent physical quantity tabulations or priced inventory listings

- Manipulating the inventory counts/compilations for locations not visited by the auditor
- Double-counting inventory in transit between locations
- Physically moving inventory and counting it at two locations
- Including in inventory merchandise recorded as sold but not yet shipped to a customer (bill and hold sales)
- Arranging for false confirmations of inventory held by others
- Including inventory receipts for which corresponding payables had not been recorded
- Overstating the stage of completion of work-in-process
- Reconciling physical inventory amounts to falsified amounts in the general ledger
- Manipulating the roll-forward of an inventory taken before the financial statement date

tests of the underlying asset or liability account. Alternatively, the auditor could compare ending accounts payable balances by major vendor to prior year balances, or to the volume of activity during the year. The auditor would expect that high-volume vendors will have relatively large accounts payable balances. In addition, if there is no balance for a vendor that in previous years was significant, the auditor would want to consider why that would be the case. When evaluating evidence regarding expense accounts, the auditor should consider that management is more likely to (1) understate rather than overstate expenses and (2) classify expense items as assets rather than vice versa. Therefore, the most relevant assertion related to expenses in the acquisition and payment cycle is also the completeness assertion. However, it is important for the auditor to understand client motivations. For example, a client may be motivated to minimize income taxes and thus would want to overstate expenses and understate income. In such cases, the auditor should concentrate on items classified as expenses that should be recorded as an asset.

Exhibit 11.12 presents the assertions and audit procedures that would typically be used to gather evidence regarding accounts payable.

Accounts Payable and Related Expense Accounts: Substantive Analytical Procedures

When the auditor has concluded that control risk is low for expense accounts, the primary substantive tests may be substantive analytical procedures. In conducting analytical procedures, the auditor should recognize that many account balances are directly related to the client's volume of activity. Stable relationships are expected between specific accounts (for example, cost of goods sold and sales) that can be investigated for unusual discrepancies. Examples of expenses that should vary directly with sales

EXHIBIT **11.12**	Assertions and Audit Procedures for Accounts Payable

Assertions	Audit Procedures
Existence/occurrence	1. Perform a cutoff test of purchases and cash disbursements
Completeness	1. Request vendors' monthly statements or send confirmations to major vendors requesting a statement of open account items
	2. Agree monthly statements and confirmations from major vendors with accounts payable list
	3. Examine a sample of cash disbursements made after the end of the year to determine whether the disbursements are for goods and services applicable to the previous year
	4. Perform analytical review of related expense accounts, such as travel and entertainment or legal expenses
Rights and obligations	1. Review long-term purchase commitments, and determine whether a loss needs to be accrued.
Valuation or allocation	1. Use GAS to verify mathematical accuracy of accounts payable, and agree to general ledger.
Presentation and disclosure	1. Review client's financial statement disclosure of: • Accounts payable • Expense accounts such as travel and entertainment

include warranty expense, sales commissions, and supplies expense. The analytical model should be built using either audited data or independently generated data. If the expense account falls within expected ranges, the auditor can be comfortable in concluding that it is not materially misstated. If the account balance is not within the expected range, the auditor develops hypotheses as to why it may differ and systematically investigates the situation through tests of details. The investigation should include inquiries of client personnel and the examination of corroborating evidence (including a detailed examination of the expense accounts, where merited). For example, sales commissions may have averaged 3% of sales over the past five years, and the auditor may expect that trend to continue. If that ratio drops to 1% this year, the auditor should examine the cause of the change. If the auditor obtains sufficient evidence through substantive analytical procedures, the extent of substantive tests of details may be decreased. The *Auditing in Practice* feature "Understatement of Liabilities and Expenses at Advanced Marketing Services" provides an example of a fraud that might have been detected earlier using substantive analytics.

Accounts Payable and Related Expense Accounts: Existence or Occurrence

Analytical Review of Related Expense Accounts This procedure is designed to determine if the accounting data indicate a potential understatement of expenses. If an understatement is likely, the auditor expands accounts payable tests by performing one or both of the two tests of details described next. Analytical review of related expense accounts is used as the primary substantive test on clients for whom control risk has been assessed as low, when no red flags are present to indicate motivation to understate payables, and when the company is not in danger of violating potential debt covenants related to maintenance of working capital.

Understatement of Liabilities and Expenses at Advanced Marketing Services

Advanced Marketing Services (AMS) is a San Diego-based wholesaler of general-interest books that provides a variety of other services, including promotional and advertising services. A scheme to fraudulently overstate earnings at AMS involved not informing retailers of credits due to them for certain advertising and promotional services that the retailers provided. Instead of contacting the retailers and reconciling amounts, AMS improperly reversed the liability for these credits and thereby decreased

expenses and increased its income. An executive at AMS profited from her participation in the fraudulent schemes through her receipt of annual bonuses and sales of AMS stock. An analytical comparison of expenses with the previous years and with sales volumes might have been a good indicator that something was wrong.

For further details on this case, see SEC Accounting and Auditing Enforcement Release (AAER) No. 2312.

Accounts Payable and Related Expense Accounts: Completeness

Testing Subsequent Disbursements The auditor examines a sample of cash disbursements made after year end to determine whether the disbursements are for goods and services applicable to the previous year—and, if so, whether a liability was recorded in the previous year. The disbursements review is followed by an examination of unrecorded vendor invoices and receiving reports to determine whether goods or services received in the previous year were properly set up as a payable. If control risk is high or there are fraud-related red flags, the auditor may review 100% of the larger subsequent disbursements.

注册会计师抽样检查期后发生的现金支出交易以确定期末记录的应付账款是否真实存在。

Reconciling Vendor Statements or Confirmations with Recorded Payables The auditor may choose to request vendors' monthly statements or send confirmations to major vendors requesting a statement of open account items. The auditor reconciles the vendor's statement or confirmation with the client's accounts payable trial balance. The method generates reliable evidence but is costly (in auditor time spent reconciling the amounts) and is used when there is a high risk that the company does not pay vendors on a timely basis.

Related Expense Accounts Some expense accounts in the acquisition and payment cycle are of intrinsic interest to the auditor simply because of the nature of the account, even though they are likely not as material as inventory, cost of goods sold, or accounts payable. These include legal expense, travel and entertainment expense, repairs and maintenance expense, and income tax expense. The legal expense account should be examined as a possible indicator of litigation that may require recording and/or disclosure. Travel and entertainment expense should be examined for questionable or non-business-related items. Repairs and maintenance expense should be examined together with fixed-asset additions to assure a proper distinction has been made between expenditures that should be expensed and those that should be capitalized. Income tax expense and related liability(s) should be examined, often by a tax specialist, to assure that tax laws and regulations have been followed. Underlying documentation should be sampled to determine the

Expenses at Rite Aid

Executives at Rite Aid conducted a wide-ranging accounting fraud that resulted in the significant inflation of Rite Aid's income. When the fraud was ultimately discovered, Rite Aid was forced to restate its pretax income by $2.3 billion and net income by $1.6 billion, the largest restatement ever recorded at that time. One aspect of the fraud involved reversals of actual expenses. Rite Aid's accounting staff reversed amounts that had been recorded for various expenses incurred and already paid (debiting accounts payable and crediting expenses). These reversals were unjustified and, in each instance, were put back on the books in the subsequent quarter. The effect was to overstate Rite Aid's income during the period in which the expenses were incurred. Specifically, entries of this nature caused Rite Aid's pretax income for one quarter to be overstated by $9 million. This example makes an important point: *Sometimes management wants to misstate only a particular quarter to keep their stock price high, with the intent that they can fix problems before year end.*

For further details on this case, see SEC AAER No. 1581 and No. 2023.

nature of the expenditure, its appropriate business use, and the correctness of the recorded item.

The most widely used approach to detailed testing of expenses is to either (a) have the client create a schedule of all larger items making up the expense account (usually done for smaller clients) to be examined, or (b) use audit software to (i) examine randomly selected items from the expense account using sampling and (ii) prepare a list of all credits to the expense items for further review. The *Auditing in Practice* feature "Expenses at Rite Aid" provides an example of a fraud related to expenses in the acquisition and payment cycle.

Accounts Payable and Related Expense Accounts: Rights and Obligations

Organizations are increasingly entering into long-term contracts to purchase inventory at fixed prices or at a fixed price plus inflation adjustments. These contracts can extend over a period of years, and there is always some risk that economic circumstances can change and the contracts may no longer be economically viable. The contracts should be examined to determine penalties associated with default, and the auditor should gain sufficient knowledge to assess the client's estimate of the probability of contract default or losses.

Accounts Payable and Related Expense Accounts: Valuation or Allocation

Substantive tests of accounts payable and related expense accounts for valuation usually involve simply verifying the mathematical accuracy of the accounts, and agreeing them to general ledger and supporting documentation.

Accounts Payable and Related Expense Accounts: Presentation and Disclosure

There is relatively little that is usually disclosed in the footnotes about accounts payable and related expense accounts. Rather, these accounts usually just appear on the face of the financial statements. An example of a typical accounts payable disclosure for Ford Motor Company is shown in Exhibit 11.13.

| EXHIBIT **11.13** | Ford Motor Company Accounts Payable Presentation on Balance Sheet from the 2011 Annual Report |

Ford Motor Company and Subsidiaries Consolidated Balance Sheet (in millions)

	December 31, 2011	December 31, 2010
Liabilities		
Payables	$ 17,724	$ 16,362
Accrued liabilities and deferred revenue (Note 16)	45,369	43,844
Debt (Note 18)	99,488	103,988
Deferred income taxes (Note 22)	696	1,135
Total liabilities	163,277	165,329

Review of Unusual Entries to Expense Accounts

The vast majority of transactions to expense accounts should be debits that are accompanied by purchases of goods or services that can be validated through independent receipts and by independent vendor invoices. The exceptions to this rule are accounts that represent estimates or accounts that are based on a relationship with specific asset or liability accounts such as fixed assets (depreciation) or bonds (interest expense). The *Auditing in Practice* feature "WorldCom and Unusual Adjusting Entries" provides an example of a fraud that was perpetrated via the use of unusual adjusting entries.

Fraud-Related Substantive Procedures for Accounts Payable and Related Expenses

In those audits where there is a heightened risk of fraud related to accounts payable and other related expenses, the auditor will want to consider performing the following procedures or, if the procedures are already being performed, altering the timing and extent of the procedures:

- Send blank confirmations to vendors that ask them to furnish information about all outstanding invoices, payment terms, payment histories, and so forth. The procedure can be expanded to include new vendors and accounts with small or zero balances.

WorldCom and Unusual Adjusting Entries

AUDITING IN PRACTICE

Management at WorldCom wanted to keep line expenses at 42% of total costs because (a) line expense was a key ratio followed by Wall Street analysts and (b) it helped to keep reported profits high. One of the processes used was to credit line expense by reducing restructuring reserves. The reserve account would be debited for a round figure, such as:

Dr. Restructuring Reserve $450,000
     Cr. Line Expense $450,000

An examination of the credits in the expense account would have provided insight into this highly unusual accounting transaction. It is recommended that repair and maintenance expense be examined at the same time as fixed asset increases. If performed as recommended for the WorldCom audit, the fraud would have been discovered much earlier.

- Scan journals for unusual or large year-end transactions and adjustments, for example, transactions that are not typical, approvals not going through standard processes, or not having the usual supporting documentation
- Review client's vendor files for unusual items. Unusual items might include non-standard forms, different delivery addresses; or vendors that have multiple addresses
- Obtain and examine documentation for payments of invoices that are for amounts just under the limit that typically requires some level of approval

Documenting Substantive Procedures

The auditor would normally include the following types of documentation related to the substantive procedures for accounts in the acquisition and payment cycle:

- Substantive analytical procedures (including fraud-related procedures) conducted, conclusions reached, and related actions that were taken
- Evidence about physical inventory observations for all material amounts
  - Include information about locations observed, counts that were made and recorded, controls over inventory observation that were used, and specific test counts taken.
  - Include information about the dollar amount (for example, $50,000) above which inventory items would have been specifically tested.
  - If the physical inventory counts were taken at an interim date, the workpapers should include evidence about the procedures that were performed between the interim date and the balance sheet date.
- Evidence about product costing, such as the audit program for auditing the standard costing system and related evidence that was obtained
- Evidence pertaining to net realizable valuable calculations
- Evidence from inventory specialists
- Summaries of evidence obtained and conclusions reached about material amounts of inventory on consignment
- Evidence from evaluating subsequent disbursements for accounts payable
- Vendor statements
- Confirmations with vendors regarding accounts payable
- Evidence regarding conducting a review of unusual entries, including documentation of such entries and the explanations for them

SUMMARY AND NEXT STEPS

The acquisition and payment cycle presents unique risks for the auditor. Inventory existence and valuation are of primary concern because by overstating ending inventory, cost of goods sold is understated and net income is overstated. Therefore, the physical existence and valuation of inventory are critical to the accuracy of reporting earnings results. This fact has been exploited by unscrupulous managers in the past, so fraudulent financial reporting in the acquisition and payment cycle should be in the forefront of the mind of a skeptical auditor. In addition, the auditor should be especially concerned about the physical controls over inventory because of the potential for frauds involving misappropriation of assets. In addition to substantive analytical procedures and tests of controls (where applicable), the auditor will conduct substantive tests of inventory, including physical observation, test counts, net realizable valuation tests, tests of costing systems, and consultation with inventory valuation experts.

In terms of accounts payable and related expense accounts, the auditor is most concerned with completeness of recording because management may have incentives to not completely record transactions relating to these accounts. In addition to evaluating controls and conducting analytical procedures, the auditor will conduct substantive tests of accounts payable, such as confirmations and subsequent cash payments, to provide evidence on whether accounts payable and other related expenses have been completely recorded. Other related expenses such as legal expense and travel and entertainment expense are important because, while likely not as material as inventory, cost of goods sold, or accounts payable, these accounts may be a possible indicator of litigation or may contain questionable or non-business-related expenditures.

Looking ahead to the next chapter, we turn to auditing the acquisition of long-lived assets. These include accounts such as buildings, goodwill and other intangibles (along with the associated depreciation, amortization, or depletion), impairments, gains or losses on disposals, and leases.

SIGNIFICANT TERMS

Automated purchasing system A networked software system that links a company's Web site to other vendors whose offerings and prices have been preapproved by appropriate management.

Cycle count Periodic testing of the accuracy of the perpetual inventory record by counting all inventories on a cyclical basis.

Inventories Items of tangible personal property that are held for sale in the ordinary course of business, that are in the process of production for such sale, or that are to be currently consumed in the production of goods or services to be available for sale.

Inventory shrinkage Reduction in inventory presumed to be due to physical loss or theft.

Periodic inventory system A system of inventory recordkeeping in which no continuous record of changes in inventory (receipts and issues of inventory items) is kept. At the end of an accounting period, the ending inventory is determined by an actual physical count of every item, and its cost is computed using a suitable method.

Perpetual inventory system A system of inventory recordkeeping where book inventory is continuously in agreement with inventory on hand within specified time periods. In some cases, book inventory and stock on hand may be reconciled with each transaction; in other systems, these two numbers may be reconciled less often. This process is useful in keeping track of the actual availability of goods and determining what the correct time to reorder from suppliers might be.

Requisition A request for the purchase of goods or services by an authorized department or function within the organization; may be documented on paper or in a computer system.

Supply chain management The management and control of materials in the logistics process from the acquisition of raw materials to the delivery of finished products to the end user (customer).

Three-way match A control in which a purchase order, receiving information, and a vendor invoice are matched to determine whether the vendor's invoice is correct and should be paid. This process can be automated or can be performed manually.

TRUE-FALSE QUESTIONS

11-1 [LO 1] The existence and presentation/disclosure assertions are usually the most relevant for inventory.

11-2 [LO 1] The most common concerns for inventory are that purchases are understated or ending inventory is overstated, both of which will result in lower cost of goods sold and higher net income.

11-3 [LO 2] The audit of inventory is complex because inventory is easily transportable, exists at multiple locations, may become obsolete, and may be difficult to value.

11-4 [LO 2] Two important complexities in auditing inventory arise because inventory accounts experience a high volume of activity and are valued according to various inventory valuation methods.

11-5 [LO 3] One of the common ways that managers have committed fraud in the acquisition and payment cycle involves inappropriately classifying assets (for example, inventory) as expenses.

11-6 [LO 3] The following are possible manipulations that may occur when fraud is perpetrated during the purchase of inventory: under-recording purchases, recording purchases in a later period, and not recording purchases.

11-7 [LO 4] A well-conceived inventory control system should assure that all purchases are authorized and that inventory transactions are recorded accurately, completely, and in a timely manner.

11-8 [LO 4] Common rationales for having a separate purchasing function in an organization include the ability of purchasing agents to exert favoritism to valuable suppliers, the reduction in the opportunity of fraud by combining the authorization to purchase with custody and recording, and the decentralization of control to enhance the application of knowledge of purchasing and inventory management.

11-9 [LO 5] In terms of preliminary analytical procedures, assume that the company has introduced a new product with a low price point and significant customer demand. The auditor would expect inventory turnover to increase, and days' sales in inventory to also increase.

11-10 [LO 5] A preliminary analytical procedure in the acquisition and payment cycle that might indicate fraud is that inventory is growing at a rate greater than sales.

11-11 [LO 6] The following mix of evidence would be appropriate for a high risk client when conducting the audit of the acquisition and payment cycle: significant tests of internal controls, significant reliance on substantive analytical procedures, and limited tests of details.

11-12 [LO 6] When considering the appropriate mix of evidence, the sufficiency and appropriateness of selected procedures vary to achieve the desired level of assurance for each relevant assertion.

11-13 [LO 7] When selecting controls to test and performing tests of controls in the acquisition cycle, the auditor might reasonably take a sample of receiving reports and trace them through the system to test controls related to the completeness assertion for inventory and accounts payable.

11-14 [LO 7] When conducting the audit of acquisition and payment cycle accounts, the auditor will likely conduct less substantive tests for companies with effective internal controls compared to companies with ineffective internal controls.

11-15 [LO 8] A substantive procedure appropriate for testing the existence of inventory would be to perform year-end cutoff tests by noting the last shipping and receiving document numbers used before the physical inventory count is taken.

11-16 [LO 8] A substantive procedure appropriate for testing rights and obligations associated with inventory would be to review vendor invoices when testing disbursements to determine that proper title is conveyed.

MULTIPLE-CHOICE QUESTIONS

11-17 [LO 1] Which of the following is not an activity associated with the acquisition and payment cycle?
a. Receive a customer purchase order.
b. Purchase of goods and services.
c. Receipt of, and accounting for, goods and services.
d. Approval of items for payment.

11-18 [LO 1] An automated purchasing system will perform which of the following tasks?
a. Apply preloaded specifications and materials lists to the system to start the process.
b. Automatically flag invoices that do not reconcile with purchase orders.
c. Create change orders and analyze variances from purchase orders.
d. All of the above.

11-19 [LO 2] Which of the following is an inherent risk relating to inventory?
a. Inventory is easily transportable.
b. Inventory may become obsolete because of technological advances even though there are no visible signs of wear.
c. Inventory is often returned by customers, so care must be taken to separately identify returned merchandise, check it for quality, and record it at net realizable value.
d. All of the above.

11-20 [LO 2] Which of the following is not an inherent risk relating to inventory?
a. Sales contracts may contain unusual terms, and revenue recognition is often complex.
b. Inventory accounts typically experience a high volume of activity.
c. Inventory accounts may be valued according to various accounting valuation methods.
d. Identifying obsolete inventory and applying the lower of cost or market principle to determine valuation are difficult.

11-21 [LO 3] Which of the following is an example of fraud in the acquisition and payment cycle?
a. Theft of inventory by an employee.
b. Employee schemes involving fictitious vendors as means to transfer payments to themselves.
c. Executives recording fictious inventory or inappropriately recording higher values for existing inventory.
d. All of the above.

11-22 **LO 3** Refer to Exhibit 11.2, and identify the possible inventory or cost of goods sold manipulation that might occur when inventory is sold.
a. Overstate returns.
b. Overcount inventory.
c. Not record cost of goods sold nor reduce inventory.
d. Under-record purchases.

11-23 **LO 4** Refer to Exhibit 11.3, and identify which of the following is a typical control associated with the requisition process for inventory purchases in a just-in-time manufacturing process.
a. The store manager's ability to issue a purchase order may be subject to overall corporate limits, usually specified in dollars.
b. An agreement is signed with the supplier whereby the supplier agrees to ship merchandise according to the production schedule set by the manufacturer.
c. Overall authorization to purchase product lines is delegated to individual buyers by the marketing manager.
d. The limits for individual goods can be exceeded only on specific approval by the marketing manager.

11-24 **LO 4** Which of the following is a legitimate rationale for centralizing the purchasing function in a separate purchasing department?
a. It promotes efficiency and effectiveness.
b. It eliminates potential favoritism that could take place if individual department heads were allowed to place orders.
c. It decentralizes control across functions.
d. a. & c.
e. a. & b.

11-25 **LO 5** Which of the following expected relationships is reasonable in terms of performing preliminary analytical procedures in the acquisition and payment cycle?
a. Assume that the company's production and pricing strategies have remained the same during the past year. Gross margin is expected to improve because of the stability.
b. Assume that the company has introduced a new product with a low price point and significant customer demand. Inventory turnover is expected to increase, and days' sales in inventory is expected to decrease.
c. Assume that the company has invested in a new manufacturing process that results in significantly less waste and overall increases in efficiency during the production process. Cost of goods sold is expected to increase, and gross margin is expected to decrease.
d. All of the above are reasonable expected relationships.

11-26 **LO 5** Which of the following analytical relationships is most suggestive of a heightened risk of fraud in the acquisition and payment cycle?
a. Unexpected increases in gross margin.
b. Unexpected decreases in gross margin.
c. Inventory that is growing at a rate slower than sales.
d. Expense accounts that have significant debit entries.

11-27 **LO 6** Which mix of evidence would be most appropriate for the following scenario? This is a client where the auditor has assessed the risk of material misstatement related to the existence of inventory at the maximum level. This client has incentives to overstate income to achieve profit targets that affect management bonuses.

Oversight of the vice president of finance is relatively weak because of a lack of supervision by top management. Other controls are designed effectively.

a. 100% tests of details.
b. 50% tests of details, 30% analytics, 20% tests of controls.
c. 30% tests of details, 40% analytics, 30% tests of controls.
d. 20% tests of details, 40% analytics, 40% tests of controls.

11-28 **L0 6** Which mix of evidence would be most appropriate for the following scenario? This is a client where the auditor has assessed the risk of material misstatement related to the existence of inventory at a relatively low level. Top management appears to possess integrity. Management has spent the resources necessary to ensure effective design, implementation, and operation of controls.

a. 100% tests of details.
b. 70% tests of details, 10% substantive analytics, 20% tests of controls.
c. 50% tests of details, 10% substantive analytics, 40% tests of controls.
d. 20% tests of details, 40% substantive analytics, 40% tests of controls.

11-29 **L0 7** Which of the following statements is false regarding obtaining evidence about internal control operating effectiveness in the acquisition and payment cycle?

a. For integrated audits, the auditor will test the operating effectiveness of important controls as of the client's year end.
b. The auditor will select controls that are important to the auditor's conclusion about whether the organization's controls adequately address the assessed risk of material misstatement in the acquisition and payment cycle.
c. Evidence of proper payment is not necessary for each purchase and payment, but is necessary for those that are material.
d. The auditor will take a sample of receiving reports and trace through the system to test controls related to the completeness assertion for accounts payable.

11-30 **L0 7** Refer to the *Auditing in Practice* feature "Inventory Controls at CSK Auto Corporation." Which of the following represents an implication of weaknesses in the company's controls over inventory?

a. The company could not adequately process and account for the disposition of inventory returns from customers.
b. The board of directors fired the CEO of CSK Auto as a result of the internal control deficiencies.
c. The company had to make adjustments to year-end inventory balances.
d. a. & c.
e. a. & b.

11-31 **L0 8** Which of the following auditing procedures would be used to test the existence or occurrence assertion for inventory?

a. Perform year-end cutoff tests by noting the last shipping and receiving document numbers used before physical inventory is taken.
b. Make inquiries of the client regarding the segregation of duties between the purchasing department and the receiving department.
c. Review the client's proposed physical inventory procedures to determine whether they are likely to result in a complete and correct physical inventory.

d. Make inquiries of the client regarding allowances made for expected returns.

e. All of the above.

11-32 [LO 8] Which of the following auditing procedures would be used to test the valuation or allocation assertion for inventory?

a. Inquire of production and warehouse personnel about the existence of obsolete inventory.

b. Test inventory cost by taking a sample of recorded inventory, and trace to source documents indicating cost of inventory.

c. Review trade journals for changes in product technology.

d. Inquire of the client about sales adjustments (markdowns) that have been offered to sell any products.

e. All of the above.

REVIEW AND SHORT CASE QUESTIONS

11-33 [LO 1] List the five primary activities involved in the acquisition and payment cycle.

11-34 [LO 1] What is an automated purchasing system? Describe the beneficial tasks that an automated purchasing system can perform.

11-35 [LO 1] Match the following assertions with their associated description: (a) existence or occurrence, (b) completeness, (c) rights and obligations, (d) valuation or allocation, (e) presentation and disclosure.

1. The company has title to the inventory as of the balance sheet date.
2. Inventory balances exist at the balance sheet date.
3. Inventory is properly classified on the balance sheet and disclosed in the notes to the financial statements.
4. Inventory balances include all inventory transactions that have taken place during the period.
5. The recorded balances reflect the true underlying economic value of those assets.

11-36 [LO 1] Match the following assertions with their associated description: (a) existence or occurrence, (b) completeness, (c) rights and obligations, (d) valuation or allocation, (e) presentation and disclosure.

1. The recorded balances reflect the true underlying economic value of those liabilities.
2. Accounts payable balances include all accounts payable transactions that have taken place during the period.
3. The company actually owes a liability for the accounts payable as of the balance sheet date.
4. Accounts payable is properly classified on the balance sheet and disclosed in the notes to the financial statements.
5. Accounts payable balances exist at the balance sheet date.

11-37 [LO 2] List at least five reasons that inventory is a complex accounting and auditing area.

11-38 [LO 2, 9] Assume that you are conducting the audit of College Ware, a publicly held manufacturer and distributor of printed, embroidered, and embossed specialty clothing and gift items marketed to college students with school-specific logos. The company pays licensing fees and manufactures products in advance of the fall and winter peak sales periods. The stores that sell the company's products have a contractual agreement that they may return a

ETHICS

NOTE: Completing Review and Short Case Questions does not require the student to reference additional resources and materials.

NOTE: For the remaining problems, we make special note of those addressing fraud, international issues, professional skepticism, and ethics.

percentage of unsold merchandise. During the current audit year, many stores in the University of Wisconsin and University of Illinois markets canceled orders just before the start of the school year because of changes in school logos. In addition, the percentage of unsold merchandise, and associated returns, was higher than normal for these stores. As a result, College Ware has made an adjusting entry to record a loss caused by market decline of inventory (Dr. loss because of market decline of inventory, Cr. allowance to reduce inventory to market value for $40,000). You as the auditor have conducted a physical inventory of the products, and, based upon sales data collected from College Ware's competitors, you are convinced that the write-down should be for $90,000 (a materially higher amount).

Another issue in the College Ware audit is that the company has started implementing plans to change its marketing strategy to include more sales of general-purpose clothes and gift items to mass-merchandising retailers. These retailers are larger, and the initial receivables payments indicate that they present a more reliable pattern of payments, with fewer uncollectible amounts. As such, management has argued that the allowance for doubtful accounts should be reduced and has made the associated adjusting entry (Dr. allowance for doubtful accounts, Cr. other revenue for $40,000).

In the past, you had questioned College Ware management about its steady increase in the allowance for doubtful accounts, which had risen by about 3% per year for each of the past five years even though the rate of customer default on receivables had remained steady over that time. However, you had never insisted that management revise its allowance downward because you considered management's estimates to be conservative (i.e., it reduced income rather than increased income). In your opinion, the allowance for doubtful accounts probably *should* be reduced, although it is hard to judge exactly the amount by which the reduction should be recorded because of the relatively recent change in the marketing strategy. In other words, it is difficult for you to dispute whether management's current adjusting entry is recorded at the correct amount.

a. Comment on why management of College Ware may have an incentive to reduce the allowance for doubtful accounts this year.
b. The overly conservative accounting estimates used by management in its valuation of accounts receivable represent what is commonly referred to as cookie jar reserves. Using this financial reporting strategy, management sets aside money in allowance accounts that it plans to remove later to cover future losses. In doing so, management allows itself discretion to report income at smoother levels than would otherwise be achieved had the cookie jar reserves not been put in place. Comment on the implications of management's financial reporting strategy.
c. Use the ethical decision making framework introduced in Chapter 4 to address the dilemmas the auditor faces regarding what the auditor should require the client to do regarding the client's inventory and accounts receivable balances. Recall that the steps in the framework are as follows:
    • Identify the ethical issue(s).
    • Determine the affected parties and identify their rights.

- Determine the most important rights.
- Develop alternative courses of action.
- Determine the likely consequences of each proposed course of action.
- Assess the possible consequences, including an estimation of the greatest good for the greatest number. Determine whether the rights framework would cause any course of action to be eliminated.
- Decide on the appropriate course of action.

11-39 [LO 3] List at least five common fraud schemes in the acquisition and payment cycle. FRAUD

11-40 [LO 3] Refer to the *Auditing in Practice* feature "Fraud in the Acquisition and Payment Cycle at WorldCom and Phar-Mor." Compare and contrast the nature of these two frauds, motivations underlying the frauds, and how management perpetrated these frauds. FRAUD

11-41 [LO 3, 4, 8] Each year Susan Riley, president of Bargon Construction, Inc., takes a three-week vacation to Hawaii and signs several checks to pay major bills during the period in which she is absent. Riley's vacation often occurs near the end of Bargon's fiscal reporting period because it is a slack time for the construction business. Jack Morgan, head bookkeeper for the company, uses this practice to his advantage. He makes out a check to himself for the amount of a large vendor's invoice and records it as a payment to the vendor for the purchase of supplies. He holds the check for several weeks to make sure the auditors will not examine the canceled check. Shortly after the first of the year, Morgan resubmits the invoice to Riley for payment approval and records the check in the cash disbursements journal. At that point, he marks the invoice as paid and files it with all other paid invoices. Morgan has been following this practice successfully for several years and feels confident that he has developed a foolproof fraud. FRAUD
a. What is the auditor's responsibility for discovering this type of fraud?
b. What deficiencies exist in the client's internal controls?
c. What substantive audit procedures are likely to uncover the fraud?

11-42 [LO 4] Following is a list of controls in the acquisition and payment cycle for inventory and cost of goods sold. Match each control with the following activities in this cycle: (1) requisition for goods and services, (2) purchase of goods and services, (3) receipt of, and accounting for, goods and services, (4) approval of items for payment, and (5) cash disbursements.
1. The receiving department electronically scans bar codes on the goods received to record quantity and visually inspects for quality.
2. Computer-generated purchase orders are reviewed by the purchasing department.
3. Management approves contracts with suppliers.
4. Management reviews payments and compares them to data such as production budgets.
5. Management requires competitive bids for large purchases.
6. An individual in a position of authority reviews the completeness of supporting documentation prior to signing a check for payment.
7. A policy exists and is enforced whereby purchase agents are rotated across product lines.

8. A requisition form is forwarded to the purchasing department by a supervisor.
9. A policy exists and is enforced whereby employees cannot purchase from vendors outside an authorized vendor database.
10. Controls exist to ensure that only authorized goods are received.
11. Controls exist to ensure that goods meet order specifications.
12. The receiving department prepares prenumbered receiving documents to record all receipts.
13. A three-way match is made between the invoice, the purchase order, and the receiving report.
14. Limits on the purchase of inventory can be exceeded only on specific approval by a manager.
15. Supporting documentation is canceled on payment to avoid duplicate payments.
16. Management monitors inventory and purchase levels.
17. Vendor disputes about payments are handled by individuals outside the purchasing department.
18. An agreement exists with the supplier whereby the supplier agrees to ship merchandise (just in time) according to the production schedule set by the manufacturer.

11-43 **LO 4, 8** The organizational structure of a manufacturing company includes the following departments: purchasing, receiving, inspecting, warehousing, and controllership. An auditor is assigned to audit the receiving department. During planning, the auditor determines the following information:

1. A copy of each purchase order is routinely sent to the receiving department by the purchasing department via intracompany e-mail. This is followed by the physical copy via regular intracompany mail. Each purchase order is filed by purchase order number. In response to a job enrichment program, everyone in the receiving department is authorized to file the purchase orders. Whoever happens to be available is expected to file any purchase orders received.

2. When a shipment of goods is delivered to the receiving dock, the shipper's invoice is signed and forwarded to the controller's office, the vendor's packing slip is filed in receiving by vendor name, and the goods are stored in the warehouse by receiving personnel. In response to a job enrichment program, all persons in the receiving department have been trained to perform all three activities independently. Whoever happens to be available when a shipment arrives is expected to perform all three of the activities associated with that shipment.

   a. What are the major deficiencies and inefficiencies in the process as described?
   b. How could the process be improved? First, consider the need for strategic production and suppliers. Second, consider how greater computerization could improve the process.
   c. Why is it important to have segregation between the purchasing, receiving, and payment functions? How is that segregation maintained when all three functions are automated?
   d. Assume the purchasing and receiving functions operate as described. What would your preliminary assessment be of control risk? What are the implications for substantive testing of the related account balances? Describe the substantive procedures the auditor should consider for inventory, expenses, payables, and other related accounts.

11-44 **LO 5** How can cross-sectional analysis performed as a preliminary analytical procedure help the auditor identify potential inventory misstatements for a multi-location retail client?

11-45 **LO 5** How might the auditor effectively use preliminary analytical procedures in the audit of various expense accounts, such as miscellaneous expenses? Give an example of how analytical procedures might be used in the audit of such accounts.

11-46 **LO 6** Refer to Exhibit 11.7. Describe the differences in the planned audit approaches for Clients A and B and the reasons for such differences.

11-47 **LO 8** Refer to the *Auditing in Practice* feature "Weaknesses in Performing Substantive Analytical Procedures: The Case of Deloitte's PCAOB Inspection Report." Describe the errors that Deloitte's auditors made with regard to conducting substantive analytical procedures for inventory. Explain the potential implications of their errors.

11-48 **LO 8** The following are the procedures that an auditor should complete when observing a client's physical inventory. Refer to Exhibit 11.9 to list these procedures in the order in which they would be completed, from step (1) to step (7).

Steps to Take When Observing a Client's Physical Inventory

_____Upon arriving at each site:

    a. Meet with client personnel, obtain a map of the area, and obtain a schedule of inventory counts to be made for each area.

    b. Obtain a list of sequential tag numbers to be used in each area.

    c. Observe the procedures the client has implemented to shut down receipt or shipment of goods.

    d. Observe that the client has shut down production.

    e. Obtain document numbers for the last shipment and receipt of goods before the physical inventory is taken. Use the information to perform cutoff tests.

_____Meet with the client to discuss the procedures, timing, location, and personnel involved in taking the annual physical inventory.

_____Review the inventory-taking procedures with all audit personnel. Familiarize them with the nature of the client's inventory; potential problems with the inventory; and any other information that will ensure that the client and audit personnel will properly recognize inventory items, high-dollar-value items, and obsolete items; and understand potential problems that might occur in counting the inventory.

_____Document your conclusion as to the quality of the client's inventory-taking process, noting any problems that could be of audit significance. Determine whether a sufficient inventory count has been taken to properly reflect the goods on hand at year end.

_____Determine whether specialists are needed to test or assist in correctly identifying inventory items.

_____Observe the counting of inventory and note the following on inventory count working papers:

    a. The first and last tag number used in the section.

    b. All tag numbers and the disposition of all tag numbers in the sequence.

    c. The product identification, product description, units of measure, and number of items on a count sheet.

    d. Items that appear to be obsolete or of questionable value.

    e. All high-dollar-value items included in inventory.

    f. Movement of goods into or out of the company during the process of inventory taking. Determine if goods are properly counted or excluded from inventory.

_____Review the client's plans for counting and tagging inventory items.

11-49 **LO 8** The following tasks are completed by the auditor while observing the physical inventory. For each task, state which assertion(s) is tested by the task: (1) existence or occurrence, (2) completeness, (3) rights and obligations, (4) valuation or allocation, or (5) presentation and disclosure.

    a. The auditor makes test counts of selected items and records the test counts for subsequent tracing into the client's inventory compilation.

    b. The auditor takes notations of all items that appear to be obsolete or that are in questionable condition; the auditor follows up on these items with inquiries of client personnel and retains the data to determine how they are accounted for in the inventory compilation.

    c. The auditor observes the handling of scrap and other material.

    d. The auditor observes whether any physical movement of goods occurs during the counting of inventory.

    e. The auditor records all high-dollar-value items for subsequent tracing into the client's records.

11-50 **LO 8** Describe the conditions under which it is acceptable to have the client take inventory before year end.

11-51 **LO 8** Determining the amount of inventory that should be written off because of obsolescence is a difficult and challenging audit task because (1) the client will usually state that most of the goods are still salable at current selling prices and (2) net realizable value is only an estimate (in other words, there is no specific, correct price at which inventory should be valued). Because of this, the auditor usually gathers corroborating evidence to provide evidence on valuation and, relatedly, obsolescence. Identify at least five sources of such corroborating evidence.

FRAUD

11-52 **LO 8** In those audits where a heightened risk of fraud exists related to inventory and cost of goods sold, the auditor will want to consider performing certain fraud-related substantive procedures. List at least five such procedures.

FRAUD

PROFESSIONAL SKEPTICISM

11-53 **LO 8** The *Auditing in Practice* feature "Examples of Fraud in the Physical Observation of Inventory" provides examples of how clients may fraudulently manipulate inventory amounts. List at least five such examples. Explain why even a professionally skeptical auditor might fall victim to a client that is perpetrating such a fraud.

11-54 **LO 8** Refer to Exhibit 11.12, which describes assertions and related auditing procedures for accounts payable. Match the following assertions with their associated auditing procedure: (a) existence or occurrence, (b) completeness, (c) rights and obligations, (d) valuation or allocation, (e) presentation and disclosure.

    1. Request vendors' monthly statements or send confirmations to major vendors requesting a statement of open account items.

    2. Review the client's financial statement disclosures of accounts payable and expense accounts such as travel and entertainment.

3. Use GAS to verify mathematical accuracy of accounts payable, or agree to the general ledger.
4. Examine a sample of cash disbursements made after the end of the year to determine whether the disbursements are for goods and services applicable to the previous year.
5. Perform a cutoff test of purchases and cash disbursements.
6. Perform analytical review of related expense accounts, for example, travel and entertainment or legal expenses.
7. Review long-term purchase commitments, and determine whether a loss needs to be accrued.
8. Agree monthly statements and confirmations from major vendors with the accounts payable list.

11-55 [LO 8] Explain why examining a sample of cash disbursements made after the end of the year is useful in determining the completeness of recorded accounts payable at year end.

11-56 [LO 8] Reviewing unusual entries to expense accounts is an important audit procedure that is sometimes overlooked, or that is not conducted with professional skepticism. Refer to the *Auditing in Practice* feature "WorldCom and Unusual Adjusting Entries," which explains how WorldCom executives used unusual journal entries to perpetrate their fraud.
a. What is unusual about the journal entry in this *Auditing in Practice* feature?
b. If confronted, do you think that management at WorldCom would have some reasonable, or at least plausible, explanation for the entry? Explain.
c. Imagine yourself as a young auditor that discovers this unusual entry and inquires about it with someone at the client. What factors might cause you to lack professional skepticism in evaluating the client's explanation?

FRAUD

PROFESSIONAL SKEPTICISM

11-57 [LO 8] During observation of a client's year-end inventory, the auditor notes that shipping document 8,702 was the last shipment for the year and that receiving report 10,163 was the last receiving slip for the year. Explain how the information gathered would be used in performing an inventory cutoff test.

11-58 [LO 8] The Northwoods Manufacturing Company has automated its production facilities dramatically during the last five years, to the extent that the number of direct-labor hours has remained steady, while production has increased fivefold. Automated equipment, such as robots, has helped increase productivity. Overhead, previously applied at the rate of $7.50 per direct-labor hour, is now being applied at the rate of $23.50 per direct-labor hour. Explain how an auditor might evaluate the reasonableness of the application of factory overhead to year-end inventory and cost of goods sold.

11-59 [LO 8] The auditor has always received good cooperation from a particular client and has no reason to question management's integrity. The controller has requested that the auditor inform her about which warehouse locations that the auditor will visit during the upcoming inventory count. In addition, the controller has requested copies of the auditor's observations on the physical inventory because she wants to make sure that a good inventory was taken. Should the auditor comply with these requests? State your rationale, including a discussion of professional skepticism.

PROFESSIONAL SKEPTICISM

11-60 [LO 8] The auditor has been assigned to the audit of Marathon Oil Company and will observe the testing of inventory at a major storage area in Ohio. The company has approximately 15 different types of fuel oils stored in various tanks. The value of the fuel varies dramatically according to its grade. Explain how the auditor might use a specialist in auditing the inventory.

11-61 `LO 8` The auditor is always concerned whether slow-moving or potentially obsolete inventory is included in inventory, and whether inventory should be reduced to a lower market value. Identify five substantive audit procedures the auditor might use to determine the existence of obsolete goods or goods whose market value is less than cost.

11-62 `LO 8` Explain how GAS could be used to help identify potentially obsolete inventory.

11-63 `LO 8` Explain the purpose of test counts and other inventory observations that the auditor notes while a physical inventory is being taken.

11-64 `LO 8` What financial statement disclosures are required for inventory? How does the auditor determine the adequacy of the client's financial statement disclosures?

11-65 `LO 8` Identify two audit approaches that might be used to gain assurance about the correctness of perpetual inventory records.

11-66 `LO 8` The following audit procedures (labeled 1. through 8. below) are found in audit programs addressing the acquisition and payment cycle. For each audit procedure described:

a. Identify the objective of the procedure or the audit assertion being tested.

b. Classify the procedure as primarily a substantive test, a test of controls, or both.

1. The auditor examines payments to vendors following year end and then reviews any open accounts payable files.

2. The auditor reviews computer-center records on changes to passwords and the client's procedures to monitor unusual amounts of access by password type. The auditor makes inquiries of purchasing agents about how often passwords are changed and whether assistants are allowed to access computer files in their absence in order to efficiently handle inquiries or process standing orders.

3. The auditor reviews a report of all accounts payable items that were not matched by the automated matching system but had been paid upon authorization of the accounts payable department. A sample of selected items is taken and traced to the vendor payment and supporting documentation.

4. The auditor uses software to prepare a report of all debits to accounts payable other than payments to vendors. A sample of the debits is selected and examined for support.

5. The auditor uses software to access all recorded receipts of merchandise that have not been matched to an open purchase order.

6. The client prepares a report from a database showing inventory write-downs by product line and by purchasing agent. The auditor reviews the report and analyzes the data in relation to sales volume by product.

7. The auditor creates a spreadsheet showing the amount of scrap generated monthly, by product line.

8. The auditor downloads client data to create a report showing monthly sales and inventory levels, by product line.

11-67 `LO 8` Auditing standards require the auditor to observe the client's physical inventory. That requirement could be met by observing the client's annual physical count of inventory and, in some circumstances, by observing inventory in connection with tests of the accuracy of the client's perpetual inventory.

a. What major purpose is served by requiring the auditor to observe the client's physical inventory count? What are the primary assertions for which the auditor gains evidence during the inventory observation?

b. Identify at least five items related to inventory that the auditor should be looking for and should document during the observation of the client's inventory.

c. How does the observation process differ when the client takes a complete physical count at or near year end versus when physical counts are taken throughout the year to test the accuracy of the perpetual records?

11-68 `LO 8` An auditor has been assigned to audit the accounts payable of a high risk audit client. Control risk is assessed as high, management integrity is marginal, and the company is near violation of important loan covenants, particularly one that requires the maintenance of a minimum working-capital ratio. Explain how the auditor should approach the year-end audit of accounts payable, including a discussion of specific audit procedures.

11-69 `LO 8` Paul Mincin, CPA, is the auditor of Raleigh Corporation. Mincin is considering the audit work to be performed in the accounts payable area for the current-year engagement. The prior-year documentation shows that confirmation requests were mailed to 100 of Raleigh's 1,000 suppliers. The selected suppliers were based on Mincin's sample that was designed to select accounts with large dollar balances. Mincin and Raleigh staff spent a substantial number of hours resolving relatively minor differences between the confirmation replies and Raleigh's accounting records. Alternative audit procedures were used for those suppliers who did not respond to the confirmation requests.

a. Identify the accounts payable management assertions that Mincin must consider in determining the audit procedures to be followed.

b. Identify situations in which Mincin should use accounts payable confirmations, and discuss whether he is required to use them.

c. Discuss why using large dollar balances as the basis for selecting accounts payable for confirmation might not be the most effective approach and indicate what more effective procedures could be followed when selecting accounts payable for confirmation.

11-70 `LO 8` The auditor often examines some expense accounts, such as legal expenses, in detail even if the account balance is not material. Explain why.

11-71 `LO 8` Why does the auditor examine travel and entertainment expenses? What would poor controls regarding executive reimbursements say about the tone at the top for purposes of evaluating and reporting on internal control?

CONTEMPORARY AND HISTORICAL CASES

FRAUD

PROFESSIONAL SKEPTICISM

11-72 **THOR INDUSTRIES, INC. AND MARK SCHWARTZHOFF, AND DELOITTE** LO **2, 3, 4, 6, 8** Refer to the *Professional Judgment in Context* feature "Thor Industries, Inc. and Mark Schwartzhoff: Fraudulent Reductions in Cost of Goods Sold Through Manipulation of Inventory Accounts." Answer the following questions.

a. List the incentives and opportunities that enabled Schwartzhoff to commit the fraud. Speculate on his possible rationalizations.

b. What do the control deficiencies imply about the approach Deloitte should have used to audit the inventory-related accounts and assertions on the Thor and Dutchmen audits? Discuss your answer in terms of the relative mix of evidence in the form of tests of details, substantive analytics, and tests of controls. Why might Deloitte auditors have lacked professional skepticism regarding the financial results of Dutchmen?

c. What substantive audit procedures (both tests of details and analytical procedures) could have detected this type of fraud earlier?

PROFESSIONAL SKEPTICISM

11-73 **ACE HARDWARE AND KPMG** LO **2, 3, 4, 5** Ace Hardware is a retailer-owned cooperative, with 4,600 hardware, home center, and building materials stores. At the time of this case, Ace was a private company that was planning to go public. In September 2007, Ace Hardware said it discovered a $154 million accounting discrepancy between its general ledger and its actual inventory. The accounting error was discovered during an internal review of financial reports. The company explained that it had found a difference between the company's 2006 general ledger balance—the company's primary method for recording financial transactions—and its actual inventory records, referred to as its perpetual inventory balance.

Ace hired a law firm and a consulting firm to investigate. The investigation cost about $10 million. As a result of the investigation, in January 2008, Ace Hardware reported that a mid-level employee in the finance department caused a $152 million accounting discrepancy between the general ledger and the actual inventory. The former finance worker made journal entries of a sizeable amount that masked a difference in numbers between the two ledger books. The ledgers looked as though they were reconciled, but were not. About one-quarter of the error dated to 1995, and the rest took place from 2002 through 2006. In its 10-K filing, the company reported that gross margins had increased by about 2% in the five years leading up to fiscal year end 2002, rising from 7.7 % to 9.4%. Home Depot, in contrast, maintained a very stable gross margin over that period, which was consistently about 30%. KPMG issued unqualified audit opinions on the company's financial statements during the period of the inventory misstatements.

Company officials stressed that the employee did not commit fraud and that no inventory or money was missing. Rather, the company suggested that the finance person was not properly trained or equipped to do the job. The company further suggested that the situation was Ace's fault, in that the finance person was not appropriately trained and that oversight and checks and balances were not in place. Company officials also blamed the error partly on the increasingly complex and competitive retail hardware industry. Specifically, systems in place were not adequate for addressing complications that arose from Ace's recent increase in product imports from Asia. Since that time, Ace has implemented a modern, point-of-sale inventory management system that has significantly improved internal controls and inventory pricing at individual retailer locations.

As a result of the discovery of the inventory problem, Ace had to put on hold its plans to issue a public offering of stock and in fact had still not issued a public offering of stock as of 2012. While we often think of inventory misstatements as due to fraud, this case illustrates that such misstatements can also be caused by errors.

a. List the inherent, control, and fraud risk factors relevant to this case.

b. State plausible reasons that KPMG audit personnel may have lacked professional skepticism in their audits of Ace Hardware.

11-74 | **VERIFONE HOLDINGS, INC.**   **FRAUD**
LO 2, 3, 4, 5, 6, 8   In 2009, the SEC charged VeriFone   **PROFESSIONAL SKEPTICISM**
Holdings, Inc., a technology company, with falsifying the company's financial statement to improve gross margins and income. VeriFone relied on gross margin as an indicator of its financial results and provided forecasts of its quarterly gross margins to investment analysts.

In early February 2007, during the quarterly closing process for the fiscal year ending January 31, 2007, preliminary financial results revealed a gross margin of 42.8%, which was about four percentage points below internal forecasts that had been communicated to analysts. Paul Periolat was a mid-level controller at VeriFone, and his responsibilities included forecasting gross margins, and making final inventory-related valuation adjustments relating to royalties, warranty reserves, and inventory obsolescence. When the CEO and CFO learned of the unexpectedly low gross margins in the preliminary financial results, they sent emails calling the issue an "unmitigated disaster" and instructed VeriFone managers beneath them to "figure it [and related low results] out."

Periolat determined that the problem in gross margin was due to incorrect accounting by a foreign subsidiary. He made a manual adjusting entry to record an increase to ending inventory of $7 million, thereby decreasing cost of goods sold and increasing gross margin. He failed to confirm the adjustments with the foreign subsidiary's controller, and knew that the adjustments were incorrect. Periolat continued to make large manual adjustments to inventory balances quarterly for which there was no reasonable basis over the next two quarters. These adjustments allowed the company to continue to meet its internal forecasts and its earnings guidance made to analysts. Periolat was able to make his unwarranted adjustments, in part, because VeriFone had few internal controls to prevent them. Neither the employee's supervisor nor any other senior manager reviewed the employee's work. Further, effective controls were not in place to prevent the person responsible for forecasting financial results from making adjustments that allowed the company to meet the forecasts.

Ultimately, when the misstatements were revealed and VeriFone restated its financial statements, the company's operating income fell from $65.6 million to $28.6 million, a reduction of 129%. When the misrepresentations were revealed in December 2007, VeriFone's stock price dropped 46%, which represented a one-day drop in market capitalization of $1.8 billion. With this much at stake, auditors need to remember to be professionally skeptical about manual entries and to require that appropriate documentation supporting the entries be available for their review. Further, in areas where internal controls are not effective, the auditor should implement appropriate substantive procedures due to the heightened risk of misstatement. For further information, see SEC AAER No. 3044, September 1, 2009.

a. List the inherent, control, and fraud risk factors relevant to this case.

b. What substantive audit procedures would have detected the fraud? Would preliminary or substantive analytics have been helpful in detecting the fraud?

PROFESSIONAL SKEPTICISM   **11-75**   **PCAOB AND GRANT THORNTON**
LO 1, 5, 6, 8, 9   On October 4, 2008, the PCAOB issued its annual inspection report of Grant Thornton LLP (PCAOB Release No. 104-2008-046). In conducting its inspections, the PCAOB focuses on audit engagements that it considers particularly risky or prone to error on the part of each audit firm. In its inspection report of Grant Thornton, the PCAOB noted the following problems in testing the inventory valuation assertion for a Grant Thornton client. The firm failed in the following respects to adequately test the valuation assertion regarding inventory:

• There was no evidence in the audit documentation, and no persuasive other evidence, that the firm had performed sufficient substantive procedures to test the raw materials and/or labor and overhead components of inventory at certain of its manufacturing locations. Analytical procedures, consisting of various high-level comparisons, including average cost, inventory balances, gross profit margins, and inventory turnover, were the firm's primary tests, but these procedures failed to meet the requirements for substantive analytical procedures. Specifically, the firm failed to develop expectations that were precise enough to provide the desired level of assurance that differences that may be potential material misstatements, individually or in the aggregate, would be identified, and failed to obtain corroboration of management's explanations of significant unexpected differences.

• The firm failed to evaluate the assumptions that management had used to determine the reserve for obsolete inventory.

a. The PCAOB report summarized a problem with Grant Thornton's testing of a client's inventory valuation assertion. Discuss why you believe the PCAOB was dissatisfied with the firm's performance.

b. Use the framework for professional decision making from Chapter 4 to determine the appropriate steps that the firm could have taken that would have ultimately been acceptable to the PCAOB. Recall that the framework is as follows:

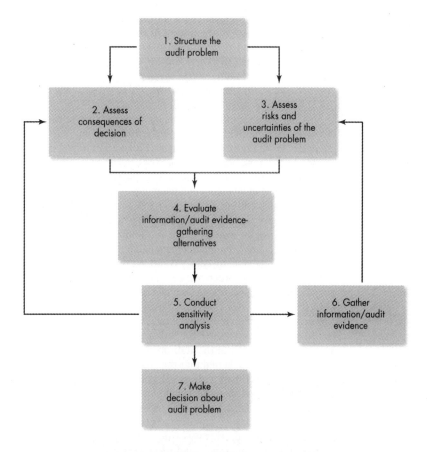

Source: Adapted from "Judgment and Choice," by Robin Hogarth.

11-76 **CENCO MEDICAL HEALTH SUPPLY CORPORATION**
LO **2, 3, 4, 6, 7, 8, 9**   Cenco
Medical Health Supply Corporation (CMH) was an SEC-registered
company that went bankrupt after it had materially misstated its
financial statements for a number of years. It inflated the reporting
of its physical inventory by 50% during two years prior to its
bankruptcy. The fraud was perpetrated by "(1) altering the quantities recorded on the pre-numbered, two-part inventory tags used in
counting the inventory; (2) altering documents reflected on a computer list prepared to record the physical count of inventory; and
(3) creating inventory tags to record quantities of nonexistent
inventory."

The SEC asserted that the auditors should have detected the fictitious inventory but did not because the audit firm "left the extent
of various observation testing to the discretion of auditors, not all
of whom were aware of significant audit planning that should have
related directly to the extent of such testing. Observation of inventory counts at year end was confined to six locations (representing
about 40% of the total CMH inventory) as opposed to nine in the
preceding year. The field auditors did not adequately control the
inventory tags and the auditor did not detect the creation of bogus
inventory tags which were inserted in the final inventory
computations." The SEC was also critical of the audit firm for

FRAUD

PROFESSIONAL SKEPTICISM

assigning interns to a significant portion of the inventory observation without training them in the nature of the client's inventory or its counting procedures. This is an example of a situation in which auditors' lack of professional skepticism led to low audit quality and a subsequent audit failure.

Source: R. W. V. Dickenson, "Why the Fraud Went Undetected," *CA Magazine April* 1977, pp. 67–69.

The SEC alleged that many deficiencies occurred during the audit of CMH. Among the complaints were the following:

1. The audit firm "left the extent of various observation testing to the discretion of auditors, not all of whom were aware of significant audit conclusions which related directly to the extent of such testing. Observations of inventory counts at year end were confined to six locations (representing about 40% of the total CMH inventory) as opposed to nine in the preceding year. The field auditors did not adequately control the inventory tags and Seidman & Seidman [the auditor] did not detect the creation of bogus inventory tags which were inserted in the final inventory computations."

2. The comparison of recorded test counts to the computer lists in the nine warehouse locations in which the inventory count was observed indicated error rates ranging from 0.9% to 38.3% of the test counts, with error rates in excess of 10% in several locations. Management attributed the differences to errors made by a keypunch operator. When the auditors asked to see the inventory tags, the CMH official stated that they had been destroyed.

3. The Seidman & Seidman auditor who performed the price testing of the CMH inventory determined that, as in previous years, in numerous instances CMH was unable to produce sufficient vendor invoices to support the purchase by CMH of the quantities being tested. This was true even though Seidman & Seidman ultimately accepted vendor invoices reflecting the purchase of the item by any CMH branch, regardless of the location of the inventory actually being price-tested.

4. A schedule of comparative inventory balances reflected significant increases from the prior year. A CMH financial officer wrote on this schedule management's explanations for the increases in inventory accounts.

5. CMH did not use prenumbered purchase orders and shipping documents.

6. Several differences exist between the tags reflected on the computer list for the Miami warehouse and the observation of the same tag numbers by Seidman & Seidman auditors. The computer list contained a series of almost 1,000 tags, covering about 20% of the tags purportedly used and more than 50% of the total reported value of the Miami inventory, which were reported as being unused on the tag control document obtained by Seidman & Seidman during its observation work.

7. Because CMH management did not provide sufficient invoices as requested, the auditors relied primarily on vendor catalogs, price lists, and vendor invoices to test the accuracy of the CMH inventory pricing representations.
   a. For each of the deficiencies identified, indicate the appropriate action that should have been taken by the auditor.
   b. What inventory information should be communicated to an auditor who is not regularly assigned to the audit of a

particular client prior to the observation of a physical inventory count?

c. How do questions of management integrity affect the approach that should be taken in planning the observation of a client's inventory-counting procedures?

d. Identify instances in which the auditors in this case did not exercise appropriate professional skepticism. For each of those instances, describe an alternative way that the auditor should have handled this situation.

e. The individual auditors conducting the audit inventory tests were lacking the appropriate training or knowledge to conduct their jobs. Assume that you and your classmates were assigned to an audit client and you find yourselves in a similar situation when you arrive to conduct an inventory observation. In particular, you are asked to observe inventory counts of products for which you are unsure of the appropriate measurement technique and are lacking in knowledge of the product itself. The client quickly describes the measurement process and offers to help you identify the different products. You are still somewhat unsure of your abilities to conduct this inventory observation. Use the framework for professional decision making from Chapter 4 to determine the appropriate steps to take.

CHAPTER

12

Auditing Long-Lived Assets: Acquisition, Use, Impairment, and Disposal

CHAPTER OVERVIEW AND LEARNING OBJECTIVES

When auditing long-lived assets, the auditor focuses on asset acquisition, use, impairment, and disposal. This chapter presents a discussion of the risks and risk responses associated with long-lived assets, such as land, property and equipment, natural resources, intangibles, and leases. In terms of the audit opinion formulation process, this chapter primarily involves Phases II, III, and IV, that is, performing risk assessment procedures, tests of controls, and substantive procedures for long-lived assets and related accounts.

Through studying this chapter, you will be able to achieve these learning objectives:

通过本章的学习，你将能够实现以下学习目标：

1. Identify the significant accounts, disclosures, and relevant assertions in auditing long-lived assets.

   在审计长期资产时识别重要的账户、披露和相关的认定。

2. Identify and assess inherent risks of material misstatement associated with long-lived assets.

   识别和评估与长期资产有关的重大错报的固有风险。

3. Identify and assess fraud risks of material misstatement associated with long-lived assets.

   识别和评估与长期资产有关的重大错报的舞弊风险。

4. Identify and assess control risks of material misstatement associated with long-lived assets.

   识别和评估与长期资产有关的重大错报的控制风险。

5. Describe how to use preliminary analytical procedures to identify possible material misstatements associated with long-lived assets.

   描述如何运用初步的分析性程序识别与长期资产有关的可能的重大错报。

6. Determine appropriate responses to identified risks of material misstatement in auditing long-lived assets.

   明确对于识别的与长期资产有关的重大错报风险如何进行适当的反应。

7. Determine appropriate tests of controls and consider the results of tests of controls in auditing long-lived assets.

   在审计长期资产时确定适当的控制测试，并且考虑控制测试的结果。

8. Determine and apply sufficient appropriate substantive audit procedures in auditing long-lived assets.

   在审计长期资产时确定和应用充分、适当的实质性审计程序。

9. Apply the frameworks for professional decision making and ethical decision making to issues involving the audit of long-lived assets.

   运用职业决策和职业道德决策框架解决与长期资产审计有关的问题。

THE AUDIT OPINION FORMULATION PROCESS

I. Making Client Acceptance and Continuance Decisions **Chapter 14**	II. Performing Risk Assessment **Chapters 3, 7 and 9–13**	III. Obtaining Evidence about Internal Control Operating Effectiveness **Chapters 8–13 and 16**	IV. Obtaining Substantive Evidence about Accounts, Disclosures and Assertions **Chapters 8–13 and 16**	V. Completing the Audit and Making Reporting Decisions **Chapters 14 and 15**

The Auditing Profession, the Risk of Fraud and Mechanisms to Address Fraud: Regulation, Corporate Governance, and Audit Quality **Chapters 1 and 2**	Professional Liability and the Need for Quality Auditor Judgments and Ethical Decisions **Chapter 4**

The Audit Opinion Formulation Process and A Framework for Obtaining Audit Evidence
Chapters 5 and 6

PROFESSIONAL JUDGMENT IN CONTEXT

Accounting Problems Related to Long-Lived Assets at Ignite Restaurant Group

Ignite Restaurant Group (IRG), the owner of various restaurants including Joe's Crab Shack, went public in May 2012. Just two months later, the company announced that it needed to restate its financial statements to correct errors related to the treatment of certain leases. The announcement resulted in a single-day stock price decline of 22%. The lease errors began in 2006 (the year of the company's origination) and continued through the first quarter of 2012. The restatement related to the leases is estimated to be between $3.4 and $3.8 million. IRG also plans a fixed-asset accounting review to assess historical asset additions, dispositions, useful lives, and depreciation from 2006 through the first quarter of 2012. IRG anticipates additional restatements of at least $1.2 million related to the accounting for its other fixed assets and related depreciation expense. As the company determines the total restatement that is needed, it has warned investors that the financial statements contained in the company's prior filings with the SEC can no longer be relied upon.

In conjunction with these restatements, the company is also reviewing the effectiveness of its internal controls over leases and other fixed assets.

As you read through this chapter, consider the following questions:

- What types of misstatements occur in long-lived asset accounts? (LO 1, 2, 3)
- What might motivate management to misstate long-lived asset accounts? (LO 3)
- What controls should be in place to mitigate misstatements associated with long-lived assets? (LO 4)
- What procedures should an auditor perform when auditing long-lived asset accounts? (LO 5, 6, 7, 8)

Significant Accounts, Disclosures, and Relevant Assertions

重要账户、披露和相关认定

Long-lived assets often represent the largest single category of assets of many organizations. Long-lived assets are noncurrent assets that are used over multiple operating cycles and include **tangible assets** of land, buildings, fixtures, and equipment. Some organizations also have natural resources, such as timber tracts, oil wells, and mineral deposits. Long-lived

LO 1 Identify the significant accounts, disclosures, and relevant assertions in auditing long-lived assets.

479

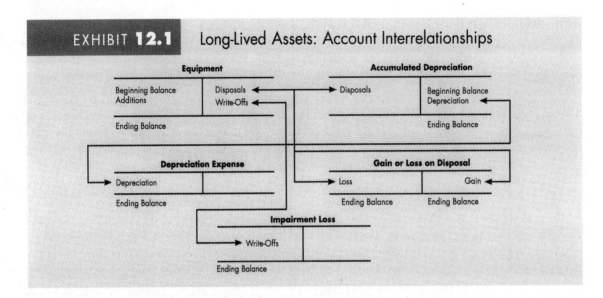

EXHIBIT **12.1** Long-Lived Assets: Account Interrelationships

assets also include **intangible assets**. For example, drug companies like Pfizer have patent costs that are capitalized as intangible assets, and companies like Coca-Cola have franchise licenses that make up a significant portion of the company's total assets. Goodwill is often a significant intangible asset of many companies. Because of significant complexities in auditing goodwill, we defer discussion of that topic until Chapter 16. An overview of the accounts typically associated with long-lived assets is shown in Exhibit 12.1.

The asset account (equipment, buildings, or similarly titled assets) represents the culmination of additions and disposals. Other accounts associated with long-lived assets include the related depreciation or impairment expense, any related gains caused by disposals, any related losses caused by disposals or impairments, and the accumulated depreciation account. For natural resources, the related expense account would be referred to as **depletion expense** (the expense associated with the extraction of natural resources). For intangible assets with a definite life, the related expense account would be referred to as **amortization expense**. Assets can also be acquired through capital leases, and organizations acquiring assets through capital leases will need to consider whether the relevant criteria for capitalizing the lease have been met.

长期资产采购与付款循环
中涉及的主要活动

Activities in the Long-Lived Asset Acquisition and Payment Cycle

The purchase of long-lived assets includes the same types of activities for purchasing current assets that we discussed in Chapter 11. The long-lived assets will be requested and purchased. The organization will approve and make payment for the asset. An important difference is that the acquisition of long-lived assets will be based on an organization's planning for long-term productive capacity.

Once the asset has been acquired, the organization will need to allocate a portion of the asset's cost as an expense—depreciation, amortization, or depletion, depending on the type of asset—in each reporting period. The organization will also review its long-lived tangible and intangible assets for possible asset impairment, and when appropriate, will recognize an impairment loss and write down the asset to its fair value. In situations when an organization disposes of its long-lived assets, it will need to determine and record the gain or loss on the asset disposal.

Relevant Financial Statement Assertions

相关的财务报表认定

The five management assertions relevant to long-lived assets are as follows:

1. *Existence or occurrence*—The long-lived assets exist at the balance sheet date. The focus is typically on additions during the year.
2. *Completeness*—Long-lived asset account balances include all relevant transactions that have taken place during the period.
3. *Rights and obligations*—The organization has ownership rights for the long-lived assets as of the balance sheet date.
4. *Valuation or allocation*—The recorded balances reflect the balances in accordance with GAAP (includes appropriate cost allocations and impairments).
5. *Presentation and disclosure*—The long-lived asset balance is reflected on the balance sheet in the noncurrent section. The disclosures for depreciation methods and capital lease terms are adequate.

The existence and valuation assertions related to long-lived assets are usually the more relevant assertions. Organizations may have incentives to overstate their long-lived assets and may do so by including fictitious long-lived assets on the financial statements. Alternatively, organizations may capitalize costs, such as repairs and maintenance costs, which should be expensed. Concerns regarding valuation include whether the organization properly and completely recorded depreciation and properly recorded any asset impairments. The valuation issues typically involve management estimates that may be subject to management bias.

Performing Risk Assessment Procedures for Long-Lived Assets

对长期资产实施风险评估程序

As part of performing risk assessment procedures, the auditor obtains information that is useful in assessing the risk of material misstatement. This includes information about inherent risks at the financial statement level (for example, the client's business and operational risks and financial reporting risks) and at the account and assertion levels, fraud risks including feedback from audit team brainstorming sessions, strengths and weaknesses in internal control, and results from preliminary analytical procedures. Once the risks of material misstatement have been identified, the auditor then determines how best to respond to them as part of the audit opinion formulation process.

LO 2 Identify and assess inherent risks of material misstatement associated with long-lived assets.

Identifying Inherent Risks

识别固有风险

Much of the inherent risk associated with long-lived assets is due to the importance of management estimates, such as estimating useful lives and residual values and determining whether asset impairment has occurred. Inherent risk related to **asset impairment** stems from the following factors:

与长期资产相关的固有风险大多源于管理层估计，如估计可使用年限、残值以及决定资产是否已经发生减值。

- Normally, management is not interested in identifying and writing down assets.
- Sometimes, management wants to write down every potentially impaired asset to a minimum realizable value (although this will cause a one-time reduction to current earnings, it will lead to higher reported earnings in the future).
- Determining asset impairment, especially for intangible assets, requires a good information system, a systematic process, effective controls, and professional judgment.

Other inherent risks associated with long-lived assets and related expenses include:

- Incomplete recording of asset disposals
- Obsolescence of assets
- Incorrect recording of assets, due to complex ownership structures
- Amortization or depreciation schedules that do not reflect economic impairment or use of the asset

The auditor will become aware of these risks through:

- Knowledge of the client's business, including industry trends and technological advances
- Review of various documents, including:
  - The business plan for major acquisitions or changes in the way the company conducts its business
  - Major contracts regarding capital investments or joint ventures with other companies
  - The minutes of board of directors' meetings
  - Company filings with the SEC describing company actions, risks, and strategies

The *Auditing in Practice* feature "Auditing of Long-Lived Assets Does Have Risks" makes the point that the audit of long-lived assets may not always be a low-risk audit area.

Inherent Risks Associated with Natural Resources Natural resources present unique risks. First, it is often difficult to identify the costs associated with discovery of the natural resource. Second, once the natural resource has been discovered, it is often difficult to estimate the amount of commercially available resources to be used in determining a depletion rate. Third, the client may be responsible for restoring the property to its original condition (reclamation) after the resources are removed. Reclamation costs may be difficult to estimate.

Inherent Risks Associated with Intangible Assets Intangible assets should be recorded at cost. However, the determination of cost for intangible assets is not as straightforward as it is for tangible assets, such as equipment. A particularly troublesome area is the cost of a patent. For example, research and development costs related to new products, such as drugs or software, should be expensed as incurred up until the point that there is a viable product and a plan to bring the product to market. Legal costs for

Auditing of Long-Lived Assets Does Have Risks   AUDITING IN PRACTICE

Many new auditors just returning from an internship believe that the audit of long-lived assets is primarily mechanical, for example, recalculating depreciation, tracing amounts to accumulated depreciation, and vouching fixed-asset additions. In some organizations, that may be the case. However, as with all other aspects of the audit, the auditor must understand the client's business strategy, current economic conditions, and potential changes in the economic value of the assets. Auditors can make serious mistakes if they act as if long-lived assets are always a low-risk audit area. The IRG example provided in the *Professional Judgment in Context* feature highlights that errors in this area can lead to companies having to restate their financial statements.

obtaining and defending a patent are capital expenditures if the defense is successful. If it is not successful, the patent has no value and any related costs should be expensed. Patents purchased from another company are capital costs. The cost of patents should be amortized over the lesser of their legal life or their estimated useful life. Minor changes to the patented item have been made by drug companies to extend the life of some patented drugs. As with tangible long-lived assets, management needs to determine if the book values of patents and other intangible assets have been impaired.

Identifying Fraud Risk Factors

One of the more common techniques used to fraudulently misstate financial statements involves the overstatement of assets through overvaluing existing assets, including fictitious assets, or capitalizing expenses. The WorldCom fraud case is a classic example illustrating some of the fraud risks relating to long-lived asset accounts. One element of the WorldCom fraud involved management reducing the accumulated depreciation account by debiting that account and crediting depreciation expense. These entries were performed on a regular basis, and, unfortunately, the auditors did not view them as unusual or otherwise worthy of separate investigation. Management also misstated assets by routinely capitalizing a line expense (in other words, cash paid to other carriers when WorldCom used their lines to transmit calls). Finally, upon making new acquisitions, management boosted the value of the assets, but it established reserves for plant closings and related expenses. When the actual expenses were less, management debited the liability and credited the expense, thereby increasing net income in subsequent periods.

Other potential fraud schemes relating to long-lived assets include:

- Sales of assets are not recorded, and proceeds are misappropriated.
- Assets that have been sold are not removed from the books.
- Inappropriate residual values or lives are assigned to the assets, resulting in miscalculation of depreciation.
- Amortization of intangible assets is miscalculated.
- Costs that should have been expensed are improperly capitalized.
- Impairment losses on long-lived assets are not recognized.
- Fair value estimates are unreasonable or unsupportable.

Identifying Control Risks

Once the auditor has obtained an understanding of the inherent and fraud risks of material misstatement related to long-lived assets, the auditor needs to understand the controls that the client has designed and implemented to address those risks. Remember, the auditor is required to gain an overall understanding of internal controls for both integrated audits and financial statement only audits. Such understanding is normally gained by means of a walkthrough of the process, inquiry, observation, and review of the client's documentation. The auditor considers both entity-wide controls and transaction controls at the account and assertion levels. This understanding provides the auditor with a basis for making an initial control risk assessment.

At the entity-wide level, the auditor considers the control environment and other entity-wide components of internal control—risk assessment, information and communication, and monitoring controls. The *Auditing in Practice* feature "WorldCom and Waste Management: Two Examples of Asset Misstatement" highlights two well-known cases involving material misstatements in long-lived assets and related expenses where there was a weakness in the control environment.

Although all the components of internal control need to be understood, the auditor typically finds it useful to focus on significant control activities related to the long-lived asset accounts. As part of this understanding, the auditor focuses on the relevant assertions for each account and identifies the

LO 3 Identify and assess fraud risks of material misstatement associated with long-lived assets.

通过高估现有资产来虚增资产是财务报表舞弊的一个重要方法，包括虚构资产或者费用资本化。

识别控制风险

LO 4 Identify and assess control risks of material misstatement associated with long-lived assets.

AUDITING IN PRACTICE

WorldCom and Waste Management: Two Examples of Asset Misstatement

The weaknesses in the control environment at these two companies allowed for management override of existing controls and ultimately the ability to commit large frauds.

WorldCom
The WorldCom bankruptcy was one of the largest in U.S. history. From the first quarter of 1999 through the first quarter of 2002, WorldCom's management improperly released approximately $984 million in depreciation reserves to increase pretax earnings by decreasing depreciation expense or increasing miscellaneous income. The depreciation reserves were created in a variety of ways, including:

- The cost of equipment returned to vendors for credit after being placed in service was credited to the reserve (accumulated depreciation), rather than the asset itself.
- Unsupported additions to an asset account were recorded with a corresponding increase in the reserve.

After the end of each fiscal quarter, management in general accounting would direct property accounting personnel to release large balances from this reserve account (debit to the accumulated depreciation account), usually to reduce depreciation expense. If it was too late in the quarterly closing process to record depreciation expense as a standard adjusting entry,

property accounting personnel were directed to prepare a draft journal entry so general accounting could make the adjustment. WorldCom also inappropriately capitalized line expense (amounts paid to other carriers such as AT&T to use their lines) as fixed assets.

Source: *Report of Investigation* by the Special Investigative Committee of the Board of Directors of WorldCom, Inc., March 31, 2003.

Waste Management
Waste Management, Inc. is the nation's largest waste disposal company. The company grew though extensive acquisitions—seemingly all dependent on ever-increasing sales and net income that fueled higher stock prices. Waste Management's previous management recognized the importance of stock prices to pay for more acquisitions, but the company was losing its profitability. Management struck on a new way to increase reported net income—simply increase the estimated useful lives of all the depreciable assets. The auditors never questioned the change even though the change accounted for virtually all of Waste Management's increase in earnings over a period of years. Finally, the SEC stepped in and pointed out these estimated useful lives simply were not realistic. Waste Management had misstated earnings by a whopping $3.5 billion. Arthur Andersen paid fines of $220 million, and the SEC fined the individual auditors on the engagement.

controls that relate to risks for these assertions. In an integrated audit or in a controls reliance audit of the financial statements, the auditor uses this understanding to identify important controls that need to be tested.

Typical controls that affect multiple assertions for long-lived assets include:

- Formal budgeting process with appropriate follow-up variance analysis
- Written policies for acquisition and disposals of long-lived assets, including required approvals
- Limited physical access to assets, where appropriate
- Periodic comparison of physical assets to subsidiary records
- Periodic reconciliations of subsidiary records with the general ledger

Controls Related to Existence/Occurrence and Valuation for Tangible Assets To provide reasonable assurance that the existence and valuation assertions for fixed assets are materially correct, controls should be in place to:

- Identify existing assets, inventory them, and reconcile the physical asset inventory with the property ledger on a periodic basis (existence)
- Provide reasonable assurance that all purchases are authorized and properly valued (valuation)

- Appropriately classify new equipment according to its expected use and estimate of useful life (valuation)
- Periodically reassess the appropriateness of depreciation categories (valuation)
- Identify obsolete or scrapped equipment and write the equipment down to scrap value (valuation)
- Review management strategy and systematically assess the impairment of assets (valuation)

Many organizations face a challenge in tracking the location, quantity, condition, maintenance, and deprecation status of their fixed assets. One approach to dealing with this challenge is to use serial numbered asset tags, often with bar codes. Then periodically, the organization takes inventory, utilizing a barcode reader.

Given the challenges related to asset impairment, the auditor needs to understand management's controls related to asset impairment judgments. Such controls should include:

- A systematic process to identify assets that are not currently in use
- Projections of future cash flows, by reporting unit, that is based on management's strategic plans and economic conditions
- Systematic development of current market values of similar assets prepared by the client

Controls over Natural Resources Most established natural resource companies have developed procedures and associated internal controls for identifying costs, and such organizations use geologists to establish an estimate of the reserves contained in a new discovery. These organizations periodically reassess the amount of reserves as more information becomes available during the course of mining, harvesting, or extracting resources.

Controls Related to Valuation and Presentation/Disclosure for Intangible Assets For intangible assets, controls should be designed to:

- Provide reasonable assurance that decisions are appropriately made as to when to capitalize or expense research and development expenditures (presentation and disclosure)
- Develop amortization schedules that reflect the remaining useful life of patents or copyrights associated with the asset (valuation)
- Identify and account for intangible-asset impairments (valuation)

Management should have a monitoring process in place to review valuation of intangible assets. For example, a pharmaceutical company should have fairly sophisticated models to predict the success of newly developed drugs and monitor actual performance against expected performance to determine whether a drug is likely to achieve expected revenue and profit goals. Similarly, a software company should have controls in place to determine whether capitalized software development costs will be realized. Exhibit 12.2 identifies examples of other controls over intangible long-lived assets that clients may have in place.

Documenting Controls Auditors need to document their understanding of internal controls for both integrated audits and financial statement only audits. Similar to other audit areas, the auditor can provide this documentation in various formats, including a control matrix, a control risk assessment questionnaire, and/or a memo.

Performing Preliminary Analytical Procedures

When planning the audit, the auditor is required to perform preliminary analytical procedures. These procedures can help auditors identify areas of

实施初步的分析性程序

LO 5 Describe how to use preliminary analytical procedures to identify possible material misstatements associated with long-lived assets.

EXHIBIT **12.2**	Examples of Controls over Intangible Long-Lived Assets

- Management authorizations are required for intangible asset transactions.
- Documentation regarding intangible assets should be maintained, and such documentation should include:
  - Manner of acquisition (for example, purchased or developed internally)
  - Basis for the capitalized amount
  - Expected period of benefit
  - Amortization method
- Amortization periods and calculations should be approved and periodically reviewed by appropriate personnel.

potential misstatements. Auditors do not look at just the numbers when performing analytical procedures. Auditors need to go through the four-step process described in Chapter 7, which begins with developing expectations for account balances, ratios, and trends.

Auditors must know the business and the economics of the business to perform meaningful analytical procedures. Consider a simple example. A local company is in the business of picking up and hauling garbage. Shouldn't the auditors have a fairly good idea of approximately how long the trucks will last? They know the mileage; they know the beating the trucks take every day; they know something about the company's policy for cleaning and repairing the trucks. What if management comes in and makes a decision to extend the depreciable life from five to twelve years when the rest of the industry is at about six years? Does this make sense? Although the auditor cannot always make a decision as to whether five years is better than six, the auditor needs to be in a position to understand whether five years is much closer to economic reality than twelve years.

Ratio and Trend Analyses   Techniques that auditors can use when performing preliminary analytical procedures include the following:

- Review and analyze gains/losses on disposals of equipment (gains indicate depreciation lives are too short; losses indicate the opposite).
- Perform an overall estimate of depreciation expense.
- Compare capital expenditures with the client's capital budget, with an expectation that capital expenditures would be consistent with the capital budget.
- Compare depreciable lives used by the client for various asset categories with those of the industry. Large differences may indicate earnings management.
- Compare the asset and related expense account balances in the current period to similar items in the prior audit and determine whether the amounts appear reasonable in relation to other information you know about the client, such as changes in operations.

Ratios that the auditor should plan to review, after developing independent expectations, include:

- *Ratio of depreciation expense to total depreciable long-lived tangible assets*—This ratio should be predictable and comparable over time unless there is a change in depreciation method, basis, or lives. The auditor should plan to analyze any unexpected deviation and assess whether any changes are reasonable.
- *Ratio of repairs and maintenance expense to total depreciable long-lived tangible assets*—This ratio may fluctuate because of changes in

management's policies (for example, maintenance expenses can be postponed without immediate breakdowns or loss of productivity). The auditor should plan to analyze any unexpected deviation with this consideration in mind.

If preliminary analytical procedures do not identify any unexpected relationships, the auditor would conclude that there is not a heightened risk of material misstatements in these accounts. If unusual or unexpected relationships exist, the planned audit procedures (tests of controls, substantive procedures) would be adjusted to address the potential material misstatements. The auditor should be aware that if a fraud is occurring in long-lived asset accounts, the financial statements usually will contain departures from industry norms, but may not differ from the expectations set by management. Therefore, the auditor should compare the unaudited financial statements with both past results and industry trends.

注册会计师应该注意，当长期资产账户发生舞弊时，财务报表可能不会偏离管理层的预期，但通常会偏离整个行业的水平。

Responding to Identified Risks of Material Misstatement

对识别的重大错报风险的反应

LO 6 Determine appropriate responses to identified risks of material misstatement in auditing long-lived assets.

Once the auditor has developed an understanding of the risks of material misstatement, the auditor can determine the appropriate audit procedures to perform. Audit procedures should be proportional to the assessed risks, with areas of higher risk receiving more audit attention and effort. Responding to identified risks typically involves developing an audit approach that contains substantive procedures (such as tests of details and, when appropriate, substantive analytical procedures) and tests of controls, when applicable. If the client's controls related to long-lived assets are effective, then the auditor can rely more extensively on substantive analytical procedures to obtain evidence on account balances. The sufficiency and appropriateness of selected procedures vary to achieve the desired level of assurance for each relevant assertion. While audit firms may have a standardized audit program for auditing long-lived assets, the auditor should customize the audit program based on the assessment of the risk of material misstatement.

Consider a client where the auditor has assessed the risk of material misstatement related to the existence of equipment at slightly below the maximum. Further, assume that incentives exist to overstate income to achieve profit targets that affect management bonuses, and oversight is relatively weak because of a lack of supervision by top management. Therefore, there is a heightened risk of capitalizing items that should be expensed. The auditor may develop an audit program that consists of first performing limited tests of operating effectiveness of controls, then performing limited substantive analytical procedures, and finally performing extensive substantive tests of details. Because of the high risk, the auditor will want to obtain a great deal of evidence directly from tests of details. In contrast, consider a client where the auditor has assessed the risk of material misstatement related to the existence of equipment as low, and believes that the client has implemented effective controls in this area. For this client, the auditor will likely perform tests of controls, gain a high level of assurance from substantive analytical procedures such as a reasonableness test, and then complete the substantive procedures by performing tests of details at a limited level.

Panel A of Exhibit 12.3 shows that because of differences in risk, the box of evidence to be filled for testing the existence of equipment at the low-risk client is smaller than that at a high-risk client. Panel B of Exhibit 12.3 illustrates the different levels of assurance that the auditor will obtain from tests of controls and substantive procedures for the two assertions. Panel B makes the point that because of the higher risk associated with the existence of equipment at Client B, the auditor will want to design the audit so that

EXHIBIT **12.3**

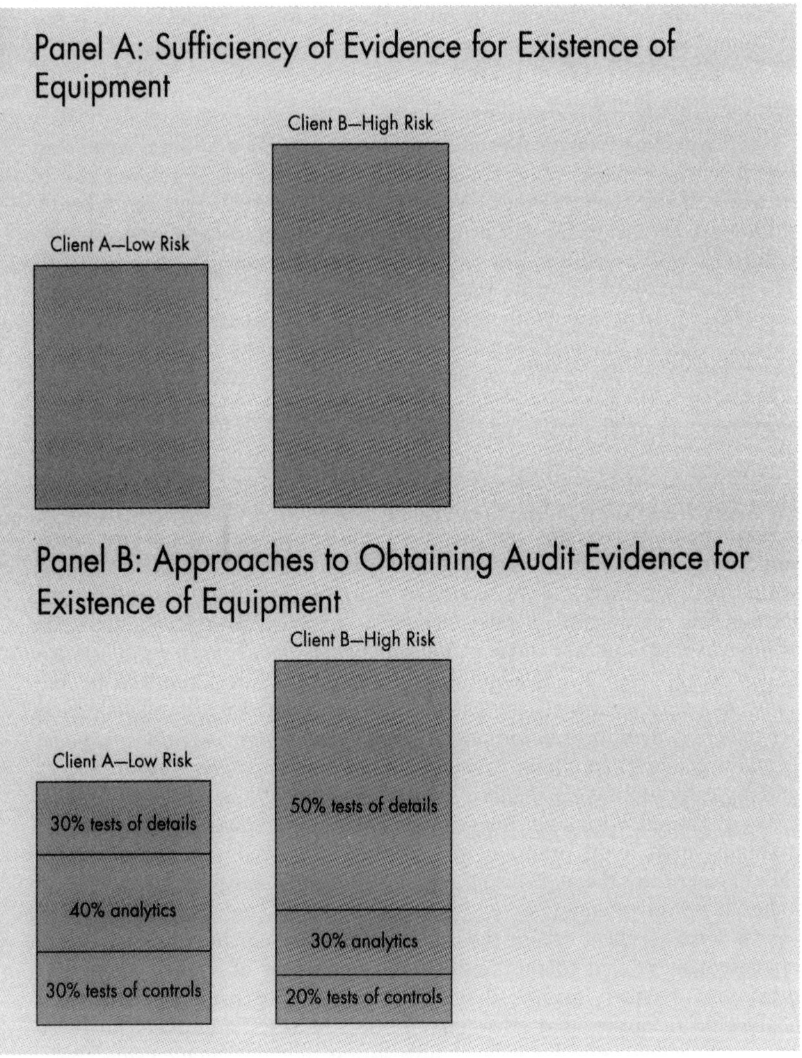

Panel A: Sufficiency of Evidence for Existence of Equipment

Client B—High Risk

Client A—Low Risk

Panel B: Approaches to Obtaining Audit Evidence for Existence of Equipment

Client B—High Risk

50% tests of details

30% analytics

20% tests of controls

Client A—Low Risk

30% tests of details

40% analytics

30% tests of controls

more of the assurance is coming from tests of details. Note that the relative percentages are judgmental in nature; the examples are simply intended to give you a sense of how an auditor might select an appropriate mix of procedures.

Additional Considerations For many organizations, long-lived assets involve only a few assets of relatively high value. In these settings, the time and effort needed to perform tests of controls in order to reduce substantive testing may exceed the time required to simply perform the substantive tests. Therefore, the most efficient approach would be to use a substantive approach, using tests of details, for obtaining evidence. However, if an organization has a high volume of long-lived asset transactions, it may be more efficient to perform tests of controls to support a moderate- or low-assessed level of control risk, and then reduce substantive testing. The auditor should always consider the unique circumstances of the client when making decisions about how to respond to identified risks of material misstatement.

Obtaining Evidence about Internal Control Operating Effectiveness for Long-Lived Asset Accounts and Related Expenses

For integrated audits, the auditor will test the operating effectiveness of important controls as of the client's year end. If the auditor wants to rely on controls for the financial statement audit, the auditor will test the operating effectiveness of those controls throughout the year.

Selecting Controls to Test and Performing Tests of Controls

The auditor selects controls that are important to the auditor's conclusion about whether the organization's controls adequately address the assessed the risk of material misstatement in the revenue cycle. The auditor selects both entity-wide and transaction controls for testing. Typical tests of transaction controls include inquiry of personnel performing the control, observation of the control being performed, inspection of documentation confirming that the control has been performed, and reperformance of the control by the auditor testing the control.

For example, assume that a client implements a policy requiring the establishment and enforcement of property management training for all personnel involved in the use, stewardship, and management of equipment. The control (the policy and its implementation) could be tested in a variety of ways, including the following:

- *Inquiry*—Select a sample of personnel required to complete such training and talk with them about whether they have completed the training and the nature of that training.
- *Observation*—Observe a training session in process or observe property management actions in process.
- *Inspection of documentation*—Review the training materials and, for a sample of personnel, review documentation showing completion of the training.

Considering the Results of Tests of Controls

The auditor will analyze the results of the tests of controls to determine additional appropriate procedures. There are two potential outcomes:

1. If control deficiencies are identified, the auditor will assess those deficiencies to determine their severity (are they significant deficiencies or material weaknesses?). The auditor would then need to modify the preliminary control risk assessment (possibly from low to moderate or high) and document the implications of the control deficiencies. Appropriate modifications to planned substantive audit procedures will be determined by the types of misstatements that are most likely to occur because of any control deficiency.
2. If no control deficiencies are identified, the auditor will likely determine that the preliminary assessment of control risk as low is still appropriate. The auditor will then determine the extent that controls can provide evidence on the correctness of account balances, and determine planned substantive audit procedures. The level of substantive testing in this situation will be less than what is required in circumstances where deficiencies in internal control were identified. From the audit risk model, we know that organizations with effective internal controls should require less substantive testing of account balances.

The strengths and deficiencies of an organization's internal controls have a significant impact on the audit of the long-lived asset accounts. Recall the IRG example in the *Professional Judgment in Context* feature at the beginning of the chapter. IRG needs to restate its financial statements because of misstatements in its lease and fixed-asset accounts, and company personnel

对长期资产账户和相关费用获取内部控制运行有效性的证据

LO 7 Determine appropriate tests of controls and consider the results of tests of controls in auditing long-lived assets.

选择要测试的控制和实施控制测试

考虑控制测试的结果

predict that they will find deficiencies in internal control that allowed those misstatements to occur. Auditors who are aware of control deficiencies will need to modify their substantive testing in response to those deficiencies or risk missing material misstatements in the financial statements.

对长期资产账户和相关费用获取账户、披露和认定的实质性证据

Obtaining Substantive Evidence about Accounts, Disclosures, and Assertions for Long-Lived Asset Accounts and Related Expenses

LO 8 Determine and apply sufficient appropriate substantive audit procedures in auditing long-lived assets.

In performing substantive procedures, the auditor wants reasonable assurance that:

- Long-lived assets reflected in the balance sheet physically exist.
- The organization has rights of ownership to recorded long-lived assets.
- Long-lived assets include all relevant items, including those that are purchased, contributed, constructed in-house or by third parties, and leases meeting the criteria for capital leases.
- Long-lived asset additions are recorded correctly.
- Items to be capitalized are identified and distinguished from repairs and maintenance expense items.
- Depreciation/amortization/depletion calculations are made and based on appropriate estimated useful lives and methods.
- Retirements, trade-ins, and unused property and equipment are identified and recorded correctly.
- Long-lived assets and related expenses, such as depreciation, amortization, or depletion, are appropriately presented in the financial statements with adequate disclosures.
- Fraudulent transactions are not included in the financial statements.

Typical substantive procedures for long-lived assets are shown in Exhibit 12.4. The extent to which substantive analytical procedures and tests of details are performed depends on a number of factors, including the risk of material misstatement and the effectiveness of controls.

实质性分析程序

Substantive Analytical Procedures

Before performing tests of details, the auditor may perform substantive analytical procedures, such as a reasonableness test. If the client's controls related to long-lived assets are effective, then the auditor can rely more extensively on substantive analytical procedures to obtain evidence on account balances. For example, substantive analytical procedures, such as a reasonableness test, can be used to estimate depreciation expense and accumulated depreciation. The auditor can use a property ledger, which should uniquely identify each asset and provide details on cost of the property, acquisition date, depreciation method used for both book and tax, estimated life, estimated scrap value (if any), and accumulated depreciation to date, to develop expectations to compare with what the company has recorded. In general, if the substantive analytical procedures do not result in unresolved issues, direct testing of account balances can be reduced.

有形资产的实质性细节测试——测试当期的增加

Substantive Tests of Details for Tangible Assets— Testing Current Period Additions

The proper recording of current period additions is important because of the long-term effect these assets have on the financial statements. Because most companies typically have relatively few long-lived asset transactions, the auditor often examines supporting documentation of individual transactions. One approach is to examine a schedule of additions (usually prepared by the client). After the schedule is agreed to the general ledger, the auditor should select a few items for testing. For example, auditors obtain documentary

EXHIBIT **12.4** Management Assertions and Substantive Procedures for Long-Lived Assets and Related Expenses

Management Assertion	Substantive Procedure
Existence/occurrence—Recorded long-lived assets exist.	1. Perform substantive analytical procedures. 2. Inspect tangible assets. 3. Vouch additions to supporting documentation. 4. Review account activity for the year and vouch significant items.
Completeness—All long-lived assets have been recorded.	1. Perform substantive analytical procedures. 2. Review capitalization policy to assure that all significant capital expenditures are properly capitalized. 3. Review entries to repair and maintenance expense to determine whether some items should have been capitalized.
Rights/obligations—The organization has legal title or similar rights of ownership to recorded long-lived assets.	1. Inquire of management as to whether long-lived assets have been pledged as collateral. 2. Examine documents of title.
Valuation/allocation—Long-lived assets are properly valued.	1. Review depreciation policy and test depreciation calculations. 2. Inquire of management about assets that are idle. 3. Test amortization expense. 4. Assess the reasonableness of carrying amounts and unamortized balances. 5. Inquire of management as to whether there has been any permanent impairment of assets. 6. Assess management's impairment estimates.
Presentation/disclosure—Long-lived assets and related expenses, such as depreciation, amortization, or depletion, are appropriately presented in the financial statements with adequate disclosures.	1. Review presentation and disclosure in the financial statements and determine whether they are in accordance with GAAP.

support (such as invoices or contracts) for additions above a certain amount or physically inspect a sample of additions made during the audit period.

The auditor also wants to determine that capitalized additions were appropriate and that none of them should have been expensed as repairs and maintenance or other costs. The *Auditing in Practice* feature "Improper Capitalization of Operating Expenses: The Case of Safety-Kleen Corporation" provides a well-known example of a company that capitalized, rather than expensed, certain costs.

Companies often have to make judgments as to whether a particular expenditure should be capitalized or expensed as a repair. Most companies have policies, usually based on materiality and the cost of bookkeeping, as to whether expenditures under a certain amount are expenses—even if they appear to be of a capital nature. Usually, the auditor starts by determining if such a policy is reasonable. Further, the auditor considers whether management might attempt to not comply with the policy because of an incentive to manipulate reported earnings, for example, decrease reported earnings in a good period and vice versa in a poor period.

If the auditor perceives that such risks are applicable to a particular client, the auditor will adjust the procedures, usually by requesting that the client prepare a schedule of both fixed-asset additions and repair and

Improper Capitalization of Operating Expenses: The Case of Safety-Kleen Corporation

Safety-Kleen Corporation (SK) is one of the leading providers of industrial waste collection and disposal services. In the late 1990s, SK was merged with another company, and SK's management made promises to investors and analysts that the merger would result in annual savings of $100 to $160 million. Unfortunately, those savings never materialized, and the company's CFO, controller, and vice president of accounting orchestrated an accounting fraud to overstate SK's revenue and earnings. One element of the fraud involved the improper capitalization and deferral of operating expenses. For example, at the end of the third quarter of 1999, they improperly capitalized $4.6 million of payroll expenses. At the end of the fourth quarter of 1999, they improperly capitalized $1.8 million of salaries and wages. Also during the fourth quarter of 1999, they recorded $7.3 million of fraudulent adjustments to capitalize the tires on the company's trucks and the fuel in the tanks. Safety-Kleen ultimately filed for bankruptcy, and the SEC pursued the company and the individuals involved.

For further details on this case, see SEC Complaint No. 17891 (December 12, 2002).

maintenance expense transactions. Selected transactions from both schedules can be vouched to vendor invoices, work orders, or other supporting evidence to determine their proper classification.

When conducting these procedures, the auditor can usually test existence, rights, and valuation assertions at the same time. Exhibit 12.5 presents an example of typical audit documentation testing fixed-asset additions. Even though the total fixed-asset account balance may be large, the audit work can be done efficiently by concentrating on the additions and then adjusting the estimates of depreciation expense and accumulated depreciation for changes made during the year.

有形资产的实质性细节测
试——测试当期的减少

Substantive Tests of Details for Tangible Assets— Testing Current Period Deletions

Exhibit 12.5 includes two disposals that occurred during the year. Similar to testing additions, the auditor typically obtains a schedule from the client of all sales or other disposals made during the year. The auditor should trace the original cost of the item and its accumulated depreciation to the supporting documentation. Proceeds from the disposal, if material, should be traced to the cash receipts journal and the bank deposit. The auditor should also recompute any gain or loss to determine whether it is accounted for in conformity with GAAP.

The auditor should also perform procedures to search for any unrecorded disposals. First, the auditor may make inquiries of the client about disposals. The auditor could obtain evidence of unrecorded retirements by examining the cash receipts journal, property tax records, insurance records, or scrap sales accounts. Another approach is to use GAS to prepare a printout of fully depreciated (or nearly fully depreciated) assets and then attempt to locate them for physical examination. Alternatively, trade-ins noted during the audit of asset additions can be traced to the removal of the old equipment from the books.

与有形资产折旧费用和累
积折旧相关的实质性程序

Substantive Procedures Related to Depreciation Expense and Accumulated Depreciation for Tangible Assets

The specific procedures used by the auditor to test depreciation of tangible assets depend on the risk of material misstatement. The auditor's primary objective in testing depreciation is to determine whether the client is following

EXHIBIT 12.5   Schedule of Long-Lived Asset Additions and Disposals

Burke Enterprises
Long-Lived Asset Additions and Disposals—Equipment
December 31, 2013

PBC
Work Performed by *AMT*
Date *1/28/2014*

Description	Date Purchased	Cost				Accumulated Depreciation			
		Beginning Balance	Additions	Disposals	Ending Balance	Beginning Balance	Depreciation Expense	Disposals	Ending Balance
Beginning balance	Various	124,350			124,350	33,429	12,435*		45,864
Additions:									
40" lathe	10/30/13	–0–	9,852†		9,852	–0–	1,250‡		1,250
1040 press	3/25/13	–0–	18,956†		18,956	–0–	1,895‡		1,895
60" lathe	5/29/13	–0–	13,903†		13,903	–0–	950‡		950
Disposals:									
Fork lift	6/2/10			7,881§	(7,881)			3,703	(3,703)
Computer	7/2/11			3,300§	(3,300)			2,625	(2,625)
Totals		124,350@	42,711**	11,181**	170,880**††	33,429@	16,530**	6,378**	43,581***††

* Estimated from last year; includes one-half year depreciation for assets disposed of during the year. See Working Paper PPE-4 for calculation of the estimate.
† Examined invoice or other supporting document, noting cost and appropriate categorization for depreciation purposes.
‡ Recalculated, noting that depreciation is in accordance with company policy and asset classification-estimated economic life.
§ Traced to asset ledger and verified that equipment had been removed. Examined sales document or scrap disposal document for the disposal of the asset.
@ Traced to December 31, 2012, audit documentation.
** Footed/cross footed.
†† Traced to trial balance.

a consistent depreciation policy and whether the client's calculations are accurate. The auditor should determine whether management's estimates, such as estimated useful lives and salvage values, are reasonable.

Low Risk: Perform Substantive Analytical Procedures In low-risk situations, the auditor tests the controls over depreciation and determines that the only additional audit procedure to be performed is substantive analytical procedures. The current estimate of depreciation of assets continuing in the business is calculated and then modified for assets added or disposed of during the year. The analytical procedures could incorporate a number of ratios and an overall test of reasonableness to help determine the reasonableness of current charges to the accounts. The ratios might include the following:

- Current depreciation expense as a percentage of the previous-year depreciation expense.
- Fixed assets (by class) as a percentage of previous-year assets—the relative increase in this percentage can be compared with the relative increase in depreciation as a test of overall reasonableness.
- Depreciation expense (by asset class) as a percentage of assets each year—this ratio can indicate changes in the age of equipment or in depreciation policy.
- Accumulated depreciation (by class) as a percentage of gross assets each year—this ratio provides information on the overall reasonableness of the account and may indicate problems of accounting for fully depreciated equipment.
- Average age of assets (by class)—this ratio provides additional insight on the age of assets and may be useful in modifying depreciation estimates.

If the corroborating factors do not support the auditor's estimation, substantive tests of details should be performed.

当控制无效、重大错报风险较高时，注册会计师首先需要对固定资产总账实施折旧的细节测试。

High Risk: Perform Substantive Tests of Details In situations where controls are not effective, that is, there is a high risk of material misstatement, the auditor needs to perform detailed tests of depreciation by starting with the fixed-asset ledger, which contains a list of all the assets, their estimated useful life, salvage value, and depreciation method. The auditor would use GAS to foot the ledger and agree it to the general ledger and then, taking a sample of items contained in the detailed property ledger, recalculate depreciation for the items chosen. The sampling procedure should be based on the same criteria introduced in Chapter 8; that is, the auditor considers materiality and risk and takes a sample based on recorded depreciation. Differences should be projected to the population as a whole. If there are significant differences, the auditor should investigate to determine the root cause of the problem and have the client correct the problem. Finally, the auditor should use GAS to identify all entries into the depreciation and accumulated depreciation accounts that come from other than the normal depreciation entries and asset disposals.

Evaluating Changes in Depreciation Methods The auditor should make sure that the depreciation methods used are consistent with the prior year unless the client has reasonable justification for changing methods. The auditor should carefully read the notes to the financial statements to be sure that all relevant information about such changes is disclosed.

自然资源和相关费用账户的实质性细节测试

Substantive Tests of Details for Natural Resources and the Related Expense Accounts

The focus for the auditor is on the costs and the estimate of reserves contained in a new discovery. The auditor normally has experience with the quality of the client's estimates and would want to evaluate the credentials of the individual making the estimates—whether it is a member of management or a specialist hired by management. The auditor may also decide to use an auditor specialist/expert to perform additional analysis and/or review the client's analysis.

The audit procedures for determining the cost of natural resources are similar to those for other fixed assets. The auditor should test the capitalization of all new natural resources and should verify the costs by examining documents, including the client's own process of documenting all the costs of exploration and drilling. Depletion expense should be based on the items extracted during the year using the units of production method. The company should have production records of daily extractions. In addition, the auditor will be able to substantiate the amount of items sold during the year. Further, the company should have procedures to estimate any changes in reserves in order to update the depletion procedures.

Substantive Tests of Details for Intangible Assets

The following substantive procedures are commonly used when testing intangible assets:

无形资产的实质性的细节测试

- Determine that the intangible assets exist by reviewing appropriate documentation, for example, legal documentation (in the case of a license or patent).
- Determine that the intangible assets are owned by the organization by inspecting relevant documentation, such as the purchase agreement or sales agreement.
- Test management's calculation of any gain or loss on the disposal of intangible assets and determine whether the carrying amounts have been properly reduced.
- For amortizable intangibles with finite lives, determine whether amortization expense is accurate and whether the amortization policy and useful lives are reasonable and consistent with prior years.
- Inquire of management about whether circumstances indicate that the carrying amounts of intangibles (which are subject to amortization) may not be recoverable. Where such circumstances exist, evaluate management's impairment testing and conclusion regarding the write-off. Exhibit 12.6 provides examples of indicators suggesting that impairment of an intangible asset might have occurred.

Substantive Procedures Related to Asset Impairment

与资产减值相关的实质性程序

Even though determining the potential impairment of fixed assets is difficult, the accumulated knowledge of industry product trends, changes in client product lines, and technological changes will assist the auditor in making necessary judgments. An asset may be impaired if it does not generate as much cash flow in future years as it has in the past. A tour of the plant may provide

EXHIBIT **12.6** Circumstances Indicating Potential Impairment of Intangible Assets

- A change in circumstances, such as the legal environment or business climate, that could affect the asset's value or cause an adverse action by a regulator
- An accumulation of costs that are significantly in excess of the amount originally expected to be needed to acquire or construct the asset
- Losses or projections indicating continuing losses associated with an asset used to generate revenue
- A current expectation that, more likely than not, an asset will be sold or otherwise disposed of significantly before the end of its previously estimated useful life.

hints that some assets are not fully utilized or are not utilized efficiently. Such observations might indicate a potential impairment in value.

The auditor needs reasonable assurance that the long-lived assets are valued at their economic benefit to the organization and that, when the value has been impaired, the organization has written down the asset reflecting the decline in economic benefit of the asset. If there is evidence that an asset has been impaired, the auditor needs to address the valuation issue. In most situations, the auditor needs to understand management's process for assessing impairment and needs to evaluate the reasonableness of management's assumptions. As indicated in the *Auditing in Practice* feature "PCAOB Identifies Audit Deficiencies Related to Asset Impairment Issues" auditors have had many challenges related to asset impairments.

与租赁相关的实质性程序 ## Substantive Procedures Related to Leases

General substantive procedures for leases include:

- Obtain copies of lease agreements, read the agreements, and develop a schedule of lease expenditures.

PCAOB Identifies Audit Deficiencies Related to Asset Impairment Issues

AUDITING IN PRACTICE

The 2010 PCAOB inspection report of Grant Thornton LLP identified the following audit deficiency:

> The Firm was aware that the issuer had determined not to test a significant portion of its property and equipment for impairment, despite indicators that the carrying amount may not be recoverable. These indicators included operating losses for the relevant segment for the last three years, substantial charges for the impairment of goodwill and other intangible assets during the year, a projected loss for the segment for the upcoming year, and reduced and delayed customer orders. The Firm failed to evaluate the effects on the financial statements of the failure to test the assets for impairment.

The 2010 PCAOB inspection report of PricewaterhouseCoopers LLP identified the following audit deficiency:

> During the year, the issuer recorded a significant impairment charge for its fixed assets, based on the assumption that all machinery and equipment that was more than four years old had a fair value of zero, while all machinery and equipment acquired within the past four years had a fair value that approximated net book value. There was no evidence in the audit documentation, and no

> persuasive other evidence, that the Firm had tested this assumption.

The 2010 PCAOB inspection report of McGladrey & Pullen LLP identified the following audit deficiency:

> The Firm failed to sufficiently evaluate the fair value, useful life, and potential impairment of an indefinite-lived intangible asset related to a marketing agreement that the issuer entered into during the current year. The Firm failed to test, beyond inquiries of management, the fair value that the issuer assigned to the intangible asset. Also, in evaluating the issuer's assertion that the intangible asset had an indefinite life, the Firm failed to consider the fact that the marketing agreement allowed both the issuer and the counterparty to terminate the agreement. Further, the Firm's testing of the issuer's assertion that there were no economic or competitive factors that could affect the useful life of the marketing agreement was limited to inquiries of management. The Firm also failed to sufficiently evaluate the issuer's conclusion that the intangible asset was not impaired, as the Firm failed to consider potential indicators of impairment, such as the issuer's recurring losses and recurring impairments of goodwill and other intangible assets during the year.

- Review the lease expense account, select entries to the account, and determine if there are entries that are not covered by the leases obtained from the client. Determine if the expenses are properly accounted for.
- Review the relevant criteria from the FASB's codified standards (ASC) to determine which leases meet the requirement of capital leases.
- For all capital leases, determine that the assets and lease obligations are recorded at their present value. Determine the economic life of the asset. Calculate amortization expense and interest expenses, and determine any adjustments to correct the financial statements.
- Develop a schedule of all future lease obligations or determine whether the client's schedule is correct by referring to underlying lease agreements.
- Review the client's disclosure of lease obligations to determine that it is in accordance with GAAP.

Performing Substantive Fraud-Related Procedures

实施与舞弊相关的实质性程序

The following fraud-related audit procedures can be used to respond to any fraud risk factors identified during the risk assessment of long-lived assets and related expense accounts:

- Physically inspect tangible assets, including major additions, and agree serial numbers with invoices or other supporting documents.
- Request that the client perform a complete inventory of long-lived assets at year end.
- Carefully scrutinize appraisals and other specialist reports that seem out of line with reasonable expectations, and challenge the underlying assumptions.
- Use the work of a specialist for asset valuations, including impairments.
- When vouching long-lived asset additions, accept only original invoices, purchase orders, receiving reports, or similar supporting documentation.
- Confirm the terms of significant additions of property or intangibles with other parties involved in the transaction.

If any of these procedures were part of the original audit program, the auditor should consider expanding the extent of testing or in some way modifying the timing or nature of testing, if significant fraud risk factors are identified.

Documenting Substantive Procedures

记录实质性程序

A number of important items should be documented when performing substantive procedures for long-lived assets and related expense accounts. For tangible assets such as property, the auditor's documentation should include:

- A summary schedule showing beginning balances, additions, deletions, and ending balances for the asset account and for accumulated depreciation (see Exhibit 12.5)
- Identification of the specific items tested (for example, all additions greater than $100,000)

For intangible assets, the documentation should include evidence supporting the evaluation and review of the reasonableness of their continuing value.

SUMMARY AND NEXT STEPS

Auditing long-lived assets is usually straightforward—perform tests of changes in account balances during the year. However, the auditor should be skeptical and therefore alert to the possibility that management is managing earnings by changing the related estimates without justification or by capitalizing costs that should be expensed. The major continuing challenge related to long-lived assets is determining asset impairment and assessing whether the record depreciation is appropriate given the economic life of the asset. Now that you have an understanding of how to perform audit procedures related to long-lived assets, in the next chapter we turn to auditing equity and debt transactions.

SIGNIFICANT TERMS

Amortization expense A process of expensing the acquisition cost minus the residual value of intangible assets over their estimated useful economic life.

Asset impairment A term used to describe management's recognition that a significant portion of fixed assets is no longer as productive as had originally been expected. When assets are so impaired, the assets should be written down to their expected economic value.

Depletion expense Expense associated with the extraction of natural resources.

Intangible Assets Nonphysical assets, such as patents, trademarks, copyrights, and brand recognition.

Long-lived assets Noncurrent assets that are used over multiple operating cycles and include tangible and intangible assets.

Tangible assets Assets that have a physical form, such as machinery, buildings, and land.

TRUE-FALSE QUESTIONS

12-1 `LO 1` Long-lived assets are typically immaterial for most organizations.

12-2 `LO 1` Patents are an example of long-lived assets.

12-3 `LO 2` The pervasiveness of management estimates is a factor that heightens the inherent risk associated with long-lived assets.

12-4 `LO 2` An inherent risk associated with intangible long-lived assets is the difficulty in determining the cost of the asset.

12-5 `LO 3` A fraud technique common for long-lived assets is the overstatement of assets though overvaluing the existing assets.

12-6 `LO 3` A fraud technique used by WorldCom management was to capitalize items that should have been expensed.

12-7 `LO 4` Auditors should expect clients to have written policies for the acquisition and disposal of long-lived assets.

12-8 `LO 4` A formal budgeting process that is tied to the acquisition of long-lived assets would not be considered a control over long-lived assets.

12-9 `LO 5` The auditor needs to understand the client's business in order to perform meaningful preliminary analytical procedures.

12-10 `LO 5` When performing preliminary analytical procedures, the auditor should not typically expect the client to use depreciable lives similar to organizations in the same industry.

12-11 `LO 6` If a client's long-lived assets involve only a few assets of relatively high value, it might be most efficient to test long-lived assets by using only substantive tests of details.

12-12 `LO 6` Assume a client setting where there are weak controls and client incentives to capitalize items that should be expensed. In such a setting, the auditor likely obtains most of the audit evidence through tests of controls.

12-13 `LO 7` When testing a control that requires training for all employees involved in equipment management, the auditor would typically reperform the control.

12-14 `LO 7` Auditors who are aware of control deficiencies that could result in the material misstatement of lease accounts need to modify their substantive testing in response to those deficiencies.

12-15 `LO 8` One procedure that can be used to test management's assertion that tangible long-lived assets exist would be to inspect the tangible asset.

12-16 `LO 8` When testing potential impairment of assets, the auditor may need to rely on work performed by a specialist/expert.

MULTIPLE-CHOICE QUESTIONS

12-17 `LO 1` Long-lived assets include which of the following?
a. Tangible assets such as equipment.
b. Intangible assets such as patents.
c. Natural resources.
d. All of the above.

12-18 `LO 1` Which of the following statements is true?
a. Existence and valuation assertions related to long-lived assets are usually the most relevant assertions.
b. A concern regarding the existence of long-lived assets relates to whether management has properly recorded deprecation.
c. Depletion expense is not an account that would be included when auditing long-lived assets.
d. All of the above statements are true.

12-19 `LO 2` Which of the following is *not* an inherent risk related to long-lived asset accounts?
a. Failing to record asset disposals.
b. Capitalizing repairs and maintenance expense.
c. Changing depreciation estimates to manage earnings.
d. All of the above.

12-20 `LO 2` Which of the following risks is an inherent risk related to asset impairment?
a. Determining asset impairment is based on management judgment.
b. It is difficult to identify the costs associated with the discovery of natural resources.
c. Management might have incentives to not record all asset disposals.
d. All of the above are inherent risks related to asset impairment.

12-21 `LO 3` Which of the following statements is false regarding fraud risk factors related to long-lived assets?
a. A potential fraud scheme involves not removing sold assets from the books.
b. Because long-lived assets are typically an audit area of low risk, auditors do not need to perform brainstorming activities related to long-lived assets.
c. Management might use unreasonably long depreciable lives in an effort to reduce expenses.
d. None of the above statements is false.

12-22 [LO 3] Which of the following techniques can be used by management to overstate long-lived assets?
a. Overvalue existing assets.
b. Include fictitious assets on the financial statements.
c. Capitalize transactions that should be expensed.
d. All of the above.

12-23 [LO 4] Which of the following controls would be most useful in providing reasonable assurance about the valuation of tangible assets?
a. A policy requiring the reconciliation of the physical asset count with the property ledger.
b. A policy requiring that deprecation categories and lives be periodically assessed.
c. A formal budgeting process.
d. Written policies requiring authorization for the acquisition of long-lived assets.

12-24 [LO 4] Which of the following controls should management have in place to provide reasonable assurance about asset impairment judgments?
a. A policy requiring the reconciliation of the physical asset count with the property ledger.
b. Limits to physical access of long-lived assets.
c. A systematic process to identify assets that are not currently in use.
d. A formal budgeting process.

12-25 [LO 5] An auditor performing preliminary analytical procedures scans the repairs and maintenance accounts. Which of the following statements is consistent with what the auditor is most likely focused on?
a. Expenditures for long-lived assets have not been charged to expense.
b. Expenditures for long-lived assets have been properly approved.
c. Expenditures for long-lived assets have been recorded in the correct period.
d. The auditor would not be performing scanning as a preliminary analytical procedure.

12-26 [LO 5] Which of the following analyses might an auditor perform as part of preliminary analytical procedures?
a. Develop an overall estimate of depreciation expense.
b. Compare capital expenditures with the client's capital budget.
c. Perform a trend analysis of the ratio of depreciation expense to total depreciable long-lived tangible assets.
d. All of the above could be performed as part of preliminary analytical procedures.

12-27 [LO 6] Assume that the auditor decides to only perform substantive tests of details when auditing the equipment account. Which of the following statements best describes the circumstances associated with the client being audited?
a. The client does not have effective controls over equipment.
b. The equipment account involves only a few assets of relatively high value.
c. Either a. or b. could be descriptive of the circumstances associated with the client being audited.
d. Neither a. nor b. would be descriptive of the circumstances associated with the client being audited.

12-28 [LO 6] Assume that a client's controls over recording retirements of long-lived tangible assets are not well designed. Which of the following procedures would the auditor plan to perform as a way of responding to the heightened risk of material misstatement?

a. Select long-lived tangible assets recorded in the property ledger and locate them for inspection.

b. Inspect long-lived tangible assets located at the client location and trace those assets to the property ledger.

c. Review the tangible long-lived asset property ledger to see if depreciation was recorded on each tangible long-lived asset.

d. The auditor would perform all of the above procedures to respond to the heightened risk of material misstatement.

12-29 `LO 7` Which of the following situations would lead an auditor to test controls over long-lived assets?

a. Substantive analytical procedures suggested that controls over long-lived assets were not effective.

b. Risk assessment procedures indicated that controls were effectively designed.

c. Tests of details identified many errors in recording long-lived asset transactions.

d. The auditor has decided that the additional effort to test controls would not exceed the potential reduction in substantive procedures.

12-30 `LO 7` To test the effectiveness of controls over asset impairment, the auditor could perform which of the following procedures?

a. Perform analytical procedures.

b. Send confirmations to the management specialist who performed work related to the impairment.

c. Inquire of management as to its process for determining assessment impairment.

d. Inspect the asset for potential impairment.

12-31 `LO 8` When auditing intangible assets, the auditor would likely recompute amortization and determine whether management's recorded amount is reasonable. When performing this procedure which assertion is the auditor primarily gathering evidence for?

a. Completeness.

b. Existence.

c. Valuation.

d. Rights and obligations.

12-32 `LO 8` As part of auditing equipment, the auditor will inspect new equipment additions selected from the client's property ledger. The procedure will provide evidence about which of the following assertions?

a. Completeness.

b. Existence.

c. Valuation.

d. Rights and obligations.

REVIEW AND SHORT CASE QUESTIONS

12-33 `LO 1` Refer to Exhibit 12.1. One of the significant and relevant accounts for this cycle is equipment. For this account, what would typically be the most relevant assertions for the auditor to consider? Why is it important for the auditor to identify the more relevant assertions?

12-34 `LO 1` Refer to Exhibit 12.1. Depreciation expense is included in the exhibit. How is depreciation expense similar to depletion expense and amortization expense?

NOTE: Completing Review and Short Case Questions does not require the student to reference additional resources and materials.

NOTE: For the remaining problems, we make special note of those addressing fraud, international issues, professional skepticism, and ethics.

12-35 [LO 1] Identify the five management assertions and describe how they are relevant to long-lived assets.

12-36 [LO 2] What is asset impairment, and what inherent risk factors are associated with asset impairment?

12-37 [LO 2] What are some inherent risks of material misstatement associated with natural resources?

12-38 [LO 2] What are some inherent risks of material misstatement associated with intangible assets?

FRAUD **12-39** [LO 3] A 2010 study on fraudulent financial reporting by COSO notes ways in which long-lived assets can be fraudulently overstated, including:
- Fictitious assets on the books (WorldCom)
- Improper and incomplete depreciation (Waste Management)
- Failure to record impairment of assets, especially goodwill (Sun Microsystems)
- Expired or worthless assets left on a company's books (Millacron)
- Assets overvalued upon acquisition, especially in the purchase of a company (WorldCom)

a. What might motivate management to overstate fixed assets?
b. What other factors should the auditor consider when assessing fraud risk related to long-lived assets?

FRAUD
PROFESSIONAL SKEPTICISM **12-40** [LO 3] Explain how a skeptical auditor might come to understand management's potential for adjusting earnings through manipulation of fixed-asset accounts.

FRAUD **12-41** [LO 3] Identify potential fraud schemes related to long-lived assets.

12-42 [LO 4] Consider the risks typically associated with tangible long-lived assets and identify the internal controls over these assets that you would expect a client to have in place.

12-43 [LO 4] Consider the risks typically associated with intangible long-lived assets and identify the internal controls over these assets that you would expect a client to have in place.

12-44 [LO 5] Identify preliminary analytical procedures related to depreciation expense that may be effective in identifying potential material misstatements.

12-45 [LO 5] Identify ratios and expected relationships that might be used when performing preliminary analytical procedures related to long-lived assets.

12-46 [LO 6] Refer to Exhibit 12.3. Describe the differences in the planned audit approaches for Clients A and B and the reasons for such differences.

12-47 [LO 6] Explain why in some audit settings relating to long-lived assets auditors may choose to perform only substantive tests of details, even though controls are designed effectively.

12-48 [LO 6] The following questions might be addressed when an auditor is completing an internal control question. For each question (labeled as 1. through 8. below):
a. Indicate the purpose of the control.
b. Indicate the impact on the planned substantive audit procedures if the answer to the question indicates weak controls.
1. Does the client periodically take a physical inventory of property and reconcile to the property ledger?

2. Does the client have a policy manual to classify property and assign an estimated life for depreciation purposes to the class of assets?
3. Does the client have a policy on minimum expenditures before an item is capitalized? If yes, what is the minimum amount?
4. Does the client have a mechanism to identify pieces of equipment that have been designated for scrap? If yes, is it effective?
5. Does the client have an acceptable mechanism to differentiate major renovations from repair and maintenance? If yes, is it effective?
6. Does the client regularly self-construct its own assets? If yes, does the client have an effective procedure to appropriately identify and classify all construction costs?
7. Does the client systematically review major classes of assets for potential impairment?
8. Does management periodically review asset disposal or the scrapping of assets as a basis for reviewing the assignment of estimated life for depreciation purposes?

12-49 `LO 7` Based on the following description, determine appropriate tests of controls for the company's controls over tangible long-lived assets.

A corporation operates a highly automated flexible manufacturing facility. The capital-intensive nature of the corporation's operations makes internal control over the acquisition and use of tangible long-lived assets important management objectives.

A tangible long-lived assets budget that indicates planned capital expenditures by department is established at the beginning of each year. Department managers request capital expenditures by completing a tangible long-lived assets requisition form, which must be approved by senior management. The firm has a written policy that establishes whether a budget request is to be considered as a capital expenditure or as a routine maintenance expenditure.

A management committee meets each month to review budget reports that compare actual expenditures made by managers to their budgeted amounts and to authorize any additional expenditures that may be necessary. The committee also reviews and approves, as necessary, any departmental request for sale, retirement, or scrapping of tangible long-lived assets. Copies of vouchers used to document department requests for sale, retirement, or scrapping of fixed assets are forwarded to the accounting department to initiate removal of the asset from the tangible long-lived assets ledger.

The accounting department is responsible for maintaining a detailed ledger of tangible long-lived assets. When a tangible long-lived asset is acquired, it is tagged for identification. The identification number, as well as the cost, location, and other information necessary for depreciation calculations, are entered into the tangible long-lived assets ledger. Depreciation calculations are made each quarter and are posted to the general ledger. Periodic physical inventories of tangible long-lived assets are taken for purposes of reconciliation to the tangible long-lived assets ledger as well as appraisal for insurance purposes.

12-50 `LO 7` Refer to Exhibit 12.2. Identify tests of controls that could be used to test the controls included in the exhibit.

FRAUD **12-51** LO 8 A 2010 study on fraudulent financial reporting by COSO notes the many ways in which long-lived assets can be fraudulently overstated, including:

- Fictitious assets on the books (WorldCom)
- Improper and incomplete depreciation (Waste Management)
- Failure to record impairment of assets, especially goodwill (Sun Microsystems)
- Expired or worthless assets left on a company's books (Millacron)
- Assets overvalued upon acquisition, especially in the purchase of a company (WorldCom)

What substantive audit procedures might have detected these frauds?

12-52 LO 8 The audit senior has asked you to perform analytical procedures to obtain substantive evidence on the reasonableness of recorded depreciation expense of the delivery vehicles of a client. Changes in the account occurred pretty much evenly during the year. The estimated useful life is six years. Estimated salvage value is 10% of original cost. Straight-line depreciation is used. Additional information:

Delivery Equipment (per General Ledger)

Beginning balance	$380,500
Additions	154,000
Disposals	(95,600)
Ending balance	$438,900

Current year depreciation expense per books = $60,500

Based on this information, estimate the amount of depreciation expense for the year using analytical procedures. Does the recorded depreciation expense seem acceptable? Explain. What is the impact of the result of this analytical procedure on other substantive procedures that the auditor may perform?

12-53 LO 8 What audit procedures might an auditor use to identify fully depreciated equipment? How might the auditor determine that such equipment is properly valued?

12-54 LO 8 A client has a policy manual that categorizes equipment by type and assigns a depreciation life based on the categorization. All equipment in a category is depreciated using the same depreciation method. How does the auditor determine the reasonableness of the client's approach?

12-55 LO 8 What evidence might an auditor gather to determine the proper valuation of an impaired asset?

12-56 LO 8 Assume that a company obtains an appraisal for equipment that may be impaired. Does the auditor need to test the appraisal? What work should the auditor perform to determine that the appraisal should be relied upon as a best estimate of the value of the assets?

12-57 LO 8 Describe the basic approach to auditing leases.

12-58 LO 8 You are performing the year-end audit of Halvorson Fine Foods, Inc. for December 31, 2014. The client has prepared the following schedule for the fixed assets and related allowance for depreciation accounts.

Halvorson Fine Foods, Inc.
Analysis of Fixed Assets
For the Year Ended December 31, 2014

Description	Final Balance, December 31, 2013	Additions	Retirements	Per Books, December 31, 2014
Assets:				
Land	$22,500	$5,000		$27,500
Buildings	120,000	17,500		137,500
Machinery and equipment	385,000	40,400	$26,000	399,400
	$527,500	$62,900	$26,000	$564,400
Allowance for depreciation:				
Building	$60,000	$5,150		$65,150
Machinery and equipment	173,200	39,220		212,470
	$233,250	$44,370		$277,620

You have compared the opening balances with your prior-year audit working papers. The following information (labeled as 1. through 6. below) is found during your audit. Review this information and do the following:

a. In addition to inquiring of the client, explain how you found each of the described items of information (labeled as 1. through 6. below) during the audit.

b. Prepare the adjusting journal entries (if necessary) with supporting computations that you would suggest at December 31, 2014, to adjust the accounts for the listed transactions. Disregard income tax implications.

1. All equipment is depreciated on a straight-line basis (no salvage value taken into consideration) based on the following estimated lives: buildings, 25 years; all other items, 10 years. The company's policy is to take one-half year's depreciation on all asset acquisitions and disposals occurring during the year.

2. On April 1 of the current year, the company entered into a 10-year lease contract for a die-casting machine with annual rentals of $5,000, payable in advance every April 1. The lease is cancelable by either party (60 days' written notice is required), and there is no option to renew the lease or buy the equipment at the end of the lease. The estimated useful life of the machine is 10 years with no salvage value. The company recorded the die-casting machine in the machinery and equipment account at $40,400, the present value at the date of the lease, and $2,020, applicable to the machine, has been included in depreciation expense for the year.

3. The company completed the construction of a wing on the plant building on June 30 of the current year. The useful life of the building was not extended by this addition. The lowest construction bid received was $17,500, the amount recorded in the buildings account. Company personnel were used to construct the addition at a cost of $16,000 (materials, $7,500; labor, $5,500; and overhead, $3,000).

4. On August 18, Halvorson paid $5,000 for paving and fencing a portion of land owned by the company for use as a parking lot for employees. The expenditure was charged to the land account.

5. The amount shown in the retirements column for the machinery and equipment asset represents cash received on September 5, on disposal of a machine purchased in July 2000 for $48,000. The bookkeeper recorded a depreciation expense of $3,500 on this machine in 2012.

6. Crux City donated land and building appraised at $10,000 and $40,000, respectively, to Halvorson for a plant. On September 1, the company began operating the plant. Because no costs were involved, the bookkeeper made no entry for the foregoing transaction.

ETHICS **12-59** `LO 8, 9` Your audit firm has been the auditor of Cowan Industries for a number of years. The company manufactures a wide range of lawn care products and typically sells to major retailers. In recent years, the company has expanded into ancillary products, such as recreation equipment, that use some of the same technology. The newer lines of business, while successful, have not been particularly profitable. The company's stock price has languished, and management has recently been replaced.

The new management team announces that it will close two factories and will phase out one of the newer lines of business. It plans to expand existing products and increase marketing efforts. Even though there is no technological obsolescence of existing products, the new management does not believe the company has a competitive advantage. It wants to take a one-time hit to the balance sheet and income statement of $15.3 million (about one-third of total assets) as a reserve for the shutdown of the plants and the disposal of a line of business. It also plans on severance pay for employees at the two plants.

a. Define the term *impairment of assets*.

b. Is management typically motivated to understate or overstate the write-down because of asset impairment? Explain.

c. Assume in this situation that the auditor believes management is overestimating the impairment charge and thus the improvement in future earnings because of reduced depreciation charges in subsequent periods. Further assume that the auditor has gathered and evaluated evidence that convincingly reveals the impairment charge should more reasonably fall in a range from $8 to $10 million, rather than management's estimate of about $15 million. Finally, assume the auditor has discussed the issue with management and it refuses to vary from its original estimate. Management has stated that its assumptions and evidence are just as convincing as the auditor's. Use the seven-step framework for ethical decision making from Chapter 4 to make a recommendation about the course of action the auditor should take. Recall that the steps are as follows: (1) identify the ethical issue; in this case the ethical issue is how to properly ensure that the review comments are taken seriously and addressed; (2) determine the affected parties and identify their rights; (3) determine the most important rights for each affected party; (4) develop alternative courses of action; (5) determine the likely consequences of each proposed course of action on each affected party; (6) assess the possible consequences; and (7) decide on an appropriate course of action.

12-60 `LO 8, 9` Novelis, Incorporated is the world's leading rolled-aluminum products producer. Items 1. through 3. below provide descriptions of issues involving asset impairments derived from the company's footnote disclosures.

1. In connection with the decision to close and sell our plant in Borgofranco, Italy, we recognized an impairment charge of $5 million to reduce the net book value of the plant's fixed assets

to zero. We based our estimate on third-party offers and nego-
tiations to sell the business.

2. We recorded an impairment charge of $65 million to reduce the
    carrying value of the production equipment at two facilities in
    Italy to their fair value of $56 million. We determined the fair
    value of the impaired assets based on the discounted future cash
    flows of these facilities using a 7% discount rate.

3. We announced that we would cease operations in Falkirk,
    Scotland. We designated certain production equipment with a
    nominal carrying value for transfer to our Rogerstone facility.
    We reduced the carrying value of the remaining fixed assets to
    zero, which resulted in an $8 million impairment charge.

Complete the first four steps of the seven-step framework for
professional decision making introduced in Chapter 4 by
answering the following questions:

a. What difficulties will the auditor of Novelis face when deciding
    whether the impairment charges that Novelis incurred are
    reasonable?

b. What are the consequences of the auditor's decisions in evalu-
    ating impairments?

c. What are the risks and uncertainties associated with Novelis's
    estimation?

d. What types of evidence should the auditor gather to evaluate
    the reasonableness of management's estimates?

Recall that the framework is as follows:

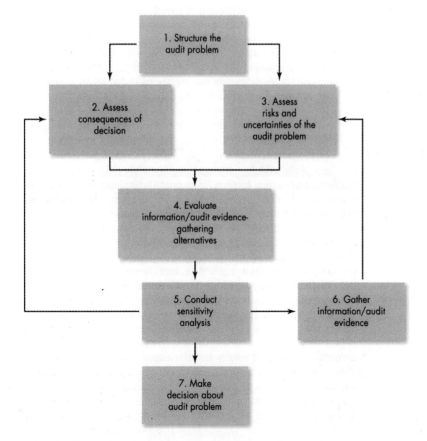

Source: Adapted from "Judgment and Choice," by Robin Hogarth.

CONTEMPORARY AND HISTORICAL CASES

12-61 **IGNITE RESTAURANT GROUP**
LO 1, 2, 3, 4, 5, 6, 7, 8 Refer to the *Professional Judgment in Context* feature "Accounting Problems Related to Long-Lived Assets at Ignite Restaurant Group." Answer the following questions:
a. What long-lived asset accounts at Ignite Restaurant Group (IRG) were misstated?
b. What might have motivated management to materially misstate the assets identified in part a.?
c. What controls should be in place at IRG to mitigate the misstatements that needed to be corrected?
d. What procedures should the auditor have performed when auditing the assets identified in part a.?

FRAUD

PROFESSIONAL SKEPTICISM

12-62 **WORLDCOM**
LO 2, 3, 8 The WorldCom bankruptcy is one of the largest in U.S. economic history. Much of the fraud was carried out by capitalizing operating expenses, such as payments to other companies for line rental, as fixed assets. Adjusting journal entries were made at the company's headquarters in Mississippi even though property accounting records were located in Dallas.
a. Would it be considered unusual to find debits to fixed assets coming from a journal entry source rather than a purchase journal? Explain.
b. Would it be considered unusual to find entries to accumulated depreciation and depreciation expense to come from a journal entry source rather than another source?
c. Assume you were auditing WorldCom, and in your sample of debits to fixed assets, you find an entry for $500,000 with the following notation: "Capitalization of line capacity per CFO, amounts were originally incorrectly recorded as an expense." Explain what you would do to complete the audit of this item. How might the professionally skeptical auditor respond? What evidence would you need to see to either corroborate or question the entry?

FRAUD

12-63 **SAFETY-KLEEN AND PRICEWATERHOUSECOOPERS**
LO 2, 3, 4 Refer to the *Auditing in Practice* feature "Improper Capitalization of Operating Expenses: The Case of Safety-Kleen Corporation." In addition to the information provided in the feature, consider the following information.

At the close of each quarter, Safety-Kleen executives met to discuss the results of operations. Typically, they discussed what the targeted earnings amount was, and then they discussed potential accounting adjustments to help them achieve the target. Although the company had always made legitimate quarterly adjusting entries in preparing its financial statements, the magnitude and nature of the adjustments changed dramatically during fiscal year 1999. As time went on, the discrepancy between the company's projected results and the actual results increased, and they made several improper adjustments each quarter to reach the earnings targets. As the following table indicates, Safety-Kleen's quarterly earnings were materially increased as a result of the accounting adjustments (in other words, the legitimate adjustments and the improper adjustments combined). In some reporting periods, the company's reported earnings were increased by more than 100%.

As an example of inappropriate entries, at the end of the third quarter of fiscal 1999, they improperly capitalized approximately $4.6 million of payroll expenses relating to certain marketing and start-up activities. At the close of the fourth quarter of fiscal 1999, they improperly capitalized $1.8 million of salaries and wages incurred in connection with the development and implementation of various software systems. Not only did this adjusting entry fail to comply with GAAP, it ultimately was recorded twice.

	Earnings Before Adjustments (in Millions)	Earnings as Reported After Adjustments (in Millions)	Total Adjustments (in Millions)	%
First Quarter FY 1999	$90.9	$127.5	$36.6	40.3
Second Quarter FY 1999	$76.7	$107.6	$30.9	40.3
Third Quarter FY 1999	$47.9	$123.4	$75.5	157.6
Fourth Quarter FY 1999	$57.3	$110.4	$53.1	92.7
First Quarter FY 2000	$47.0	$116.8	$69.8	148.5
Total	$319.8	$585.7	$265.9	83.1

On March 6, 2000, after Safety-Kleen's board of directors had received information concerning possible accounting irregularities, the company announced that it had initiated an internal investigation of its previously reported financial results and certain of its accounting policies. On March 10, 2000, Safety-Kleen filed a Form 8-K stating that the company's independent accounting firm, PricewaterhouseCoopers LLP, had withdrawn its audit reports on the financial statements for fiscal years 1997, 1998, and 1999.

In 2005, a lawsuit brought by a group of institutional investors against former officers of Safety-Kleen Corporation ended with a $200 million judgment against two former officers and more than $84 million in settlements against the company's former auditor and directors. PricewaterhouseCoopers, Safety-Kleen's former auditors, agreed to settle and pay $48 million, and the directors agreed to pay $36 million.

a. What were likely factors contributing to the fraud?
b. What audit procedures might have identified the inappropriate adjustments?

CHAPTER

13
Auditing Debt Obligations and Stockholders' Equity Transactions

CHAPTER OVERVIEW AND LEARNING OBJECTIVES

In terms of the audit opinion formulation process, this chapter primarily involves Phases II, III, and IV, that is, performing risk assessment procedures, tests of controls, and substantive procedures for accounts, disclosures, and relevant assertions related to debt obligations and stockholders' equity transactions.

Through studying this chapter, you will be able to achieve these learning objectives:

通过本章的学习，你将能够实现以下学习目标：

1. Identify the significant accounts, disclosures, and relevant assertions in auditing debt obligations and stockholders' equity transactions.

   在审计负债和股东权益交易时识别重要的账户、披露和相关的认定。

2. Identify and assess inherent risks of material misstatement associated with debt obligations and stockholders' equity transactions.

   识别和评估与负债和股东权益交易有关的重大错报的固有风险。

3. Identify and assess fraud risks of material misstatement associated with debt obligations and stockholders' equity transactions.

   识别和评估与负债和股东权益交易有关的重大错报的舞弊风险。

4. Identify and assess control risks of material misstatement associated with debt obligations and stockholders' equity transactions.

   识别和评估与负债和股东权益交易有关的重大错报的控制风险。

5. Describe how to use preliminary analytical procedures to identify possible material misstatements associated with debt obligations and stockholders' equity transactions.

   描述如何运用初步的分析性程序识别与负债和股东权益交易有关的可能的重大错报。

6. Determine appropriate responses to identified risks of material misstatement in auditing debt obligations and stockholders' equity transactions.

   在审计负债和股东权益交易时，明确对于识别的重大错报风险如何进行适当的反应。

7. Determine appropriate tests of controls and consider the results of tests of controls in auditing debt obligations and stockholders' equity transactions.

   在审计负债和股东权益交易时，确定适当的控制测试，并且考虑控制测试的结果。

8. Determine and apply sufficient appropriate substantive audit procedures in auditing debt obligations and stockholders' equity transactions.

   在审计负债和股东权益交易时，确定和应用充分、适当的实质性审计程序。

9. Apply the frameworks for professional decision making and ethical decision making to issues involving the audit of debt obligations and stockholders' equity transactions.

   运用职业决策和职业道德决策框架解决涉及负债和股东权益交易审计的问题。

THE AUDIT OPINION FORMULATION PROCESS

I. Making Client Acceptance and Continuance Decisions
Chapter 14

II. Performing Risk Assessment
Chapters 3, 7 and 9–13

III. Obtaining Evidence about Internal Control Operating Effectiveness
Chapters 8–13 and 16

IV. Obtaining Substantive Evidence about Accounts, Disclosures and Assertions
Chapters 8–13 and 16

V. Completing the Audit and Making Reporting Decisions
Chapters 14 and 15

The Auditing Profession, the Risk of Fraud and Mechanisms to Address Fraud: Regulation, Corporate Governance, and Audit Quality
Chapters 1 and 2

Professional Liability and the Need for Quality Auditor Judgments and Ethical Decisions
Chapter 4

The Audit Opinion Formulation Process and A Framework for Obtaining Audit Evidence
Chapters 5 and 6

PROFESSIONAL JUDGMENT IN CONTEXT

Deficiencies in Auditing Debt Obligations and Stockholders' Equity Accounts: Insights from SEC Releases

Debt Obligations: Federico Quinto, Jr., CPA

In August 2012, the SEC issued an Accounting and Auditing Enforcement Release in the matter of Federico Quinto, Jr., CPA. Quinto was an audit engagement partner for Soyo Group, Inc., in 2007. During 2007 and the first three quarters of 2008, Soyo booked over $47 million in fictitious revenues. At the same time, Soyo was financing its business with debt from United Commercial Bank (UCB). As of December 31, 2007, Soyo's debt with UCB was approximately $27.8 million, which represented 63% of Soyo's total liabilities. Because of Soyo's struggling business, the company often found itself in violation of its debt covenants with UCB. Quinto's audit team conducted an analysis that identified that Soyo was not in compliance with three of its six debt covenants with UCB as of December 31, 2007. Because of the debt covenant violations, UCB could take action that would force Soyo into bankruptcy, as Soyo needed the financing to fund its business operations. The audit team did not follow up on the identified debt covenant violations and did not obtain any evidence indicating whether a waiver had been granted by UCB. The audit work papers did not provide any

evidence that the audit team considered whether these violations could impact the going concern status of Soyo. Further, the audit report for 2007 included an unqualified opinion, although Soyo did not make the required disclosures regarding noncompliance with its debt covenants.

Source: Securities and Exchange Commission, Accounting and Auditing Enforcement Release No. 3403, August 31, 2012, available at *http://www.sec.gov/litigation/admin/2012/34-67767.pdf*

Adjustments to Stockholders' Equity Accounts: Delphi Corporation

In 2006, the Securities and Exchange Commission outlined its case of allegations involving Delphi Corporation and certain of its senior officers, accounting staff, and treasury staff. The allegations involve a pattern of violations of federal securities laws from 2000 through 2004. One of the alleged violations related to Delphi improperly accounting for an increase in warranty reserves related to warranty claims made by its former parent company. Delphi recorded the reserve increase as a direct adjustment to retained earnings rather than as an expense. There was no basis for Delphi to record the reserve adjustment as an adjustment to retained earnings. The SEC further alleged that Delphi disclosed the adjustment in an intentionally and materially misleading way. Specifically, the disclosure suggested, falsely, that the adjustment primarily related to certain pension and other postemployment benefit ("OPEB") matters and Delphi failed to disclose highly material information concerning the reserve increase and the former parent company's warranty claim. The misclassification of the reserve increase as a direct adjustment to equity, rather than as an expense item, resulted in Delphi materially overstating its net income for 2000 by $69 million.

Source: SEC Accounting and Auditing Enforcement Release No. 2504, October 30, 2006. A related SEC complaint in this matter is available at *http://www.sec.gov/litigation/complaints/2006/comp19891.pdf*

As you read through this chapter, consider the following questions:

- What are the risks of material misstatement associated with debt obligations and stockholders' equity accounts? (LO 2, 3, 4)
- What are the typical substantive procedures that auditors should perform when auditing debt obligations and stockholders' equity accounts? (LO 8)
- How could a lack of appropriate professional skepticism by auditors lead to material misstatements related to debt obligations and stockholders' equity accounts? (LO 2, 3, 5, 6, 8)

重要账户、披露和相关认定

LO 1 Identify the significant accounts, disclosures, and relevant assertions in auditing debt obligations and stockholders' equity transactions.

负债

负债审计的总体目标是判断是否所有的负债均已记录，并进行恰当的分类和披露。注册会计师主要关注负债的低估，因此完整性认定的审计是重点。

Significant Accounts, Disclosures, and Relevant Assertions

An organization uses many approaches to meet its long-term financing needs. Two common approaches are through issuing debt or equity.

Debt Obligations

Bonds are issued to finance major expansions or to refinance existing debt. Organizations also obtain financing through notes or mortgages. An organization typically has only a few debt transactions, but each transaction is usually highly material to the financial statements. Relevant accounts when auditing debt obligations include:

- Bonds payable
- Interest expense
- Gains or losses on refinancing debt
- Notes payable
- Mortgages payable

The overall objective of the audit of debt obligations is to determine whether all obligations are recorded and properly classified and disclosed. The auditor is primarily concerned with understatement and, therefore, focuses on the completeness assertion. Other relevant assertions in auditing bonds or other long-term debt include:

- Proper valuation of premium or discount (includes amortization)
- Valuation of gains or losses on refinancing debt
- Proper presentation and disclosure, including important restrictions contained in the debt obligations

Activities Related to Debt Obligations

Bond Issuance and Amortization Schedules Most bonds are marketed through an underwriter, with the proceeds going to the issuer after deducting the underwriter's commission. The authorization to issue a bond is usually limited to the board of directors. A bond premium/discount amortization spreadsheet can be used to help assure that the bond is appropriately valued and disclosed in the financial statements. A **bond indenture** provides important information regarding the bond, including the time period before repayment, amount of interest paid, if the bond is convertible (and if so, at what price or what ratio), if the bond is callable, and the amount of money that is to be repaid.

Periodic Payments and Interest Expense Most organizations have agreements with bond trustees to handle the registration of current bond-holders and to make the periodic interest payments. The organization issuing the bond makes interest payments to the trustee, plus a fee for the trustee's service, and the trustee disburses the individual payments to the bondholders.

Debt Covenants Debt covenants are written to protect bondholders against possible financial decline or against the subordination of the value of the debt by the issuance of other debt. Common restrictions include maintenance of a minimum level of retained earnings before dividends can be paid, maintenance of a minimum working-capital ratio, specification of a maximum debt-equity ratio, and specific callable provisions that identify procedures for calling and retiring debt at prespecified prices and dates.

Stockholders' Equity

所有者权益

Relevant accounts when auditing stockholders' equity activities include:

- Stock accounts (common, preferred, and treasury)
- Additional paid-in capital
- Dividend accounts
- Retained earnings

Activities Related to Stockholders' Equity

Common transactions affecting stockholders' equity include:

- New stock issuances
- Purchase of treasury stock
- Declaration and payment of dividends
- Grants of stock options and warrants
- Exercises and expirations of stock options and warrants
- Transfer of net income to retained earnings
- Recording of prior-period adjustments to retained earnings

In auditing equity accounts, the auditor primarily focuses on whether the securities are accurately valued (valuation assertion) and are properly classified and appropriately presented and disclosed (presentation and disclosure assertion).

Valuation Most stock issuances do not present valuation problems because most stock is issued for cash. However, not all stock is issued for cash. In those instances, valuation difficulties can occur in determining (1) whether the market value of the stock issued or the market value of the asset acquired is a better representation of value and (2) the proper accounting for an exchange of stock to acquire another business. Further, stock is also issued in the form of stock options and the exercise of those options. The stock option is an expense that is measured at the fair value of the option—usually measured by the Black-Scholes method. Companies then purchase stock on the open market to fulfill the exercise of those options.

Presentation and Disclosure Disclosure includes a proper description of (1) each class of stock outstanding and the number of shares authorized, issued, and outstanding and special rights associated with each class,

EXHIBIT **13.1**	Balance Sheet Disclosure of Stockholders' Equity

Papa John's International, Inc. and Subsidiaries Consolidated Balance Sheets

	(In thousands, except per share amounts)	
	December 25, 2011	December 26, 2010
Stockholders' equity:		
Preferred stock ($.01 par value per share; authorized 5,000 shares, no shares issued)		
Common stock ($.01 par value per share; authorized 50,000 shares, issued 36,656 in 2011 and 36,084 in 2010)	367	361
Additional paid-in capital	262,456	245,380
Accumulated other comprehensive income	1,849	849
Retained earnings	298,807	243,152
Treasury stock (12,637 shares in 2011 and 10,645 shares in 2010, at cost)	(353,826)	(291,048)
Total stockholders' equity, net of noncontrolling interests	209,653	198,694

(2) stock options outstanding, (3) convertible features, and (4) existence of stock warrants. Any restrictions or appropriations of retained earnings should be disclosed, as well as prior-period adjustments and other comprehensive income adjustments.

Exhibit 13.1 provides Papa John's International, Inc. balance sheet disclosure related to stockholders' equity. Note that the balance sheet disclosure includes information related to preferred stock, the amount of additional paid-in capital, accumulated other comprehensive income, retained earnings, and treasury stock. Papa John's footnote disclosures provide additional details on stock repurchases and stock options activity, including the number outstanding, granted, exercised, and cancelled.

The potential dilutive effect of convertible debt or preferred stock, stock options, and warrants should be disclosed in accordance with relevant accounting guidance in computing primary and fully diluted earnings per share. Exhibit 13.2 provides Papa Johns' earnings per share income statement disclosure, assuming dilution.

对负债和股东权益交易
实施风险评估程序

Performing Risk Assessment Procedures for Debt Obligations and Stockholders' Equity Transactions

LO 2 Identify and assess inherent risks of material misstatement associated with debt obligations and stockholders' equity transactions.

As part of performing risk assessment procedures, the auditor obtains information that is useful in assessing the risk of material misstatement. This includes information about inherent risks at the financial statement level (for example, the client's business and operational risks, financial reporting risks) and at the account and assertion levels, fraud risks including feedback from audit team brainstorming sessions, strengths and weaknesses in internal control, and results from preliminary analytical procedures. Once the risks of material misstatement have been identified, the auditor then determines how best to respond to them as part of the audit opinion formulation process.

EXHIBIT **13.2**	Income Statement Disclosure of Earnings per Share, Assuming Dilution

Papa John's International, Inc. and Subsidiaries Consolidated Statements of Income

	(In thousands, except per share amounts) Years Ended		
	December 25, 2011	December 26, 2010	December 27, 2009
Basic earnings per common share	$ 2.22	$ 1.97	$ 2.07
Earnings per common share - assuming dilution	$ 2.20	$ 1.96	$ 2.06
Basic weighted average shares outstanding	25,043	26,328	27,738
Diluted weighted average shares outstanding	25,310	26,468	27,909

Identifying Inherent Risks

Identifying Inherent Risks—Debt Obligations

Inherent risks related to debt obligations primarily concern the authorization of debt, receipt of funds, recording of debt transactions, and compliance with any debt covenants. For authorization, inherent risks include incurring debt that is not properly authorized or reviewed. Similarly, there are risks that new debt, debt extinguishments, or debt payment transactions are not properly authorized. In terms of recording debt transactions, risks include interest expense not being properly recorded or accrued and debt not being classified or recorded in accordance with GAAP. Regarding debt covenant compliance issues, inherent risks relate to whether debt covenants are calculated accurately and whether compliance with debt covenants is appropriately reviewed and disclosed.

Identifying Inherent Risks—Stockholders' Equity Transactions

Inherent risks related to stockholders' equity transactions vary across the specific activities. Exhibit 13.3 outlines some of the common inherent risks associated with typical stockholders' equity activities.

Identifying Fraud Risk Factors

Auditing standards require the auditor to identify and assess the risks of material misstatement due to fraud at the financial statement level and at the assertion level. As part of brainstorming activities, the auditor should identify possible frauds that could occur.

Identifying Fraud Risk Factors—Debt Obligations

Recall the case of Federico Quinto, Jr., CPA presented in the *Professional Judgment in Context* feature. The client involved in that case, Soyo Group, acted fraudulently by not accurately disclosing violations of its debt covenants. Other potential frauds related to debt obligations include the following:

- Debt obligations are not properly authorized.
- Long-term or short-term debt is misclassified.
- Interest expense is recorded in the wrong period, at the wrong amount, not recorded at all, or is misclassified.
- Entire loan payments are charged to either principal or interest.

识别固有风险

与负债相关的固有风险主要集中于债务的授权、资金的收取、债务交易的记录和债务契约的遵循。

识别舞弊风险因素

LO 3 Identify and assess fraud risks of material misstatement associated with debt obligations and stockholders' equity transactions.

EXHIBIT **13.3**	Inherent Risks Associated with Stockholders' Equity Activities

Stock Sales and Issuances

Assertion	Inherent Risk
Existence	Issuances/sales are not authorized in accordance with organization's bylaws. Proceeds are not received. Stock issuances/sales are recorded in the wrong period.
Valuation	Stock issued in exchange for goods/services is not properly valued.
Presentation and disclosure	Equity activities are not properly disclosed in accordance with GAAP.

Purchase of Treasury Stock

Assertion	Inherent Risk
Completeness	All stock repurchased is not recorded as treasury stock. Treasury stock transactions are recorded in the wrong period.
Valuation	The cost of treasury stock that is subsequently retired is not properly allocated among the appropriate accounts.

Dividends

Assertion	Inherent Risk
Existence	Dividends may be recorded and paid before being declared. Dividends may not be properly approved before being declared. Dividends are recorded in the wrong period.

Stock Options and Warrants

Assertion	Inherent Risk
Existence	Options/warrants are granted without being properly approved. Inadequate records as to options/warrants issued but not exercised.
Rights/obligations	Options exercised or expired remain on the organization's books.
Valuation	Option/warrant grants are not properly valued due to inappropriate assumptions or models. Inappropriate amortization methods are used. Inaccurate period of service is used.

Identifying Fraud Risk Factors—Stockholders' Equity

Recall the case of Delphi Corporation presented in the *Professional Judgment in Context* feature. Delphi and members of its management and staff acted fraudulently by charging expenses directly to retained earnings rather than to the appropriate expense accounts. Other potential frauds related to stockholders' equity accounts include the following:

- Stock sales or issuances are not authorized.
- Stock sales or issuances violate debt covenants.
- Stock sales or issuances are not recorded.

- Stock options exercised are not authorized or are not in accordance with the terms of options granted.
- Stock options are backdated.
- Dividends are paid in violation of restrictive covenants.
- Dividends are paid to wrong parties or at incorrect amounts.
- Proceeds from stock sales are misappropriated.

Identifying Control Risks

Once the auditor has obtained an understanding of the inherent and fraud risks of material misstatement associated with debt obligations and stockholders' equity transactions, the auditor needs to understand the controls that the client has designed and implemented to address those risks. Remember, the auditor is required to gain an overall understanding of internal controls for both integrated audits and financial statement only audits. Such understanding is normally gained by means of a walkthrough of the process, inquiry, observation, and review of the client's documentation. The auditor considers both entity-wide controls and transaction controls at the account and assertion levels. This understanding provides the auditor with a basis for making an initial control risk assessment.

At the entity-wide level, the auditor considers the control environment, including such principles as a commitment to financial accounting competencies and the independence of the board of directors. The auditor also considers the remaining components of internal control that are typically entity-wide—risk assessment, information and communication, and monitoring controls. Although all the components of internal control need to be understood, the auditor typically finds it useful to focus on significant control activities, and focuses on the relevant assertions for each account and identifies the controls that relate to risks for these assertions. In an integrated audit or in a controls reliance audit, this understanding is used to identify important controls that need to be tested.

Controls—Debt Obligations

Given the typical inherent and fraud risks described earlier, the auditor would expect an organization to have some of the following controls in place:

- The board of directors approves all new debt.
- Debt and interest accounts are updated and reconciled to the general ledger on a monthly basis.
- Top management and the board of directors review draft financial statements prior to issuance for proper disclosure of debt obligations.
- A debt amortization schedule is prepared for each new debt obligation, updated as appropriate, and is reviewed by appropriate personnel.

Controls—Stockholders' Equity Transactions

Given the typical inherent and fraud risks described earlier, the auditor would expect an organization to have some of the following controls in place:

- The board of directors approves all stock transactions (including options and warrants).
- The CEO and CFO authorize all stock transactions (including options and warrants) approved by the board of directors.
- Stockholders' equity accounts are updated and reconciled to the general ledger on a timely basis.
- Top management and the board of directors review draft financial statements prior to issuance for proper disclosure of equity accounts.

识别控制风险

LO 4 Identify and assess control risks of material misstatement associated with debt obligations and stockholders' equity transactions.

- An outside party, such as an attorney, maintains details of shares issued, repurchased, and cancelled.
- The organization's accountant researches and analyzes proper accounting for stock option grants, and the organization's legal counsel and CFO review and approve the analysis.

Documenting Controls

Auditors need to document their understanding of internal controls for both integrated audits and financial statement only audits. Similar to other audit areas, the auditor can provide this documentation in various formats, including a control matrix, a control risk assessment questionnaire, and/or a memo.

实施初步的分析性程序

LO 5 Describe how to use preliminary analytical procedures to identify possible material misstatements associated with debt obligations and stockholders' equity transactions.

Performing Preliminary Analytical Procedures

When planning the audit, the auditor is required to perform preliminary analytical procedures. These procedures can help auditors identify areas of potential misstatements. Auditors do not look at just the numbers when performing analytical procedures. Auditors need to go through the four-step process described in Chapter 7, which begins with developing expectations for account balances, ratios, and trends.

The following are examples of typical analytical procedures related to debt obligations:

- Perform a trend analysis of the balances in notes payable, interest expense, and accrued interest with prior periods, considering known client activities related to debt.
- Estimate interest expense based on average interest rates and average debt outstanding.
- Calculate debt-to-equity ratios and perform a trend analysis with prior periods.
- Calculate the times interest earned ratio and perform a trend analysis with prior periods.

The primary preliminary analytical procedure for stockholders' equity accounts is a comparison of current year account balances with prior-year account balances. The auditor should have an expectation as to the nature and magnitude of any account balance changes.

If preliminary analytical procedures do not identify any unexpected relationships, the auditor would conclude that a heightened risk of material misstatement does not exist in these accounts. If unusual or unexpected relationships exist, the planned audit procedures (tests of controls, substantive procedures) would be adjusted to address the potential material misstatements.

对识别的重大错报风险的反应

LO 6 Determine appropriate responses to identified risks of material misstatement in auditing debt obligations and stockholders' equity transactions.

在审计股东权益交易时，注册会计师通常使用实质性方法。这种方法对权益交易审计来说是适用的，因为该类交易的数量通常较小。

Responding to Identified Risks of Material Misstatement

Once the auditor has developed an understanding of the risks of material misstatement, including inherent risks, fraud risks, and control risks, the auditor can determine the appropriate audit procedures to perform. Typically, when determining the appropriate audit procedures to perform for debt accounts, the auditor usually decides to test debt obligations, including interest, using only substantive procedures. This approach is often appropriate because the number of transactions is relatively small and the dollar amounts involved are usually quite material.

Similarly, when auditing stockholders' equity transactions, the auditor commonly uses a substantive approach. This approach is often appropriate because the number of equity transactions with outside parties is usually small. In fact, a substantive approach using only tests of details is most commonly used to audit equity accounts.

For both debt accounting and stockholders' equity accounts, the boxes of evidence would typically be filled only with evidence obtained through substantive procedures.

Obtaining Evidence about Internal Control Operating Effectiveness for Debt Obligations and Stockholders' Equity Transactions

For integrated audits, the auditor tests the operating effectiveness of important controls as of the client's year end. The auditor selects controls that are important to the auditor's conclusion about whether the organization's controls adequately address the assessed risk of material misstatement for the relevant debt and equity accounts. The auditor selects both entity-wide and transaction controls for testing. Typical tests of transaction controls include inquiry of personnel performing the control, observation of the control being performed, inspection of documentation confirming that the control has been performed, and reperformance of the control by the auditor testing the control. If testing results in identified control deficiencies, the auditor assesses those deficiencies to determine their severity (are they significant deficiencies or material weaknesses?) and their impact on the opinion on internal control effectiveness.

If the auditor wants to rely on controls for the financial statement audit, the auditor would test the operating effectiveness of those controls throughout the year. However, for financial statement audit purposes, when auditing debt obligations and stockholders' equity transactions, the auditor most likely performs a substantive audit and therefore does not perform tests of controls for the debt and equity accounts.

Obtaining Substantive Evidence in Auditing Debt Obligations and Stockholders' Equity Transactions

The audits of debt obligations and stockholders' equity transactions typically involve only substantive procedures. Debt obligations accounts are tested with both substantive analytical procedures and tests of details. In contrast, only tests of details are typically used to audit stockholders' equity accounts. Further, the transactions in the stockholders' equity accounts are typically tested 100% because they are usually so few, and yet they are highly material.

Substantive Analytical Procedures—Debt Obligations

When auditing debt obligations, the primary substantive analytical procedure would involve the auditor developing an independent expectation of interest expense. This expectation would be based on average debt outstanding and average interest rates. When performing this analysis as a substantive procedure, the auditor would use disaggregated data—likely disaggregated by type of debt. If the auditor's expectation is similar to what the client has recorded, additional substantive testing of interest expense and accrued interest would not be necessary. Exhibit 13.4—Panel A notes that in this situation the box of evidence obtained by the auditor would include evidence only from substantive analytical procedures.

If there is a significant difference between the auditor's estimate and what the client has recorded, the auditor needs to perform additional substantive test of details to determine the reason for the difference. For example, if

对负债和股东权益交易获取内部控制运行有效性的证据

LO 7 Determine appropriate tests of controls and consider the results of tests of controls in auditing debt obligations and stockholders' equity transactions.

在审计负债和股东权益交易时获取实质性证据

LO 8 Determine and apply sufficient appropriate substantive audit procedures in auditing debt obligations and stockholders' equity transactions.

实质性分析程序——负债

EXHIBIT **13.4**	Panel A: Substantive Analytical Procedures Approach to Obtaining Audit Evidence for Completeness of Interest Expense

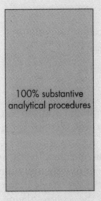

100% substantive
analytical procedures

Panel B: Substantive Analytical Procedures and Tests of Details Approach to Obtaining Audit Evidence for Completeness of Interest Expense

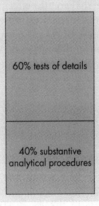

60% tests of details

40% substantive
analytical procedures

interest expense recorded by the client is significantly lower than the auditor's expectation, it may mean that interest payments have not been properly recorded, possibly having been charged to principal. Exhibit 13.4—Panel B notes that in this situation the box of evidence obtained by the auditor would include evidence from substantive analytical procedures and tests of details. Note that the relative percentages are judgmental in nature; the examples are simply intended to give you a sense of how an auditor might select an appropriate mix of procedures.

Why Tests of Controls Might Not Be Performed When substantive analytical procedures are performed, they are typically performed only after the relevant controls have been tested. However, when performing the substantive analytical procedure related to interest expense, the auditor will likely not test controls. The primary reason is that the information being used to perform the analytical procedure (loan amounts and interest rates) is typically confirmed with an independent outside party. Therefore, the effectiveness of the client's controls is not as important a concern as in other areas where the information being used for the substantive analytical procedures is not subject to external independent confirmation.

Substantive Tests of Details—Debt Obligations

实质性细节测试——负债

Typical substantive procedures include:

- Reading new loan agreements
- Determining what changes, if any, have been made to prior loan agreements
- Confirming with relevant outside parties the significant factors and transactions that have occurred

As a starting point for these procedures, the auditor will have the client provide a schedule of debt obligations and interest. The client should also have a bond premium/discount amortization schedule that the auditor can review in assessing whether bonds are appropriately valued and disclosed in the financial statements. For additions to debt, the auditor traces the proceeds into the cash receipts records and the bank statement. The auditor might also examine the debt instrument and obtain assurance regarding board approval of the debt through review of board meeting minutes. For debt reductions, the auditor examines payments through the cash disbursements records, possibly including canceled checks. Also, for notes or mortgages that have been paid in full, the auditor should examine the canceled notes.

Typical substantive procedures for relevant assertions related to debt obligations are shown in Exhibit 13.5.

Debt and Bond Covenants

The auditor should obtain an understanding of the procedures the client uses to determine whether they are in compliance with their debt covenants. The auditor should then independently determine if the client is in compliance. Consider a covenant that requires the client to maintain a current ratio that does not fall below a specified level. If the auditor determines that the client's current ratio is below that level, the auditor should assess the effects of the violation. If the violation is not waived by the creditor and the loan is in default, the creditor may declare the outstanding balance immediately due and payable. In that case, the auditor generally would assume that the debt would need to be reclassified as short-term debt. In addition, the

---

EXHIBIT 13.5 **Relevant Management Assertions and Substantive Procedures for Debt Obligations**

Management Assertion	Substantive Procedure
Completeness—Recorded debt obligations include all debt obligations.	1. Perform substantive analytical procedures. 2. Confirm debt obligations. 3. Vouch additions and deletions to debt obligations.
Valuation/allocation—Debt obligations and related expenses are recorded correctly, including account, amount, and period	1. Perform substantive analytical procedures to analyze interest expense and recalculate accrued interest.
Presentation/disclosure—Debt obligations are properly classified in the balance sheet between current and noncurrent liabilities, and adequate disclosures are made in accordance with GAAP requirements.	1. Review debt agreements for the restrictive covenants and consider their effect on disclosures in the financial statements. 2. Inquire of management. 3. Examine balance sheet for proper disclosure of current and noncurrent portions, related parties, and restrictions resulting from debt. 4. Read all disclosures for appropriateness, consistency, and clarity. (The *Auditing in Practice* feature "SEC Focus on Debt Presentation and Disclosure" provides additional discussion.)

SEC Focus on Debt Presentation and Disclosure AUDITING IN PRACTICE

In Deloitte (2011) *SEC Comment Letters*, the audit firm makes the following statement regarding the SEC's focus on debt presentation and disclosure:

> The SEC staff has frequently commented on the appropriate balance sheet classification of outstanding debt amounts. When presenting a classified balance sheet, registrants must determine whether outstanding debt should be classified as current or noncurrent. This determination becomes even more involved when debt arrangements include certain provisions or clauses that may accelerate the maturity of the debt, generally requiring the registrant to classify its outstanding debt as current. As a result, registrants should consider ASC 470-10-45-9 through 45-12 when debt arrangements include provisions that result in the debt's being due on demand (i.e.,

callable by the creditor). Registrants should also consider ASC 470-10-45-2 and ASC 470-10-50-3 when debt agreements contain subjective acceleration clauses, which accelerate the scheduled maturities of the obligation if certain events occur that are not objectively determinable.

> In addition, the SEC staff has focused on the disclosures required when a violation of debt covenants has been waived by the creditor. Regulation S-X, Rule 4-08(c), requires that an entity disclose the amount of the obligation and the period of the waiver if the creditor has waived its right for a stated period.

Source: Deloitte (2011). *SEC Comment Letters—Including Industry Insights Improving Transparency*. Available at *http://www.deloitte. com/assets/Dcom-UnitedStates/Local%20Assets/Documents/AERS/ ASC/us_aers_seccommentletterbook.pdf*

auditor must consider what financial statement disclosures will be required and how the events of default will affect the audit opinion. For example, could the default suggest going concern issues that would need to be identified in the audit opinion?

实质性细节测试——股东
权益交易

Substantive Tests of Details—Stockholders' Equity Transactions

As a starting point for testing capital stock and equity transactions, the auditor should review a copy of the client's articles of incorporation. This document provides relevant information with respect to each class of stock. The auditor can agree that information to the disclosures included in the client's financial statements. The auditor will also prepare, or ask the client to prepare, an analysis of all capital stock transactions.

The auditor will inspect documentation related to the client's record keeping of capital stock and contributed capital. This documentation may be maintained by the client or held by a **transfer agent**. Review of this documentation provides the auditor with evidence related to the existence and completeness of capital.

To obtain evidence related to the valuation of capital stock, the auditor should review the minutes of the board of directors meetings and examine the stock records books (or confirm with the registrar and transfer agent) to determine issuance and repurchase of capital stock. The auditor would typically obtain evidence for all capital stock transactions. For example, if stock is sold, the auditor traces the proceeds to the cash receipts journal and reviews documentation indicating that the proper amount was recorded in the stock and paid-in capital accounts. The auditor may also have instances when capital stock was issued in a nonmonetary transaction. For those instances, the auditor needs to determine that the client has properly recorded the issuance in accordance with GAAP.

Deficiencies in Substantive Procedures Related to Stockholders' Equity Transactions: Insights From the PCAOB

On October 22, 2007, the Public Company Accounting Oversight Board (PCAOB) issued a report outlining findings in its 2004, 2005, and 2006 inspections. The PCAOB noted identified deficiencies related to inadequate testing of stockholders' equity transactions, including:

- The auditors failed to evaluate whether the audit clients had appropriately determined the fair values assigned to equity-based transactions and to test the reasonableness of such fair values.
- The auditors failed to evaluate the adequacy of the disclosure of equity transactions in the notes to the financial statements and to determine whether the equity transactions were recorded in the proper period.
- The auditors failed to properly address and evaluate the substance, business purpose, or significant terms of the equity arrangements.
- The auditors failed to consider the accounting principles potentially applicable to the equity transactions.

For further details, see PCAOB Release No. 2007-010, Report on the PCAOB's 2004, 2005, and 2006 Inspections of Domestic Triennially Inspected Firms, available at http://pcaobus.org/Inspections/Documents/2007_10-22_4010_Report.pdf.

For those clients with treasury stock, the auditor will examine documentation supporting changes in the number of shares since the prior year. This documentation might include obtaining confirmation from the stock transfer agent and tracing the transaction through the cash receipts or cash disbursements journals.

对于有库存股的客户，注册会计师将检查自上一年以来支持股票份额变更的记录。

While the substantive audit procedures related to capital stock and equity activities are somewhat straightforward, the *Auditing in Practice* feature "Deficiencies in Substantive Procedures Related to Equity Transactions: Insights from the PCAOB" identifies areas posing potential difficulties in auditing stockholders' equity transactions.

Dividends The auditor examines the minutes of the board of directors meetings for authorization of the dividend per share amount and the dividend record date. For those clients who maintain their own records and pay the dividends, the auditor recalculates the amount of the dividends and agrees that amount to the cash disbursements journal. If a client uses a transfer agent, the auditor traces the payment to a cash disbursement made by the client to the agent. The auditor may also confirm the amount with the agent.

The auditor will also want to obtain evidence as to whether the payment was made to the stockholders who owned the stock as of the dividend record date. The auditor can trace the payee's name on the canceled check to the dividend records to make sure the payee was to have received the dividend.

The auditor also needs to be aware of restrictions related to dividend payments and determine that the restrictions are adequately disclosed in the financial statements. The *Auditing in Practice* feature "SEC Focus on Disclosure of Restrictions Related to Dividend Payments" highlights the importance for the auditor of determining that relevant dividend payment restrictions are appropriately disclosed in the client's financial statements.

Retained Earnings The auditor typically examines all transactions recorded in the retained earnings account during the audit period. The

SEC Focus on Disclosure of Restrictions Related to Dividend Payments

In Deloitte (2011) *SEC Comment Letters*, the audit firm makes the following statement regarding the SEC's focus on disclosure of restrictions related to dividend payments:

> The SEC staff has issued a number of comment letters focusing on the disclosure requirements in Rule 4-08(e) for restrictions imposed on a registrant's ability to pay dividends. Typically, these restrictions arise when loan agreements prohibit the registrant from paying cash dividends without the consent of a third party (i.e., the lender). In addition, in certain circumstances, these restrictions exist

at a subsidiary-company level such that the registrant's subsidiary companies may not transfer amounts to the registrant without the consent of a third party. A registrant must disclose the nature of any restrictions on the ability of the registrant or any of its subsidiaries to pay dividends and the amounts subject to such restrictions.

Source: Deloitte (2011) *SEC Comment Letters—Including Industry Insights Improving Transparency.* Available at *http://www.deloitte.com/assets/Dcom-UnitedStates/Local%20Assets/Documents/AERS/ASC/us_aers_seccommentletterbook.pdf*

common entries include net income or loss. These amounts would be tested through substantive audit procedures related to revenues and expenses. The other common entry includes dividends. If there are additional entries, the auditor examines documentation supporting that the entries should be included. For example, if there is a correction of an error from a prior period, the auditor determines that the correction is made in accordance with relevant accounting standards.

实施与舞弊相关的实质性
程序

Performing Substantive Fraud-Related Procedures

If the auditor identifies a risk of material misstatement due to fraud related to debt obligations or stockholders' equity accounts, the auditor needs to determine the appropriate responses, potentially including changing the nature, timing, and extent of audit procedures.

Fraud-Related Substantive Procedures for Debt Obligations

In those audits where there is a heightened risk of fraud related to debt obligations, the auditor should consider performing the following procedures or, if the procedures are already being performed, altering the timing and extent of the procedures:

- Search public records to identify debt obligations
- Vouch and trace loan proceeds and debt payments
- Send confirmations to lenders and creditors, including confirmation of compliance with any debt covenants
- Require original supporting documents rather than copies
- Agree detail of debt terms to authorization in minutes of board meetings

Fraud-Related Substantive Procedures for Stockholders' Equity Accounts

In those audits where there is a heightened risk of fraud related to stockholders' equity accounts, the auditor should consider performing the following procedures or, if the procedures are already being performed, altering the timing and extent of the procedures:

- Confirm terms of equity arrangements and shares held directly with shareholders
- Confirm with shareholders whether there are any side agreements
- Employ an appropriate level of professional skepticism and carefully analyze transactions to determine whether the terms and substance of the transactions indicate that the proceeds should be recorded as debt or as equity
- Confirm with the transfer agent information on issued stock
- Account for and vouch all proceeds from stock issues

Documenting Substantive Procedures

记录实质性程序

A number of important items should be documented when performing substantive procedures for debt obligations and capital stock and equity activities. For debt obligations, the auditor's documentation should include:

- Copies of the debt agreements
- Identification of the specific items tested
- Schedule of debt obligations and interest
- A summary of the calculations supporting compliance with debt covenants
- Confirmations or documentation of alternative procedures performed

For stockholders' equity transactions, the auditor's documentation should include:

- Client's articles of incorporation
- A summary of changes in equity accounts
- Verification of authorization with respect to any changes in capitalization or declaration of dividends
- Confirmations with transfer agent or shareholders

SUMMARY AND NEXT STEPS

Auditing debt obligations and stockholders' equity transactions is usually straightforward—perform substantive tests of the few, but typically material, transactions recorded during the audit period. However, the auditor should be skeptical, and therefore alert to the possibility that management is managing earnings by not appropriately recording expenses, such as charging expenses directly to retained earnings or underrecording interest expense. Further, management may attempt to avoid appropriate disclosures related to these accounts, especially disclosures related to debt covenants and possible covenant violations. Now that you understand how to perform audit procedures for many of the accounts included on the income statement and balance sheet, in the next chapter we turn to the remaining audit steps conducted prior to completing the audit, each designed to assure that the audit has been conducted in a quality manner and that the ultimate audit opinion is appropriate.

SIGNIFICANT TERMS

Bond indenture A contract between an issuer of bonds and the bondholder stating the time period before repayment, amount of interest paid, if the bond is convertible (and if so, at what price or what ratio), if the bond is callable, and the amount of money that is to be repaid.

Debt covenants Restrictions in debt agreements aimed at protecting the lender (creditor, debt holder, or investor) by restricting the activities of the borrower (debtor).

Transfer agent An organization such as a trust company, bank, or other financial institution that is used by an organization to maintain records of investors and account balances and transactions, to cancel and issue certificates, and to process investor mailings.

TRUE-FALSE QUESTIONS

13-1 [LO 1] An organization typically has many debt transactions during the year, with each individual transaction being immaterial.

13-2 [LO 1] Typically, the most relevant assertion related to debt obligations is completeness.

13-3 [LO 2] Recording the purchases of treasury stock is straightforward and therefore does not pose any inherent risk of material misstatement.

13-4 [LO 2] An inherent risk associated with debt obligations is that management might try to avoid complete and accurate disclosure of debt covenants and potential violations.

13-5 [LO 3] A potential fraud risk associated with debt obligations is the intentional misclassification of short-term debt as long-term debt.

13-6 [LO 3] Charging expenses directly to retained earnings rather than to the appropriate expense account is potential fraud risk associated with stockholders' equity accounts.

13-7 [LO 4] Because the auditor is likely not testing controls related to stockholders' equity transactions, the auditor does not need to have an understanding of controls over stockholders' equity transactions.

13-8 [LO 4] A reconciliation of debt and interest accounts to the general ledger is a control designed to mitigate the risks of material misstatement associated with debt obligations.

13-9 [LO 5] The primary preliminary analytical procedure for stockholders' equity accounts is a comparison of current year account balances with prior-year account balances, after considering the auditor's expectations.

13-10 [LO 5] Trend analyses would not typically be used as preliminary analytical procedures related to debt obligations.

13-11 [LO 6] When responding to identified risks of material misstatements associated with stockholders' equity accounts, the auditor often decides to rely heavily on tests of controls.

13-12 [LO 6] When testing debt obligations, the auditor typically uses a substantive audit approach.

13-13 [LO 7] When auditing debt obligations, the auditor may test controls at the year end for the audit opinion on internal controls, but choose not test controls for the financial statement audit.

13-14 [LO 7] When auditing stockholders' equity transactions, the auditor may test controls at the year end for the audit opinion on internal controls, but choose not test controls for the financial statement audit.

13-15 [LO 8] Confirmations can be used as a substantive procedure designed to obtain evidence on the completeness of debt obligations.

13-16 `LO 8` If there is a heightened risk of fraud related to the completeness of debt obligations, the auditor may choose to search public records to identify debt obligations.

MULTIPLE-CHOICE QUESTIONS

13-17 `LO 1` Which of the following can be used by organizations for obtaining financing?
a. Notes.
b. Mortgages.
c. Bonds.
d. All of the above.

13-18 `LO 1` Which of the following accounts would not typically be included in the audit of debt obligations?
a. Interest income.
b. Interest expense.
c. Bonds payable.
d. Notes payable.

13-19 `LO 2` Inherent risks related to debt obligations primarily include which of the following?
a. Debt is not properly authorized.
b. Interest expense is not properly accrued.
c. Debt covenants are not properly disclosed.
d. Debt is not appropriately classified as short or long term.
e. All of the above are inherent risks related to debt obligations.

13-20 `LO 2` Which of the following is not an inherent risk typically associated with the existence of dividends?
a. Dividends are recorded before being declared.
b. Dividends are not properly amortized.
c. Dividends have not been approved before being declared.
d. Dividends are recorded in the wrong period.

13-21 `LO 3` Which of the following most accurately describes the nature of fraud related to debt obligations described in the case of Federico Quinto, Jr., CPA presented in the *Professional Judgment in Context* feature?
a. Interest expense was recorded in the wrong period.
b. Entire loan payments were charged to principal.
c. Debt covenants and potential violations were not appropriately presented and disclosed.
d. Long-term debt was misclassified as short-term debt.

13-22 `LO 3` Which of the following most accurately describes the nature of fraud related to stockholders' equity accounts described in the case of Delphi Corporation presented in the *Professional Judgment in Context* feature?
a. Stock options were back dated.
b. Stock sales were not authorized.
c. Proceeds from stock sales were misappropriated.
d. Expenses were charged directly to retained earnings rather than to the appropriate expense accounts.

13-23 [LO 4] Which of the following would an auditor typically not perform as part of gaining an understanding of the client's controls related to debt obligations?

a. Review the client's documentation of controls.

b. Recalculate interest expense.

c. Inquire of management about the process for reviewing compliance with debt covenants.

d. Review policies related to approval required for new debt.

13-24 [LO 4] Which of the following is a control the auditor would expect a client to have related to stockholders' equity transactions?

a. A policy requiring approval by the board of directors for all stock transactions.

b. Reconciliation of equity accounts to the general ledger.

c. CFO and CEO authorization of all stock transaction approved by the board of directors.

d. The auditor would typically expect all of the above controls to be in place.

13-25 [LO 5] Which of the following statements is true regarding preliminary analytical procedures for debt obligations and stockholders' equity transactions?

a. Because there are typically only a few stockholders' equity transactions, the auditor is not required to perform preliminary analytical procedures for stockholders' equity accounts.

b. Trend analysis would not typically be performed for debt obligations.

c. The long-term debt to equity ratio could be considered by the auditor as part of the preliminary analytical procedures.

d. All of the above statements are true.

13-26 [LO 5] Which of the following are typical preliminary analytical procedures related to debt obligations?

a. Estimate interest expense based on average interest rates and average debt outstanding.

b. Calculate the total debt-to-equity ratio and perform a trend analysis with prior periods.

c. Calculate the long-term debt-to-equity ratio and perform a trend analysis with prior periods.

d. Calculate the times interest earned ratio and perform a trend analysis with prior periods.

e. All of the above could be performed as preliminary analytical procedures related to debt obligations.

13-27 [LO 6] How does an auditor typically respond to identified risks of material misstatement associated with debt obligations?

a. The auditor will plan to perform a controls reliance approach to the audit.

b. An approach that uses only substantive procedures would typically be appropriate.

c. The auditor does not need to respond to identified fraud risks since the risk of fraud related to debt obligations is typically minimal.

d. Because of the low level of risk of material misstatement, the auditor would only rely on preliminary analytical procedures.

13-28 **LO 6** How does an auditor typically respond to identified risks of material misstatement associated with stockholders' equity accounts?
a. The auditor will plan to perform a controls reliance approach to the audit.
b. An approach that uses only substantive procedures would typically be appropriate.
c. The auditor does not need to respond to identified fraud risks since the risk of fraud related to stockholders' equity accounts is typically minimal.
d. Because of the low level of risk of material misstatement, the auditor would only rely on preliminary analytical procedures.

13-29 **LO 7** Which of the following best describes the auditor's typical approach to testing controls related to debt obligations?
a. Controls would be tested for integrated audit purposes, but not for financial statement audit purposes.
b. Controls would be tested for financial statement audit purposes, but not for integrated audit purposes.
c. Controls would be tested for both the integrated audit and financial statement audit.
d. Controls would not be tested for either the integrated audit or financial statement audit.

13-30 **LO 7** Which of the following best describes the auditor's typical approach to testing controls related to stockholders' equity accounts?
a. Controls would be tested for integrated audit purposes, but not for financial statement audit purposes.
b. Controls would be tested for financial statement audit purposes, but not for integrated audit purposes.
c. Controls would be tested for both the integrated audit and financial statement audit.
d. Controls would not be tested for either the integrated audit or financial statement audit.

13-31 **LO 8** The auditor's audit program for long-term debt should include which of the following procedures?
a. Verification of the existence of the bondholders.
b. Review debt loan agreements.
c. Inspection of the accounts payable master file.
d. Investigation of credits to the bond interest income account.

13-32 **LO 8** When a client does not maintain its own stock records, the auditor should obtain written confirmation from the stock transfer agent concerning which of the following?
a. Restrictions on the payment of dividends.
b. The number of shares issued and outstanding.
c. Guarantees of preferred stock liquidation value.
d. The number of shares subject to agreements to repurchase.

NOTE: Completing Review and Short Case Questions does not require the student to reference additional resources and materials.

REVIEW AND SHORT CASE QUESTIONS

13-33 **LO 1** What are the relevant accounts when auditing debt obligations, and what is the auditor's primary objective?

13-34 **LO 1** What are the relevant accounts related to stockholders' equity transactions?

13-35 **LO 1** Identify common transactions affecting stockholders' equity accounts.

NOTE: For the remaining problems, we make special note of those addressing fraud, international issues, professional skepticism, and ethics.

13-36 [LO 1] Review Exhibits 13.1 and 13.2. Describe the disclosures related to stockholders' equity provided by Papa John's International, Inc.

13-37 [LO 2] Identify common inherent risks associated with debt obligations.

13-38 [LO 2] Review Exhibit 13.3 and identify inherent risks associated with typical stockholders' equity transactions.

FRAUD **13-39** [LO 3] Identify fraud risks associated with debt obligations.

FRAUD **13-40** [LO 3] Identify fraud risks associated with stockholders' equity accounts.

FRAUD **13-41** [LO 4] Given typical inherent and fraud risks related to material misstatement of debt obligations, identify controls that an auditor would expect a client to have implemented.

FRAUD **13-42** [LO 4] Given typical inherent and fraud risks related to material misstatement of stockholders' equity accounts, identify controls that an auditor would expect a client to have implemented.

13-43 [LO 5] What are typical preliminary procedures related to debt obligations?

13-44 [LO 5] What are typical preliminary procedures related to stockholders' equity accounts?

13-45 [LO 6] What type of audit approach is typically planned for debt obligations? Why is this most often the most appropriate approach?

13-46 [LO 6] What type of audit approach is typically planned for stockholders' equity accounts?

13-47 [LO 6] An audit firm is engaged in the examination of the financial statements of Zeitlow Corporation for the year ended December 31, 2013. Zeitlow Corporation's financial statements and records have never been audited. The stockholders' equity section of Zeitlow Corporation's balance sheet at December 31, 2013, follows:

Stockholders' Equity:

Capital stock—10,000 shares of $10 par value authorized:	
5,000 shares issued and outstanding	$ 50,000
Capital contributed in excess of par value of capital stock	58,800
Retained earnings	105,000
Total stockholders' equity	$213,800

Founded in 2005, Zeitlow Corporation has 10 stockholders and serves as its own registrar and transfer agent. It has no capital stock subscription contracts in effect. Prepare the detailed audit program for the examination of the three accounts composing the stockholders' equity section of Zeitlow Corporation's balance sheet. (Do not include in the audit program for the verification of the results of the current-year operations.)

13-48 [LO 7] Describe the evidence typically obtained from tests of controls when auditing debt obligations or stockholders' equity accounts.

13-49 `LO 8` Review the two panels in Exhibit 13.4. Describe the two alternative approaches to auditing interest expense and the reason for the difference in approaches.

13-50 `LO 8` Refer to Exhibit 13.5 and identify typical substantive procedures for relevant assertions related to debt obligations.

13-51 `LO 8` Review the *Auditing in Practice* feature "SEC Focus on Debt Presentation and Disclosure" and identify potential audit problems related to presentation and disclosure of debt.

13-52 `LO 8` Identify substantive procedures that the auditor should perform related to dividends.

13-53 `LO 8` Retained earnings is a component of stockholders' equity. What substantive procedures will the auditor typically perform related to retained earnings?

13-54 `LO 8` What important items should be documented related to substantive procedures performed for debt obligations and stockholders' equity accounts?

13-55 `LO 8` What information should the auditor note when reading a bond indenture? How is the information used in the audit?

13-56 `LO 8` After all other account balances on the balance sheet have been audited, it might appear that the retained earnings figure is a balancing figure and requires no further audit procedures. Why would an auditor still choose to audit retained earnings?

13-57 `LO 8` Assume your audit client declared a 5% stock dividend. Identify the evidence you would examine to determine whether the stock dividend was accounted for properly.

13-58 `LO 8` Explain how a bond amortization spreadsheet might be used to audit interest expense over the life of a bond.

13-59 `LO 8` The auditor should review the bond indenture at the time a bond is issued and anytime subsequent changes are made to it.
a. Briefly identify the information the auditor would expect to obtain from a bond indenture. List at least five specific pieces of information that would be relevant to the conduct of the audit.
b. Because auditors are especially concerned with the potential understatement of liabilities, should they confirm the existence of the liability with individual bondholders? State your rationale.
c. A company issued bonds at a discount. Explain how the amount of the discount is computed and how the auditor could determine whether the amount is properly amortized each year.
d. Explain how the auditor could verify that semiannual interest payments are made on the bond each year.
e. The company has a 15-year, $20 million loan that is due on September 30 of next year. It is the company's intent to refinance the bond before it is due, but it is waiting for the best time to issue new debt. Because its intent is to issue the bond next year, the company believes that the existing $20 million bond need not be classified as a current liability. What evidence should the auditor gather to determine the appropriate classification of the bond?

13-60 `LO 8` The following covenants are extracted from a bond indenture. The indenture provides that failure to comply with its terms in any respect automatically advances the due date of the loan to the date of noncompliance (the maturity date is 20 years hence). Identify the audit steps that should be taken or reporting requirements necessary in connection with each one of the following independent scenarios:

a. The debtor company shall endeavor to maintain a working capital ratio of 2 to 1 at all times, and, in any fiscal year following a failure to maintain the said ratio, the company shall restrict compensation of the CEO and executive officers to a total of no more than $500,000. Executive officers for this purpose shall include the chairman of the board of directors, the president, all vice presidents, the secretary, and the treasurer.

b. The debtor company shall insure all property that is security for this debt against loss by fire to the extent of 100% of its actual value. Insurance policies securing this protection shall be filed with the trustee.

c. The debtor company shall pay all taxes legally assessed against the property that serves as security for this debt within the time provided by law for payment without penalty and shall deposit receipted tax bills or equally acceptable evidence of payment of the same with the trustee.

d. A sinking fund shall be deposited with the trustee by semiannual payments of $300,000, from which the trustee shall, at her discretion, purchase bonds of this issue.

13-61 LO 8 The following long-term debt documentation (indexed K-l), and presented on the next page, was prepared by client personnel and audited by AA, an audit assistant, during the calendar year 2013 audit of American Widgets, Inc., a continuing audit client. The engagement supervisor is thoroughly reviewing the working papers. Identify the deficiencies in the audit documentation (shown on the next page) that the engagement supervisor should discover.

CONTEMPORARY AND HISTORICAL CASES

FRAUD

PROFESSIONAL SKEPTICISM

ETHICS

13-62 **(FEDERICO QUINTO, JR., CPA AND SOYO GROUP LO 1, 2, 3, 4, 6, 8, 9)** Refer to the *Professional Judgment in Context* feature "Deficiencies in Auditing Debt Obligations and Stockholders' Equity Accounts: Insights from SEC Releases" and review the panel related to Federico Quinto, Jr., CPA. Answer the following questions:

a. What risks of material misstatement were present in the case?

b. What are the auditor's responsibilities related to debt covenants? What would you consider to be the most relevant assertions related to debt covenants, and what substantive procedures should the auditor have performed?

c. Identify ways in which the audit team appeared to have a lack of appropriate professional skepticism.

d. Assume that you were part of the audit team for the Soyo Group 2007 audit and you were aware that the appropriate disclosures related to debt covenants had not been made in the financial statements. Use the framework for ethical decision making presented in Chapter 4 to determine the actions you should take. Recall that the steps are as follows: (1) identify the ethical issue, (2) determine the affected parties and identify their rights, (3) determine the most important rights, (4) develop alternative courses of action, (5) determine the likely consequences of each proposed course of action, (6) assess the possible consequences, and (7) decide on an appropriate course of action.

13-61 CONTINUED

Long-term Debt
December 31, 2013

Prepared by / Approved by

Initials AA   Date 2/10/14

Lender	Interest Rate	Payment Terms	Collateral	Balance December 31, 2012	2013 Borrowings	2013 Reductions	Balance December 31, 2013	Interest Paid to	Accrued Interest Payable December 31, 2013	Comments
First Commercial Bank*	12%	Interest only on 25th of month, principal due in full 1/1/17, no prepayment penalty	Inventories	$ 50,000†	$300,000‡ 1/31/13	$100,000§ 6/30/13	$ 250,000‖	12/25/13	$2,500**	Dividend of $80,000 paid 9/2/13 (W/P N-3) violates a provision of the debt agreement, which thereby permits lender to demand immediate payment; lender has refused to waive this violation
Lender's Capital Corp.*	Prime plus 1	Interest only on last day of month, principal due in full 3/5/17	Second mortgage on Park St. building	100,000†	50,000‡ 2/29/13	–	200,000†	12/31/13		Prime rate was 8% to 9% during the year
Gigantic Building & Loan Association*	12%	$5,000 principal plus interest due on 5th of month, due in full 12/31/12	First mortgage on Park St. building	720,000†	–	60,000‡‡	660,000††	12/5/13	5,642§§	Reclassification entry for current portion proposed (See RJE-3)
J. Lott, majority stockholder*	0%	Due in full 12/31/14	Unsecured	300,000†	–	100,000‖‖ 12/31/13	200,000††	–	–	Borrowed additional $100,000 from J. Lott on 1/7/12
				$1,170,000†††	$350,000†††	$260,000 12/31/13 †††	$ 1,310,000 †††		$8,142*** †††	

Interest costs from long-term debt

Interest expense for year	$ 281,333***
Average loan balance outstanding	$1,406,667§§

Five-year maturities (for disclosure purposes)

Year-end 12/31/14	$ 60,000
12/31/15	260,000
12/31/16	260,000
12/31/17	310,000
12/31/18	60,000
Thereafter	360,000
	$1,310,000
	†††

†† Readded, foots correctly
† Confirmed without exception, W/P K-2
‖ Confirmed with exception, W/P K-3
** Does not recompute correctly
‡ Agreed to loan agreement, validated bank deposit ticket, and board of directors' authorization, W/P W-7
‡‡ Agreed to canceled checks and lender's monthly statements
‖‖ Agreed to cash disbursements journal and canceled check dated 12/31/13, clearing 1/8/14
*** Traced to working trial balance
† Agreed to 12/31/12 working papers
* Agreed interest rate, term, and collateral to copy of note and loan agreement
§ Agreed to canceled check and board of directors' authorization, W/P W-7

Overall Conclusions
Long-term debt, accrued interest payable, and interest expense are correct and complete at 12/31/13.

FRAUD

PROFESSIONAL SKEPTICISM

13-63 **DELPHI CORPORATION** **LO 2, 3, 4, 6, 8** Refer to the *Professional Judgment in Context* feature "Deficiencies in Auditing Debt Obligations and Stockholders' Equity Accounts: Insights from SEC Releases" and review the panel related to Delphi Corporation. Answer the following questions:

a. What risks of material misstatement were present in the case?
b. What are the auditor's responsibilities related to auditing retained earnings? What procedures should the auditor have performed?
c. Identify ways in which the audit team appeared to have a lack of appropriate professional skepticism.

14

Activities Required in Completing a Quality Audit

CHAPTER OVERVIEW AND LEARNING OBJECTIVES

Auditors must accomplish certain tasks prior to completing the audit, each designed to help assure that the audit has been conducted in a quality manner and that the ultimate audit opinion is appropriate. These activities fall into three general categories: (1) review activities, (2) communications with the audit committee and management, and (3) issues relating to audit firm portfolio management (client acceptance and continuance decisions), audit partner rotation, and audit firm rotation. In terms of the audit opinion formulation process, this chapter focuses on Phases I and V—making client acceptance and continuance decisions and completing the audit.

Through studying this chapter, you will be able to achieve these learning objectives:

通过本章的学习，你将能够实现以下学习目标：

1. Review, summarize, and resolve detected misstatements and identified control deficiencies.
   复核、总结和解决已经发现的错报和已经识别的控制缺陷。

2. Review and assess the appropriateness of the client's accounting for and disclosure of loss contingencies.
   复核和评估客户对或有损失说明和披露的适当性。

3. Review and assess the appropriateness of the client's significant accounting estimates.
   复核和评估客户重要会计估计的适当性。

4. Review the adequacy of disclosures.
   复核披露的充分性。

5. Review and assess the implications of noncompliance with laws and regulations.
   复核和评估不遵循法律和法规的潜在影响。

6. Review the appropriateness of the going-concern assumption using relevant professional guidance.
   利用有关的专业指导复核持续经营假设的适当性。

7. Perform final analytical review procedures.
   实施最终的分析性复核程序。

8. Review management representations in certifications required under the Sarbanes-Oxley Act (for public clients) and describe the contents of a management representation letter.
   复核《萨班斯—奥克斯利法案》(对公众)要求认证的管理层声明，描述管理层声明书的内容。

9. Review subsequent events that occur after the balance sheet date and assess proper treatment.
   复核期后事项，评估合适的处理方式。

10. Determine how to address situations in which omitted audit procedures come to the auditor's attention after the audit report has been issued.
    确定如何解决在出具审计报告后发现遗漏审计程序的情形。

11. Assess the adequacy of supervision and perform an engagement quality review.
    评估监管的充分性，实施项目质量控制复核。

12. Identify issues to communicate to the audit committee.
    识别应与审计委员会沟通的问题。

13. Identify issues to communicate to management via a management letter.
    通过管理建议书识别应与管理层沟通的问题。

14. Describe the process by which audit firms make client acceptance and continuance decisions.
    描述会计师事务所做出客户接受与保留决策的过程。

15. Identify the requirements concerning mandatory partner rotation and mandatory audit firm rotation for publicly traded audit clients.
    对于公开上市的审计客户，识别强制审计合伙人变更和强制会计师事务所变更的要求。

16. Apply the frameworks for professional decision making and ethical decision making to issues involved in completing the audit.
    运用职业决策和职业道德决策框架解决涉及完成审计的问题。

THE AUDIT OPINION FORMULATION PROCESS

I. Making Client Acceptance and Continuance Decisions **Chapter 14**	II. Performing Risk Assessment **Chapters 3, 7 and 9–13**	III. Obtaining Evidence about Internal Control Operating Effectiveness **Chapters 8–13 and 16**	IV. Obtaining Substantive Evidence about Accounts, Disclosures and Assertions **Chapters 8–13 and 16**	V. Completing the Audit and Making Reporting Decisions **Chapters 14 and 15**

The Auditing Profession, the Risk of Fraud and Mechanisms to Address Fraud: Regulation, Corporate Governance, and Audit Quality **Chapters 1 and 2**	Professional Liability and the Need for Quality Auditor Judgments and Ethical Decisions **Chapter 4**

The Audit Opinion Formulation Process and A Framework for Obtaining Audit Evidence
Chapters 5 and 6

PROFESSIONAL JUDGMENT IN CONTEXT

A Case of Poor Review Quality and Improper Professional Conduct

Stephen Nardi, the Practice Office Assurance Director for BDO's Philadelphia office, was responsible for providing technical guidance to other partners and managers, coordinating the office's quality control procedures, overseeing personnel assignments to engagements, supervising managers in the office, and making promotion decisions. During fall 2004, Nardi assigned an audit manager to the audit of Hemispherx Biopharma Incorporated. Shortly after the manager completed the planning phase of the engagement, Nardi directed her to cease work on the Hemispherx audit and to begin work on another public company audit engagement because the Philadelphia office was, at the time, very short-staffed. The audit senior on the Hemispherx audit completed the remainder of the work without supervision or review by the manager. Nardi signed the audit opinion, but no one reviewed the final audit workpapers, and the manager did not sign the work papers to indicate that she had performed the required review procedures.

In late spring 2005, Nardi was informed that BDO would perform an internal inspection of certain Philadelphia office engagements during August 2005, which was a normal part of the firm's internal quality control process. On Thursday,

August 11, 2005, Nardi learned that the Hemispherx audit had been selected for inspection by BDO's internal quality control review team. Over the following weekend, Nardi directed one of his subordinates to examine the Hemispherx workpapers, and the subordinate informed Nardi that there were no initials or signatures on the workpapers to indicate that the audit had been reviewed. The manager had been on vacation the previous week and she arrived back at the office on Monday, August 15, 2005, which was the first day of the internal quality control review. Soon after arriving, Nardi entered her office and demanded that she initial and sign the workpapers so that it would appear to the review team that she had, in fact, performed the review of the workpapers earlier in the spring. At first, the manager protested and refused to sign. However, Nardi ultimately convinced her to sign the workpapers, and she entered the signatures and used dates that would give the impression that she had performed the review in the spring prior to the issuance of the audit report. It is unclear how the PCAOB learned of the deception, but ultimately the PCAOB barred Nardi from performing audits of public companies for at least one year.

For further details on this case, see PCAOB Release No. 105-2007-008.
As you read through this chapter, consider the following questions:

• During the conduct of the audit engagement, reviews of work performed by lower-level staff are necessary to be sure that necessary audit steps have been completed and that they have been completed competently. Toward the end of the audit, what other types of reviews should be conducted? (LO 1, 2, 3, 4, 5, 6, 7, 8, 9, 10, 11)

• Why are engagement quality reviews important? (LO 11)
• Why were Nardi's actions harmful to BDO and to the Hemispherx audit? (LO 11, 16)
• What was the ethical dilemma faced by the manager? (LO 16)
• What alternative courses of action could Nardi have taken when he discovered that the engagement had not been reviewed and that it was about to be inspected during the engagement quality review? (LO 10, 11, 16)

复核活动 | Review Activities

LO 1 Review, summarize, and resolve detected misstatements and identified control deficiencies.

复核、总结和解决已发现的错报

Review activities towards the end of the audit are quite varied. In the following sections, we describe these activities, which relate to Learning Objectives 1 through 11. These activities are critical because they provide one last opportunity for the auditor to make adjustments to the financial statements or to the audit process so that the ultimate audit opinion is appropriate.

Reviewing, Summarizing, and Resolving Detected Misstatements

The auditor needs to summarize misstatements found during the audit to determine whether they are material and need to be recorded and corrected. A misstatement may be a difference between the amount reported in the financial statements versus what should be reported under generally accepted accounting principles (GAAP), or the omission of an amount that should be disclosed in accordance with GAAP. Misstatements are categorized as known misstatements, projected misstatements, and judgmental misstatements. **Known misstatements** are those that have been specifically identified and about which there is no doubt; known misstatements are also referred to as **factual misstatements**. **Projected misstatements** are those that are the auditor's best estimate of the misstatements in a given population, and that are a projection of the misstatements identified in an audit sample to the entire population from which the sample was drawn. **Judgmental misstatements** are those that arise from differences in judgments of management concerning accounting estimates that the auditor considers unreasonable, or the selection or application of accounting policies that the auditor considers inappropriate.

判断错报
(judgmental misstatements)
是注册会计师和管理层对会计估计值的判断差异以及对会计政策选择的判断差异。当注册会计师认为管理层做出的会计估计不合理，或者选择和运用的会计政策不恰当时，就会导致注册会计师与管理层之间的判断差异。

Misstatements are likely to be detected that individually are not material, and the auditor may temporarily pass on asking the client to make those adjustments. Those misstatements should not be forgotten, however. Most audit firms use a schedule to accumulate the known and projected misstatements and the carryover effects of prior-year uncorrected misstatements. See Exhibit 14.1 for an example of a summary of possible adjustments related to known misstatements. At the end of the audit, management and the auditor discuss which possible adjustments will be booked, that is, corrected in the financial statements, and which will be waived, that is, left uncorrected. Only immaterial misstatements may be waived.

In Exhibit 14.1, the first adjustment reflects a pricing error detected by confirming a sample of receivables. The known misstatement is $972, as shown in the first section of the schedule. However, when projected to the population, the projected misstatement for the unknown and unexamined part of the population was $13,493, as shown in the second section of the schedule. If these were corrected, both sales and accounts receivable would be reduced by $14,465 ($972 + $13,493), resulting in a reduction of pretax

EXHIBIT **14.1**	Summary of Possible Adjustments

	Debit (Credit)					
	Assets		Liabilities		Retained	
W/P Account Description	Current	Noncurrent	Current	Noncurrent	Earnings	Net Earnings
Uncorrected Known Misstatements						
Sales						972
Accounts receivable	(972)					
Misstatement from A/R confirmations ($972 known misstatement and $13,493 additional projected misstatement)						
Accounts payable			1,500			
Cash	(1,500)					
Unrecorded check # 14,389						
Projected Misstatements						
Sales						
Accounts receivable	(13,493)					13,493
Projected pricing misstatements from sample						
Carryover Effect of Prior Year Misstatements						
Retained earnings					6,900	
Salary expense						(6,900)
Under accrual of prior year's salaries						
Subtotal: income before taxes						7,565
Tax Adjustment						
Income taxes payable ((13,493+972) × 0.34)			4,918			
Income tax expense (7,565 × 0.34)						(2,572)
Retained earnings (6,900 × 0.34)					(2,346)	
Total Misstatements	(15,965)	0	6,418	0	4,554	4,993
Balance from trial balance	19,073,000	1,997,000	(3,346,000)	(13,048,000)	(4,676,000)	1,678,000
Total misstatement as % of balance	0.08%	0.0%	0.19%	0.0%	0.1%	0.3%

Conclusion: In my opinion, the total likely misstatements are not material to the financial statements taken as a whole. The projected misstatements are quantitatively immaterial and do not reflect material weaknesses in internal control. Therefore, no adjustments are required, nor is any additional audit work needed for these account balances.

Marginal tax rate: 34%

PREPARED BY:	KMJ	DATE	10-17-13
REVIEWED BY:	AAG	DATE	10-17-13

earnings and current assets. The second adjustment involves an unrecorded check for $1,500. The third adjustment involves the carryover effects of understating last year's accrued salaries and salary expense ($6,900). Because the carryover effect is to overstate this year's salary expense, the correction is shown as a reduction in the current year's salary expense, thereby resulting in an increase in pretax earnings and a reduction in the beginning balance of retained earnings.

The income-tax effects are then entered into the schedule to show the total effects of correcting these misstatements. Near the end of the audit, these possible adjustments should be reviewed in the aggregate to determine whether the combined effect is material. The auditor compares the total misstatements (the sum of known and projected misstatements) to each significant segment of the financial statements, such as total current assets, total noncurrent assets, total current liabilities, total noncurrent liabilities, owners' equity, and pretax income, to determine if they are, in aggregate, material to the financial statements. The total misstatement as a percentage of these segments is clearly immaterial, and that conclusion is noted in the work paper. The materiality of a misstatement is based not only on the quantitative amount of the misstatement—the auditor should also consider the nature of the misstatement to determine if there are qualitative features that would make it material. For example, if the misstatement reflects negatively on management, or if correcting the misstatement would have the effect of changing a positive earnings trend to a negative earnings trend.

Management's incentives may bias their willingness to book, or correct, these detected misstatements. For example, in some cases detected misstatements are material, and if management wishes to show higher net income, they may argue with the auditor against correcting an income-reducing misstatement. In such a situation, the auditor might feel some pressure to acquiesce to management's demands in order to preserve a harmonious working relationship. It is in these situations in which audit firm culture, an important driver of audit quality, is important. It is critical that the auditor is confident that the audit firm will support a decision insisting that management correct a misstatement, even if management does not want to do so. Thus, audit firm culture that emphasizes doing the right thing encourages auditors to take sufficient time to deal with difficult issues. A culture that emphasizes that the audit firm's long-term reputation is more important than the immediate satisfaction of client preferences encourages quality actions by its auditors. Likewise, a culture that encourages auditors to seek consultation with other members of the audit firm helps ensure that the auditor does not feel isolated in making difficult decisions; this is critical when the auditor is pressured by inappropriate or aggressive client behavior regarding detected misstatements. The *Auditing in Practice* feature, "The PCAOB Position on Management Bias in Correcting Detected Misstatements," provides insight into management bias in the correction of misstatements.

Additional Considerations for an Integrated Audit In an integrated audit, the auditor assesses whether the financial statement misstatements identified during the audit were the result of significant deficiencies or material weaknesses in internal control. Recall that if one or more material weaknesses exist, the auditor needs to issue an adverse opinion on internal control over financial reporting.

Throughout the audit, the auditor evaluates the severity of each individual control deficiency to determine whether that deficiency is a material weakness. However, deficiencies less severe than material weaknesses should not be forgotten, but instead are accumulated on a summary work sheet. At the end of the engagement, the auditor assesses whether the combination of identified deficiencies results in a material weakness. The auditor should

The PCAOB Position on Management Bias in Correcting Detected Misstatements

The PCAOB's AS 14 provides important insight that auditors must consider as they decide whether management's refusal to correct a detected misstatement is indicative of intentional bias. The PCAOB notes that the following are forms of management bias in this setting:

> The selective correction of misstatements brought to management's attention during the audit (for example, correcting misstatements that have the effect of increasing reported earnings but not correcting misstatements that have the effect of decreasing reported earnings).
>
> The identification by management of additional adjusting entries that offset misstatements accumulated by the auditor. If such adjusting entries are identified, the auditor should perform procedures to determine why the underlying

misstatements were not identified previously and evaluate the implications on the integrity of management and the auditor's risk assessments, including fraud risk assessments. The auditor also should perform additional procedures as necessary to address the risk of further undetected misstatement. (AS 14, paragraph 25).

If the auditor identifies this type of management bias in the resolution of misstatements, the auditor should determine whether the bias, along with its effect, on the overall financial statements, is material. In addition, this type of management bias should lead auditors to reevaluate their risk assessments, particularly those related to management integrity and the risk of fraud. We further discuss the more complex issues related to the resolution of detected misstatements and the book or waive decision in Chapter 16.

---

determine whether individual control deficiencies that affect the same significant account or disclosure, or relevant assertion collectively result in a material weakness. Consider a scenario where an auditor identified several control deficiencies in the revenue cycle. When considered individually, none of the deficiencies were considered to be material weaknesses. However, multiple deficiencies in the same cycle increase the likelihood of misstatement in that cycle, and may, in combination, constitute a material weakness. The auditor needs to complete this evaluation before determining the appropriate opinion on internal control.

Reviewing Contingencies

In Accounting Standards Codification (ASC) 450 (formerly Statement of Financial Accounting Standard (SFAS) No. 5, "Accounting for Contingencies"), the Financial Accounting Standards Board (FASB) provides the standard for accruing and disclosing three categories of potential losses that can be reasonably estimated. Those categories reflect the contingent (not known for sure) nature of those losses and the guiding criteria are organized around probability of outcomes classified as (1) probable, (2) reasonably possible, and (3) remote. ASC 450 requires the accrual and disclosure of contingent losses that can be both reasonably estimated and that are probable. It also requires the disclosure of a contingent loss if there is at least a reasonable possibility that a loss may have been incurred and either an accrual has not been made or an exposure exists that is greater than the amount accrued. Examples of loss contingencies include the following:

复核或有事项

LO 2 Review and assess the appropriateness of the client's accounting for and disclosure of loss contingencies.

- Threat of expropriation of assets in a foreign country
- Litigation, claims, and assessments
- Guarantees of debts of others

Contingent Liabilities at British Petroleum

In July 2010, BP released its second quarter 2010 earnings report. The report discussed the risks associated with the ongoing events and cleanup effort in the Gulf of Mexico due to the oil spill associated with BP. It also included an income statement with a $32 billion pretax charge and a notation that "second quarter and first half 2010 include a charge of $32,192 million in production and manufacturing expenses, and a credit of $10,003 million in taxation in relation to the Gulf of Mexico oil spill." In conducting the annual audit, BP's auditors should have obtained assurance that the contingency in connection with the oil spill was accurately reported and disclosed.

- Obligations of banks under standby letters of credit
- Agreements to repurchase receivables that have been sold
- Purchase and sale commitments

Responsibilities Related to Contingencies

Management is responsible for designing and maintaining policies and procedures to identify, evaluate, and account for contingencies. Auditors are responsible for determining that the client has properly identified, accounted for, and disclosed material contingencies. The *Auditing in Practice* feature, "Contingent Liabilities at British Petroleum," provides an example of the type of situation requiring disclosure of a contingent liability.

Sources of Audit Evidence of Contingencies

The primary source of evidence concerning contingencies is the client's management. The auditor should obtain the following from management:

- A description and evaluation of contingencies that existed at the balance sheet date or that arose prior to the end of the fieldwork, and for which matters were referred to legal counsel, including correspondence and invoices from lawyers
- Assurance that the accounting and disclosure requirements concerning contingent liabilities have been met
- Information about major contracts in which contingencies may be present, such as the sale of receivables
- Documentation of communication with internal and external legal counsel of the client
- Documentation of contingent liabilities contained in corporate minutes, correspondence from governmental agencies, and bank confirmations

Letter of Audit Inquiry The primary source of corroborative evidence concerning litigation, claims, and assessments is the client's legal counsel. The auditor should ask the client to send a **letter of audit inquiry** to its legal counsel asking counsel to confirm information about asserted claims and those claims that are probable of assertion. Attorneys are hesitant to provide much information to auditors because their communications with clients are usually privileged. As a result, the American Bar Association and the AICPA have agreed that the letter of audit inquiry should include the following:

- Identification of the company, its subsidiaries, and the date of the audit
- Management's list (or a request by management that the lawyer prepare a list) that describes and evaluates the contingencies to which the lawyer has devoted substantial attention

- A request that the lawyer furnish the auditor with the following:
  1. A comment on the completeness of management's list and evaluations
  2. For each contingency:
     a. A description of the nature of the matter, the progress to date, and the action the company intends to take
     b. An evaluation of the likelihood of an unfavorable outcome and an estimate of the potential loss or range of loss
  3. Any limitations on the lawyer's response, such as not devoting substantial attention to the item or that the amounts are not material

Legal counsel should be instructed by the client to respond directly to the auditors. The auditor and client should agree on what is material for this purpose. If a lawyer refuses to furnish the requested information, it is considered a scope limitation and the auditor would not be able to issue an unqualified audit opinion (see discussion on this issue in Chapter 15).

Reviewing Significant Estimates

Financial statement balances include many judgmental estimates, including the following:

- Fair value of many assets
- Net realizable values of inventory and receivables
- Property and casualty insurance loss reserves
- Revenues from contracts accounted for by the percentage-of-completion method
- Warranty expenses and associated liabilities
- Depreciation and amortization methods
- Impairment of depreciable assets and goodwill
- Useful lives and residual values of productive facilities, natural resources and intangibles
- Valuation and classification of financial instruments, pensions, and other postretirement benefits
- Compensation in stock option plans

Auditors need to take special care to review these types of significant estimates because management sometimes tries to manage or smooth earnings by using estimates to create hidden reserves in unusually good years that can be used in years when real profits do not meet expectations. Alternatively, management sometimes underestimates liabilities or impairment of asset values to achieve reported earning goals in years when real profits do not meet expectations. Auditors should be alert to period-end adjusting journal entries that relate to accounts with significant estimates. Ultimately, the auditor is responsible for providing reasonable assurance that:

- The estimates are reasonable.
- The estimates are presented in conformity with GAAP.
- The disclosure about estimates is adequate.

Accounting estimates are based on management's knowledge and experience of past and current events, as well as its assumptions about conditions that it expects to exist and courses of action it expects to take. Estimates are based on both subjective and objective factors; there is potential for bias in both. Of course, the auditor evaluates estimates in these accounts during the conduct of the audit. However, the auditor should also take time at the end of the audit to consider whether, taken together, the estimates made in these accounts are reasonable; that is, that they do not result in overly conservative or overly aggressive financial reporting. Events or transactions occurring after the balance sheet date, but before the audit report date, can be useful in identifying and evaluating the reasonableness of estimates.

复核重要的估计

L0 3 Review and assess the appropriateness of the client's significant accounting estimates.

由于管理层可能管理会计估计或者平滑盈余，所以注册会计师需要特别关注重要的会计估计是否是合理的，会计估计的披露是否遵循公认会计原则的要求，以及披露是否充分。

Examples of these events include collection of receivables, sale of inventory or financial instruments, and the purchase of inventory under a purchase commitment for which an estimated loss was or should have been accrued.

In evaluating the reasonableness of an estimate, the auditor normally concentrates on key factors and assumptions that are:

- Significant to the accounting estimate
- Sensitive to variations
- Deviations from historical patterns
- Subjective and susceptible to misstatement and bias
- Inconsistent with current economic trends

The auditor should consider the historical experience of the client in making past estimates. However, changes in facts, circumstances, or the client's procedures may cause factors different from those considered in the past to become significant to the estimate. For example, economic changes may occur that increase or decrease the ability of customers to make timely payments, or the client may have changed its credit policies, providing for a longer or shorter time before payment is due. Auditors may be reluctant to challenge management estimates that result in current-period reductions in income (such as increases in bad debt expense) and associated increases in reserve accounts (such as allowance for doubtful accounts). However, it is important for auditors to remember that management may try to tap into these reserves in the future to improve an otherwise weak level of earnings at that time. Ultimately, the auditor should review management's judgments and decisions to determine whether possible management bias affected the estimation process. The *Auditing in Practice* feature, "PCAOB Fines Ernst & Young for an Issue

PCAOB Fines Ernst & Young for an Issue Involving Accounting Estimates

AUDITING IN PRACTICE

Medicis Pharmaceutical Corporation sells pharmaceutical products that have time-sensitive expiration dates. Medicis' return policy gave customers the right to return a product anywhere from four months before the expiration date up to 12 months after the expiration date. Medicis' revenue recognition policy violated GAAP because the policy provided for establishing the reserve for returned products at the original sales price rather than at replacement cost. In 2005, for example, if Medicis had estimated the reserve at replacement cost rather than sales price, the company's reserve and related expense would have increased over $54 million. Medicis' management convinced the audit partners at Ernst & Young that their revenue recognition policy was acceptable under GAAP because of an exception in the relevant financial accounting standard.

The PCAOB took issue with Ernst & Young's acceptance of Medicis' revenue recognition policy and its related estimate of product returns. Further, the PCAOB took issue with Ernst & Young's

willingness to agree with Medicis' lack of disclosure of its policies in this regard. The improper accounting and disclosure existed for several years, and at one point Ernst & Young national-level consultation experts suggested to the partners involved in the Medicis audit that they were incorrect in allowing Medicis' accounting and disclosure policy. Still, Ernst & Young auditors signed the audit report with an unqualified opinion.

Ultimately, the issue was investigated, and on November 10, 2008, Medicis filed restated financial statements for the years ending December 31, 2005, 2006, and 2007. In the restatement, Medicis increased the returns reserve by $94.6 million (585%), $52.1 million (148%) and $58.9 million (600%) as of 2005, 2006, and 2007, respectively. The PCAOB imposed a penalty of $2,000,000 on Ernst & Young and penalties ranging from $25,000 to $50,000 on the individual partners on the Medicis engagement.

For further details on this case, see PCAOB Release No. 105-2012-001.

Involving Accounting Estimates," provides an example of a situation in which auditors failed to exercise professional skepticism in their audit of an important accounting estimate.

Reviewing the Adequacy of Disclosures

The auditor's report covers the basic financial statements, which include the balance sheet, income statement, statement of cash flows, a statement of changes in stockholders' equity or retained earnings, and the related notes. If the auditor determines that informative disclosures are not reasonably adequate, the auditor must identify that fact in the auditor's report. Disclosures can be made on the face of the financial statements (in the form of classifications or parenthetical notations), or they can be made in the notes to the statements. See the *Auditing in Practice* feature, "Related Party Disclosures at OAO Gazprom," for an example of disclosures in the footnotes

复核披露的充分性

LO 4 Review the adequacy of disclosures.

Related Party Disclosures at OAO Gazprom   AUDITING IN PRACTICE

OAO Gazprom produces natural gas and is the largest company in Russia. The company's 2010 International Financial Reporting Standards (IFRS)-based disclosures to the financial statements state the following with respect to related parties:

> "For the purpose of these consolidated financial statements, parties are considered to be related if one party has the ability to control the other party or exercise significant influence over the other party in making financial and operational decisions as defined in IAS 24 'Related Party Disclosures'. Related parties may enter into transactions which unrelated parties might not, and transactions between related parties may not be effected on the same terms, conditions, and amounts as transactions between unrelated parties."

The disclosures go on to state that:

> "The Government of the Russian Federation is the ultimate controlling party of OAO Gazprom and has a controlling interest (including both direct and indirect ownership) of over 50% in OAO Gazprom" and that "As a condition of privatization in 1992, the Government imposed an obligation on the Group to provide an uninterrupted supply of gas to customers in the Russian Federation at government controlled prices."

Of interest, however, is the relative lack of detail in terms of specific related parties or specific related-party transactions that are contained in the notes to the financial statements. This is in contrast to related-party disclosures at companies such as Ford Motor Company, which describe individual Ford family members, their relationships with the company, and the exact nature of their related-party transactions with the company.

PwC found out just how difficult it can be to conduct an audit of a company in the Russian Federation, particularly because of the complex nature of related-party transactions and high-level interrelationships between executives in companies operating in the Federation. Of particular importance, top members of management at OAO Gazprom have friends or relatives that transact in a related-party context with the company. For example, in one transaction, Gazprom sold natural gas to a related company at $2 per cubic meter, and then the related company sold the gas to European customers for more than $40 per cubic meter. In doing so, the related company (and its management owners) essentially siphoned profits out of Gazprom and into their personal accounts. Gazprom entered into a very significant number of such transactions, but PwC did not require the company to disclose them in its audited financial statements. Minority shareholders of Gazprom were very outspoken in their objections to these types of transactions and to PwC's audits of the company. Ultimately, the political pressure on PwC led to Gazprom putting the audit engagement up for bid. In addition, Hermitage Capital filed multiple lawsuits against PwC in 2002 related to the firm's audits of Gazprom. Those lawsuits were ultimately dismissed, and PwC was retained by the Company as its auditor. As of the date of this writing, PwC is still Gazprom's auditor, so the firm appears to have weathered the political storm of the early 2000s.

EXHIBIT **14.2**   Excerpt of IFRS Disclosure Checklist

Disclosure checklists help auditors identify items needing disclosure. Below is an excerpt from Deloitte's International Financial Reporting Standards (IFRS) Checklist (June 2011) related to goodwill disclosures. The checklists are usually organized to first include a question, and to then list the relevant professional guidance. Some of the questions in Deloitte's checklist are:

- "Is the 'aggregate amount of goodwill' presented as a separate line item in the statement of financial position? [ASC 350-20-45-1]
- Is the 'aggregate amount of goodwill impairment losses' presented 'as a separate line item in the income statement before...income from continuing operations (or similar caption) unless a goodwill impairment loss is associated with discontinued operation'? [ASC 350-20-45-2]
- Is 'a goodwill impairment loss' related to a discontinued operation 'included (on a net of tax basis) within the results of discontinued operations'? [ASC 350-20-45-3]
- Are 'changes in the carrying amount of goodwill during the period' disclosed properly showing separately all the items in ASC 350-20-50-1 as applicable? [ASC 350-20-50-1"

and the problems that PwC experienced in conducting an audit of the company. When assessing the adequacy of disclosures, the auditor should have reasonable assurance that:

- Disclosed events and transactions have occurred and pertain to the entity.
- All disclosures that should have been included are included.
- The disclosures are understandable to users.
- The information is disclosed accurately and at appropriate amounts.

The excerpt of an IFRS disclosure checklist in Exhibit 14.2 is an example of a checklist that helps remind the auditor of matters that should be considered for disclosure. The checklist is also a convenient documentation format for evidence that the auditor adequately evaluated the client's disclosures. Of course, there may be items that should be disclosed but that are not covered by the audit firm's checklist. The auditor, therefore, should not blindly follow a checklist, but use good audit judgment when there are unusual circumstances of which the users should be aware.

The auditor should consider matters for disclosure while gathering evidence during the course of the audit, not just at the end of the audit. For example, during the audit of receivables, the auditor should be aware of the need to separately disclose receivables from officers, employees, or other related parties, as well as the pledging of receivables as collateral for a loan. One of the key disclosures is a summary of significant accounting policies used by the company. In evaluating this summary, the auditor is guided by the substantive nature of transactions as well as the evolving nature of business, as opposed to simply reviewing relevant accounting guidance.

Finally, it is important to note that the auditor's report does not specifically cover the statements made by management in the Management Discussion and Analysis (MD&A) section of the annual report. However, auditors routinely review the MD&A to provide reasonable assurance that it does not contain information that is factually inaccurate or inconsistent with the audited portion of the financial statements and accompanying footnotes.

注册会计师对客户违反法律法规行为的责任

LO 5   Review and assess the implications of noncompliance with laws and regulations.

Auditors' Responsibilities Regarding Clients' Noncompliance with Laws and Regulations

Management and those charged with governance must be sure that the entity's operations and financial reporting are conducted in accordance with laws and regulations. **Noncompliance** involves "acts of omission or commission by the entity, either intentional or unintentional, which are contrary to the prevailing laws or regulations" (AU-C 250). Auditors are responsible for obtaining reasonable assurance that the financial statements are free from material misstatements. In responding to this responsibility, auditors should consider the applicable legal and regulatory frameworks that apply to the entity. However, auditing standards recognize that there are inherent limitations in an auditor's ability to detect material misstatements relating to the entity's compliance with laws and regulations. These limitations include:

- Laws and regulations often relate to operational issues within the entity that do not necessarily relate to the financial statements, so the information systems relating to financial reporting may not capture noncompliance.
- Management may act to conceal noncompliance, or may override controls, or may intentionally misrepresent facts to the auditor.
- The legal implications of noncompliance are ultimately a matter for legal authorities to resolve, and are not a matter the auditor can resolve.

In reviewing for potential noncompliance, obtaining an understanding of the entity's internal controls that are designed to achieve proper compliance with laws and regulations is important. If management or those charged with governance do not demonstrate a commitment to internal control over noncompliance, then the auditor should expend additional effort in reviewing for instances of noncompliance. See the *Auditing in Practice* feature, "Triton Energy and Noncompliance with Laws and Regulations," for a historically important case involving noncompliance with the Foreign Corrupt Practices Act of 1977 (FCPA). The FCPA was written to respond to SEC

Triton Energy and Noncompliance with Laws and Regulations

AUDITING IN PRACTICE

Triton Energy engages in the exploration and production of crude oil and natural gas in many areas around the world. Triton has traditionally operated in areas in relatively high-risk, politically unstable areas where larger and better-known producers do not operate. Top Triton Indonesia officials (President, CFO, Commercial Manager, and Controller) were investigated by the SEC for violations of the Foreign Corrupt Practices Act. These violations included:

- Improper payments were made to a middle-man who used the funds to reduce Triton Indonesia's tax liability.
- Improper payments were made to a middle-man who used the funds to ensure a favorable governmental audit.
- Improper payments were made to a middle-man who used the funds to obtain from government officials corporate tax refunds.
- The recording of false journal entries by Triton Indonesia's Commercial Manager and Controller were made to cover up the improper payments.

These improper payments and false journal entries were facilitated because Triton's CEO, Bill Lee, was an aggressive top manager who provided weak tone at the top in terms of his failure to encourage compliance with applicable laws and regulations, failure to discourage improper payments, and failure to implement internal controls to deter improper payments. Triton was ultimately fined $300,000 related to the scandal.

If an auditor becomes aware of violations of law, the auditor should notify the audit committee about the violations, their circumstance, and the effect on the financial statements. Further, the auditor should consider whether risk assessments made prior to knowledge of violations are still appropriate.

For further details on this case, see the SEC's Securities Exchange Act of 1934 Release No. 38343 and Accounting and Auditing Enforcement Release No. 889, February 27, 1997.

investigations in the 1970s revealing that over 400 companies had made questionable or illegal payments of over $300 million to foreign officials, politicians, and political parties. The payments involved bribery of foreign officials to facilitate business operations in their respective foreign countries. The main provisions of the FCPA include:

- No U.S. person or company that has securities listed on U.S. markets may make a payment to a foreign official for the purpose of obtaining or retaining business. This provision is commonly called the anti-bribery provision of the FCPA.
- Companies that have securities listed on U.S. markets must make and keep financial records that accurately and fairly reflect the transactions of the company and must design and maintain an adequate system of internal accounting controls.
- Certain payments to foreign officials are acceptable. These include grease payments, which are payments made to an official to expedite the performance of the duties that the official would already be bound to perform.

评估持续经营假设

LO 6 Review the appropriateness of the going-concern assumption using relevant professional guidance.

2012年11月，美国会计准则委员会规定，评估公司的持续经营能力是公司管理层的责任，注册会计师的责任是评估管理层对持续经营能力评估的适当性。

Evaluating the Going-Concern Assumption

Business failures result from a variety of causes, such as inadequate financing, cash-flow problems, poor management, product obsolescence, natural disasters, loss of a major customer or supplier, and competition. Investors and creditors become upset when a business fails, particularly when it happens shortly after the auditor has issued an unqualified opinion. However, investors need to realize that an audit opinion is not a guarantee that the business is a going concern. Still, auditors are required to evaluate the likelihood of each client continuing as a going concern for a **reasonable period of time**. In addition, in November 2012 the FASB ruled that assessing a company's going concern status is the responsibility of management, and that the auditor's responsibility is to evaluate the appropriateness of that assessment. Exhibit 14.3 highlights the important actions that the auditor takes in making a going-concern assessment.

The going-concern evaluation is based on information obtained from normal audit procedures performed to test management's assertions; no separate procedures are required unless the auditor believes that there is substantial doubt about the client's ability to continue as a going concern. However, because the public expects auditors to evaluate the going-concern assumption, many audit firms use bankruptcy prediction models in analyzing whether a particular client might have a going-concern problem. If there is substantial doubt about the ability of the client to remain a going concern, the auditor identifies and assesses management's plans to overcome the problems. If, after reviewing management's plans, the auditor concludes that substantial doubt about the entity's ability to continue as a going concern has been alleviated, the auditor considers the disclosure of the conditions or events that initially caused the auditor to believe there was substantial doubt. The auditor should consider the possible effects of such conditions or events, and any mitigating factors, including management's plans. Alternatively, if the auditor concludes that substantial doubt about the entity's ability to continue as a going concern for a reasonable period of time remains, the auditor should include an emphasis-of-matter paragraph in the auditor's report to reflect that conclusion. The audit report will use of the phrase *substantial doubt about the entity's ability to continue as a going concern* or similar wording that includes the terms *substantial doubt* and *going concern*. We discuss these report modifications in Chapter 15.

Management often resists a going-concern modification, making the argument that such a qualification will cause investors, lenders, and customers to lose faith in the business and thus cause it to fail. Auditors also may be reluctant to issue a going-concern audit opinion because it can be a self-fulfilling prophecy that the company will, indeed, go bankrupt. In other words, if an audit firm

EXHIBIT **14.3**   Going-Concern Process

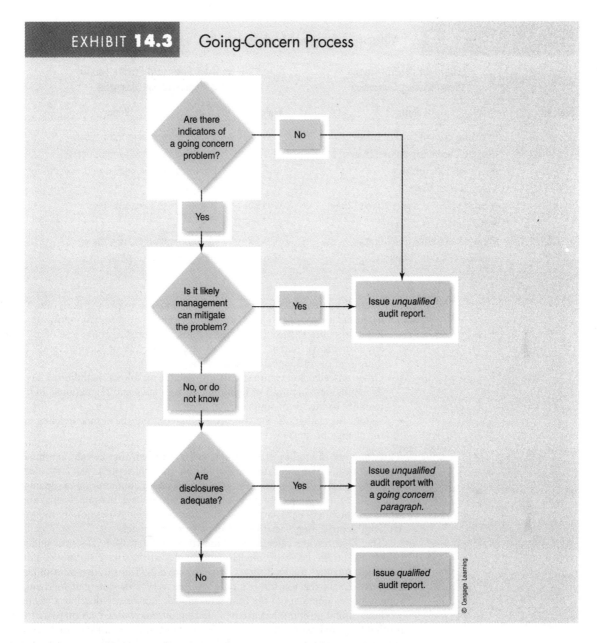

issues a report stating that the company may not be a going concern, lenders and customers may become so worried that they stop lending money or doing business with the company, thereby hastening its demise. In addition, auditors may be reluctant to issue a going concern opinion because it is simply very difficult to know beforehand whether a financially distressed client will actually cease operations or will somehow pull itself away from that outcome.

Indicators of Potential Going-Concern Problems

Auditors must carefully analyze all the factors that indicate a going-concern problem and determine if management has a viable plan to address the problems. Potential indicators of going-concern problems include the following:

- Negative trends, such as recurring losses, working-capital deficiencies, negative cash flows from operating activities, and adverse key financial ratios

EXHIBIT **14.4**   Altman Z-Score Models

Z-Score for Publicly Owned Manufacturing Companies		Z-Score for Public and Private Service and Manufacturing Companies	
Weight	Ratio	Weight	Ratio
1.2 ×	Working capital to total assets	6.56 ×	Working capital to total assets
+ 1.4 ×	Retained earnings to total assets	+ 3.26 ×	Retained earnings to total assets
+ 3.3 ×	Return on total assets	+ 6.72 ×	Earnings before interest and taxes to total assets
+ 0.99 ×	Sales to total assets	+ 1.05 ×	Net worth to total liabilities
+ 0.6 ×	Market value of equity to total debt		
	Interpretation of Z-Score		
< 1.81	High potential for bankruptcy	< 1.1	High potential for bankruptcy
> 2.99	Little potential for bankruptcy	> 2.6	Little potential for bankruptcy

- Internal matters, such as loss of key personnel, employee strikes, out-dated facilities and products, and uneconomic long-term commitments
- External matters, such as new legislation, pending litigation, loss of a key franchise or patent, loss of a principal customer or supplier, and uninsured or underinsured casualty loss
- Other miscellaneous matters, such as default on a loan, inability to pay dividends, restructuring of debt, violation of laws and regulations, and inability to buy from suppliers on credit
- Significant changes in the competitive market and the competitiveness of the client's products

A number of studies of bankruptcies have shown that certain combinations of ratios can indicate the likelihood of bankruptcy. Two Altman Z-scores—a five-ratio model for publicly owned manufacturing companies and a four-ratio model for public or privately owned manufacturing and service companies—are available for auditor use, with newer models available representing variations of these original models.[1]

The Z-scores are calculated as shown in Exhibit 14.4. Z-scores falling below 1.81 in the five-ratio model or below 1.1 in the four-ratio model indicate high potential for bankruptcy. Scores above 2.99 in the five-ratio model or above 2.6 in the four-ratio model indicate very little potential for bankruptcy. For example, using the four-ratio model, a company that has a strong working-capital position, has accumulated significant retained earnings, and is profitable would score above the 2.6 threshold and be unlikely to have a going-concern problem. Although a low Z-score (or a similar score using a different bankruptcy prediction model) does not in itself indicate that the company will fail, it does provide presumptive evidence that there is a going-concern problem. Research has shown that these models are better predictors of problems than are the auditor's qualifications of audit reports.

Mitigating Factors

If the auditor concludes that there may be a going-concern problem, management's plans to overcome this problem should be identified and assessed. Management may plan to sell nonessential assets, borrow money or restructure existing debt, reduce or delay unnecessary expenditures, and/or increase owner

---

[1] E. Altman, *Corporate Financial Distress* (New York: John Wiley & Sons, 1983).

investments. The auditor should identify those factors that are most likely to resolve the problem and gather independent evidence to determine the likely success of such plans. For example, if financial projections are an integral part of the solution, the auditor should ask management to provide that information and the underlying assumptions. The auditor should then consider, and independently test, the adequacy of support for the major assumptions. As another example, if management indicates that their major financial institution is willing to renegotiate the terms of an outstanding loan to provide more favorable terms, the auditor should consider this when evaluating management's recovery plans. Of course, the auditor should confirm the new terms with the bank, through obtaining corroborating evidence directly from the bank rather than relying on management's verbal representations. The auditor should also evaluate the reasonableness of other assumptions made by management, including some of the following:

- Management's assumption about increasing prices or market share should be analyzed in relationship to current industry developments.
- Management's assumptions about cost savings related to a reduction in work force should be recomputed and evaluated to determine if there are hidden costs (such as pension obligations) that were overlooked by management.
- Management's assumptions about selling off assets—either a division or specifically identified assets—should be evaluated in relationship to current market prices.

After considering these factors, the auditor will assess whether management can mitigate the going-concern problem, and reporting decisions will follow based upon that assessment and possible disclosures that may be necessary.

Performing Analytical Review of the Financial Statements

实施财务报表的分析性复核

LO 7 Perform final analytical review procedures.

Analytical procedures help auditors assess the overall presentation of the financial statements. Auditing standards require the use of analytical procedures in the final review phase of the audit to assist in identifying anything unusual in the ending account relationships. At the final review phase of the audit, the audit team analyzes the data from an overall business perspective. The auditors are looking not only at the trends and ratios, but are asking hard questions about whether the company's results make sense in relationship to industry and economic trends. By performing a final analytical review, the audit firm identifies any unusual, unexpected, or unexplained relationships that should be resolved before the issuance of the audit report. The auditor's expectations in final analytical procedures can be less precise than those for substantive analytics, but the same basic four-step process for using analytical procedures still applies: (1) develop an expectation, (2) define when the difference between the auditor's expectation and the client's balance would be considered significant, (3) compute the difference between the auditor's expectation and the client's balance, and (4) follow up on significant differences.

Analytical procedures provide evidence on whether certain relationships make sense in light of the knowledge obtained during the audit. Such procedures may indicate that further audit work needs to be performed before rendering the audit opinion. Ratio analysis, common-size analysis, and analysis of the dollar and percentage changes in each income statement item over the previous year are useful for this purpose. The auditor should have accumulated sufficient appropriate evidence during the audit to explain any unusual changes, such as changes when none are expected, no changes when they are expected, or changes that are not of the expected size or direction. For example, if the client paid more attention to quality control and order processing during the current year, then sales returns and allowances should have decreased as a percentage of sales. As another example, if a client increased its market share by substantially reducing prices for the last three months of the year and undertaking a massive advertising campaign, a decrease in the gross profit margin should be expected. If these expected changes are not reflected in the accounting records, the audit documentation should contain adequate evidence, supplementing the explanations of management to corroborate those explanations. Otherwise, the auditor should investigate more to determine the reason for the discrepancies in the data, as they could represent account balances that are misstated.

Ultimately, analytical procedures conducted during the final review phase of the audit should corroborate conclusions formed during the audit, which enables the auditor to draw conclusions upon which to base the audit opinion. If analytical procedures conducted during the final review phase of the audit identify a previously unrecognized risk of material misstatement, the auditor must go back and revise the original risk assessment and conduct additional procedures to address the risk. The need for additional audit procedures is particularly relevant when management is unable to provide an explanation for the previously unrecognized risk identified through the analytical procedures. See Exhibit 14.5 for an example of the financial data and some relevant ratios for Koss Corporation, including concerns that seem relevant in terms of analytical review of the financial position of the company.

EXHIBIT **14.5** Identifying Risks at Koss Corporation Using Analytical Procedures

The fraud at Koss Corporation perpetrated by the Company's CFO, Sue Sachdeva, occurred during the period 2005–2009. In this Exhibit, you will see the audited financial statements of Koss during that period (prior to restatement). Put yourself in the position of the auditor conducting an analytical review of the financial statements during the final review phase of the 2009 audit. After analyzing the financial results and ratios below and using your knowledge of analytical review procedures, consider the following patterns in the data:

- Cash balances have declined to their lowest level since FYE 2004.
- Sales increased over the period, but have returned to about FYE 2004 levels.
- Cost of goods sold as a percentage of sales has risen sharply over the period, with a particularly significant increase from FYE 2008 to 2009.
- Relatedly, gross profit has decreased sharply over the period, with a particularly significant decrease from FYE 2008 to 2009.
- SG&A as a percentage of sales has risen sharply over the period, with a particularly significant increase from FYE 2008 to 2009.
- Net income as a percentage of sales has decreased sharply over the period, with a particularly significant decrease from FYE 2008 to 2009.
- Accounts receivable as a percentage of sales has remained relatively stable over the period, so there do not appear to be problems in billing or collections.
- Current liabilities as a percentage of sales has remained relatively stable over the period, so there do not appear to be problems in the purchasing cycle.

Account ($ millions)	FYE 2009	FYE 2008	FYE 2007	FYE 2006	FYE 2005	FYE 2004
Net sales	38,185	46,943	46,202	50,892	40,287	40,493
Cost of goods sold	24,917	29,152	28,285	31,095	25,217	24,531
Gross profit	13,267	17,792	17,917	19,796	15,070	15,962
SG&A	10,653	10,792	10,066	10,064	8,544	8,090
Net income	1,977	4,494	5,157	6,222	4,494	5,448
Cash	1,664	3,323	4,188	6,147	5,219	2,111
Accounts receivable	8,680	10,149	7,939	6,820	8,764	9,340

| EXHIBIT **14.5** | Identifying Risks at Koss Corporation Using Analytical Procedures (*continued*) |

Account ($ millions)	FYE 2009	FYE 2008	FYE 2007	FYE 2006	FYE 2005	FYE 2004
Inventory	9,763	9,374	9,924	10,522	7,596	7,315
Net PP&E	4,076	2,746	2,567	3,038	2,994	2,697
Current liabilities	3,619	5,587	4,130	9,149	6,034	3,480
Ratios:						
COGS/Sales	65%	62%	61%	61%	63%	61%
Gross profit %	35%	38%	39%	39%	37%	39%
SG&A/Sales	28%	23%	22%	20%	21%	20%
Net income/Sales	5%	10%	11%	12%	11%	13%
Accts. receiv./Sales	23%	22%	17%	13%	22%	23%
Inventory/Sales	26%	20%	21%	21%	19%	18%
Current liab./Sales	9%	12%	9%	18%	15%	9%

Taken together, these financial data and ratios signal a very significant shift in performance from FYE 2008 to 2009. Concerns that should be investigated by the auditor related to the analytical procedures include:

- Why is cash showing such a decline? What are controls over cash?
- Are costs being inappropriately allocated to cost of goods sold or SG&A? Who has oversight over allocations and journal entries to these accounts? Is that individual adequately supervised?
- Gross margins are usually relatively stable; what is management's explanation for the significant change?
- While sales seem to be slowing, perhaps due to the recession, profitability has declined even more substantially. What is the explanation for this unexpected relationship?

Of course, hindsight makes these trends appear consistent with the fraud that was ultimately discovered. It is unclear why the audit team and engagement partner did not exercise professional skepticism to better understand these puzzling analytics. Ultimately, the fraud was exposed when American Express employees recognized that Sachdeva was paying her credit card bills with large wire transfers from a Koss bank account. They alerted Koss CEO, Michael Koss, and at that point the FBI confronted Sachdeva. So, no individual charged with governance at Koss appears to have ever seriously challenged the declining and unusual financial results at Koss. In fact, because of situations like this, the PCAOB issued *Staff Audit Practice Alert No. 10: Maintaining and Applying Professional Skepticism in Audits* on December 4, 2012 urging auditors to be vigilant in exercising appropriate professional skepticism.

Evaluating Management Representations

The auditor will evaluate management representations made in certifications required under the Sarbanes-Oxley Act of 2002 (SOX) and certifications made in the management representation letter.

Certifications Required under SOX for Public Companies

Section 302 of the Sarbanes-Oxley Act requires the signing officers of publicly traded companies (usually the CEO and CFO) to certify, among other things, that the financial statements are fairly presented in accordance with generally accepted accounting principles. Most CEOs and CFOs have internal processes to help them meet their primary responsibility for the reliability of the financial statements. In a quality audit, the auditor reviews management's processes for certification to provide reasonable assurance that those processes are adequate and that they can be relied upon. Exhibit 14.6 provides an excerpt of a management certification at Groupon. An interesting point to note is the discussion about management's responsibility regarding internal controls, along with the subsequent 8-K disclosure of a restatement and notification that Groupon has a material weakness in its internal controls.

评估管理层声明

LO 8 Review management representations in certifications required under the Sarbanes-Oxley Act (for public clients) and describe the contents of a management representation letter.

EXHIBIT **14.6**	Management Certifications at Groupon

GROUPON CERTIFICATION OF CHIEF EXECUTIVE OFFICER

I, Andrew D. Mason, certify that:

1. I have reviewed this Annual Report on Form 10-K of Groupon, Inc.;
2. Based on my knowledge, this report does not contain any untrue statement of a material fact or omit to state a material fact necessary to make the statement made, in light of the circumstances under which such statements were made, not misleading, with respect to the periods covered by this report;
3. Based on my knowledge, the financial statements, and other financial information included in this report, fairly represent in all material respects the financial condition, results of operations and cash flows of the registrant as of, and for, the periods presented in this report;
4. The registrant's other certifying officer and I are responsible for establishing and maintaining disclosure controls and procedures (as defined in Exchange Act Rules 13a-15(e) and 15d-15(e)) for the registrant and have:
   (a) Designed such disclosure controls and procedures, or caused such disclosure controls and procedures to be designed under our supervision, to ensure that material information relating to the registrant, including its consolidated subsidiaries, is made known to us by others within those entities, particularly during the period in which this report is being prepared;
   (b) [Omitted pursuant to Exchange Act Rules 13a-14(a) and 15d-15(a).]
   (c) Evaluated the effectiveness of the registrant's disclosure controls and procedures and presented in this report our conclusions about the effectiveness of the disclosure controls and procedures, as of the end of the period covered by this report based on such evaluation; and
   (d) Disclosed in this report any change in the registrant's internal control over financial reporting that occurred during the registrant's most recent fiscal quarter (the registrant's fourth fiscal quarter in the case of an annual report) that has materially affected, or is reasonably likely to materially affect, the registrant's internal control over financial reporting; and
5. The registrant's other certifying officer(s) and I have disclosed, based on our most recent evaluation of internal control over financial reporting, to the registrant's auditors and the audit committee of the registrant's board of directors (or persons performing the equivalent functions):
   (a) All significant deficiencies and material weaknesses in the design or operation of internal control over financial reporting which are reasonably likely to adversely affect the registrant's ability to record, process, summarize and report financial information; and
   (b) Any fraud, whether or not material, that involves management or other employees who have a significant role in the registrant's internal control over financial reporting.

Date: March 30, 2012   /s/ Andrew D. Mason

Andrew D. Mason
Chief Executive Officer

Of particular interest, on the same date, Groupon issued an 8-K form announcing a restatement of its fourth quarter 2011 financial results. In the 8-K, management stated the following:

> In conjunction with the completion of the audit of Groupon's financial statements for the year ended December 31, 2011 by its independent auditor, Ernst & Young LLP, the Company included a statement of a material weakness in its internal controls over its financial statement close process in its Annual Report on Form 10-K for year ended December 31, 2011. The Company has been working for several months with another global accounting firm in preparation for reporting on the effectiveness of its internal controls by the end of 2012, as required following Groupon's initial public offering last year. The Company continues to implement process improvement initiatives and augment its staffing, and is expanding the accounting firm's engagement scope to address the underlying causes of the material weakness.

Taken together, these two disclosures alert users that Groupon management is (a) responsible for maintaining internal controls for the company, and (b) has fallen short of its responsibility. Not surprisingly, Groupon's stock price fell 17% upon the release of the restatement news.

Management Representation Letter

Auditors should obtain a **management representation letter** at the end of each audit. The letter is part of audit evidence, but is not a substitute for audit procedures that are performed to corroborate the information contained in the letter. The purposes of the letter are to help promote audit quality by doing the following:

- Reminding management of its responsibility for the financial statements
- Confirming oral responses obtained by the auditor earlier in the audit and the continuing appropriateness of those responses
- Reducing the possibility of misunderstanding concerning the matters that are the subject of the representations

The letter is prepared on the client's letterhead, is addressed to the auditor, and should be signed by the chief executive officer and the chief financial officer. The auditor usually prepares the letter for the client to read and sign. The contents depend on the circumstances of the audit and the nature and basis of presentation of the financial statements. It may be limited to matters that are considered material to the financial statements and should include representations about known fraud involving management or employees. If management refuses to sign the representation letter, it means that they are not willing to stand by their verbal representations when asked to do so in writing; in short, it would imply that management was being untruthful in verbal representations. Management's refusal to sign the management representation letter is considered a scope limitation sufficient to preclude the issuance of an unqualified opinion; see Chapter 15 for further details. Exhibit 14.7 contains an example management representation letter from AU-C 580.

管理层声明书
(management representation letter)
是来自被审计单位内部的一种证据，不具有独立性，证明力较弱，其本身不能构成充分、适当的审计证据，也不能作为发表审计意见的基础。注册会计师不应以管理层声明书替代能够合理预期获取的其他审计证据。

EXHIBIT 14.7 | Management Representation Letter Example from AU-C 580 "Management Representations"

(Entity Letterhead)

(To Auditor) (Date)

This representation letter is provided in connection with your audit of the financial statements of ABC Company, which comprise the balance sheet as of December 31, 20XX, and the related statements of income, changes in stockholders' equity, and cash flows for the year then ended, and the related notes to the financial statements, for the purpose of expressing an opinion on whether the financial statements are presented fairly, in all material respects, in accordance with accounting principles generally accepted in the United States (U.S. GAAP).

Certain representations in this letter are described as being limited to matters that are material. Items are considered material, regardless of size, if they involve an omission or misstatement of accounting information that, in the light of surrounding circumstances, makes it probable that the judgment of a reasonable person relying on the information would be changed or influenced by the omission or misstatement.

Except where otherwise stated below, immaterial matters less than $[*insert amount*] collectively are not considered to be exceptions that require disclosure for the purpose of the following representations. This amount is not necessarily indicative of amounts that would require adjustment to or disclosure in the financial statements.

We confirm that to the best of our knowledge and belief, having made such inquiries as we considered necessary for the purpose of appropriately informing ourselves [as of (date of auditor's report),]:

Financial Statements

- We have fulfilled our responsibilities, as set out in the terms of the audit engagement dated [*insert date*], for the preparation and fair presentation of the financial statements in accordance with U.S. GAAP.
- We acknowledge our responsibility for the design, implementation, and maintenance of internal control relevant to the preparation and fair presentation of financial statements that are free from material misstatement, whether due to fraud or error.

(continued)

EXHIBIT 14.7 Management Representation Letter Example from AU-C 580 "Management Representations" (*continued*)

- We acknowledge our responsibility for the design, implementation, and maintenance of internal control to prevent and detect fraud.
- Significant assumptions used by us in making accounting estimates, including those measured at fair value, are reasonable.
- Related party relationships and transactions have been appropriately accounted for and disclosed in accordance with the requirements of U.S. GAAP.
- All events subsequent to the date of the financial statements and for which U.S. GAAP requires adjustment or disclosure have been adjusted or disclosed.
- The effects of uncorrected misstatements are immaterial, both individually and in the aggregate, to the financial statements as a whole. A list of the uncorrected misstatements is attached to the representation letter.
- The effects of all known actual or possible litigation and claims have been accounted for and disclosed in accordance with U.S. GAAP.

Information Provided

We have provided you with:

- Access to all information, of which we are aware that is relevant to the preparation and fair presentation of the financial statements such as records, documentation and other matters;
- Additional information that you have requested from us for the purpose of the audit; and
- Unrestricted access to persons within the entity from whom you determined it necessary to obtain audit evidence.
- All transactions have been recorded in the accounting records and are reflected in the financial statements.
- We have disclosed to you the results of our assessment of the risk that the financial statements may be materially misstated as a result of fraud.
- We have [*no knowledge of any*][*disclosed to you all information that we are aware of regarding*] fraud or suspected fraud that affects the entity and involves:
  - Management;
  - Employees who have significant roles in internal control; or
  - Others when the fraud could have a material effect on the financial statements
- We have [*no knowledge of any*][*disclosed to you all information that we are aware of regarding*] allegations of fraud, or suspected fraud, affecting the entity's financial statements communicated by employees, former employees, analysts, regulators or others.
- We have disclosed to you all known instances of noncompliance or suspected noncompliance with laws and regulations whose effects should be considered when preparing financial statements.
- We [*have disclosed to you all known actual or possible*][*are not aware of any pending or threatened*] litigation and claims whose effects should be considered when preparing the financial statements [*and we have not consulted legal counsel concerning litigation or claims*]
- We have disclosed to you the identity of the entity's related parties and all the related party relationships and transactions of which we are aware.

[*Name of Chief Executive Officer and Title*]

[*Name of Chief Financial Officer and Title*]

复核期后事项和期后发现的事实

LO 9 Review subsequent events that occur after the balance sheet date and assess proper treatment.

Reviewing Subsequent Events and Subsequently Discovered Facts

This section presents two situations relating to events occurring after the balance sheet date that require special audit attention:

1. Those that provide evidence of conditions that existed at the date of the financial statements
2. Those that provide evidence of conditions that arose after the date of the financial statements

The timeline in Exhibit 14.8 illustrates these situations. Every audit includes procedures to review events and transactions that occur during

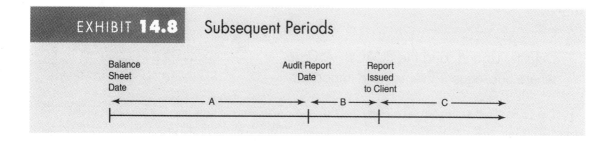

EXHIBIT **14.8** Subsequent Periods

period A, known as the subsequent period, which is the period between the balance sheet date and the audit report date. The auditor has no responsibilities to continue obtaining audit evidence after the audit report date: periods B and C.

Review of Subsequent Events

Two types of events occurring in Period A in Exhibit 14.8 have been identified in the professional literature as subsequent events that may require dollar adjustments to the financial statements and/ or disclosure: Type I subsequent events and Type II subsequent events. **Subsequent events** are events occurring between the date of the financial statements and the date of the auditor's report. A **subsequent events review** is a review of events occurring in the period between the balance sheet date and the audit report date to determine their possible effect on the financial statements.

Type I Subsequent Events Type I subsequent events provide evidence about conditions that existed at the balance sheet date. The financial statement numbers should be adjusted to reflect this information. Footnote disclosure may also be necessary to provide additional information. The following are examples:

- A major customer files for bankruptcy during the subsequent period because of a deteriorating financial condition, which the client and auditor were unaware of until learning about the bankruptcy filing. This information should be considered in establishing an appropriate amount for the allowance for doubtful accounts and in making an adjustment if the allowance is not sufficient to cover this potential loss.
- A lawsuit is settled for a different amount than was accrued.
- A stock dividend or split that takes place during the subsequent period should be disclosed. In addition, earnings-per-share figures should be adjusted to show the retroactive effect of the stock dividend or split.
- A sale of inventory below carrying value provides evidence that the net realizable value was less than cost at year end.
- Information becomes available that provides evidence about the valuation of an estimate or reserve that had been accrued at year end. For an example of this situation, see the *Auditing in Practice* feature, "Deloitte, Ligand, and the PCAOB: A Case where Subsequent Events were Important."

Type II Subsequent Events Type II subsequent events indicate conditions that did not exist at the balance sheet date, but that may require disclosure. The events that should be considered for disclosure are financial in nature and are material. The following are examples:

- An uninsured casualty loss that occurred after the balance sheet date causes a customer's bankruptcy during the subsequent period. Because the customer was able to pay at the balance sheet date, the allowance

Deloitte, Ligand, and the PCAOB: A Case where Subsequent Events were Important

Deloitte was fined $1,000,000 in December 2007 as a penalty for a low quality audit of Ligand Pharmaceuticals' 2003 financial statements. The fundamental problem in the audit was that an unqualified audit partner, James Fazio, oversaw the engagement and signed the audit opinion. Most surprisingly, Deloitte had identified Fazio as a quality risk and was in the process of forcing him to resign from the firm. The specific audit issue that led to a material misstatement of Ligand's financial statements concerned significant product returns from three large wholesalers that distributed Ligand's products. Deloitte knew that the pharmaceutical products that Ligand sold to these wholesalers were relatively new products, there was a lack of return history, and there were significant increases in or excess levels of inventory in the distribution channel. These factors made the valuation of the reserve for product returns very risky to audit. At year end, Ligand employees developed an estimate for product returns that turned out to be materially too low. Deloitte personnel did not address significant differences between historical actual returns and Ligand's estimate for product returns. The audit plan provided for the evaluation of subsequent events related to product returns after year end, but before the completion of the audit. However, the plan was not executed by Deloitte personnel, nor was the estimate adequately reviewed by Fazio. Ultimately, Deloitte resigned from the Ligand engagement in 2004 and Ligand was subsequently forced to restate its 2002, 2003, and some of its 2004 financial statements. Fazio was denied the ability to audit public companies for at least two years. This case highlights the importance of professional competence and the need to carefully consider events occurring during the period subsequent to year end when auditing important financial statement estimates.

For additional details, see PCAOB Releases Nos. 105-2007-005 and 105-2007-106.

for doubtful accounts should not be adjusted, but the information should be disclosed.

- A significant lawsuit is initiated relating to an incident that occurred after the balance sheet date.
- Because of a natural disaster such as fire, earthquake, or flood, a company loses a major facility after the balance sheet date.
- Major decisions are made during the subsequent period, such as to merge, discontinue a line of business, or issue new securities.
- A material change occurs in the value of investment securities.

The financial statement account balances should not be adjusted for these events, but they should be considered for disclosure.

Audit Procedures Concerning the Review of Subsequent Events

Some of the procedures discussed in previous chapters relate to subsequent events, such as cutoff tests, review of subsequent collections of receivables, and the search for unrecorded liabilities. Additional procedures related to subsequent events include the following:

- Read the minutes of the meetings of the board of directors, stockholders, and other authoritative groups. The auditor should obtain written assurance that minutes of all such meetings through the audit report date have been made available. This can be included in the management representation letter described earlier in this chapter.
- Read interim financial statements and compare them to the audited financial statements, noting and investigating significant changes.
- Inquire of management concerning:
  - Any significant changes noted in the interim statements

- The existence of significant contingent liabilities or commitments at the balance sheet date or date of inquiry, which should be near the audit report date
- Any significant changes in working capital, long-term debt, or owners' equity
- The status of items for which tentative conclusions were drawn earlier in the audit
- Any unusual adjustments made to the accounting records after the balance sheet date

Dual Dating

When the auditor becomes aware of an event that occurs after the audit report date but before the report release date (period B in Exhibit 14.8), and the event is disclosed in the footnotes, the auditor has two options for dating the audit report:

1. Use the date of this event as the date of the audit report.
2. Dual-date the report, using the dates of the original audit report and the date of the event, to disclose the work done only on that event after the original audit report date.

As an example, consider a situation in which the original audit report date is February 27, 2013, and a fire destroyed the client's main manufacturing plant and warehouse on March 2, 2013. This event is disclosed in Note 14 to the financial statements. The audit report release date was March 5. The auditor may date the report March 2, 2013, or dual-date it as "February 27, 2013, except for Note 14, as to which the date is March 2, 2013." The auditor is assuming less responsibility by dual-dating the report. The only event occurring after the original audit report date for which the auditor is taking responsibility is disclosed in Note 14. If the report were dated March 2, 2013, the auditor would be taking responsibility for all events occurring during period B. In that case, the auditor should perform audit procedures to identify other significant subsequent events that occurred between February 27 and March 2.

Subsequently Discovered Facts That Become Known to the Auditor after the Report Release Date

Facts may come to the auditor's attention after the report release date (period C in Exhibit 14.8) that may have affected the financial statements and auditor's report, had the facts been known at the report release date. Such facts may come to the auditor's attention through news reports, performing another service for the client, other business contacts, or a subsequent audit. If such facts had been known at the report date, and therefore would have been investigated during the audit, the auditor should determine the following:

- The reliability of the new information
- Whether the development or event had occurred by the report date, as issuance of revised financial statements and an audit report is not required when the development or event occurs after the report date.
- Whether users are likely to still be relying on the financial statements
- Whether the audit report would have been affected had the facts been known to the auditor at the report date

If the auditor decides that steps should be taken to prevent further reliance on the financial statements and audit report, the client is advised to make appropriate and timely disclosure of these new facts. The key action is to notify users as soon as possible so they do not continue to rely on information that is now known to be incorrect. The appropriate action depends on the circumstances:

- If the revised financial statements and audit report can be quickly prepared and distributed, the reasons for the revision should be described in a footnote and referred to in the auditor's report.
- Revision and explanation can be made in the subsequent-period audited financial statements if their distribution is imminent.
- If it will take an extended amount of time to develop revised financial statements, the client should immediately notify the users that the previously distributed financial statements and auditor's report should no longer be relied on, and that revised statements and report will be issued as soon as possible.

The auditor should make sure the client takes the appropriate action. If the client will not cooperate:

- The auditor should notify the client and any regulatory agency having jurisdiction over it, such as the SEC, that the audit report should no longer be associated with the client's financial statements.
- The auditor should notify users known to the auditor that the audit report should no longer be relied on. Auditors typically do not know all the users who receive the report. Therefore, the appropriate regulatory agency should be requested to take whatever steps are needed to disclose this situation.

对报告日后发现的遗漏程序的考虑

LO 10 Determine how to address situations in which omitted audit procedures come to the auditor's attention after the audit report has been issued.

如果在出具审计报告后，注册会计师发现了被遗漏的审计程序，此时，注册会计师应判断在考虑遗漏的审计程序后是否依然支持之前发布的审计报告。如果认为不能支持，那么注册会计师需要执行和记录遗漏的审计程序或者替代性的审计程序。

实施项目质量控制复核

LO 11 Assess the adequacy of supervision and perform an engagement quality review.

Consideration of Omitted Procedures Discovered after the Report Date

After the audit report has been issued, the auditor may discover an **omitted procedure**, which is an important audit procedure that was not performed. For example, an auditor may have failed to follow up on a material accounts receivable confirmation response indicating a difference between the client's recorded balance and the customer's recorded balance. Such an omission may be discovered when audit documentation is reviewed as part of an external or internal review program. In this case, the auditor should decide whether the previously issued audit report can still be supported in light of the omitted procedures. If not, the omitted or alternative procedures should be promptly performed and documented.

For example, if the auditor failed to confirm receivables when that should have been done, it may be too late to confirm now. In that case, the auditor could extend the previous work done on subsequent collections to help determine that the receivables existed and were properly valued at the balance sheet date. If the results indicate that the previously issued statements and audit report should be modified, the guidance in the previous section of this chapter should be followed. Otherwise, no further action is necessary.

Performing an Engagement Quality Review

As part of a quality audit for public companies, the audit firm must have policies and procedures in place for conducting an internal quality review of each audit before issuing the audit opinion. Auditors of privately held companies generally perform these reviews even though they are not explicitly required. An experienced reviewer who was not a part of the audit team, but who has appropriate competence, independence, integrity, and objectivity, should perform this independent review, referred to as a **concurring partner review** or **engagement quality review**. The purpose of these reviews is to provide reasonable assurance that the audit and audit documentation are complete and support the audit opinion on the financial statements and, for integrated audits, on the client's internal controls.

The engagement quality review is a risk-based review, where the reviewer evaluates the significant judgments made by the engagement team and the conclusions that the engagement team reached. Some of the procedures the reviewer should perform as part of the review process include:

- Discussing with the audit team any significant matters related to the financial statements and internal controls, including the audit team's identification of material weaknesses and audit procedures to address significant risks
- Evaluating judgments about materiality and the disposition of corrected and uncorrected identified misstatements
- Reviewing the engagement team's evaluation of the firm's independence in relation to the engagement
- Reviewing the related audit documentation to determine its sufficiency
- Reading the financial statements, management's report on internal control, and auditor's report
- Confirming with the lead audit partner that there are no significant unresolved matters
- Determining if appropriate consultations have taken place on difficult or contentious matters
- Evaluating whether the auditor documentation supports the conclusions reached by the engagement team with respect to the matters reviewed
- Assessing whether appropriate matters have been communicated to audit committee members, management, and other appropriate parties
- Evaluating whether appropriate levels of supervision and reviews of individual audit tasks were completed adequately during the audit

Documentation of an Engagement Quality Review

The audit documentation should include evidence on the performance of the engagement quality review. This documentation should include the following information:

- Who performed the engagement quality review
- Documents reviewed by the engagement quality reviewer
- Date the engagement quality reviewer provided concurring approval of issuance

Communicating with Management and the Audit Committee (And Those Charged with Governance)

与管理层和审计委员会（以及治理层）的沟通

As the auditor completes the audit, various types of reporting and communication activities are conducted to provide reasonable assurance that the client's financial statements are materially correct and to promote audit quality. These reporting and communication activities include the following:

- Identifying issues to communicate to the audit committee
- Identifying issues to communicate to management via a management letter

Responsibilities of External Auditors to Communicate with the Audit Committee

外部注册会计师与审计委员会沟通的责任

 Identify issues to communicate to the audit committee.

It is important that the external auditor have a constructive and detailed dialogue with the audit committee. This communication is important because the audit committee serves as an independent subcommittee of the board of directors. The audit committee can also assist the auditor should a disagreement occur between the auditor and management. The audit committee must be assured that the auditor is free of any restrictions and has not been inappropriately influenced by management during the course of the audit. The following are typical communications between the auditor and the audit committee:

- *Auditor's Responsibility under Generally Accepted Auditing Standards.* The auditor must clearly communicate the audit firm's responsibility to perform the audit according to relevant auditing standards and independently assess the fairness of the financial statements, to assess the quality of the entity's internal controls over financial reporting, and to design the audit to detect material misstatements. The auditor should communicate that the audit of the financial statements does not relieve management of its financial reporting responsibilities.
- *Overview and Planned Scope of the Audit.* The auditor needs to communicate the planned scope of the audit engagement to the audit committee and have a discussion with it on the adequacy of the planned scope.
- *Independence.* The auditor should affirm that the engagement team and others in the audit firm have complied with relevant independence requirements.
- *Significant Accounting Policies.* The auditor should inform the audit committee about the initial selection of, and changes in, significant accounting policies or their application, and discuss the quality of accounting principles used. SOX requires that the auditor communicate all alternative treatments of financial information within GAAP that have been discussed with management, ramifications of using alternative treatments or disclosures, and the treatment that the audit firm prefers.
- *Management Judgments and Accounting Estimates.* Many corporate failures have involved manipulation of accounting estimates such as loan loss reserves. The auditor should inform the audit committee of the processes used by management in making sensitive accounting estimates and should convey the auditor's assessment of those processes and accompanying estimates.
- *Significant Audit Adjustments.* Significant audit adjustments may reflect on the stewardship and accountability of management. The audit committee should be made aware of such adjustments, even if management readily agrees to make them. Significant adjustments, by definition, suggest that there have been internal control failures that must be communicated to management and to the audit committee. The auditor should also communicate about any uncorrected misstatements.
- *Judgments about the Quality of the Company's Accounting Principles.* The auditor needs to discuss with the audit committee the quality of the company's financial statements and provide reasonable assurance that they are acceptable under GAAP. Auditors should be prepared to have a frank discussion about differences in assessments of the quality of the financial statements. In other words, the auditor should be prepared to discuss the quality, not just the acceptability, of significant accounting policies. See the *Auditing in Practice* feature, "Guidance on Assessing the Quality, Not Just the Acceptability, of Significant Accounting Policies," for further insights on this important professional judgment.
- *Other Information in Annual Reports.* The auditor should briefly describe his or her responsibility to review other information contained in an annual report and whether such information is consistent with the audited financial statements.
- *Disagreements with Management.* All major accounting disagreements with management, even if eventually resolved, should be discussed with the audit committee. This requirement is intended to insulate the auditors from management pressure to change or bend accounting treatments to suit management and should remove any hints that the

Guidance on Assessing the Quality, Not Just the Acceptability, of Significant Accounting Policies

Objective criteria for evaluating the quality of the client's accounting policies is not available, so assessing the quality, not just the acceptability of significant accounting policies is a matter of professional judgment. The AICPA has issued a tool that provides guidance in this regard, "Discussions to Expect From the Independent Auditor" (AICPA 2008). That guidance encourages auditors to consider the following in making this judgment:

- What is the consistency of the organization's accounting principles and their application?
- What is the clarity of the financial statements and related disclosures?
- What is the completeness of the financial statements and related disclosures?

- Are there any items that have a significant impact on the representational faithfulness, verifiability, and neutrality of the accounting information included in the financial statements? For example, are there:
  - Selection of new accounting policies or changes to current ones
  - Estimates, judgments, and uncertainties
  - Unusual transactions
  - Accounting policies relating to significant financial statement items, including the timing of transactions and the period in which they are recorded
- Is the company using accounting practices that are not specifically addressed in the accounting literature, such as industry-specific practices?

audit firm may be replaced because it disagrees with management's proposed accounting treatments.
- *Major Issues Discussed with Management Before Retention.* During the proposal and hiring stages of the engagement, management and the auditor discuss issues related to accounting principles and audit standards. These issues should be discussed with the audit committee.
- *Internal Control over Financial Reporting.* The auditor should discuss the quality of internal controls and any deficiencies therein (including material weaknesses, significant deficiencies, and those deficiencies that are less severe than significant deficiencies), even if they were remediated, prior to year end. The audit committee needs to understand these issues in order to help assess the elements of the Committee of Sponsoring Organizations (COSO) framework, and to engage in remediation discussions. For integrated audit clients, the auditor must provide these communications in writing to management and the audit committee prior to issuing the auditor's report on internal control over financial reporting.

Communicating with Management via the Management Letter

通过管理建议书与管理层沟通

Auditors often notice things that could help management do a better job. The auditor generally reports these observations in a **management letter** as a constructive part of the audit. Such a letter should not be confused with a management representation letter. The management letter is not required, but it is used to make significant operational or control recommendations to the client. The letter helps to provide management comfort that the auditor has done a quality job and that the auditor knows and understands the client's business. Many audit firms consider management's inattention to addressing comments in the letter to be an important risk factor in subsequent-year audits. See the *Auditing in Practice* feature, "An Example Management Letter to a College Foundation," for details on the contents and structure of a typical management letter.

LO 13 Identify issues to communicate to management via a management letter.

An Example Management Letter to a College Foundation

Below, we provide an example management letter from the audit firm of Johnstone & Gramling LLP related to the June 30, 2011, audit of the Bucky Badger College Foundation. You should note the following features of the letter:

- It contains the auditor's observations and recommendations to management.
- It contains management's response.
- It addresses the issue of whether/how management responded to the management letter related to the prior year's audit.

Bucky Badger College Foundation
Addendum A

Financial System Reporting

Observation
Currently, the financial reporting system used by the college and the Foundation produces various reports that must be printed and manually reclassified to properly report amounts in the financial statements. Efficiencies could be gained by accounting personnel if the financial reporting system were updated.

Recommendation
We recommend that management work with IT support at the College to develop an updated financial reporting system.

Management's Response
We agree with the recommendation. The current system will be updated, and adequate funds are available to accomplish the update.

Allowance for Doubtful Accounts

Observation
Currently the Foundation reviews the pledge accounts receivables from promised gifts by donors to determine the appropriateness of the allowance for doubtful accounts. This process has produced reasonable estimates in the past. The Foundation is beginning a new capital campaign to donors, which should result in increased pledges over the next several years. These pledges and associated receivables should be carefully and separately tracked from those amounts arising from prior capital campaigns.

Recommendation
We recommend that management develop a process to estimate and track the collectability of campaign pledge receivables from the new campaign, and to allocate sufficient staffing resources to do so.

Management's Response
We agree with the recommendation. A multi-pledge campaign evaluation process will be developed and implemented for future financial reporting.

Disposition of Prior Year Comments
In our management letter for the year ended June 30, 20XX, we made several comments and recommendations intended to improve the Foundation's internal controls. During our current year audit, we reviewed these comments to determine if the recommendations were implemented.

Pledge Receivable

Observation
During our audit it became apparent that the Foundation recorded as a pledge receivable the death benefit of an insurance policy in which it was named the beneficiary. However, accounting rules state that it does not meet the criteria to be recorded as a pledge receivable because the Foundation was only a named beneficiary.

Recommendation
We recommend that management review similar insurance policies to determine if the accounting is proper for these accounts.

Management's Response
We agree with the recommendation. We have initiated an internal review process to track and properly record pledge receivables.

Investment Income

Observation
During our audit, it came to our attention that unrealized gains and losses are allocated to individual fund balances yearly rather than semi-annually, resulting in potential inaccuracies during the year.

Recommendation
We recommend that unrealized gains and losses be posted to individual fund balances on a semi-annual basis, or quarterly if possible.

Management's Response
We agree with the recommendation. Unrealized gains or losses will be posted for each fund on a semi-annual basis beginning with the period ending December 31, 20XX.

In Summary
The comments relating to the prior year audit have been adequately addressed.

Issues Relating to Audit Firm Portfolio Management, Audit Partner Rotation, and Audit Firm Rotation

与会计师事务所客户组合管理、审计合伙人轮换和会计师事务所轮换相关的问题

After the auditor completes the current audit or anticipates a new audit engagement, several issues become important in considering the subsequent year audit. These include:

- Audit firm portfolio management: Deciding whether to continue providing audit services to the client—the client continuance decision, or deciding whether to begin providing services to a new client—the client acceptance decision
- Considering mandatory partner rotation and mandatory audit firm rotation requirements for publicly traded audit clients

Client Acceptance and Continuance Decisions

客户接受与保留决策

LO 14 Describe the process by which audit firms make client acceptance and continuance decisions.

Client acceptance and continuance decisions (sometimes called client retention decisions), which audit firms and individual engagement partners make either immediately before agreeing to conduct an audit or immediately after completing the audit, are just a part of an audit firm's overall portfolio management activities. In essence, one can view an individual audit client like an individual stock in an investment portfolio. That is, some stocks (clients) are more risky, but yield better returns; some stocks (clients) are less risky, but yield weaker returns. Still other stocks (clients) do not present a clear picture of their risk-return profile. In the context of auditing, better returns does not just mean higher audit fees, but instead may also include the upside potential of a client that may become publicly traded, the reputational visibility that an audit firm gains when they audit a superior and well-known company, and so forth. In Chapter 1, we introduced you to client acceptance and continuance decisions; at this point we provide a more theoretical description of how clients come into an audit firm's portfolio and how they move out of that portfolio. Accomplishing portfolio management, of which client acceptance and continuance decisions are just one part, is the key to an audit firm's long-run survival and its ability to offer high-quality audit services to its clients. Audit firm culture plays a role in audit firm portfolio management, in that some audit firms are more willing to provide service to risky clients than are other audit firms.

As depicted in Exhibit 14.9, an audit firm begins each period with a given number of clients in its portfolio. Some clients voluntarily depart from the audit firm, such as in the case of a company going bankrupt or merging with another company; other reasons include fee issues, service issues, changes in location, poor working relationships, and so on. Other clients are newly accepted into the audit firm's portfolio based on the **client acceptance decision**. These clients are evaluated based upon their relative risk and audit fee profile. The audit firm makes a proposal (and in some cases a formal bid) to the client if the audit firm decides the client is acceptable; if the client accepts, the audit firm adds the client to its portfolio.

为了控制审计风险，在首次接受审计委托时，注册会计师需要执行针对建立有关客户关系和具体审计业务的质量控制程序；而在连续审计时，注册会计师需要执行针对保持客户关系和具体审计业务的质量控制程序。

Existing clients for which the audit firm provided services in the preceding period are evaluated by the audit firm and individual engagement partner at the completion of the audit to determine whether the audit firm should continue to provide services again in the next period. The process by which this decision is made is called the **client continuance decision**. In short, the engagement partner and the audit firm must decide, based on what they know about the client, whether it is worthwhile to retain the client in the firm's portfolio. Like the client acceptance decision, the client continuance decision is made based on a consideration of the client's relative risk and audit fee profile. Discontinued clients are those the audit firm

EXHIBIT **14.9**   Audit Firm Portfolio Management

```
                    ┌───────────────────────────────────┐
                    │  Begining-of-Period Client Portfolio│◄──────────┐
                    └───────────────────────────────────┘            │
                                                                      │
 ┌──────────────┐  ┌──────────────────────┐  ┌──────────────────────┐ │
 │Client-Initiated│ │**Client-Continuance**  │  │**Client-Acceptance**   │ │
 │ Departures    │ │**Decisions Assess:**   │  │**Decisions Assess:**   │ │
 │(e.g., bankruptcies,│ │• Risk (e.g., mgt. integrity│ │• Risk (e.g., mgt. integrity│ │
 │ mergers,      │ │  and other characteristics,│ │  and other characteristics,│ │
 │ dissatisfaction)│ │  financial health, control│ │  financial health, control│ │
 └──────────────┘  │  quality, governance, etc.)│ │  quality, governance, etc.)│ │
                    │• Audit Fees           │  │• Audit Fees           │ │
                    │                       │  │                       │ │
                    │  Should the audit firm │  │  Should the audit firm │ │
                    │  continue to provide   │  │  submit a bid to perform│ │
                    │  services for an existing│ │  services for a potential│ │
                    │       client?          │  │       client?         │ │
                    └──────────────────────┘  └──────────────────────┘ │
```

| Client-Initiated Departures (e.g., bankruptcies, mergers, dissatisfaction) | **Client-Continuance Decisions Assess:** • Risk (e.g., mgt. integrity and other characteristics, financial health, control quality, governance, etc.) • Audit Fees   Should the audit firm continue to provide services for an existing client? | **Client-Acceptance Decisions Assess:** • Risk (e.g., mgt. integrity and other characteristics, financial health, control quality, governance, etc.) • Audit Fees   Should the audit firm submit a bid to perform services for a potential client? |

If YES, and if the client accepts the bid

If YES   If NO

| Continuing Clients | Discontinued Clients | Newly Accepted Clients |

Audit Firm's End-of-Period Client Portfolio

© Cengage Learning

eliminates from its portfolio based on the client continuance decision; the clients will be informed that the firm will no longer be associated with them after the current period audit report is issued. Continuing clients are those the audit firm will continue its ongoing relationship with; the firm will continue to be associated with them once the current period audit report is issued.

Client Acceptance and Continuance-Related Risks

The following are some of the key types of risk that audit firms consider when they make client acceptance and client continuance decisions:

- *Client entity characteristics.* For example, a history of earnings management or of making unrealistic promises to analysts; failing to meet market expectations or consistently just meeting those expectations; difficulties in relationships with prior professional service providers, such as attorneys; and high-risk business models, such as Internet gaming.

- *Independence risk factors.* For example, the engagement partner has a business or family relationship with the client; client management was a former employee of the audit firm; the client purchases consulting services from the audit firm; or the audit firm has some other independence-related conflict with the client.
- *Third party /due diligence risk factors.* For example, the reason for the client to change auditors is unknown or is due to negative relationship factors, the predecessor audit firm is unwilling to discuss the reasons for the client's departure, there have been significant changes in the ownership structure of the entity or evidence that key members of management have prior histories of financial fraud or other types of legal difficulties.
- *Quantitative risk factors.* For example, the client is in significant financial stress, is having difficulty raising capital or paying its existing debts, or is experiencing significant cash flow problems.
- *Qualitative risk factors.* For example, the industry in which the client operates is in either the early development stage or is late in its product life cycle, there are minimal barriers to entry to the client's business model, the business model is weak or untested, there are low profit margins, the client's products have multiple viable substitutes, there are significant supply chain risks, there is significant production or operational complexity, or there are risks related to strong union presence.
- *Entity organizational or governance risks.* For example, the organizational structure is inappropriate for the business operations of the entity, there are weak internal controls, there is weak governance, management is unqualified or lacks integrity, and the internal audit function is weak or nonexistent.
- *Financial reporting risks.* For example, the client uses inappropriate estimates in its financial reporting judgments, management has a history of misrepresentations or unwillingness to correct detected misstatements, the financial statement line items involve a significant amount of judgment or complexity, there are large or unusual transactions that management records at quarter or year-end, or the prior audit report is other than an unqualified report.

In addition to these risk factors, an important consideration in client continuance decisions involves the audit firm's growth strategy. Audit firms may discontinue serving a client because the client does not fit the profile the firm is hoping to achieve. For example, a Big 4 firm may discontinue serving a smaller client because it is not sufficiently profitable, or the client may not be in an industry the firm wants to emphasize. On the other hand, some smaller audit firms may discontinue serving a larger client because they do not have the size or expertise to serve the client as the client grows larger, becomes more geographically dispersed, or increases in complexity. See the *Auditing in Practice* feature, "Why Might an Audit Firm Refuse to Continue Providing Services to a Client? The Case of Longtop Financial and Deloitte," for an example of auditor resignation due to suspicions of fraud.

Audit firm portfolio management decisions, which include client acceptance and continuance decisions, are critical to achieve audit quality. If an audit firm accepts or continues to provide service to a potentially problematic client such as a client that is in very weak financial condition, a client that has very poor internal controls, a client that is perpetrating a fraud, or a client with poor management integrity, it may be difficult for the audit

Why Might an Audit Firm Refuse to Continue Providing Services to a Client? The Case of Longtop Financial Technologies and Deloitte

Deloitte audited the financial statements of Longtop Financial Technologies (Longtop) both before and after the company's 2007 initial public offering. In May 2011, Deloitte resigned from the Longtop engagement, citing concerns about management fraud. The allegations are that Longtop's top management, including the chief operating officer, interfered with the audit confirmation process. In fact, there is currently widespread concern that significant collusion has been taking place between Chinese companies and their banks, including evidence that banks are signing false confirmations of their clients' cash accounts. The reason for the false confirmations is that the Chinese companies, including Longtop, had been recording fictitious revenues and recording fictitious inflows of cash to agree with the revenues. When Deloitte personnel confronted Longtop management, the auditors were subject to seizure of their audit workpapers and were faced with physical threats to try to prevent the auditors from leaving the property. Below is the resignation letter from Deloitte Shanghai to the Longtop Audit Committee on May 22, 2011:

"BY EMAIL & BY REGISTERED MAIL

The Audit Committee
Longtop Financial Technologies Limited
No. 61 Wanghai Road, Xiamen Software Park
Xiamen, Fujian Province
People's Republic of China

Attention: Mr. Thomas Gurnee, Chairman of the Audit Committee

Dear Sirs,

Longtop Financial Technologies Limited (the "Company") and together with its subsidiaries (the "Group") Audit for the Year Ended 31 March 2011

We hereby give you formal notice of our resignation as auditor of the Company.

Background and significant issues encountered by Deloitte Touche Tohmatsu CPA Ltd. (China) ("Deloitte")

As part of the process for auditing the Company's financial statements for the year ended 31 March 2011, we determined that, in regard to bank confirmations, it was appropriate to perform follow up visits to certain banks. These audit steps were recently performed and identified a number of very serious defects including: statements by bank staff

that their bank had no record of certain transactions; confirmation replies previously received were said to be false; significant differences in deposit balances reported by the bank staff compared with the amounts identified in previously received confirmations (and in the books and records of the Group); and significant bank borrowings reported by bank staff not identified in previously received confirmations (and not recorded in the books and records of the Group).

In the light of this, a formal second round of bank confirmation was initiated on 17 May. Within hours however, as a result of intervention by the Company's officials including the Chief Operating Officer, the confirmation process was stopped amid serious and troubling new developments including: calls to banks by the Company asserting that Deloitte was not their auditor; seizure by the Company's staff of second round bank confirmation documentation on bank premises; threats to stop our staff leaving the Company premises unless they allowed the Company to retain our audit files then on the premises; and then seizure by the Company of certain of our working papers.

In that connection, we must insist that you promptly return our documents.

Then on 20 May the Chairman of the Company, Mr. Jia Xiao Gong called our Eastern Region Managing Partner, Mr. Paul Sin, and informed him in the course of their conversation that "there were fake revenue in the past so there were fake cash recorded on the books". Mr. Jia did not answer when questioned as to the extent and duration of the discrepancies. When asked who was involved, Mr. Jia answered: "senior management".

We bring these significant issues to your attention in the context of our responsibilities under Statement on Auditing Standards No. 99 "Consideration of Fraud in a Financial Statement Audit" issued by the American Institute of Certified Public Accountants.

Reasons for our resignation
The reasons for our resignation include: 1) the recently identified falsity of the Group's financial records in relation to cash at bank and loan balances (and also now seemingly in the sales revenue); 2) the deliberate interference by the management in our audit process; and 3) the unlawful detention of our audit files. These recent developments undermine our ability to rely on the representations of the management which is an essential element of the audit process; hence our resignation.

AUDITING IN PRACTICE

Why Might an Audit Firm Refuse to Continue Providing Services to a Client? The Case of Longtop Financial Technologies and Deloitte (*continued*)

Prior periods' financial reports and our reports thereon

We have reached the conclusion that we are no longer able to place reliance on management representations in relation to prior period financial reports. Accordingly, we request that the Company take immediate steps to make the necessary 8-K filing to state that continuing reliance should no longer be placed on our audit reports on the previous financial statements and moreover that we decline to be associated with any of the Company's financial communications during 2010 and 2011.

Our consent

We hereby consent to a copy of this letter being supplied to the SEC and the succeeding auditor to be appointed.

Section 10A of the Securities Exchange Act of 1934 (U.S.)

In our view, without providing any legal conclusion, the circumstances mentioned above could constitute illegal acts for purposes of Section 10A of the Securities Exchange Act of 1934. Accordingly, we remind the Board of its obligations under Section 10A of the Securities Exchange Act, including the notice requirements to the U.S. Securities and Exchange Commission. You may consider taking legal advice on this.

Yours faithfully,

/s/ Deloitte Touche Tohmatsu CPA Ltd.

c.c.: The Board of Directors"

Ultimately, the SEC delisted Longtop because the company failed to file its annual report for FYE March 31, 2011. Similar delistings occurred at other Chinese companies with stock traded in U.S. markets, including Advanced Battery Technologies, China MediaExpress Holdings, and Shengda Tech. These examples serve as a serious warning to audit firms as they enter high-risk international markets and as they make their client continuance decisions.

Source: Deloitte Shanghai, May 22 2011.

---

firm to provide a quality audit. For example, a client in weak financial condition may be unable to pay a reasonable audit fee, and so the audit firm may find itself in a position of not having enough budgeted audit hours to do a quality audit. Or a client with weak internal controls may be difficult to audit because of unreliable financial data. Similarly, a client perpetrating a fraud, or one with weak management integrity, may present financial information that is intentionally unreliable, and so again the audit may be difficult to conduct in a way that results in an accurate audit opinion. Given the importance of client acceptance and continuance decisions to audit quality, audit firms with strong cultures of quality place great emphasis on developing, maintaining, and monitoring systems of quality control that yield good decisions in this regard.

Partner Rotation and Audit Firm Rotation

In Chapter 1, you learned about the AICPA's conceptual framework on independence. That framework describes seven categories of threats to independence, which are circumstances that could lead to an auditor lacking independence in fact or in appearance. Of most relevance to the issue

合伙人轮换与会计师事务所轮换

LO 15 Identify the requirements concerning mandatory partner rotation and mandatory audit firm rotation for publicly traded audit clients.

当会计师事务所或者审计项目合伙人的任期比较长时，审计项目合伙人或对审计项目有重大影响的事务所其他人员容易与被审计单位管理层建立密切的私人关系，而这种关系会损害注册会计师公正无偏地评估审计证据的意愿和能力。

of mandatory partner or audit firm rotation is the familiarity threat, which occurs when the auditor has a longstanding relationship with an important person associated with the client, such as the CEO or the CFO. Having a longstanding relationship with the client could aid audit quality because of the knowledge that the partner and members of the engagement team gain through time. However, in terms of independence, the concern is that an individual audit partner or members of the audit firm may have developed very close personal relationships with top management; such relationships

---

KPMG and General Electric Company: A Relationship that has Lasted over 100 Years

AUDITING IN PRACTICE

It may surprise you to learn that KPMG (or its former member firms prior to the latest merger that created KPMG) has audited General Electric Company for over 100 years. While the Company and audit firm clearly appear to appreciate the long-standing relationship, some users of the financial statements question it very strongly. In fact, the United Brotherhood of Carpenters Pension Fund, a shareholder of the Company's, filed the letter and proposal below to General Electric requesting that the Company consider implementing an audit firm rotation policy whereby the Company would rotate audit firms after seven years. Text of the letter and proposal appear below. Ultimately, the proposal was ignored by General Electric, and was not put to a vote of the shareholders. Thus, it appears that General Electric and KPMG are not supportive of mandatory audit firm rotation.

November 9, 2011

Bracken B. Denniston III
Secretary
General Electric Company 3135 Easton Turnpike
Fairfield, Connecticut 06828

Dear Mr. Denniston:

On behalf of the United Brotherhood of Carpenters Pension Fund ("Fund"), I hereby submit the enclosed shareholder proposal ("Proposal') for inclusion in the General Electric Company ("Company") proxy statement to be circulated to Company shareholders in conjunction with the next annual meeting of shareholders. The Proposal relates to audit firm rotation, and is submitted under Rule 14(a)~8 (Proposals of secutity Holders) of the U.S. Securities and Exchange Commission proxy regulations.

The Fund is the beneficial owner of 136,086 shares of the Company's common stock that have been held continuously for more than a year prior to this date of submission. The Fund intends to hold the shares through the date of the Company's next annual meeting of shareholders. The record holder of the stock will provide the appropriate verification of the Fund's beneficial ownership by separate letter. Either the undersigned or a designated representative will present the proposal for consideration at the annual meeting of shareholders.

Sincerely,
Douglas J. McCarron Fund Chairman
cc. Edward J. Durkin

Audit Firm Rotation Policy Proposal

"Be it Resolved: That the shareholders of General Electric Company ("Company") hereby request that the Company's Board Audit Review Committee establish an Audit Firm Rotation Policy that requires that at least every seven years the Company's audit firm rotate off the engagement for a minimum of three years.

Supporting Statement: Audit independence is fundamentally important to the integrity of the public company financial reporting system that underpins our nation's capital markets. In a system in which audit clients pay for-profit accounting firms to perform financial statement audits, every effort must be made to ensure accounting firm independence. One important reform to advance the independence, skepticism, and objectivity accounting firms have toward their audit clients is a mandatory auditor rotation requirement

KPMG and General Electric Company: A Relationship that has Lasted Over 100 Years (*continued*)

Information gathered on the current terms of engagement between audit firms and client corporations indicates that at the largest 500 companies based on market capitalization long-term auditor-client relationships are prevalent: for the largest 100 companies auditor tenure averages 28 years, while the average tenure at the 500 largest companies is 21 years. These long-term financial relationships result in the payment to the audit firm of hundreds of millions of dollars over the average period of engagement. According to its recent proxy statements, General Electric has paid its audit firm, KPMG LLP, a total of $801,600,000 in total fees over the last 7 years alone.

Auditor independence is described by the Public Company Accounting Oversight Board (PCAOB), an organization established to set and monitor accounting standards and practices, as "both a description of the relationship between auditor and client and the mindset with which the auditor must approach his or her duty to serve the public." (PCAOB Release No. 2011-055, August 16, 2011). One measure of an independent mindset is the auditor's ability to exercise "professional skepticism," which is an attitude that includes a questioning mind and a critical assessment of audit evidence." PCAOB standards require an auditor to conduct an audit engagement with a mindset that recognizes the possibility that a material misstatement due to fraud could be present, regardless of any past experience with the entity and regardless of the auditor's belief about management's honesty and integrity.

Instances of systemic accounting fraud in the market have prompted various legislative and regulatory reforms to the audit process, including audit partner rotation requirements, limits on the non-audit services that can be provided by accounting firms to audit clients, and enhanced responsibilities for board audit committees. Despite these important reforms, recent PCAOB Investigations often reveal audit deficiencies that may be attributable to a failure to exercise the required professional skepticism and objectivity.

We believe that an important next step in improving the integrity of the public company audit system is to establish a mandatory audit firm rotation requirement of seven years. The periodic audit firm rotation by public company clients would limit long-term client-audit firm relationships that may compromise the independence of the audit firm's work."

Source: Reprinted by permission of THE UNITED BROTHERHOOD OF CARPENTERS AND JOINERS OF AMERICA.

could impair their willingness or ability to perform an unbiased assessment of the audit evidence. See the *Auditing in Practice* feature, "KPMG and General Electric Company: A Relationship that has Lasted Over 100 Years." This example highlights the fact that shareholders are now beginning to question long-standing relationships between a given company and its auditor.

Rules differ internationally in terms of mandatory partner rotation and mandatory audit firm rotation. Differences exist in terms of whether rotation is required, the length of time the auditor or audit firm may serve before rotation, and the length of time of a cooling off period. A **cooling off period** is the number of years after which the individual auditor or audit firm may resume its prior role with the audit client. During the cooling off period, the individual or audit firm may not engage in any meaningful audit-related interactions with the client. Exhibit 14.10 summarizes these differences.

| EXHIBIT **14.10** | U.S. and International Guidance on Mandatory Audit Partner Rotation and Mandatory Audit Firm Rotation |

Times and requirements vary internationally in terms of mandatory audit partner and mandatory audit firm rotation. The U.S. differs from the European Union countries dramatically in terms of not supporting the idea of mandatory audit firm rotation. There is more commonality in terms of mandatory audit partner rotation, but with differing time periods and cooling off periods by jurisdiction. These differences are outlined below.

AICPA Auditing Standards Board (ASB)

Mandatory Partner Rotation
- Not required

Mandatory Audit Firm Rotation
- Not required

Public Company Accounting Oversight Board (PCAOB)

Mandatory Partner Rotation (SOX Section 203)
- Required after five years for engagement partner and engagement quality review (concurring) partner
- Cooling off period of five years

Mandatory Audit Firm Rotation
- Not required, but the PCAOB has considered requiring mandatory audit firm rotation

International Auditing and Assurance Standards Board (IAASB) International Federation of Accountants (IFAC)

Mandatory Partner Rotation (Code of Ethics Section 290)
- Required after seven years for engagement partner and engagement quality review (concurring) partner
- Cooling off period of two years

Mandatory Audit Firm Rotation (European Union Reform of the Audit Market Proposal)
- Proposal includes required audit firm rotation after six years
- Proposal includes cooling off period of four years

SUMMARY AND NEXT STEPS

Before issuing an audit opinion, the auditor must determine whether the financial statements are presented fairly in all material respects, whether they contain adequate disclosures, and whether they properly reflect events that have occurred up to the audit report date. In short, many activities must be completed prior to issuing the audit report. These activities are designed to provide reasonable assurance that the audit was conducted in a quality manner. Now that you understand these steps, Chapter 15 will describe in detail the various types of audit opinions that auditors may express based upon their audit procedures and related conclusions.

SIGNIFICANT TERMS

Altman Z-score   A series of ratios that have predictive power in indicating the likelihood of bankruptcy. This score is named for the person that first introduced the concept and associated measurement.

Client acceptance decision   The process by which a new client is evaluated by the audit firm and individual engagement partner prior to being accepted into the audit firm's portfolio of clients.

Client continuance decision The process by which existing clients for which the audit firm provided services in the preceding period are evaluated by the audit firm and individual engagement partner at the completion of the audit to determine whether the audit firm should continue to provide services again in the next period.

Concurring partner review See engagement quality review.

Cooling off period The number of years after which the individual auditor or audit firm may resume its prior role with the audit client.

Engagement quality review A review at the end of each audit conducted by an experienced auditor, usually a partner, who was not a part of the audit team, but who has appropriate competence, independence, integrity, and objectivity. The purposes are to help make sure that the audit and audit documentation are complete and support the audit opinion on the financial statements and, for public companies, on the client's internal controls.

Factual misstatement See known misstatement; misstatements about which there is no doubt.

Judgmental misstatement A misstatement that arises from differences in judgments of management concerning accounting estimates that the auditor considers unreasonable, or the selection or application of accounting policies that the auditor considers inappropriate.

Known misstatement A misstatement that has been specifically identified; known misstatements are also referred to as factual misstatements.

Letter of audit inquiry A letter that the auditor asks the client to send to its legal counsel to gather corroborative evidence concerning litigation, claims, and assessments.

Management letter A letter from the auditor to the client identifying any problems and suggested solutions that may help management improve its effectiveness or efficiency.

Management representation letter A letter to the auditors that the client's chief executive and chief financial officers are required to sign that specifies management's responsibility for the financial statements and confirms oral responses given to the auditor during the audit.

Noncompliance This involves acts of omission or commission by the entity, either intentional or unintentional, which are contrary to the prevailing laws or regulations.

Omitted procedures After the audit report has been issued, the auditor may discover that an important audit procedure was not performed; these are called omitted procedures.

Projected misstatement A misstatement that is the auditor's best estimate of the misstatement in a given population, and that is a projection of the misstatement identified in an audit sample to the entire population from which the sample was drawn.

Reasonable period of time A period of time not to exceed one year beyond the date of the financial statements being audited.

Report release date The date the auditor grants the entity permission to use the auditor's report in connection with the financial statements.

Subsequent events Events occurring between the date of the financial statements and the date of the auditor's report.

Subsequent events review A review of events occurring in the period between the balance sheet date and the audit report date to determine their possible effect on the financial statements.

Type I subsequent events Events that existed at the balance sheet date.

Type II subsequent events Events that did not exist at the balance sheet date, but that may require disclosure.

TRUE-FALSE QUESTIONS

14-1 LO 1 The auditor should consider only quantitative factors when assessing the materiality of detected misstatements.

14-2 LO 1 The PCAOB provides guidance that auditors must consider as they decide whether management's refusal to correct a detected misstatement is indicative of intentional bias.

14-3 LO 2 The auditor is responsible for designing and maintaining policies and procedures to identify, evaluate, and account for contingencies; management is responsible for determining that the auditor has properly identified, accounted for, and disclosed material contingencies.

14-4 LO 2 One source of evidence concerning contingencies is management; a primary source of corroborative evidence concerning contingencies is the client's legal counsel which is obtained in the management representation letter.

14-5 LO 3 With regard to reviewing significant estimates, the auditor is responsible for providing reasonable assurance that the estimates are reasonable.

14-6 LO 3 Auditors should not challenge management estimates that result in current-period reductions in income and associated increases in reserve accounts.

14-7 LO 4 The audit report contains attestation covering information contained in the MD&A section of the annual report.

14-8 LO 4 One of the key disclosures in the annual report is a summary of significant accounting policies used by the company.

14-9 LO 5 Auditing standards recognize that there are inherent limitations in an auditor's ability to detect material misstatements relating to the entity's compliance with laws and regulations.

14-10 LO 5 The legal implications of a company's noncompliance with laws and regulations are ultimately a matter for the auditor to resolve before the audit opinion can be issued.

14-11 LO 6 The going-concern evaluation is based on information obtained from normal audit procedures performed to test management's assertions; no separate procedures are required, unless the auditor believes that there is substantial doubt about the client's ability to continue as a going concern.

14-12 `LO 6` Auditors should not issue a going-concern audit opinion if it would be a self-fulfilling prophecy that the company will, indeed, go bankrupt.

14-13 `LO 7` Performing analytical review procedures in the final review phase of the audit is optional.

14-14 `LO 7` The auditor's expectations when performing final analytical review procedures can be less precise than those for substantive analytics.

14-15 `LO 8` Section 404 of SOX requires the signing officers of publicly traded companies (usually the CEO and CFO) to certify, among other things, that the financial statements are fairly presented in accordance with GAAP.

14-16 `LO 8` One of the purposes of a management representation letter is to confirm oral responses obtained by the auditor earlier in the audit and the continuing appropriateness of those responses.

14-17 `LO 9` Type I subsequent events provide evidence about conditions that existed at the balance sheet date, while Type II subsequent events provide evidence about conditions that did not exist at the balance sheet date, but that may require disclosure.

14-18 `LO 9` An example of a Type I subsequent event would be when a significant lawsuit is initiated relating to an incident that occurred after the balance sheet date.

14-19 `LO 10` If after the audit report date the auditor discovers that an important audit procedure was not performed, then SOX requires that the auditor file a Form 8K with the SEC.

14-20 `LO 10` An example of a situation in which the auditor discovers omitted procedures after the report date would be one in which the auditor failed to confirm receivables and this fact comes to light as part of an internal review program.

14-21 `LO 11` The terms engagement quality review and concurring partner review are synonymous.

14-22 `LO 11` An engagement quality review is required for publicly traded companies, so engagement quality reviews for privately held company audits rarely happen.

14-23 `LO 12` The auditor is required to communicate certain issues with the audit committee; this communication is important because the audit committee serves as an independent subcommittee of the board of directors, and the audit committee can also assist the auditor should a disagreement occur between the auditor and management.

14-24 `LO 12` One of the issues that the auditor is required to communicate to the audit committee is the competence, training, and industry specialization of each of the highest ranking members of the engagement team (the partner, manager, and audit senior).

14-25 `LO 13` The management representation letter and the management letter are both required for the audits of publicly traded companies.

14-26 `LO 13` The management letter helps to provide management comfort that the auditor has done a quality job and that the auditor knows and understands the client's business.

14-27 `LO 14` Existing clients for which the audit firm provided services in the preceding period are evaluated by the audit firm and by the individual engagement partner at the completion of the audit to determine whether the audit firm should continue to provide services again in the next period; the process by which this evaluation occurs is called the client continuance decision.

14-28 [LO 14] Audit firms may discontinue serving a client because the client does not fit the profile or growth strategy of the audit firm.

14-29 [LO 15] KPMG has audited General Electric Company for over 100 years.

14-30 [LO 15] Audit firm rotation is relatively common across the world, whereas audit partner rotation is less common and is not required for audits of publicly traded companies in the U.S.

MULTIPLE-CHOICE QUESTIONS

14-31 [LO 1] The auditor discovers various errors in the client's financial statements during the audit. At the end of the audit, these misstatements are analyzed to determine if they need to be recorded and corrected. In which situation could management and the auditor decide not to correct the misstatement?
a. If, by correcting the misstatement, net income would increase rather than decrease.
b. If, by correcting the misstatement, net income would decrease rather than increase.
c. If the misstatement is material.
d. If the misstatement is immaterial.

14-32 [LO 1] The PCAOB's AS 14 provides insight that auditors must consider as they decide whether management's refusal to correct a detected misstatement is indicative of intentional bias. Which of the following is a form of management bias in this setting?
a. Refusal on the part of management to allow the auditor to communicate with the audit committee about the misstatement.
b. The identification by management of additional adjusting entries that offset misstatements accumulated by the auditor.
c. Refusal on the part of management to allow the auditor to collect additional evidence to evaluate the materiality of the misstatement.
d. The identification by management of procedures that the auditor omitted during the audit, which yield information about the misstatement.

14-33 [LO 2] In obtaining evidence about loss contingencies, which of the following are sources of evidence that the auditor should obtain from management?
a. A description and evaluation of contingencies that existed at the balance sheet date.
b. Assurance that the accounting and disclosure requirements concerning contingent liabilities have been met.
c. Documentation of communication with internal and external legal counsel of the client.
d. All of the above.

14-34 [LO 2] In completing the audit, the auditor must obtain a letter of audit inquiry. Which of the following is an accurate description of a letter of audit inquiry?
a. A letter that is the primary source of corroborative evidence concerning litigation, claims, and assessments, which is received from the client's legal counsel.
b. A letter that is the primary source of corroborative evidence concerning cash valuation, which is received from the client's bank.

   c. A letter that is the primary source of corroborative evidence concerning accounts receivable valuation, which is received from the client's customer.

   d. A letter that is the primary source of corroborative evidence concerning inventory valuation, which is received from the client's supplier.

14-35 `LO 3` In completing the audit, the auditor should review management's significant accounting estimates. In this setting, the auditor is responsible for providing reasonable assurance about which of the following?

   a. The estimates are reasonable.

   b. The estimates are presented in conformity with GAAP.

   c. The disclosure about the estimates is adequate.

   d. All of the above.

14-36 `LO 3` In evaluating the reasonableness of significant accounting estimates, the auditor should consider which of the following?

   a. The significance of the estimate.

   b. The sensitivity of the estimate to variations.

   c. The sensitivity of the estimate to misstatement and bias.

   d. All of the above.

14-37 `LO 4` In completing the audit, the auditor should review the adequacy of the disclosures in the financial statements. When assessing the disclosures, the auditor should have reasonable assurance that which of the following are characteristic of the disclosures?

   a. The disclosed events and transactions have occurred and pertain to the entity.

   b. All the disclosures that should have been included are included.

   c. The disclosures are understandable to users.

   d. All of the above.

14-38 `LO 4` The auditor's report does not provide assurance about which of the following elements of the client's financial reporting?

   a. The 10-K.

   b. The MD&A.

   c. The financial statements.

   d. The disclosures in the footnotes to the financial statements.

14-39 `LO 5` The auditor has responsibility regarding clients' noncompliance with laws and regulations. Obviously, management may try to hide acts involving noncompliance, which limits the auditor's ability to detect such acts. Which of the following are inherent limitations in the audit that limit the auditor's ability to detect acts involving noncompliance?

   a. Laws and regulations often relate to operational issues within the entity that do not necessarily relate to the financial statements, so the information systems relating to financial reporting may not capture noncompliance.

   b. Management may act to conceal noncompliance, or may override controls, or may intentionally misrepresent facts to the auditor.

   c. The legal implications of noncompliance are ultimately a matter for legal authorities to resolve, and are not a matter about which the auditor can resolve.

   d. All of the above.

14-40 `LO 5` Which of the following is an important provision of the Foreign Corrupt Practices Act?

   a. Auditors of clients operating in foreign countries must hire a joint auditor in the foreign country to provide assurance that laws and regulations have been followed by the client.

    b. Auditors of clients operating in foreign countries must ensure that any inventory observations that occur in the foreign country are observed by at least some audit personnel from the U.S.; this requirement is in place because fraud often occurs in inventory accounts.

    c. Companies that have securities listed on U.S. markets must make and keep financial records that accurately and fairly reflect the transactions of the company and must design and maintain an adequate system of internal accounting controls.

    d. Companies that have securities listed on U.S. markets must adhere to the internal control requirements of both the U.S. and the applicable foreign country.

14-41 **LO 6** In evaluating whether the client is a going concern, the auditor should ask which of the following questions?

    a. Are there indicators of going concern problems?

    b. Is it likely that management can mitigate the problems?

    c. Are disclosures about the problems adequate?

    d. All of the above.

14-42 **LO 6** The Altman Z-Score is a model used to help assess the likelihood that a company will go bankrupt. The model contains which of the following ratios?

    a. Working capital to total assets.

    b. Working capital to total sales.

    c. Sales to total debt.

    d. Sales to total accounts receivable.

14-43 **LO 7** Which of the following statements concerning analytical review procedures at the completion of the audit is false?

    a. Analytical procedures help auditors assess the overall presentation of the financial statements.

    b. The auditor's expectations in final analytical procedures should be more precise than those for substantive analytics.

    c. Auditing standards require the use of analytical procedures in the final review phase of the audit to assist in identifying ending account relationships that are unusual.

    d. Ratio analysis, common-size analysis, and analysis of the dollar and percentage changes in each income statement item over the previous year are useful for performing final analytical procedures.

14-44 **LO 7** The analytical procedures of the financial statements of Koss Corporation that are depicted in Exhibit 14.5 reveal which of the following indicators of the fraud?

    a. Cash balances had declined to their lowest level since FYE 2004.

    b. Cost of goods sold as a percentage of sales had risen sharply over the period, with a particularly significant increase from FYE 2008 to 2009.

    c. Net income as a percentage of sales had decreased sharply over the period, with a particularly significant decrease from FYE 2008 to 2009.

    d. All of the above.

14-45 **LO 8** In completing the audit, the auditor must obtain a management representation letter. Which of the following statements about the management representation letter is false?

    a. The management representation letter is intended to remind management about its responsibility for the financial statements.

b. The management representation letter is prepared on the client's letterhead, is addressed to the auditor, and should be signed by the CEO and the CFO.

c. Management's refusal to sign the management representation letter is considered such a violation of ethics and professionalism that auditors of publicly traded clients must resign from the engagement immediately and require the client to file a Form 8K with the SEC.

d. The contents of the management representation letter may be limited to matters that are considered material to the financial statements and should include representations about known fraud involving management or employees.

14-46 [10 8] In completing the audit, the auditor must assess management's representations, including certifications required under SOX for public companies. Which of the following statements is true concerning this certification?

a. Section 302 of SOX requires the signing officers of publicly traded companies (usually the CEO and CFO) to certify, among other things, that the financial statements are fairly presented in accordance with GAAP.

b. Section 302 of SOX requires the auditor of publicly traded companies to certify, among other things, that the financial statements are fairly presented in accordance with GAAP.

c. Section 302 of SOX requires the signing officers of publicly traded companies (usually the CEO and CFO) to certify, among other things, that no material fraud has taken place within the entity for a period not to exceed one year prior to the issuance of the financial statements.

d. Section 302 of SOX requires the auditor of publicly traded companies to certify, among other things, that no material fraud has taken place within the entity for a period not to exceed one year prior to the issuance of the financial statements.

14-47 [10 9] Which of the following is an example of a Type II subsequent event?

a. A lawsuit is settled for a different amount than was accrued.

b. A sale of inventory below carrying value provides evidence that the net realizable value was less than cost at year end.

c. Information becomes available that provides evidence about the valuation of an estimate or reserve that had been accrued at year end.

d. None of the above.

14-48 [10 9] After the report release date, the auditor may become aware of facts that may have affected the financial statements and auditor's report, had the facts been known at the time of issuance. With regard to this situation, which of the following statements is true?

a. Because such facts become known after the report release date, the auditor cannot reasonably be held accountable for these issues; no action is required on the part of the auditor.

b. If the auditor decides that steps should be taken to prevent further reliance on the financial statements and audit report, the client is advised to make appropriate and timely disclosure of these new facts.

c. If such facts would have been investigated had they been known at the report date, the auditor should determine whether engagement personnel are competent and qualified to perform audits; action is required on the part of the auditor to assess whether engagement personnel should be retained to work on the engagement in the subsequent year.

d. If the auditor decides that steps should be taken to prevent further reliance on the financial statements and audit report, the auditor should notify the audit committee immediately; no action beyond this is required on the part of the auditor because of confidentiality concerns.

14-49 **LO 10** Which of the following statements is true when considering omitted audit procedures discovered after the report date?

a. After the audit report has been issued, the auditor may discover that an important audit procedure was not performed.

b. Such an omission may be discovered when audit documentation is reviewed as part of an external or internal review program.

c. The auditor should decide whether the previously issued audit report can still be supported in light of the omitted procedures.

d. All of the above.

14-50 **LO 10** If it is discovered after the report date that the auditor failed to confirm receivables, which of the following statements is true?

a. The auditor should try to examine subsequent collections of accounts receivable to help determine whether the accounts receivables existed and whether they were properly valued at the balance sheet date.

b. The auditor must resign immediately.

c. The auditor must notify the SEC immediately.

d. The auditor must notify users of the financial statements immediately.

14-51 **LO 11** Which of the following statements is false concerning engagement quality reviews?

a. The purpose of the engagement quality review is to provide reasonable assurance that the audit and audit documentation are complete and that they support the audit opinion on the financial statements.

b. The engagement quality review must be documented, and the documentation should include who performed the review, which documents were reviewed, and the date the engagement quality reviewer provided approval of the issuance of the audit opinion.

c. Engagement quality reviews are required for both publicly traded companies and private companies in the U.S.

d. One of the procedures that would be performed during the engagement quality review is to determine if appropriate consultations have taken place on difficult or contentious matters.

14-52 **LO 11** Which of the following is not a procedure that would be performed during an engagement quality review?

a. Evaluating whether or not to continue providing audit services to the client in the subsequent year, based on information gained during the current period audit.

b. Discussing significant matters related to the financial statements and internal controls.

c. Evaluating judgments about materiality and the disposition of corrected and uncorrected identified misstatements.

d. Reviewing the engagement team's evaluation of the firm's independence in relation to the engagement.

14-53 [LO 12] Which of the following is not a typical communication between the auditor and the audit committee?

a. Discussion of the auditor's responsibility under GAAS.

b. Discussion of the client continuance decision.

c. Discussion about auditor independence.

d. Discussion about management judgments and accounting estimates.

14-54 [LO 12] Which of the following is not a typical communication between the auditor and the audit committee?

a. Discussion of the cash confirmation process.

b. Discussion of significant audit adjustments.

c. Discussion of significant accounting policies.

d. Discussion about the quality of the company's accounting principles.

14-55 [LO 13] In completing the audit, the auditor communicates with management via the management letter. Which of the following is false about management letters?

a. The management letter is used to make significant operational or control recommendations to management.

b. Many audit firms consider management's inattention to addressing comments in the letter to be an important risk factor in subsequent-year audits.

c. The management letter is required for publicly traded companies in the U.S., but not privately held companies.

d. All of the above are false.

14-56 [LO 13] In the *Auditing in Practice* feature, "An Example Management Letter to a College Foundation," which of the following items is not present in the management letter?

a. The auditor's observations and recommendations to management.

b. Management's response.

c. The issue of whether/how management responded to the management letter related to the prior year's audit.

d. What actions the auditor will take in the subsequent year audit to help management address the identified weaknesses.

14-57 [LO 14] With regard to client continuance decisions, which of the following is false?

a. Client continuance decisions are one part of the audit firm's overall portfolio management activities.

b. The primary driver of the client continuance decision is the level of audit fees that can be charged to the client.

c. One can view an individual audit client like an individual stock in an investment portfolio.

d. Existing clients for which the audit firm provided services in the preceding period are evaluated by the audit firm and individual engagement partner at the completion of the audit to determine whether the audit firm should continue to provide services again in the next period.

14-58 [LO 14] Which of the following is an example of a risk relevant to the client continuance decision?

a. Client entity characteristics.

b. Independence risk factors.

c. Third party/due diligence risk factors.

d. All of the above.

14-59 [LO 15] Which of the following statements is true regarding audit partner rotation and audit firm rotation?

a. Having a longstanding relationship with the client management could impair the willingness or ability to perform an unbiased assessment of audit evidence.

b. Rules are essentially the same around the world in terms of requirements regarding audit partner rotation and audit firm rotation.

c. A cooling off period is put in place when there is a disagreement between client management and the auditor; it is required to be one year for publicly traded companies according to SOX.

d. The IAASB requires mandatory audit firm rotation after 10 years.

14-60 **LO 15** In the *Auditing in Practice* feature, "KPMG and General Electric Company: A Relationship that has Lasted Over 100 Years," there is a letter from the United Brotherhood of Carpenters Pension Fund to General Electric. In this letter, the Fund requests that General Electric establish an audit firm rotation policy that requires that at least every seven years the Company's audit firm rotate off the engagement for a minimum of three years. Which of the following is not a rationale used in that letter?

a. One important reform to advance the independence, skepticism, and objectivity accounting firms have toward their audit clients is a mandatory auditor rotation requirement.

b. For the largest 100 companies based on market capitalization, auditor tenure averages 28 years. These long term financial relationships result in the payment to audit firms of substantial amounts of dollars over the average period of the engagement.

c. General Electric paid KPMG over $900 million in total fees over the last 7 years.

d. There is substantive evidence that the large audit fees paid to KPMG have resulted in low audit quality.

REVIEW AND SHORT CASE QUESTIONS

PROFESSIONAL SKEPTICISM

NOTE: Completing Review and Short Case Questions does not require the student to reference additional resources and materials.

NOTE: For the remaining problems, we make special note of those addressing fraud, international issues, professional skepticism, and ethics.

14-61 **LO 1** What is an audit adjustment, and why is the resolution of such adjustments important to audit quality? What role should professional skepticism play when management disagrees with the auditor about making an audit adjustment to correct a misstatement? What types of management bias might be revealed in this type of setting?

14-62 **LO 1** How does a summary of possible adjustments help the auditor determine whether the financial statements are fairly presented? What information might it contain? How might an analysis of the summary affect the auditor's internal control report on a public company?

14-63 **LO 1** Why is audit firm culture important in ensuring that individual audit engagement partners resolve audit adjustments in a quality manner?

14-64 **LO 1** During the course of the audit of Nature Sporting Goods, the auditor discovered the following:

• The accounts receivable confirmation work revealed one pricing misstatement. The book value of $12,955.68 should be $11,984.00. The total misstatement based on this difference is $14,465, which includes a $972 known misstatement and an unknown projected misstatement of $13,493.

• Nature Sporting Goods had understated the accrued vacation pay by $13,000. A review of the prior-year documentation indicates the following uncorrected misstatements:

- Accrued vacation pay was understated by $9,000.
- Sales and accounts receivable were overstated by an estimated $60,000 because of cutoff errors.

Prepare a summary of a possible adjustments schedule and draw your conclusion about whether the aggregate effect of these misstatements is material. Use the trial balance numbers shown in Exhibit 14.1, but ignore the misstatements shown in the exhibit. The income tax rate is 40% for the current and prior year. *Note*: Materiality must be considered in developing your answer.

14-65 **LO 1, 16** Refer to the *Auditing in Practice* feature, "The PCAOB Position on Management Bias in Correcting Detected Misstatements." The PCAOB guidance alerts auditors to situations in which management may resist auditor attempts to convince them to correct misstatements, including biases in which:

(1) management selectively corrects misstatements to achieve a financial reporting objective (such as correcting only those that result in increases to net income) and in which
(2) management searches for offsetting misstatements after the auditor has identified existing misstatements.

How do such actions and biases on the part of management reflect on their integrity and ethics? What would management likely use as an explanation for such actions, particularly in the second case? How would management's actions affect the auditor's professional skepticism?

14-66 **LO 2** What is the primary source of information about litigation, claims, and assessments? What is the primary source of corroborative evidence in this regard?

14-67 **LO 2** Why might client lawyers be hesitant to disclose information to auditors?

14-68 **LO 2** Who sends the letter of audit inquiry to the client's lawyers? To whom should the lawyer send the response to that letter?

14-69 **LO 2** What is the effect on the auditor's report of a lawyer's refusal to furnish the information requested in the letter of audit inquiry?

14-70 **LO 2** Each of the following is an independent situation related to a contingency. Describe what the auditor should do in each case.
a. The lawyer refused to furnish the requested information.
b. The lawyer was unable to form an opinion on the probability or amount of a pending lawsuit, but the auditor believes that the amount could be material.
c. The client stated that it had not consulted lawyers during the past year.
d. The client refuses to accrue for, or disclose, a pending lawsuit related to the infringement of a patent that is the basis of its major product. It is afraid that it will lose customers. The plaintiff is suing for $2,500,000, which represents 50% of owners' equity. The lawyer believes that the case can be settled for less than the damages claimed.

14-71 **LO 2** An audit client is being sued for $500,000 for discriminatory hiring practices. Indicate the appropriate action the auditor should take for each of the following independent responses to the letter of audit inquiry:
a. The lawyer stated that there is only a remote chance that the client will lose. The client did not accrue any contingent loss or disclose this situation.

    b. The lawyer stated that the client will probably lose, and the amount of loss could be anywhere between $250,000 and $500,000, with no amount within that range being more likely than another. The client disclosed this situation but did not accrue a loss.

    c. The lawyer stated that there is a reasonable possibility that the client will lose. The client disclosed this situation but did not accrue a loss.

    d. The lawyer stated that the client will probably lose between $250,000 and $500,000, but most likely will lose $400,000. The client accrued a $250,000 contingent loss and disclosed the situation.

PROFESSIONAL SKEPTICISM   **14-72** [LO 3] Why should the auditor exercise heightened professional skepticism concerning accounting estimates? What key factors and assumptions should the auditor consider in evaluating the reasonableness of an estimate?

PROFESSIONAL SKEPTICISM   **14-73** [LO 3] Consider the following areas in which estimates are made in the preparation of financial statements:

    a. Pension obligation

    b. Warranty liability and related expenses

    c. Allowance for uncollectible accounts (manufacturing company)

    d. Allowance for returned goods (such as at a catalog company like Lands' End or L.L. Bean which have a guaranteed-period warranty on catalog sales)

    1. Identify the factors inherent in each account that might significantly affect the dollar estimate of the account balance.

    2. For each factor identified, briefly discuss the importance of the item to the overall account estimate. For example, how important is the interest rate assumption to the overall estimate of the pension liability? *(Hint:* You may want to perform a sensitivity analysis to assess the importance of each factor.)

    3. For each factor identified, briefly describe audit evidence that should be gathered to determine how the factor should be used in making the accounting estimate. For example, how should the auditor determine the proper interest rate assumption in estimating the account balance?

    4. Assuming there are differences between the auditor's estimate and management's estimate, indicate how a professionally skeptical auditor can determine whether management is attempting to manage or smooth earnings or that there is a genuine disagreement on the correct factor to be used in making the estimate.

14-74 [LO 4] How is a disclosure checklist helpful? What precautions should the auditor take when using such a checklist?

14-75 [LO 4] When assessing disclosures, about what matters regarding disclosures should the auditor have reasonable assurance?

14-76 [LO 4] Refer to the *Auditing in Practice* feature, "Related Party Disclosures at OAO Gazprom." What risks do the related party transactions with the Russian government pose for PwC in its audits of the company? Why might companies without such government ownership be less sensitive about their related party disclosures?

14-77 [LO 5] What are the inherent limitations in an auditor's ability to detect material misstatements relating to the client's compliance with laws and regulations?

14-78 `LO 5` What are the main provisions of the Foreign Corrupt Practices Act?

14-79 `LO 5` Refer to the *Auditing in Practice* feature, "Triton Energy and Noncompliance with Laws and Regulations." How did Triton Energy violate the provisions of the Foreign Corrupt Practices Act? What are the auditor's responsibilities when they become aware of violations of law at their client?

14-80 `LO 6` Are auditors required to evaluate the likelihood of a client remaining a going concern as a part of each audit? What types of conditions and factors should auditors consider when making this evaluation?

14-81 `LO 6` An Altman Z-score indicates the possibility that a client will go bankrupt. What effect could this score have on the audit report? Explain.

14-82 `LO 6` List various factors that may indicate that a client may not remain a going concern. For each, indicate the degree of subjectivity and judgment that would be required in determining if the indicator would, in fact, result in the company going bankrupt (use the following categories: high, medium, low). Be prepared to discuss your rationale for the subjectivity and judgment assessment.

14-83 `LO 6` This is the third year audit of GreenLawns. The company has carved out a new market niche on the Web for the delivery of lawn and garden supplies, including links with local companies that provide lawn services. The company issued stock two years ago and raised sufficient capital to continue operations through this year. The company is currently trading at five times revenue. The company showed no profits in its first three years. Revenue growth has been 100%, 65%, and 30%, respectively, over each of the last three years. The current year revenue is at $220 million. The auditor has audited current cash flow and has serious reservations about the ability of the company to remain a going concern without either some profitability or an infusion of cash. The company has responded with the following management plan:
- Another public offering of stock to raise $200 million in capital, which will be equal to 30% of the existing stock outstanding
- Sign an agreement with at least fifty more local distributors during the year
- Improve warehousing and distribution to cut at least 20% off the distribution costs
- Increase sales by 50% through more advertising, coupons, and better marketing to existing customers
- Improve profit margins by using its purchase power to sign more attractive purchase agreements with vendors, but stay away from major-brand vendors such as Scott's, Ortho products, and so forth
    a. What is the auditor's responsibility to evaluate the effectiveness of management's plan? What action should the auditor take if he or she does not believe that management's plan will be effective?
    b. Assume that the auditor modifies the opinion on the financial statements. What does this action say to the users of the financial statements about confidence in management's ability to remain a going concern?
    c. What is the required disclosure regarding management's plans?

d. For each element in management's plan, indicate the auditor's responsibility to assess the element. Indicate audit procedures that should be performed to assess each part of management's plans.

14-84 [LO 7] What is the purpose of performing analytical procedures in completing the audit?

14-85 [LO 7] The audit of GolfDay Company, a manufacturer of bicycle racks and golf carts, is almost finished. Krista Heiss is the most experienced auditor on this audit and is in charge of performing final analytical procedures. The company ships most of its products to a combination of distributors and retailers. The business in totally within the United States at the present time and is seasonal.
a. Why is it important that final analytical procedures be performed by experienced auditors?
b. What are some analytical procedures that Heiss might perform?
c. How can these procedures be useful at this stage of the audit to help ensure audit quality?

[FRAUD]

[PROFESSIONAL SKEPTICISM]

14-86 [LO 7] Refer to Exhibit 14.5, "Identifying Risks at Koss Corporation Using Analytical Procedures." Review the analytical procedure results and trends. Presumably, Sue Sachdeva knew that the auditors might ask pointed questions about the financial results and odd analytics apparent in the data from FYE 2004-FYE 2009. For each of the trends listed below, describe how you think Sachdeva might have tried to explain away the issue (because, of course, she would not admit to the fraud). Indicate how a professionaly skeptical auditor might have responded to her explanations.

Financial Trend	CFO's Likely Explanation
Cash balances have declined to their lowest level since FYE 2004.	
Sales increased over the period, but have returned to about FYE 2004 levels.	
Cost of goods sold as a percentage of sales has risen sharply over the period, with a particularly significant increase from FYE 2008 to 2009.	
Relatedly, gross profit has decreased sharply over the period, with a particularly significant decrease from FYE 2008 to 2009.	
SG&A as a percentage of sales has risen sharply over the period, with a particularly significant increase from FYE 2008 to 2009.	
Net income as a percentage of sales has decreased sharply over the period, with a particularly significant decrease from FYE 2008 to 2009.	
Accounts receivable as a percentage of sales has remained relatively stable over the period, so there do not appear to be problems in billing or collections.	
Current liabilities as a percentage of sales has remained relatively stable over the period, so there do not appear to be problems in the purchasing cycle.	

14-87 `LO 8` What is a management representation letter? Who prepares it? Who should sign it? When should it be dated? How does it differ from the CEO and CFO certification of financial statements?

14-88 `LO 8` What are the implications if management refuses to sign a management representation letter? If management signs a management representation letter, is that a good indication that all of management's statements described in the letter are actually true? What is the importance of professional skepticism in assessing the management representation letter as audit evidence?

PROFESSIONAL SKEPTICISM

14-89 `LO 8` Refer to Exhibit 14.7, "Management Representation Letter Example from AU-C 580." What role does materiality play in the contents of the management representation letter? Is the same level of materiality applied to the audited financial statements as to the management representation letter?

14-90 `LO 9` What are the types of subsequent events the auditor should identify and evaluate as part of performing an audit? Give an example of each type of subsequent event. How should each type be handled in the financial statements?

14-91 `LO 9` What audit procedures should be performed to search for subsequent events?

14-92 `LO 9` Explain the auditor's responsibilities when it is discovered that facts existed at the date of the audit report that were not known to the auditor until after the report release date.

14-93 `LO 9` Refer to the *Auditing in Practice* feature, "Deloitte, Ligand, and the PCAOB: A Case where Subsequent Events were Important." How did James Fazio fail in his duty to evaluate subsequent events? What were the implications of his failure in this regard?

14-94 `LO 9` What is dual dating in terms of the audit report? Assume the following facts: The original audit report is dated March 18, 2013. The company entered into a definitive agreement to discontinue a material line of business on March 22, 2013. This event is disclosed in Note 22 to the financial statements. The report release date was March 25, 2013. On which dates may the auditor date the report? Which dating convention yields the least responsibility for the auditor?

14-95 `LO 9` The auditor is auditing financial statements for the year ended December 31, 2013, and is completing the audit in early March 2014. The following situations have come to the auditor's attention. Indicate and explain whether the financial statements should be adjusted only, adjusted and disclosed, disclosed only, or neither adjusted nor disclosed.
1. On February 12, 2014, the client agreed to an out-of-court settlement of a property damage suit resulting from an accident caused by one of its delivery trucks. The accident occurred on November 20, 2013. An estimated loss of $30,000 was accrued in the 2013 financial statements. The settlement was for $50,000.
2. Same facts as in part 1, except the accident occurred January 1, 2014, and no loss was accrued.
3. The client is a bank. A major commercial loan customer filed for bankruptcy on February 26, 2014. The bankruptcy was caused by an adverse court decision on February 15, 2014, involving a product liability lawsuit initiated in 2012 arising from products sold in 2012.

4. The client purchased raw materials that were received just before year end. The purchase was recorded based on its estimated value. The invoice was not received until January 31, 2014, and the cost was substantially different than was estimated.

5. On February 2, 2014, the board of directors took the following actions:
   (a) Approved officers' salaries for 2014.
   (b) Approved the sale of a significant bond issue.
   (c) Approved a new union contract containing increased wages and fringe benefits for most of the employees. The employees had been on strike since January 2, 2014.

6. A major customer was killed in a boating accident on January 25, 2014. The customer had pledged his boat as collateral against a loan that he took out in 2013. The boat, which was destroyed in the accident, was not insured. The allowance for doubtful accounts is not adequate to cover the anticipated loss.

14-96 `LO 10` During the course of an interoffice quality review, it was discovered that the auditors had failed to consider whether inventory costs of a wholesale client exceeded their market value. The review took place six months after the audit report had been issued. Some prices had apparently been falling near year end. Inventory is a major item in the financial statements, but the auditors do not know whether the market price declines were material.

a. What procedures could the auditors now perform to resolve this audit problem?

b. What should the auditors do if it turns out that inventory was materially overstated?

14-97 `LO 10` What is the auditor's responsibility if, after the report release date, the auditor discovers that an important audit procedure was not performed?

14-98 `LO 11` What are the purposes of the engagement quality review (concurring partner review)? What procedures should the reviewer perform as part of the review process?

14-99 `LO 11` Consistent quality in the performance of an audit is one of the major concerns of all audit firms. However, internal inspections by audit firms themselves, along with external inspections by peer review teams and the PCAOB, point out that although effective audit policies and procedures are generally in place, they are sometimes not consistently performed. The result is that audit quality may sometimes be compromised, yet audit firm management is unaware of which particular audits are of low quality.

a. What audit documentation should engagement quality review partners retain to provide evidence that they have properly evaluated the consistent quality of the audit work performed?

b. Assume that an auditor concludes that all the assumptions regarding warranties are appropriate. What documentation would an engagement quality review partner expect to see to support such a conclusion?

`ETHICS` **14-100** `LO 11, 16` Review the *Professional Judgment in Context* feature, "A Case of Poor Review Quality and Improper Professional Conduct."

a. Why were Nardi's actions harmful to BDO and to the Hemispherx audit?

b. What was the ethical dilemma faced by the manager?

c. What alternative courses of action could Nardi have taken when he discovered that the engagement had not been reviewed and that it was about to be inspected as part of the firm's internal review process?

14-101 [LO 12] Each of the following are typical communications between the auditor and the audit committee. Explain why each is important.
- Auditor's responsibility under GAAP
- Overview and planned scope of the audit
- Auditor independence
- Significant accounting policies
- Management judgments and accounting estimates
- Significant audit adjustments
- Judgments about the quality of the company's accounting principles
- Other information in annual reports
- Disagreements with management
- Major issues discussed with management before retention
- Internal control over financial reporting

14-102 [LO 12] Refer to the *Auditing in Practice* feature, "Guidance on Assessing the Quality, Not Just the Acceptability, of Significant Accounting Policies." Assessing the quality of accounting policies is a matter of professional judgment. What considerations are relevant in making this judgment?

14-103 [LO 13] Describe the purpose of a management letter, and distinguish it from a management representation letter. Refer to the *Auditing in Practice* feature, "An Example Management Letter to a College Foundation." What are the major observations made by the auditor? What is the tone of management's responses? How does management plan to address the observations, and what does this say about management's commitment to financial reporting quality?

14-104 [LO 14] Describe how individual audit clients are both similar to and different from individual stocks in an investment portfolio. What is the difference between a client acceptance decision and a client continuance decision? In which decision-making setting does the auditor have the benefit of deeper knowledge of the client?

14-105 [LO 14] Refer to Exhibit 14.9. What are the three possibilities that may happen to the clients in the audit firm's beginning-of-period client portfolio? What are the two main factors that auditors consider in making client acceptance and continuance decisions?

14-106 [LO 14] The following are the key types of risk that audit firms consider when they make client acceptance and continuance decisions. Provide examples of each of these types of risk.
- Client entity characteristics
- Independence risk factors
- Third party/due diligence risk factors
- Quantitative risk factors
- Qualitative risk factors
- Entity organizational or governance risks
- Financial reporting risks

14-107 [LO 14] Refer to the *Auditing in Practice* feature, "Why Might an Audit Firm Refuse to Continue Providing Services to a Client? The Case of Longtop Financial Technologies and Deloitte." Read the e-mail that Deloitte sent to Longtop management describing their reasons for resigning from the engagement. Briefly describe

INTERNATIONAL

Deloitte's main complaints. Deloitte and other large audit firms would like very much to operate in the China market. What risks do you think might be unique to accepting and retaining clients in a foreign country that is not necessarily supportive of U.S. interests?

14-108 `LO 15` What is audit partner rotation? What is audit firm rotation? What is the fundamental rationale for rotation of either type? What is the primary problem associated with rotation of either type?

14-109 `LO 15` Refer to the *Auditing in Practice* feature, "KPMG and General Electric Company: A Relationship that has Lasted over 100 Years." What are the key arguments put forth by the United Brotherhood of Carpenters Pension Fund (the Fund) supporting audit firm rotation for General Electric? General Electric and KPMG essentially ignored the request by the Fund, and KPMG continues to provide audit services to the company. Do you agree with the Fund, or with General Electric and KPMG? Explain your rationale.

`INTERNATIONAL` **14-110** `LO 15` Refer to Exhibit 14.10. Describe the partner rotation and audit firm rotation rules of the following groups:
- Auditing Standards Board of the AICPA
- PCAOB
- IAASB

CONTEMPORARY AND HISTORICAL CASES

`ETHICS` **14-111** `ERNST & YOUNG`
`LO 1, 16` One of the fundamental changes brought about by the Sarbanes-Oxley Act of 2002 is that the audit profession is no longer self-regulated for audits of public companies. Now, the Public Company Accounting Oversight Board (PCAOB) has the authority to assess whether audit firms are conducting quality audits. To make that assessment, the PCAOB conducts formal inspections of audits completed by audit firms registered with the PCAOB, and the result of those inspections is made public on the PCAOB's website (*www.pcaob.org*; follow the links to inspection reports). The inspection teams select certain high-risk areas for review, inspect the engagement team's workpapers, and interview engagement personnel regarding those areas. In addition, the inspection teams analyze potential adjustments to the issuer's financial statements that had been identified during the audit but not recorded in the financial statements.

The reports that have been released to the public contain a variety of examples of audit engagements in which auditors have had difficulty dealing with potential adjustments to client financial statements. One example of such an audit quality problem is evident in the inspection report of Ernst & Young LLP (November 17, 2005), which states:

> The Firm proposed a judgmental audit adjustment (which the issuer recorded) to increase the issuer's reserve for excess and obsolete inventory, even though the Firm's work papers did not include documentation supporting percentages used to estimate this reserve. After the Firm proposed this audit adjustment, the issuer's chief executive officer proposed an adjustment to increase the value of inventory received in a bankruptcy settlement, which was contrary

to the issuer's earlier conclusion that the bankruptcy settlement accounting would result in no gain or loss. This adjustment was equal to and offset the excess and obsolete inventory adjustment described above. The Firm failed to assess, or failed to include evidence in the work papers that it assessed, whether the offsetting adjustments described above and another set of offsetting year-end adjustments relating to the accounting for major construction contracts (which in total approximated 24% of the issuer's pre-tax income) indicated a bias in management's estimates that could result in material misstatement of the financial statements, and/or a need for the Firm to reevaluate planned audit procedures.

a. Comment on the PCAOB's inspection process, focusing on (1) why it may be needed to assure audit quality and (2) how it may improve audit quality.
b. Review the issue outlined in the preceding inspection report. Summarize the actions of the client and the corresponding actions of Ernst & Young. Discuss the income statement implications of the journal entries that are at the center of this inspection comment.
c. What were the major concerns of the PCAOB about this issue?
d. Assume that you were the audit manager on the Ernst & Young audit engagement detailed in the inspection report. Assume also that you knew the audit partner had agreed to allow the client to pursue the offsetting series of journal entries that are the subject of this case. Using the framework for ethical decision making from Chapter 4, develop an appropriate course of action to pursue.

14-112 DELL INC.
LO 4, 11 In July 2010, the SEC issued a complaint against senior management at Dell Inc. including the company's chairman, CEO, and CFO. The complaint includes allegations that Dell engaged in fraud during the period 2002-2006 by failing to disclose a significant relationship with its major vendor (Intel) that led to Intel's making payments back to Dell. According to the complaint, Intel agreed to make cash payments to Dell in exchange for Dell's promise that it would not purchase microprocessors from Intel's arch-rival, Advanced Micro Devices (AMD). The cash payments were very large, ranging from 10% to 76% of operating income over the period of the fraud. In March 2006, Dell announced that it would begin using AMD as a vendor, and Intel immediately retaliated by ceasing to make its usual cash payments to Dell, thereby resulting in a 36% drop in Dell's quarterly income. In the quarterly earnings conference call, Michael Dell attributed the drop to pricing pressures in the face of slowing demand and to component costs that declined less than expected; of course, these statements were false.

Consider the difficulty that this scheme posed for Dell's auditors, PwC. The most senior members of the management team were actively involved in this deception and had no intention of making full and fair disclosures to investors or the auditors. However, should the auditors have otherwise known of the payments? This question is at the heart of a continuing debate about auditing versus forensic accounting (looking for fraud). The auditors, heretofore, had not seen any reason to question management's integrity, but economic situations and motivations change. Further, instituting a standard audit procedure in which audit software is used to search for cash receipts from major vendors (where only cash disbursements are expected) would have likely uncovered the cash received

FRAUD

PROFESSIONAL SKEPTICISM

from Intel. Should such procedures—even when fraud is not expected—be performed on every audit, simply because such fraud can occur? Perhaps so, but this would also mean that audit firms would have to systematically think about a host of situations that may occur with all clients and add the standard software analysis to the audits—thereby driving up audit costs (maybe without an increase in audit fees).

This example illustrates the difficulty that auditors sometimes face in their obligation to review the adequacy of disclosures—when faced with fraud, intentional concealment, and collusion among the perpetrators, it is very difficult for the auditors to reach an accurate conclusion regarding their audit work. Critics of PwC might say that the audit was conducted in a low-quality manner, thereby resulting in a failure to detect the fraud.

a. Why were Dell's recording and disclosure of the payments from Intel materially false and misleading?

b. What changes in the economic environment, or in the management culture of Dell, might have led PwC to become more skeptical of the company and therefore to expand audit procedures?

c. Should using audit software to identify significant cash receipts from vendors be a normal part of every audit engagement? Explain your rationale and consider such things as audit cost and expectations of the audit.

d. Assume that instead of negotiating payments from Intel, Dell would have negotiated a long-term supply contract with Intel that resulted in lower prices for Intel chips as long as Dell agreed not to use a competitor's chips in its products. Should the amount of the price reduction be disclosed as a separate item in the financial statements under GAAP? Why or why not?

e. Assume the company negotiated lower prices with Intel as described in part d. How would the auditor become aware of the lower prices? Consider that, especially in tougher economic times, almost all companies are negotiating lower prices from their suppliers.

f. Assume the role of the engagement quality review partner. What kinds of review and analysis might have alerted you to the size and nature of the Intel payments?

g. Considering this case and the many ways in which the payments (or price reductions) from Intel could have occurred, how would you decide that the judgments and decisions made by management moves from aggressive accounting to outright fraud?

FRAUD

ETHICS

PROFESSIONAL SKEPTICISM

14-113 MCA FINANCIAL
LO 4, 11, 16   The facts of this case are drawn from the SEC's Accounting and Auditing Enforcement Release No. 2076 (August 5, 2004).

The Company Perpetrating the Fraud This case involves a fraud perpetrated by MCA Financial Corporation, which was incorporated in 1989 as a holding company for four wholly owned subsidiaries, with 45 branch offices in seven states. MCA primarily was involved in the residential mortgage banking business. MCA's fraudulent scheme was accomplished through related-party transactions and involved the following steps.

1. MCA purchased distressed rental properties in the city of Detroit, sold them to the Related Limited Partnerships at inflated prices, advanced the Related Limited Partnerships small

down payments (usually 10% or 20%), and accepted executed mortgages or land contracts for the remainder of the purchase prices.

2. MCA established the prices at which it sold the rental properties to the Related Limited Partnerships by calculating the value each property would have after substantial rehabilitation, even though rehabilitation work had not been completed or even begun. MCA then recognized the entire gain on each sale as revenue, even though MCA knew that the Related Limited Partnerships could not afford to pay for the properties because of the inflated sales prices and the prevailing rental rates. In fact, the Related Limited Partnerships failed to make most of the required loan payments to MCA for the properties.

3. MCA recorded the money owing from the Related Limited Partnerships as a result of advancing the down payments on the asset side of its balance sheet under the heading of Accounts Receivable-Related Parties. MCA carried those receivables without any valuation allowance, despite the Related Limited Partnerships' inability to repay the receivables.

4. MCA fraudulently sold some related-party mortgages and land contracts to the pools and carried the remainder at cost or with an inadequate allowance for loan losses under the headings of Mortgages Held for Resale or Land Contracts Held for Resale, despite the Related Limited Partnerships' inability to repay and the inadequate collateral. The collateral for these mortgages and land contracts was the real estate that MCA had sold to the Related Limited Partnerships at inflated prices. As a result, MCA knew that foreclosing on the collateral would not result in MCA receiving the full principal amount of the loans. MCA did not disclose in its financial statements that a material amount of its mortgages and land contracts held for resale were related-party mortgages and land contracts.

The Auditors Grant Thornton LLP was one of two firms that jointly provided audit services to MCA and jointly signed reports containing unqualified opinions on MCA's annual financial statements from 1993 through 1998. Doerun Mayhew & Co. P.C., a Michigan accounting firm, was the other firm that jointly provided audit services to MCA and jointly signed reports containing unqualified opinions on MCA's annual financial statements from 1993 through 1998.

Peter Behrens is a CPA who served as an engagement partner for Grant Thornton's joint audits of MCA. Marvin Morris is a CPA who served as an engagement partner for Doeren Mayhew's joint audits of MCA. Benedict Rybicki is a CPA who served as the engagement manager for Doeren Mayhew's joint audits of MCA. Morris obtained personal mortgages through MCA in July 1994 for approximately $344,000 and in July 1995 for approximately $200,000. The 1994 mortgage was discharged when the 1995 mortgage was executed. Morris did not review the auditors' work papers for several key portions of the 1998 MCA audit, including the work papers for mortgages and land contracts held for resale and gains on sale of real estate. As late as 2001, Morris stated that he had only ever read the first 13 of the approximately 150 Statements of Financial Accounting Standards. Reading the Statements of Financial Accounting Standards was not "what [Morris did] for a living." Rather, he considered himself a "salesperson."

As the engagement manager, Rybicki signed a work paper in connection with the 1998 MCA audit (a) confirming that the entire MCA engagement had been performed in accordance with professional standards; (b) confirming that related parties or unusual transactions and relationships were properly disclosed and documented in MCA's financial statements; and (c) agreeing with the issuance of the report containing an unqualified opinion. Rybicki socialized with Alexander Ajemian, MCA's controller, during the time that Doeren Mayhew acted as one of MCA's auditors. Rybicki first met Ajemian in approximately 1987, when both were staff accountants at the Detroit office of Pannell Kerr & Forster. Rybicki and Ajemian both played on Pannell Kerr's softball team. They continued playing on the same team even after each had left Pannell Kerr, including while Ajemian was MCA's controller and Rybicki was the engagement manager for the MCA audits. Rybicki, Ajemian, and the remainder of the softball team often ate and drank together after the games.

Between 1993 and 1998, Rybicki and Ajemian occasionally spent weekends in Petosky, Michigan, where they stayed at a lakefront condominium owned by MCA. During the same time period, Rybicki and Ajemian spoke socially on the telephone, ate together, water-skied, and traveled to the Kentucky Derby. After MCA filed for bankruptcy in 1999 and Ajemian pled guilty in 2001 to federal criminal charges in connection with his conduct at MCA, Rybicki and Ajemian continued socializing. They dined together, attended sporting events, played on the same softball team, and traveled together.

While acting as MCA's auditors, Doeren Mayhew and Grant Thornton personnel, including Behrens, Morris, and Rybicki, sometimes attended a party, known as the "Bean Counters Bash," held by Ajemian annually at his home and paid for by MCA. This party was held to celebrate the completion of the annual audit. MCA executives provided Doeren Mayhew and Grant Thornton auditors with free tickets to Detroit Red Wings hockey games and University of Michigan football games. MCA executives also invited the auditors to tailgate parties paid for by MCA at the football games. Rybicki obtained a personal mortgage through MCA for approximately $59,000 to purchase his house in the early 1990s.

During the 1998 MCA audit, Behrens, Morris, and Rybicki knew that millions of dollars of the mortgages and land contracts held for resale reported in MCA's 1998 annual financial statements consisted of related-party mortgages and land contracts. Behrens, Morris, and Rybicki obtained this knowledge through their preparation of the 1998 MCA audit plan, their review of the 1998 audit work papers and other materials, their performance of audit procedures during the 1998 audit, their communications with MCA executives, and/or their knowledge of MCA's business from prior audits.

Specifically with respect to the work papers, Behrens and Rybicki reviewed them as part of the 1998 MCA audit, which showed that MCA sold approximately $10.8 million in real estate to the Related Limited Partnerships in fiscal year 1998. Those work papers also showed that MCA advanced the Related Limited Partnerships a small down payment for the real estate and accepted an executed mortgage or land contract for the remaining portion of the purchase price. Those work papers further calculated that approximately $4.9 million of those related-party mortgages and land contracts had not been sold as of MCA's balance sheet date and thus were included in the total mortgages or land contracts held for resale as reported in MCA's 1998 annual financial statements. Rybicki prepared, and Behrens and Morris reviewed, a work paper in connection with the 1998 MCA audit entitled Audit Planning. In this work paper, Rybicki assessed the audit risk on the MCA engagement as high. Later in the work paper, Rybicki noted that the reasons for the high-risk assessment were that MCA had "significant and/or frequent difficult-to-audit transactions or balances" and "material, related-party transactions on a recurring basis." Behrens and Rybicki also reviewed work papers as part of the 1998 MCA audit that contained balance sheets for the Related Limited Partnerships reflecting approximately $57.3 million in liabilities under the heading of Mortgages and Land Contracts Payable. Behrens and Rybicki additionally reviewed workpapers as part of the 1998 MCA audit that showed approximately $4 million of MCA's land contracts held for resale, those that had been pledged as collateral for one of MCA's debenture offerings, were related-party land contracts.

During the 1998 MCA audit, Behrens, Morris, and Rybicki read MCA's 1998 annual financial statements. Those financial statements did not disclose any related-party mortgages or land contracts held for resale or state the total amount of such mortgages and land contracts held for resale. Grant Thornton and Doeren Mayhew issued a report, dated April 28, 1998, containing an unqualified opinion on MCA's 1998 annual financial statements, even though Behrens, Morris, and Rybicki knew that MCA had failed to disclose material, related-party mortgages, and land contracts.

a. Summarize the nature of the fraud perpetrated by MCA involving related-entity transactions, and describe the problems with the lack of disclosure and engagement review.
b. Summarize the nature of the inappropriate relationships between MCA and its auditors.
c. Discuss how the concepts of auditor independence, ethics, and professional skepticism are related, with an emphasis on the facts in this case. Discuss the issue of what personal relationships are or are not acceptable between an audit firm and the client.
d. Recommend changes that these audit firms should make to improve their quality-control procedures.

15

Audit Reports on Financial Statements

CHAPTER OVERVIEW AND LEARNING OBJECTIVES

Auditing standards for financial statement and integrated audits require auditors to provide **positive assurance**—that is, an explicit statement as to whether the financial statements are presented fairly and, for larger U.S. public companies, whether internal control over financial reporting is effective. The professional auditing standards provide the rules that the auditors should follow when making reporting decisions, and there exist some differences in audit report requirements across the standards of the AICPA, PCAOB, and IAASB.

With respect to the financial statements, the expectation of both the auditor and the client is usually that the report includes an **unqualified**

opinion (sometimes referred to as an **unmodified opinion**); that is, the auditor has no reservations about the fairness of presentation. However, the auditor may have reasons for reservations about the fairness of presentation, or the auditor may have been precluded from gathering sufficient appropriate evidence to render an opinion. For other engagements, the auditor may be able to provide an unqualified opinion, but will also include additional explanatory language as part of the audit report.

In terms of the audit opinion formulation process, this chapter focuses on the reporting decision component of Phase V.

Through studying this chapter, you will be able to achieve these learning objectives:

通过本章的学习，你将能够实现以下学习目标：

1. Identify and describe the principles underlying audit reporting on financial statements.
   识别和描述财务报表审计报告的基本原则。

2. Describe the information that is included in a standard unqualified audit report on financial statements and list the requirements for issuing a standard unqualified report on financial statements.
   描述财务报表标准无保留审计报告中应包含的信息，列示出具财务报表标准无保留审计报告的要求。

3. Describe financial statement audits requiring an unqualified report with explanatory language and identify the appropriate audit report modifications.
   描述注册会计师出具带解释性说明的无保留意见的情形，识别恰当的审计报告修正。

4. Describe financial statement audits requiring a qualified report and identify the appropriate audit report modifications.
   描述注册会计师出具保留意见的情形，识别恰当的审计报告修正。

5. Describe financial statement audits requiring an adverse report and identify the appropriate audit report modifications.
   描述注册会计师出具否定意见的情形，识别恰当的审计报告修正。

6. Describe financial statement audits requiring a disclaimer of opinion and identify the communication the auditor is required to provide.
   描述注册会计师出具无法表示意见的情形，识别注册会计师需要提供的沟通事项。

7. Assess various reporting situations requiring other than a standard unqualified report and determine the appropriate audit report that should be issued.
   评估除标准无保留审计报告之外的各种需要的报告情形，确定发布的审计报告是恰当的。

8. Describe the information that is included in a standard unqualified audit report on internal control over financial reporting and identify the appropriate audit report modifications for situations requiring other than an unqualified report on internal control over financial reporting.
   描述财务报告内部控制标准无保留审计报告中应包含的信息，对于财务报告内部控制无保留审计报告外的其他情形，识别恰当的审计报告修正。

9. Apply the frameworks for professional decision making and ethical decision making to issues involving audit reporting situations.
   运用职业决策和职业道德决策框架解决涉及审计报告的问题。

THE AUDIT OPINION FORMULATION PROCESS

I. Making Client Acceptance and Continuance Decisions
Chapter 14

II. Performing Risk Assessment
Chapters 3, 7 and 9–13

III. Obtaining Evidence about Internal Control Operating Effectiveness
Chapters 8–13 and 16

IV. Obtaining Substantive Evidence about Accounts, Disclosures and Assertions
Chapters 8–13 and 16

V. Completing the Audit and Making Reporting Decisions
Chapters 14 and 15

The Auditing Profession, the Risk of Fraud and Mechanisms to Address Fraud: Regulation, Corporate Governance, and Audit Quality
Chapters 1 and 2

Professional Liability and the Need for Quality Auditor Judgments and Ethical Decisions
Chapter 4

The Audit Opinion Formulation Process and A Framework for Obtaining Audit Evidence
Chapters 5 and 6

PROFESSIONAL JUDGMENT IN CONTEXT

Investors, Auditors, and Standard Setters Debate Changes in Audit Reports

A report issued by CFA Institute in 2010 indicated that investment professionals wanted additional information included in an audit report. A November 2011 article in *Compliance Week* discussed investors' interest in an expanded standard unqualified audit report, as well as disclosure of audit partner names in the audit report. For the last several years, both the Public Company Accounting Oversight Board (PCAOB) and the International Auditing and Assurance Standards Board (IAASB) have been considering possible changes to the standard unqualified audit report. Changes being debated by auditing standard setters and investors include:

- Addition of auditor commentary on matters significant to users' understanding of the audited financial statements, or of the audit, including:
  - the level of materiality applied by the auditor to perform the audit
  - areas of significant difficulty encountered during the audit and their resolution

  - areas of risk of material misstatement of the financial statements identified by the auditor
  - perceptions about the entity and the quality of its financial reporting based on the work done for the financial statement audit
  - information about estimates and judgments, as well as sensitivity analysis around significant judgment areas, unusual transactions, restatements, and accounting policies and practice
- More frequent use of Emphasis of Matter paragraphs
- Disclosure of which engagement partner at the firm supervised the audit and who from outside the audit firm participated in the audit (for example, valuation specialists)

The PCAOB and IAASB have indicated that they will issue proposed standards on the auditor reporting model that may address some of these additional disclosures.

As you read through this chapter, consider the following questions:

- What information is currently included in the standard unqualified audit report? (LO 2)
- How does the standard unqualified audit report issued for U.S. public companies differ from the standard report issued in other parts of the world or for U.S. nonpublic companies? (LO 2)
- What types of additional information could be included in the standard unqualified audit report? (LO 2)
- What circumstances require a deviation from the standard unqualified audit report? (LO 3, 4, 5, 6)

审计报告的基本原则

LO 1 Identify and describe the principles underlying audit reporting on financial statements.

Principles Underlying Audit Reporting

The auditor needs to form an opinion on the financial statements based on an evaluation of the audit evidence obtained, and express clearly that opinion through a written report. The American Institute of Certified Public Accountant's (AICPA) first and seventh principles governing an audit conducted in accordance with generally accepted auditing standards (GAAS) describe the principles underlying audit reporting (AICPA, *Preface to* Codification of Statements on Auditing Standards, *Principles Underlying an Audit Conducted in Accordance With Generally Accepted Auditing Standards*).

Principle 1. "The purpose of an audit is to provide financial statement users with an opinion by the auditor on whether the financial statements are presented fairly, in all material respects, in accordance with the applicable financial reporting framework. An auditor's opinion enhances the degree of confidence that intended users can place in the financial statements."

Principle 7. "Based on an evaluation of the audit evidence obtained, the auditor expresses, in the form of a written report, an opinion in accordance with the auditor's findings, or states that an opinion cannot be expressed. The opinion states whether the financial statements are presented fairly, in all material respects, in accordance with the applicable financial reporting framework."

In essence, these principles require auditors either to express an unqualified opinion on the entire set of financial statements and related footnotes, including all years presented for comparative purposes, or to state the reasons that such an opinion cannot be expressed. If the auditor has reservations about the fairness of presentation, the reason(s) must be stated in the auditor's report. Further, if there is a material departure from generally accepted accounting principles (GAAP), the auditor should explicitly state the nature of the departure and the dollar effects (if such amounts are determinable by the auditor) so that a user can appropriately modify the financial statements to determine what the result would be if they had been fairly presented.

财务报表的标准无保留审计报告

LO 2 Describe the information that is included in a standard unqualified audit report on financial statements and list the requirements for issuing a standard unqualified report on financial statements.

标准无保留审计报告：美国公众公司

Standard Unqualified Audit Reports on Financial Statements

Standard unqualified audit reports on financial statements differ depending on whether the report is issued for a U.S. public company, a U.S. nonpublic company, or a non-U.S. company.

Standard Unqualified Audit Reports: U.S. Public Companies

Audit reports are designed to promote clear communication between the auditor and the financial statement user by delineating:

- What was audited and the relative responsibilities of the client and the auditor (introductory paragraph)

- The nature of the audit process (scope paragraph)
- The auditor's opinion on the fairness of the financial statements (opinion paragraph)

For large U.S. public companies, the auditor's report also refers to the audit of internal control over financial reporting. The auditor may issue a separate report on internal controls or a combined report on both the financial statements and internal controls. If a separate report is issued, the report on the financial statements includes a paragraph after the scope paragraph (before the opinion paragraph) indicating that an audit of internal controls was performed and providing an opinion. If a combined report on both the financial statements and internal control is issued, it includes two additional paragraphs:

- Definition paragraph (after the scope paragraph) that defines what is meant by internal control over financial reporting
- Inherent limitations paragraph (following the definition paragraph) that discusses why internal control may not prevent or detect misstatements

Other important components of an audit report include:

- A title that includes the word *independent*
- An addressee, which for public companies would be the board of directors or shareholders of the organization, but varies depending on the circumstances of the engagement
- An audit report date that is no earlier than the date on which the auditor has obtained sufficient appropriate evidence to support the opinion
- Signature of audit firm
- The city and state from which the auditor's report has been issued

Panel A of Exhibit 15.1 shows an example of an unqualified audit opinion on financial statements when the auditor issues a separate unqualified report on the effectiveness of internal control. The fourth paragraph in Panel A of Exhibit 15.1 (audit report for The Coca-Cola Company) summarizes and refers to a separate report on the client's internal controls.

Panel B of Exhibit 15.1 (audit report for Diageo plc) provides a similar report for a foreign-domiciled U.S. public company. Both reports indicate that the auditors conducted the audit in accordance with PCAOB standards and that the internal control criteria was *Internal Control–Integrated Framework* issued by the Committee of Sponsoring Organizations of the Treadway Commission. The primary difference is that the Diageo report references International Financial Reporting Standards (IFRS) as the reporting framework and the International Accounting Standards Board (IASB) as the relevant accounting standard setter, whereas the Coca-Cola report references U.S. GAAP as the financial accounting reporting framework. The audit opinion formulation process used by auditors reporting on IFRS-based financial statements is generally similar to the process described in this text. However, the criteria on which auditors assess whether financial statements are fairly presented are IFRS.

SEC Requirements for Timeliness of Reporting

The timeliness of the audit report matters. The Security and Exchange Commission (SEC) wants organizations—and their auditors—to provide timely financial information to investors while allowing for enough time to gather sufficient appropriate audit evidence. The SEC also recognizes that smaller companies may not have the same resources to report on a timely fashion compared to larger companies. Therefore, the requirements vary by the size of the organization, as shown in Exhibit 15.2.

| EXHIBIT **15.1** | Examples of Unqualified Audit Reports |

Panel A: Unqualified Report on an Integrated Audit for a U.S. Public Company: The Coca-Cola Company

Report of Independent Registered Public Accounting Firm

Board of Directors and Shareowners
The Coca-Cola Company

We have audited the accompanying consolidated balance sheets of The Coca-Cola Company and subsidiaries as of December 31, 2011 and 2010, and the related consolidated statements of income, shareowner' equity, and cash flows for each of the three years in the period ended December 31, 2011. These financial statements are the responsibility of the Company's management. Our responsibility is to express an opinion on these financial statements based on our audits.

We conducted our audits in accordance with the standards of the Public Company Accounting Oversight Board (United States). Those standards require that we plan and perform the audit to obtain reasonable assurance about whether the financial statements are free of material misstatement. An audit includes examining, on a test basis, evidence supporting the amounts and disclosures in the financial statements. An audit also includes assessing the accounting principles used and significant estimates made by management, as well as evaluating the overall financial statement presentation. We believe that our audits provide a reasonable basis for our opinion.

In our opinion, the financial statements referred to above present fairly, in all material respects, the consolidated financial position of The Coca-Cola Company and subsidiaries at December 31, 2011 and 2010, and the consolidated results of their operations and their cash flows for each of the three years in the period ended December 31, 2011, in conformity with U.S. generally accepted accounting principles.

We also have audited, in accordance with the standards of the Public Company Accounting Oversight Board (United States), The Coca-Cola Company and subsidiaries' internal control over financial reporting as of December 31, 2011, based on criteria established in Internal Control–Integrated Framework issued by the Committee of Sponsoring Organizations of the Treadway Commission and our report dated February 23, 2012 expressed an unqualified opinion thereon.

Ernst & Young LLP

Atlanta, Georgia
February 23, 2012

Source: The Coca-Cola Company. Form 10-K, p. 145, via EDGAR, accessed February 2012. *http://www.sec.gov/Archives/edgar/data/21344/000002134412000007/a2011123110-k.htm#s96424D7AA547AB58D3335FE75818FBAC*

Panel B: Unqualified Report on an Integrated Audit for a Foreign-Domiciled U.S. Public Company: Diageo plc

Report of Independent Registered Public Accounting Firm

The board of directors and shareholders
Diageo plc:

We have audited the accompanying consolidated balance sheets of Diageo plc and subsidiaries as of 30 June 2011 and 2010, and the related consolidated income statements, consolidated statements of comprehensive income, consolidated statements of changes in equityand consolidated statements of cash flows for each of the years in the three-year period ended 30 June 2011 on pages 140 to 233, and including the disclosures identified as 'part of the audited financial statements' within the 'Critical accounting policies' section on pages 83 to 85 and the 'Principal group companies' on page 234. These consolidated financial statements are the responsibility of the company's management. Our responsibility is to express an opinion on these consolidated financial statements based on our audits.

EXHIBIT **15.1**	Examples of Unqualified Audit Reports (*continued*)

We conducted our audits in accordance with the standards of the Public Company Accounting Oversight Board (United States). Those standards require that we plan and perform the audit to obtain reasonable assurance about whether the financial statements are free of material misstatement. An audit includes examining, on a test basis, evidence supporting the amounts and disclosures in the financial statements. An audit also includes assessing the accounting principles used and significant estimates made by management, as well as evaluating the overall financial statement presentation. We believe that our audits provide a reasonable basis for our opinion.

In our opinion, the consolidated financial statements referred to above present fairly, in all material respects, the financial position of Diageo plc and subsidiaries as of 30 June 2011 and 2010, and the results of their operations and their cash flows for each of the years in the three-year period ended 30 June 2011, in conformity with International Financial Reporting Standards (IFRS) as issued by the International Accounting Standards Board and IFRS as adopted by the European Union.

We also have audited, in accordance with the standards of the Public Company Accounting Oversight Board (United States), Diageo plc's internal control over financial reporting as of 30 June 2011, based on criteria established in *Internal Control–Integrated Framework* issued by the Committee of Sponsoring Organisations of the Treadway Commission (COSO), and our report dated 24 August 2011 expressed an unqualified opinion on the effectiveness of the company's internal control over financial reporting.

KPMG Audit Plc

KPMG Audit Plc
London, England
24 August 2011

Source: DIAGEO plc. Form 20-F, p. 139, via EDGAR, accessed February 2012. *http://www.sec.gov/Archives/edgar/data/835403/000104746911007990/a2205476z20-f.htm*

EXHIBIT **15.2**	SEC Reporting Requirements

Size of Filer	Form 10-K (Annual Report)
Large accelerated filer—Market capitalization greater than $700 million	60 days after year end
Accelerated filer—Market capitalization greater than $75 million, but less than $700 million	75 days after year end
Nonaccelerated filer—Market capitalization less than $75 million	90 days after year end

Requirements for a Standard Unqualified Audit Report on the Financial Statements for U.S. Public Companies

Standard unqualified audit reports on financial statements following the PCAOB's reporting standards are illustrated in Panels A and B of Exhibit 15.1. Such reports can be issued for public companies only if:

- There are no material violations of GAAP.
- Disclosures are adequate.
- The auditor was able to perform all of the necessary procedures.
- There was no change in accounting principles that had a material effect on the financial statements.
- The auditor does not have significant doubt about the client remaining a going concern.
- The auditor is independent.

注册会计师能够实施所有必要的审计程序意味着注册会计师已经按照审计准则的规定计划和实施审计工作，在审计过程中未受到限制。

When these conditions are not present, the auditor needs to modify the standard unqualified report in one of the following ways, each of which is discussed later in the chapter:

- Issue an unqualified opinion with explanatory language
- Qualify the audit opinion
- Issue an adverse opinion
- Issue a disclaimer

标准无保留审计报告：美国非公众公司和非美国公司

Standard Unqualified Audit Reports: U.S. Nonpublic Companies and Non-U.S. Companies

U.S. Nonpublic Companies

The components of the audit report for U.S. nonpublic companies are similar to those described for public companies. However, there are some formatting differences because of requirements for specific headings included in the AICPA auditing standards and additional disclosures. Audit reports for U.S. nonpublic companies detail:

- What was audited (introductory paragraph)
- Responsibilities of client management (management's responsibility paragraph; should include the heading "Management's Responsibility for the Financial Statements")
- Responsibilities of the auditor and the nature of the audit process (scope paragraph; should include the heading "Auditor's Responsibility")
- The auditor's opinion on the fairness of the financial statements (opinion paragraph; should include the heading "Opinion")

The language contained in the management's responsibility paragraph is:

> Management is responsible for the preparation and fair presentation of these consolidated financial statements in accordance with accounting principles generally accepted in the United States of America; this includes the design, implementation, and maintenance of internal control relevant to the preparation and fair presentation of consolidated financial statements that are free from material misstatement, whether due to fraud or error. (AICPA, AU-C Section 700, Appendix A)

The language contained in the auditor's responsibility paragraph is:

> Our responsibility is to express an opinion on these consolidated financial statements based on our audits. We conducted our audits in accordance with auditing standards generally accepted in the United States of America. Those standards require that we plan and perform the audit to obtain reasonable assurance about whether the consolidated financial statements are free from material misstatement.
>
> An audit involves performing procedures to obtain audit evidence about the amounts and disclosures in the consolidated financial statements. The procedures selected depend on the auditor's judgment, including the assessment of the risks of material misstatement of the consolidated financial statements, whether due to fraud or error. In making those risk assessments, the auditor considers internal control relevant to the entity's preparation and fair presentation of the consolidated financial statements in order to design audit procedures that are appropriate in the circumstances, but not for the purpose of expressing an opinion on the effectiveness of the entity's internal control. Accordingly, we express no such opinion. An audit also includes evaluating the appropriateness of accounting policies used and the reasonableness of significant accounting estimates made by management, as well as evaluating the overall presentation of the consolidated financial statements.
>
> We believe that the audit evidence we have obtained is sufficient and appropriate to provide a basis for our audit opinion. (AICPA, AU-C Section 700, Appendix A)

Multiple Sets of Auditing Standards For some engagements, the financial statements might be audited in accordance with multiple auditing standards, for example, those generally accepted in the United States of America (GAAS) and International Standards on Auditing (ISA). For those engagements, the auditor's responsibility section should include the following language:

> We conducted our audits in accordance with auditing standards generally accepted in the United States of America and in accordance with International Standards on Auditing. (AICPA, AU-C Section 700, Appendix A)

Non-U.S. Companies

Auditors following the ISAs would refer to ISA 700 for relevant guidance, which is generally consistent with the AICPA's AU-C 700, although there are terminology differences. These differences, however, do not create differences between the applications of the two sets of auditing standards.

One terminology difference of note is that ISA 700 indicates that the description in the auditor's report can refer to either the preparation and fair presentation of the financial statements or the preparation of financial statements that give a true and fair view. U.S. auditing standards do not include any references to the term *true and fair view* because such wording has not historically been used in the United States; GAAS continues to require the use of the term *present fairly, in all material respects* in the auditor's report.

Unqualified Audit Reports with Explanatory Language

带解释性说明的无
保留审计报告

L0 3 Describe financial statement audits requiring an unqualified report with explanatory language and identify the appropriate audit report modifications.

增加解释性说明的情况包括：合理
偏离公认会计原则、公认会计原则
的非连续应用、对客户的持续经营
能力产生重大疑虑、强调事项以及
提及其他注册会计师。

There are five situations in which an auditor may choose to issue an unqualified audit report with explanatory language. Explanatory language would be used to explain the following:

- A justified departure from GAAP
- Inconsistent application of GAAP
- Substantial doubt about the client being a going concern
- The emphasis of some matter, such as unusually important subsequent events, risks, or uncertainties associated with contingencies or significant estimates
- Reference to other auditors

Explanatory Language: Justified Departure from GAAP

解释性说明：合理偏离公
认会计原则

In rare circumstances, the client may have a justified departure from GAAP. Rule 203 of the AICPA Code of Professional Conduct permits the auditor to issue an unqualified opinion when there has been a material departure from GAAP if the client can demonstrate, and the auditor concurs, that due to unusual circumstances, the financial statements would have been misleading had GAAP been followed. What constitutes unusual circumstances is a matter of professional judgment. Examples include new legislation or the evolution of a new form of business transaction.

When a client has a justified departure from GAAP, the auditor should add an informational paragraph, either before or after the opinion paragraph, to describe the departure from GAAP, its approximate effects (if they can be practicably determined), and the reasons for which compliance with GAAP would result in misleading statements. Exhibit 15.3 provides an example of possible audit report language that could be used to describe a justified departure from GAAP.

Explanatory Language: Inconsistent Application of GAAP

解释性说明：公认会计原
则的非连续应用

Changes in accounting principles should be fully disclosed so that a user can make comparisons over time and between companies. A change in

EXHIBIT **15.3**	Example of Possible Audit Report Language Describing a Justified Departure from GAAP

[Standard introductory and scope paragraphs would be followed by the explanatory paragraph provided below. The opinion paragraph would provide the standard unqualified opinion.]

As described in Note 3, in May 20X4, the company exchanged shares of its common stock for $5,060,000 of its outstanding public debt. The fair value of the common stock issued exceeded the carrying amount of the debt by $466,000, which has been shown as an extraordinary loss in the 20X4 statement of operations. Because a portion of the debt exchanged was convertible debt, a literal application of FASB ASC Topic 470 "Debt" would have resulted in a further reduction in net income of $3,611,000, which would have been offset by a corresponding $3,611,000 credit to additional paid-in capital; accordingly, there would have been no net effect on stockholders' investments. In the opinion of company management, with which we agree, a literal application of accounting litera-ture would have resulted in misleading financial statements that do not properly portray the economic consequences of the exchange.

accounting principles includes a change from one GAAP to another, such as from FIFO to LIFO. A change from non-GAAP to GAAP—such as from the cash basis to the accrual basis—is accounted for as a correction of an error, but is treated by the auditor as a change in accounting principle requiring an explanatory paragraph. Both changes would require the auditor to add an explanatory paragraph to the audit report. If there is a change in reporting entity that is not due to a transaction or event, for example, a change to present consolidated statements rather than the statements of an individual company, the auditor would address this change by adding an explanatory paragraph. However, if the change in reporting entity arises from a transac-tion or event such as an acquisition, the auditor would not add an explana-tory paragraph. Changes in accounting estimates and accounting for new transactions are not considered changes in accounting principles. However, a change in estimate affected by an accounting principle does require explan-atory language in the audit report. An accounting change does not include a correction of an error in previously audited financial statements. However, AS 6 does require an additional paragraph for the correction of an error not involving an accounting principle for public companies.

If the client has changed an accounting principle, has reasonable justifi-cation for the change, and has followed GAAP in accounting for and dis-closing this change, the explanatory paragraph serves as a flag directing the user's attention to the relevant footnote disclosure. This flag can be very use-ful. For example, consider a company that reported a 22% increase in net income and highlighted the increase several times in its annual report to shareholders. But only by noting the additional paragraph in the auditor's report and carefully reading the financial statements and footnotes would the user have seen that the increase in net income would have been only 6% had there not been a change in an accounting principle.

If the change in accounting principle is not justified or accounted for correctly, or there is inadequate disclosure, the auditor is dealing with a departure from GAAP. As we note later, a GAAP departure leads to either a qualified audit opinion or, in some cases, an adverse audit opinion.

解释性说明：对客户的持
续经营能力产生重大疑虑

Explanatory Language: Substantial Doubt About the Client Being a Going Concern

As discussed in Chapter 14, the auditor has a responsibility to evaluate whether there is substantial doubt about the client's ability to continue as a going concern for a reasonable period of time. If there is substantial doubt about the client's ability to remain a going concern, the auditor should issue an unqualified opinion that contains an explanatory paragraph following the opinion paragraph, as illustrated in Exhibit 15.4 for Imperial Sugar Company. The explanatory paragraph should be clearly worded to indicate the auditor has *substantial doubt* about the client's continuing as a *going concern* and refer to management's footnote(s) explaining the problems and plans to overcome the problems. Exhibit 15.4 provides the auditor's explanatory paragraph in Panel A, along with management's explanation of the going-concern issue in Panel B.

For some going-concern situations in which the client is experiencing severe financial distress, the auditor may not feel comfortable expressing any opinion. As discussed later in the chapter, in such cases, the auditor may issue a disclaimer of opinion. Finally, if the auditor is convinced that the company will be liquidated, then the auditor should indicate that liquidation values would be more appropriate.

Explanatory Language: Emphasis of a Matter

解释性说明：强调事项

Auditors have the option of including a paragraph with an unqualified opinion to emphasize a matter regarding the financial statements. The choice to emphasize a matter is strictly one of auditor judgment. Examples of such matters that have been emphasized by audit firms in their reports include:

- Significant transactions with related entities
- Important subsequent events, such as a board-of-director decision to divest a major segment of the business
- Important risks or uncertainties associated with contingencies or significant estimates

Exhibit 15.5 illustrates an added paragraph for a change in fiscal year end for Morgan Stanley.

Emphasis-of-Matter Paragraphs and Other-Matter Paragraphs in the Independent Auditor's Report for U.S. Nonpublic Companies

The auditing standards for U.S. nonpublic companies describe an emphasis-of-matter paragraph as a paragraph included in the auditor's report that is required by GAAS, or is included at the auditor's discretion, and that refers to a matter appropriately presented or disclosed in the financial statements that, in the auditor's professional judgment, is of such importance that it is fundamental to users' understanding of the financial statements.

When the auditor includes an emphasis-of-matter paragraph in the auditor's report, the auditor should include it immediately after the opinion paragraph in the auditor's report and use the heading "Emphasis of Matter" or other appropriate heading. Further, the auditor should include in the paragraph a clear reference to the matter being emphasized and to where relevant disclosures that fully describe the matter can be found in the financial statements. Finally, the auditor should indicate that the auditor's opinion is not modified with respect to the matter being emphasized.

AU-C 706 also refers to an other-matter paragraph, which is a paragraph included in the auditor's report that is required by GAAS, or is included at the auditor's discretion, and that refers to a matter other than those presented or disclosed in the financial statements that, in the auditor's professional judgment, is relevant to users' understanding of the audit, the auditor's responsibilities, or the auditor's report. If the auditor chooses to use this type of paragraph, the auditor should do so in a paragraph in the auditor's report with the heading "Other Matter" or other appropriate heading. The auditor should include this paragraph immediately after the opinion paragraph and any emphasis-of-matter paragraph.

EXHIBIT 15.4 Unqualified Report with a Going-Concern Paragraph for Imperial Sugar Company

Panel A: Auditor Reporting on Going-Concern Issue

[The audit report on the 2011 financial statements of Imperial Sugar Company includes introductory, scope, and opinion paragraphs, along with the following going-concern explanatory paragraph.]

The accompanying consolidated financial statements have been prepared assuming that the Company will continue as a going concern. As discussed in Note 1 to the consolidated financial statements, the Company's operating losses, pension plan contributions and capital expenditures have consumed a significant amount of the Company's liquidity. As a result, the Company could trigger the applicability of the financial covenants and other restrictions under the credit agreement for which it will need to seek a waiver from its lenders in order to avoid an event of default under the credit agreement. These conditions raise substantial doubt about the Company's ability to continue as a going concern. Management's plans concerning these matters are also discussed in Note 1 to the consolidated financial statements. The consolidated financial statements do not include any adjustments that might result from the outcome of this uncertainty.

Panel B: Management's Explanation of the Going-Concern Issue in the Notes to the Consolidated Financial Statements

The consolidated financial statements have been prepared on the going concern basis, which contemplates the realization of assets and satisfaction of liabilities in the ordinary course of business. However events and circumstances described below create substantial doubt about the Company's ability to continue as a going concern.

The Company's revolving credit agreement requires the maintenance of certain minimum availability levels or requires the Company to meet a financial covenant related to a minimum earnings level. Operating losses, pension plan contributions and capital expenditures have consumed a significant amount of the Company's liquidity. While the minimum availability levels under the credit agreement have not been breached, future cash needs, including capital expenditures, pension contributions and margin requirements of the commodity futures program, as well as the need to fund possible future operating losses in the event current margin pressures continue, the Company's borrowing availability in fiscal 2012 and beyond may be reduced to levels that would trigger the applicability of the financial covenants and other restrictions under the credit agreement. In such an event, it is possible that the Company will not be in compliance with such covenants and will need to seek a waiver from its lenders in order to avoid an event of default under the credit agreement. There is no assurance that such a waiver will be obtained from our lenders or that the lenders would not condition a waiver on the Company's agreement to terms that could materially limit the Company's ability to make additional borrowings or that could be otherwise disadvantageous.

The Company is attempting to enhance operating cash flow by increasing sales prices and improving operating efficiencies, and is reviewing opportunities to improve its liquidity, including potential sale of assets. In December 2011 the Company sold its one-third interest in Louisiana Sugar Refining, LLC ("LSR") rather than make additional capital contributions necessitated by the financial condition of the venture. The sales price for the Company's one-third interest and certain other assets was $18.0 million with $14.2 million received at closing and the balance payable over the next 21 months. The Company is exploring with its partner the potential of selling their interests in Wholesome Sweeteners, Inc. ("Wholesome") to a third party. Pursuant to the Wholesome joint venture agreement, if a third party agrees to pay a specified minimum price for Wholesome, subject to certain conditions, both the Company and its joint venture partner could be required to sell their interests. However, there is no assurance that these steps will be successful or will improve the Company's financial condition sufficiently to avoid the consequences under the bank credit agreement described above.

The Company's continuation as a going concern is dependant upon its ability to generate sufficient cash flows from operations or increase its liquidity through asset sales in order to meet its obligations as they become due. The consolidated financial statements do not include any adjustments relating to the recoverability and reclassification of recorded assets or amounts and reclassification of liabilities that may result from these uncertainties should the Company be unable to continue as a going concern.

Source: Imperial Sugar Company. 2011 Annual Report, pp. 44, 50, via EDGAR, accessed February 2012. http://www.sec.gov/Archives/edgar/data/831327/000119312512003953/d251187d10k.htm

EXHIBIT **15.5**	Unqualified Report with Emphasis of Important Matter: Morgan Stanley

As discussed in Note 1 to the consolidated financial statements, the Company changed its fiscal year end from November 30 to December 31.

[This paragraph followed the opinion paragraph in Deloitte & Touche's unqualified report on Morgan Stanley's 2010 financial statements and preceded the paragraph describing the opinion on internal control effectiveness.]

/s/ Deloitte & Touche LLP
New York, New York
February 28, 2011

Source: Morgan Stanley. 2010 Annual Report, p. 119, via EDGAR, accessed November 2011. *http://www.sec.gov/Archives/edgar/data/895421/000119312511050049/d10k.htm*

Explanatory Language: Reference to Other Auditors

解释性说明：提及其他注册会计师

The audit client may have branches, warehouses, factories, or subsidiaries at various locations around the country or overseas, and so another audit firm may perform part of the audit. The principal auditor (also referred to as group engagement partner) needs to decide whether to mention the other auditor in the overall audit report. As described in Exhibit 15.6, reporting requirements do differ across the AICPA, PCAOB, and the IAASB. Most notably, international standards do not permit the auditor's report to make reference to another auditor unless required by law or regulation.

Audit firms may require that they audit the whole entity or will refrain from accepting the client. Care must be taken when relying on other auditors' reports because inadequate audits performed by other auditors can lead to legal and regulatory action against the principal auditor as well as the other audit firm. Further, it is very important for the principal auditor to have participated in the audit at a sufficient level, rather than solely relying on the work of the other auditor. However, regardless of whether reference is made in the auditor's report to the report of another auditor, the principal auditor is responsible for the overall opinion. The *Auditing in Practice* feature "Possible Problems When Serving as a Principal Auditor: Insights from the PCAOB" identifies potential problems when serving as a principal auditor.

If the principal audit firm chooses to mention the other firm in the audit report, the wording of the standard report is modified, and no additional paragraph is needed. The resulting opinion is unqualified unless there are other reasons for expressing a different opinion. The most extensive change appears in the introductory paragraph to indicate the shared responsibility for the overall opinion, including the magnitude of the amounts audited by the other firm. The scope and opinion paragraphs are also modified to reference the other auditor. For nonpublic clients, the extensive change would appear in the auditor's responsibility section; and the opinion paragraph would include a reference to the other auditor. The name of the other audit firm is mentioned only with its express permission and if its report is also included in the document.

If the other auditor's report is qualified, the principal auditor must consider whether the subject of the qualification is of such nature and significance in relation to the overall financial statements that it would affect the overall opinion. What was material to the segment audited by the other auditor may not be significant to the overall financial statements.

EXHIBIT **15.6**	Reporting Requirements When Part of an Audit Is Performed by Other Independent Auditors

AICPA Auditing Standards Board (ASB)

AU-C 600 addresses this topic and is essentially the same guidance as is found in ISA 600, which is discussed below. An important point of difference, however, is that AU-C 600 allows for the auditor's report to make reference to another auditor, while ISA 600 does not permit the auditor's report to make reference to another auditor unless required by law or regulation.

Public Company Accounting Oversight Board (PCAOB)

AU 543 discusses the use of the work of other auditors during an audit. This standard notes that the principal auditor has to determine whether his or her involvement in and knowledge of the audit are sufficient to allow him or her to be the principal auditor. The principal auditor then has to decide whether to make reference to the work of any other independent auditors in the audit report.

Reference to the other auditor is generally appropriate when the portion of the financial statements audited by the other auditor is material in relation to the whole. The principal auditor's report should clearly indicate the degree of shared responsibility and the portions of the financial statements audited by each. Therefore, modifications should be made to the introductory, scope, and opinion paragraphs.

References to the other audit firm will likely not be made when:

- The other firm is an associated or correspondent firm.
- The other firm is hired by the principal audit firm that directs the work of the other firm.
- The other firm is hired by the client and the principal auditors are able to satisfy themselves that the work done by the other firm meets their own requirements.
- The amounts audited by the other firm are not material to the combined or consolidated financial statements.

If the principal auditor decides to accept responsibility for the other auditor's work, the principal auditor's standard report is issued without modification. In such a case, the principal auditor's report expresses an opinion on the financial statements as if he or she had conducted the entire audit; no reference is made to the other auditor, or the other auditor's work, in the principal auditor's report.

International Auditing and Assurance Standards Board (IAASB)

ISA 600 discusses the use of a component auditor's work as part of a group audit. A group engagement partner is the partner or other person in the firm who is responsible for the group audit engagement and its performance, and for the auditor's report on the group financial statements that is issued on behalf of the firm. The term group refers to all the components whose financial information is included in the group financial statements. A group always has more than one component. ISA 600 requires that the report of the principal auditor not refer to a component auditor, unless required by law or regulation to include such reference. If such reference is required by law or regulation, the auditor's report shall indicate that the reference does not diminish the group engagement partner's or the his or her firm's responsibility for the group audit opinion, which is the audit opinion on the group financial statements.

The terminology in ISA 600 is somewhat different than that in the PCAOB standard in that ISA 600 refers to a group audit, which is an audit of group financial statements. Group financial statements are those that include the financial information of more than one component. The term group financial statements also refers to combined financial statements aggregating the financial information prepared by components that have no parent but are under common control.

Problems When Serving as a Principal Auditor: Insights from the PCAOB

In July 2010, the PCAOB issued Staff Audit Practice Alert No. 6, *Auditor Considerations Regarding Using the Work of Other Auditors and Engaging Assistants from Outside the Firm*. The report notes:

> The PCAOB staff has observed that a number of registered public accounting firms located in the United States ("U.S.") have been issuing audit reports on financial statements filed by issuers that have substantially all of their operations outside of the U.S. Although there is nothing inherently inappropriate about this, observations from the Board's inspection process suggest that some firms may not be conducting those audits in accordance with PCAOB standards. Specifically, some firms may be issuing audit reports based on the work of another firm, or by using the work of assistants engaged from outside of the firm, without complying with relevant PCAOB standards.

The report describes one situation where a U.S. audit firm was engaged to audit an issuer with substantially all of its operations in China. The U.S. firm retained an audit firm in China to perform audit procedures. Personnel from the U.S. firm did not travel to China during the audit, and the audit procedures performed by the other firm represented substantially all of the audit procedures on the issuer's financial statements. The firm in the China region did not issue a report; the U.S. firm issued an audit report stating that it had audited the financial statements and expressed an unqualified opinion on the financial statements. The PCAOB staff, however, concluded that it was inappropriate for the firm to serve as principal auditor and use the work of the other auditor. A firm cannot serve as principal auditor (and, accordingly, may not sign the audit report on the issuer's financial statements) unless the firm's own participation in the audit is sufficient. The Staff Audit Practice Alert notes:

> If an issuer has no significant operations other than those in another country, a registered public accounting firm that plays no significant part in the audit of the foreign operations is highly unlikely to have sufficient participation in the audit to serve as the issuer's principal auditor. A lack of sufficient participation cannot be overcome by using the work of the other auditor, even if the firm assumes responsibility for that work.

Source: *http://pcaobus.org/Standards/QandA/2010-07-12_APA_6.pdf*

Qualified Reports, Adverse Reports, and Disclaimers

保留意见报告、否定意见报告和无法表示意见报告

Occasionally, circumstances are such that the auditor alters the wording of the standard unqualified report in a manner that affects the type of opinion expressed. In these situations, the auditor cannot issue an unqualified opinion. The issuance of other than unqualified opinions is unusual. The SEC, with limited exceptions, will not accept financial statements for which the audit opinion is other than unqualified. As a result, the auditor has significant leverage to encourage the client to make corrections that would allow for an unqualified audit opinion. When the auditor is not able to give an unqualified opinion, the auditor will provide a **modified opinion**, which could include a qualified opinion, an adverse opinion, or a disclaimer of opinion. In the following sections, we describe these circumstances and the resulting reports for U.S. public companies. The *Auditing in Practice* feature "Language in Modified Reports for U.S. Nonpublic Companies" describes terminology and formatting differences for U.S. nonpublic companies. The guidance discussed in this *Auditing in Practice* feature is generally consistent with the guidance provided in the ISAs.

Language in Modified Reports for U.S. Nonpublic Companies

When the auditor modifies the opinion on the financial statements, the auditor should include a basis for modification paragraph in the auditor's report that provides a description of the matter giving rise to the modification. The auditor should place this paragraph immediately before the opinion paragraph in the auditor's report and use a heading that includes "Basis for Qualified Opinion," "Basis for Adverse Opinion," or "Basis for Disclaimer of Opinion," as appropriate.

Further, when the auditor modifies the audit opinion, the auditor should use a heading that includes "Qualified Opinion," "Adverse Opinion," or "Disclaimer of Opinion," as appropriate, for the opinion paragraph.

When the auditor expresses a qualified or an adverse opinion, the auditor should amend the description of the auditor's responsibility to state that the auditor believes that the audit evidence the auditor has obtained is sufficient and appropriate to provide a basis for the auditor's modified audit opinion.

保留意见审计报告

LO 4 Describe financial statement audits requiring a qualified report and identify the appropriate audit report modifications.

出具保留意见的情形包括：
（1）错报单独或者累计起来对财务报表影响重大，但不具有广泛性；
（2）披露不充分，但不具有广泛性；
（3）由于审计范围受限，以至于未发现的错报（如存在）可能对财务报表产生重大影响，但不具有广泛性。

Qualified Audit Reports

There are three situations in which an auditor will issue a qualified report. These situations occur when there is

- A material unjustified departure from GAAP that is not pervasive
- Inadequate disclosure that is not pervasive
- A scope limitation such that the possible effects on the financial statements of undetected misstatements, if any, could be material but not pervasive

Qualified Report: Material Unjustified Departure from GAAP That is Not Pervasive

If a client has a departure from GAAP that can be isolated to one item, a qualified opinion will usually be expressed. For example, if a client expensed the acquisition cost of some assets that should have been capitalized and depreciated over their useful lives, a qualified opinion would be appropriate. For this example, the opinion paragraph would be modified to state the following:

> In our opinion, except for the effects of not capitalizing the acquisition costs of some assets as discussed in the preceding paragraph, the financial statements referred to above state fairly, ...

The report would also include an explanatory paragraph that, if practicable, would include the effects of the subject matter of the qualification. For the above qualification, the explanatory paragraph would describe how the balance sheet and income statement, including individual line items, would be different if the financial statements did not contain the GAAP departure.

As described later, more **pervasive** GAAP departures, generally affecting more than one item, would result in an adverse opinion.

Qualified Report: Inadequate Disclosure

It is presumed that financial statements include all the necessary disclosures to comply with accounting standards and, perhaps more important, include disclosures designed to keep the financial statements from potentially being misleading. If the client refuses to make the appropriate disclosures, the auditor should express a qualified or adverse opinion, depending on the pervasiveness of the omitted disclosures, and provide the omitted information in the audit report, if practicable. The auditor is not, however, required to prepare and present a basic financial statement, such as an omitted cash-flow statement or segment information.

The introductory and scope paragraphs of the auditor's report are not affected by this situation. The explanatory paragraph should describe the nature of the omitted disclosures, and the opinion paragraph should be modified to describe the nature of the qualification. Exhibit 15.7 provides the qualified opinion for Honda Motor Co., Ltd. because of inadequate disclosure.

Qualified Report: Scope Limitation

An unqualified opinion can be given only when the auditor has been able to conduct the audit in accordance with professional auditing standards. Restrictions on the scope of the audit, whether imposed by the client or by circumstances beyond the auditor's or client's control, may require the auditor to qualify an opinion. In some situations, as discussed below, the circumstances may be such that a disclaimer would be more appropriate.

Examples of circumstances that may limit the audit scope are the timing of the fieldwork, such as being engaged to do the audit after year end, the inability to gather sufficient appropriate evidence, or an inadequacy in the accounting records. For example, when a company is audited for the first time, the audit firm is often appointed during the year to be audited. In such a case, the auditor may not be able to obtain sufficient appropriate evidence concerning the fairness of the beginning inventory, which affects the current year's income, or of the accounting principles used in the prior year. This may be a scope limitation that is beyond the auditor's control. If the auditor can gather sufficient appropriate evidence without being engaged prior to the beginning of the year, then the scope limitation no longer exists, and the auditor can render whatever would be the appropriate audit opinion.

Exhibit 15.8 presents an opinion that is qualified because of an inability to obtain evidence that could impact the valuation of the allowance for loan losses. The scope paragraph refers to the scope limitation, which is then described in an explanatory paragraph. Note that the exception in the opinion paragraph refers to the possible misstatements rather than to the scope limitation.

EXHIBIT 15.7 Opinion Qualification Because of Inadequate Disclosure: Honda Motor Co., Ltd.

[Introductory and scope paragraphs are followed by these explanatory and opinion paragraphs.]

The Company's consolidated financial statements do not disclose certain information required by Statement of Financial Accounting Standards No. 131, "Disclosures about Segments of an Enterprise and Related Information." In our opinion, disclosure of this information is required by U.S. generally accepted accounting principles.

In our opinion, *except for the omission of the segment information referred to in the preceding paragraph,* the consolidated financial statements referred to above present fairly, in all material respects, the financial position of Honda Motor Co., Ltd. and subsidiaries as of March 31, 2005 and 2006, and the results of their operations and their cash flows for each of the years in the three-year period ended March 31, 2006 in conformity with U.S. generally accepted accounting principles.

/S/ KPMG AZSA & Co.
Tokyo, Japan June 23, 2006
[Emphasis added.]

Source: 20-F 1 d20f.htm ANNUAL REPORT, p. F-3, http://www.sec.gov/Archives/edgar/data/715153/000119312506140213/d20f. htm#toc17446_63

| EXHIBIT **15.8** | Opinion Qualification Because of a Scope Limitation: Tennessee Commerce Bancorp, Inc. |

Report of Independent Registered Public Accounting Firm

To the Board of Directors and Shareholders
Tennessee Commerce Bancorp, Inc.

We have audited the accompanying consolidated balance sheets of Tennessee Commerce Bancorp, Inc. and Subsidiaries (collectively, the "Company") as of December 31, 2010 and 2009, and the related consolidated statements of income, changes in shareholders' equity, and cash flows for each of the three years in the period ended December 31, 2010. These consolidated financial statements are the responsibility of the Company's management. Our responsibility is to express an opinion on these consolidated financial statements based on our audits.

Except as discussed in the following paragraph, we conducted our audits in accordance with the standards of the Public Company Accounting Oversight Board (United States). Those standards require that we plan and perform the audit to obtain reasonable assurance about whether the financial statements are free of material misstatement. An audit includes examining, on a test basis, evidence supporting the amounts and disclosures in the financial statements. An audit also includes assessing the accounting principles used and significant estimates made by management, as well as evaluating the overall financial statement presentation. We believe that our audits provide a reasonable basis for our opinion.

Due to an unresolved report of examination from the Federal Deposit Insurance Corporation and Tennessee Department of Financial Institutions that could require adjustments to the allowance for loan losses as discussed in Note 12, we were unable to satisfy ourselves about the valuation of the Company's allowance for loan losses as of December 31, 2010.

In our opinion, except for the effects of such adjustments, if any, as might be determined necessary based on the outcome of the regulatory examination discussed in Note 12, the consolidated financial statements referred to above present fairly, in all material respects, the financial position of Tennessee Commerce Bancorp, Inc. and Subsidiaries as of December 31, 2010 and 2009, and the results of their operations and their cash flows for each of the three years in the period ended December 31, 2010, in conformity with U.S. generally accepted accounting principles.

We were not engaged to examine management's assessment of the effectiveness of Tennessee Commerce Bancorp, Inc. and Subsidiaries' internal control over financial reporting as of December 31, 2010, in accordance with the standards of the Public Company Accounting Oversight Board, included in the accompanying Management's Report on Internal Control Over Financial Reporting and, accordingly, we do not express an opinion thereon.

/s/ KraftCPAs PLLC
Nashville, Tennessee
April 15, 2011

Source: Tennessee Commerce Bankcorp, Inc. 2010 Annual Report, p. F-3, via EDGAR, accessed February 2012. *http://www.sec.gov/Archives/edgar/data/1323033/000104746911003740/a2203054z10-k.htm*

否定意见审计报告

LO 5 Describe financial statement audits requiring an adverse report and identify the appropriate audit report modifications.

如果认为错报单独或累计起来对财务报表的影响重大且具有广泛性，以及披露不充分且对财务报表具有广泛的影响，那么注册会计师应发表否定意见。

Adverse Audit Reports

An auditor issues an adverse report when the financial statements contain a pervasive and material unjustified departure from GAAP, including a lack of important disclosures that is pervasive. An adverse opinion should be expressed when the auditor believes that the financial statements taken as a whole are not presented fairly in conformity with GAAP. This can happen when a significant number of items in the financial statements violate GAAP. For example, if the auditor believes the client is no longer a going concern, GAAP may require the financial statements to reflect liquidation values. If the items are presented in accordance with normal going-concern accounting, the statements are not fairly presented. Such opinions are very

EXHIBIT **15.9**	Example of Possible Audit Report Language Describing a Justified Departure from GAAP

Except as discussed in the following paragraph, we conducted our audits in accordance with the standards of the Public Company Accounting Oversight Board (United States). Those standards require that we plan and perform the audit to obtain reasonable assurance about whether the financial statements are free of material misstatement. An audit includes examining, on a test basis, evidence supporting the amounts and disclosures in the financial statements. An audit also includes assessing the accounting principles used and significant estimates made by management, as well as evaluating the overall financial statement presentation. We believe that our audits provide a reasonable basis for our opinion.

As discussed in Note 2 to the consolidated financial statements, the Company has presented its consolidated financial statements on the going-concern basis, which states assets and liabilities at historical amounts. Because of the magnitude and complexity of the matters discussed in Note 2 (certain of which are not within the direct control of the Company), including the Company's losses from operations, net stockholders' capital deficiency, defaults or other violations of debt covenants, restrictions on its access to the use of a significant proportion of its remaining liquid assets, its present financial inability to complete development of its land held for resale and land held for rental, and the lack of a significant market for its land held for resale and land held for rental, we believe that the Company can no longer carry out its plans and intentions, which are also discussed in Note 2, and cannot convert or otherwise dispose of its assets in the normal course of its business operations. In these circumstances, it is our opinion that generally accepted accounting principles require the Company's assets and liabilities to be stated at their liquidating values. The effect of this departure from generally accepted accounting principles cannot be reasonably determined; however, amounts ultimately received upon liquidation of the assets and amounts ultimately paid to settle liabilities may be different from the amounts stated in the accompanying consolidated financial statements.

In our opinion, *because of the effects of the matters discussed in the preceding paragraph,* the consolidated financial statements *do not present fairly,* in conformity with accounting principles generally accepted in the United States of America, the financial position of the Company, Inc. and its subsidiaries at December 31, 19X5 and 19X4 or the results of their operations or their cash flows for the years then ended.

Note: *Emphasis* added.

rare. Exhibit 15.9 provides possible wording that could be used to reflect a situation when there is a material departure from GAAP. When issuing an adverse opinion, the opinion paragraph should refer to a separate paragraph that provides the basis for the adverse opinion.

Adverse Report: Lack of Important Disclosures That Is Pervasive

While an auditor would typically issue a qualified opinion when the client's financial statements lack disclosures, the auditor could issue an adverse opinion if the omitted disclosures are such that in the judgment of the auditor, the financial statements taken as a whole are not presented fairly in conformity with GAAP.

Audit Reports with a Disclaimer of Opinion

An auditor issues a disclaimer of opinion report in the following situations:

- A scope limitation exists
- Substantial doubt exists about the client being a going concern
- The auditor lacks independence

Disclaimer: Scope Limitation

When the client imposes substantial restrictions on the scope of the audit, there is a significant risk that the client is trying to hide important evidence, and the auditor should ordinarily disclaim an opinion. If scope limitations

无法表示意见审计报告

LO 6 Describe financial statement audits requiring a disclaimer of opinion and identify the communication the auditor is required to provide.

出具无法表示意见的情形包括：
（1）由于审计范围受到限制，以至于未发现的错报（如存在）可能对财务报表产生的影响重大且具有广泛性；
（2）对客户的持续经营能力产生重大疑虑；（3）注册会计师缺乏独立性。

caused by circumstances are such that it is not possible to form an opinion, a disclaimer should also be issued. The wording of the introductory paragraph is modified for a scope limitation, the scope paragraph is omitted, an additional paragraph is inserted to describe the scope limitation(s), and the last paragraph clearly states that no opinion can be expressed.

The introductory paragraph is modified from *We have audited ...* to *We were engaged to audit ...* An example of appropriate language for the last paragraph follows:

> Because of the significance of matters discussed in the preceding paragraph, the scope of our work was not sufficient to enable us to express, and we do not express, an opinion on the financial statements referred to in the first paragraph.

Non-U.S. Companies One difference of note between U.S. auditing standards and ISAs is that ISA 705 requires the auditor to withdraw from the audit when the auditor is unable to obtain sufficient appropriate audit evidence because of a management-imposed scope limitation, and the auditor concludes that the possible effects on the financial statements of undetected misstatements, if any, could be both material and pervasive so that a qualification of the opinion would be inadequate to communicate the gravity of the situation. The U.S. standards have a requirement that the auditor should consider withdrawal from the engagement under such circumstances. However, the auditor is not required to withdraw from an engagement but, rather, should consider whether to withdraw or disclaim an opinion on the financial statements.

Disclaimer: Substantial Doubt About the Client Being a Going Concern

In some reporting situations, doubt about the client continuing as a going concern is such that the auditor does not believe that an additional paragraph to an unqualified opinion is appropriate. In such cases, the auditor may issue a disclaimer of opinion. Such was the case in the auditor's report on the 2010 financial statements of Majestic Capital, Ltd., as shown in Exhibit 15.10.

Disclaimer: Auditor Lacking Independence

When auditors lack independence with respect to a client, they, by definition, cannot perform an audit in accordance with professional auditing standards and are precluded from expressing an opinion on the financial statements. In such cases, a one-paragraph disclaimer should be issued stating the lack of independence, but omitting the reasons for the lack of independence. By omitting the reasons for the lack of independence, the auditor is avoiding the possibility of the user second-guessing the auditor as to independence or lack thereof. The report would have no title or salutation. The following language would be appropriate for a disclaimer report:

> We are not independent with respect to MMM Company and the accompanying balance sheets of the Company as of March 31, 2014 and 2013 and the related statements of operations, stockholders' equity and cash flows for the years then ended were not audited by us, and accordingly, we do not express an opinion on them.

Such a situation should rarely occur. It could happen, for example, when it is discovered late in the audit that one of the auditors on the engagement had a financial interest in the client.

EXHIBIT 15.10 Disclaimer Due to Substantial Doubt About the Client Being a Going Concern—Majestic Capital, Ltd.

Report of Independent Registered Public Accounting Firm

To the Board of Directors and Shareholders
Majestic Capital, Ltd.

We have audited the accompanying consolidated balance sheets of Majestic Capital, Ltd. as of December 31, 2010 and 2009, and the related statements of operations and comprehensive loss, shareholders' equity, and cash flows for the years then ended. Our audit also included the supplemental schedules listed in the Index at Item 15. These financial statements and supplemental schedules are the responsibility of the Company's management. Our responsibility is to report on these financial statements and supplemental schedules based on our audits.

We conducted our audits in accordance with the standards of the Public Company Accounting Oversight Board (United States). Those standards require that we plan and perform the audit to obtain reasonable assurance about whether the financial statements are free of material misstatement. We were not engaged to perform an audit of the Company's internal control over financial reporting. Our audits included consideration of internal control over financial reporting as a basis for designing audit procedures that are appropriate in the circumstances, but not for the purpose of expressing an opinion on the effectiveness of the Company's internal control over financial reporting. Accordingly, we express no such opinion. An audit also includes examining, on a test basis, evidence supporting the amounts and disclosures in the financial statements, assessing the accounting principles used and significant estimates made by management, and evaluating the overall financial statement presentation. We believe that our audits provide a reasonable basis for our report.

The accompanying consolidated financial statements have been prepared assuming the Company will continue as a going concern. As shown in the financial statements, the Company has incurred losses of $44.8 million and $41.6 million for the years ended December 31, 2010 and 2009, respectively. These losses have significantly weakened the Company's financial position and its ability to fund its operations and, at December 31, 2010, the Company's accumulated deficit is $59.8 million. As further discussed in Notes 1 and 24, the following events have limited the sources of cash available to the Company: (1) termination of the Company's previously announced merger with a third party; (2) the conservation and rehabilitation of Majestic Insurance Company, the Company's principal operating subsidiary, by the California Department of Insurance; and (3) the restrictions of the Bermuda Monetary Authority on Twin Bridges, the Company's Bermuda reinsurance subsidiary. Furthermore, as discussed in Note 4, the Company is in violation of covenants governing certain of its contractual obligations. As discussed in Note 1, based on the above factors, the Company may be forced to seek relief through a filing under the U.S. Bankruptcy Code or Bermuda Companies Act (bankruptcy filing). A bankruptcy filing would result in the violation of one or more legal and financial covenants of the Company's debt and other contractual obligations. All of these matters raise substantial doubt about the Company's ability to continue as a going concern. The financial statements do not include any adjustments to reflect the possible future effects on the recoverability and classification of assets or the amounts or classifications of liabilities that may result from the outcome of this uncertainty.

Because of the possible material effects on the financial statements and supplemental schedules referred to above of the matters described in the preceding paragraph, we are unable to, and do not, express an opinion on these financial statements and supplemental schedules as of and for the year ended December 31, 2010.

In our opinion, the 2009 financial statements referred to above present fairly, in all material respects, the consolidated financial position of Majestic Capital, Ltd. at December 31, 2009, and the consolidated results of its operations and its cash flows for the year ended December 31, 2009, in conformity with U.S. generally accepted accounting principles. Also, in our opinion, the related 2009 supplemental schedules, when considered in relation to the basic financial statements taken as a whole, present fairly in all material respects the information set forth therein.

/s/ Ernst & Young LLP
New York, New York
April 21, 2011

Source: Majestic Capital, Ltd. Form 10-K, p. 96, via EDGAR, accessed April 2012. *http://www.sec.gov/Archives/edgar/data/1338949/ 000143774911002503/majestic_10k-123110.htm*

非标准无保留审计报告
间的比较

Comparisons of Modifications to the Standard Unqualified Audit Report

L0 7 Assess various reporting situations requiring other than a standard unqualified report and determine the appropriate audit report that should be issued.

Exhibit 15.11 summarizes the major conditions leading to a modification to the standard unqualified audit report. Deciding on the type of opinion is a judgment that should not be taken lightly. This is particularly true of the decisions based on the materiality level and pervasiveness of GAAP violations, the significance of scope limitations, and the likelihood of the entity being a going concern. Issuing an inappropriate opinion can lead to legal problems. Because of its importance, the decision is often made after consultation with other professionals within the firm.

财务报告内部控制审计
报告

Audit Reports on Internal Control Over Financial Reporting

L0 8 Describe the information that is included in a standard unqualified audit report on internal control over financial reporting and identify the appropriate audit report modifications for situations requiring other than an unqualified report on internal control over financial reporting.

In determining the appropriate opinion on internal control over financial reporting (ICFR), the auditor evaluates identified control deficiencies individually, and in the aggregate, to assess whether there is a material weakness in ICFR. The auditor's assessment, as well as whether there were any scope limitations, will influence the nature of the auditor's opinion. The auditor will issue an unqualified opinion when the auditor determines that there are no material weaknesses in ICFR (refer to Exhibit 1.1 in Chapter 1), and will issue an adverse opinion when the auditor has identified one or more material weaknesses in ICFR (refer to Exhibit 5.13 in Chapter 5).

PCAOB AS 5 identifies five situations in which the auditor will modify the audit report on ICFR effectiveness. These situations include the following:

EXHIBIT 15.11 Summary of Audit Report Modifications for U.S. Public Companies

Condition (Exhibit Number)	Unqualified	Qualified	Adverse	Disclaimer
Justified departure from GAAP (15.3)	1 or 2			
Inconsistent application of GAAP	1			
Substantial doubt about going-concern (15.4,10)*	1			2
Emphasis of a matter (15.5)	1 or 2			
Reference to other auditors (15.6)	3			
Inadequate Disclosure (15.7)**		2	2	
Scope limitation (15.8)***		2 & 4		2 & 5
Unjustified GAAP violation (15.9)**		2	2	
Auditor lacks independence				6

1. Explanatory paragraph *after* opinion paragraph
2. Explanatory paragraph *before* opinion paragraph
3. Modify wording of all three paragraphs
4. Modify scope paragraph
5. Modify introductory paragraph and replace scope paragraph with explanatory paragraph
6. One paragraph disclaimer

*The explanatory paragraph in an unqualified report is adequate. However, the auditor is not precluded from issuing a disclaimer.
**The choice depends on materiality and pervasiveness considerations.
***The choice depends on the importance of the omitted procedures to the auditor's ability to form an opinion. If it is a significant scope limitation imposed by the client, a disclaimer should ordinarily be issued.

- Elements of management's annual report on internal control are incomplete or improperly presented.
- There is a restriction on the scope of the engagement.
- The auditor decides to refer to the report of other auditors as the basis, in part, for the auditor's own report.
- There is other information contained in management's annual report on ICFR.
- Management's annual certification pursuant to section 302 of the Sarbanes-Oxley Act is misstated.

Elements of Management's Annual Report on Internal Control Are Incomplete or Improperly Presented

管理层年度内部控制报告的要素不完整或者披露不恰当

In reviewing management's report, the auditor may conclude that the report is not complete or is improperly presented or does not fairly describe an identified material weakness. If the auditor determines that the report is incomplete or not properly presented, the auditor's report will include an explanatory paragraph that describes the reasons for this determination.

Restriction on the Scope of the Engagement

审计范围受限

The auditor is able to express an opinion on ICFR only if the auditor is able to perform all procedures deemed necessary. If there are restrictions placed on the scope of the engagement, the auditor will either withdraw from the engagement or disclaim an opinion (thereby stating that the auditor does not express an opinion on ICFR effectiveness). Exhibit 15.12 provides an example of such a report.

Auditor Refers to the Report of Other Auditors as the Basis, in Part, for the Auditor's Own Report

注册会计师引用其他注册会计师的报告以为自己的报告提供部分基础

In certain situations, the audit report on ICFR may include a reference by the auditor to work performed by another auditor. Such a reference would occur if the auditor were relying on work of another auditor who might be performing the ICFR audit work at a subsidiary, division, branch, or component of the company. The decision about whether to make reference to another auditor in the report on the audit of ICFR might differ from the corresponding decision as it relates to the audit of the financial statements. For example, the audit report on the financial statements may make reference to the audit of a significant equity investment performed by another auditor, but the report on ICFR might not make a similar reference because management's assessment of ICFR did not include controls at the equity method investee.

Other Information Contained in Management's Annual Report on ICFR

ICFR下包括在管理层年度内部控制报告中的其他信息

In some instances, management may choose to include information in its report on ICFR in addition to the information required to be provided. If management chooses to provide this additional disclosure, the auditor will disclaim an opinion on that additional information.

Management's Annual Certification Pursuant to Section 302 of the Sarbanes-Oxley Act Is Misstated

管理层依据《萨班斯-奥克斯利法案》302条款的要求提供的年度认证包含虚假陈述

In some situations, matters may come to the auditor's attention as a result of the audit of ICFR that would cause the auditor to believe that modifications to the disclosures about changes in ICFR (addressing changes in ICFR

EXHIBIT **15.12**   Disclaimer of Opinion on ICFR Due to Scope Limitation: Taro Pharmaceutical Industries Ltd.

Report of Independent Registered Public Accounting Firm

Board of Directors and Stockholders
Taro Pharmaceutical Industries Ltd.
Yakum, Israel

We have audited the internal control over financial reporting of Taro Pharmaceutical Industries Ltd. and its subsidiaries (the "Company") as of December 31, 2007, based on criteria established in *Internal Control–Integrated Framework* issued by the Committee of Sponsoring Organizations of the Treadway Commission (the COSO criteria). The Company's management is responsible for maintaining effective internal control over financial reporting and for its assessment on the effectiveness of internal control over financial reporting, included in the accompanying Report on Internal Control Over Financial Reporting. Our responsibility is to express an opinion on the Company's internal control over financial reporting based on our audit.

We conducted our audit in accordance with the standards of the Public Company Accounting Oversight Board (United States). Those standards require that we plan and perform the audit to obtain reasonable assurance about whether effective internal control over financial reporting was maintained in all material respects. Our audit included obtaining an understanding of internal control over financial reporting, assessing the risk that a material weakness exists, testing and evaluating the design and operating effectiveness of internal control based on that risk, and performing such other procedures as we considered necessary in the circumstances. We believe that our audit provides a reasonable basis for our opinion.

A company's internal control over financial reporting is a process designed to provide reasonable assurance regarding the reliability of financial reporting and the preparation of financial statements for external purposes in accordance with generally accepted accounting principles. A company's internal control over financial reporting includes those policies and procedures that (1) pertain to the maintenance of records that, in reasonable detail, accurately and fairly reflect the transactions and dispositions of the assets of the company; (2) provide reasonable assurance that transactions are recorded as necessary to permit preparation of financial statements in accordance with generally accepted accounting principles, and that receipts and expenditures of the company are being made only in accordance with authorizations of management and directors of the company; and (3) provide reasonable assurance regarding prevention or timely detection of unauthorized acquisition, use, or disposition of the company's assets that could have a material effect on the financial statements.

Because of its inherent limitations, internal control over financial reporting may not prevent or detect misstatements. Also, projections of any evaluation of effectiveness to future periods are subject to the risk that controls may become inadequate because of changes in conditions, or that the degree of compliance with the policies or procedures may deteriorate.

Since management was unable to complete all of its testing of internal controls and we were unable to apply other procedures to satisfy ourselves as to the effectiveness of the Company's internal control over financial reporting, the scope of our work was not sufficient to enable us to express, and we do not express, an opinion on the effectiveness of the Company's internal control over financial reporting.

Nevertheless, we draw attention to management conclusion that the Company has at least the following material weaknesses in internal control over financial reporting as of December 31, 2007:

- Control Activities Associated with Financial Statement Closing Processes. The Company identified material weaknesses in its financial statement closing processes arising from the potential for a material error in the financial statements from consideration of the following deficiencies:
  - Estimating certain accounts receivable reserves and sales deductions including rebates and other sales deductions.
  - Significant, complex and non-routine transactions, including the area of taxation and certain other accounting items.
  - Ensuring adequate preparation, timely review and documented approval of account reconciliations, journal entries, both recurring and non-recurring and certain information primarily in the form of spreadsheets that supports our financial reporting process, and consistent communication among the various

EXHIBIT **15.12** Disclaimer of Opinion on ICFR Due to Scope Limitation: Taro Pharmaceutical Industries Ltd. (*continued*)

finance and non-finance organizations across the Company on the terms of our commercial arrangements.

- Revenue. The Company lacks the proper procedures and controls in estimating its rebate and other deductions reserves, including indirect and Medicaid rebates. Specifically, the Company is dependent on manual processes and experienced turnover in the roles responsible for certain estimates and lacked sufficient time and resources to properly and fully estimate these reserves. As a result, the Company did not consistently and accurately record the provision at the time of the sale.
- Inventory. The Company found that adjustments of inventory and cost of goods sold were necessary and mainly relate to errors in the assessment of inventory valuation. Inventory valuation adjustments primarily resulted due to the errors identified in the accounts receivable reserves, which impacted the computation of the Company's net selling prices which resulted in changes to inventory valuation.
- Income Taxes. The Company did not maintain adequate policies and procedures and related internal controls or employ adequate resources with sufficient technical expertise, on a global basis, in the area of accounting for income taxes to ensure the completeness, accuracy, and timely preparation and review of our consolidated income tax provision, related account balances and disclosures sufficient to prevent a material misstatement of related account balances. In addition, the Company was unable to finalize its tax provision due to the lack of audited financial statements for prior years.

These material weaknesses, identified by management, were considered in determining the nature, timing, and extent of audit tests applied in our audit of the consolidated financial statements as of and for the year ended December 31, 2007, of the Company and this report does not affect our report dated June 29, 2011, on those financial statements.

We also have audited, in accordance with the standards of the Public Company Accounting Oversight Board (United States) the consolidated balance sheets of Taro Pharmaceutical Industries Ltd. as of December 31, 2007, and the related consolidated statements of income and comprehensive income, stockholders' equity, and cash flows for the year end December 31, 2007 and our report dated June 29, 2011 expressed an unqualified opinion thereon.

/s/ Ziv Haft
Ziv Haft
Certified Public Accountants (Isr)
BDO Member Firm
June 29, 2011

Tel Aviv: Tel: 972(0)3-6386868 Fax: 972(0)3-6394320 **Jerusalem:** Tel: 972(0)2-6546200 Fax: 972(0)2-6526633
Haifa: Tel: 972(0)4-8680600 Fax: 972(0)4-8620866 **Be'er Sheva:** Tel: 972(0)77-6900700 Fax: 972(0)3-6368714
Kiryat Shmona: Tel: 972(0)4-6951389 Fax: 972(0)4-6950004 **Be'ne Braq:** Tel: 972(0)73-7145300 Fax: 972(0)73-7145317

BDO Israel, an Israeli partnership, is a member of BDO International Limited, a UK company limited by guarantee, and forms part of the international BDO network of independent member firms. BDO is the brand name for the BDO network and for each of the BDO Member Firms

occurring during the fourth quarter) are necessary for the annual certifications to be accurate and to comply with the requirements of Section 302 of Sarbanes-Oxley. The auditor should modify the report on ICFR to include an explanatory paragraph describing the reasons the auditor believes management's disclosures should be modified.

SUMMARY AND NEXT STEPS

With the completion of this chapter, you have now worked through all the audit activities in the audit opinion formulation process. Determining the appropriate audit report to issue is an important part of that process as the audit report is the primary means that the auditor has of communicating the results of the audit to the users of the financial statements. While it is typically expected that the auditor will issue an unqualified opinion on the financial statements and internal control, this chapter describes situations in which modifications to the reports including those opinions are warranted.

Although you have completed all of the phases of the audit opinion formulation process, the next chapter covers some complex judgments that you might encounter at various points in the audit process.

SIGNIFICANT TERMS

Component   An entity or business activity for which group or component management prepares financial information that is required by the applicable financial reporting framework to be included in the group financial statements.

Component auditor   An auditor who performs work on the financial information of a component that will be used as audit evidence for the group audit. A component auditor may be part of the group engagement partner's firm, a network firm of the group engagement partner's firm, or another firm.

Group   All the components whose financial information is included in the group financial statements. A group always has more than one component.

Group audit   The audit of group financial statements.

Group audit opinion   The audit opinion on the group financial statements.

Group engagement partner   The partner or other person in the firm who is responsible for the group audit engagement and its performance, and for the auditor's report on the group financial statements that is issued on behalf of the firm.

Group financial statements   Financial statements that include the financial information of more than one component. The term *group financial statements* also refers to combined financial statements aggregating the financial information prepared by components that have no parent but are under common control.

Modified opinion   A qualified opinion, an adverse opinion, or a disclaimer of opinion.

Pervasive   A term used in the context of misstatements to describe the effects or the possible effects on the financial statements of misstatements that are undetected due to an inability to obtain sufficient appropriate audit evidence.

Positive assurance   An explicit statement as to whether the financial statements are presented fairly.

Unmodified opinion   See unqualified opinion.

Unqualified opinion   The opinion expressed by the auditor when the auditor concludes that the financial statements are presented fairly, in all material respects, in accordance with the applicable financial reporting framework.

TRUE-FALSE QUESTIONS

15-1   `LO 1`   The auditor should provide an opinion on the financial statements only if the opinion indicates that the financial statements are fairly stated in all material respects.

15-2   `LO 1`   The auditor's opinion should be provided in a written report.

15-3   `LO 2`   The audit opinion for a U.S. public company includes an introductory paragraph that identifies what was audited and the relative responsibilities of management and the auditor.

15-4   `LO 2`   If an auditor conducts an audit in accordance with multiple auditing standards, only one set of standards can be mentioned in the audit report.

15-5   `LO 3`   If an auditor decides to include explanatory language in the audit report because of concerns about the client's ability to remain a going concern, the explanatory paragraph should include the terms *material doubt* and *going concern*.

15-6   `LO 3`   International auditing standards generally permit the auditor to refer to other auditors in the auditor's report, while the U.S. auditing standards allow this reference only if required by law or regulation.

15-7   `LO 4`   A qualified audit report would usually be issued when the client's financial statements contain a justified departure from GAAP.

15-8   `LO 4`   An auditor's inability to obtain evidence that could impact the allowance for loan losses would likely lead to a qualified audit opinion.

15-9   `LO 5`   The primary reason for issuing an adverse audit opinion is that the client's financial statements contain a pervasive and material unjustified departure from GAAP.

15-10   `LO 5`   An adverse opinion would contain language indicating that the financial statements are not presented fairly in accordance with GAAP.

15-11   `LO 6`   If the auditor issues a disclaimer because of a scope limitation, the scope paragraph of the report is moved to the beginning of the report.

15-12   `LO 6`   When the auditor issues a disclaimer because of a lack of independence, the audit report should state the lack of independence, and describe the reasons for the lack of independence.

15-13   `LO 7`   When the financial statements contain a justified departure from GAAP, the auditor can choose between an unqualified and qualified opinion.

15-14   `LO 7`   If the auditor lacks independence, the auditor can choose between an adverse opinion and a disclaimer of opinion.

15-15   `LO 8`   The auditor issues an adverse opinion on ICFR if the client has one or more significant deficiencies in ICFR.

15-16   `LO 8`   If there are restrictions placed on the scope of the engagement being conducted for purposes of issuing an opinion on ICFR, the auditor either withdraws from the engagement or disclaims an opinion.

MULTIPLE-CHOICE QUESTIONS

15-17 [LO 1] Which of the following statements is false regarding audit reporting?
   a. The auditor's opinion should be expressed in a written report.
   b. The auditor should provide an opinion in accordance with the auditor's findings or state that an opinion cannot be expressed.
   c. The opinion should state whether the financial statements are presented fairly, in all material respects, in accordance with the applicable financial reporting framework.
   d. None of the above statements are false.

15-18 [LO 1] Which of the following statements is true regarding the auditor's responsibilities related to reporting?
   a. Sufficient appropriate evidence should be obtained to afford a reasonable basis for the opinion regarding the financial statements under audit.
   b. The audit opinion relates only to the client's financial statements, and does not relate to the required footnote disclosures.
   c. If the auditor has reservations about the fairness of presentation of the financial statements, the auditor does not need to provide the reason for this reservation, but needs to only state that the financial statements are not fairly presented.
   d. All of the above statements are true.

15-19 [LO 2] In which of the following situations would an auditor ordinarily issue an unqualified audit opinion without an explanatory paragraph?
   a. The auditor wishes to emphasize that the entity had significant related-party transactions.
   b. The auditor decides to refer to the report of another auditor as a basis, in part, for the auditor's opinion.
   c. The entity issues financial statements that present financial position and results of operations but omits the statement of cash flows.
   d. The auditor has substantial doubt about the entity's ability to continue as a going concern, but the circumstances are fully disclosed in the financial statements.

15-20 [LO 2] Which of the following describes a situation when an auditor cannot typically issue a standard unqualified audit opinion?
   a. The client has prepared its financial statements using IFRS as the financial reporting framework.
   b. The auditor has complied with the auditing standards of both the AICPA and the IAASB.
   c. The auditor is not independent.
   d. The auditor believes that the client will remain a going concern for a reasonable period of time.

15-21 [LO 3] In which of the following situations would an auditor typically issue an unqualified opinion, but include explanatory language?
   a. The client has changed an accounting principle, has reasonable justification for the change, and has followed GAAP in accounting for and disclosing the change.
   b. The auditor has substantial doubt about the client being a going concern.
   c. The client has had significant transactions with related entities that the auditor wants to emphasize.
   d. An auditor would typically issue an unqualified opinion, but include explanatory language, in all of the above situations.

15-22 [LO 3] Eagle Company's financial statements contain a departure from GAAP because, due to unusual circumstances, the statements would otherwise be misleading. Which of the following audit opinions should the auditor provide?

a. Unqualified, but not mention the departure in the auditor's report.
b. Unqualified, and describe the departure in a separate paragraph of the audit report.
c. Qualified, and describe the departure in a separate paragraph of the audit report.
d. Qualified or adverse, depending on materiality, and describe the departure in a separate paragraph of the audit report.

15-23 `LO 4` Tech Company has an uncertainty because of pending litigation. The auditor's decision to issue a qualified opinion rather than an unqualified opinion most likely would be determined by which of the following?

a. Lack of sufficient evidence.
b. Inability to estimate the amount of loss.
c. The client's lack of experience with such litigation.
d. Adequacy of the disclosures.

15-24 `LO 4` Which of the following phrases should not be used when the auditor is qualifying the audit opinion?

a. With the exception of
b. Except for
c. Subject to
d. Any of the above phrases would be appropriate.

15-25 `LO 5` In which of the following circumstances would an auditor be most likely to express an adverse opinion on a company's financial statements?

a. Information comes to the auditor's attention that raises substantial doubt about the company's ability to continue as a going concern.
b. The auditor is denied access to minutes of board of directors' meetings by the client.
c. Tests of controls indicate that the organization's ICFR is ineffective.
d. The financial statements are not in conformity with FASB requirements regarding the capitalization of leases.

15-26 `LO 5` When an auditor issues an adverse opinion, which of the following should be included in the opinion paragraph?

a. The reasons that the financial statements are misleading.
b. A reference to a separate paragraph that describes the reason for the adverse opinion.
c. A statement that indicates that the financial statements are fairly stated except for a reason that is described in the separate paragraph.
d. The financial statement effects of the departure from GAAP.

15-27 `LO 6` When disclaiming an opinion because of a client-imposed scope limitation, which of the following is false regarding changes that would be made to the audit report?

a. The auditor would indicate in a separate paragraph why the audit did not comply with professional auditing standards.
b. The auditor would omit the scope paragraph.
c. The auditor would modify the introductory paragraph.
d. The auditor would omit the opinion paragraph.

15-28 `LO 6` In which of the following situations would a disclaimer of opinion not be appropriate?

a. The auditor is not independent.
b. The client imposed a substantial restriction on the scope of the audit.
c. The financial statements have a departure from GAAP that is not justified.
d. A disclaimer of opinion would be appropriate in all of the above situations.

15-29 [LO 7] In which of the following situations would an auditor usually choose between issuing a qualified opinion and issuing a disclaimer of opinion?
a. Departure from GAAP.
b. Inadequate disclosure of accounting policies.
c. Inability to obtain sufficient appropriate evidence for a reason other than a management-imposed scope restriction.
d. Unreasonable justification for a change in accounting principles.

15-30 [LO 7] Tread Corp. accounts for the effect of a material accounting change prospectively, when the inclusion of the cumulative effect of the change is required in the current year. The auditor would choose which of the following opinions?
a. Qualified opinion or a disclaimer of opinion.
b. Disclaimer of opinion or an unqualified opinion with an explanatory paragraph.
c. Unqualified opinion with an explanatory paragraph or an adverse opinion.
d. Qualified opinion or an adverse opinion.

15-31 [LO 8] The auditor of a large U.S. public company has determined that a material weakness exists in the client's ICFR. Which of the following statements is true?
a. Such a weakness requires an adverse opinion of the financial statements.
b. The auditor should express an adverse opinion on internal controls only if a material misstatement was found in the financial statements.
c. The auditor should express an adverse opinion on internal controls, even though no material misstatements were found in the financial statements.
d. The auditor is not required to express an opinion on internal controls.

15-32 [LO 8] In which of the following situations would the auditor modify the audit report on ICFR?
a. The auditor identifies multiple unrelated significant deficiencies in ICFR.
b. The auditor concludes that management's report on ICFR is not complete or is improperly presented.
c. The auditor relies on the work of other auditors, but decides not to include a reference to the other auditors.
d. The auditor would modify the audit report on ICFR in all of the above situations.

REVIEW AND SHORT CASE QUESTIONS

Note: Completing Review and Short Case Questions does not require the student to reference additional resources and materials.

Note: For the remaining problems, we make special note of those addressing fraud, international issues, professional skepticism, and ethics.

15-33 [LO 1] Why is the audit report important to the audit opinion formulation process?

15-34 [LO 1] What are the requirements of the AICPA's Principles 1 and 7 regarding audit reporting?

15-35 [LO 2] Under what circumstances may an auditor express an unqualified opinion when the related financial statements contain a material departure from a FASB standard?

15-36 [LO 2] What conditions must be present for an auditor to be able to issue a standard unqualified audit report similar to the ones presented in Exhibit 15.1?

15-37 [LO 2] Review Exhibit 15.2 and identify the timing requirements for U.S. public companies to file audited financial statements with the SEC.

15-38 [LO 2] List the components of a standard unqualified audit report for a U.S. public company.

15-39 [LO 2] Identify the primary difference in auditor reporting terminology between AU-C 700 and ISA 700. INTERNATIONAL

15-40 [LO 2] How would the auditor's opinion differ if the financial statements of a company that was a foreign private issuer were prepared in conformity with IFRS and filed with the SEC rather than prepared in conformity with U.S. GAAP? INTERNATIONAL

15-41 [LO 2] Refer to Panel A of Exhibit 15.1. What words and phrases in an unqualified audit report imply that there is a risk that the audited financial statements may contain a material misstatement?

15-42 [LO 3] Refer to Exhibit 15.6. Under what circumstances might the auditor choose not to refer to other auditors who worked on a part of the audit? How do the requirements differ under international auditing standards? INTERNATIONAL

15-43 [LO 3] You are in charge of the audit of the financial statements of Parat, Inc. and consolidated subsidiaries, covering the two years ended December 31, 2014. Another public accounting firm is auditing Nuam, Inc., a major subsidiary of Parat that accounts for total assets, revenue, and net income of 30%, 26%, and 39%, respectively, for 2013, and 28%, 20%, and 33% for 2014.
   a. What is meant by the term *principal auditor?* What term can be used in place of *principal auditor?*
   b. Write the audit report referring to the other audit firm and expressing an unqualified opinion.

15-44 [LO 3] The following audit report was drafted by a staff accountant of Turner & Turner, CPAs, at the completion of the audit of the financial statements of Lyon Computers, Inc. (a public company) for the year ended March 31, 2014. It was submitted to the engagement partner, who reviewed matters thoroughly and properly concluded that Lyon's disclosures concerning its ability to continue as a going concern for a reasonable period of time were adequate, but there is substantial doubt about Lyon being a going concern. Identify the deficiencies contained in the audit report as drafted by the staff accountant. Group the deficiencies by paragraph. Do not redraft the report.

To the Board of Directors of Lyon Computers, Inc.:

We have audited the accompanying balance sheet of Lyon Computers, Inc. as of March 31, 2014, and the other related financial statements for the year then ended. Our responsibility is to express an opinion on these financial statements based on our audit.

We conducted our audit in accordance with standards that require that we plan and perform the audit to obtain reasonable assurance about whether the financial statements are in conformity with generally accepted accounting principles. An audit includes examining, on a test basis, evidence supporting the amounts and disclosures in the financial statements. An audit also includes assessing the accounting principles used and significant estimates made by management.

The accompanying financial statements have been prepared assuming that the Company will continue as a going concern. As discussed in Note X to the financial statements, the Company has suffered recurring losses from operations and has a net capital deficiency that raises substantial doubt about its ability to continue as a going concern. We believe that management's plans in regard to these matters, which are also described in Note X, will permit the Company to continue as a going concern beyond a reasonable period of time. The financial statements do not include any adjustments that might result from the outcome of this uncertainty.

In our opinion, subject to the effects on the financial statements of such adjustments, if any, as might have been required had the outcome of the uncertainty referred to in the preceding paragraph been known, the financial statements referred to above present fairly, in all material respects, the financial position of Lyon Computers, Inc., and the results of its operations and its cash flows in conformity with generally accepted accounting principles applied on a basis consistent with that of the preceding year.

Turner & Turner, CPAs
April 28, 2014

15-45 [L0 3] The accounting and auditing literature discusses several different types of accounting changes. For each of the changes listed below (a. through e.), indicate whether the auditor should add a paragraph to the audit report, assuming that the change had a material effect on the financial statements and was properly justified, accounted for, and disclosed. Assume that the organization is a U.S. nonpublic company.

a. Change from one GAAP to another GAAP

b. Change in accounting estimate not affected by a change in accounting principle

c. Change in accounting estimate affected by a change in accounting principle

d. Correction of an error

e. Change from non-GAAP to GAAP (a special case of correction of an error)

15-46 [L0 3] Various types of accounting changes can affect the auditor's report.

a. Briefly describe the rationale for having accounting changes affect the auditor's report and the auditor's responsibility in such cases.

b. For each of the changes listed below (1. through 8.), indicate the type of change and its effect on the audit report.

1. A change from the completed-contract method to the percentage-of-completion method of accounting for long-term construction contracts.

2. A change in the estimated useful life of previously recorded fixed assets. (The change is based on newly acquired information.)

3. Correction of a mathematical error in inventory pricing made in a prior period.

4. A change from full absorption costing to direct costing for inventory valuation (which is non-GAAP).

5. A change from presentation of statements of individual companies to presentation of consolidated companies.

6. A change from deferring and amortizing preproduction costs to recording such costs as an expense when incurred, because future benefits of the costs have become doubtful. (The new accounting method was adopted in recognition of the change in estimated future benefits.)

7. A change from amortizing goodwill to testing for impairment each year. (The change was in response to an accounting pronouncement from the FASB.)

8. A change from including the employer's share of FICA taxes with other taxes to including the employer's share of FICA taxes as retirement benefits on the income statement.

15-47 [L0 3] Under what circumstances must the audit report refer to the consistency, or the lack of consistency, in the application of GAAP? What is the purpose of such reporting?

15-48 [L0 3] When a client has a justified departure from GAAP, how should the auditor modify the audit report?

15-49 [LO 3] Provide examples of matters that auditors may choose to emphasize when issuing an unqualified opinion.

15-50 [LO 4] Identify the situations in which an auditor issues a qualified opinion.

15-51 [LO 4] On February 28, 2014, Stu & Dent, LLP completed the audit of Shylo Ranch, Inc. (a public company) for the year ended December 31, 2013. A recent fire destroyed the accounting records concerning the cost of Shylo's livestock. These were the only records destroyed. The auditors are unable to obtain adequate evidence concerning the cost of the livestock, which represents about 8% of total assets. These are GAAP-based financial statements, and the auditors found no other problems during the audit. The audit report is to cover the 2013 financial statements only. The audit partner has indicated that a qualified opinion is more appropriate than an adverse opinion. Prepare a draft of the audit report for review by the audit partner.

15-52 [LO 4] You are a senior auditor working for Fuhremann & Fuhremann, CPAs. Your staff assistant has drafted the following audit report of a publicly traded U.S. company. You believe the scope limitation is significant enough to qualify the opinion, but not to disclaim an opinion. Identify the deficiencies in this draft and state how each deficiency should be corrected. Organize your answer around the components of the audit report (introductory paragraph, scope paragraph, and so on).

To Joseph Halberg, Controller
Billings Container Company, Inc.

We have audited the accompanying balance sheet of Billings Container Company and the related statements of income, retained earnings, and statement of changes in financial position as of December 31, 2014. These financial statements are the responsibility of the Company's management.

Except as discussed in the following paragraph, we conducted our audit in accordance with accounting principles generally accepted in the United States of America. Those standards require that we plan and perform the audit to obtain assurance about whether the financial statements are free of misstatement. An audit includes examining evidence supporting the amounts and disclosures in the financial statements. An audit also includes assessing the accounting principles used as well as evaluating the overall financial statement presentation. We believe that our audit provides a reasonable basis for our opinion.

We were unable to obtain sufficient appropriate evidence of the fair market value of the Company's investment in a real estate venture due to the unique nature of the venture. The investment is accounted for using the equity method and is stated at $450,000 and $398,000 at December 31, 2014 and 2013, respectively.

In our opinion, except for the above-mentioned limitation on the scope of our audit, the financial statements referred to above present fairly the financial position of Billings Container Company as of December 31, 2014 and 2013, and the results of its operations and its cash flows for the year then ended in conformity with auditing standards generally accepted in the United States of America.

/s/ Kristen Fuhremann, CPA
Madison, WI
December 31, 2014

15-53 LO 4 Refer to Exhibit 15.7. What is the nature of the qualification of the audit report for Honda Motor Company? How was the audit report modified?

15-54 LO 5 In what situations would an auditor issue an adverse opinion?

15-55 LO 6 What is the purpose of a disclaimer of opinion? In what situations would an auditor issue a disclaimer of opinion?

15-56 LO 6 Why should the auditor ordinarily disclaim an opinion if the client imposes significant scope limitations on the audit procedures?

15-57 LO 7 Identify the basic types of audit reports other than a standard unqualified audit report and explain the circumstances under which each type of report is appropriate.

15-58 LO 7 The following table outlines various scenarios in which an auditor will determine the appropriate audit opinion to issue. Note that the auditor's professional judgment about the nature of the matter giving rise to the modification and the pervasiveness of its effects or possible effects on the financial statements affects the type of opinion to be expressed. Complete the following table to identify the report that should be issued by the auditor.

Nature of Matter Giving Rise to the Modification	Auditor's Professional Judgment About the Pervasiveness of the Effects or Possible Effects on the Financial Statements	
	Material but Not Pervasive	**Material and Pervasive**
Financial statements are materially misstated		
Inability to obtain sufficient appropriate audit evidence		

15-59 LO 7 Several independent audit situations are presented here. Assume that everything other than what is described would have resulted in an unqualified opinion on the company's financial statements. Indicate the type of opinion you believe should be expressed in each situation and explain your choice. If an explanatory paragraph is needed, indicate whether it should precede or follow the opinion paragraph.

a. The auditor was unable to obtain confirmations from two of the client's major customers that were included in the sample. These customers wrote on the confirmation letters that they were unable to confirm the balances because of their accounting systems. The auditor was able to achieve satisfaction through other audit procedures.

b. The client treated a lease as an operating lease, but the auditor believes it should have been accounted for as a capital lease. The effects are material.

c. The client changed from FIFO to LIFO this year. The effect is material. Address the following two situations:
   (i) The change was properly accounted for, justified, and disclosed.
   (ii) The change was properly accounted for and disclosed, but was not properly justified.

d. The client restricted the auditor from observing the physical inventory. Inventory is a material item.

e. The client is engaged in a product liability lawsuit that is properly accounted for and adequately described in the footnotes.

The lawsuit does not threaten the going-concern assumption, but an adverse decision by the court could create a material obligation for the client.

f. The status of the client as a going concern is extremely doubtful. The problems are properly described in the footnotes.

g. One of your client's subsidiaries was audited by another audit firm, whose opinion was qualified because of a GAAP violation. You do not believe that the GAAP violation is material to the consolidated financial statements on which you are expressing an opinion.

h. You are convinced that your client is violating another company's patent in the process of manufacturing its only product. The client will not disclose this because it does not want to wave a red flag and bring this violation to the other company's attention. A preliminary estimate is that the royalty payments required would be material to the financial statements.

i. The client, with reasonable justification, has changed its method of accounting for depreciation for all factory and office equipment. The effect of this change is not material to the current-year financial statements, but is likely to have a material effect in future years. The client's management will not disclose this change because of its immaterial effect on the current-year statements. You have been unable to persuade management to make the disclosure.

15-60 [LO 7] The following are independent audit situations for which you are to recommend an appropriate audit report. For each situation listed as 1. through 6. below, identify the appropriate type of audit report from the list below (a. through f.) and briefly explain the rationale for selecting the report.

Appropriate type of audit report:

a. Unqualified, standard
b. Unqualified, explanatory paragraph
c. Qualified opinion because of departure from GAAP
d. Qualified scope and opinion
e. Disclaimer
f. Adverse

Audit Situations

1. An audit client has a significant amount of loans receivable outstanding (40% of assets), but has an inadequate internal control system over the loans. The auditor cannot locate sufficient information to prepare an aging of the loans or to identify the collateral for about 75% of the loans, even though the client states that all loans are collateralized. The auditor sent out confirmations to verify the existence of the receivables, but only 10 of the 50 sent out were returned. The auditor attempts to verify the other loans by looking at subsequent payments, but only eight had remitted payments during the month of January, and the auditor wants to wrap up the audit by February 15. The auditor estimates that if only 10 of the 50 loans were correctly recorded, loans would need to be written down by $7.5 million.

2. During the audit of a large manufacturing company, the auditor did not observe all locations of physical inventory. The auditor chose a random number of sites to visit, and the company's internal auditors visited the other sites. The auditor has confidence in the competence and objectivity of the internal auditors. The auditor personally observed only about 20% of the total inventory, but neither the auditor nor the internal auditors noted any exceptions in the inventory process.

3. During the past year, Network Computer, Inc. devoted its entire research and development efforts to develop and market an enhanced version of its state-of-the-art telecommunications system. The costs, which were significant, were all capitalized as research and development costs. The company plans to amortize these capitalized costs over the life of the new product. The auditor has concluded that the research to date will likely result in a marketable product. A full description of the research and development, and the costs, is included in a note. The note also describes that basic research costs are expensed as incurred, and the auditor has verified the accuracy of the statement.

4. During the course of the audit of Sail-Away Company, the auditor noted that the current ratio had dropped to 1.75. The company's loan covenant requires the maintenance of a current ratio of 2.0, or the company's debt is all immediately due. The auditor and the company have contacted the bank, which is not willing to waive the loan covenant because the company has been experiencing operating losses for the past few years and has an inadequate capital structure. The auditor has substantial doubt that the company can find adequate financing elsewhere and may encounter difficulties staying in operation. Management, however, is confident that it can overcome the problem. The company does not deem it necessary to include any additional disclosure because management members are confident that an alternative source of funds will be found by pledging their personal assets.

5. The Wear-Ever Wholesale Company has been very profitable. It recently received notice of a 10% price increase for a significant portion of its inventory. The company believes it is important to manage its products wisely and has a policy of writing all inventory up to current replacement cost. This assures that profits will be recognized on sales sufficient to replace the assets and realize a normal profit. This operating philosophy has been very successful, and all salespeople reference current cost, not historical cost, in making sales. Only inventory has been written up to replacement cost, but inventory is material because the company carries a wide range of products. The company's policy of writing up the inventory and its dollar effects is adequately described in a footnote to the financial statements. For the current year, the net effect of the inventory write-up increased reported income by only 3% and assets by 15% above historical cost.

6. The audit of NewCo was staffed primarily by three new hires and a relatively inexperienced audit senior. The manager found numerous errors during the conduct of the audit and developed very long to-do lists for all members of the audit to complete before the audit was concluded. Although the manager originally doubted the staff's understanding of the audit procedures, by the time the audit was finished, he concluded that the new auditors did understand the company and the audit process and that no material errors existed in the financial statements.

15-61 **LO 7** Audit situations 1. through 8. presented below describe various independent factual situations an auditor might encounter in conducting an audit. List A represents the types of opinions the auditor ordinarily would issue, and List B represents the report modifications (if any) that would be necessary. For each situation, select one response from List A and one from List B. Select, as the best answer for each item, the action the auditor normally would take. Items from either list may be selected once, more than once, or not at all.

Assume the following:

- The auditor is independent.
- The auditor previously expressed an unqualified opinion on the prior-year financial statements.
- Only single-year (not comparative) statements are presented for the current year.
- The conditions for an unqualified opinion exist unless contradicted in the factual situations.
- The conditions stated in the factual situations are material.
- No report modifications are to be made except in response to the factual situation.

Factual Audit Situations

1. The financial statements present fairly, in all material respects, the financial position, results of operations, and cash flows in conformity with GAAP.
2. In auditing the long-term investments account, an auditor is unable to obtain audited financial statements for an investee located in a foreign country. The auditor concludes that sufficient appropriate evidence regarding this investment cannot be obtained, but is not significant enough to disclaim an opinion.
3. Because of recurring operating losses and working-capital deficiencies, an auditor has substantial doubt about an organization's ability to continue as a going concern for a reasonable period of time. However, the financial statement disclosures concerning these matters are adequate.
4. The principal auditor decides to refer to the work of another auditor who audited a wholly owned subsidiary of the organziation and issued an unqualified opinion.
5. An organziation issues financial statements that present the financial position and results of operations but omits the related statement of cash flows. Management discloses in the notes to the financial statements that it does not believe the statement of cash flows to be a useful statement.
6. An organziation changes its depreciation method for production equipment from the straight-line to a units-of-production method based on hours of utilization. The auditor concurs with the change, although it has a material effect on the comparability of the entity's financial statements.
7. An organziation is a defendant in a lawsuit alleging infringement of certain patent rights. However, management cannot reasonably estimate the ultimate outcome of the litigation. The auditor believes that there is a reasonable possibility of a significant material loss, but the lawsuit is adequately disclosed in the notes to the financial statements.
8. An organziation discloses certain lease obligations in the notes to the financial statements. The auditor believes that the failure to capitalize these leases is a departure from GAAP that is not justified.

List A—Types of Opinions

a. A qualified opinion
b. An unqualified opinion
c. An adverse opinion
d. A disclaimer of opinion
e. Either a qualified opinion or an adverse opinion
f. Either a disclaimer of opinion or a qualified opinion
g. Either an adverse opinion or a disclaimer of opinion

List B—Report Modifications

h. Describe the circumstances in an explanatory paragraph *preceding* the opinion paragraph *without modifying* the three standard paragraphs.

i. Describe the circumstances in an explanatory paragraph *following* the opinion paragraph *without modifying* the three standard paragraphs.

j. Describe the circumstances in an explanatory paragraph *preceding* the opinion paragraph and *modifying the opinion* paragraph.

k. Describe the circumstances in an explanatory paragraph *following* the opinion paragraph and *modifying the opinion* paragraph.

l. Describe the circumstances in an explanatory paragraph *preceding* the opinion paragraph and *modifying the scope and opinion* paragraphs.

m. Describe the circumstances in an explanatory paragraph *following* the opinion paragraph and *modifying the scope and opinion* paragraphs.

n. Describe the circumstances within the *scope* paragraph without adding an explanatory paragraph.

o. Describe the circumstances within the *opinion* paragraph without adding an explanatory paragraph.

p. Describe the circumstances within the *scope and opinion* paragraphs without adding an explanatory paragraph.

q. Describe the circumstances in the *introductory* paragraph without adding an explanatory paragraph and modify the wording of the *scope and opinion* paragraphs.

r. Issue the *standard* auditor's report *without modification*.

15-62 **LO 7** Each of the following phrases (1. through 5.) is from a paragraph in an auditor's report. Assume that except for the information indicated in the phrase, the report would have been a standard unqualified report. Select from the following list (a. through d.) the most likely report for the indicated phrase. Each choice in the list may be used once, more than once, or not at all.

List

a. Unqualified
b. Qualified
c. Adverse
d. Disclaimer

   1. In our opinion, except for the omission of the statement of cash flows ...
   2. We are not independent with respect to KC Company ...
   3. ... based on our audit and the report of other auditors ...
   4. ... presents fairly, in all material respects ...
   5. ... the scope of our work was not sufficient to enable us ...

ETHICS **15-63** **LO 7, 9** Assume that you are in a situation where you had doubts about your client's ability to continue as a going concern. Further, assume you have decided that, after performing all the required audit procedures, you can issue an unqualified opinion but need to modify the audit opinion to indicate substantial doubt about the client's ability to continue as a going concern. You have to let the CFO, who is a longtime friend of yours, know of your decision. When you do this, the CFO tries to explain to you that if the company receives a going-concern opinion, it will go under—that the opinion is a self-fulfilling prophecy. The CFO tries to convince you that if your firm does not issue a going-concern opinion, it is very likely the company will be able to weather its financial difficulties and survive. Further, the CFO notes that this is really a matter of professional judgment and believes that many other auditors would not see the need to issue a going-concern opinion. Should you issue a standard unqualified audit report or an unqualified audit report with a going-concern explanatory paragraph?

Use the framework for ethical decision making introduced in Chapter 4 to address the dilemma you face regarding what type of opinion to issue. Recall that the steps in the framework are as follows: (1) identify the ethical issue(s), (2) determine who are the affected parties and identify their rights, (3) determine the most important rights, (4) develop alternative courses of action, (5) determine the likely consequences of each proposed course of action, (6) assess the possible consequences, including an estimation of the greatest good for the greatest number, and (7) decide on the appropriate course of action.

15-64 `LO 8` Under what circumstances must the auditor of a public company express an adverse opinion on the client's ICFR?

15-65 `LO 8` Identify the conditions under which an auditor would modify the opinion on ICFR (for situations other than the presence of a material weakness).

CONTEMPORARY AND HISTORICAL CASES

15-66 `XL LEISURE GROUP, MOVIELINK`
`LO 3` In September 2008, XL Leisure Group, Britain's third-largest tour operator, filed for bankruptcy. A few months prior to filing for bankruptcy, the company had issued its audited financial statements. Neither the financial statements nor the auditor's opinion contained any explicit warning that the company was in financial difficulty.

`INTERNATIONAL`

`PROFESSIONAL SKEPTICISM`

In contrast, in 2007 the auditors of MovieLink expressed substantial doubt that MovieLink, which offers movies that can be downloaded from the Internet, would be able to continue as a going concern. The basis for the auditors' concern included MovieLink's recurring losses from operations, negative cash flows from operating activities, and an accumulated deficit that had risen to $145 million.

A company's financial statements are prepared and audited under the assumption that the company is a going concern, meaning that that company will continue to operate for a reasonable period of time, for example, one year. However, during times of financial crisis, it is expected that many companies will find themselves facing financial difficulties, even to the point of filing for bankruptcy. Financial difficulties can arise when companies fund their operations through debt, ranging from overdrafts to credit lines to large loans. If companies need these sources of funds to continue to operate, yet banks are unwilling to commit to providing these loans, many companies face the prospect of not being able to continue their operations. During times of financial crisis, banks may not be willing to continue providing the lending they have in the past or to commit to new lending. In these situations, auditors may have substantial doubt about a company's ability to continue as a going concern.

a. How does the auditor's substantial doubt about a client's ability to remain a going concern affect the format of the audit opinion?

b. What are the implications to the company and to the audit firm when the audit firm's report expresses substantial doubt about a company's ability to remain a going concern?

    c. Why might the auditors of XL Leisure Group and MovieLink have arrived at two different decisions?

    d. How might professional skepticism impact the auditor's decision to issue a going-concern opinion?

FRAUD   **15-67**   **SEC, MICHAEL B. JOHNSON**
LO 3, 7, 9   The SEC issued Accounting and Auditing Enforcement Release (AAER) No. 2393 on March 8, 2006. The Enforcement Release related to the matter of Michael B. Johnson and Michael Johnson & Co. and concerns the audits of Winners. The following facts about Johnson and Co.'s audit of Winners are included in the AAER:

- Johnson, age 56, is a resident of Littleton, Colorado. Johnson has been the manager and sole member of Johnson & Co. and a licensed certified public accountant in Colorado since 1975. He also is a licensed certified public accountant in Florida and Mississippi.
- Johnson & Co. is an accounting firm located in Denver, Colorado. Johnson is the only member of, and the only certified public accountant affiliated with, the firm.
- Johnson & Co., through the participation of Johnson, audited the financial statements of Winners Internet Network, Inc. (Winners) for the years ended December 31, 1997 and 1998. Johnson supervised the audits and compilations of these financial statements and signed the audit reports for the 1997 and 1998 audits on behalf of Johnson & Co.
- Winners' December 31, 1999, financial statements were prepared and audited by Johnson and Johnson & Co.
- Johnson & Co. issued audit reports accompanying Winners' year-end financial statements for 1997 and 1998 that contained a going-concern modification and an unqualified audit report for 1999. These financial statements contained material misstatements, some of which related to entries made by Johnson or under the direction of Johnson. These reports falsely stated that the financial statements were presented fairly in all material respects in conformity with GAAP and that the audits of these financial statements were conducted in accordance with GAAS. These statements were false, since portions of the underlying financial statements were not presented in conformity with GAAP, which, in turn, rendered false the statements that the audits were conducted in accordance with GAAS, since the failure to address a deviation from GAAP in an audit report is a violation of GAAS.

a. Given the nature of Johnson & Co.'s work on Winners' financial statements for 1997–1999, what type of audit opinion should have been issued?

b. In considering this decision, answer the following questions by completing the first four steps of the seven-step framework for professional decision making introduced in Chapter 4:

    1. What difficulties might Johnson have faced when deciding what type of opinion to issue? Why might Johnson have not issued the appropriate opinions?

    2. What are the consequences of Johnson's decisions in this case?

    3. What are the risks and uncertainties associated with this decision?

    4. In deciding on whether to issue a going-concern modification, what types of evidence should the auditor gather to evaluate the reasonableness of the going-concern assumption?

Recall that the framework is as follows:

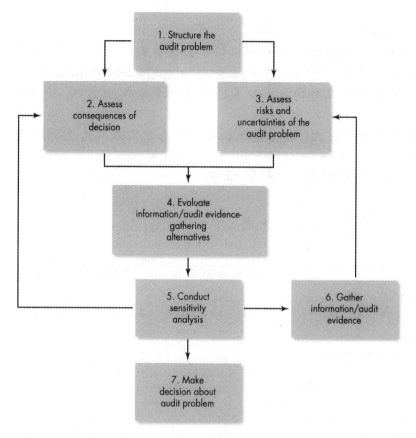

Source: Adapted from "Judgment and Choice," by Robin Hogarth.

教 学 支 持 服 务

圣智学习出版集团（Cengage Learning）作为为终身教育提供全方位信息服务的全球知名教育出版集团，为秉承其在全球对教材产品的一贯教学支持服务，将为采用其教材图书的每位老师提供教学辅助资料。任何一位通过Cengage Learning北京代表处注册的老师都可直接下载所有在线提供的、全球最为丰富的教学辅助资料，包括教师用书、PPT、习题库等。

鉴于部分资源仅适用于老师教学使用，烦请索取的老师配合填写如下情况说明表。

教学辅助资料索取证明

兹证明_____大学_____系/院_____学年(学期)开设的_____名
学生□主修 □选修的_____课程，采用如下教材作为□主要教材 或 □参
考教材：

书名：_____

作者：_____　□英文影印版　　□中文翻译版

出版社：_____

学生类型：□本科1/2年级　　□本科3/4年级　　□研究生　□MBA □EMBA　□在职培训

任课教师姓名：_____

职称/职务：_____

电话：_____

E-mail：_____

通信地址：_____

邮编：_____

对本教材的建议：_____

系/院主任：_____（签字）

（系/院办公室章）

_____年_____月_____日

----

*相关教辅资源事宜敬请联络圣智学习出版集团北京代表处。

北京大学出版社
PEKING UNIVERSITY PRESS

经济与管理图书事业部
北京市海淀区成府路205号　100871
联系人：徐 冰 张 燕
电　话：**010-62767312 / 62767348**
传　真：**010-62556201**
电子邮件：em@pup.cn　em_pup@126.com
Q　Q：552063295
新浪微博：@北京大学出版社经管图书
网　址：http://www.pup.cn

CENGAGE Learning™

Cengage Learning Beijing Office
圣智学习出版集团北京代表处
北京市海淀区科学院南路2号融科资讯中心C座南楼1201室
Tel: (8610) 8286 2095 / 96 / 97　Fax: (8610) 8286 2089
E-mail: asia.infochina@cengage.com
www.cengageasia.com